C++

for Engineers and Scientists

Third Edition

Gary J. Bronson

G.J. Borse
Contributing Editor
Lehigh University

COURSE TECHNOLOGY
CENGAGE Learning

Australia • Brazil • Japan • Korea • Mexico • Singapore • Spain • United Kingdom • United States

COURSE TECHNOLOGY
CENGAGE Learning™

C++ for Engineers and Scientists, Third Edition

Gary J. Bronson

Managing Editor: Marie Lee

Acquisitions Editor: Amy Jollymore

Senior Product Manager: Alyssa Pratt

Developmental Editor: Lisa M. Lord

Content Product Manager: Matt Hutchinson

Marketing Manager: Bryant Chrzan

Editorial Assistant: Julia Leroux-Lindsey

Art Director: Marissa Falco

Compositor: GEX Publishing Services

For product information and technology assistance, contact us at
Cengage Learning Customer & Sales Support, 1-800-354-9706

For permission to use material from this text or product, submit all requests online at **www.cengage.com/permissions**
Further permission questions can be e-mailed to
permissionrequest@cengage.com

International Student Edition:
ISBN-13: 978-1-4390-3950-2
ISBN-10 : 1-4390-3950-X

Course Technology
20 Channel Center Street
Boston, Massachusetts 02210
USA

Cengage Learning is a leading provider of customized learning solutions with office locations around the globe, including Singapore, the United Kingdom, Australia, Mexico, Brazil, and Japan. Locate your local office at: **international.cengage.com/region**

Cengage Learning products are represented in Canada by Nelson Education, Ltd.

For your lifelong learning solutions, visit **www.cengage.com**

Purchase any of our products at your local college store or at our preferred online store **www.ichapters.com**

Some of the product names and company names used in this book have been used for identification purposes only and may be trademarks or registered trademarks of their respective manufacturers and sellers.

Any fictional data related to persons or companies or URLs used throughout this book is intended for instructional purposes only. At the time this book was printed, any such data was fictional and not belonging to any real persons or companies.

The programs in this book are for instructional purposes only.

They have been tested with care but are not guaranteed for any particular intent beyond educational purposes. The author and the publisher do not offer any warranties or representations, nor do they accept any liabilities with respect to the programs.

Printed in Canada
1 2 3 4 5 6 7 14 13 12 11 10

Part 1
Fundamentals of C++ Programming

6 Contents

Contents

The C++ programming language, which includes C as a proper subset, has become the preeminent programming language in the engineering and scientific fields. For most engineers and scientists, however, using the full potential of C++, which is a hybrid language containing both structured and object-oriented features, involves a gradual refinement of programming skills from a structured approach to an object-oriented one. One reason for this is that many engineering and scientific problems can be solved efficiently and conveniently by using only C++'s structured elements.

The refinement approach, from structural to object-oriented programming, is the one *C++ for Engineers and Scientists, Third Edition*, takes. Therefore, like the first two editions, this new edition begins by providing a strong foundation in structured programming. This foundation is then expanded to a complete object orientation in a pedagogically sound and achievable progression. Additionally, to keep it current with the current ANSI/ISO C++ standard, this edition has several important changes and added features, including the following:

- Restructuring Part One to include both arrays and files, which allows using Part One as the basis for a complete semester course in C++
- Adding more than 40 new engineering and scientific exercises that incorporate the fields of electrical engineering, mechanical engineering thermodynamics, structural engineering, numerical applications, physics, heat transfer, chemistry, and fluid mechanics
- Adding a section on performing a unit analysis
- Adding a new introduction to the Standard Template Library
- Adding a section that introduces the fundamentals of the Unified Modeling Language (UML)
- Restructuring the case studies throughout the book to emphasize specific engineering or scientific applications
- Adding end-of chapter programming projects that supplement the exercises at the end of each section
- Labeling all exercises and programming projects as to application type

The following features have been retained from the second edition:

- Fundamentals of software engineering are discussed from both procedural and object-oriented viewpoints.
- Common Programming Errors sections have been retained. These sections anticipate problems that novice C++ programmers encounter.
- The ANSI/ISO C++ `iostream` library and namespace mechanism are used in all programs.
- Exception handling is discussed in a complete section, with practical applications of exception handling included throughout the book.
- The new C++ `string` class is covered.
- A thorough discussion is included of input data validation and functions to check the numerical data type of input items and to allow reentering invalid numerical types.

In practical terms, this book has been written to support both a one- and two-semester technical C++ programming course; the only prerequisite is that students should be familiar with fundamental algebra. This book is constructed to be flexible enough so that professors can mold the book to their preferences for topic presentations. This flexibility is achieved in the following ways.

Excluding Chapter 1, which includes computer literacy material for those who require this background, Part One presents the basic structured syntax, flow control, and modularity topics needed for a thorough understanding of C++'s structural features. With the topics of arrays (Chapter 7) and files (Chapter 8) having been moved to Part One, this part now provides a comprehensive one-semester course. As Chapters 7 and 8 have been written specifically to depend only on Chapters 1 through 6, their order of presentation in the classroom is entirely up to the professor's discretion. With time permitting, the basics of classes, introduced in Chapter 10, can also be covered to complete a one-semester course. Additionally, depending on time and inclination, the numerical techniques discussed in Chapter 14 can be presented at any point after Part One has been completed. Figure 1 illustrates this one-semester topic dependency.

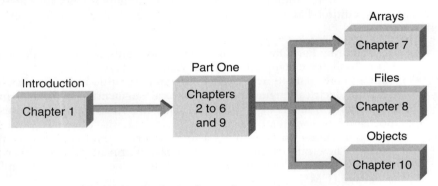

Figure 1   Topic dependency for a one-semester course

An important feature of this book is that Part Two, on object-oriented programming, and Part Three, on data structures, are interchangeable. So if you want to cover object-oriented programming early, follow a Part One–Part Two–Part Three progression. On the other hand, if you want to continue with additional structured programming reinforcement and discuss object-oriented programming at the end of the course or the start of a second semester, follow the sequence Part One–Part Three–Part Two. In either case, the material on arrays in Chapter 7, files in Chapter 8, classes in Chapter 10, and numerical techniques in Chapter 14 can be introduced at any time after covering the first six chapters. Figure 2 shows the topic dependency chart for the complete book and illustrates the flexibility of introducing different topics under the umbrella of procedural programming, object-oriented programming, and data structures.

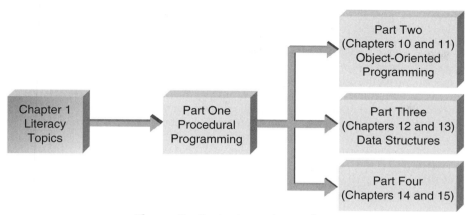

Figure 2 Topic dependency chart

Distinctive Features of This Book

Writing Style One thing I have found to be essential in my own classes is that after the professor sets the stage in class, the assigned book must continue to encourage, nurture, and assist students in acquiring and "owning" the material. To do this, the book must be written in a manner that makes sense to students. My primary concern, and one of the distinctive features of this book, is that it has been written for students. Therefore, I believe the writing style used to convey the concepts is one of the most important aspects of this book.

Modularity To produce readable and maintainable programs, modularity is essential. C++, by its nature, is a modular language. Therefore, the connection between C++ functions and modules is made early in Chapter 2 and sustained throughout the book. Similarly, the idea of parameter passing into modules is discussed early in Chapter 3, using C++'s mathematical library. Explaining these concepts early introduces students to function and argument passing as natural programming techniques. With the introduction of object-oriented programming techniques in Chapter 10, students can build on the basic concept of encapsulating both data and functions, which strengthens this modular emphasis.

Software Engineering Rather than simply introduce students to programming in C++, this book introduces students to the fundamentals of software engineering from both a structured and object-oriented viewpoint. Chapter 1 introduces the software development procedure, which incorporates one of this book's main themes: emphasizing problem-solving techniques. Therefore, the importance of understanding and defining a problem, selecting and refining a solution, and understanding the relationship between analysis, design, coding, and testing is stated early and followed through with practical examples in all subsequent case studies.

Case Studies Starting with Chapter 2, most chapters contain a case study. These case studies demonstrate and reinforce effective problem solving in the context of the software development procedure explained in Chapter 1 and are extended to object-oriented development when classes are introduced in Chapter 10.

Program Testing   Every C++ program in this book has been compiled and run successfully and has been quality assurance tested with Microsoft Visual C++ .NET. Source code for all programs can be found on the Course Technology Web site (*www.cengage.com/coursetechnology*). Using the source code permits students to experiment with and extend the existing programs and modify them more easily, as required for a number of end-of-section exercises.

Pedagogical Features

To facilitate the goal of making C++ accessible as a first-level course, the following pedagogical features have been incorporated into this book.

End-of-Section Exercises   Almost every section in the book contains numerous and diverse skill-building and programming exercises. Each exercise is identified as to type (practice, desk check, and so forth) or application (such as electrical engineering, heat transfer, environmental, and so on). Additionally, solutions to all exercises are provided in the Instructor Downloads section on *www.cengage.com/coursetechnology*.

End-of-Chapter Programming Projects   Each chapter includes several programming projects that combine all elements of C++ covered in previous sections and chapters. Projects are identified as to type (practice, desk check, and so forth) or application (electrical engineering, heat transfer, environmental, and so on).

Common Programming Errors and Chapter Summary   Each chapter ends with a section on common programming errors and a summary of the main topics covered in the chapter.

Enrichment Sections   Given the many different emphases that can be used in teaching C++, several chapters include an enrichment section called "A Closer Look." These sections allow you to provide varying emphases with different students in C++ classes.

Point of Information Boxes   These boxes present additional clarification of commonly used or difficult concepts, such as abstraction, lvalues and rvalues, values versus identities, flags, and stream formatting. In addition, many Point of Information boxes explain alternative and advanced programming techniques, useful technical points, programming tips, and programming tricks used by professional programmers.

Pseudocode Descriptions   Pseudocode is used throughout the book. Flowchart symbols are introduced but are used only in illustrating flow-of-control constructs.

Engineering and Scientific Disciplines   Many chapters have a box at the end with information on several engineering and scientific fields, such as electrical, chemical, mechanical, and aeronautical engineering.

Appendixes This book includes four appendixes on operator precedence, ASCII character codes, floating-point number storage, and command-line arguments. Additionally, Course Technology provides tutorials for using various C++ compilers at *www.cengage.com/coursetechnology*.

Supplemental Materials

The following supplemental materials are available when this book is used in a classroom setting:

Electronic Instructor's Resources. The Instructor's Resources that accompany this book include the following:

- Additional instructional material to assist in class preparation, including suggestions for lecture topics
- Solutions to all the end-of-chapter materials, including the programming projects

ExamView®. This book is accompanied by ExamView, a powerful testing software package that allows instructors to create and administer printed, computer (LAN-based), and Internet exams. ExamView includes hundreds of questions that correspond to the topics covered in this book, enabling students to generate detailed study guides that include page references for further review. These computer-based and Internet testing components allow students to take exams at their computers and save instructors time because each exam is graded automatically. The Test Bank is also available in WebCT and Blackboard formats.

PowerPoint Presentations. This book comes with Microsoft PowerPoint slides for each chapter. They are included as a teaching aid for classroom presentations, to make available to students on the network for chapter review, or to be printed for classroom distribution. Instructors can add their own slides for additional topics they introduce to the class.

Source Code. The source code for this book is available at *www.cengage.com/coursetechnology* and is also available on the Teaching Tools CD.

Solution Files. The solution files for all programming exercises and projects are available at *www.cengage.com/coursetechnology* and on the Teaching Tools CD.

To Rochelle, Jeremy, David, and Matthew Bronson

Acknowledgments

The writing of this third edition is a direct result of the success (and limitations) of the previous two editions. In this regard, my most heartfelt acknowledgment and appreciation is to the instructors and students who found the previous editions to be of service in their quests to teach and learn C++.

Next, I would like to thank Alyssa Pratt, my Senior Product Manager at Course Technology. In addition to her continuous faith and encouragement, her ideas and partnership were instrumental in creating this book. After the writing process was completed, the task of turning the final manuscript into a book depended on many people other than myself. For this, I especially want to thank my developmental editor, Lisa Lord, who provided an outstanding job. Her editing so dovetailed with both the spirit and idiosyncrasies of my own writing style that it was an absolute pleasure working with her. She stayed true to what I was attempting to achieve while patiently going through both the technical and grammatical content. A truly incredible feat! This editing was supplemented by the equally detailed work of my colleague, Professor Joan Zucker Hoffman, with structural engineering applications provided by Professors Andy Gregg and Al Branchi and moral support provided by Dr. John Becker of the Theology Department. Finally, I would like to thank the testers at Course Technology's MQA Department as well as GEX Publishing Services, especially the interior designer, and Camille Kiolbasa, the copyeditor. The dedication of this team of people was extremely important to me and I am very grateful to them.

The following reviewers provided extensive, extremely useful, and detailed information and corrections that made this edition better and more accurate. No matter how careful I was, each reviewer pointed out something that I missed or could be stated better. I am very thankful to them. Naturally, all errors rest squarely on my shoulders, but these reviewers made the load much easier: Hyder Ali, California State University, Northridge, and Robert Baird, Salt Lake Community College. In addition, I'd like to thank the following instructors who reviewed the proposal for this edition and offered valuable feedback: Randy Bower, Jacksonville University; Helen Darcey, Cleveland State Community College; Akira Kawaguchi, The City College of New York; Cynthia Lester, Tuskegee University; and Sherman Wong, Baruch University.

As with the first edition, special acknowledgement goes to Dr. G.J. Borse of Lehigh University, who provided material that was adapted for this book. Specifically, his contribution includes almost all of Chapter 14, which Dr. Borse graciously permitted me to adapt from his FORTRAN 77 text (copyright held by PWS Publishing). I would also like to acknowledge, with extreme gratitude, the wonderful academic environment for learning and teaching created at Fairleigh Dickinson University—starting with the President, Dr. Michael Adams, followed through in the academic departments by the university and campus provosts, Dr. Joseph Kiernan and Dr. Kenneth Greene, and finally to the direct encouragement and support provided by my dean, Dr. William Moore, and my chairperson, Dr. Paul Yoon. Without their support, this book could not have been written.

Finally, I deeply appreciate the patience, understanding, and love provided by my friend, wife, and partner, Rochelle.

Gary Bronson
2009

Part

One

Fundamentals of C++ Programming

Although C++ is an object-oriented language, it was developed as an extension to C, a procedural-oriented language. As such, C++ is a hybrid language having both procedural and object features. Because of this hybrid nature, not only is it possible to write a complete C++ program using just procedural code, but also it's impossible to write an object-oriented program in C++ that doesn't include procedural elements. Therefore, a proper start to learning C++ requires familiarity with its procedural aspects.

Chapter 1

Preliminaries

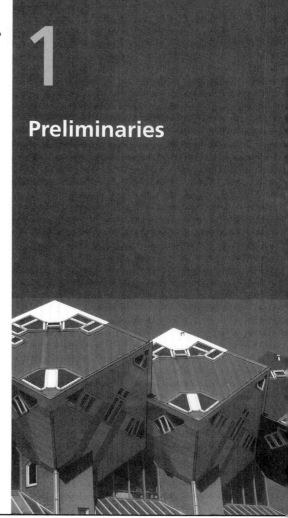

Programming scientific and engineering applications requires a number of basic skills, both in understanding the underlying applications and in understanding the fundamentals of the programming process itself. On the applications side, a knowledge of numerical measurements and their corresponding units, as well as a familiarity with performing calculations, are assumed. Using consistent sets of units and knowing how to convert between units is a basic prerequisite of these applications.

Additionally, the programming process assumes the programmer starts with a preliminary set of skills. As you develop your programming abilities in C++, a clear understanding of how programs are developed, in general, is important. This understanding includes what constitutes a "good" program and what an algorithm is.

This chapter covers these preliminary requirements and can be used as an introduction or a review.

1.1 Preliminary One: Unit Analysis

In all fields of study, using consistent and correct units when making computations is crucial. As a simple example, consider calculating the area of a rectangle by using this formula:

$$Area = length \times width \qquad \text{[Eq. 1-1]}$$

When using this formula, the units for length and width must be the same. Therefore, if the length is given as 2 feet and the width as 3 inches, at least one of these units must be converted to ensure that both length and width are in the same units before the area is calculated. Converting the length to inches, the rectangle's area is computed as follows:

$$Area = 2 \, ft \left(\frac{12 \, in}{1 \, ft} \right) \times 3 \, in = 36 \, in^2 \qquad \text{[Eq. 1-1a]}$$

Similarly, if you choose to convert the width from 3 inches to its equivalent feet, the calculation becomes the following:

$$Area = 2 \, ft \times 3 \, in \left(\frac{1 \, ft}{12 \, in} \right) = 0.25 \, ft^2 \qquad \text{[Eq. 1-1b]}$$

In the same manner, if one side of the rectangle is given in centimeters and the other in meters, a conversion is necessary to compute the area.

Notice that in Equations 1-1a and 1-1b, units for both length and width *as well as* units for the conversion factor ([12 in/1 ft] in Eq. 1-1a and [1 ft/12 in] in Eq. 1-1b) are included in the formula. The reason is that the terms for units can be multiplied and divided to provide the final unit result. In many cases, this technique is a powerful one for selecting a correct conversion factor and ensuring that a computation is being calculated correctly.

To see why, continue with the area example. Use Eq. 1-1a, but include only the unit terms, which yields the following:

$$Area = ft \left(\frac{in}{ft} \right) \times in \qquad \text{[Eq. 1-1c]}$$

Now a unit of *ft* divided by a unit of *ft* is 1. That is, you can cancel the *ft* units in Eq. 1-1c as follows, which yields the final units as *in* multiplied by *in*, or *in²*, which is a correct unit for the area:

$$Area = \cancel{ft} \left(\frac{in}{\cancel{ft}} \right) \times in = in^2$$

Including only the units and conversion factors in an equation, and canceling out corresponding units in the numerator and denominator, is referred to as performing a **unit analysis**. As an example of a unit analysis for selecting a correct form of a conversion factor, assume you need to convert miles (symbol mi) to kilometers (symbol km), and you have the information that 1 kilometer = 0.6214 miles. As a conversion factor, this equality can be written as either of the following fractions:

$$\frac{1 \, km}{0.6214 \, mi} \quad \text{or} \quad \frac{0.6214 \, mi}{1 \, km}$$

Deciding which conversion factor to use in converting miles to kilometers is easy when you consider units. To see why, try both factors with miles, canceling the units that occur in both the numerator and denominator and concerning yourself only with the final resulting units:

$$\cancel{mi} \times \left(\frac{1\,km}{0.6214\,\cancel{mi}} \right) = km$$

and

$$mi \times \left(\frac{0.6214\,mi}{.1\,km} \right) = \frac{mi^2}{km}$$

Because the first factor (1 km/0.6214 mi) provides the correct final units of kilometers, it's the form of the conversion factor that must be applied to convert miles to kilometers.

For a slightly more complicated example of performing a unit analysis for selecting correct conversion factors, consider converting days to seconds. You can determine the correct form of each conversion factor easily by including the units with each conversion factor, as you change days to hours, then hours to minutes, and finally minutes to seconds, performing each conversion one at a time and canceling units as you proceed with each conversion, as follows:

1st conversion:
days to hours
(cross out the days)

$$\cancel{days} \times \frac{24\,hr}{\cancel{day}}$$

The next conversion changes the units of hours to minutes, using the conversion factor 60 min/hr, as follows:

1st conversion:
days to hours
(cross out the days)

2nd conversion:
hours to minutes
(cross out the hours)

$$\cancel{days} \times \frac{24\,\cancel{hr}}{\cancel{day}} \times \frac{60\,min}{\cancel{hr}}$$

The final conversion is used to convert minutes to seconds:

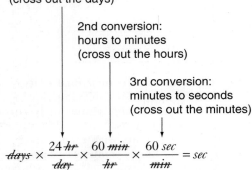

1st conversion:
days to hours
(cross out the days)

2nd conversion:
hours to minutes
(cross out the hours)

3rd conversion:
minutes to seconds
(cross out the minutes)

$$\cancel{days} \times \frac{24\ \cancel{hr}}{\cancel{day}} \times \frac{60\ \cancel{min}}{\cancel{hr}} \times \frac{60\ sec}{\cancel{min}} = sec$$

In a single line, the complete conversion appears as follows:

$$\cancel{days} \times \frac{24\ \cancel{hr}}{\cancel{day}} \times \frac{60\ \cancel{min}}{\cancel{hr}} \times \frac{60\ sec}{\cancel{min}} = sec$$

Before showing how a unit analysis can help ensure that a complete computation is being calculated correctly, it's useful to first summarize the systems of units in common use.

Engineering and Scientific Units

Two unit systems are commonly used in engineering and scientific work: the English Engineering system and the International System (SI). Both are used in this book. Table 1.1 lists the units used in these two systems.

Table 1.1   Commonly Used Physical Quantities

Quantity	Symbol	International System (SI) Units	English Engineering Units	Conversion Equalities
Time	t	seconds (s)	seconds (sec)	
Length	l	meters (m)	feet (ft)	1 m = 3.2808 ft
Area	A	sq. meters (m^2)	sq. feet (ft^2)	1 m^2 = 10.76 ft^2
Volume	V	cubic meters (m^3)	cubic feet (ft^3)	1 m^3 = 35.31 ft^3
Mass	m	kilograms (kg)	pounds-mass (lbm)	1 kg = 2.19 lbm
Force	F	Newton (1 N = 1 kg-m/s^2)	pounds-force (lbf = lbm-ft/sec^2)	1 lbf = 4.448 N
Weight	W	Newton (N)	pounds-force (lbf)	1 lbf = 4.448 N
Density	ρ	kilograms/cubic meters (kg/m^3)	pounds-mass/cubic ft (lbm/ft^3)	1 lbf/ft^3 = 16.02 kg/m3
Velocity	v	meters/sec (m/s)	feet/sec (ft/sec)	1 m/s = 3.2808 ft/sec
Acceleration	a	meters/sec^2 (m/s^2)	feet/sec^2 (ft/sec^2)	1 m/s^2 = 3.2808 ft/sec^2

Table 1.1 Commonly Used Physical Quantities (continued)

Quantity	Symbol	International System (SI) Units	English Engineering Units	Conversion Equalities
Pressure	P	Pascal (Pa) (1 Pa = 1 N/m²)	lbf/ft²	1 lbf/ft² = 47.88 Pa
Heat transfer	Q	Joules (J) (1 J = 1 N.m)	British Thermal Unit (BTU)	1 BTU = 1055 J
Heat flux	Q	Joules/sec (J/s) (1 J/s = 1 Watt)	BTU/sec	1 BTU/sec = 1055 J/s
Work	W	Joules (J)	ft-lbf	1 ft-lbf = 1.356 J
Power	W	Watts (W) (1 W = 1 J/s)	ft-lbf/sec	1 ft-lbf/sec = 1.356 W
Temperature	T	degrees Celsius (C) and degrees Kelvin (K)	degrees Fahrenheit (F) and degrees Rankin (R)	

The following conversion formulas show the relationships between the various temperature scales:

$°F = 1.8°C + 32 = 9/5°C + 32$

$°C = (°F - 32)/1.8 = 5/9 (°F - 32)$

$°K = °C + 273.15$

$°R = °F + 459.67$

$°R = 1.8°K$

$°C = (°R - 491.67) / 1.8 = 5/9 (°R - 491.67)$

Using these conversion formulas provides the equivalent boiling and freezing points of water for each of the temperature scales listed in the following chart:

	°C	°F	°K	°R
Freezing point of water	0	32	273.15	491.67
Boiling point of water	100	212	373.15	671.67

As an example, using the conversion equalities in Table 1.1 (last column), consider calculating Newton's Second Law for a mass of 5 kilograms and an acceleration of 32.2 ft/sec². Newton's Second Law states that

Force = Mass × Acceleration

Assuming SI units are used, the calculation becomes

$$Force = 5\,kg \times \frac{32.2\; ft}{sec^2} \left(\frac{1\; m}{3.2808\; ft} \right) = \frac{49.07\; kg\,m}{sec^2} = 49.07\; N$$

Notice from the information in Table 1.1 that 1 m = 3.2808 ft is used to create this conversion factor

$$\left(\frac{1\ m}{3.2808\ ft} \right)$$

rather than this conversion factor

$$\left(\frac{3.2808\ ft}{1\ m} \right)$$

because the first form achieves the desired cancelation of units. If you mistakenly use the second conversion factor, you would end up with the following final units, which immediately alert you that an incorrect result would occur:

$$Force = 5\ kg \times \frac{32.2\ ft}{sec^2} \left(\frac{3.2808\ ft}{1\ m} \right) = \frac{kg\ ft^2}{sec^2\ m}$$

Finally, you could also achieve the correct conversion by using the following set of conversions:

1st conversion:
feet to inches
(cross out the ft)

2nd conversion:
inches to centimeters
(cross out the in)

3rd conversion:
centimeters to meters
(cross out the cm)

$$Force = 5\ kg \times \frac{32.2\ ft}{sec^2} \times \frac{12\ in}{ft} \times \frac{2.54\ cm}{in} \times \frac{1\ m}{100\ cm} = 49.073\ kg\ m/s^2$$

Frequently, when you don't know the final conversion factor, making intermediate conversions, as in this last calculation, can get you to the correct result easily. Notice that by applying one conversion factor at a time and canceling units as you go along, you avoid the common mistake of multiplying or dividing by the wrong conversion factor. If the final units, by themselves, *do not* yield the correct resulting units, then the resulting numerical answer *must be incorrect*. Correspondingly, if correct conversion factors *and* correct individual measurements are used, the result will be correct in both numerical and unit terms. Using the correct units and doing a unit analysis certainly can't protect you against using incorrect numbers in a calculation or making calculation errors, but by itself, a unit analysis can ensure that you're on the right path to computing a final numerical result correctly.

EXERCISES 1.1

1. **(Practice) a.** To convert inches (in) to feet (ft), the number of inches should be multiplied by which of the following conversion factors?

    i.   12 in/1 ft   **ii.**   1 ft/12 in

    b. To convert meters (m) to kilometers (km), the number of meters should be multiplied by which of the following conversion factors?

    i.   1000 m/1 km   **ii.**   1 km/1000 m

    c. To convert minutes (min) to seconds (sec), the number of minutes should be multiplied by which of the following conversion factors?

    i.   60 sec/1 min   **ii.**   1 min/60 sec

    d. To convert seconds (sec) to minutes (min), the number of seconds should be multiplied by which of the following conversion factors?

    i.   60 sec/1 min   **ii.**   1 min/60 sec

2. **(Practice) a.** To convert feet (ft) to meters (m), the number of feet should be multiplied by which of the following conversion factors?

    i.   1 m/3.28 ft   **ii.**   3.28 ft/1 m

    b. To convert sq.in to sq.ft, the number of sq.in should be multiplied by which of the following conversion factors?

    i.   144 sq.in/1 sq.ft   **ii.**   1 sq.ft/144 sq.in

    c. To convert sq.yd to sq.ft, the number of sq.yd should be multiplied by which of the following conversion factors?

    i.   1 sq.yd/9 sq.ft   **ii.**   9 sq.ft/1 sq.yd

3. **(Practice)** Determine the final units of the following expression:

    $9.8 \text{ m/s}^2 \times 100 \text{ cm/1 m} \times 1 \text{ in/2.54 cm} \times 1 \text{ ft/12 in}$

4. **(Practice) a.** Determine the conversion factors that can be used to convert miles per gallon (mpg = mi/gal) to kilometers per liter (km/liter), given that 1 liter = 0.22 gallons and 1 kilometer = 0.6214 miles.

    b. Using the conversion factors you determined in Exercise 4a, convert 25 mpg into km/liter.

5. **(Automotive) a.** An automobile engine's performance can be determined by monitoring its rotations per minute (rpm). Determine the conversion factors that can be used to convert rpm to frequency in Hertz (Hz), given that 1 rotation = 1 cycle, 1 minute = 60 seconds, and 1 Hz = 1 cycle/sec.

    b. Using the conversion factors you determined in Exercise 5a, convert 2000 rpm into Hertz.

6. **(Chemistry) a.** Determine the final units of the following expression, which provides the molecular weight of 1.5 moles of hydrogen peroxide:

    1.5 moles $\times$ 34.0146 grams/mole

    b. Determine the final units of the following expression, which provides the molecular weight of 5.3 moles of water:

5.3 moles × 18 grams/mole

7. **(Oceanography)** The pressure, P, exerted on an underwater object can be determined by this formula:

$P = \rho g h$

    ρ is the density of water, which is 100 kg/m^3.
    g is the acceleration caused by Earth's gravity, which is 9.8 m/s^2.
    h is the depth of the object in the water in meters.

    a. Determine the units of P by calculating the units resulting from the right side of the formula. Check that your answer corresponds to the units for pressure listed in Table 1.1.

    b. Determine the pressure on a submarine operating at a depth of 500 meters.

8. **(Thermodynamics)** The work, W, performed by a single piston in an engine can be determined by this formula:

$W = F d$

    F is the force provided by the piston in Newtons.
    d is the distance the piston moves in meters.

    a. Determine the units of W by calculating the units resulting from the right side of the formula. Check that your answer corresponds to the units for work listed in Table 1.1.

    b. Determine the work performed by a piston that provides a force of 1000 N over a distance of 15 centimeters.

1.2   Preliminary Two: Exponential and Scientific Notations

Many engineering and scientific applications require dealing with extremely large and extremely small numbers. For example, Avogadro's number, used in chemistry, has the value 602,214,179,000,000,000,000,000; the universal gravitational constant used in aerospace and rocketry applications has the value 0.0000000000667428. To make entering these numbers in a computer program easier, they can be written in a more compact form known as **exponential notation**. Similarly, in performing hand calculations for verification purposes, an equivalent representation known as **scientific notation** is typically used.

    The following examples illustrate how numbers with decimals can be expressed in both exponential and scientific notation:

Decimal Notation	Exponential Notation	Scientific Notation
1625.	1.625e3	1.625×10^3
63421.	6.3421e4	6.3421×10^4
.00731	7.31e-3	7.31×10^{-3}
.000625	6.25e-4	6.25×10^{-4}

In exponential notation, the letter e stands for exponent. The number following the e represents a power of 10 and indicates the number of places the decimal point should be moved to obtain the standard decimal value. The decimal point is moved to the right if the number after e is positive, or it's moved to the left if the number after e is negative. For example, the e3 in 1.625e3 means move the decimal place three places to the right, so the number becomes 1625. The e-3 in 7.31e-3 means move the decimal point three places to the left, so 7.31e-3 becomes .00731. Using these representations, Avogadro's number is written as 6.02214179e23 and $6.02214179 \times 10^{23}$ in exponential and scientific notation, and the universal gravitational constant is written as 6.67428e-11 in exponential notation and 6.67428×10^{-11} in scientific notation.

As noted previously, exponential notation is used to enter very large or very small numbers in a C++ program and will be used in Section 2.6, where very large numbers are required for the given application.

Using Scientific Notation

An essential part of engineering and scientific programming is understanding what formulas are to be used and verifying calculations, typically by hand. For evaluating formulas that use very large or very small numbers, which isn't uncommon in the applications you'll be programming, scientific notation is convenient. The reason is that scientific notation permits using the following two basic exponential rules, as they apply to the powers of 10:

Rule 1: $10^n \times 10^m = 10^{n+m}$ for any values, positive or negative, of n and m
Examples: $10^2 \times 10^5 = 10^7$ (that is, $100 \times 100,000 = 10,000,000$)
$\quad\quad\quad\quad 10^{-2} \times 10^5 = 10^3$ (that is, $.01 \times 100,000 = 1,000$)
$\quad\quad\quad\quad 10^2 \times 10^{-5} = 10^{-3}$ (that is, $100 \times .00001 = .001$)
$\quad\quad\quad\quad 10^{-2} \times 10^{-5} = 10^{-7}$ (that is, $.01 \times .00001 = .0000001$)
$\quad\quad\quad\quad 10^{-23} \times 10^{34} = 10^{11}$

Rule 2: $\dfrac{1}{10^{-n}} = 10^n$ for any positive or negative value of n

Examples: $\dfrac{1}{10^{-2}} = 10^2$ (that is, $\dfrac{1}{.01} = 100$)

$\quad\quad\quad\quad \dfrac{1}{10^2} = 10^{-2}$ (that is, $\dfrac{1}{100} = .01$)

$\quad\quad\quad\quad \dfrac{1}{10^{-3}} = 10^3$ (that is, $\dfrac{1}{.001} = 1000$)

$\quad\quad\quad\quad \dfrac{1}{10^4} = 10^{-4}$ (that is, $\dfrac{1}{10,000} = .0001$)

Notice that in scientific notation (as in exponential notation), if the exponent is positive, it represents the actual number of zeros that follow the 1, but if the exponent is negative, is represents one less than the number of zeros after the decimal point and before the 1.

After you understand the basic rules of using scientific notation, you can combine them easily, as shown in this computation:

$$\frac{10^2 \times 10^5}{10^4} = \frac{10^7}{10^4} = 10^7 \times 10^{-4} = 10^3$$

If scientific notation were concerned only with powers of 10, as in the preceding example, its usefulness would be extremely limited. Fortunately, however, this notation can be used with any decimal number. For example, take a look at this computation:

$$\frac{236,000 \times .345 \times 1,345,000}{67.8 \times .000007}$$

This computation is calculated more easily by first converting each number to its equivalent scientific notation, and then combining exponents (using Rules 1 and 2) as follows:

$$\frac{2.36 \times 10^5 \times 3.45 \times 10^{-1} \times 1.345 \times 10^6}{6.78 \times 10^1 \times 7.0 \times 10^{-6}} =$$

$$\frac{2.36 \times 3.45 \times 1.345 \times 10^{10}}{6.78 \times 7.0 \times 10^{-5}} =$$

$$\frac{2.36 \times 3.45 \times 1.345 \times 10^{15}}{6.78 \times 7.0}$$

Finally, the remaining numbers in the numerator can be multiplied and then divided by the numbers in the denominator to yield a final result of $.2307 \times 10^{15} = 2.307 \times 10^{14}$.

Whenever a formula contains one or more extremely small or large numbers, use the technique of first, converting the number to scientific notation, and second, dealing with the exponents and remaining numbers individually. This technique can be of great help in the final computation. (Note that converting all the numbers isn't necessary.) You'll make use of this technique often in performing hand calculations to validate results during the testing phase of a program.

Scientific Notational Symbols   Certain scientific notations occur frequently enough in science and engineering applications that they have their own symbols. The most commonly used are listed in Table 1.2.

Table 1.2   Scientific Notational Symbols

Scientific Notation	Symbol	Name
10^{-12}	p	pico
10^{-9}	n	nano
10^{-6}	μ	micro
10^{-3}	m	milli
10^3	k	kilo
10^6	M	mega
10^9	G	giga
10^{12}	T	tera

For example, the storage capacities of computer disks and thumb drives are currently specified in megabytes (MB) and gigabytes (GB), which means they contain millions (10^6) and billions (10^9) of bytes, respectively. (See Section 1.5 for the definition of a byte.)Similarly, computer processing speeds are specified in the nanosecond (nsec) range, which means a billionth (10^{-9}) of a second.

EXERCISES 1.2

1. **(Practice)** Convert the following numbers from exponential form into standard decimal form:
   a. 6.34e5

   b. 1.95162e2

   c. 8.395e1

   d. 2.95e-3

   e. 4.623e-4

2. **(Practice)** Convert the following numbers from scientific notation into standard decimal form:
   a. 2.67×10^3

   b. 2.67×10^{-3}

   c. 1.872×10^9

   d. 1.872×10^{-9}

   e. 2.67×10^3

   f. 6.6256×10^{-34} (known as Planck's constant)

3. **(Practice)** Write the following decimal numbers using scientific notation:
   a. 126

   b. 656.23

   c. 3426.95

   d. 4893.2

   e. .321

   f. .0123

   g. .006789

4. **(Practice)** Compute the following:
   a. $10^4 \times 10^{-6} \times 10^{-3} \times 10^{12}$

   b. $\dfrac{1}{10^4 \times 10^{-6} \times 10^{-3} \times 10^{12}}$

   c. $\dfrac{10^2 \times 10^7 \times 10^4}{10^4 \times 10^{-6} \times 10^{-3} \times 10^{12}}$

   d. $\dfrac{10^3 \times 10^{-7} \times 10^4}{10^{-6} \times 10^5}$

5. **(Practice)** Compute the following:
   a. $2.8 \times 10^4 \times 1.6 \times 10^{-6} \times 3.2 \times 10^{-3}$

   b. $\dfrac{1}{4.5 \times 10^4 \times 1.8 \times 10^{-6} \times 6.7 \times 10^{-3}}$

   c. $\dfrac{1.4 \times 10^2 \times 2.5 \times 10^7 \times 5.310^4}{3.2 \times 10^4 \times 1.8 \times 10^{-6} \times 2.7 \times 10^{-3}}$

   d. $\dfrac{7.1 \times 10^3 \times 8.45 \times 10^{-7} \times 3.6710^4}{9.89 \times 10^{-6} \times 6.28 \times 10^5}$

6. **(Aeronautics)** The initial acceleration, a, of a rocket fired from earth, with an initial thrust, T, is given by this formula:

$$a = \frac{T - mg}{m}$$

   a is the initial acceleration.
   T is the thrust in Newtons.
   m is the mass in kg.
   g is the acceleration caused by gravity in m/s^2.

   a. Determine the units of the initial acceleration by calculating the units resulting from the right side of the equation. (*Hint:* As listed in Table 1.1, a Newton is $N = kg - m/s^2$.)

   b. Determine the initial acceleration of a rocket having a mass of 5×10^4 kg and an initial thrust of 6×10^5 Newtons. The value of g is 9.81 m/s^2.

7. **(Heat Transfer)** The energy radiated from the surface of the sun or a planet in the solar system can be calculated by using Stephan-Boltzmann's Law:

   $E = \sigma\, T^4$

   E is the energy radiated.
   σ is Stephan-Boltzmann's constant (5.6697×10^{-8} Watts/m^{2}K^4).
   T is the surface temperature in degrees Kelvin ($^\circ K = {}^\circ C + 273$).

   a. Determine the units of E by calculating the units resulting from the right side of the formula.

   b. Determine the energy radiated from the sun's surface, given that the sun's average temperature is approximately 6,000°K.

1.3   Preliminary Three: Software Development

A computer is a machine, and like other machines, such as an automobile or a lawnmower, it must be turned on and then driven, or controlled, to perform the task it was meant to do. In an automobile, for example, control is provided by the driver, who sits inside the car and directs it. In a computer, the driver is a set of instructions called a program. More formally, a **computer program** is a self-contained set of instructions used to operate a computer to produce a specific result. Another term for a program or set of programs is software, and both terms are used interchangeably throughout this book.[1]

At its most basic level, a program is a solution developed to solve a particular problem, written in a form that can be executed on a computer. Therefore, writing a program is almost the last step in a process that first determines the problem to be solved and the method to be used in the solution. Each field of study has its own name for the systematic method of designing solutions to solve problems. In science and engineering, the approach is referred to as the **scientific method**, and in quantitative analysis, the approach is called the **systems approach**. Professional software developers use the **software development procedure** for

---

[1]More inclusively, the term "software" is also used to denote both the programs and the data on which programs operate.

understanding the problem to be solved and for creating an effective, appropriate software solution. This procedure, illustrated in Figure 1.1, consists of three overlapping phases:

1. Development and design
2. Documentation
3. Maintenance

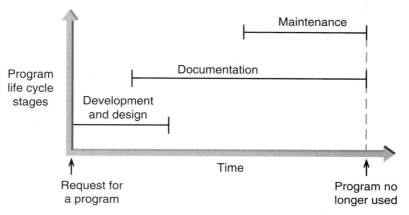

Figure 1.1   The three phases of program development

As a discipline, **software engineering** is concerned with creating readable, efficient, reliable, and maintainable programs and systems, and it uses the software development procedure to achieve this goal.

Phase I: Development and Design

Phase I begins with a statement of a problem or a specific request for a program, which is referred to as a **program requirement**. After a problem has been stated or a specific request for a program solution has been made, the development and design phase begins. This phase consists of four well-defined steps, as illustrated in Figure 1.2.

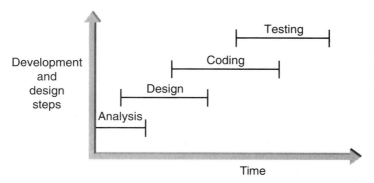

Figure 1.2   The development and design steps

Step 1 Analyze the Problem

The analysis of a problem can consist of up to two parts. The first part is a **basic analysis** that must be performed on all problems; it consists of extracting the complete input and output information supplied by the problems. For this analysis, you must

1. Determine and understand the output items the program must produce.
2. Determine the input items.

Together, these two items are referred to as the problem's **input/output (I/O)**. Only after determining a problem's I/O can you select specific steps for transforming inputs into outputs. At this point, doing a hand calculation to verify that the output(s) can indeed be obtained from the inputs is sometimes necessary and/or useful. Clearly, if you have a formula that relates inputs to the output, you can omit this step. If the required inputs are available and the desired outputs can be produced, the problem is said to be clearly defined and can be solved.

For a variety of reasons, completing a basic analysis might not be possible. If so, an extended analysis might be necessary. An **extended analysis** simply means you must gather more information about the problem so that you thoroughly understand what's being asked for and how to achieve the result. In this book, any additional information required to understand the problem is supplied along with the problem statement.

Step 2 Develop a Solution

In this step, you select the exact set of steps, called an "algorithm," to be used to solve the problem. Typically, you find the solution by a series of refinements, starting with the initial solution you find in the analysis step, until you have an acceptable and complete solution. This solution must be checked, if it wasn't done in the analysis step, to make sure it produces the required outputs correctly. The check is usually carried out by doing one or more hand calculations that haven't been done already.

For small programs, the selected solution might be extremely simple and consist of only one or more calculations. More typically, you need to refine the initial solution and organize it into smaller subsystems, with specifications for how the subsystems interface with each other. To achieve this goal, the solution's description starts from the highest level (top) requirement and proceeds downward to the parts that must be constructed to meet this requirement. To make this explanation more meaningful, consider a computer program that must track the number of parts in inventory. The required output for this program is a description of all parts carried in inventory and the number of units of each item in stock; the given inputs are the initial inventory quantity of each part, the number of items sold, the number of items returned, and the number of items purchased.

For these specifications, a designer could initially organize the program's requirements into the three sections illustrated in Figure 1.3. This figure is referred to as both a **top-level structure diagram** and a **first-level structure diagram** because it represents the first overall structure of the program the designer has selected.

After an initial structure is developed, it's refined until the tasks in the boxes are completely defined. For example, the data entry and report modules shown in Figure 1.3 would be refined further. The data entry module certainly must include provisions for entering data. Because planning for contingencies and human error is the system designer's responsibility, provisions must also be made for changing incorrect data after an entry is made and for deleting previous entries. Similar subdivisions for the report module can be made.

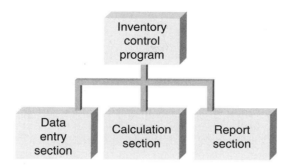

Figure 1.3   A first-level structure diagram

Figure 1.4 illustrates a **second-level structure diagram** for an inventory tracking system that includes these further refinements.

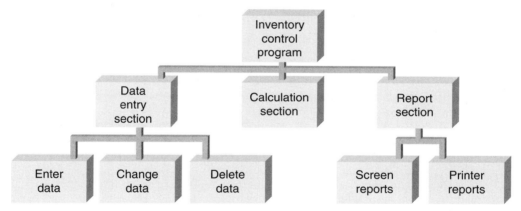

Figure 1.4   A second-level structure diagram

The process of refining a solution continues until the smallest requirement is included. Notice that the design produces a treelike structure, in which the levels branch out as you move from the top of the structure to the bottom. When the design is finished, each task designated in a box is typically coded with separate sets of instructions that are executed as they're called on by tasks higher up in the structure.

Step 3   Code the Solution (Write the Program)

This step consists of actually writing a C++ program that corresponds to the solution developed in Step 2. If the analysis and solution steps have been performed correctly, the coding step becomes rather mechanical in nature. In a well-designed program, the statements making up the program, however, conform to certain well-defined patterns or structures that have been defined in the solution step. These structures control how the program executes and consist of the following types:

- Sequence
- Selection

- Iteration
- Invocation

Sequence defines the order in which the program executes instructions. Specifying which instruction comes first, which comes second, and so on is essential if the program is to achieve a well-defined purpose.

Selection provides the capability to make a choice between different operations, depending on the result of some condition. For example, the value of a number can be checked before a division is performed: If the number is not zero, it can be used as the denominator of a division operation; otherwise, the division isn't performed and the user is issued a warning message.

Iteration, also referred to as "looping" and "repetition," makes it possible to repeat the same operation based on the value of a condition. For example, grades might be entered and added repeatedly until a negative grade is entered. In this case, the entry of a negative grade is the condition that signifies the end of the repetitive input and addition of grades. At that point, an average for all grades entered could be calculated.

Invocation involves invoking, or summoning, a set of statements as it's needed. For example, computing a person's net pay involves the tasks of obtaining pay rates and hours worked, calculating the net pay, and providing a report or check for the required amount. Each task is typically coded as a separate unit that's called into execution, or invoked, as it's needed.

Step 4   Test and Correct the Program

The purpose of testing is to verify that a program works correctly and actually fulfills its requirements. In theory, testing would reveal all existing program errors. (In computer terminology, a program error is called a **bug**.[2]) In practice, finding all errors would require checking all possible combinations of statement execution. Because of the time and effort required, this goal is usually impossible, except for extremely simple programs. (Section 4.8 explains why this goal is generally considered impossible.)

Because exhaustive testing isn't feasible for most programs, different philosophies and methods of testing have evolved. At its most basic level, however, testing requires a conscious effort to make sure a program works correctly and produces meaningful results. This effort means giving careful thought to what the test is meant to achieve and to the data used in the test. If testing reveals an error (bug), the process of debugging, which includes locating, correcting, and verifying the correction, can be initiated. Realize that although testing might reveal the presence of an error, *it doesn't necessarily indicate the absence of one.* Therefore, the fact that a test revealed one bug *does not indicate that another one isn't lurking somewhere else in the program.*

To catch and correct errors in a program, developing a set of test data for determining whether the program gives correct answers is important. In fact, often an accepted step in formal software development is to plan test procedures and create meaningful test data *before* writing the code. Doing this step first helps you be more objective about what the program must do because it circumvents the subconscious temptation after coding to avoid test data that would reveal a problem with your program. The procedures for testing a program should examine every possible situation in which the program will be used. The program should be tested with data in a reasonable range as well as at the limits and in areas where the program

---

[2]The derivation of this term is rather interesting. When a program stopped running on the Mark I at Harvard University in September 1945, Grace Hopper traced the malfunction to a dead insect that had gotten into the electrical circuits. She recorded the incident in her logbook as "Relay #70. . . . (moth) in relay. First actual case of bug being found."

should tell the user that the data is invalid. Developing good test procedures and data for sophisticated problems can be more difficult than writing the program code itself.

Table 1.3 lists the comparative amount of effort that's typically expended on each development and design step in large commercial programming projects. As this listing shows, coding is not the major effort in Phase I. Many new programmers have trouble because they spend the majority of their time writing the program and don't spend enough time understanding the problem or designing an appropriate solution. To help you avoid making the same mistake, remember the programming proverb, "It is impossible to write a successful program for a problem or application that's not fully understood." An equally valuable proverb is, "The sooner you start coding a program, the longer it usually takes to complete."

Table 1.3 Effort Expended in Phase I

Step	Effort
Analyze the problem	10%
Develop a solution	20%
Code the solution (write the program)	20%
Test the program	50%

Phase II: Documentation

Because of inadequate documentation, so much work becomes useless or lost and many tasks must be repeated, so documenting your work is one of the most important steps in problem solving. Many critical documents are created during the analysis, design, coding, and testing steps. Completing the documentation phase requires collecting these documents, adding user-operating material, and presenting documentation in a form that's most useful to you and your organization.

Although not everybody classifies them in the same way, there are five main documents for every problem solution:

- Program description
- Algorithm development and changes
- Well-commented program listing
- Sample test runs
- Users' manual

Putting yourself in the shoes of a person who might use your work—anyone from secretaries to programmers/analysts and management—should help you strive to make the content of important documentation clear. The documentation phase formally begins in the development and design phase and continues into the maintenance phase.

Phase III: Maintenance

This phase is concerned with the ongoing correction of problems, revisions to meet changing needs, and addition of new features. Maintenance is often the major effort, the primary source of revenue, and the longest lasting of the engineering phases. Development might take days or months, but maintenance could continue for years or decades. The better the documentation is, the more efficiently maintenance can be performed, and the happier customers and end users will be.

Backup

Although not part of the formal design process, making and keeping backup copies of the program at each step of the programming and debugging process are critical. Deleting or changing a program's current working version beyond recognition is all too easy. With backup copies, you can recover the last stage of work with little effort. The final working version of a useful program should be backed up at least twice. In this regard, another useful programming proverb is, "Backup is unimportant if you don't mind starting over again."

Many organizations keep at least one backup on site, where it can be retrieved easily, and another backup copy in a fireproof safe or at a remote location.

EXERCISES 1.3

N O T E | **Note:** In each of these exercises, a programming problem is given. Read the problem statement first, and then answer the questions pertaining to the problem. **Do not** attempt to write a program to solve the problems. Instead, simply answer the questions following the program specifications.

1. **(Electrical Eng.)** You've been asked to write a C++ program to calculate the total resistance of a series circuit. In this circuit, the total resistance is the sum of all individual resistance values. The circuit consists of a number of 56-ohm, 33-ohm, and 15-ohm resistors.

   a. For this programming problem, how many outputs are required?

   b. How many inputs does this problem have?

   c. Determine a formula for converting input items into output items. The number of 56-ohm resistors is m, the number of 33-ohm resistors is n, and the number of 15-ohm resistors is p.

   d. Test the formula written for Exercise 1c, using the following sample data: $m = 17$, $n = 24$, and $p = 12$.

2. **(Physics)** You've been asked to write a program to calculate the value of distance, in miles, given this relationship:

   distance = rate × elapsed time

   a. For this programming problem, how many outputs are required?

   b. How many inputs does this problem have?

   c. Determine a formula for converting input items into output items.

   d. Test the formula written for Exercise 2c, using the following sample data: *rate* is 55 miles per hour and *elapsed time* is 2.5 hours.

   e. How must the formula you determined in Exercise 2c be modified if the elapsed time is given in minutes instead of hours?

3. **(Electrical Eng.)** You've been asked to write a program that outputs the following specifications:

Voltage amplification: 35

Power output: 2.5 Watts

Bandwidth: 15 KHz

  a. For this programming problem, how many lines of output are required?

  b. How many inputs does this problem have?

  c. Determine a formula for converting input items into output items.

4. **(Physics)** You've been asked to write a C++ program to determine how far a car has traveled after 10 seconds, assuming the car is initially traveling at 60 mph and the driver applies the brakes to decelerate at a uniform rate of 12 mi/sec^2. Use the following formula:

$distance = st - (1/2)dt^2$

  s is the initial speed of the car.

  d is the deceleration.

  t is the elapsed time.

  a. For this programming problem, how many outputs are required?

  b. How many inputs does this problem have?

  c. Determine a formula for converting input items into output items.

  d. Test the formula written for Exercise 4c, using the data given in the problem.

5. **(General Math)** Consider the following programming problem: In 1627, Manhattan Island was sold to Dutch settlers for $24. If the proceeds of that sale had been deposited in a Dutch bank paying 5% interest, compounded annually, what would the principal balance be at the end of 2002? The following display is required: "Balance as of December 31, 2002 is: xxxxxx"; xxxxxx is the amount calculated by your program.

  a. For this programming problem, how many outputs are required?

  b. How many inputs does this problem have?

  c. Determine a formula for converting input items into output items.

  d. Test the formula written for Exercise 5c, using the data given in the problem statement.

6. **(Electrical Eng.)** You've been asked to write a program that calculates and displays the output voltages of two electrical circuits and the sum of the two voltages. The output voltage for the first circuit is given by this formula:

$$\frac{150\,V}{0.38\,f}$$

The output voltage for the second circuit is given by this formula:

$$\frac{230\,V}{\sqrt{56^2 + (0.98\ f)^2}}$$

  V is the input voltage to the circuit.

  f is the frequency in Hertz.

    a. For this programming problem, how many outputs are required?

    b. How many inputs does this problem have?

    c. Determine a formula for converting input items into output items.

    d. Test the formula written for Exercise 6c, using the following sample data: The first circuit is operated with an input voltage of 1.2 volts at a frequency of 144 Hertz, and the second circuit is operated with an input voltage of 2.3 volts at 100 Hertz.

7. (Statistics) Consider the following programming problem: This is the formula for the standard normal deviate, z, used in statistical applications:

$$z = (X - \mu)/\sigma$$

    X is a single value.

    μ refers to an average value.

    σ refers to a standard deviation.

Using this formula, you need to write a program that calculates and displays the value of the standard normal deviate when $X = 85.3$, $\mu = 80$, and $\sigma = 4$.

    a. For this programming problem, how many outputs are required?

    b. How many inputs does this problem have?

    c. Determine a formula for converting input items into output items.

    d. Test the formula written for Exercise 7c, using the data given in the problem.

8. (Electrical Eng.) Read the following problem statement: The electrical resistance, r, of a metal wire, in ohms, is given by this formula:

$$r = \frac{ml}{a}$$

    m is the resistivity of the metal.

    l is the length of the wire in feet.

    a is the cross-sectional area of the wire in circular mils.

Using this information, you need to write a C++ program to calculate the resistance of a wire that's 125 feet long, has a cross-sectional area of 500 circular mils, and is copper. The resistivity of copper, m, is 10.4.

    a. Determine the outputs required of the program.

    b. What inputs does the program require?

    c. What is the formula for obtaining the outputs from the inputs?

1.4 Preliminary Four: Algorithms

Before a program is written, the programmer must clearly understand what data are to be used, the desired result, and the procedure used to produce this result. As mentioned previously, the procedure, or solution, selected is referred to as an algorithm. More precisely, an **algorithm** is defined as a step-by-step sequence of instructions that must terminate and that describe how the data is to be processed to produce the desired outputs. In essence, an algorithm answers the question "What method will you use to solve this problem?"

Only after you clearly understand the data you'll be using and select an algorithm (the specific steps required to produce the desired result) can you code the program. Seen in this light, programming is the translation of a selected algorithm into a language the computer can use.

To understand how an algorithm works, consider a simple problem: A program must calculate the sum of all whole numbers from 1 through 100. Figure 1.5 illustrates three methods you could use to find the required sum. Each method constitutes an algorithm.

Method 1 - Columns: Arrange the numbers from 1 to 100 in a column and add
them

$$
\begin{array}{r}
1 \\
2 \\
3 \\
4 \\
. \\
. \\
. \\
98 \\
99 \\
+100 \\
\hline
5050
\end{array}
$$

Method 2 - Groups: Arrange the numbers in groups that sum to 101 and multiply
the number of groups by 101

$$
\left.
\begin{array}{l}
1 + 100 = 101 \\
2 + 99 = 101 \\
3 + 98 = 101 \\
4 + 97 = 101 \\
\quad . \quad . \\
\quad . \quad . \\
49 + 52 = 101 \\
50 + 51 = 101
\end{array}
\right\} \text{50 groups}
$$

$$(50 \times 101 = 5050)$$

Method 3 - Formula: Use the formula

$$\text{sum} = \frac{n(a + b)}{2}$$

where

n= number of terms to added (100)
a= first number to be added (1)
b= last number to be added (100)

$$\text{sum} = \frac{100(1 + 100)}{2} = 5050$$

Figure 1.5   Summing the numbers 1 through 100

Clearly, most people wouldn't bother to list the possible alternatives in a detailed step-by-step manner, as shown in Figure 1.5, and then select one of the algorithms to solve the problem. Most people, however, don't think algorithmically; they tend to think heuristically. For example, if you have to change a flat tire on your car, you don't think of all the steps required—you simply change the tire or call someone else to do the job. This is an example of heuristic thinking.

Unfortunately, computers don't respond to heuristic commands. A general statement such as "add the numbers from 1 to 100" means nothing to a computer because it can respond only to algorithmic commands written in a language it understands, such as C++. To program a computer successfully, you must understand this difference between algorithmic and heuristic commands. A computer is an "algorithm-responding" machine; it's not an "heuristic-responding" machine. You can't tell a computer to change a tire or to add the numbers from 1 through 100. Instead, you must give the computer a detailed, step-by-step set of instructions that collectively form an algorithm. For example, the following set of instructions forms a detailed method, or algorithm, for determining the sum of the numbers from 1 through 100:

Set n equal to 100
Set a = 1
Set b equal to 100
Calculate sum = n(a + b)/2
Print the sum

These instructions are not a computer program. Unlike a program, which must be written in a language the computer can respond to, an algorithm can be written or described in various ways. When English-like phrases are used to describe the steps in an algorithm, as in this example, the description is called **pseudocode**. When mathematical equations are used, the description is called a **formula**. When diagrams with the symbols shown in Figure 1.6 are used, the description is referred to as a **flowchart**. Figure 1.7 illustrates using these symbols to depict an algorithm for determining the average of three numbers.

Symbol	Name	Description
	Terminal	Indicates the beginning or end of a program
	Input/output	Indicates an input or output operation
	Process	Indicates computation or data manipulation
	Flow lines	Used to connect the other flowchart symbols and indicate the logic flow
	Decision	Indicates a program branch point
	Loop	Indicates the initial, limit, and increment values of a loop
	Predefined process	Indicates a predefined process, as in calling a function
	Connector	Indicates an entry to, or exit from, another part of the flowchart or a connection point
	Report	Indicates a written output report

Figure 1.6   Flowchart symbols

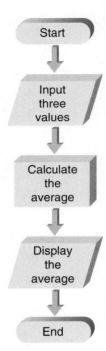

Figure 1.7   Flowchart for calculating the average of three numbers

   Because flowcharts are cumbersome to revise and can support unstructured programming practices easily, they have fallen out of favor by professional programmers. Using pseudocode to express the logic of algorithms has gained increasing acceptance. Short English phrases are used to describe an algorithm with pseudocode. Here's an example of acceptable pseudocode for describing the steps to compute the average of three numbers:

Input the three numbers into the computer's memory
Calculate the average by adding the numbers and dividing the sum by three
Display the average

As stated previously, before you can write an algorithm by using computer-language statements, you must select an algorithm and understand the required steps. Writing an algorithm by using computer-language statements is called coding the algorithm, which is the third step in the program development procedure shown in Figure 1.8. Most of Part One of this book is devoted to showing you how to develop and code algorithms into C++.

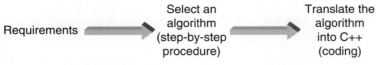

Figure 1.8   Coding an algorithm

EXERCISES 1.4

Note: There's no one correct answer for each task. This exercise is designed is to give you practice in converting heuristic commands into equivalent algorithms and making the shift between the processes involved in these two types of thinking.

1. **(Practice)** Determine a step-by-step procedure (list the steps) to do the following tasks:
   a. Fix a flat tire.
   b. Make a telephone call.
   c. Log on to a computer.
   d. Roast a turkey.

2. **(Practice)** Are the procedures you developed for Exercise 1 algorithms? Discuss why or why not.

3. **(Practice)** Determine and write an algorithm (list the steps) to interchange the contents of two cups of liquid. Assume that a third cup is available to hold the contents of either cup temporarily. Each cup should be rinsed before any new liquid is poured into it.

4. **(Electrical Eng.)** Write a detailed set of instructions in English to calculate the resistance of the following resistors connected in series: n resistors, each having a resistance of 56 ohms; m resistors, each having a resistance of 33 ohms; and p resistors, each having a resistance of 15 ohms. Note that the total resistance of resistors connected in series is the sum of all individual resistances.

5. **(Numerical)** Write a set of detailed, step-by-step instructions in English to find the smallest number in a group of three integer numbers.

6. **(Numerical) a.** Write a set of detailed, step-by-step instructions in English to calculate the fewest number of dollar bills needed to pay a bill of amount TOTAL. For example, if TOTAL is $97, the bills would consist of one $50 bill, two $20 bills, one $5 bill, and two $1 bills. (For this exercise, assume that only $100, $50, $20, $10, $5, and $1 bills are available.)
   b. Repeat Exercise 6a, but assume the bill is to be paid only in $1 bills.

7. **(Data Processing) a.** Write an algorithm to locate the first occurrence of the name JEAN in a list of names arranged in random order.
   b. Discuss how you could improve your algorithm for Exercise 7a if the list of names were arranged in alphabetical order.

8. **(Data Processing)** Determine and write an algorithm to determine the total occurrences of the letter e in any sentence.

9. **(Numerical)** Determine and write an algorithm to sort four numbers into ascending (from lowest to highest) order.

1.5   A Closer Look: Software, Hardware, and Computer Storage[3]

The process of writing a program, or software, is called **programming**, and the set of instructions used to construct a program is called a **programming language**. Programming languages come in a variety of forms and types.

Machine Language

At their most fundamental level, the only programs that can actually be used to operate a computer are **machine-language programs**. These programs, also referred to as executable programs (executables, for short), consist of a sequence of instructions composed of binary numbers, such as:[4]

```
11000000 000000000001 000000000010
11110000 000000000010 000000000011
```

Machine-language instructions consist of two parts: an instruction and an address. The instruction part, referred to as the **opcode** (short for operation code), is usually the leftmost set of bits and tells the computer the operation to be performed, such as add, subtract, multiply, and so on. The rightmost bits specify the memory addresses of the data to be used. For example, assume that the eight leftmost bits of the first instruction contain the opcode to add, and the next two groups of 12 bits are the addresses of the two operands to be added. This instruction would be a command to "add the data in memory location 1 to the data in memory location 2." Similarly, assuming that the opcode 11110000 means multiply, the next instruction is a command to "multiply the data in memory location 2 by the data in location 3."

Assembly Languages

Because each class of computers—such as IBM, Apple, and Hewlett-Packard—has its own particular machine language, writing machine-language programs is tedious and time consuming.[5] One of the first advances in programming was substituting word-like symbols, such as ADD, SUB, and MUL, for binary opcodes and using decimal numbers and labels for memory addresses. Using these symbols and decimal values for memory addresses, the previous two machine-language instructions can now be written as follows:

```
ADD 1, 2
MUL 2, 3
```

Programming languages using this type of symbolic notation are referred to as **assembly languages**. Because computers can execute only machine-language programs, the instructions in an assembly-language program must be translated into a machine-language program before they can be executed on a computer (see Figure 1.9). Translator programs that perform this function for assembly-language programs are known as **assemblers**.

---

[3]This topic can be omitted on first reading without loss of subject continuity.
[4]Converting binary to decimal numbers is explained at the end of this section.
[5]In actuality, the machine-level language is defined for the processor around which the computer is constructed.

A Closer Look: Software, Hardware,
and Computer Storage

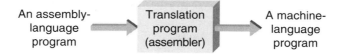

Figure 1.9   Assembly-language programs must be translated

Low- and High-Level Languages

Both machine-level and assembly languages are classified as **low-level languages** because they use instructions that are tied to one type of computer. Therefore, an assembly-language program is limited to being used only with the specific computer type for which it's written. These programs do, however, permit using special features of a particular computer type and generally execute at the fastest level possible.

In contrast, a **high-level language** uses instructions resembling written languages, such as English, and can be run on a variety of computer types. Visual Basic, C, C++, and Java are examples of high-level languages. Using C++, an instruction to add two numbers and multiply the sum by a third number can be written as follows:

```
result = (first + second) * third;
```

Programs written in a computer language (high- or low-level) are referred to as both **source programs** and **source code**. Like a low-level assembly program, after a program is written in a high-level language, it must be translated into the machine language of the computer on which it will run. This translation can be done in two ways.

When each statement in a high-level source program is translated separately and executed immediately after translation, the programming language is called an **interpreted language**, and the program doing the translation is an **interpreter**.

When all statements in a high-level source program are translated as a complete unit before any statement is executed, the programming language is called a **compiled language**. In this case, the program doing the translation is a **compiler**. Both compiled and interpreted versions of a language can exist, although one typically predominates. C++ is predominantly a compiled language.

Figure 1.10 illustrates the relationship between a C++ source program and its compilation into a machine-language executable program. As shown, the source program is entered by using an editor program, which is a word-processing program that's part of the development environment the compiler supplies. Remember, however, that you can begin entering code only after you have analyzed an application and planned the program's design carefully.

Translating the C++ source program into a machine-language program begins with the compiler. The output the compiler produces is called an **object program**, which is a machine-language version of the source code. Source code almost always makes use of existing preprogrammed code—code you have written previously or code the compiler provides, such as mathematical code for finding a square root. Additionally, a large C++ program might be stored in two or more separate program files. Any additional code must be combined with the object program before the program can be executed. It's the task of the **linker** to perform this step. The result of the linking process is a machine-language (executable) program that contains all the code your program requires and is ready for execution. The last step in the process is to load the machine-language program into the computer's main memory for actual execution.

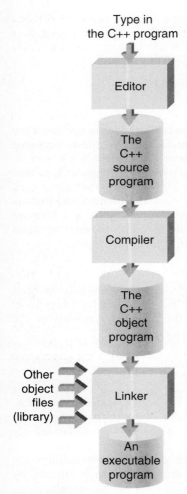

Type in
the C++ program

Editor

The
C++
source
program

Compiler

The
C++
object
program

Other
object
files
(library)

Linker

An
executable
program

Figure 1.10   Creating an
executable C++ program

Procedural and Object Orientations

In addition to being classified as high- or low-level, programming languages are classified by orientation—procedural or object oriented. In a **procedural language**, the instructions are used to create self-contained units, referred to as **procedures**. The purpose of a procedure is to accept data as input and transform the data in some manner to produce a specific result as an output. Until the 1990s, most high-level programming languages were procedural.

Currently, object orientation has taken center stage. One motivation for **object-oriented languages** was the development of graphical screens and support for graphical user interfaces (GUIs), capable of displaying windows containing both graphical shapes and text. In a GUI environment, each window can be considered an object with associated characteristics, such as color, position, and size. In an object-oriented approach, a program must first define the objects it's manipulating. This definition includes a description of the objects' general characteristics, such as initial size, shape, and color. Additionally, specific code must be supplied to manipulate each object, such as changing its size and position, and transferring data between objects. Object-oriented languages have also become more prominent because they support reusing existing code more easily, which removes the need to revalidate and retest new or modified code.

C++, which is classified as an object-oriented language, contains features of both procedural and object-oriented languages. In this book, you design and develop both types of code, which is how most current C++ programs are written. Because object-oriented C++ code always contains some procedural code, and many simple C++ programs are written entirely in procedural code, this type of code is presented in Part One of this book.

Application and System Software

Two logical categories of computer programs are application software and system software. **Application software** consists of programs written to perform particular tasks that users require. All the programs in this book are examples of application software.

System software is the collection of programs that must be readily available to any computer system for it to operate. In the computer environments of the 1950s and 1960s, users had to load system software by hand to prepare the computer to do anything at all. This software was loaded by using rows of switches on a front panel, and the commands entered by hand were said to "boot" the computer, an expression derived from "pulling yourself up by your bootstraps." Today, the so-called **bootstrap loader** is a permanent, automatically executed component of a computer's system software.

Collectively, the set of system programs used to operate and control a computer is called the **operating system (OS)**. Tasks handled by modern OSs include memory management; allocation of CPU time; control of input and output units, such as keyboards, screens, and printers; and management of secondary storage devices. Many OSs handle large programs as well as multiple users concurrently by dividing programs into segments that are moved between the disk and memory as needed. With these OSs, referred to as **multiuser systems**, more than one user can run a program on the computer. Additionally, many OSs, including most windowed environments, enable each user to run multiple programs and are called **multiprogrammed** and **multitasking** systems.

The Development of C++

The purpose of most application programs is to process data to produce specific results. In a procedural language, a program is constructed from sets of instructions, with each set referred to as a procedure, as noted previously. Each procedure moves the data one step closer to the final desired output along the path shown in Figure 1.11.

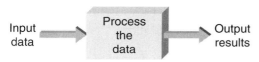

Figure 1.11 Basic procedural operations

The programming process in Figure 1.11 mirrors the input, processing, and output hardware units used to construct a computer (discussed later in "Computer Hardware"). This mirroring isn't accidental because early programming languages were designed to match and to control corresponding hardware units.

The first procedural language, FORTRAN (derived from FORmula TRANslation), was introduced in 1957 and remained popular until the early 1970s. FORTRAN has algebra-like instructions that concentrate on the processing phase shown in Figure 1.11. It was developed for scientific and engineering applications that required high-precision numerical outputs, accurate to many decimal places. For example, calculating a rocket's trajectory or the bacterial concentration level in a polluted pond, as illustrated in Figure 1.12, requires evaluating a mathematical equation to a high degree of numerical accuracy and is typical of FORTRAN-based applications.

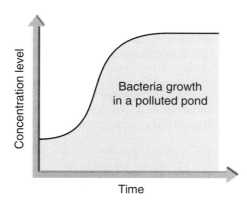

Figure 1.12 FORTRAN was developed for scientific and engineering applications

The next important high-level application language was COBOL (COmmon Business-Oriented Language), which was introduced in the 1960s and remained a major procedural language throughout the 1980s. This language had features geared toward business applications, which required simpler mathematical calculations than those for engineering applications. One of COBOL's main benefits was providing extensive output formats that made it easy to create reports containing columns of neatly formatted monetary amounts, as illustrated in Figure 1.13. It forced programmers to construct well-defined, structured procedures that followed a more consistent pattern than was required in FORTRAN.

Part No.	Description	Quantity	Price
12225	#4 Nails, Common	25 boxes	1.09
12226	#6 Nails, Common	30 boxes	1.09
12227	#8 Nails, Common	65 boxes	1.29
12228	#10 Nails, Common	57 boxes	1.35
12229	#12 Nails, Common	42 boxes	
12230	#16 Nails, Common		

Figure 1.13   COBOL was developed for business applications

Another language, BASIC (Beginners All-purpose Symbolic Instruction Code), was developed at Dartmouth College in the 1960s. BASIC was a scaled-down version of FORTRAN intended as an introductory language for college students. It was a fairly straightforward, easy-to-understand language that didn't require detailed knowledge of a specific application. Its main drawback was that it didn't require or enforce a consistent, structured approach to creating programs.

To remedy this drawback and make understanding and reusing code easier, the Pascal language (named after the 17th-century mathematician Blaise Pascal) was developed in 1971. It gave students a firmer foundation in structured programming design than early versions of BASIC did.

Structured programs are created by using a set of well-defined structures organized into separate programming sections. Each section performs a specific task that can be tested and modified without disturbing other program sections. The Pascal language was so rigidly structured, however, that escapes from the structured sections didn't exist, even when escapes would be useful. This limitation was unacceptable for many real-world projects and is one of the reasons Pascal didn't become widely accepted in scientific and engineering fields. Instead, the C language became the dominant engineering applications language of the 1980s. Ken Thompson, Dennis Ritchie, and Brian Kernighan of AT&T Bell Laboratories developed this structured, procedural language in the 1970s. C's extensive capabilities allow writing programs in a high-level language yet still accessing a computer's machine-level features directly.

Finally, C++ was developed in the early 1980s, when Bjarne Stroustrup (also at AT&T) used his simulation language background to create an object-oriented programming language. A central feature of simulation languages is that they model real-life situations as objects. This object orientation, which was ideal for graphical screen objects such as rectangles, circles, and windows, was combined with existing C features to form the C++ language. Therefore, C++ retained the extensive structured and procedural capabilities of C but added its object orientation to become a true general-purpose programming language. C++ can be used for everything from simple, interactive programs to sophisticated, complex engineering and scientific programs, within the context of a truly object-oriented structure.

A Closer Look: Software, Hardware,
and Computer Storage

Computer Hardware

All computers, from large supercomputers to desktop PCs, must be capable of at least the
following:

- Accepting input
- Displaying output
- Storing information in a logical, consistent format (traditionally binary)
- Performing arithmetic and logic operations on input or stored data
- Monitoring, controlling, and directing the computer's overall operation and sequencing

Figure 1.14 illustrates the computer components that support these capabilities and
collectively form a computer's **hardware**.

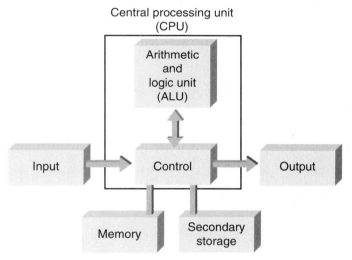

Figure 1.14   Basic hardware units of a computer

The **arithmetic and logic unit (ALU)** performs all arithmetic and logic functions, such as
addition and subtraction.

The **control unit** directs and monitors the computer's overall operation. It keeps track of
the next instruction's location in memory, issues the signals for reading data from and writing
data to other units, and controls execution of all instructions.

The **memory unit** stores information in a logical, consistent format. Typically, both
instructions and data are stored in memory, usually in separate areas.

The **input and output (I/O) units** provide the interface where peripheral devices, such as
keyboards, monitors, printers, and card readers, are attached.

Because memory in very large quantities is still expensive and volatile (meaning the
information is lost when power is turned off), it's not practical as a permanent storage area for
programs and data. **Secondary** (or auxiliary) **storage** is used for this purpose. Media such as
punched cards were used in the past, but secondary storage is now on magnetic tape,
magnetic disks, USB/flash drives, and CDs/DVDs.

In the first commercially available computers of the 1950s, hardware units were built by
using relays and vacuum tubes. These computers were enormous pieces of equipment
capable of thousands of calculations per second and cost millions of dollars.

The introduction of transistors in the 1960s reduced the size and cost of computer hardware. The transistor's small size—about one-twentieth the size of vacuum tubes—allowed manufacturers to combine the ALU with the control unit into a single unit called the **central processing unit (CPU)**. Combining the ALU and control unit made sense because most control signals that a program generates are directed to the ALU in response to arithmetic and logic instructions in the program. Combining the ALU with the control unit also simplified the interface between these two units and improved processing speed.

Integrated circuits (ICs) were introduced in the mid-1960s, which resulted in another major reduction in the space required to produce a CPU. Initially, ICs were manufactured with up to 100 transistors on a single square-centimeter chip of silicon and were called small-scale integrated (SSI) circuits. Current versions of these chips, called very large-scale integrated (VLSI) chips, can contain more than a million transistors. With VLSI chip technology, the giant computers of the 1950s could be transformed into today's desktop and notebook PCs. Each unit required to form a computer (CPU, memory, and I/O) is now manufactured on a single VLSI chip, and a single-chip CPU is referred to as a **microprocessor**. Figure 1.15 illustrates how these chips are connected internally in current desktop PCs.

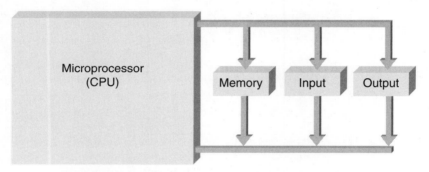

Figure 1.15   VLSI chip connections for a desktop PC

Concurrent with the remarkable reduction in hardware size has been a dramatic decrease in cost and increase in processing speeds. Computer hardware that cost more than a million dollars in 1950 can now be purchased for less than $100. If the same reductions occurred in the automobile industry, for example, a Rolls Royce could now be purchased for $10! Similarly, current computers' processing speeds have increased by a factor of thousands over their 1950s predecessors, with computational speeds now being measured in millions of instructions per second (MIPS) and billions of instructions per second (BIPS).

Computer Storage

The physical components used in manufacturing a computer preclude using the same symbols people use for numbers and letters. For example, the number 126 isn't stored with the symbols 1, 2, and 6, nor is the letter you recognize as an *A* stored with this symbol. In this section, you see why and learn how computers store numbers. In Chapter 2, you see how letters are stored.

A Closer Look: Software, Hardware,
and Computer Storage

The smallest and most basic data item in a computer is called a bit. Physically, a **bit** is actually a switch that can be open or closed. The convention followed in this book is that the open position is represented as a 0, and the closed position is represented as a 1.[6]

A single bit that can represent the values 0 and 1 has limited usefulness. All computers, therefore, group a set number of bits together for storage and transmission. Grouping 8 bits to form a larger unit, called a **byte**, is an almost universal computer standard. A single byte consisting of 8 bits, with each bit being a 0 or 1, can represent any one of 256 distinct patterns. These patterns consist of 00000000 (all eight switches open) to 11111111 (all eight switches closed) and all possible combinations of 0s and 1s in between. Each pattern can be used to represent a letter of the alphabet, a character (such as a dollar sign or comma), a single digit, or a number containing more than one digit. The collection of patterns used to represent letters, single digits, and other characters is called a **character code**. (One character code, called ASCII, is discussed in Section 2.1.) The patterns used to store numbers are called **number codes**, one of which is explained in the next section.

Twos Complement Numbers   The most common number code for storing integer values in a computer is called the **twos complement** representation. Using this code, the integer equivalent of any bit pattern, such as 10001101, is easy to determine and can be found for positive or negative integers with no change in the conversion method. For convenience, assume byte-sized bit patterns consisting of 8 bits each, although the procedure carries over to larger bit patterns.

The easiest way to determine the integer each bit pattern represents is to construct a simple device called a **value box**. Figure 1.16 shows a value box for a single byte. Mathematically, each value in this box represents an increasing power of two. Because twos complement numbers must be capable of representing both positive and negative integers, the leftmost position, in addition to having the largest absolute magnitude, has a negative sign.

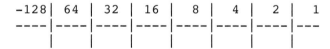

Figure 1.16   An 8-bit value box

To convert any binary number, such as 10001101, simply insert the bit pattern into the value box and add the values having 1s under them. Therefore, as illustrated in Figure 1.17, the bit pattern 10001101 represents the integer number -115.

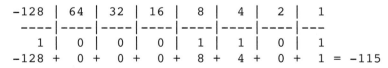

Figure 1.17   Converting 10001101 to a base 10 number.

The value box can also be used in reverse to convert a base 10 integer number into its equivalent binary bit pattern. Some conversions, in fact, can be made by inspection. For

---

[6]This convention, unfortunately, is rather arbitrary, and you often encounter the reverse, in which the open and closed positions are represented as 1 and 0, respectively.

example, the base 10 number -125 is obtained by adding 3 to -128. Therefore, the binary representation of -125 is 10000011, which equals -128 + 2 + 1. Similarly, the twos complement representation of the number 40 is 00101000, which is 32 + 8.

Although the value box conversion method is deceptively simple, it's related to the underlying mathematical basis of twos complement binary numbers. The original name of the twos complement code was the **weighted-sign code**, which correlates to the value box. As the name "weighted sign" implies, each bit position has a weight, or value, of two raised to a power and a sign. The signs of all bits except the leftmost bit are positive, and the sign of the leftmost bit is negative.

In reviewing the value box, you can see that any twos complement binary number with a leading 1 represents a negative number, and any bit pattern with a leading 0 represents a positive number. Using the value box, it's easy to determine the most positive and negative values capable of being stored. The most negative value that can be stored in a single byte is the decimal number -128, which has the bit pattern 10000000. Any other non-zero bit simply adds a positive amount to the number. Additionally, a positive number must have a 0 as its leftmost bit. From this, you can see that the largest positive 8-bit twos complement number is 01111111, or 127.

Words and Addresses   One or more bytes can be grouped into larger units, called **words**, to facilitate faster and more extensive data access. For example, retrieving a word consisting of 4 bytes from a computer's memory results in more information than retrieving a word of a single byte. This type of retrieval is also faster than four separate 1-byte retrievals. Achieving this increase in speed and capacity, however, requires increasing the computer's cost and complexity.

Early personal computers, such as the Apple IIe and Commodore, stored and transmitted words consisting of single bytes. The first IBM PCs used word sizes of 2 bytes, and more current PCs store and process words of 4 to 16 bytes each.

The number of bytes in a word determines the maximum and minimum values the word can represent. Table 1.4 lists these values for 1-, 2-, and 4-byte words (derived by using 8-, 16-, and 32-bit value boxes, respectively).

Table 1.4   Word Size and Integer Values

Word Size	Maximum Integer Value	Minimum Integer Value
1 byte	127	-128
2 bytes	32,767	-32,768
4 bytes	2,147,483,647	-2,147,483,648

In addition to representing integer values, computers must also store and transmit numbers containing decimal points, which are mathematically referred to as real numbers. The codes for real numbers, which are more complex than those for integers, are in Appendix C.

1.6 Common Programming Errors

The most common errors associated with the material in this chapter are as follows:

1. Forgetting to check that all units for numerical values used in a calculation are consistent.
2. Using an incorrect form of a conversion factor.
3. Rushing to write and run a program before fully understanding what's required, including the algorithms used to produce the required result. A symptom of this haste to get a program entered into the computer is the lack of any documentation, even a program outline or a written program. Many problems can be caught by checking a written copy of the program or even checking a description of the algorithm written in pseudocode.
4. Not backing up a program. Almost all new programmers make this mistake until they lose a program that has taken considerable time to code.
5. Not understanding that computers respond only to explicitly defined algorithms. Telling a computer to add a group of numbers is quite different from telling a friend to add the numbers. The computer must be given precise instructions in a programming language to perform the addition.

1.7 Chapter Summary

1. For a calculation to produce a correct and useful numerical value, the units corresponding to the numerical value must also be correct.

2. To determine correct forms of a conversion factor, perform a unit analysis. This means multiplying, dividing, and canceling units in the same manner as numerical values are processed.

3. The programs used to operate a computer are also referred to as software.

4. A computer program is a self-contained unit of instructions and data used to operate a computer to produce a specific result.

5. As a discipline, software engineering is concerned with creating readable, efficient, reliable, and maintainable programs and systems.

6. The software development procedure consists of three phases: program development and design, documentation, and maintenance.

7. The program development and design phase consists of four well-defined steps:

   - Analyze the problem.

   - Develop a solution.

   - Code the solution (write the program).

   - Test and correct the solution.

8. An algorithm is a step-by-step procedure that must terminate; it describes how a computation or task is to be performed.

9. The four control structures used in coding a program are sequence, selection, iteration, and invocation.

Preprogramming Projects for Chapter 1

1. (General Math) The volume of a sphere can be determined by using this formula:

$$V = 4/3\pi r^3$$

V is the volume of the sphere.

π is the dimensionless number (no units) having the value 3.1416, accurate to four decimal places.

r is the radius in centimeters (cm) of the sphere.

a. Determine the units of *V* by calculating the units resulting from the right side of the formula. Check that your answer corresponds to the units for work listed in Table 1.1.

b. Determine the volume of a sphere having a radius of 4 cm.

c. If you were required to write a computer program to determine the volume of a sphere, what inputs, outputs, and algorithm would you use?

2. (Civil Eng.) The stress placed on the fixed end of a symmetrical steel I-beam, shown in Figure 1.18, can be determined by this formula:

$$S = \frac{Ldc}{I}$$

S is the stress.

L is weight, in lbs, of the load placed on the beam.

I is the beam's rectangular moment of inertia in units of in^4.

d is the distance, in inches, the load is placed from the fixed end of the beam (technically referred to as the "moment arm").

c is one half the height, in inches, of a symmetrical beam.

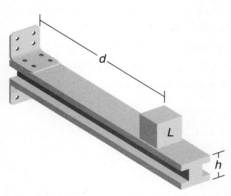

Figure 1.18 Determining the stress on an I-beam

a. Determine the units of stress, S, by calculating the units resulting from the right side of the formula.

b. For a steel beam having a rectangular moment of inertia of 21.4 in^4 and a height of 6 inches, determine the stress for a load of 700 lbs placed 8 feet from the fixed end.

c. If you were required to write a computer program to determine the stress placed on a symmetrical beam, what inputs, outputs, and algorithm would you use?

3. **(Physics)** Typically, most objects that radiate heat do so at many different wavelengths (see the Technical Note in Section 3.5 for a description of wavelength). The wavelength at which an object emits its maximum heat energy can be found by using Wein's Law:

$\lambda_{max} = W/T$

λ_{max} is the maximum wavelength.

T is the object's temperature in °K.

W is Wein's constant (2897 microns/°K).

a. Determine the units of λ_{max} by calculating the units resulting from the right side of the formula.

b. Determine the maximum heat-radiating wavelength for the sun, assuming a temperature of 6000°K.

c. If you were required to write a computer program to determine the heat radiated from a planet, what inputs, outputs, and algorithm would you use?

4. **(Physics)** The energy, E, of a photon can be determined by using this formula:

$$E = \frac{h\,c}{\lambda}$$

E is the energy of the photon.

h is known as Planck's constant and has the value 6.6256×10^{-34} Joules/sec.

c is the speed of light, which is 299,792,458 m/s.

λ is the wavelength of the light in meters.

a. Determine the units of a photon's energy, E, by calculating the units resulting from the right side of the formula.

b. Determine the energy of violet light, which has a wavelength of 5.9×10^{-6} meters.

c. If you were required to write a computer program to determine the energy of a photon of different light wavelengths (such as red, green, and so forth), what inputs, outputs, and algorithm would you use?

5. **(Eng. Mechanics)** The minimum radius, r, required of a cylindrical rod, such as that used on a bicycle pedal (see Figure 1.19), to provide enough support for the pressure exerted by the rider's foot, yet not exceed the stress placed on the crank arm's sprocket attachment, is determined by this formula:

$$r^3 = \frac{d\,P}{\pi\,S}$$

r is the radius of the cylindrical rod in inches.

d is the length of the crank arm in inches.

P is the weight placed on the pedal in lbs.

S is the stress in lbs/in^2.

a. Determine the value of r for a crank arm that's 7 inches long, must accommodate a maximum weight of 300 lbs, and be able to sustain a stress of 10,000 lbs/in^2.

b. If you were asked to write a computer program to determine the radius of the cylindrical rod for a bicycle's crank arm, what inputs, outputs, and algorithm would your program require?

Figure 1.19   Determining the radius of a bicycle's crank arm

6. **(Heat Transfer)** The following formula is used to determine the heat transferred through a flat substance, such as a wall, with its two sides maintained at different temperatures:

$$q = -k\left(\frac{T_2 - T_1}{d}\right)$$

q is the heat transfer.

k is the thermal conductivity of the substance in Watts/m°C.

T_2 is the higher temperature on one side of the substance in °C.

T_1 is the lower temperature on the other side of the wall in °C.

d is the thickness of the substance in meters.

a. Determine the units of q by calculating the units resulting from the right side of the formula.

b. For a glass window with a thickness of 0.5 centimeters, a thermal conductivity of 0.77 Watts/m°C, and outside and inside temperatures of 36.6°C and 22.2°C, respectively, determine the value of q.

c. If you were asked to write a computer program to determine the heat transfer through a substance, what inputs, outputs, and algorithm would your program require?

Engineering and Scientific Disciplines

Aeronautical/Aerospace Engineering

Among the youngest of the engineering fields, aeronautical/aerospace engineering is concerned with all aspects of designing, producing, testing, and using vehicles or devices that fly in air (aeronautical) or space (aerospace), from hang gliders to space shuttles. Because the science and engineering principles involved are so broad, aeroengineers usually specialize in a subarea that might overlap with other engineering fields, such as mechanical, metallurgical/materials, chemical, civil, or electrical engineering. These subareas include the following:

- Aerodynamics: The study of flight characteristics of various structures or configurations. Typical considerations are the drag and lift associated with airplane design or the onset of turbulent flow. A knowledge of fluid dynamics is essential. Modeling and testing all forms of aircraft are part of this subarea.
- Structural design: Designing, producing, and testing aircraft and spacecraft to withstand the wide range of in-flight demands on these vehicles, such as underwater vessels, are in the structural engineer's province.
- Propulsion systems: The design of internal combustion, jet, and liquid- and solid-fuel rocket engines and their coordination in the vehicle's overall design. Rocket engines, especially, require innovative engineering to accommodate the extreme temperatures of storing, mixing, and burning fuels such as liquid oxygen.
- Instrumentation and guidance: The aerospace industry has been a leader in developing and using solid-state electronics in the form of microprocessors to monitor and adjust the operations of hundreds of aircraft and spacecraft functions. This field uses the expertise of both electrical engineers and aeroengineers.
- Navigation: Computing orbits within and outside the atmosphere and determining the orientation of a vehicle with respect to points on Earth or in space.

Chapter

2

Problem Solving Using C++

An integral part of a building's design is its structure, and the same is true for a program. Constructing well-designed C++ programs depends on careful planning and execution, if the final design is to ensure that the completed program accomplishes its intended purpose. A central element of this planning is using modular program design, which is explained in Section 2.1. In this chapter, you also learn about different types of data and how to process them in the context of a complete C++ program.

2.1 Introduction to C++

A well-designed program is constructed by using a design philosophy similar to one for constructing a well-designed building. It doesn't just happen; it depends on careful planning and execution, if the final design is to accomplish its intended purpose.

As with buildings, an integral part of designing a program is its structure. Programs with a structure consisting of interrelated segments (called **modules**), arranged in a logical, easily understandable order to form an integrated and complete unit, are referred to as **modular**

programs (see Figure 2.1). Modular programs are easier to develop, correct, and modify than programs constructed in some other manner.

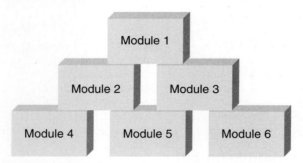

Figure 2.1   A well-designed program is built by using modules

Each module is designed and developed to perform a specific task and is actually a small subprogram. A complete C++ program is constructed by combining as many modules as necessary to produce the desired result. The advantage of modular construction is that you can develop the program's overall design before writing any modules. After finalizing requirements for each module, you can then program the modules and integrate them into the overall program as they're completed.

In C++, modules can be classes or functions. It helps to think of a **function** as a small machine that transforms the data it receives into a finished product. For example, Figure 2.2 illustrates a function that accepts two numbers as inputs and multiplies the two numbers to produce one output. The process of converting inputs to results is encapsulated and hidden in the function. In this regard, the function can be thought of as a single unit providing a special-purpose operation.

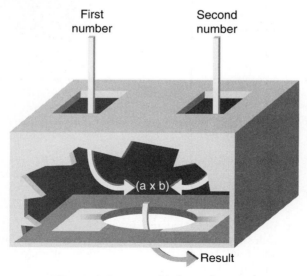

Figure 2.2   A multiplying function

A similar analogy is suitable for a **class**, although it's a more complicated unit because it contains both data and functions for manipulating the data. Unlike a function, used to encapsulate a set of operations, a class encapsulates both data and sets of operations. Each class contains all the elements required for input, output, and processing its objects and can be thought of as a small factory containing raw material (the data) and machines (the functions). In the first part of this book, however, you're focusing on the more basic function module. Although you'll also use capabilities provided by classes, it's in Part Two that you learn how to construct and program your own classes.

An important requirement for designing a good function is giving it a name that conveys some idea of what the function does. The names allowed for functions are also used to name other elements of the C++ language and are collectively referred to as **identifiers**. Identifiers can be made up of any combination of letters, digits, or underscores (_) selected according to the following rules:

1. The first character of the name must be a letter or an underscore.
2. Only letters, digits, or underscores can follow the first letter. Also, blank spaces aren't allowed to separate words in a function name; either use the underscore to separate words, or capitalize the first letter of words after the first word.
3. A function name can't be one of the keywords listed in Table 2.1. (A **keyword** is a word the language sets aside for a special purpose and can be used only in a specified manner.[1])
4. The maximum number of characters in a function name is 1024.[2]

Table 2.1 Keywords in C++

auto	delete	goto	public	this
break	do	if	register	template
case	double	inline	return	typedef
catch	else	int	short	union
char	enum	long	signed	unsigned
class	extern	new	sizeof	virtual
const	float	overload	static	void
continue	for	private	struct	volatile
default	friend	protected	switch	while

Examples of valid C++ identifiers are the following:

```
degToRad     intersect    addNums     slope
bessel1      multTwo      findMax     density
```

These are examples of invalid identifiers:

```
1AB3          Begins with a number, which violates rule 1.
E*6           Contains a special character, which violates rule 2.
while         Consists of a keyword, which violates rule 3.
```

---

[1] Keywords in C++ are also reserved words, which means they must be used only for their specified purpose. Attempting to use them for any other purpose generates an error message.
[2] The ANSI standard requires that C++ compilers provide at least this number of characters.

In addition to conforming to C++'s identifier rules, a C++ function name must always be followed by parentheses. Also, a good function name should be a **mnemonic** (pronounced "knee-*mon*-ic"), which is a word designed as a memory aid. For example, the function name degToRad() is a mnemonic for a function that converts degrees to radians. The name helps identify what the function does. Function names that aren't mnemonics should not be used because they convey no information about what the function does. Here are some examples of valid function names that aren't mnemonics:

```
easy()    c3po()    r2d2()    theForce()    mike()
```

Function names can also consist of mixed uppercase and lowercase letters, as in theForce(). This convention is becoming increasingly common in C++, although it's not necessary. Identifiers in all uppercase letters are usually reserved for symbolic constants, covered in Section 3.5.

If you do mix uppercase and lowercase letters, be aware that C++ is a **case-sensitive** language, meaning the compiler distinguishes between uppercase and lowercase letters. Therefore, in C++, the names TOTAL, total, and TotaL are three different identifiers.

The **main()** Function

As mentioned, a distinct advantage of using functions—and, as you see in Part Two, classes—is that you can plan the program's overall structure in advance. You can also test and verify each function's operation separately to make sure it meets its objectives.

For functions to be placed and executed in an orderly fashion, each C++ program must have one, and only one, function named main(). The main() function is referred to as a **driver function** because it tells other functions the sequence in which they execute (see Figure 2.3).[3]

Figure 2.4 shows the main() function's structure. The first line of the function—in this case, int main()—is referred to as a **function header**. This line is always the first line of a function and contains three pieces of information:

- What type of data, if any, is returned from the function
- The name of the function
- What type of data, if any, is sent to the function

The keyword before the function name defines the type of value the function returns when it has finished operating. When placed before the function's name, the keyword int (listed in Table 2.1) means the function returns an integer value. Similarly, when the parentheses following the function name are empty, no data is transmitted to the function when it runs. (Data transmitted to a function at runtime is referred to as **arguments** of the function.) The braces, { and }, determine the beginning and end of the function body and enclose the statements making up the function. The statements inside the braces determine what the function does, and each statement must end with a semicolon (;).

You'll be naming and writing many of your own C++ functions. In fact, the rest of Part One is primarily about the statements required to construct useful functions and how to combine functions and data into useful classes and programs. Each program, however, must have one and only one main() function. Until you learn how to pass data to a function and return data from

---

[3]Functions executed from main() can, in turn, execute other functions. Each function, however, always returns to the function that initiated its execution. This is true even for main(), which returns control to the operating system that was in effect when main() was initiated.

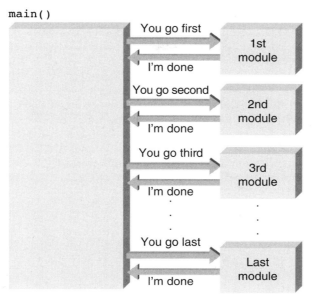

Figure 2.3 The `main()` function directs all other functions

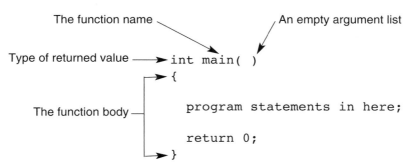

Figure 2.4 The structure of a `main()` function

a function (the topics of Chapter 6), the function header shown in Figure 2.4 serves for all the programs you need to write. For simple programs, the first two lines

```
int main()
{
```

simply designate that "the program begins here," and the last two lines

```
return 0;
}
```

designate the end of the program. Fortunately, many useful functions and classes have already been written for you. Next, you see how to use an object created from one of these classes to create your first working C++ program.

The cout Object

One of the most versatile and commonly used C++ resources is an object named cout (pronounced "see out" and derived from *c*onsole *out*put).[4] It's an output object that sends data it receives to the standard display device. For most systems, this display device is a computer screen. For example, if the data Hello there world! is sent to cout, this data is displayed on your screen. To send the data Hello there world! to the cout object, enclose the text in quotation marks ("text in here") and place the insertion symbol, <<, after the object's name and before the message, as shown in this line:

```
cout << "Hello there world!";
```

Now you see how to put all this together into a working C++ program, Program 2.1, that can be run on your computer.

Program 2.1

```
#include <iostream>
using namespace std;

int main()
{
  cout << "Hello there world!";

  return 0;
}
```

The first line of the program is a preprocessor command that uses the reserved word include:

```
#include <iostream>
```

Preprocessor commands begin with a pound sign (#) and perform some action before the compiler translates the source program into machine code. Specifically, the #include preprocessor command causes the contents of the named file—in this case, iostream—to be inserted wherever the #include command appears in the program. The iostream file is part of the standard library that contains, among other code, two classes: istream and ostream. These two classes provide data declarations and methods for data input and output, respectively. The iostream file is called a **header file** because a reference to it is always placed at the top, or head, of a C++ program by using the #include command. You might be wondering what the iostream file has to do with this simple program. The answer is that the cout object is created from the ostream class. Therefore, the iostream header file must be included in all programs using cout. As shown in Program 2.1, preprocessor commands don't end with a semicolon.

---

[4]The cout object is formally created for the ostream class, which is described in detail in Chapter 8.

Point of Information

What Is Syntax?

A programming language's **syntax** is the set of rules for formulating statements that are grammatically correct for the language. In practice, it means a C++ statement with correct syntax has the proper form specified for the compiler. If statements are in the proper form, the compiler accepts them and doesn't generate an error message.

Note, however, that a statement or program can be syntactically correct yet logically incorrect. In other words, the statement or program is structured correctly but produces an incorrect result. It's similar to an English statement that's grammatically correct but makes no sense, such as "The tree is a ragged cat."

Following the preprocessor `#include` command is a statement containing the reserved word `using`. The following statement, for example, tells the compiler where to look to find header files in the absence of an explicit designation:

```
using namespace std;
```

You can think of a **namespace** as a section of source code the compiler accesses when it's looking for prewritten classes or functions. Because the `iostream` header file is contained in a namespace named `std` (for the standard library), the compiler automatically uses `iostream`'s `cout` object from this namespace whenever `cout` is referenced. By using namespaces, you can create your own classes and functions with the same names the standard library provides and place them in differently named namespaces. You can then tell the program which class or function to use by specifying the namespace where you want the compiler to look for the class or function. In Chapter 9, you learn how to create your own namespaces. For now, you'll use the classes and functions provided by the `std` namespace.

The `using` statement is followed by the start of the program's `main()` function, which begins with the function header described previously. The body of the function, enclosed in braces, consists of only two statements. The first statement in `main()` sends one message to the `cout` object: the string `"Hello there world!"`.

Because `cout` is an object of a prewritten class, you don't have to create it; it's available for use just by activating it correctly. Like all C++ objects, `cout` can perform only certain well-defined actions. For `cout`, the action is to assemble data for output display. When a string of characters is sent to `cout`, the object makes sure the string is displayed onscreen correctly, as shown in this output from Program 2.1:

```
Hello there world!
```

Strings in C++ are any combination of letters, numbers, and special characters enclosed in quotation marks (`"string in here"`). The quotation marks delimit (mark) the beginning and ending of the string and aren't considered part of the string. Therefore, the string of characters making up the message sent to cout must be enclosed in quotation marks, as was done in Program 2.1.

Now examine another program to understand cout's versatility. Read Program 2.2 to determine what it does.

 Program 2.2

```
#include <iostream>
using namespace std;

int main()
{
    cout << "Computers, computers everywhere";
    cout << "\n   as far as I can C";

    return 0;
}
```

When Program 2.2 is run, the following is displayed:

```
Computers, computers everywhere
    as far as I can C
```

You might be wondering why the \n didn't appear in the output. The characters \ and n, when used together, are called a **newline escape sequence**. They tell cout to send instructions to the display device to move to the beginning of a new line. Otherwise, the second cout statement would simply append its characters to the previous statement's characters; it doesn't start on a new line by itself. In C++, the backslash (\) character provides an "escape" from the normal interpretation of the character following it and alters its meaning—in this case, the n. If the backslash were omitted from the second cout statement in Program 2.2, the n would be printed as the letter "n" and the program would output the following:

```
Computers, computers everywheren   as far as I can C
```

Newline escape sequences can be placed anywhere in the message sent to cout. See whether you can determine the display Program 2.3 produces.

Program 2.3

```cpp
#include <iostream>
using namespace std;

int main()
{
  cout << "Computers everywhere\n as far as\n\nI can see";

  return 0;
}
```

This is the output for Program 2.3:

```
Computers everywhere
 as far as

I can see
```

EXERCISES 2.1

1. **(Practice)** State whether the following are valid function names and if so, whether they're mnemonic names that convey some idea of the function's purpose. If they are invalid names, state why.

power	density	m1234	newamp	1234	abcd
total	tangent	absval	computed	b34a	34ab
volts$	a2B3	while	minVal	sine	$sine
cosine	speed	netdistance	sum	return	stack

2. **(Practice)** Assume the following functions have been written:

   getLength(), getWidth(), calcArea(), displayArea()

   a. From the functions' names, what do you think each function might do?

   b. In what order do you think a main() function might execute these functions (based on their names)?

3. **(Practice)** Assume the following functions have been written:

   speed(), distance(), acceleration()

   From the functions' names, what do you think each function might do?

4. (Practice) Determine names for functions that do the following:

   a. Find the average of a set of numbers.

   b. Find the area of a rectangle.

   c. Find the minimum value in a set of numbers.

   d. Find the density of a steel door.

   e. Sort a set of numbers from lowest to highest.

5. (Program) a. Using cout, write a C++ program that displays your name on one line, your street address on a second line, and your city, state, and zip code on a third line.

   b. Run the program you have written for Exercise 5a. (*Note*: You must understand the procedures for entering and running a C++ program on the particular computer installation you're using.)

6. (Program) a. Write a C++ program to display the following output:

```
The cosecant of an angle
   is equal to one over
      the sine of the angle.
```

   b. Compile and run the program you have written for Exercise 6a.

7. (Program) a. How many cout statements would you use to display the following output?

```
Degrees    Radians
0          0.0000
90         1.5708
180        3.1416
270        4.7124
360        6.2832
```

   b. What's the minimum number of cout statements that could be used to print the output in Exercise 7a?

   c. Write a complete C++ program to produce the output shown in Exercise 7a.

   d. Run the program you have written for Exercise 7c.

8. (Program) a. Assuming your compiler isn't case sensitive, determine which of these program unit names are equivalent:

```
AVERAG    averag    MODE    BESSEL    Mode
Total     besseL    TeMp    Densty    TEMP
denSTY    MEAN      total   mean      mode
```

   b. Redo Exercise 8a, assuming a case-sensitive compiler.

Project Structuring Exercises

Most projects, both programming and nonprogramming, can usually be structured into smaller subtasks or units of activity. These smaller subtasks can often be delegated to different people so that when all the tasks are finished and integrated, the project or program is completed. For Exercises 9 through 14, determine a set of subtasks that, performed together, complete the project. Be aware that each exercise has many possible solutions. The only requirement is that the set of subtasks, when performed together, complete the required task.

> **Note:** The purpose of these exercises is to have you consider the different ways that complex tasks can be structured. Although there's no one correct solution to these exercises, there are incorrect solutions and solutions that are better than others. An incorrect solution is one that doesn't fully specify the task. One solution is better than another if it more clearly or easily identifies what must be done.

9. **(Practice)** You're given the task of wiring and installing lights in your attic. Determine a set of subtasks to accomplish this task. (*Hint*: The first subtask is determining the placement of light fixtures.)

10. **(Practice)** You're given the job of preparing a complete meal for five people next weekend. Determine a set of subtasks to accomplish this task. (*Hint*: One subtask, not necessarily the first, is buying the food.)

11. **(Practice)** You're a sophomore in college and are planning to go to graduate school for a master's degree in electrical engineering after you graduate. List a set of major objectives you must fulfill to meet this goal. (*Hint*: One subtask is "Determine the correct courses to take.")

12. **(Practice)** You're given the job of planting a vegetable garden. Determine a set of subtasks to accomplish this task. (*Hint*: One subtask is planning the garden's layout.)

13. **(Practice)** You're responsible for planning and arranging the family camping trip this summer. List a set of subtasks to accomplish this task. (*Hint*: One subtask is selecting the campsite.)

14. **(Data Processing) a.** A national medical testing laboratory wants a new computer system to analyze its test results. The system must be capable of processing each day's results as well as retrieving and outputting a printed report of all results meeting certain criteria, such as all results for a particular doctor or for hospitals in a certain state. Determine three or four major program units into which this system could be separated. (*Hint*: One possible program unit is "Prepare Daily Results" to create each day's reports.)

    b. Suppose someone enters incorrect data for a test result, and the error is discovered after the system has entered and stored the data. What program unit is needed to correct this problem? Discuss why such a program unit might or might not be required by most systems.

    c. Assume a program unit exists that allows users to change data that has been entered and stored incorrectly. Discuss the need for including an "audit trail" that would allow reconstructing the changes later as well as when they were made and who made them.

2.2 Programming Style

C++ programs start execution at the beginning of the `main()` function. Because a program can have only one starting point, every C++ program must contain one and only one `main()` function. As you have seen, all the statements making up the `main()` function are then included within the braces following the function name. Although the `main()` function must be present in every C++ program, C++ doesn't require placing the word `main`, the parentheses, or the braces in any particular form. The form used in the previous section

```
int main()
{
  program statements in here;

  return 0;
}
```

was chosen strictly for clarity and ease in reading the program but is not required. For example, the following general form of a `main()` function would also work:

```
int main
  (
  ) { first statement;second statement;
          third statement;fourth
statement;
return 0;}
```

Notice that you can put more than one statement on a line or place a statement on more than one line. Except for strings, quotation marks, identifiers, and keywords, C++ ignores all **white space**. (White space refers to any combination of blank spaces, tabs, or new lines.) For example, changing the white space in Program 2.1 and making sure not to split the string Hello there world! across two lines results in the following valid program:

```
#include <iostream>
using namespace std;
int main
(
){
cout <<
"Hello there world!";
  return 0;
}
```

Although this version of `main()` does work, it's an example of poor programming style because it's difficult to read and understand. For readability, the `main()` function should always be written in this standard form:

```
int main()
{
  program statements in here;

  return 0;
}
```

In this standard form, the function name starts at the left margin (call this column 1) and is placed with the required parentheses on a line by itself. The opening brace of the function body follows in column 1 on the next line, directly under the first letter of the line containing the function's name. Similarly, the closing function brace is placed by itself in column 1 (lined up with the opening brace) as the last line of the function. This structure highlights the function as a single unit.

Within the function, all program statements are indented at least two spaces. Indentation is another sign of good programming practice, especially if the same indentation is used for similar groups of statements. Review Program 2.2 to see that the same indentation was used for both `cout` statements.

As you progress in your understanding and mastery of C++, you'll develop your own indentation standards. Just keep in mind that the final form of your programs should be consistent and always aid others in reading and understanding your programs.

Comments

Comments are explanatory remarks made in a program. When used carefully, comments can be helpful in clarifying the overall program's purpose, explaining what a group of statements is meant to accomplish, or explaining what one line is intended to do. C++ supports two types of comments: line and block. Both types can be placed anywhere in a program and have no effect on program execution. The compiler ignores all comments—they are there strictly for the convenience of anyone reading the program.

A **line comment** begins with two slashes (//) and continues to the end of the line. For example, the following examples are line comments:

```
// this is a comment
// this program prints out a message
// this program calculates a square root
```

The symbols //, with no white space between them, designate the start of the line comment. The end of the line on which the comment is written designates the end of the comment. A line comment can be written on a line by itself or at the end of the line containing a program statement. Program 2.4 shows using line comments in a program.

Program 2.4

```
// this program displays a message
#include <iostream>
using namespace std;

int main()
{
   cout << "Hello there world!"; // this produces the display

   return 0;
}
```

The first comment appears on a line by itself at the top of the program, and this location is a good one for a comment describing the program's purpose. If more comments are required, they can be placed one per line, as with the comment after the cout statement. When a comment is too long to be contained on one line, it can be separated into two or more line comments, with each comment preceded by the // symbol. For example, the following comment generates a C++ error message because the second line doesn't start with the // symbol:

```
// this comment is invalid because it
   extends over two lines
```

This comment is correct, written as follows:

```
// this comment is used to illustrate a
// comment that extends across two lines
```

Comments that span two or more lines are, however, more conveniently written as C-type **block comments**, which begin with the symbols /* and end with the symbols */, as in this example:

```
/* This is a block comment that
   spans
   three lines */
```

In C++, a program's structure is intended to make it readable and understandable, so extensive comments aren't necessary. This guideline is reinforced by carefully selecting function names to convey their purpose, as discussed previously. However, if the program element's purpose still isn't clear from its structure, name, or context, include comments where clarification is needed.

Obscure code with no comments is a sure sign of bad programming, especially when other people must maintain or read the program. Similarly, excessive comments are a sign of bad programming because not enough thought was given to making the code self-explanatory. Typically, any program you write should begin with comments including a short program description, your name, and the date the program was written or last modified. For space considerations and because all programs in this book were written by the author, these initial comments are used only for short program descriptions when they aren't provided as part of the accompanying text.

EXERCISES 2.2

1. **(Debug) a.** Will the following program work?

```
#include <iostream>
using namespace std;
int main() {cout << "Hello there world!"; return 0;}
```

b. Even if the program in Exercise 1a works, explain why it's not a good program.

2. **(Modify)** Rewrite the following programs to conform to good programming practice and correct syntax:

   a.
```
#include <iostream>
   int main(
   ) {
   cout            <<
   "The time has come"
   ; return 0;}
```

   b.
```
#include <iostream>
   using namespace std;   int main
       (    ) {cout << "Newark is a city\n";cout <<
```

```
      "In New Jersey\n"; cout <<
      "It is also a city\n"
      ; cout << "In Delaware\n"
      ; return 0;}
```

c.
```
   #include <iostream>
   using namespace std;
    int main() {cout << Reading a program\n";cout <<
    "is much easier\n"
    ; cout << "if a standard form for main is used\n")
    ; cout
    <<"and each statement is written\n";cout
    <<           "on a line by itself\n")
    ; return 0;}
```

d.
```
   #include <iostream.h>
   using namespace std;
    int main
    (     ){ cout << "Every C++ program"
    ; cout
    <<"\nmust have one and only one"
    ;
    cout << "main function"
    ;
    cout <<
    "\n the escape sequence of characters")
    ; cout <<
       "\nfor a newline can be placed anywhere"
    ; cout
    <<"\n within the message passed to cout"
    ; return 0;}
```

3. **(For Thought) a.** When used in a message, the backslash character alters the meaning of the character immediately following it. If you want to print the backslash character, you have to tell cout to escape from the way it normally interprets the backslash. What character do you think is used to alter the way a single backslash character is interpreted?

   b. Using your answer to Exercise 3a, write the escape sequence for printing a backslash.

4. **(For Thought) a.** A **token** of a computer language is any sequence of characters, with no intervening characters or white space, that taken as a unit has a unique meaning. Using this definition of a token, determine whether escape sequences, function names, and the keywords listed in Table 2.1 are tokens of the C++ language.

   b. Discuss whether adding white space to a message alters the message and whether messages can be considered tokens of C++.

   c. Using the definition of a token in Exercise 4a, determine whether the following statement is true: "Except for tokens of the language, C++ ignores all white space."

2.3 Data Types

The objective of all programs is to process data, be it numerical, alphabetical, audio, or video. Central to this objective is classifying data into specific types. For example, calculating a rocket's trajectory requires mathematical operations on numerical data, and alphabetizing a list of names requires comparison operations on character-based data. Additionally, some operations aren't applicable to certain types of data. For example, it makes no sense to add names together. To prevent programmers from attempting to perform an inappropriate operation, C++ allows performing only certain operations on certain data types.

The types of data permitted and the operations allowed for each type are referred to as a **data type**. Formally, a data type is defined as a set of values and a set of operations that can be applied to these values. For example, the set of all integer (whole) numbers constitutes a set of values, as does the set of all real numbers (numbers containing a decimal point). These two sets of numbers, however, don't constitute a data type until a set of operations is included—in these examples, mathematical and comparison operations. The combination of a set of values plus operations becomes a true data type.

C++ categorizes data types in two basic groupings: class data types and built-in data types. A **class data type** (referred to as a "class," for short) is a programmer-created data type, which means the programmer defines the acceptable values and operations, using C++ code. This data type is discussed in Part Two.

A **built-in data type** is provided as part of the C++ compiler and requires no external C++ code. Therefore, a built-in data type can be used without supplementary additions, such as the `iostream` header file for the `cout` object. Built-in data types, also referred to as **primitive types**, consist of the basic numerical types shown in Figure 2.5 and the operations listed in Table 2.2. As shown in this table, most operations for built-in data types are designated as symbols. For class data types, most operations are provided as functions.

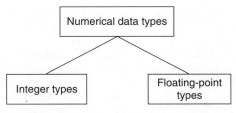

Figure 2.5 Built-in data types

Table 2.2 Built-in Data Type Operations

Built-in Data Type	Operations
Integer	`+, -, *, /, %, =, ==, !=, <=, >=, sizeof()`, and bit operations (see Chapter 15)
Floating point	`+, -, *, /, =, ==, !=, <=, >=, sizeof()`

To introduce C++'s built-in data types, literals are used. A **literal** is an acceptable value for a data type. The term "literal" in this context means the value identifies itself. (Another name for a literal is a **literal value** or **constant**.) For example, all numbers, such as 2, 3.6, and -8.2, are referred to as literal values because they literally display their values. Text, such as `"Hello World!"`, is also a literal value because the text is displayed. You have been using literal values throughout your life but have known them as numbers and words. In Section 2.5, you see some examples of non-literal values—those that don't display themselves but are stored and accessed by using identifiers.

Integer Data Types

C++ provides nine built-in integer data types, as shown in Figure 2.6. The essential difference between these integer data types is the amount of storage used for each type, which affects the range of values each type is capable of representing. The three most important and common types used in most applications are int, char, and bool. The other types were provided to accommodate special situations (such as a small or large range of numbers) and have been retained for historical reasons. They enabled programmers to maximize memory usage by selecting the data type using the smallest amount of memory, consistent with an application's requirements. When computer memories were small, compared with today's computers, and expensive, the amount of memory used was a major concern. Although no longer a concern for most programs, these types still allow programmers to optimize memory usage when necessary, typically in special-purpose digital control systems used in home appliances and automobiles.

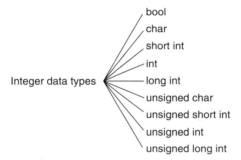

Integer data types

- bool
- char
- short int
- int
- long int
- unsigned char
- unsigned short int
- unsigned int
- unsigned long int

Figure 2.6 C++ integer data types

The int Data Type The values supported by the int data type are whole numbers, mathematically known as **integers**. An integer value consists of digits only and can optionally be preceded by a plus (+) or minus (-) sign. Therefore, an integer value can be the number 0 or any positive or negative number without a decimal point, as shown in these examples of valid integers:

```
0    5    -10    +25    1000    253    -26351    +36
```

As these examples illustrate, integers can contain a sign. However, no commas, decimal points, or special symbols, such as the dollar sign, are allowed, as in these examples of invalid integers:

```
$255.62    2,523    3.    6,243,892    1,492.89    +6.0
```

Compilers differ in their internal limits on the largest (most positive) and smallest (most negative) integer values that can be stored in each data type.[5] The most common storage

---

[5]The limits imposed by the compiler are found in the limits header file and defined as the hexadecimal constants int_max and int_min.

allocation is 4 bytes for the int data type, which restricts the values used to represent integers from -2,147,483,648 to 2,147,483,647.[6]

The char Data Type   The char data type is used to store single characters, including the letters of the alphabet (uppercase and lowercase), the digits 0 through 9, and special symbols, such as + $. , - and !. A character value is any single letter, digit, or special symbol enclosed by single quotation marks, as shown in these examples:

'A'   '$'   'b'   '7'   'y'   '!'   'M'   'q'

Character values are typically stored in a computer by using ASCII or Unicode codes. The ASCII (American Standard Code for Information Interchange, pronounced "*as*-key") code provides codes for the English-language character set plus codes for printer and display control, such as newline and printer paper eject codes. Each character code is contained in a single byte, which provides 256 distinct codes. Table 2.3 lists the ASCII byte codes for uppercase letters.

Additionally, C++ provides for the newer Unicode code that uses 2 bytes per character and can represent 65,536 characters. This code is used for international applications because it includes character sets for other languages in addition to English. As the first 256 Unicode codes have the same numerical value as the 256 ASCII codes (the additional byte is coded with all 0s), you needn't be concerned with which storage code to use with English-language characters.

Table 2.3   The ASCII Uppercase Letter Codes

Letter	ASCII Code	Letter	ASCII Code
A	01000001	N	01001111
B	01000010	O	01001110
C	01000011	P	01010000
D	01000100	Q	01010001
E	01000101	R	01010010
F	01000110	S	01010011
G	01000111	T	01010100
H	01001000	U	01010101
I	01001001	V	01010110
J	01001010	W	01010111
K	01001011	X	01011000
L	01001100	Y	01011001
M	01001101	Z	01011010

Using Table 2.3, you can determine how the characters 'B', 'A', 'R', 'T', 'E', and 'R', for example, are stored in a computer by using ASCII codes. This sequence of six characters requires 6 bytes of storage (1 byte for each letter) and is stored as illustrated in Figure 2.7.

---

[6]The most negative number is always one higher than the most positive number. Effectively, the "lost" positive number is used for the number 0. (See the twos complement method of integer storage, described in Section 1.6.)

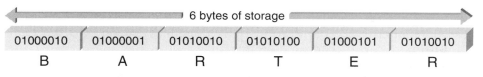

Figure 2.7 The letters BARTER stored in a computer

The Escape Character As you've seen in Section 2.1, the backslash (\) has a special meaning in C++ as the escape character. When a backslash is placed in front of a group of characters, it tells the compiler to escape from the way these characters are normally interpreted. The combination of a backslash and these characters is called an **escape sequence**. Table 2.4 lists C++'s most common escape sequences.

Table 2.4 Escape Sequences

Escape Sequence	Character Represented	Meaning	ASCII Code
\n	Newline	Move to a new line	00001010
\t	Horizontal tab	Move to the next horizontal tab setting	00001001
\v	Vertical tab	Move to the next vertical tab setting	00001011
\b	Backspace	Move back one space	00001000
\r	Carriage return	Move the cursor to the start of the current line; used for overprinting	00001101
\f	Form feed	Issue a form feed	00001100
\a	Alert	Issue an alert (usually a bell sound)	00000111
\\	Backslash	Insert a backslash character (used to place an actual backslash character in a string)	01011100
\?	Question mark	Insert a question mark character	00111111
\'	Single quotation	Insert a single-quote character (used to place an inner single quote within a set of outer single quotes)	00100111

Table 2.4   Escape Sequences (continued)

Escape Sequence	Character Represented	Meaning	ASCII Code
\ "	Double quotation	Insert a double-quote character (used to place an inner double quote within a set of outer double quotes)	00100010
\nnn	Octal number	Consider the number nnn (n is a digit) an octal number	Dependent on nnn
\xhhhh	Hexadecimal number	Consider the number hhhh (h is a digit) a hexadecimal number	Dependent on hhhh
\0	Null character	Insert the null character, which is defined as having the value 0	00000000

Although each escape sequence in Table 2.4 is made up of two characters, the combination of these characters, with no intervening white space, causes the compiler to create the single ASCII code listed in the table.

The bool Data Type   In C++, the bool data type is used to represent Boolean (logical) data, so it's restricted to one of two values: true or false. This data type is most useful when a program must examine a condition and take a prescribed course of action, based on whether the condition is true or false. For example, in a sales application, the condition being examined might be "is the total purchase for $100 or more." Only when this condition is true is a discount applied. Because the bool data type uses an integer storage code, however, it has useful implications that most professional C++ programmers utilize. The practical uses of Boolean conditions are covered in Chapter 4, so the bool data type is discussed in more detail in that chapter.

Determining Storage Size

A unique feature of C++ is that you can see where and how values are stored. As an example, the C++ operator sizeof() provides the number of bytes used to store values for the data type named in the parentheses. (Review Section 1.6 if you're unfamiliar with the concept of a byte.) This built-in operator doesn't use an arithmetic symbol to perform its operation. Program 2.5 uses this operator to determine the amount of storage reserved for the int, char, and bool data types.

Point of Information

The Character '\n' and the String "\n"

The compiler recognizes both '\n' and "\n" as containing the newline character. The difference is in the data type used. Formally, '\n' is a character literal, and "\n" is a string literal. From a practical standpoint, both cause the same thing to happen: A new line is forced in the output display. In encountering the character value '\n', however, the compiler translates it by using the ASCII code 00001010 (see Table 2.4). In encountering the string value "\n", the compiler translates it by using the correct character code but also adds an end-of-string character, which is '\0'.

Good programming practice requires ending the last output display with a newline escape sequence. This practice ensures that the first line of output from one program doesn't end up on the last line displayed by the previously executed program.

 Program 2.5

```
#include <iostream>
using namespace std;

int main()
{
  cout << "\nData Type  Bytes"
       << "\n---------  -----"
       << "\nint        " << sizeof(int)
       << "\nchar       " << sizeof(char)
       << "\nbool       " << sizeof(bool)
       << '\n';

     return 0;
}
```

In reviewing Program 2.5, notice that a single character value is inserted in the display by cout by enclosing it in single quotation marks, as in the escape sequence '\n' at the end of the cout statement. In the first five displayed lines, this character is included in each output string. Each time the compiler encounters the newline escape sequence, as a single character or as part of a string, it's translated as a single character that forces the display to start at the beginning of a new line. Although quotation marks can be used for the final newline insertion, as "\n", they designate a string. When only a single character is being transmitted, and to emphasize that single characters are designated by using single quotation marks, '\n' is used instead of "\n". From a practical standpoint, however, both notations force a new line in the display.

Point of Information

Object-Oriented and Procedural Programs

Except for the `bool` type, all of C++'s built-in data types are direct carryovers from the C procedural language. Not surprisingly, programs using only built-in data types can't be object-oriented programs. Instead, as in Program 2.5, they become procedural programs, those based primarily on procedures, such as `main()`.

Only when built-in data types are bundled together to form a packet of data, which becomes an object, can an object-oriented program come into existence.

The output of Program 2.5 is compiler dependent, meaning each compiler reports the amount of storage it provides for the data type under consideration. When run on a computer using Microsoft's current Visual C++ .NET compiler, for example, the following output is produced:

```
Data Type  Bytes
---------  -----
int          4
char         1
bool         1
```

For this output, which is the typical storage almost all current C++ compilers provide, you can determine the range of values that can be stored in each data type. To do so, however, requires understanding the difference between a signed and an unsigned data type, discussed next.

Signed and Unsigned Data Types

A **signed data type** permits storing negative values in addition to 0 and positive values, so `int` is a signed data type. An **unsigned data type** provides for only non-negative values (that is, 0 and positive values). Some applications require only unsigned numerical values. For example, many date applications store dates in the numerical form *yearmonthday* (storing 12/25/2007 as 20071225, for example) and are concerned only with dates after 0 CE. For these applications, which never require a negative value, an unsigned data type can be used.

All unsigned integer types, such as `unsigned int`, provide a range of positive values that, for all practical purposes, is double the range for their signed counterparts. This extra positive range is made available by using the negative range of its signed version for additional positive numbers.

With an understanding of the difference between signed and unsigned data types, you can use Table 2.5 to determine the range of integer values supported by current C++ compilers. As you can see, a `long int` uses the same amount of storage (4 bytes) as an `int`. The only requirement of the ANSI C++ standard is that an `int` must provide at least as much storage as a `short int`, and a `long int` must provide at least as much storage as an `int`. On early desktop computers with a memory capacity limited to thousands of bytes, a `short int` typically used 1 byte of storage, an `int` 2 bytes, and a `long int` 4 bytes. This storage limited the range of `int` values from -32,768 to +32,767 and `unsigned int` values from 0 to 65,535, thus doubling the number of possible positive values, which was significant. With the current range of `int` values in the -2 to +2 billion range, doubling positive values is rarely a consideration. Additionally, a `long int` is unnecessary now because it is uses the same storage capacity as an `int`.

Table 2.5 Integer Data Type Storage

Name of Data Type	Storage Size	Range of Values
char	1	256 characters
bool	1	true (considered as any positive value) and false (which is a 0)
short int	2	-32,768 to +32,767
unsigned short int	2	0 to 65,535
int	4	-2,147,483,648 to +2,147,483,647
unsigned int	4	0 to 4,294,967,295
long int	4	-2,147,483,648 to +2,147,483,647
unsigned long int	4	0 to 4,294,967,295

Floating-Point Types

A **floating-point number**, more commonly known as a **real number**, can be the number 0 or any positive or negative number containing a decimal point, as shown in these examples:

```
+10.625    5.    -6.2    3251.92    0.0    0.33    -6.67    +2.
```

Therefore, the numbers 5., 0.0, and +2. are classified as floating-point values, but the same numbers written without a decimal point (5, 0, +2) are integer values. As with integer values, special symbols such as the dollar sign and comma aren't permitted in real numbers, as shown in these examples of invalid real numbers:

```
5,326.25    24    6,459    $10.29    7.007.645
```

C++ supports three floating-point data types: `float`, `double`, and `long double`. The difference between these data types is the amount of storage the compiler uses. Most compilers use twice the amount of storage for `doubles` as for `floats`, which allows a `double` to have approximately twice the precision of a `float`. For this reason, a `float` value is sometimes referred to as a **single-precision number** and a `double` value as a **double-precision number**. The actual storage allocation for each data type, however, depends on the compiler. The ANSI C++ standard requires only that a `double` have at least the same amount of precision as a `float`, and a `long double` have at least the same amount of storage as a `double`. Currently, most C++ compilers allocate 4 bytes for `floats` and 8 bytes for `doubles` and `long doubles`, which produces the range of numbers listed in Table 2.6.

Table 2.6 Floating-Point Data Types

Type	Storage	Absolute Range of Values (+ and -)
float	4 bytes	$1.40129846432481707 \times 10^{-45}$ to $3.40282346638528860 \times 10^{38}$
double and long double	8 bytes	$4.94065645841246544 \times 10^{-324}$ to $1.79769313486231570 \times 10^{308}$

Point of Information

What Is Precision?

In numerical theory, the term **precision** typically refers to numerical accuracy. In this context, the statement "This computation is accurate, or precise, to the fifth decimal place" means the fifth digit after the decimal point has been rounded, and the number is accurate to within ±0.00005.

In computer programming, "precision" can refer to the accuracy of a number or the amount of significant digits in the number; **significant digits** are defined as the number of clearly correct digits plus 1. For example, if the number 12.6874 has been rounded to the fourth decimal place, it's correct to say that this number is precise to the fourth decimal place. In other words, all digits in the number are accurate except the fourth decimal digit, which has been rounded. Similarly, this same number has a precision of six digits, which means the first five digits are correct and the sixth digit has been rounded. Another way of saying this is that the number 12.6874 has six significant digits.

The significant digits in a number need not have any relation to the number of displayed digits. For example, if the number 687.45678921 has five significant digits, it's accurate only to the value 687.46; the last digit is assumed to be rounded. Similarly, dollar values in large financial applications are often rounded to the nearest hundred thousand dollars. In these applications, a displayed dollar value of $12,400,000, for example, isn't accurate to the closest dollar. If this value is specified as having three significant digits, it's accurate only to the hundred-thousand digit.

In compilers using the same amount of storage for double and long double numbers, these two data types are identical. (The sizeof() operator in Program 2.5 can always be used to determine the amount of storage your compiler reserves for these data types.) A float literal is indicated by appending an f or F to the number, and a long double is created by appending an l or L to the number. In the absence of these suffixes, a floating-point number defaults to a double. For example, take a look at the following:

9.234 indicates a double literal
9.234F indicates a float literal
9.234L indicates a long double literal

The only difference in these numbers is the amount of storage the computer can use for them. Appendix C describes the binary storage format used for floating-point numbers and its impact on number precision.

EXERCISES 2.3

1. **(Practice)** Determine data types appropriate for the following data:
   a. The average of four grades
   b. The number of days in a month

    c. The length of the Golden Gate Bridge

    d. The numbers in a state lottery

    e. The distance from Brooklyn, N.Y. to Newark, N.J.

    f. The single-character prefix that specifies a component type

2. **(Practice)** Compile and execute Program 2.5.

3. **(Modify)** Modify Program 2.5 to determine the storage your compiler uses for all the C++ integer data types.

4. **(Practice)** Show how the name KINGSLEY is stored in a computer that uses the ASCII code by drawing a diagram similar to Figure 2.7, shown previously.

5. **(Practice)** Repeat Exercise 4 using the letters of your own last name.

6. **(Modify)** Modify Program 2.5 to determine how many bytes your compiler assigns to the `float`, `double`, and `long double` data types.

7. **(For Thought)** Because computers use different representations for storing integer, floating-point, double-precision, and character values, discuss how a program might alert the computer to the data types of various values it will be using.

8. **(For Thought)** Although you have concentrated on operations involving integer and floating-point numbers, C++ allows adding and subtracting characters and integers. (These operations are possible with characters because they're integer data types and are stored by using integer codes.) Therefore, characters and integers can be mixed in arithmetic expressions. For example, if your computer uses ASCII code, the expression `'a'` + 1 equals `'b'` and `'z'` – 1 equals `'y'` is valid. Similarly, `'A'` + 1 is `'B'` and `'Z'` – 1 is `'Y'`. With this information as background, determine the character results of the following expressions. (Assume all characters are stored by using ASCII codes.)

    a. `'m'` – 5

    b. `'m'` + 5

    c. `'G'` + 6

    d. `'G'` – 6

    e. `'b'` – `'a'`

    f. `'g'` – `'a'` + 1

    g. `'G'` – `'A'` + 1

N O T E | **Note:** To complete the following exercise, you need to understand basic computer storage concepts. Specifically, if you're unfamiliar with the concepts of bytes and words, refer to Section 1.6 before doing the next exercise.

9. **(Practice)** Although the total number of bytes varies from computer to computer, memory sizes of 65,536 to more than several million bytes are common. In computer language, the letter K represents the number 1024, which is 2 raised to the 10th power, and M represents the number 1,048,576, which is 2 raised to the 20th power. Therefore, a memory size of 640 KB is really 640 times 1024 (655,360 bytes), and a memory size of 4 MB is really 4 times

1,048,576 (4,194,304 bytes). Using this information, calculate the actual number of bytes in the following:

a. A memory containing 512 MB

b. A memory consisting of 256 MB words, where each word consists of 2 bytes

c. A memory consisting of 256 MB words, where each word consists of 4 bytes

d. A thumb drive that specifies 2 MB

e. A disk that specifies 250 MB

f. A disk that specifies 8 GB (*Hint:* See Table 1.2.)

2.4   Arithmetic Operations

The previous section presented the data values corresponding to C++'s built-in data types. This section explains the arithmetic operations that can be applied to these values.

Integers and real numbers can be added, subtracted, multiplied, and divided. Although it's usually better not to mix integers and real numbers when performing arithmetic operations, you can get predictable results when using different data types in the same arithmetic expression. Surprisingly, you can add and subtract character data and mix it with integer data to produce useful results. (For example, 'A' + 1 results in the character 'B'.) These operations are possible because characters are stored by using integer codes.

The operators used for arithmetic operations are called **arithmetic operators** and are as follows:

Operation	Operator
Addition	+
Subtraction	−
Multiplication	*
Division	/
Modulus division[7]	%

These operators are also called **binary operators**, which means the operator requires two operands to produce a result. An **operand** can be a literal value or an identifier with an associated value. A **simple binary arithmetic expression** consists of a binary operator connecting two literal values in this form:

literalValue   operator   literalValue

Examples of simple binary arithmetic expressions are the following:

```
3 + 7
8 - 3
12.62 + 9.8
0.08 * 12.2
12.6 / 2
```

---

[7]Don't be concerned at this stage if you do not understand the term "modulus division." You learn more about this operator later in "Integer Division."

The spaces around arithmetic operators in these examples are inserted strictly for clarity and can be omitted without affecting the value of the expression. However, an expression in C++ must be entered in a straight-line form, as shown in these examples. For example, the C++expression equivalent to 12.6 divided by 2 must be entered as 12.6 / 2, not as the algebraic expression shown here:

$$\frac{12.6}{2}$$

You can use cout to display the value of any arithmetic expression onscreen. To do this, the value must be sent to the object. For example, the following statement yields the display 21:

```
cout << (6 + 15);
```

Strictly speaking, the parentheses surrounding the expression 6 + 15 aren't required to indicate that the value of the expression (that is, 21) is being displayed.[8] In addition to displaying a numerical value, cout can display a string identifying the output, as was done in Section 2.1. For example, the following statement sends two pieces of data, a string and a value, to cout:

```
cout << "The sum of 6 and 15 is " <<  (6 + 15);
```

Each set of data sent to cout must be preceded by its own insertion operator, <<. In the preceding example, the first data sent for display is the string "The sum of 6 and 15 is ", and the second item sent is the value of the expression 6 + 15. This statement produces the following display:

```
The sum of 6 and 15 is 21
```

The space between the word "is" and the number 21 is caused by the space in the string sent to cout. As far as cout is concerned, its input is a set of characters sent to be displayed in the order they're received. Characters from the input are queued, one behind the other, and sent to the screen for display. Placing a space in the input makes the space part of the stream of characters that's displayed. For example, the statement

```
cout << "The sum of 12.2 and 15.754 is " <<  (12.2 + 15.754);
```

yields the following display:

```
The sum of 12.2 and 15.754 is 27.954
```

When multiple insertions are sent to cout, the code can be spread across multiple lines. Only one semicolon, however, must be used, which is placed after the last insertion and terminates the complete statement. Therefore, the preceding display is also produced by the following statement, which spans two lines:

```
cout << "The sum of 12.2 and 15.754 is "
     <<  (12.2 + 15.754);
```

However, when you allow a statement to span multiple lines, two rules must be followed: A string contained in quotation marks can't be split across lines, and the terminating semicolon should appear only on the last line. You can always place multiple insertion symbols in a line.

---

[8]The parentheses aren't required because the + operator has a higher precedence than the << operator; therefore, the addition is performed before the insertion.

If floating-point numbers have six or fewer decimal digits, they're displayed with enough decimal places to accommodate the fractional part of the number. If the number has more than six decimal digits, the fractional part is rounded to six decimal digits, and if the number has no decimal digits, neither a decimal point nor any decimal digits are displayed.[9]

Program 2.6 illustrates using cout to display the results of arithmetic expressions in the statements of a complete program.

Program 2.6

```cpp
#include <iostream>
using namespace std;

int  main()
{
  cout << "15.0 plus 2.0 equals "        << (15.0 + 2.0) << endl
       << "15.0 minus 2.0 equals "       << (15.0 - 2.0) << endl
       << "15.0 times 2.0 equals "       << (15.0 * 2.0) << endl
       << "15.0 divided by 2.0 equals " << (15.0 / 2.0) << endl;

  return 0;
}
```

The output of Program 2.6 is the following:

```
15.0 plus 2.0 equals 17
15.0 minus 2.0 equals 13
15.0 times 2.0 equals 30
15.0 divided by 2.0 equals 7.5
```

The only new item used in Program 2.6 is the term endl, which is an example of a C++ manipulator. A **manipulator** is an item used to change how the output stream of characters is displayed. In particular, the endl manipulator first causes a newline character ('\n') to be inserted in the display, and then forces all current insertions to be displayed immediately, instead of waiting for more data. (Section 3.2 lists the most commonly used manipulators.)

Expression Types

An **expression** is any combination of operators and operands that can be evaluated to yield a value. An expression containing only integer values as operands is called an **integer expression**, and the result of the expression is an integer value. Similarly, an expression containing only floating-point values (single-precision and double-precision) as operands is called a **floating-point expression** (also referred to as a "real expression"), and the result of the

[9]None of this output is defined as part of the C++ language. Rather, it's defined by a set of classes and routines provided with each C++ compiler.

Point of Information

The **endl** Manipulator

On many systems, the endl manipulator and the \n escape sequence are processed in the same way and produce the same effect. The one exception is on systems where output is accumulated internally until enough characters collect to make it advantageous to display them all in one burst onscreen. In these systems, referred to as "buffered," the endl manipulator forces all accumulated output to be displayed immediately, without waiting for additional characters to fill the buffer area before being printed. As a practical matter, you wouldn't notice a difference in the final display. As a general rule, however, use the \n escape sequence whenever it can be included in an existing string, and use the endl manipulator whenever a \n would appear by itself or to formally signify the end of a specific group of output.

expression is a floating-point value. An expression containing integer and floating-point values is called a **mixed-mode expression**. Although it's usually better not to mix integer andfloating-point values in an arithmetic operation, the data type of each operation is determined by the following rules:

- If both operands are integers, the result of the operation is an integer.
- If one operand is a real value, the result of the operation is a double-precision value.

The result of an arithmetic expression is never a single-precision (float) number. This is because during execution, a C++ program temporarily converts all single-precision numbers to double-precision numbers when an arithmetic expression is evaluated.

Integer Division

The division of two integer values can produce rather strange results for the unwary. For example, the expression 15/2 yields the integer result 7. Because integers can't contain a fractional part, a value of 7.5 can't be obtained. The fractional part resulting when two integers are divided—the remainder—is always dropped (truncated). Therefore, the value of 9/4 is 2 and 20/3 is 6.

Often, however, you need to retain the remainder of an integer division. To do this, C++ provides the **modulus operator** (also referred to as the "remainder operator"), which has the symbol %. This operator captures the remainder when an integer is divided by an integer; using a non-integer value with the modulus operator results in a compiler error. The following examples show how the modulus operator is used:

9   % 4 is 1 (the remainder when 9 is divided by 4 is 1)
17 % 3 is 2 (the remainder when 17 is divided by 3 is 2)
15 % 4 is 3 (the remainder when 15 is divided by the 4 is 3)
14 % 2 is 0 (the remainder when 14 is divided by 2 is 0)

Negation

In addition to binary operators, C++ provides **unary operators**, which operate on a single operand. One of these unary operators uses the same symbol as binary subtraction (–). With this unary operator, the minus sign in front of a single numerical value negates (reverses the sign of) the number.

Table 2.7 summarizes the six arithmetic operations described so far and lists the data type for the result each operator produces, based on the data type of the operands involved.

Table 2.7   Summary of Arithmetic Operators

Operation	Operator Symbol	Type	Operand(s)	Result
Addition	+	Binary	Both are integers One operand is not an integer	Integer Double-precision
Subtraction	–	Binary	Both are integers One operand is not an integer	Integer Double-precision
Multiplication	*	Binary	Both are integers One operand is not an integer	Integer Double-precision
Division	/	Binary	Both are integers One operand is not an integer	Integer Double-precision
Modulus	%	Binary	Both are integers One operand is not an integer	Integer Double-precision
Negation	–	Unary	Integer or double	Same as operand

Operator Precedence and Associativity

In addition to simple expressions, such as 5 + 12 and .08 * 26.2, you can create more complex arithmetic expressions. C++, like most other programming languages, requires following certain rules when writing expressions containing more than one arithmetic operator:

- Two binary operator symbols must never be placed side by side. For example, 5 * % 6 is invalid because two operators, * and %, are placed next to each other.
- Parentheses can be used to form groupings, and all expressions enclosed in parentheses are evaluated first. In this way, you can use parentheses to alter the evaluation to any desired order. For example, in the expression (6 + 4) / (2 + 3), the 6 + 4 and 2 + 3 are evaluated first to yield 10 / 5. The 10 / 5 is then evaluated to yield 2.
- Parentheses can be enclosed by other parentheses. For example, the expression (2 * (3 + 7)) / 5 is valid and evaluates to 4. When parentheses are included within parentheses, expressions in the innermost parentheses are always evaluated first. The evaluation continues from innermost to outermost parentheses until all expressions in parentheses have been evaluated. The number of closing parentheses,), must always equal the number of opening parentheses, (, so that no unpaired sets exist.

- Parentheses can't be used to indicate multiplication; instead, the multiplication operator, *, must be used. For example, the expression (3 + 4) (5 + 1) is invalid. The correct expression is (3 + 4) * (5 + 1).

Parentheses should specify logical groupings of operands and indicate clearly, to the compiler and programmers, the intended order of arithmetic operations. Although expressions in parentheses are always evaluated first, expressions containing multiple operators, whether enclosed in parentheses or not, are evaluated by the priority, or **precedence**, of the operators. There are three levels of precedence:

1. P1—All negations are done first.
2. P2—Multiplication, division, and modulus operations are computed next. Expressions containing more than one multiplication, division, or modulus operator are evaluated from left to right as each operator is encountered. For example, in the expression 35 / 7 % 3 * 4, all operations have the same priority, so the operations are performed from left to right as each operator is encountered. The division is done first, yielding the expression 5 % 3 * 4. The modulus operation, 5 % 3, is performed next, yielding a result of 2. Finally, the expression 2 * 4 is computed to yield 8.
3. P3—Addition and subtraction are computed last. Expressions containing more than one addition or subtraction are evaluated from left to right as each operator is encountered.

In addition to precedence, operators have an **associativity**, which is the order in which operators of the same precedence are evaluated, as described in rule P2. For example, does the expression 6.0 * 6 / 4 yield 9.0, which is (6.0 * 6) / 4, or 6.0, which is 6.0 * (6 / 4)? The answer is 9.0 because C++'s operators use the same associativity as in general mathematics, which evaluates multiplication from left to right, as rule P2 indicates.

Table 2.8 lists the precedence and associativity of the operators discussed in this section. As you have seen, an operator's precedence establishes its priority in relation to all other operators. Operators at the top of Table 2.8 have a higher priority than operators at the bottom of the table. In expressions with multiple operators of different precedence, the operator with the higher precedence is used before an operator with lower precedence. For example, in the expression 6 + 4 / 2 + 3, because the division operator has a higher precedence (P2) than the addition operator, the division is done first, yielding an intermediate result of 6 + 2 + 3. The additions are then performed, left to right, to yield a final result of 11.

Table 2.8 Operator Precedence and Associativity

Operator	Associativity
Unary –	Right to left
* / %	Left to right
+ –	Left to right

Finally, take a look at using Table 2.8 and the precedence rules to evaluate an expression containing operators of different precedence, such as 8 + 5 * 7 % 2 * 4. Because the multiplication and modulus operators have a higher precedence than the addition operator, these two operations are evaluated first (P2), using their left-to-right associativity, before the addition is evaluated (P3). Therefore, the complete expression is evaluated as the following:

```
8 + 5 * 7 % 2 * 4 =
    8 + 35 % 2 * 4 =
            8 + 1 * 4 =
                8 + 4 = 12
```

EXERCISES 2.4

1. **(Practice)** For the following correct algebraic expressions and corresponding incorrect C++ expressions, find the errors and write corrected C++ expressions:

Algebra	**C++ Expression**
a. (2)(3) + (4)(5)	(2)(3) + (4)(5)
b. $\dfrac{6+18}{2}$	6 + 18 / 2
c. $\dfrac{4.5}{12.2 - 3.1}$	4.5 / 12.2 - 3.1
d. 4.6 (3.0 + 14.9)	4.6 (3.0 + 14.9)
e. (12.1 + 18.9) (15.3 - 3.8)	(12.1 + 18.9) (15.3 - 3.8)

2. **(Practice)** Determine the values of the following integer expressions:

  a. 3 + 4 * 6   **f.** 20 - 2 / 6 + 3

  b. 3 * 4 / 6 + 6   **g.** 20 - 2 / (6 + 3)

  c. 2 * 3 / 12 * 8 / 4   **h.** (20 - 2) / 6 + 3

  d. 10 * (1 + 7 * 3)   **i.** (20 - 2) / (6 + 3)

  e. 50 % 20   **j.** (10 + 3) % 4

3. **(Practice)** Determine the value of the following floating-point expressions:

  a. 3.0 + 4.0 * 6.0

  b. 3.0 * 4.0 / 6.0 + 6.0

  c. 2.0 * 3.0 / 12.0 * 8.0 / 4.0

  d. 10.0 * (1.0 + 7.0 * 3.0)

  e. 20.0 - 2.0 / 6.0 + 3.0

  f. 20.0 - 2.0 / (6.0 + 3.0)

  g. (20.0 - 2.0) / 6.0 + 3.0

  h. (20.0 - 2.0) / (6.0 + 3.0)

4. **(Practice)** Evaluate the following mixed-mode expressions and list the data type of the result. In evaluating the expressions, be aware of the data types of all intermediate calculations.

  a. 10.0 + 15 / 2 + 4.3

    b. `10.0 + 15.0 / 2 + 4.3`

    c. `3.0 * 4 / 6 + 6`

    d. `3 * 4.0 / 6 + 6`

    e. `20.0 - 2 / 6 + 3`

    f. `10 + 17 * 3 + 4`

    g. `10 + 17 / 3. + 4`

    h. `3.0 * 4 % 6 + 6`

    i. `10 + 17 % 3 + 4`

5. **(Practice)** Assume that `amount` stores the integer value 1, `m` stores the integer value 50, `n` stores the integer value 10, and `p` stores the integer value 5. Evaluate the following expressions:

    a. `n / p + 3`

    b. `m / p + n - 10 * amount`

    c. `m - 3 * n + 4 * amount`

    d. `amount / 5`

    e. `18 / p`

    f. `-p * n`

    g. `-m / 20`

    h. `(m + n) / (p + amount)`

    i. `m + n / p + amount`

6. **(Practice)** Repeat Exercise 5, assuming that `amount` stores the value 1.0, `m` stores the value 50.0, `n` stores the value 10.0, and `p` stores the value 5.0.

7. **(Practice)** Enter, compile, and run Program 2.6.

8. **(Desk Check)** Determine the output of the following program:

```
#include <iostream>
using namespace std;
int main()  // a program illustrating integer truncation
{
  cout << "answer1 is the integer " << 9/4;
  cout << "\nanswer2 is the integer " << 17/3;

  return 0;
}
```

9. **(Desk Check)** Determine the output of the following program:

```
#include <iostream>
using namespace std;
int main()  // a program illustrating the % operator
{
  cout << "The remainder of 9 divided by 4 is " << 9 % 4;
  cout << "\nThe remainder of 17 divided by 3 is " << 17 % 3;
```

```
    return 0;
}
```

10. **(Program)** Write a C++ program that displays the results of the expressions `3.0 * 5.0`, `7.1 * 8.3 - 2.2`, and `3.2 / (6.1 * 5)`. Calculate the value of these expressions manually to verify that the displayed values are correct.

11. **(Program)** Write a C++ program that displays the results of the expressions `15 / 4`, `15 % 4`, and `5 * 3 - (6 * 4)`. Calculate the value of these expressions manually to verify that the displayed values are correct.

2.5   Variables and Declaration Statements

All integer, floating-point, and other values used in a program are stored and retrieved from the computer's memory. Conceptually, locations in memory are arranged like the rooms in a large hotel. Like room numbers in a hotel, each memory location has a unique address. Before high-level languages such as C++, memory locations were referenced by their addresses. For example, storing the integer values 45 and 12 in the memory locations 1652 and 2548 (see Figure 2.8) required instructions equivalent to the following:

Put a 45 in location 1652
Put a 12 in location 2548

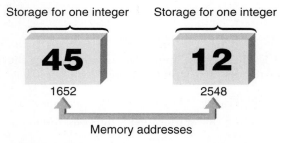

Figure 2.8   Enough storage for two integers

To add the two numbers just stored and save the result in another memory location, such as 3000, you need an instruction such as the following:

Add the contents of location 1652
to the contents of location 2548
and store the result in location 3000

Clearly, this method of storage and retrieval is cumbersome. In high-level languages such as C++, symbolic names, called **variables**, are used in place of memory addresses. A variable is simply a name the programmer assigns to refer to computer storage locations. The term "variable" is used because the value stored in the memory locations assigned to the variable can change, or vary. For each name the programmer uses, the computer keeps track of the memory address corresponding to that name. In the hotel room analogy, it's equivalent to putting a name on a room's door and referring to the room by this name, such as calling it the Blue Room instead of Room 205.

In C++, the selection of variable names is the programmer's choice, as long as the rules listed in Section 2.1 for selecting identifier names are observed. These rules are summarized in the following list:

1. The variable name must begin with a letter or underscore (_) and can contain only letters, underscores, or digits. It can't contain blank spaces, commas, or special symbols, such as ( ) & , $ # . ! \ ?.
2. A variable name can't be a keyword (see Table 2.1).
3. A variable name can't consist of more than 1024 characters.

Additionally, variable names should be mnemonics that give some indication of the variable's purpose. For a variable used to store a value that's the total of other values, a good name is sum or total. Variable names giving no indication of the value stored, such as r2d2, linda, and getum, shouldn't be used. As with function names, variable names can consist of uppercase and lowercase letters.

Assume the first memory location shown in Figure 2.9, which has the address 1652, is given the name num1. The memory location 2548 is given the variable name num2, and memory location 3000 is given the variable name total.

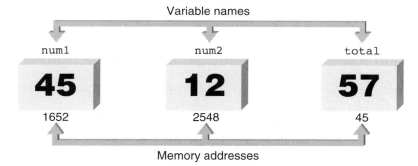

Figure 2.9 Naming storage locations

Using these variable names, the operation of storing 45 in location 1652, storing 12 in location 2548, and adding the contents of these two locations is accomplished by these C++ statements:

```
num1 = 45;
num2 = 12;
total = num1 + num2;
```

Each of these statements is called an **assignment statement** because it tells the computer to assign (store) a value in a variable. Assignment statements always have an equal sign (=) and one variable name immediately to the left of the =. The value to the right of the equal sign is determined first; this value is then assigned to the variable to the left of the equal sign. The blank spaces in assignment statements are inserted for readability. Assignment statements are explained in more detail in Chapter 3, but for now, just know that you can use them to store values in variables.

A variable name is useful because it frees programmers from having to think about where data is physically stored in the computer. You simply use the variable name and let the compiler worry about where in memory the data is actually stored. Before storing a value in a variable, however, C++ requires clearly declaring the type of data to be stored in it. You must tell the compiler, in advance, the names of variables used for characters, the names used for integers, and the names used to store other C++ data types.

Declaration Statements

To name a variable and specify the data type that can be stored in it, you use **declaration statements**, which have this general form

dataType   variableName;

where *dataType* designates a valid C++ data type, and *variableName* is the name you select for the variable. For example, variables used to hold integer values are declared by using the keyword int to specify the data type and have this form:

int *variableName;*

Therefore, the following declaration statement declares sum as the name of a variable capable of storing an integer value:

int sum;

In addition, the keyword long is used to specify a long integer.[10] For example, the statement

long datenum;

declares datenum as a variable used to store a long integer. When you're using the long qualifier, you can also include the keyword int, so the previous declaration can also be written as follows:

long int datenum;

Variables used to hold single-precision values are declared by using the keyword float, and variables used to hold double-precision values are declared by using the keyword double. For example, the statement

float firstnum;

declares firstnum as a variable used to store a single-precision number. Similarly, the statement

double secnum;

declares that the variable secnum is used to store a double-precision number.

Although declaration statements can be placed anywhere in a function, typically they're grouped together and placed after the function's opening brace. However, a variable must *always* be declared before using it, and like all C++ statements, declaration statements must

---

[10]Additionally, the keywords unsigned int are used to specify an integer that can store only non-negative numbers, and the keyword short specifies a short integer.

Point of Information

Atomic Data

All the variables declared so far have been used to store atomic data values. An **atomic data value** is considered a complete entity and can't be decomposed into a smaller data type supported by the language. For example, although an integer can be decomposed into individual digits, C++ doesn't have a numerical digit type. Instead, each integer is regarded as a complete value and, therefore, is considered atomic data. Because the integer data type supports only atomic data values, it's said to be an **atomic data type**. As you might expect, `doubles`, `chars`, and `bools` are atomic data types, too.

---

end with a semicolon. A simple `main()` function containing declaration statements right after the opening function brace has this general form:

```cpp
#include <iostream>
using namespace std;

int main()
{
  // declaration statements;

  // other statements;

  return 0;
}
```

Program 2.7 uses this form in declaring and using four double-precision variables, with the `cout` object used to display the contents of one of the variables.

Program 2.7

```cpp
#include <iostream>
using namespace std;

int main()
{
   double grade1;   // declare grade1 as a double variable
   double grade2;   // declare grade2 as a double variable
   double total;    // declare total as a double variable
   double average;  // declare average as a double variable

   grade1 = 85.5;
   grade2 = 97.0;
   total = grade1 + grade2;
   average = total/2.0;   // divide the total by 2.0
   cout << "The average grade is " << average << endl;

   return 0;
}
```

The placement of the declaration statements in Program 2.7 is straightforward, although you'll see shortly that these four declarations can be combined into a single declaration. When Program 2.7 runs, the following output is displayed:

```
The average grade is 91.25
```

Notice that when a variable name is inserted in a cout statement, the value stored in the variable is placed on the output stream and displayed.

Just as integer and real (single-precision, double-precision, and long double) variables must be declared before they can be used, a variable used to store a single character must also be declared. Character variables are declared by using the keyword char. For example, the following declaration specifies that ch is a character variable:

```
char ch;
```

Program 2.8 illustrates this declaration and the use of cout to display the value stored in a character variable.

Program 2.8

```cpp
#include <iostream>
using namespace std;

int main()
{
  char ch;       // this declares a character variable

  ch = 'a';      // store the letter a in ch
  cout << "The character stored in ch is " << ch << endl;
  ch = 'm';      // now store the letter m in ch
  cout << "The character now stored in ch is "<< ch << endl;

  return 0;
}
```

When Program 2.8 runs, this output is produced:

```
The character stored in ch is a
The character now stored in ch is m
```

Notice in Program 2.8 that the first letter stored in the variable ch is a and the second letter stored is m. Because a variable can be used to store only one value at a time, assigning m to the variable overwrites the a value automatically.

Multiple Declarations

Variables of the same data type can always be grouped together and declared by using a single declaration statement, which has this common form:

dataType   variableList;

For example, the four separate declarations used in Program 2.7

```cpp
double grade1;
double grade2;
double total;
double average;
```

can be replaced with this single declaration statement:

```cpp
double grade1, grade2, total, average;
```

Similarly, the two character declarations

```cpp
char ch;
char key;
```

can be replaced with this single declaration statement:

```
char ch, key;
```

Declaring multiple variables in a single declaration statement requires giving the data type of variables only once, separating all variable names by commas, and using only one semicolon to terminate the declaration. The space after each comma is inserted for readability and isn't required.

Declaration statements can also be used to store a value in declared variables. For example, the declaration statement

```
int num1 = 15;
```

both declares the variable num1 as an integer variable and sets the value of 15 in the variable. When a declaration statement is used to store a value in a variable, the variable is said to be **initialized**. Therefore, in this example, it's correct to say the variable num1 has been initialized to 15. Similarly, the declaration statements

```
double grade1 = 87.0;
double grade2 = 93.5;
double total;
```

declare three double-precision variables and initialize two of them. When initializations are used, good programming practice dictates declaring each initialized variable on a line by itself. Constants, expressions using only constants (such as 87.0 + 12 - 2), and expressions using constants and previously initialized variables can be used as initializers for variables declared within a function. For example, Program 2.7 with declaration initialization becomes Program 2.7a.

Program 2.7a

```
#include <iostream>
using namespace std;

int main()
{
  double grade1 = 85.5;
  double grade2 = 97.0;
  double total, average;

  total = grade1 + grade2;
  average = total/2.0;   // divide the total by 2.0
  cout << "The average grade is " << average << endl;

  return 0;
}
```

Notice the blank line after the last declaration statement. Inserting a blank line after variable declarations placed at the top of a function body is a good programming practice. It improves a program's appearance and readability.

An interesting feature of C++ is that variable declarations can be intermixed and even contained in other statements; the only requirement is that a variable must be declared before its use. For example, the variable `total` in Program 2.7a could have been declared when it was first used with the statement `double total = grade1 + grade2`. In restricted situations (such as debugging, described in Section 3.7, or in a `for` loop, described in Section 5.4), declaring a variable at its first use can be helpful. In general, however, it's preferable not to spread out declarations; instead, group them as concisely and clearly as possible at the top of each function.

Memory Allocation

The declaration statements you have seen so far have performed both software and hardware tasks. From a software perspective, declaration statements always provide a list of variables and their data types. In this software role, variable declarations also help control an otherwise common and troublesome error caused by misspelling a variable's name in a program. For example, a variable named `distance` is declared and initialized by using this statement:

```
int distance = 26;
```

Later in the program, the variable is inadvertently misspelled in this statement:

```
mpg = distnce / gallons;
```

In languages that don't require variable declarations, the program treats `distnce` as a new variable and assigns it an initial value of 0 or uses whatever value happens to be in the variable's storage area. In either case, a value is calculated and assigned to `mpg`, and finding the error or even knowing an error occurred could be difficult. These errors are impossible in C++, however, because the compiler flags `distnce` as an undeclared variable. The compiler can't, of course, detect when one declared variable is mistakenly typed in place of another declared variable.

In addition to their software role, declaration statements can also perform a hardware task. Because each data type has its own storage requirements, the computer can allocate enough storage for a variable only after knowing the variable's data type. Variable declarations provide this information, so they can be used to force the compiler to reserve enough physical memory storage for each variable. Declaration statements used for this hardware task are also called **definition statements** because they define or tell the compiler how much memory is needed for data storage.

All the declaration statements you have encountered so far have also been definition statements. Later, you'll see declaration statements that don't allocate storage and are used simply to alert the program to the data types of variables created elsewhere in the program.

Figures 2.10a through 2.10d illustrate the operations set in motion by definition statements. The figures show that definition statements (or declaration statements that also allocate memory) "tag" the first byte of each set of reserved bytes with a name. This name is, of course, the variable's name, and the computer uses it to locate the starting point of a variable's reserved memory area.

After a variable has been declared in a program, typically a programmer uses it to refer to the variable's contents (its value). The value's memory location is generally of little concern to programmers. The compiler, however, must know where each value is stored and

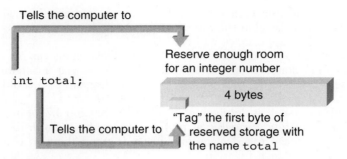

Figure 2.10a   Defining the integer variable named `total`

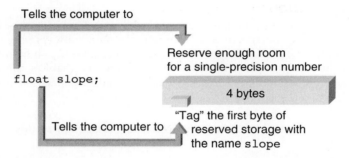

Figure 2.10b   Defining the floating-point variable named `slope`

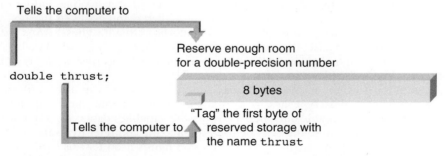

Figure 2.10c   Defining the double-precision variable named `thrust`

locate each variable correctly. For this task, the compiler uses the variable name to locate the first byte of storage previously allocated to the variable. Knowing the variable's data type then allows the compiler to store or retrieve the correct number of bytes.

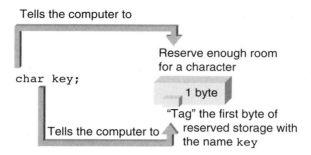

Figure 2.10d Defining the character variable named `key`

Displaying a Variable's Address[11]

Every variable has three major items associated with it: its data type, the value stored in it, and its address. The value stored in the variable is referred to as the variable's contents, and the address of the first memory location used for the variable constitutes its address. The number of locations actually used for the variable, as you have just seen, depends on the variable's data type. Figure 2.11 illustrates the relationship between these three items (type, contents, and location).

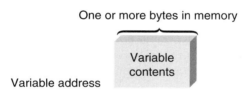

Figure 2.11 A typical variable

Programmers are usually concerned only with the value assigned to a variable (its contents) and give little attention to where the value is stored (its address). For example, take a look at Program 2.9.

---

[11]This topic can be omitted on first reading without loss of subject continuity.

Program 2.9

```cpp
#include <iostream>
using namespace std;

int main()
{
    int num;

    num = 22;
    cout << "The value stored in num is " << num << endl;

    return 0;
}
```

The following output is displayed when Program 2.9 is run:

```
The value stored in num is 22
```

Program 2.9 merely prints the value 22, which is the contents of the variable num. You can go further, however, and ask "Where is the number 22 actually stored?" Although the answer is "in num," it's only half the answer. The variable name num is simply a convenient symbol for actual memory locations, as shown in Figure 2.12.

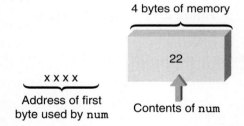

Figure 2.12 The variable num stored somewhere in memory

To determine the address of num, you can use C++'s address operator, &, which means "the address of." Except when used in an expression, the address operator placed in front of a variable's name refers to the variable's address.[12] For example, &num means "the address of num." Program 2.10 shows you an example of using the address operator.

---

[12] When used in declaration statements that create a reference variable or reference argument (see Chapter 6), the ampersand refers to the data type *preceding* it. Therefore, the declaration double &num is read as "num is the address of a double" or, more commonly, "num is a reference to a double."

Program 2.10

```cpp
#include <iostream>
using namespace std;

int main()
{
  int num;

  num = 22;
  cout << "The value stored in num is " << num << endl;
  cout << "The address of num = " << &num << endl;

  return 0;
}
```

This is the output of Program 2.10:

```
The value stored in num is 22
The address of num = 0012FED4
```

Figure 2.13 illustrates the additional address information provided by Program 2.10's output.

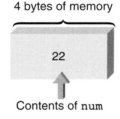

4 bytes of memory

22

0012FED4

Address of first byte used by num

Contents of num

Figure 2.13 A more complete picture of the variable num

Clearly, the address output by Program 2.10 depends on the computer used to run the program. Every time Program 2.10 runs, however, it displays the address of the first memory location used to store num. As Program 2.10's output shows, the address display is in hexadecimal notation. This display has no effect on how the program uses addresses internally; it merely gives you a means of displaying addresses that's helpful in understanding them. As you'll see in Chapters 6 and 12, using addresses, instead of just displaying them, is an important and powerful programming tool.

EXERCISES 2.5

1. **(Practice)** State whether the following variable names are valid. If they are invalid, state the reason.

```
prod_a   c1234    abcd      _c3      12345
newamp   watts    $total    new$al   a1b2c3d4
9ab6     sum.of   average   volts1   finvolt
```

2. **(Practice)** State whether the following variable names are valid. If they are invalid, state the reason. Also, indicate which of the valid variable names shouldn't be used because they convey no information about the variable.

```
current     a243    r2d2     firstnum    cc_a1
harry       sue     c3p0     total       sum
maximum     okay    a        awesome     goforit
3sum        for     tot.a1   c$five      netpower
```

3. **(Practice) a.** Write a declaration statement to declare that the variable count will be used to store an integer.

   b. Write a declaration statement to declare that the variable volt will be used to store a floating-point number.

   c. Write a declaration statement to declare that the variable power will be used to store a double-precision number.

   d. Write a declaration statement to declare that the variable keychar will be used to store a character.

4. **(Practice)** Write declaration statements for the following variables:

   a. num1, num2, and num3 used to store integer number

   b. amps1, amps2, amps3, and amps4 used to store double-precision numbers

   c. volts1, volts2, and volts3 used to store double-precision numbers

   d. codeA, codeB, codeC, codeD, and codeE used to store characters

5. **(Practice)** Write declaration statements for the following variables:

   a. firstnum and secnum used to store integer

   b. speed, acceleration, and distance used to store double-precision numbers

   c. thrust used to store a double-precision number

6. **(Modify)** Rewrite each of these declaration statements as three separate declarations:

   a. int month, day = 30, year;

   b. double hours, volt, power = 15.62;

   c. double price, amount, taxes;

   d. char inKey, ch, choice = 'f';

7. **(Desk Check) a.** Determine what each statement causes to happen in the following program:

```cpp
#include <iostream>
using namespace std;

int main()
{
   int num1, num2, total;

   num1 = 25;
```

```
     num2 = 30;
     total = num1 + num2;
     cout << "The total of " << num1 << " and "
          << num2 << " is " << total << endl;

     return 0;
}
```

    b. What output will be printed when the program in Exercise 7a runs?

8. (Practice) What are the three items associated with every variable?

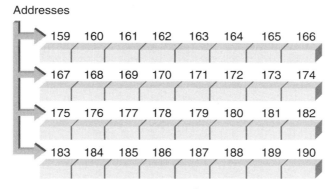

N O T E   ***Note*** for Exercises 9 to 11: Assume that a character requires 1 byte of storage, an integer requires 4 bytes, a single-precision number requires 4 bytes, and a double-precision number requires 8 bytes. Variables are assigned storage in the order they're declared. (Review Section 1.6 if you're unfamiliar with the concept of a byte.) Refer to Figure 2.14 for these exercises.

Addresses

159	160	161	162	163	164	165	166
167	168	169	170	171	172	173	174
175	176	177	178	179	180	181	182
183	184	185	186	187	188	189	190

Figure 2.14 *Memory bytes for Exercises 9 to 11*

9. (Practice) a. Using Figure 2.14 and assuming the variable name `rate` is assigned to the byte at memory address 159, determine the addresses corresponding to each variable declared in the following statements. Also, fill in the correct number of bytes with the initialization data included in the declaration statements. (Use letters for the characters, not the computer codes that would actually be stored.)

```
float rate;
char ch1 = 'M', ch2 = 'E', ch3 = 'L', ch4 = 'T';
double taxes;
int num, count = 0;
```

    b. Repeat Exercise 9a, but substitute the actual byte patterns that a computer using the ASCII code would use to store characters in the variables `ch1`, `ch2`, `ch3`, and `ch4`. (*Hint*: Use Appendix B.)

10. (Practice) a. Using Figure 2.14 and assuming the variable named `cn1` is assigned to the byte at memory address 159, determine the addresses corresponding to each variable declared in the following statements. Also, fill in the correct number of bytes with the initialization data included in the declaration statements. (Use letters for the characters, not the computer codes that would actually be stored.)

```
char cn1 = 'P', cn2 = 'E', cn3 = 'R', cn4 = 'F', cn5 = 'E';
char cn6 = 'C', cn7 = 'T', key = '\\', sch = '\'', inc = 'A';
char inc1 = 'T';
```

   b. Repeat Exercise 10a, but substitute the actual byte patterns a computer using the ASCII code would use to store characters in each of the declared variables. (*Hint*: Use Table 2.3.)

11. **(Practice)** Using Figure 2.14 and assuming the variable name `miles` is assigned to the byte at memory address 159, determine the addresses corresponding to each variable declared in the following statements:

```
float miles;
int count, num;
double dist, temp;
```

2.6   A Case Study: Radar Speed Traps

In this section, the software development procedure explained in Section 1.3 is applied to a specific programming problem. Although each problem you explore in the case studies in Part One is different, you'll see that this software development procedure works for all of them to produce a complete program. It forms the foundation for all programs developed in Part One of this book.

A highway-patrol speed detection radar emits a beam of microwaves at a frequency designated as f_e. The beam is reflected off an approaching car, and the radar unit picks up and analyzes the reflected beam, f_r. The reflected beam's frequency is shifted slightly from f_e to f_r because of the car's motion. The relationship between the speed of the car, v, in miles per hour (mph), and the two microwave frequencies is

$$v = \left(6.685 \times 10^8\right)\left(\frac{f_r - f_e}{f_r + f_e}\right)mph$$

where the emitted waves have a frequency of $f_e = 2 \times 10^{10} \, sec^{-1}$. Using the given formula, you'll write a C++ program, using the software development procedure, to calculate and display the speed corresponding to a received frequency of $2.000004 \times 10^{10} \, sec^{-1}$.

Step 1   Analyze the Problem

For this problem, a single output is required: the speed of the car. The input items required to solve for the speed are the emitted frequency, f_e, and the received frequency, f_r.

Step 2   Develop a Solution

The algorithm for transforming the three input items into the required output item is given by the formula $v = 6.685 \times 10^8 (f_r - f_e) / (f_r + f_e)$. Therefore, the complete algorithm for the program solution is as follows:

Assign values to f_r and f_e
Calculate the speed using the formula v = 6.685 × 10⁸(f_r - f_e) / (f_r + f_e)
Display the speed

A hand calculation, using the data $f_e = 2 \times 10^{10}$ sec^{-1} and $f_r = 2.000004 \times 10^{10}$ sec^{-1}, yields a speed of 66.85 mph.

Step 3   Code the Solution

Program 2.11 provides the necessary code.

Program 2.11

```cpp
#include <iostream>
using namespace std;

int main()
{
  double speed, fe, fr;

  fe = 2e10;
  fr = 2.0000004e10;

  speed = 6.685e8 * (fr - fe) / (fr + fe);
  cout << "The speed is " << speed << " miles/hour " << endl;

  return 0;
}
```

Program 2.11 begins with an `#include` preprocessor command followed by a `main()` function. The `main()` function in Program 2.11 contains one declaration statement, three assignment statements, and one output statement. The assignment statements `fe = 2e10;` and `fr = 2.0000004e10;` are used to initialize the `fe` and `fr` variables. The assignment statement

```cpp
speed = 6.685e8 * (fr - fe) / (fr + fe);
```

calculates a value for the variable `speed`. When Program 2.11 is compiled and executed, the following output is produced:

```
The speed is 66.85 miles/hour
```

Step 4   Test and Correct the Program

The last step in the development procedure is to test the output. Because the single calculation and displayed value agree with the previous hand calculation, you have verified that the program operates correctly. Now you can use the program for different values of received frequencies. Note that if the parentheses weren't placed correctly in the assignment statement that calculates a value for `speed`, the displayed value wouldn't agree with your previous hand calculation. This would alert you to the fact that there's an error in the program.

EXERCISES 2.6

1. **(Modify) a.** Modify Program 2.11 to calculate the speed of a car whose received radar frequency is $2.00000035 \times 10^{10}$ sec^{-1}.

   b. Compile and execute the program written for Exercise 1a.

2. **(Modify) a.** Modify Program 2.11 to determine the frequency returned by a car traveling at 55 mph. Your program should produce the following display (replacing the underlines with the values your program calculates):

   The returned frequency corresponding to 55 mph is _____

   b. Compile and execute the program written for Exercise 2a. Make sure to do a hand calculation so that you can verify the results your program produces.

   c. After verifying the results of the program written in Exercise 2a, modify the program to calculate the return frequency of a car traveling at 75 mph.

3. **(Telephony)** In a directly connected telephone network, all telephones are directly connected and don't require a central switching station to establish calls between two telephones. The number of lines needed to maintain a directly connected network for n telephones is given by this formula:

   $$\textit{no. of lines needed} = \frac{n(n-1)}{2}$$

   For example, directly connecting four telephones requires six separate lines (see Figure 2.15). Adding a fifth telephone to this network requires an additional 4 lines, for a total of 10 lines.

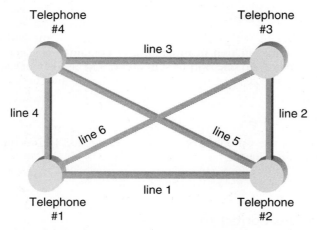

Figure 2.15   Directly connecting four telephones

    a. Using the given formula, write a C++ program that determines the number of lines required for directly connecting 100 telephones. The input for this problem is the number of telephones, denoted as *n* in the formula, and the output is the total number of lines required to directly connect the input number of telephones.

    b. Compile and execute the program written for Exercise 3a.

4. **(Modify)** Modify the program you wrote for Exercise 3 and include a new variable to represent the additional number of telephones to be connected to an existing network, and initialize this variable to 10. For this program, two outputs are required: the number of direct lines for 100 telephones and the additional number of lines needed when 10 telephones are added to the existing network.

5. **(Conversion) a.** Design, write, compile, and execute a C++ program to convert temperature in degrees Fahrenheit to degrees Celsius. This is the equation for this conversion:

Celsius = 5.0/9.0 (Fahrenheit - 32.0)

Have your program convert and display the Celsius temperature corresponding to 98.6 degrees Fahrenheit. Your program should produce the following display (replacing the underlines with the correct values):

```
For a Fahrenheit temperature of ___ degrees,
   the equivalent Celsius temperature is ___ degrees.
```

    b. Check the values computed by your program by hand. After verifying that your program is working correctly, modify it to convert 86.5 degrees Fahrenheit to its equivalent Celsius value.

6. **(Electrical Eng.) a.** Write, compile, and execute a C++ program to calculate the resistance of a series circuit consisting of twelve 56-ohm, twenty 39-ohm, thirty-two 27-ohm, and twenty-seven 15-ohm resistors. The total resistance of a series circuit is the sum of all individual resistances. Your program should produce the following display (replacing the xxxx with the actual resistance value your program calculates):

```
The total resistance, in ohms, is xxxx
```

    b. Manually check the values computed by your program. After verifying that your program is working correctly, modify it to calculate the resistance of a series circuit consisting of seventeen 39-ohm resistors, nineteen 27-ohm resistors, and forty-two 15-ohm resistors.

7. **(Thermodynamics) a.** Design, write, compile, and execute a program that determines the work performed by a piston engine providing a force of 1000 N over a distance of 15 centimeters. The following formula is used to determine the work, *W*, performed:

$W = F\,d$

    F is the force provided by the piston in Newtons.

    d is the distance the piston moves in meters.

    b. Manually check the values computed by your program. After verifying that your program is working correctly, modify it to determine the work performed by six pistons, each providing a force of 1500 N over a distance of 20 centimeters.

8. **(Civil Eng.) a.** Design, write, compile, and execute a program that determines the stress on a steel I-beam having a rectangular moment of inertia of 21.4 in^4, and a height of 6 inches,

when a load of 700 lbs is placed 8 feet from the fixed end. The stress placed on the fixed end of a symmetrical steel I-beam, as shown in Figure 2.16, can be determined by this formula:

$$S = \frac{L\,d\,c}{I}$$

S is the stress in lbs/in^2.

L is the weight, in lbs, of the load placed on the beam.

I is the beam's rectangular moment of inertia in units of in^4.

d is the distance in inches the load is placed from the fixed end of the beam (technically referred to as the "moment arm").

c is one-half the height in inches of a symmetrical beam.

b. Check the values computed by your program by hand. After verifying that your program is working correctly, modify it to determine the stress when the same load is placed at the end of an 8-foot 2" x 4" wooden beam, with a rectangular moment of inertia of 10.67 in^4.

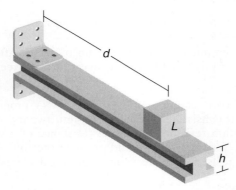

Figure 2.16   Determining the stress on a symmetrical I-beam

2.7   Common Programming Errors

Part of learning any programming language is making the elementary mistakes commonly encountered when you begin using the language. These mistakes tend to be quite frustratingbecause each language has its own set of common programming errors waiting for the unwary. When you start programming in C++, common errors include the following.

1. Omitting the parentheses after `main()`.
2. Omitting or incorrectly typing the opening brace, {, that signifies the start of a function body.
3. Omitting or incorrectly typing the closing brace, }, that signifies the end of a function.
4. Misspelling the name of an object or function, such as typing `cot` instead of `cout`.
5. Forgetting to enclose a string sent to `cout` with quotation marks.

6. Forgetting to separate data streams sent to cout with an insertion symbol, <<.
7. Omitting the semicolon at the end of each C++ statement.
8. Adding a semicolon at the end of the #include preprocessor command.
9. Forgetting the \n to indicate a new line.
10. Incorrectly typing the letter O for the number 0 or vice versa. Incorrectly typing the letter l for the number 1 or vice versa.
11. Forgetting to declare all variables used in a program. The compiler detects this error, and an error message is generated for all undeclared variables.
12. Storing an inappropriate data type in a declared variable. The compiler detects this error, and the assigned value is converted to the data type of the variable it's assigned to.
13. Using a variable in an expression before a value has been assigned to the variable. The value that happens to be in the variable when the variable is used is the value that's used when the expression is evaluated. As such, the result of the expression is meaningless.
14. Dividing integer values incorrectly. This error is usually hidden in a larger expression and can be troublesome to detect. For example, the expression

```
3.425 + 2/3 + 7.9
```

yields the same result as the expression

```
3.425 + 7.9
```

because the integer division of 2/3 is 0.
15. Mixing data types in the same expression without clearly understanding the effect. Because C++ allows expressions with "mixed" data types, understanding the order of evaluation and the data type of all intermediate calculations is important. As a general rule, it's better never to mix data types in an expression unless you want a specific effect.

Errors 3, 5, 7, 8, and 9 in this list are the most common with beginning programmers, and even experienced programmers occasionally make error 10. A worthwhile practice is writing a program and introducing each error, one at a time, to see what error messages, if any, your compiler produces. When these error messages appear because of inadvertent mistakes, you'll have had experience in understanding the messages and correcting the errors.

A major error that all beginning programmers make is rushing to code and running a program before fully understanding its requirements and the algorithms and procedures used to produce the desired result. A symptom of this haste is the lack of a written program or even a program outline. Many problems can be caught just by checking a copy of the program (handwritten or onscreen) before it's compiled.

2.8 Chapter Summary

1. A C++ program consists of one or more modules called functions. One of these functions must be called main(). The main() function identifies the starting point of a C++ program.

2. The simplest C++ program consists of the single function main().

3. Following the function name, the body of a function has the following general form:

```
{
    All C++ statements in here;
}
```

4. All C++ statements must be terminated by a semicolon.

5. Four types of data were introduced in this chapter: integer, floating-point, character, and Boolean. C++ recognizes each of these data types, in addition to other types you learn about in later chapters.

6. The cout object can be used to display all C++ data types.

7. When the cout object is used in a program, the preprocessor command #include <iostream> and the statement using namespace std; must be placed at the top of the program. The #include <iostream> preprocessor command does not end with a semicolon.

8. Every variable in a C++ program must be declared and the type of value it can store must be specified. Declaration statements can be placed anywhere in the function, although a variable can be used only after it's declared. Variables can also be initialized when they are declared. Additionally, variables of the same type can be declared with a single declaration statement. Variable declaration statements have this general form:

```
dataType   variableName(s);
```

9. A simple C++ program containing declaration statements has this typical form:

```
#include <iostream>
using namespace std;

int main()
{
  // declaration statements;
  // other statements;

  return 0;
}
```

10. Declaration statements always play the software role of informing the compiler of a function's valid variable names. When a variable declaration also causes the computer to set aside memory locations for the variable, the declaration statement is called a definition statement. (All declarations used in this chapter have also been definition statements.)

11. The sizeof() operator can be used to determine the amount of storage reserved for variables.

Programming Projects for Chapter 2

1. **(General Math) a.** Design, write, compile, and execute a C++ program that calculates and displays the perimeter of a two-dimensional triangle with sides a = 1 in, b = 1.5 in, and c = 2 in, as shown in Figure 2.17. The perimeter is given by this formula:

perimeter = a + b + c

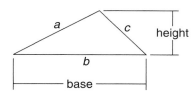

Figure 2.17 A two-dimensional triangle

b. Manually check the values computed by your program. After verifying that your program is working correctly, modify it to determine the perimeter of a two-dimensional triangle with sides a = 1.62 in, b = 2.13 in, and c = 3.2 in.

2. **(General Math) a.** Design, write, compile, and execute a C++ program that calculates and displays the area of a two-dimensional triangle, such as the one in Figure 2.17, with a base of 1 in and a height of 1.5 in. The area is given by this formula:

Area = ½ (base) × (height)

b. Manually check the values computed by your program. After verifying that your program is working correctly, modify it to determine the area of a two-dimensional triangle with a base of 2 in and a height of 1.67 in.

3. **(General Math) a.** Design, write, compile, and execute a C++ program to calculate the volume of a sphere with a radius, r, of 3 in. The volume is given by this formula:

$$Volume = \frac{4\pi r^3}{3}$$

b. Manually check the values computed by your program. After verifying that your program is working correctly, modify it to determine the volume of a cube with a radius of 1.67 in.

4. **(Physics) a.** Design, write, compile, and execute a C++ program to calculate the elapsed time it takes to make a 183.67 mile trip. This is the formula for computing elapsed time:

elapsed time = total distance / average speed

The average speed during the trip is 58 mph.

b. Manually check the values computed by your program. After verifying that your program is working correctly, modify it to determine the elapsed time it takes to make a 372-mile trip at an average speed of 67 mph.

5. **(Numerical) a.** Design, write, compile, and execute a C++ program to calculate the sum of the integers from 1 to 100. This is the formula for calculating this sum:

sum = (n/2) (2 × a + (n - 1)d)

n is the number of integers to be added.

a is the first number.

d is the difference between each number.

b. Manually check the values computed by your program. After verifying that your program is working correctly, modify it to determine the sum of the integers from 100 to 1000.

6. **(Physics and Electrical)** The energy, E, of a photon, in Joules, J, is provided by this formula:

$$E = P \times f$$

P is 6.6256×10^{-34} Joules/sec (known as Planck's constant).

f is frequency in Hertz (Hz) of the photon.

a. Given that the photon frequency of visible light is in the 3.84×10^{14} Hz to 7.69×10^{14} Hz range, design, write, compile, and execute a C++ program to calculate the energy of light with a photon frequency of 5.7×10^{14}. Verify the result produced by your program with a hand calculation.

b. After verifying that your program is working correctly, use it to determine the photon energy output of a 60 Hz power line.

7. **(Physics) a.** The weight of an object on Earth is a measurement of the downward force on the object caused by Earth's gravity. The formula for this force is determined by using Newton's Second Law:

$$F = M \times A_e$$

F is the object's weight.

M is the object's mass.

A_e is the acceleration caused by Earth's gravity (32.2 ft/sec^2 = 9.82 m/s^2).

Given this information, design, write, compile, and execute a C++ program to calculate the weight in lbf of a person having a mass of 4 lbm. Verify the result produced by your program with a hand calculation.

b. After verifying that your program is working correctly, use it to determine the weight, on Earth, of a person having a mass of 3.2 lbm.

8. **(Physics) a.** Rewrite the program you wrote for Exercise 7 to provide the mass of a person as an output, given his or her weight as an input to the program. Use your program to determine the mass of a person who weighs 140 lbf on Earth.

b. Modify the program written for Exercise 7a to also output the person's weight on Mars and the moon. The pull of gravity on Mars is 12.54 ft/sec^2 = 3.728 m/s^2, and on the moon is 5.33 ft/sec^2 = 1.625 m/s^2.

9. **(Civil Eng.)** The maximum load that can be placed at the end of a symmetrical wooden beam, such as the rectangular beam shown in Figure 2.18, can be calculated as the following:

$$L = \frac{S \times I}{d \times c}$$

L is the maximum weight in lbs of the load placed on the beam.

S is the stress in lbs/in^2.

I is the beam's rectangular moment of inertia in units of in^4.

d is the distance in inches that the load is placed from the fixed end of the beam (the "moment arm").

c is one-half the height in inches of the symmetrical beam.

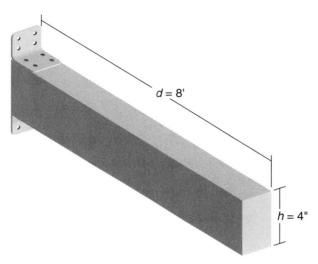

Figure 2.18   Calculating a symmetrical wooden beam's maximum load

For a 2" x 4" wooden beam, the rectangular moment of inertia is given by this formula:

$$I = \frac{base \times height^3}{12} = \frac{2 \times 4^3}{12} = 10.67$$

c = ½(4 in) = 2 in

a. Using this information, design, write, compile, and execute a C++ program that computes the maximum load in lbs that can be placed at the end of an 8-foot 2" x 4" wooden beam so that the stress on the fixed end is 3000 lb/in^2.

b. Use the program developed in Exercise 9a to determine the maximum load in lbs that can be placed at the end of a 3" x 6" wooden beam so that the stress on the fixed end is 3000 lbs/in^2.

10. (**Civil Eng.**) Modify the program written for Exercise 9 to determine the maximum load that can be placed at the end of an 8-foot I-beam, shown in Figure 2.19, so that the stress on the fixed end is 20,000 lbs/in^2. Use the fact that this beam's rectangular moment of inertia is 21.4in^4 and the value of c is 3 in.

11. (**Mechanical Eng.**) The minimum radius required for a cylindrical rod, such as one supporting a bicycle pedal (see Figure 2.20), to provide enough support for the pressure

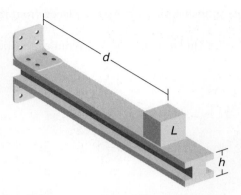

Figure 2.19   Calculating an I-beam's maximum load

exerted by the rider's foot yet not exceed the stress placed on the crank arm's sprocket attachment, is provided by this formula:

$$r^3 = \frac{d \times P}{\pi \times S}$$

r is the radius of the cylindrical rod in inches.
d is the length of the crank arm in inches.
P is the weight placed on the pedal in lbs.
S is the stress in lbs/in^2.

Figure 2.20   Determining the minimum radius of a bicycle's crank arm

Using this information, design, write, compile, and execute a C++ program that computes the value of r for a crank arm that is 7 inches long, accommodates a maximum weight of 300 lbs, and is able to sustain a stress of 10,000 lbs/in^2.

Engineering and Scientific Disciplines

Thermal Science

Thermal science is the field of engineering that includes both thermodynamics and heat transfer. **Thermodynamics** developed as a science, starting in the early 19th century, in response to the development of steam engines at that time. The intent was to understand the physical laws governing these engines in an effort to increase their efficiency. This led to analyzing and understanding the effects of temperature, pressure, and volume on steam engines and how heat moved from a hot boiler to a colder condenser and the maximum amount of work that could be generated from this flow. It now constitutes a science that includes four basic laws, known as the 0th, 1st, 2nd, and 3rd laws of thermodynamics.

Using these four laws, thermodynamics more broadly applies to large-scale systems, such as a class of engines (diesel, gas turbine, jet, rocket, and so forth) or the complete solar system. The central concept of these thermodynamic laws is energy, which is the ability to do work, and the relationship between heat, energy, and work. The fields of chemistry, chemical engineering, aerospace, mechanical engineering, biomedical engineering, material science, fluid mechanics, and physics make use of thermodynamic effects.

Heat transfer, a field derived from the 1st and 2nd laws of thermodynamics, is technically defined as the movement of energy between substances of different temperatures. Central to heat transfer is the concept of temperature, which is a measurement of the motion of atoms and molecules in a substance. Temperature determines the direction of heat flow between two objects placed in contact. If no heat flow occurs, the two objects have the same temperature (a consequence of the 1st law); otherwise, heat flows from the hotter object to the colder object (a consequence of the 2nd law). Heat transfer uses these three modes of transfer:

- **Conduction** is the transfer of heat through a substance caused by molecular movement in the substance. Examples are the transfer of heat through a metal rod if one side of the rod is at a higher temperature than the other, and heat loss through a heated house when the outside temperature is colder than the inside.
- **Convection** is the transfer of heat by the motion of a heated fluid, such as water or air. An example is the expansion of hot air into cooler air.
- **Radiation** is the transfer of heat away from an object emitting electromagnetic waves. An example is the electromagnetic waves emitted by the sun.

Each transfer occurs over time, so heat transfer calculations are typically concerned with determining the rate of transfer initially. Given the rate, the total amount of heat transferred over a fixed interval of time can always be calculated.

Chapter 3

Assignment, Formatting, and Interactive Input

In Chapter 2, you explored how results are displayed with C++'s cout statement and how numerical data is stored and processed by using variables and assignment statements. In this chapter, you complete your introduction to C++ by learning about additional processing and input capabilities.

3.1 Assignment Operations

You learned about simple assignment statements in Chapter 2. An assignment statement is the most basic C++ statement for assigning values to variables and performing computations. This statement has the following syntax:

variable = expression;

The simplest expression in C++ is a single constant. In the following assignment statements, the operand to the right of the equal sign is a constant:

```
length = 25;
width = 17.5;
```

In these assignment statements, the value of the constant to the right of the equal sign is assigned to the variable on the left of the equal sign. Note that the equal sign in C++ doesn't have the same meaning as an equal sign in algebra. The equal sign in an assignment statement tells the computer first to determine the value of the operand to the right of the equal sign, and then to store (or assign) that value in the locations associated with the variable to the left of the equal sign. For example, the C++ statement `length = 25;` is read "`length` is assigned the value 25." The blank spaces in the assignment statement are inserted for readability only.

Recall that a variable can be initialized when it's declared. If an initialization isn't done in the declaration statement, the variable should be assigned a value with an assignment statement or input operation before it's used in any computation. Subsequent assignment statements can, of course, be used to change the value assigned to a variable. For example, assume the following statements are executed one after another, and `slope` wasn't initialized when it was declared:

```
slope = 3.7;
slope = 6.28;
```

The first assignment statement assigns the value of 3.7 to the variable named `slope`.[1] The next assignment statement causes the computer to assign a value of 6.28 to `slope`. The 3.7 that was in `slope` is overwritten with the new value of 6.28 because a variable can store only one value at a time. Sometimes it's useful to think of the variable to the left of the equal sign as a temporary parking spot in a huge parking lot. Just as a parking spot can be used by only one car at a time, each variable can store only one value at a time. "Parking" a new value in a variable automatically causes the program to remove any value parked there previously.

In addition to being a constant, the operand to the right of the equal sign in an assignment statement can be a variable or any other valid C++ expression. An expression is any combination of constants, variables, and function calls that can be evaluated to yield a result. Therefore, the expression in an assignment statement can be used to perform calculations by using the arithmetic operators introduced in Section 2.4. The following are examples of assignment statements using expressions containing these operators:

```
sum = 3 + 7;
diff = 15 - 6;
product = .05 * 14.6;
tally = count + 1;
newtotal = 18.3 + total;
taxes = .06 * amount;
totalWeight = factor * weight;
average = sum / items;
slope = (y2 - y1) / (x2 - x1);
```

---

[1]Because it's the first time a value is explicitly assigned to this variable, it's often referred to as an "initialization." This term stems from historical usage that said a variable was initialized the first time a value was assigned to it. Under this usage, it's correct to say that "slope is initialized to 3.7." From an implementation viewpoint, however, this statement is incorrect because the C++ compiler handles an assignment operation differently from an initialization; an initialization can happen only when a variable is created by a declaration statement. This difference is important only when using C++'s class features and is explained in detail in Section 10.1.

As always in an assignment statement, the program first calculates the value of the expression to the right of the equal sign, and then stores this value in the variable to the left of the equal sign. For example, in the assignment statement `totalWeight = factor * weight;`, the arithmetic expression `factor * weight` is evaluated first to yield a result. This result, which is a number, is then stored in the variable `totalWeight`.

In writing assignment expressions, you must be aware of two important considerations. Because the expression to the right of the equal sign is evaluated first, all variables used in the expression must previously have been given valid values if the result is to make sense. For example, the assignment statement `totalWeight = factor * weight;` causes a valid number to be stored in `totalWeight` only if the programmer takes care to assign valid numbers first to `factor` and then to `weight`. Therefore, the following sequence of statements tells you the values used to obtain the result that will be stored in `totalWeight`:

```
factor = 1.06;
weight = 155.0;
totalWeight = factor * weight;
```

Figure 3.1 illustrates the values stored in the variables `factor`, `weight`, and `totalWeight`.

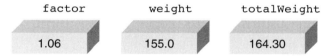

factor weight totalWeight

1.06 155.0 164.30

Figure 3.1 Values stored in variables

The second consideration is that because the value of an expression is stored in the variable to the left of the equal sign, only one variable can be listed in this position. For example, the assignment statement

```
amount + 1892 = 1000 + 10 * 5;
```

is invalid. The expression on the right evaluates to the integer 1050, which can only be stored in a variable. Because `amount + 1892` isn't a valid variable name, the compiler doesn't know where to store the calculated value.

Program 3.1 illustrates using assignment statements to calculate the volume of a cylinder. As shown in Figure 3.2, the volume of a cylinder is determined by the formula $volume = \pi r^2 h$, where r is the radius of the cylinder, h is the height, and π is the constant 3.1416 (accurate to four decimal places).

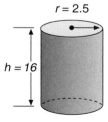

$r = 2.5$

$h = 16$

Figure 3.2 Determining the volume of a cylinder

Program 3.1

```
// this program calculates the volume of a cylinder,
// given its radius and height
#include <iostream>
using namespace std;

int main()
{
   double radius, height, volume;

   radius = 2.5;
   height = 16.0;
   volume = 3.1416 * radius * radius * height;
   cout << "The volume of the cylinder is " << volume << endl;

   return 0;
}
```

When Program 3.1 is compiled and executed, this is the output:

```
The volume of the cylinder is 314.16
```

Take a look at the flow of control the computer uses in executing Program 3.1. Program execution begins with the first statement in the body of the main() function and continues sequentially, statement by statement, until the closing brace of main() is encountered.

This sequential flow of control is true for all programs. The computer works on one statement at a time, executing that statement with no knowledge of what the next statement will be. This sequential execution explains why all operands used in an expression must have values assigned to them before the expression is evaluated. When the computer executes this statement in Program 3.1,

```
volume = 3.1416 * radius * radius * height;
```

it uses whatever value is stored in the variables radius and height at the time the assignment statement is executed.[2] If no values have been specifically assigned to these variables before they're used in the assignment statement, the computer uses whatever values happen to occupy these variables when they are referenced. (Most C++ compilers initialize all variables to zero automatically.) The computer doesn't "look ahead" to see whether you assign values to these variables later in the program.

In C++, the equal sign, =, used in assignment statements is an operator, which differs from the way most other high-level languages process this symbol. In C++ (as in C), the = symbol is called the **assignment operator**, and an expression using this operator, such as interest = principal * rate, is an **assignment expression**. Because the assignment

---

[2]Because C++ doesn't have an exponentiation operator, the square of the radius is obtained by the term radius * radius. Section 3.3 introduces C++'s power function pow(), which allows you to raise a number to a power.

operator has a lower precedence than any other arithmetic operator, the value of any expression to the right of the equal sign is evaluated first, before the assignment.

Like all expressions, an assignment expression has a value, which is the value assigned to the variable on the left of the assignment operator. For example, the expression a = 5 assigns a value of 5 to the variable a and results in the expression also having a value of 5. The expression's value can always be verified by using a statement such as the following:

```
cout << "The value of the expression is " << (a = 5);
```

This statement displays the value of the expression, not the contents of the variable a. Although both the variable's contents and the expression have the same value, it's worth realizing that you're dealing with two distinct entities.

From a programming perspective, it's the actual assignment of a value to a variable that's important in an assignment expression; the final value of the assignment expression is of little consequence. However, the fact that assignment expressions have a value has implications that must be considered when you learn about C++'s relational operators, which are explained in the next chapter (Section 4.1).

Any expression terminated by a semicolon becomes a C++ statement. The most common example is the assignment statement, which is simply an assignment expression terminated with a semicolon. For example, terminating the assignment expression a = 33 with a semicolon results in the assignment statement a = 33;, which can be used in a program on a line by itself.

Because the equal sign is an operator in C++, multiple assignments are possible in the same expression or its equivalent statement. For example, in the expression a = b = c = 25, all the assignment operators have the same precedence. Because the assignment operator has a right-to-left associativity, the final evaluation proceeds in this sequence:

```
c = 25
b = c
a = b
```

This sequence of expressions, which has the effect of assigning the number 25 to each variable, can be represented as:

```
a = (b = (c = 25))
```

Appending a semicolon to the original expression results in this multiple assignment statement:

```
a = b = c = 25;
```

This statement assigns the value 25 to the three variables, equivalent to the following order:

```
c = 25;
b = 25;
a = 25;
```

Coercion

When working with assignment statements, keep in mind the data type assigned to values on both sides of the expression because data type conversions occur across assignment operators. In other words, the value of the expression to the right of the assignment operator is converted to the data type of the variable to the left of the assignment operator. This type

---

Point of Information

lvalues and rvalues

The terms `lvalue` and `rvalue` are often used in programming technology. These terms are language independent and are used to designate the following: An `lvalue` can have a value assigned to it, but an `rvalue` can't.

In both C and C++, an `lvalue` can appear on both the left and right sides of an assignment operator, but an `rvalue` can appear only to the right of an assignment operator. All the variables you have encountered can be an `lvalue` or `rvalue`, but a number can be only an `rvalue`. Not all variables, however, can be `lvalues` and `rvalues`. For example, an array type, introduced in Chapter 7, can't be an `lvalue` or `rvalue`, but elements in an array can be both.

---

of conversion is called a **coercion** because the value assigned to the variable on the left side of the assignment operator is forced into the data type of the variable to which it's assigned.

An example of a coercion occurs when an integer value is assigned to a real variable; this assignment causes the integer to be converted to a real value. Similarly, assigning a real value to an integer variable forces conversion of the real value to an integer, which always results in losing the fractional part of the number because of truncation. For example, if temp is an integer variable, the assignment temp = 25.89 causes the integer value 25 to be stored in the integer variable temp.[3]

A more complete example of data type conversions, which includes both mixed-mode and assignment conversion, is the evaluation of the expression

```
a = b * d
```

where a and b are integer variables and d is a single-precision variable. When the mixed-mode expression b * d is evaluated,[4] the value of d used in the expression is converted to a double-precision number for purposes of computation. (The value stored in d remains a single-precision number.) Because one of the operands is a double-precision variable, the value of the integer variable b is converted to a double-precision number for the computation. (Again, the value stored in b remains an integer.) The resulting value of the expression b * d is a double-precision number. Finally, data type conversion across the assignment operator comes into play. Because the left side of the assignment operator is an integer variable, the double-precision value of the expression (b * d) is truncated to an integer value and stored in the variable a.

Assignment Variations

Although only one variable is allowed immediately to the left of the equal sign in an assignment expression, the variable to the left of the equal sign can also be used to the right. For example, the assignment expression sum = sum + 10 is valid. Clearly, as an algebraic equation, sum could never be equal to itself plus 10. In C++, however, sum = sum + 10 is *not* an equation—it's an expression evaluated in two major steps: First, the value of sum

---

[3]The correct integer portion is retained only when it's within the range of integers the compiler allows.
[4]Review the precedence and associativity rules in Section 2.4 for the evaluation of mixed-mode expressions, if necessary.

+ 10 is calculated, and second, the computed value is stored in sum. See whether you can determine the output of Program 3.2.

Program 3.2

```cpp
#include <iostream>
using namespace std;

int main()
{
    int sum;

    sum = 25;
    cout << "The number stored in sum is " << sum << endl;
    sum = sum + 10;
    cout << "The number now stored in sum is " << sum << endl;

    return 0;
}
```

In Program 3.2, the assignment statement sum = 25; tells the computer to store the number 25 in sum, as shown in Figure 3.3.

sum

Figure 3.3   The integer 25 is stored in sum

The first cout statement displays the value stored in sum with the message The number stored in sum is 25. The second assignment statement, sum = sum + 10;, causes the program to retrieve the 25 stored in sum and add 10 to this number, yielding 35. The number 35 is then stored in the variable to the left of the equal sign, which is the variable sum. The 25 that was in sum is simply overwritten with the new value of 35 (see Figure 3.4).

sum

Old value is overwritten   25   New value (35) is stored

Figure 3.4   sum = sum + 10; causes a new value to be stored in sum

Assignment expressions such as sum = sum + 25, which use the same variable on both sides of the assignment operator, can be written by using the following shortcut **assignment operators**:

```
+=    -=    *=    /=    %=
```

For example, the expression sum = sum + 10 can be written as sum += 10. Similarly, the expression price *= rate is equivalent to the expression price = price * rate. In using these new assignment operators, note that the variable to the left of the assignment operator is applied to the complete expression on the right. For example, the expression price *= rate + 1 is equivalent to the expression price = price * (rate + 1), not price = price * rate + 1.

Accumulating

Assignment expressions, such as sum += 10 or its equivalent, sum = sum + 10, are common in programming. These expressions are required in accumulating subtotals when data is entered one number at a time. For example, if you want to add the numbers 96, 70, 85, and 60 in calculator fashion, the following statements could be used:

Statement	Value in sum
sum = 0;	0
sum = sum + 96;	96
sum = sum + 70;	166
sum = sum + 85;	251
sum = sum + 60;	311

The first statement initializes sum to 0, which removes any number stored in sum that would invalidate the final total (a "garbage value"). As each number is added, the value stored in sum is increased accordingly. After completion of the last statement, sum contains the total of all the added numbers. Program 3.3 illustrates the effect of these statements by displaying sum's contents after each addition.

Program 3.3

```cpp
#include <iostream>
using namespace std;

int main()
{
  int sum;

  sum = 0;
  cout << "The value of sum is initially set to " << sum << endl;
  sum = sum + 96;
  cout << "   sum is now " << sum << endl;
  sum = sum + 70;
  cout << "   sum is now " << sum << endl;
  sum = sum + 85;
  cout << "   sum is now " << sum   << endl;
  sum = sum + 60;
  cout << "   The final sum is " << sum << endl;

  return 0;
}
```

Program 3.3 displays this output:

```
The value of sum is initially set to 0
   sum is now 96
   sum is now 166
   sum is now 251
   The final sum is 311
```

Although Program 3.3 isn't a practical program (because adding the numbers by hand is easier), it does illustrate the subtotaling effect of repeated use of statements having this form:

variable = variable + newValue;

This type of statement is called an **accumulation statement**. You'll find many uses for accumulation statements when you become more familiar with the repetition statements introduced in Chapter 5.

Counting

The **counting statement**, which is an assignment statement similar to the accumulating statement, has the following form:

variable = variable + fixedNumber;

Examples of counting statements are as follows:

```
i = i + 1;
n = n + 1;
count = count + 1;
j = j + 2;
m = m + 2;
kk = kk + 3;
```

In these examples, the same variable is used on both sides of the equal sign. After the statement is executed, the value of the variable is increased by a fixed amount. In the first three examples, the variables i, n, and count have been increased by one. In the next two examples, the variables have been increased by two, and in the final example, the variable kk has been increased by three.

For the case in which a variable is increased or decreased by only one, C++ provides two unary operators: increment and decrement operators. Using the increment operator,[5] ++, the expression variable = variable + 1 can be replaced by the expression variable++ or the expression ++variable. Here are examples of the increment operator:

Expression	Alternative
i = i + 1	i++ or ++i
n = n + 1	n++ or ++n
count = count + 1	count++ or ++count

Program 3.4 illustrates the use of the increment operator.

---

[5]As a historical note, the ++ in C++'s name was inspired by the increment operator symbol. It was used to indicate that C++ was the next increment to the C language.

Program 3.4

```
#include <iostream>
using namespace std;

int main()
{
  int count;

  count = 0;
  cout << "The initial value of count is " << count << endl;
  count++;
  cout << "    count is now " << count << endl;
  count++;
  cout << "    count is now " << count << endl;
  count++;
  cout << "    count is now " << count << endl;
  count++;
  cout << "    count is now " << count << endl;

  return 0;
}
```

This is the output displayed by Program 3.4:

```
The initial value of count is 0
    count is now 1
    count is now 2
    count is now 3
    count is now 4
```

When the ++ operator appears before a variable, it's called a **prefix increment operator**; when it appears after a variable, it's called a **postfix increment operator**. The distinction between a prefix and postfix increment operator is important when the variable being incremented is used in an assignment expression. For example, k = ++n, which uses a prefix increment operator, does two things in one expression: The value of n is incremented by one, and then the new value of n is assigned to the variable k. Therefore, the statement k = ++n; is equivalent to these two statements:

```
n = n + 1;    // increment n first
k = n;        // assign n's value to k
```

The assignment expression k = n++, which uses a postfix increment operator, reverses this procedure. A postfix increment operator works after the assignment is completed. Therefore, the statement k = n++; first assigns the current value of n to k, and then increments the value of n by one. This process is equivalent to these two statements:

```
k = n;          // assign n's value to k
n = n + 1;      // and then increment n
```

C++ also provides the decrement operator, --, in prefix and postfix variations. As you might expect, both the expressions variable-- and --variable are equivalent to the expression variable = variable - 1. Here are examples of the decrement operator:

Expression	Alternative
i = i - 1	i-- or --i
n = n - 1	n-- or --n
count = count - 1	count-- or --count

When the -- operator appears before a variable, it's called a **prefix decrement operator**. When this operator appears after a variable, it's called a **postfix decrement operator**. For example, both the expressions n-- and --n reduce the value of n by one and are equivalent to the longer expression n = n - 1.

As with the increment operators, however, the prefix and postfix decrement operators produce different results when used in assignment expressions. For example, the expression k = --n first decrements the value of n by one before assigning the value of n to k, and the expression k = n-- first assigns the current value of n to k, and then reduces the value of n by one.

EXERCISES 3.1

1. **(General Math)** Write an assignment statement to calculate the circumference of a circle having a radius of 3.3 inches. The formula for determining the circumference, c, of a circle is $c = 2\pi r$, where r is the radius and π equals 3.1416.

2. **(General Math)** Write an assignment statement to calculate the area of a circle. The formula for determining the area, a, of a circle is $a = \pi r^2$, where r is the radius and $\pi = 3.1416$.

3. **(Conversion)** Write an assignment statement to convert temperature in degrees Fahrenheit to degrees Celsius. The formula for this conversion is *Celsius = 5/9 (Fahrenheit - 32)*.

4. **(General Math)** Write an assignment statement to calculate the round-trip distance, d, in feet, of a trip that's s miles long one way.

5. **(Physics)** Write an assignment statement to calculate the elapsed time, in minutes, it takes to make a trip. The formula for computing elapsed time is *elapsed time = total distance / average speed*. Assume the distance is in miles and the average speed is in miles per hour (mph).

6. **(Numerical)** Write an assignment statement to calculate the nth term in an arithmetic sequence. This is the formula for calculating the value, v, of the nth term:
$v = a + (n - 1)d$

d is the difference between any two numbers in the sequence.

a is the first number in the sequence.

7. **(Civil Eng.)** Write an assignment statement to calculate the linear expansion in a steel beam as a function of temperature increase. The formula for linear expansion, l, is as follows:

$l = l_0[1 + \alpha\,(T_f - T_0)]$

l_0 is the length of the beam at temperature T_0.

α is the coefficient of linear expansion.

T_f is the final temperature of the beam.

8. **(Physics)** Coulomb's Law states that the force, F, acting between two electrically charged spheres is given by this formula:

$$F = \frac{k\,q_1\,q_2}{r^2}$$

q_1 is the charge on the first sphere.

q_2 is the charge on the second sphere.

r is the distance between the centers of the two spheres.

k is a proportionality constant.

Write an assignment statement to calculate the force, F.

9. **(Civil Eng.)** Write an assignment statement to determine the maximum bending moment, M, of a beam, given this formula:

$$M = \frac{X\,W\,(L - X)}{L}$$

X is the distance from the end of the beam that a weight, W, is placed.

L is the length of the beam.

10. **(Desk Check)** Determine the output of the following program:

```cpp
#include <iostream>
using namespace std;

int main() // a program illustrating integer truncation
{
    int num1, num2;

    num1 = 9/2;
    num2 = 17/4;
    cout << "the first integer displayed is " << num1 << endl;
    cout << "the second integer displayed is " << num2 << endl;
    return 0;
}
```

11. **(Debug)** Determine and correct the errors in the following programs.

a.
```cpp
#include <iostream>
using namespace std;
int main()
{
  width = 15
  area = length * width;
  cout << "The area is " << area

}
```

b.
```cpp
#include <iostream>
using namespace std;
int main()
{
  int length, width, area;
  area = length * width;
  length = 20;
  width = 15;
  cout << "The area is " << area;

  return 0;
```

c.
```cpp
#include <iostream.h>

int main()
{
  int length = 20; width = 15, area;
  length * width = area;
  cout << "The area is " , area;

  return 0;
}
```

12. **(Debug)** By mistake, a student reordered the statements in Program 3.3 as follows:

```cpp
#include <iostream>
using namespace std;

int main()
{
  int sum;
  sum = 0;
  sum = sum + 96;
  sum = sum + 70;
  sum = sum + 85;
  sum = sum + 60;
  cout << "The value of sum is initially set to " << sum << endl;
  cout << "   sum is now " << sum << endl;
  cout << "   sum is now " << sum << endl;
  cout << "   sum is now " << sum << endl;
  cout << "   The final sum is " << sum << endl;

  return 0;
}
```

Determine the output this program produces.

13. **(General Math)** Using Program 3.1, complete the following chart by determining the volume of cylinders having these radii and heights:

Radius (in)	Height (in)	Volume
1.62	6.23	
2.86	7.52	
4.26	8.95	
8.52	10.86	
12.29	15.35	

14. **(General Math)** The area of an ellipse (see Figure 3.5) is given by this formula:

$Area = \pi\, a\, b$

Using this formula, write a C++ program to calculate the area of an ellipse having a minor axis, a, of 2.5 inches and a major axis, b, of 6.4 inches.

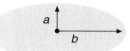

Figure 3.5 The minor axis, a, and the major axis, b, of an ellipse

15. **(Modify)** Modify Program 3.1 to calculate the weight, in pounds, of the steel cylinder whose volume was determined in that program. This is the formula for determining the weight:

$weight = 0.28\,(\pi)(r^2)(h)$

r is the radius (in inches).
h is the height (in inches) of the cylinder.

3.2 Formatting Numbers for Program Output

Besides displaying correct results, a program should present its results attractively. Most programs are judged on the perceived ease of data entry and the style and presentation of the output. For example, displaying a monetary result as 1.897 isn't in keeping with accepted report conventions. The display should be $1.90 or $1.89, depending on whether rounding or truncation is used.

To control the format of numbers displayed by cout, you can include **field width manipulators** in an output stream. Table 3.1 lists the most common stream manipulators for this purpose.[6]

Table 3.1   Commonly Used Stream Manipulators

Manipulator	Action
setw(n)	Set the field width to n.
setprecision(n)	Set the floating-point precision to n places. If the fixed manipulator is designated, n specifies the total number of displayed digits after the decimal point; otherwise, n specifies the total number of significant digits displayed (integer plus fractional digits).
setfill('x')	Set the default leading fill character to x. (The default leading fill character is a space, which is used to fill the beginning of an output field when the field width is larger than the value being displayed.)
setiosflags (flags)	Set the format flags. (See Table 3.3 for flag settings.)
scientific	Set the output to display real numbers in scientific notation.
showbase	Display the base used for numbers. A leading 0 is displayed for octal numbers and a leading 0x for hexadecimal numbers.
showpoint	Always display six digits total (combination of integer and fractional parts). Fill with trailing zeros, if necessary. For larger integer values, revert to scientific notation.
showpos	Display all positive numbers with a leading + sign.
boolalpha	Display Boolean values as true and false rather than 1 and 0.
dec	Set the output for decimal display, which is the default.
endl	Output a newline character and display all characters in the buffer.
fixed	Always show a decimal point and use a default of six digits after the decimal point. Fill with trailing zeros, if necessary.
flush	Display all characters in the buffer.
left	Left-justify all numbers.
hex	Set the output for hexadecimal display.
oct	Set the output for octal display.
uppercase	Display hexadecimal digits and the exponent in scientific notation in uppercase.
right	Right-justify all numbers (the default).
noboolalpha	Display Boolean values as 1 and 0 rather than true and false.
noshowbase	Don't display octal numbers with a leading 0 and hexadecimal numbers with a leading 0x.

---

[6]As noted in Chapter 2, the endl manipulator inserts a new line and then forces all current insertions to be displayed immediately, called "flushing the stream."

Table 3.1 Commonly Used Stream Manipulators (continued)

Manipulator	Action
noshowpoint	Don't use a decimal point for real numbers with no fractional parts, don't display trailing zeros in the fractional part of a number, and display a maximum of six decimal digits only.
noshowpos	Don't display leading + signs (the default).
nouppercase	Display hexadecimal digits and the exponent in scientific notation in lowercase.

For example, the statement cout << "The sum of 6 and 15 is" << setw(3) << 21; creates this printout:

```
The sum of 6 and 15 is 21
```

The setw(3) field width manipulator included in the data stream sent to cout is used to set the displayed field width. The 3 in this manipulator sets the default field width for the next number in the stream to be three spaces. This field width setting causes the 21 to beprinted in a field of three spaces, which includes one blank and the number 21. As shown in this output, integers are right-justified in the specified field.

Field width manipulators are useful in printing columns of numbers so that the numbers align correctly in each column. For example, Program 3.5 shows how a column of integers aligns in the absence of field width manipulators.

Program 3.5

```cpp
#include <iostream>
using namespace std;

int main()
{
  cout << 6 << endl
       << 18 << endl
       << 124 << endl
       << "---\n"
       << (6+18+124) << endl;

  return 0;
}
```

The output of Program 3.5 is the following:

```
6
18
124
---
148
```

Because no field width manipulators are used in Program 3.5, cout allocates enough space for each number as it's received. Forcing numbers to align on the units digit requires a field width wide enough for the largest displayed number, which is three for the numbers in Program 3.5. Program 3.6 shows the use of this field width.

 ## Program 3.6

```cpp
#include <iostream>
#include <iomanip>
using namespace std;

int main()
{
  cout << setw(3) << 6 << endl
       << setw(3) << 18 << endl
       << setw(3) << 124 << endl
       << "---\n"
       << (6+18+124) << endl;

  return 0;
}
```

The output of Program 3.6 is as follows:

```
  6
 18
124
---
148
```

The field width manipulator must be included for each occurrence of a number inserted in the data stream sent to cout; the manipulator applies only to the next insertion of data immediately following it, and the other manipulators remain in effect until they're changed.

When a manipulator requiring an argument is used, the iomanip header file must be included as part of the program. To do this, you use the preprocessor command #include <iomanip>, which is the second line in Program 3.6.

Formatting Numbers for Program Output

Formatting floating-point numbers requires using three field width manipulators. The first manipulator sets the total width of the display, the second manipulator forces the display of a decimal point, and the third manipulator determines how many significant digits are displayed to the right of the decimal point. (See the "Point of Information" box in Chapter 2 for a review of significant digits.) For example, examine the following statement:

```
cout << "|" << setw(10) << fixed << setprecision(3) << 25.67 << "|";
```

It causes the following printout:

```
|    25.670|
```

The bar symbol, |, in this example is used to delimit (mark) the beginning and end of the display field. The `setw` manipulator tells `cout` to display the number in a total field of 10. (With real numbers, the decimal point takes up one of these field locations.) The `fixed` manipulator forces the display of a decimal point and specifies using the `setprecision` manipulator to designate the number of digits displayed after the decimal point. In this case, `setprecision` specifies a display of three digits after the decimal point. Without the explicit designation of a decimal point (which can also be designated as `setiosflags(ios::fixed)`, explained shortly), the `setprecision` manipulator specifies the total number of displayed digits, which includes the integer and fractional parts of the number.

For all numbers (integers, single-precision, and double-precision), `cout` ignores the `setw` manipulator specification if the total specified field width is too small, and it allocates enough space for printing the integer part of the number. The fractional part of single-precision and double-precision numbers is displayed up to the precision set with the `setprecision` manipulator. (In the absence of `setprecision`, the default precision is set to six decimal places.) If the fractional part of the number to be displayed contains more digits than are called for in the `setprecision` manipulator, the number is rounded to the indicated number of decimal places; if the fractional part contains fewer digits than specified, the number is displayed with fewer digits. Table 3.2 shows the effect of several format manipulator combinations. For clarity, the bar symbol delimits the beginning and end of output fields.

Table 3.2 Effect of Format Manipulators

Manipulators	Number	Display	Comments
setw(2)	3	| 3|	Number fits in the field.
setw(2)	43	|43|	Number fits in the field.
setw(2)	143	|143|	Field width is ignored.
setw(2)	2.3	|2.3|	Field width is ignored.
setw(5) fixed setprecision(2)	2.366	| 2.37|	Field width of five with two decimal digits.
setw(5) fixed setprecision(2)	42.3	|42.30|	Number fits in the field with the specified precision. Note that the decimal point takes up one location in the field width.
setw(5) setprecision(2)	142.364	|1.4e+002|	Field width is ignored, and scientific notation is used with the setprecision manipulator.

Table 3.2   Effect of Format Manipulators (continued)

Manipulators	Number	Display	Comments
`setw(5) fixed` `setprecision(2)`	142.364	|142.36|	Field width is ignored, but precision specification is used. The `setprecision` manipulator specifies the number of fractional digits.
`setw(5) fixed` `setprecision(2)`	142.366	|142.37|	Field width is ignored, but precision specification used. The `setprecision` manipulator specifies the number of fractional digits. (Note the rounding of the last decimal digit.)
`setw(5) fixed` `setprecision(2)`	142	| 142|	Field width is used; `fixed` and `setprecision` manipulators are irrelevant because the number is an integer that specifies the total number of significant digits (integer plus fractional digits).

In addition to the `setw` and `setprecision` manipulators, a field justification manipulator is available. As you have seen, numbers sent to `cout` are normally right-justified in the display field, and strings are left-justified. To alter the default justification for a stream of data, you use the `setiosflags` manipulator. For example, the statement

```
cout << "|" << setw(10) << setiosflags(ios::left) << 142 << "|";
```

causes the following left-justified display:

```
|142       |
```

Because data sent to `cout` can be continued across multiple lines, the previous display is also produced by this statement:

```
cout << "|" << setw(10)
     << setiosflags(ios::left)
     << 142 << "|";
```

As always, the field width manipulator is in effect only for the next set of data displayed by `cout`. To right-justify strings in a stream, you use the `setiosflags(ios::right)` manipulator. The letters "ios" in the function name and the `ios::right` argument come from the first letters of the words "input output stream."

In addition to the `left` and `right` flags that can be used with `setiosflags()`, other flags can be used to affect output. Table 3.3 lists the most commonly used flags for this manipulator function. The flags in this table provide another way of setting the manipulators listed in Table 3.1.

Point of Information

What Is a Flag?

In current programming usage, the term **flag** refers to an item, such as a variable or argument, that sets a condition usually considered active or nonactive. Although the exact origin of this term in programming is unknown, it probably came from using real flags to signal a condition, such as the Stop, Go, Caution, and Winner flags commonly used at car races.

In a similar manner, each flag argument for the `setiosflags()` manipulator function activates a specific condition. For example, the `ios::dec` flag sets the display format to decimal, and the `ios::oct` flag activates the octal display format. Because these conditions are mutually exclusive (only one can be active at a time), activating this type of flag deactivates the other flags automatically.

Flags that aren't mutually exclusive, such as `ios::dec`, `ios::showpoint`, and `ios::fixed`, can be set simultaneously. You can do this by using three separate `setiosflag()` calls or combining all arguments into one call as follows:

```
cout << setiosflags(ios::dec | ios::fixed | ios::showpoint);
```

Table 3.3   Format Flags for Use with `setiosflags()`

Flag	Meaning
`ios::fixed`	Always show the decimal point with six digits after the decimal point. Fill with trailing zeros after the decimal point, if necessary. This flag takes precedence if it's set with the `ios::showpoint` flag.
`ios::scientific`	Use exponential display in the output.
`ios::showpoint`	Always display a decimal point and six significant digits total (combination of integer and fractional parts). Fill with trailing zeros after the decimal point, if necessary. For larger integer values, revert to scientific notation unless the `ios::fixed` flag is set.
`ios::showpos`	Display a leading + sign when the number is positive.
`ios::left`	Left-justify the output.
`ios::right`	Right-justify the output.

Because the flags in Table 3.3 are used as arguments to `setiosflags()` and the terms "argument" and "parameter" are synonymous, another name for a manipulator method that uses arguments is a **parameterized manipulator**. The following is an example of a parameterized manipulator method:

```
cout << setiosflags(ios::showpoint) << setprecision(4);
```

This statement forces all subsequent floating-point numbers sent to the output stream to be displayed with a decimal point and four decimal digits. If the number has fewer than four decimal digits, it's padded with trailing zeros.

In addition to outputting integers in decimal notation, the oct and hex manipulators are used for conversions to octal and hexadecimal; Program 3.7 uses these flags. Because decimal is the default display, the dec manipulator isn't required in the first output stream.

Program 3.7

```cpp
// a program that illustrates output conversions
#include <iostream>
#include <iomanip>
using namespace std;

int main()
{
  cout << "The decimal (base 10) value of 15 is " << 15 << endl;
  cout << "The octal (base 8) value of 15 is "
       << showbase << oct << 15 <<endl;
  cout << "The hexadecimal (base 16) value of 15 is "
        << showbase << hex << 15 << endl;

  return 0;
}
```

The output produced by Program 3.7 is the following:

```
The decimal (base 10) value of 15 is 15
The octal (base 8) value of 15 is 017
The hexadecimal (base 16) value of 15 is 0xf
```

The display of integer values in one of three possible number systems (decimal, octal, and hexadecimal) doesn't affect how the number is stored in a computer. All numbers arestored by using the computer's internal codes. The manipulators sent to cout tell the object how to convert the internal code for output display purposes.

Besides displaying integers in octal or hexadecimal form, they can also be written in a program in these forms. To designate an octal integer, the number must have a leading zero. The number 023, for example, is an octal number in C++. Hexadecimal numbers are denoted with a leading 0x. Program 3.8 shows how octal and hexadecimal integer numbers are used and produces the following output:

```
The decimal value of 025 is 21
The decimal value of 0x37 is 55
```

Point of Information

Formatting cout Stream Data

Floating-point data in a cout output stream can be formatted in precise ways. For example, a common format requirement is to display monetary amounts with two digits after the decimal point, such as 123.45. You can do this with the following statement:

```
cout << setiosflags(ios::fixed)
     << setiosflags(ios::showpoint)
     << setprecision(2);
```

The first manipulator flag, ios::fixed, forces all floating-point numbers in the cout stream to be displayed in decimal notation. This flag also prevents using scientific notation. The next flag, ios::showpoint, tells the stream to always display a decimal point. Finally, the setprecision manipulator tells the stream to always display two digits after the decimal point. Instead of using manipulators, you can use the cout stream methods setf() and precision(). For example, the previous formatting can also be accomplished with this code:

```
cout.setf(ios::fixed);
cout.setf(ios::showpoint);
cout.precision(2);
```

Note the syntax: The name of the object, cout, is separated from the method with a period. This format is the standard way of specifying a method and connecting it to a specific object.

Additionally, the flags used in both the setf() method and the setiosflags() manipulator method can be combined by using the bitwise OR operator, | (explained in Section 15.2). Using this operator, the following two statements are equivalent:

```
cout <<  setiosflags(ios::fixed | ios::showpoint);
cout.setf(ios::fixed | ios::showpoint);
```

The statement you select is a matter of personal preference or a predefined imposed standard.

Program 3.8

```cpp
#include <iostream>
using namespace std;

int main()
{
  cout << "The decimal value of 025 is " << 025 << endl
       << "The decimal value of 0x37 is "<< 0x37 << endl;

  return 0;
}
```

The relationship between input, storage, and display of integers is illustrated in Figure 3.6.

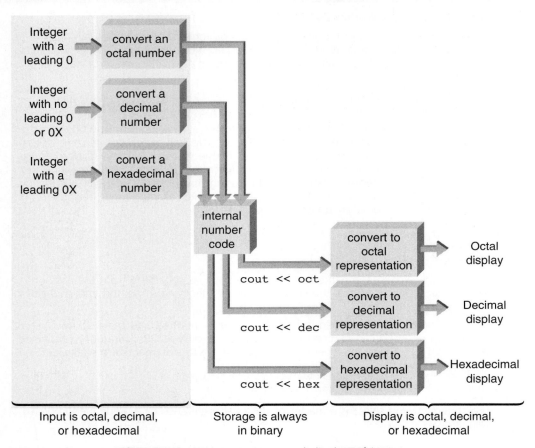

Figure 3.6 Input, storage, and display of integers

Finally, you can set the manipulators listed in Tables 3.1 and 3.2 by using the `ostream` class functions listed in Table 3.4.

Table 3.4 `ostream` Class Functions

Method	Comment	Example
`precision(n)`	Equivalent to `setprecision()`	`cout.precision(2)`
`fill('x')`	Equivalent to `setfill()`	`cout.fill('*')`
`setf(ios::fixed)`	Equivalent to `cout.setf(ios::fixed)`	`setiosflags(ios::fixed)`
`setf(ios::showpoint)`	Equivalent to `cout.setf(ios::showpoint)`	`setiosflags(ios::showpoint)`
`setf(iof::left)`	Equivalent to `left`	`cout.setf(ios::left)`

Table 3.4 ostream Class Functions (continued)

Method	Comment	Example
`setf(ios::right)`	Equivalent to `right`	`cout.setf(ios::right)`
`setf(ios::flush)`	Equivalent to `endl`	`cout.setf(ios::flush)`

In the Example column of Table 3.4, the name of the object, `cout`, is separated from the function with a period. As mentioned, this format is the standard way of calling a class function and providing it with an object to operate on.

EXERCISES 3.2

1. **(Desk Check)** Determine the output of the following program:

```cpp
#include <iostream>
using namespace std;

int main()  // a program illustrating integer truncation
{
  cout << "answer1 is the integer " <<  9/4
       << "\nanswer2 is the integer " <<  17/3 << endl;

  return 0;
}
```

2. **(Desk Check)** Determine the output of the following program:

```cpp
#include <iostream>
using namespace std;
int main()  // a program illustrating the % operator
{
  cout << "The remainder of 9 divided by 4 is " <<  9 % 4
       << "\nThe remainder of 17 divided by 3 is " <<  17 % 3 << endl;
  return 0;
}
```

3. **(Practice)** Write a C++ program that displays the results of the expressions `3.0 * 5.0`, `7.1 * 8.3 - 2.2`, and `3.2 / (6.1 * 5)`. Calculate the value of these expressions manually to verify that the displayed values are correct.

4. **(Practice)** Write a C++ program that displays the results of the expressions `15 / 4`, `15 % 4`, and `5 * 3 - (6 * 4)`. Calculate the value of these expressions manually to verify that the display your program produces is correct.

5. **(Debug)** Determine the errors in the following statements:

   a. `cout << "\n << " 15)`

   b. `cout << "setw(4)" << 33;`

   c. `cout << "setprecision(5)" << 526.768;`

   d. `"Hello World!" >> cout;`

   e. `cout << 47 << setw(6);`

   f. `cout << set(10) << 526.768 << setprecision(2);`

6. **(Desk Check)** Determine and write out the display produced by the following statements:

   a. `cout << "|" << 5 <<"|";`

   b. `cout << "|" << setw(4) << 5 << "|";`

   c. `cout << "|" << setw(4) << 56829 << "|";`

   d. `cout << "|" << setw(5)  << setiosflags(ios::fixed)`
       `<< setprecision(2) << 5.26 << "|";`

   e. `cout << "|" << setw(5)  << setiosflags(ios::fixed)`
       `<< setprecision(2) << 5.267 << "|";`

   f. `cout << "|" << setw(5)  << setiosflags(ios::fixed)`
       `<< setprecision(2) << 53.264 << "|";`

   g. `cout << "|" << setw(5)  << setiosflags(ios::fixed)`
       `<< setprecision(2) << 534.264 << "|";`

   h. `cout << "|" << setw(5)  << setiosflags(ios::fixed)`
       `<< setprecision(2) << 534. << "|";`

7. **(Desk Check)** Write out the display produced by the following statements:

   a. `cout << "The number is " << setw(6) << setiosflags(ios::fixed)`
       `<< setprecision(2)  << 26.27 << endl;`
   `cout << "The number is " << setw(6) << setiosflags(ios::fixed)`
       `<< setprecision(2)  << 682.3 << endl;`
   `cout << "The number is " << setw(6) << setiosflags(ios::fixed)`
       `<< setprecision(2)  << 1.968 << endl;`

   b. `cout << setw(6) << setiosflags(ios::fixed)`
       `<< setprecision(2) << 26.27 << endl;`
   `cout << setw(6) << setiosflags(ios::fixed)`
       `<< setprecision(2) << 682.3 << endl;`
   `cout << setw(6) << setiosflags(ios::fixed)`
       `<< setprecision(2) << 1.968 << endl;`
   `cout << "------\n";`
   `cout << setw(6) << setiosflags(ios::fixed)`
       `<< setprecision(2)`
       `<< 26.27 + 682.3 + 1.968 << endl;`

c. ```
cout << setw(5) << setiosflags(ios::fixed)
     << setprecision(2) << 26.27 << endl;
cout << setw(5) << setiosflags(ios::fixed)
     << setprecision(2) << 682.3 << endl;
cout << setw(5) << setiosflags(ios::fixed)
     << setprecision(2) << 1.968 << endl;
cout << "-----\n";
cout << setw(5) << setiosflags(ios::fixed)
     << setprecision(2)
     << 26.27 + 682.3 + 1.968 << endl;
```

d. ```
cout << setw(5) << setiosflags(ios::fixed)
     << setprecision(2) << 36.164 << endl;
cout << setw(5) << setiosflags(ios::fixed)
     << setprecision(2) << 10.003 << endl;
cout << "-----" << endl;
```

8. **(Desk Check)** The following chart lists the equivalent octal and hexadecimal representations for the decimal numbers 1 through 15:

```
    Decimal: 1  2  3  4  5  6  7  8   9   10  11  12  13  14  15
      Octal: 1  2  3  4  5  6  7  10  11  12  13  14  15  16  17
Hexadecimal: 1  2  3  4  5  6  7  8   9   a   b   c   d   e   f
```

Using this chart, determine the output of the following program:

```cpp
#include <iostream>
#include <iomanip>
using namespace std;

int main()
{
  cout << "\nThe value of 14 in octal is " << oct << 14
       << "\nThe value of 14 in hexadecimal is " << hex << 14
       << "\nThe value of 0xA in decimal is " << dec << 0xA
       << "\nThe value of 0xA in octal is " << oct << 0xA
       << endl;

  return 0;
}
```

9. **(Electrical Eng.)** The combined resistance of three resistors connected in parallel, as shown in Figure 3.7, is given by this formula:

$$\textit{Combined resistance} = \frac{1}{\left(\dfrac{1}{R_1} + \dfrac{1}{R_2} + \dfrac{1}{R_3}\right)}$$

Using this formula, write a C++ program to calculate and display the combined resistance when the three resistors $R_1 = 1000$, $R_2 = 1000$, and $R_3 = 1000$ are connected in parallel. The output should produce this display:

```
The combined resistance is xxxx.xx ohms
```

The `xxxx.xx` denotes placing the calculated value in a field width of seven columns, with two positions to the right of the decimal point.

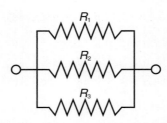

Figure 3.7   Three resistors connected in parallel

10. **(General Math)** Write a C++ program to calculate and display the value of the slope of the line connecting two points with the coordinates (3,7) and (8,12). Use the fact that the slope between two points at the coordinates (x_1,y_1) and (x_2,y_2) is slope $= (y_2 - y_1) / (x_2 - x_1)$. Your program should produce this display:

```
The value of the slope is xxx.xx
```

The `xxx.xx` denotes placing the calculated value in a field wide enough for three places to the left of the decimal point and two places to the right of it.

11. **(General Math)** Write a C++ program to calculate and display the midpoint coordinates of the line connecting the two points with coordinates of (3,7) and (8,12). Use the fact that the midpoint coordinates between two points with the coordinates (x_1,y_1) and (x_2,y_2) are $((x_1 + x_2)/2, (y_1 + y_2)/2)$. Your program should produce this display:

```
The x coordinate of the midpoint is xxx.xx
The y coordinate of the midpoint is xxx.xx
```

The `xxx.xx` denotes placing the calculated value in a field wide enough for three places to the left of the decimal point and two places to the right of it.

12. **(Civil Eng.)** Write a C++ program to calculate and display the maximum bending moment, M, of a beam that's supported on both ends (see Figure 3.8). The formula is $M = XW (L - X) / L$, where X is the distance from the end of the beam that a weight, W, is placed, and L is the length of the beam. Your program should produce this display:

```
The maximum bending moment is xxxx.xxxx
```

The `xxxx.xxxx` denotes placing the calculated value in a field wide enough for four places to the right and left of the decimal point. For your program, assign the values 1.2, 1.3, and 11.2 to X, W, and L.

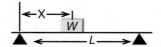

Figure 3.8   Calculating the maximum bending moment

3.3   Using Mathematical Library Functions

As you have seen, assignment statements can be used to perform arithmetic computations. For example, the following assignment statement multiplies the value in `current` by the value in `resistance` and assigns the resulting value to `volts`:

```
volts = resistance * current;
```

Although addition, subtraction, multiplication, and division are accomplished easily with C++'s arithmetic operators, no operators exist for raising a number to a power, finding a number's square root, or determining trigonometric values. To perform these calculations,C++ provides standard preprogrammed functions that can be included in a program. Before using one of C++'s mathematical functions, you need to know the following:

- The name of the mathematical function
- What the mathematical function does
- The type of data the mathematical function requires
- The data type of the result the mathematical function returns
- How to include the mathematical library

To illustrate the use of C++'s mathematical functions, take a look at the mathematical function `sqrt()`, which calculates a number's square root and uses this form:

```
sqrt(number)
```

The function's name, in this case `sqrt`, is followed by parentheses containing the number for which the square root should be calculated. The purpose of the parentheses after the function name is to provide a funnel through which data can be passed to the function (see Figure 3.9). The items passed to the function through the parentheses are called arguments of the function and constitute its input data. For example, the following expressions are used to compute the square root of the arguments 4., 17.0, 25., 1043.29, and 6.4516:

```
sqrt(4.)
sqrt(17.0)
sqrt(25.)
sqrt(1043.29)
sqrt(6.4516)
```

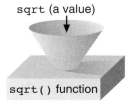

Figure 3.9   Passing data to the `sqrt()` function

Notice that the argument to the `sqrt()` function must be a real value, which is an example of C++'s function overloading capabilities. **Function overloading** permits using the same function name for arguments of different data types.[7] There are actually three functions named sqrt()—defined for float, double, and long double arguments. The correct sqrt() function is called depending on the type of value passed to the function when the call is made. When one of the functions named sqrt() is called (again, the selection isautomatic, based on the passed argument), the function determines the square root of its argument and returns the result as a double. The previous expressions return these values:

Expression	Value Returned
sqrt(4.)	2.
sqrt(17.0)	4.12311
sqrt(25.)	5.
sqrt(1043.29)	32.2
sqrt(6.4516)	2.54

In addition to the sqrt() function, Table 3.5 lists commonly used mathematical functions provided in C++. Accessing these functions in a program requires including the mathematical header file cmath, which contains declarations for mathematical functions. To use this header file, place the following preprocessor statement at the top of any program using a mathematical function:

```
#include <cmath>
```

Although some mathematical functions in Table 3.5 require more than one argument, all functions, by definition, can return at most one value. Additionally, all the functions listed are overloaded, which means the same function name can be used with integer and real arguments. Table 3.6 shows the value returned by selected functions, using sample arguments.

Table 3.5 Common C++ Functions

Function Name	Description	Returned Value
abs(a)	absolute value	Same data type as argument
pow(a1,a2)	a1 raised to the a2 power	Same data type as argument a1
sqrt(a)	square root of a real number	Double-precision
sin(a)	sine of a (a in radians)	Double
cos(a)	cosine of a (a in radians)	Double
tan(a)	tangent of a (a in radians)	Double

---

[7]If it weren't for overloading, three separate square root functions, each with a different name, would have to be defined—one for each type of argument.

Table 3.5   Common C++ Functions (continued)

Function Name	Description	Returned Value
log(a)	natural logarithm of a	Double
log10(a)	common log (base 10) of a	Double
exp(a)	e raised to the a power	Double

Table 3.6   Selected Function Examples

Example	Returned Value
abs(-7.362)	7.362
abs(-3)	3
pow(2.0,5.0)	32.
pow(10,3)	1000
log(18.697)	2.92836
log10(18.697)	1.27177
exp(-3.2)	0.040762

Each time a mathematical function is used, it's called into action by giving the name of the function and passing to it any data in the parentheses following the function's name (see Figure 3.10).

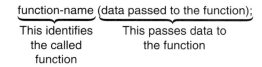

Figure 3.10   Using and passing data to a function

The arguments passed to a function need not be single constants. Expressions can also be arguments, provided the expression can be computed to yield a value of the required data type. For example, the following arguments are valid for the given functions:

```
sqrt(4.0 + 5.3 * 4.0)          abs(2.3 * 4.6)
sqrt(16.0 * 2.0 - 6.7)         sin(theta - phi)
sqrt(x * y - z/3.2)            cos(2.0 * omega)
```

The expressions in parentheses are evaluated first to yield a specific value. Therefore, values have to be assigned to the variables theta, phi, x, y, z, and omega before their use in the preceding expressions. After the value of the argument is calculated, it's passed to the function.

Functions can also be included as part of larger expressions, as shown in this example:

```
4 * sqrt(4.5 * 10.0 - 9.0) - 2.0
=   4 * sqrt(36.0) - 2.0
=   4 * 6.0 - 2.0
=   24.0 - 2.0
=   22.0
```

The step-by-step evaluation of an expression such as

```
3.0 * sqrt(5 * 33 - 13.71) / 5
```

is as follows:

Step	Result
1. Perform multiplication in the argument.	`3.0 * sqrt(165 - 13.71) / 5`
2. Complete the argument calculation.	`3.0 * sqrt(151.29) / 5`
3. Return a function value.	`3.0 * 12.3 / 5`
4. Perform the multiplication.	`36.9 / 5`
5. Perform the division.	`7.38`

Program 3.9 illustrates using the `sqrt()` function to determine the time it takes a ball to hit the ground after it has been dropped from an 800-foot tower. This is the mathematical formula for calculating the time in seconds it takes to fall a given distance in feet:

$$time = sqrt(2 \times distance \,/\, g)$$

where g is the gravitational constant, equal to 32.2 ft/sec^2.

Program 3.9

```cpp
#include <iostream>   // this line can be placed second instead of first
#include <cmath>      // this line can be placed first instead of second
using namespace std;

int main()
{
  int height;
  double time;

  height = 800;
  time = sqrt(2 * height / 32.2);
  cout << "It will take " << time << " seconds to fall "
       << height << " feet.\n";

  return 0;
}
```

Program 3.9 produces this output:

```
It will take 7.04907 seconds to fall 800 feet.
```

As used in Program 3.9, the value the `sqrt()` function returns is assigned to the variable `time`. In addition to assigning a function's returned value to a variable, the returned value can be included in a larger expression or even used as an argument to another function. For example, the following expression is valid:

```
sqrt( sin( abs(theta) ) )
```

Because parentheses are present, the computation proceeds from the inner to outer pairs of parentheses. Therefore, the absolute value of `theta` is computed first and used as anargument to the `sin()` function. The value the `sin()` function returns is then used as an argument to the `sqrt()` function.

Note that the arguments of all trigonometric functions (`sin()`, `cos()`, and so forth) must be in radians. Therefore, to calculate the sine of an angle given in degrees, the angle must be converted to radians first. You can do this easily by multiplying the angle by the term (3.1416/180.). For example, to obtain the sine of 30 degrees, use the expression `sin (30 * 3.1416/180.)`.

Casts

You have already seen the conversion of an operand's data type in mixed-mode arithmetic expressions (Section 2.4) and with different operators (Section 3.1). In addition to the implicit data type conversions made automatically in mixed-mode arithmetic and assignment expressions, C++ provides for explicit user-specified type conversions. The operator used to force converting a value to another type is the **cast operator**. C++ provides compile-time and runtime cast operators. The compile-time cast is a unary operator with this syntax:

dataType (expression)

The *dataType* is the data type to which the expression in parentheses is converted. For example, the following expression

```
int (a * b)
```

converts the value of the expression `a * b` to an integer value.[8]

With the introduction of the latest C++ standard, runtime casts are included. In this type of cast, the requested type conversion is checked at runtime and applied if the conversion results in a valid value. Although four types of runtime casts are available, the most commonly used cast and the one corresponding to the compile-time cast has the following syntax:

staticCast<data-type> (expression)

For example, the runtime cast `staticCast<int>(a * b)` is equivalent to the compile-time cast `int (a* b)`.

---

[8]The C type cast syntax, in this case `(int)(a * b)`, also works in C++.

EXERCISES 3.3

1. **(Practice)** Write function calls to determine the following:

   a. The square root of 6.37

   b. The square root of x - y

   c. The sine of 30 degrees

   d. The sine of 60 degrees

   e. The absolute value of a^2 - b^2

   f. The value of e raised to the third power

2. **(Practice)** For a = 10.6, b = 13.9, and c = -3.42, determine the following values:

   a. `int (a)`

   b. `int (b)`

   c. `int (c)`

   d. `int (a + b)`

   e. `int (a) + b + c`

   f. `int (a + b) + c`

   g. `int (a + b + c)`

   h. `float (int (a)) + b`

   i. `float (int (a + b))`

   j. `abs(a) + abs(b)`

   k. `sqrt(abs(a - b))`

3. **(Practice)** Write C++ statements for the following:

   a. $b = \sin x - \cos x$

   b. $b = \sin^2 x - \cos^2 x$

   c. $area = (c \times b \times \sin a)/2$

   d. $c = \sqrt{a^2 + b^2}$

   e. $p = \sqrt{|m - n|}$

   f. $sum = \dfrac{a(r^n - 1)}{r - 1}$

4. **(Numerical)** Write, compile, and execute a C++ program that calculates and returns the fourth root of the number 81.0, which is 3. After verifying that your program works correctly, use it to determine the fourth root of 1,728.896400. Your program should make use of the `sqrt()` function.

5. **(General Math)** Write, compile, and execute a C++ program to calculate the distance between two points with the coordinates (7, 12) and (3, 9). Use the fact that the distance between two points with the coordinates (x_1, y_1) and (x_2, y_2) is given by this formula:

$$distance = \sqrt{\left(x^2 + y^2\right)}$$

After verifying that your program works correctly by calculating the distance between the two points manually, use your program to determine the distance between the points (-12, -15) and (22, 5).

6. **(General Math)** If a 20-foot ladder is placed on the side of a building at a 85-degree angle, as shown in Figure 3.11, the height at which the ladder touches the building can be calculated as *height* = 20 × sin 85°. Calculate this height by hand, and then write, compile, and execute a C++ program that determines and displays the value of the height. After verifying that your program works correctly, use it to determine the height of a 25-foot ladder placed at an angle of 85 degrees.

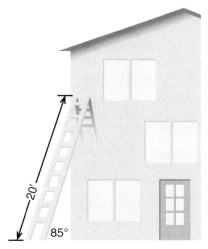

Figure 3.11   Calculating the height of a ladder against a building

7. **(Physics)** The maximum height reached by a ball thrown with an initial velocity, *v*, in meters/sec, at an angle of θ is given by this formula:

height = *(.5 × v² × sin² θ) / 9.8*

Using this formula, write, compile, and execute a C++ program that determines and displays the maximum height reached when the ball is thrown at 5 mph at an angle of 60 degrees. (*Hint*: Make sure to convert the initial velocity into the correct units. There are 1609 meters in a mile.) Calculate the maximum height manually, and verify the result your program produces. After verifying that your program works correctly, use it to determine the height reached by a ball thrown at 7 mph at an angle of 45 degrees.

8. **(Numerical)** For small values of x, the value of $\sin(x)$ can be approximated by this power series:

$$x - \frac{x^3}{3!} + \frac{x^5}{5!} - \frac{x^7}{7!} + \dots$$

As with the `sin()` function, the value of x must be in radians. Using this power series, write, compile, and execute a C++ program that approximates the sine of 180/3.1416 degrees, which equals one radian. Additionally, have your program use the `sin()` function to calculate the sine and display both calculated values and the absolute difference of the two results. Manually verify the approximation your program produces. After verifying that your program is working correctly, use it to approximate the value of the sine of 62.2 degrees.

9. **(Conversion)** The polar coordinates of a point consist of the distance, r, from a specified origin and an angle, θ, with respect to the x-axis. The point's x and y coordinates are related to its polar coordinates by these formulas:

$x = r\ cos\ \theta$

$y = r\ sin\ \theta$

Using these formulas, write a C++ program to calculate the x and y coordinates of a point with the polar coordinates $r = 10$ and $\theta = 30$ degrees. Verify the results your program produces by calculating the results manually. After verifying that your program is working correctly, use it to convert the polar coordinates $r = 12.5$ and $\theta = 67.8$ degrees into rectangular coordinates.

10. **(Ecology)** A model of worldwide population growth, in billions of people, since 2000 is given by this formula:

Population = 6.0 $e^{0.02[Year\ -\ 2000]}$

Using this formula, write, compile, and execute a C++ program to estimate the worldwide population in the year 2012. Verify the result your program produces by calculating the answer manually. After verifying that your program is working correctly, use it to estimate the world's population in the year 2019.

11. **(Physics)** A model to estimate the number of grams of a radioactive isotope left after t years is given by this formula:

remaining material = (original material) $e^{-0.00012t}$

Using this formula, write, compile, and execute a C++ program to determine the amount of radioactive material remaining after 1000 years, assuming an initial amount of 100 grams. Verify the display your program produces by using a hand calculation. After verifying that your program is working correctly, use it to determine the amount of radioactive material remaining after 275 years, assuming an initial amount of 250 grams.

12. **(Physics)** The number of years it takes for an isotope of uranium to decay to one-half an original amount is given by this formula, where λ, the decay constant (which is equal to the inverse of the mean lifetime), equals 0.00012:

half-life = ln(2) / λ

Using this formula, write, compile, and execute a C++ program that calculates and displays the half-life of this uranium isotope. Verify the result your program produces by using a hand calculation. After verifying that your program is working correctly, use it to determine the half-life of a uranium isotope with $\lambda = 0.00026$.

3.4 Program Input Using `cin`

Data for programs that are going to be executed only once can be included in the program. For example, if you want to multiply the numbers 30.0 and 0.05, you could use Program 3.10.

Program 3.10

```
#include <iostream>
using namespace std;

int main()
{
  double num1, num2, product;

  num1 = 30.0;
  num2 = 0.05;
  product = num1 * num2;
  cout << "30.0 times 0.05 is " << product << endl;

  return 0;
}
```

Program 3.10 produces this output:

```
30.0 times 0.05 is 1.5
```

Program 3.10 can be shortened, as shown in Program 3.11. Both programs, however, suffer from the same basic problem: They must be rewritten to multiply different numbers. Both programs lack the capability to enter different numbers on which to operate.

Program 3.11

```
#include <iostream>
using namespace std;

int main()
{
  cout << "30.0 times 0.05 is " << 30.0 * 0.05 << endl;

  return 0;
}
```

Except for the programming practice provided by writing, entering, and running the program, programs that do the same calculation only once, on the same set of numbers, clearly aren't very useful. After all, using a calculator to multiply two numbers is simpler than entering and running Program 3.10 or 3.11.

This section explains the cin statement, used to enter data in a program while it's running. Just as a cout statement displays the value stored in a variable, cin allows users to enter a value at the keyboard (see Figure 3.12), and then the value is stored in a variable.

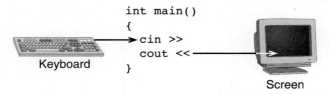

```
                              int main()
                              {
                           →  cin >>
                              cout <<  ───────→
Keyboard                      }
```

Keyboard   Screen

Figure 3.12 cin is used to enter data; cout is used to display data

When a statement such as cin >> num1; is encountered, the computer stops program execution and accepts data from the keyboard. When a data value is typed, cin causes the value to be stored in the variable listed after the extraction ("get from") operator, >>. The program then continues execution with the next statement after the cin statement. To see how cin works, take a look at Program 3.12.

Program 3.12

```cpp
#include <iostream>
using namespace std;

int main()
{
  double num1, num2, product;

  cout << "Please type in a number: ";
  cin  >> num1;
  cout << "Please type in another number: ";
  cin  >> num2;
  product = num1 * num2;
  cout << num1 << " times " << num2 << " is " << product << endl;

  return 0;
}
```

The first cout statement in Program 3.12 displays a string that tells the person at the keyboard what should be typed. When an output string is used in this manner, it's called a **prompt**. In this case, the prompt tells the user to type a number. The computer then executes the next statement, which uses `cin`. The `cin` statement puts the computer in a temporary pause (or wait) state while the user types a value. Then the user signals `cin` that data entry is finished by pressing the Enter key. The entered value is stored in the variable to the right of the extraction operator (num1), and the computer is taken out of its paused state.

Program execution proceeds with the next statement, which in Program 3.12 is another `cout` statement that displays a prompt asking the user to type another number. The next statement uses `cin` again to put the computer in a temporary wait state while the user types a second value (stored in the variable num2).

The following sample run was made using Program 3.12:

```
Please type in a number: 30
Please type in another number: 0.05
30 times 0.05 is 1.5
```

In Program 3.12, each time `cin` is invoked, it's used to store one value in a variable. A `cin` statement, however, can be used to enter and store as many values as there are extraction operators and variables to hold the entered data. For example, the statement

```
cin >> num1 >> num2;
```

results in two values being read from the keyboard and assigned to the variables num1 and num2. If the data entered at the keyboard is

```
0.052 245.79
```

the variables num1 and num2 contain the values 0.052 and 245.79, respectively. Notice that there must be at least one space between numbers when they're entered to clearly indicate where one number ends and the next begins. Inserting more than one space between numbers has no effect on `cin`.

The same spacing also applies to entering character data; the extraction operator skips blank spaces and stores the next nonblank character in a character variable. For example, in response to the statements,

```
char ch1, ch2, ch3;   // declare three character variables
cin >> ch1 >> ch2 >> ch3;   // accept three characters
```

the input

```
a   b   c
```

causes the letter a to be stored in the variable ch1, the letter b to be stored in the variable ch2, and the letter c to be stored in the variable ch3. Because a character variable can be used to store only one character, however, the following input, without spaces, can also be used:

```
abc
```

You can use any number of `cin` statements in a program, and any number of values can be entered with a single `cin` statement. Program 3.13 shows using a `cin` statement to input three numbers from the keyboard. The program then calculates and displays the average of the entered numbers.

Program 3.13

```cpp
#include <iostream>
using namespace std;

int main()
{
    int num1, num2, num3;
    double average;

    cout << "Enter three integer numbers: ";
    cin >> num1 >> num2 >> num3;
    average =  (num1 + num2 + num3) / 3.0;
    cout << "The average of the numbers is " << average << endl;

    return 0;
}
```

The following sample run was made using Program 3.13:

```
Enter three integer numbers: 22 56 73
The average of the numbers is 50.3333
```

The data entered at the keyboard for this sample run consists of 22 56 73. In response to this stream of input, Program 3.13 stores the value 22 in the variable num1, the value 56 in the variable num2, and the value 73 in the variable num3 (see Figure 3.13). Because the average of three integer numbers can be a floating-point number, the variable average, used to store the average of all entered numbers, is declared as a floating-point variable (a double). Note also that parentheses are needed in the assignment statement average = (num1 + num2 + num3)/3.0;. Without the parentheses, the only value divided by 3 would be the integer in num3 (because division has a higher precedence than addition).

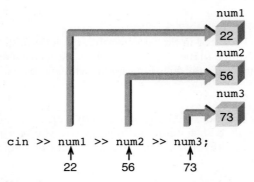

Figure 3.13   Inputting data in the variables num1, num2, and num3

The extraction operator, >>, like the insertion operator, <<, is "clever" enough to make a few data type conversions. For example, if an integer is entered instead of a double-precision number, the integer is converted to the correct data type.[9] Similarly, if a double-precision number is entered when an integer is expected, only the integer part of the number is used. For example, assume the following numbers are typed in response to the statement `cin >> num1 >> num2 >> num3;`, where `num1` and `num3` have been declared as double-precision variables and `num2` is an integer variable:

```
56   22.879   33.923
```

The 56 is converted to 56.0 and stored in the variable `num1`. The extraction operation continues, extracting data from the input stream and expecting an integer value. As far as the << operator is concerned, the decimal point in 22.879 indicates the end of an integer and the start of a decimal number. Therefore, the number 22 is assigned to `num2`. Continuing to process its input stream, the next << operator takes the .879 as the next floating-point number and assigns it to `num3`. As far as `cin` is concerned, 33.923 is extra input and is ignored. If, however, you don't enter enough data initially, the insertion operator causes the computer to pause, waiting until enough data has been entered.

A First Look at User-Input Validation

A well-constructed program should validate user input and ensure that a program doesn't crash or produce nonsensical output caused by unexpected input. The term **validate** means checking that the entered value matches the data type of the variable it's assigned to in a `cin` statement and checking that the value is within an acceptable range for the application. Programs that detect and respond effectively to unexpected user input are formally referred to as **robust programs** and informally as "bulletproof" programs. One of your goals as a programmer is to produce robust programs. As written, Programs 3.12 and 3.13 aren't robust programs, and in the following discussion, you see why.

The first problem with these programs becomes evident when a user enters a non-numerical value. For example, examine the following sample run using Program 3.13:

```
Enter three integer numbers: 10 20.68 20
The average of the numbers is -2.86331e+008
```

This output occurs because the conversion of the second entered number results in assigning the integer value 20 to `num2` and the value -858993460 to `num3`.[10] The -858993460 value results because an invalid character, the decimal point, is assigned to a variable that expects an integer. The average of the numbers 10, 20, and -858993460 is computed correctly as -286331143.3, which is displayed in scientific notation with six significant digits as -2.86331e+008. Most users, however, would report this result as a program error.

This same problem occurs when a non-integer value is entered for either of the first two inputs. (It doesn't occur for any numerical value entered as the third input because the integer part of the last input is accepted, and the remaining input ignored.) Your first response might be "The program clearly asks you to enter integer values." Programmers with more experience, however, understand that their responsibility is to make sure a program

---

[9]Strictly speaking, what comes in from the keyboard isn't any data type, such as an `int` or a `double`, but is simply a sequence of characters. The extraction operation handles the conversion from the character sequence to a defined data type.
[10]Some C++ runtime systems accept the .68 as the third input and convert it to the integer value of zero. In all cases, the last value of 20 is ignored.

anticipates and appropriately handles all inputs users might enter. To achieve this goal, think about what can go wrong with your program as you develop it, and then have another person or group test the program.

The basic approach to handling invalid data input is called **user-input validation**, which means checking the entered data during or immediately after it has been entered, and then giving users a way to reenter invalid data. User-input validation is an essential part of any commercially viable program; if done correctly, it protects a program from attempting to process data that can cause computational problems. You see how to do this type of validation in Chapters 4 and 5, when you learn about C++'s selection and repetition statements.

EXERCISES 3.4

1. **(Practice)** For the following declaration statements, write a `cin` statement that causes the computer to pause while the user enters the appropriate data:

   a. `int firstnum;`

   b. `double grade;`

   c. `double secnum;`

   d. `char keyval;`

   e. `int month, years;`
   `double average;`

   f. `char ch;`
   `int num1, num2;`
   `double grade1, grade2;`

   g. `double interest, principal, capital;`
   `double price, yield;`

   h. `char ch, letter1, letter2;`
   `int num1, num2, num3;`

   i. `double temp1, temp2, temp3;`
   `double volts1, volts2;`

2. **(Practice) a.** Write a C++ program that first displays the following prompt:

   `Enter the temperature in degrees Celsius:`

   Have your program accept a value entered from the keyboard and convert the temperature entered to degrees Fahrenheit, using this formula:

   Fahrenheit = (9.0 / 5.0) × Celsius + 32.0

   Your program should then display the temperature in degrees Fahrenheit with an appropriate message.

b. Compile and execute the program written for Exercise 2a. To verify your program, use the following test data and calculate the Fahrenheit equivalents by hand, and then use your program to see whether you get the same results:

Test data set 1: 0 degrees Celsius
Test data set 2: 50 degrees Celsius
Test data set 3: 100 degrees Celsius

When you're sure your program is working correctly, use it to complete the following chart:

Celsius	Fahrenheit
45	
50	
55	
60	
65	
70	

3. **(Practice)** Write, compile, and execute a C++ program that displays the following prompt:

```
Enter the radius of a circle:
```

After accepting a value for the radius, your program should calculate and display the area of the circle. (*Hint*: Area = $3.1416 \times radius^2$.) For testing purposes, verify your program byusing an input radius of 3 inches. After manually determining that your program's result is correct, use your program to complete the following chart:

Radius (in)	Area (sq. in)
1.0	
1.5	
2.0	
2.5	
3.0	
3.5	

4. **(Practice) a.** Write, compile, and execute a C++ program that displays the following prompts:

```
Enter the miles driven:
Enter the gallons of gas used:
```

After each prompt is displayed, your program should use a `cin` statement to accept data from the keyboard for the displayed prompt. After the number for gallons of gas used has been entered, your program should calculate and display the miles per gallon (mpg). This value should be included in a message and calculated by using the formula *miles per gallon = miles / gallons used*. Verify your program by using the following test data:

Test data set 1: miles = 276, gas = 10 gallons
Test data set 2: miles = 200, gas = 15.5 gallons

After finishing your verification, use your program to complete the following chart. (Make sure to convert the miles driven to kilometers driven and gallons used to liters used, and then compute the kilometers per liter.)

Miles Driven	Gallons Used	MPG	Km Driven	Liters Used	Km/L
250	16.00				
275	18.00				
312	19.54				
296	17.39				

b. For the program written for Exercise 4a, determine how many verification runs are required to make sure the program is working correctly, and give a reason to support your answer.

5. (Practice) a. Write, compile, and execute a C++ program that displays the following prompts:

```
Enter a number:
Enter a second number:
Enter a third number:
Enter a fourth number:
```

After each prompt is displayed, your program should use a `cin` statement to accept a number from the keyboard for the displayed prompt. After the fourth number has been entered, your program should calculate and display the average of the numbers. The average should be included in an output message. Check the average your program calculates by using the following test data:

Test data set 1: 100, 100, 100, 100
Test data set 2: 100, 0, 100, 0

After finishing your verification, use your program to complete the following chart:

Numbers	Average
92, 98, 79, 85	
86, 84, 75, 86	
63, 85, 74, 82	

b. Repeat Exercise 5a, making sure you use the same variable name, `number`, for each number input. Also, use the variable `sum` for the sum of the numbers. (*Hint*: To do this, you can use the statement `sum = sum + number` after each number is accepted. Review the material on accumulating in Section 3.1.)

6. **(General Math) a.** Write, compile, and execute a C++ program to compute and display the value of the second-order polynomial $ax^2 + bx + c$ for any user-entered values of the coefficients a, b, and c and the variable x. Have your program display a message first to inform users what the program does, and then display suitable prompts to alert users to enter the data. (*Hint*: Use a prompt such as `Enter the coefficient of the x-squared term:`.)

b. Check the result of your program written for Exercise 6a by using the following test data:

> Test data set 1: $a = 0$, $b = 0$, $c = 22$, $x = 56$
> Test data set 2: $a = 0$, $b = 22$, $c = 0$, $x = 2$
> Test data set 3: $a = 22$, $b = 0$, $c = 0$, $x = 2$
> Test data set 4: $a = 2$, $b = 4$, $c = 5$, $x = 2$

After finishing your verification, use your program to complete the following chart:

a	b	c	x	Polynomial Value
2.0	17.0	-12.0	1.3	
3.2	2.0	15.0	2.5	
3.2	2.0	15.0	-2.5	
-2.0	10.0	0.0	2.0	
-2.0	10.0	0.0	4.0	
-2.0	10.0	0.0	5.0	
-2.0	10.0	0.0	6.0	
5.0	22.0	18.0	8.3	
4.2	-16	-20	-5.2	

7. **(General Math)** The roads of Kansas are laid out in a rectangular grid at exactly one-mile intervals, as shown in Figure 3.14. Pete drives his pickup x miles east and y miles north to get to his friend Joe's farm. Both x and y are integer numbers. Using this information, write, test, and run a C++ program that prompts the user for the values of x and y, and then uses this formula to find the shortest driving distance across the fields to Joe's farm:

$$distance = \sqrt{\left(x^2 + y^2\right)}$$

Round the answer to the nearest integer value before it's displayed.

8. **(Numerical)** Write, compile, and execute a program that calculates and displays the square root value of a user-entered real number. Verify your program by calculating the square roots of this test data: 25, 16, 0, and 2. After finishing your verification, use your program to determine the square roots of 32.25, 42, 48, 55, 63, and 79.

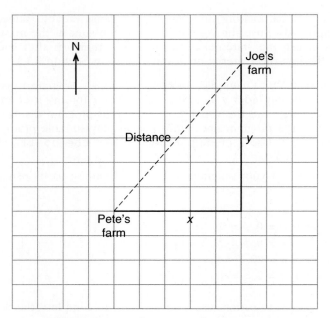

Figure 3.14   Illustration for Exercise 7

9. (**Numerical**) Write, compile, and execute a program to calculate and display the fourth root of a user-entered number. Recall from elementary algebra that you find the fourth root of a number by raising the number to the 1/4 power. (*Hint:* Don't use integer division—can you see why?) Verify your program by calculating the fourth roots of this test data: 81, 16, 1, and 0. When you're finished, use your program to determine the fourth roots of 42, 121, 256, 587, 1240, and 16,256.

10. (**Electrical Eng.**) For the series circuit shown in Figure 3.15, the voltage drop, V_2, across resistor R_2 and the power, P_2, delivered to this resistor are given by the formulas $V_2 = I\,R_2$ and $P_2 = I\,V_2$, where $I = E\,/\,(R_1 + R_2)$. Using these formulas, write, compile, and execute a C++ program that prompts users for values of E, R_1, and R_2; calculates the voltage drop and power delivered to R_2; and displays the results. Check your program by using the test data E = 10 volts, R_1 = 100 ohms, and R_2 = 200 ohms. After finishing your verification, use your program to complete the following chart:

E (Volts)	R$_1$ (Ohms)	R$_2$ (Ohms)	Voltage Drop (Volts)	Power Delivered (Watts)
10	100	100		
10	100	200		
10	200	200		
20	100	100		
20	100	200		
20	200	200		

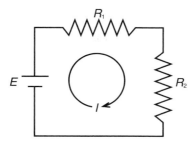

Figure 3.15   Calculating the voltage drop

11. **(Data Processing)** Program 3.12 prompts users to input two numbers; the first value entered is stored in num1, and the second value is stored in num2. Using this program as a starting point, write a program that swaps the values stored in the two variables.

12. **(Data Processing)** Write a C++ program that prompts users to enter a number. Have your program accept the number as an integer and display the integer immediately by using a cout statement. Run your program three times. The first time, enter a valid integer number; the second time, enter a double-precision number; and the third time, enter a character. Using the output display, see what number your program actually accepted from the data you entered.

13. **(Data Processing)** Repeat Exercise 12, but have your program declare the variable used to store the number as a double-precision variable. Run the program three times. The first time, enter an integer; the second time, enter a double-precision number; and the third time, enter a character. Using the output display, keep track of what number your program actually accepted from the data you entered. What happened, if anything, and why?

14. **(For Thought) a.** Why do you think successful programs contain extensive data-input validity checks? (*Hint*: Review Exercises 12 and 13.)

  b. What do you think is the difference between a data-type check and a data-reasonableness check?

  c. Assume that a program requests users to enter a month, day, and year. What are some checks that could be made on the data entered?

3.5   Symbolic Constants

Certain constants used in a program have more general meanings that are recognized outside the program's context. Examples of these types of constants include the number 3.1416, which is π accurate to four decimal places; 32.2 ft/sec^2, which is the gravitational constant;

and the number 2.71828, which is Euler's number accurate to five decimal places. The following list shows other commonly used scientific and engineering constants:

Avagadro's number = $6.02214179 \times 10^{23}$/mole
Boltzmann's constant = 1.3806×10^{-23} Joules/K
Planck's constant = 6.6256×10^{-34} Joule/sec
Stephan-Boltzmann's constant = 5.6697×10^{-8} Watts/m^{2}K^4
Universal gas constant = 8.6314472×10^{7} Joules/Kmole
Universal gravitational constant = 6.67428×10^{-11} N m^2/kg^2

Certain other constants in a program are defined in the context of the application being programmed. For example, in a program determining the weight of different sized objects, the density of an object's material takes on a special significance. By themselves, density numbers are quite ordinary, but in this application, they have a special meaning. Programmers sometimes refer to these types of numbers as **magic numbers**. When a magic number appears repeatedly in a program, it becomes a potential source of error if it has to be changed. If just one instance of the magic number is overlooked and not changed, when the program runs the result will be incorrect, and the source of the error will be difficult to locate.

To avoid the problem of having a magic number occur in many places in a program and to identify universal constants, such as π, clearly, C++ enables programmers to give these constants symbolic names. Then the symbolic name, instead of the magic number, can be used throughout the program.

If the number ever has to be changed, the change need be made only once, where the symbolic name is equated to the actual numerical value. To equate numbers to symbolic names, you use the `const` declaration qualifier, which specifies that the declared identifier is read-only after it's initialized; it can't be changed. Examples of using this qualifier are as follows:

```
const double PI = 3.1416;
const double PLANCK = 6.6256e-34;
const double DENSITY = 0.238;
const int MAXNUM = 100;
```

The first declaration statement creates a double-precision constant named `PI` and initializes it to 3.1416, and the second declaration statement creates a double-precision constant named `PLANCK` and initializes it to Planck's constant (accurate to four decimal places). The third declaration statement creates a constant named `DENSITY` and initializes it to 0.238. Finally, the fourth declaration creates an integer constant named `MAXNUM` and initializes it with the value 100.

After a `const` identifier is created and initialized, the value stored in it can't be changed. For all practical purposes, the name of the constant and its value are linked for the duration of the program that declares them.

Although the `const` identifiers have been shown in uppercase letters, lowercase letters could have been used. In C++, however, it's common to use uppercase letters for `const` identifiers to identify them easily. When programmers see uppercase letters in a program, they know a symbolic name is being used, and its value can't be changed later in the program.

After it's declared, a const identifier can be used in any C++ statement in place of the number it represents. For example, both these assignment statements are valid:

```
circum = 2 * PI * radius;
weight = DENSITY * volume;
```

These statements must, of course, appear after the declarations for all their variables. Because a const declaration equates a constant value to an identifier, and the identifier can be used as a replacement for its initializing constant, these identifiers are commonly referred to as **symbolic constants**, **named constants**, or simply **constants**. These terms are used interchangeably in this book.

Placement of Statements

At this stage, you have been introduced to a variety of statement types. The general rule in C++ for statement placement is simply that a variable or symbolic constant must be declared before it can be used. Although this rule permits placing both preprocessor directives and declaration statements throughout a program, doing so results in a poor program structure. For good programming form, the following statement ordering should be used:

```
preprocessor directives

int main()
{
  // symbolic constants
  // variable declarations

  // other executable statements

  return value;
}
```

As new statement types are introduced, this placement structure will be expanded to accommodate them. Note that comment statements can be intermixed anywhere within this basic structure. Program 3.14 illustrates this basic structure and uses a symbolic constant to calculate the weight of a steel cylinder. The density of the steel is 0.284 lb/in^3 (= 7.738 × 10^3 kg/m^{-3}).

Program 3.14

```cpp
// This program determines the weight of a steel cylinder
//   by multiplying the volume of the cylinder times its density.
// The volume of the cylinder is given by the formula PI * pow(radius,2) * height.
#include <iostream>
#include <iomanip>
#include <cmath>
using namespace std;

int main()
{
   const double PI = 3.1416;
   const double DENSITY = 0.284;
   double radius, height, weight;

   cout << "Enter the radius of the cylinder (in inches): ";
   cin  >> radius;
   cout << "Enter the height of the cylinder (in inches): ";
   cin  >> height;
   weight = DENSITY * PI * pow(radius,2) * height;
   cout << setiosflags(ios:: fixed)
        << setiosflags(ios::showpoint)
        << setprecision(4)
        << "The cylinder weighs " << weight << " pounds" << endl;

   return 0;
}
```

Notice in Program 3.14 that two symbolic constants have been defined: PI and DENSITY. The following run was made to determine the weight of a cylinder with a radius of 3 inches and a height of 12 inches.

```
Enter the radius of the cylinder (in inches): 3
Enter the height of the cylinder (in inches): 12
The cylinder weighs 96.3592 pounds
```

The advantage of using the named constant PI in Program 3.14 is that it clearly identifies the value of 3.1416 in terms most people recognize. The advantage of using the named constant DENSITY is that the programmer can change the value of the density for another material without having to search through the program to see where DENSITY is used. If, of course, many different materials are used, DENSITY should be changed from a symbolic constant to a variable. A natural question, then, is asking what the difference is between symbolic constants and variables.

Symbolic Constants

A variable's value can be altered anywhere in a program. By its nature, a named constant is a fixed value that must not be altered after it's defined. Naming a constant rather than assigning the value to a variable ensures that the value in the constant can't be altered later. Whenever a named constant appears in an instruction, it has the same effect as the constant it represents. Therefore, DENSITY in Program 3.14 is simply another way of representing the number 0.284. Because DENSITY and the number 0.284 are equivalent, the value of DENSITY can't be subsequently changed in the program. After DENSITY has been defined as a constant, an assignment statement such as

```
DENSITY = 0.156;
```

is meaningless and results in an error message because DENSITY is not a variable. Because DENSITY is only a stand-in for the value 0.284, this statement is equivalent to writing the invalid expression 0.284 = 0.156.

In addition to using a const statement to name constants, as in Program 3.14, you can also use this statement to equate the value of a constant expression to a symbolic name. A **constant expression** consists of operators and constants only. For example, the statement

```
const double DEG_TO_RAD = 3.1416/180.0;
```

equates the value of the constant expression 3.1416/180.0 to the symbolic name DEG_TO_RAD.

The symbolic name, as always, can be used in any statement following its definition. For example, because the expression 3.1416/180.0 is required for converting degrees to radians, the symbolic name for this conversion factor can be used conveniently whenever this conversion is required. For example, in the assignment statement

```
height = distance * sin(angle * DEG_TO_RAD);
```

the symbolic constant DEG_TO_RAD is used to convert the value in angle to a radian measure.

A previously defined named constant can also be used in a subsequent const statement. For example, the following sequence of statements is valid:

```
const double PI = 3.1416;
const double  DEG_TO_RAD = PI / 180.0;
```

Because the constant 3.1416 has been equated to the symbolic name PI, it can be used legitimately in any subsequent definition, even in another const statement. Program 3.15 uses the named constant DEG_TO_RAD to convert a user-entered angle, in degrees, to its equivalent radian measure for use by the sin() function.

Program 3.15

```cpp
#include <iostream>
#include <iomanip>
#include <cmath>
using namespace std;

int main()
{
  const double PI = 3.1416;
  const double DEG_TO_RAD = PI/180.0;
  double angle;

  cout << "Enter the angle (in degrees): ";
  cin >> angle;
  cout << setiosflags(ios:: fixed)
       << setiosflags(ios::showpoint)
       << setprecision(4)
       << "The sine of the angle is " << sin(angle * DEG_TO_RAD)
       << endl;

  return 0;
}
```

The following sample run was made using Program 3.15:

```
Enter the angle (in degrees): 30
The sine of the angle is 0.5000
```

Although the const qualifier has been used to construct symbolic constants, you'll see this qualifier again in Chapter 6, where you learn it's useful as a function argument to make sure the argument isn't modified in the function.

Technical Note

Frequency, Period, and Wavelength

A wave is a repeating pattern in time and space. Examples are sound waves, ocean waves, and light waves. Figure 3.16 shows a typical wave, which is usually described with one of these related terms: frequency, period, or wavelength.

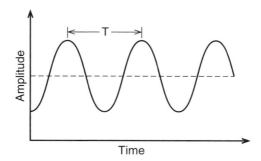

Figure 3.16   A typical wave

In science and engineering fields, a wave's frequency is denoted by the letter f, its period by the letter T, and its wavelength by the Greek letter λ (lamda). The frequency of a wave is the number of repetitions of the wave occurring in one second. For example, the frequency of the musical note middle C on a piano is 261.64 repetitions per second, typically denoted as 261.64 cycles/sec. In the SI measurement system, the synonym for cycles/sec is Hertz (Hz). Therefore, 261.64 cycles/sec = 261.64 Hz, which means there are 261.64 repetitions of the wave in one second. Audio, radio, and power line waves are described in terms of their frequencies.

Extremely low frequency waves, such as ocean waves, are typically described by their period, T, which is the inverse of the wave's frequency. So mathematically, you have the following:

T = 1 / f

Therefore, a wave's period is the time it takes to complete one cycle. For example, an ocean surface wave with a period of 3 sec/cycle means it takes 3 seconds to complete one wave cycle. What this means is that a person at a fixed location in the ocean sees a wave crest pass by every 3 seconds. The corresponding frequency of this wave is $1/T$, or 1/3 cycles per second, which equals 0.33 Hz.

Extremely high frequency waves, such as light and x-rays, are typically described by their wavelength. Wavelength, λ, and frequency, f, are related by this formula

λ = *speed of the wave / f*

where the speed of the wave is the wave's velocity in the medium through which it's traveling. For light traveling in a vacuum, the speed of a light wave is 299,792,458 m/s $\approx$ 2.998×10^8 m/s. For sound waves traveling in air, the speed of the wave is 345 m/s.

continued...

Technical Note

Frequency, Period, and Wavelength (continued)

Following is a description of waves encountered in science and engineering fields:

Wave Type	Frequency or Period	Wavelength
Ocean waves	Period = 1 to 5 seconds	Not used
European household current	50 Hz	5.996×10^6 m
American household current	60 Hz	4.996×10^6 m
Radio frequencies		
Low frequency (LF)	3×10^4 to 3×10^5 Hz (30 to 300 kilohertz, KHz)	10^4 to 10^3 m (10 to 1 km)
Medium frequency (MF)	3×10^5 to 3×10^6 Hz (.3 to 3 megahertz, MHz)	10^3 to 10^2 m (1 to .1 km)
High frequency (HF)	3×10^6 to 3×10^7 Hz (3 to 30 MHz)	100 to 10 m
Very high frequency (VHF)	3×10^7 to 3×10^9 Hz (30 to 300 MHz)	10 to 1 m
Ultra high frequency (UHF)	3×10^9 to 3×10^{12} Hz (300 to 3000 MHz)	1 to .1 m
Body heat	3×10^{11} Hz	1×10^{-3} m (1 millimeter)
Infrared light	0.04×10^{15} to $.3 \times 10^{15}$ Hz	750×10^{-9} to 100×10^{-9} nm (750 to 100 nanometers)
Red visible light	384×10^{12} to 482×10^{12} Hz	78×10^{-9} to 62×10^{-9} nm (78 to 62 nanometers)
Violet visible light	659×10^{12} to 769×10^{12} Hz	45×10^{-9} to 39.8×10^{-9} nm (45 to 39 nanometers)
Ultraviolet light	1×10^{15} to 1.5×10^{15} Hz	300×10^{-9} to 200×10^{-9} nm (300 to 200 nanometers)
X-rays	30×10^{15} to 30×10^{18} Hz	9.9×10^{-9} to $.99 \times 10^{-9}$ m

EXERCISES 3.5

1. **(Practice)** Modify Program 3.9 to use the named constant GRAV in place of the value 32.2 used in the program. Compile and execute your program to verify that it produces the same result shown in the text.

2. **(Modify)** Rewrite the following program to use the named constant FACTOR in place of the expression (5.0/9.0) used in the program:

```cpp
#include <iostream>
using namespace std;

int main()
{
  double fahren, celsius;
  cout << "Enter a temperature in degrees Fahrenheit: ";
  cin  >> fahren;
  celsius = (5.0/9.0) * (fahren - 32.0);
  cout << "The equivalent Celsius temperature is "
       << celsius << endl;

  return 0;
}
```

3. **(Modify)** Rewrite the following program to use the symbolic constant PRIME in place of the value 0.04 used in the program:

```cpp
#include <iostream>
using namespace std;

int main()
{
  float prime, amount, interest;
  prime = 0.04;       // prime interest rate
  cout << <Enter the amount: ";
  cin  >> amount;
  interest = prime * amount;
  cout << "The interest earned is"
       << interest << " dollars" << endl;

  return 0;
}
```

4. **(Modify)** Rewrite the following program so that the variable volts is changed to a symbolic constant:

```cpp
#include <iostream>
using namespace std;

int main()
{
  double current, resistance, volts;
```

```
    volts = 12;
    cout << " Enter the resistance: ";
    cin >> resistance;
    current = volts / resistance;
    cout << "The current is " << current << endl;

    return 0;
}
```

5. **(Heat Transfer)** Typically, all objects radiating heat do so at many different wavelengths. (See the Technical Note in Section 3.5 for a description of wavelength.) The wavelength at which an object emits its maximum heat energy can be found by using Wein's Law:

$$\lambda_{max} \, T = W$$

λ_{max} is the maximum wavelength.
T is the object's temperature in °K.
W is Wein's constant = 2897 microns/°K.

a. Using Wein's Law, write a C++ program that accepts an object's temperature in degrees Celsius and outputs the wavelength at which the object radiates its maximum energy. Have your program declare Wein's constant as the symbolic constant named WEINCONSTANT.

b. After verifying that your program is working, use it to determine the maximum heat-radiating wavelength for the sun, Earth, and Mars, with surface temperatures of 5727, 14, and 0.46 degrees Celsius, respectively.

3.6   A Case Study: Acid Rain

The use of coal as the major source of steam power began with the Industrial Revolution. Currently, coal is one of the principal sources of electrical power generation in many industrialized countries. Since the middle of the 19th century, it has been known that the oxygen used in the burning process combines with the carbon and sulfur in coal to produce carbon dioxide and sulfur dioxide. When these gases are released into the atmosphere, sulfur dioxide combines with water and oxygen in the air to form sulfuric acid, which is transformed into separate hydronium ions and sulfates (see Figure 3.17). The hydronium ions in the atmosphere that fall to Earth as components of rain are what change the acidity levels of lakes and forests.

The acid level of rain and lakes is measured on a pH scale by using this formula:

pH = - log_{10} (concentration of hydronium ions)

The concentration of hydronium ions is measured in units of moles/liter. A pH value of 7 indicates a neutral value (neither acidic nor alkaline), whereas levels below 7 indicate the presence of an acid, and levels above 7 indicate the presence of an alkaline substance. For example, sulfuric acid has a pH value of approximately 1, lye has a pH value of approximately 13, and distilled water typically has a pH value of 7. Marine life usually can't survive in water with a pH level below 4.

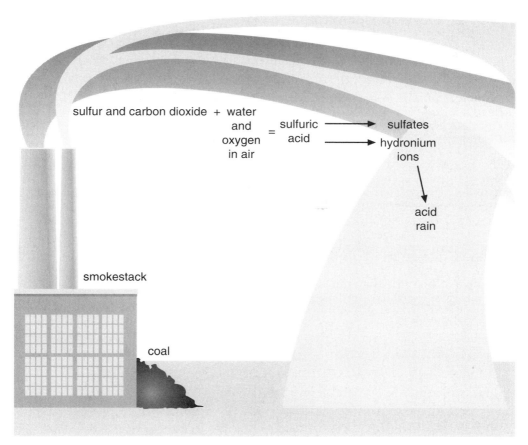

Figure 3.17 The formation of acid rain

Using the formula for pH, you'll write a C++ program, using the software development procedure described in Chapter 2, that calculates the pH level of a substance based on a user input value for the concentration of hydronium ions.

Step 1   Analyze the Problem

Although the problem statement provides technical information on the composition of acid rain, from a programming viewpoint, this problem is rather simple. You have only one required output (a pH level) and one input (the concentration of hydronium ions).

Step 2   Develop a Solution

The algorithm for transforming the input to the required output is a straightforward use of the pH formula. The pseudocode representation of the algorithm for entering input data, processing data to produce the required output, and displaying output is as follows:

Display a prompt to enter an ion concentration level.
Read a value for the concentration level.
Calculate a pH level, using the given formula.
Display the calculated value.

To make sure you understand the formula used in the algorithm, do a hand calculation. You can then use the result of this calculation to verify the result the program produces. Assuming a hydronium concentration of 0.0001 (although any value would do), the pH level is calculated as $-\log_{10} 10^{-4}$. Either by knowing that the logarithm of 10 raised to a power is the power itself or by using a log table, the value of this expression is -(-4) = 4.

Step 3   Code the Solution

Program 3.16 shows using the algorithm in C++. The variable names were chosen to convey the variables' meanings in this application.

Program 3.16

```
#include <iostream>
#include <cmath>
using namespace std;

int main()
{
  double hydron, pHlevel;

  cout << "Enter the hydronium ion concentration: ";
  cin  >> hydron;
  pHlevel = -log10(hydron);
  cout << "The pH level is " << pHlevel << endl;

  return 0;
}
```

Program 3.16 begins with two #include preprocessor statements, followed by the main() function. Within main(), a declaration statement declares two floating-point variables, hydron and pHlevel. The program then displays a prompt requesting input data from the user. After the prompt is displayed, a cin statement is used to store the entered data in the variable `hydron`. Finally, a value for `pHlevel` is calculated, using the logarithmic library function, and displayed. As always, the program is terminated with a closing brace.

Step 4 Test and Correct the Program

A test run using Program 3.16 produced the following:

```
Enter the hydronium ion concentration level: 0.0001
The pH level is 4
```

Because the program performs a single calculation, and the result of this test run agrees with your previous hand calculation, the calculation portion of the program has been tested completely. It can now be used to calculate the pH level of other hydronium concentrations with confidence that the results produced are accurate.

EXERCISES 3.6

1. **(Practice)** Enter, compile, and run Program 3.16 on your computer system.

2. **(General Math)** The value of π can be approximated by this series:

$$4\left(1 - \frac{1}{3} + \frac{1}{5} - \frac{1}{7} + ...\right)$$

Using this formula, write a program that calculates and displays the value of π, using 2, 3, and 4 terms of the series.

3. **(General Math)** The exponential function e^x, where e is known as Euler's number (and has the value 2.718281828459045 . . .) appears many times in descriptions of natural phenomena. For example, radioactive decay, population growth, and the normal (bell-shaped) curve used in statistical applications can be described by using this function. The value of e^x can be approximated by using this series:

$$1 + \frac{x}{1!} + \frac{x^2}{2!} + \frac{x^3}{3!} + \frac{x^4}{4!} + \frac{x^5}{5!} + \frac{x^6}{6!} + ...$$

Using this formula, write a program that calculates and displays the value of Euler's number, using 1, 2, 3, and 4 terms of the series.

4. **(General Math)** The volume of oil stored in an underground 200-foot deep cylindrical tank is determined by measuring the distance from the top of the tank to the surface of the oil. Knowing this distance and the radius of the tank, the volume of oil in the tank can be determined by using this formula:

volume = π radius^2 (200 - distance)

Using this information, write, compile, and execute a C++ program that accepts the radius and distance measurements, calculates the volume of oil in the tank, and displays the two input values and the calculated volume. Verify the results of your program by doing a hand calculation using the following test data: *radius* = 10 feet and *distance* = 12 feet.

5. **(General Math)** The circumference of an ellipse (review Figure 3.5) is given by this formula:

$$Circumference = \pi\sqrt{\left(a+b\right)^2}$$

Using this formula, write a C++ program to calculate the circumference of an ellipse with a minor radius, *a*, of 2.5 inches and a major radius, *b*, of 6.4 inches. (*Hint*: The square root can be taken by raising the quantity $2[a^2 + b^2]$ to the 0.5 power.)

6. **(General Math)** The perimeter, approximate surface area, and approximate volume of an in-ground pool are given by the following formulas:

perimeter = 2(length + width)

volume = length × width × average depth

underground surface area = 2(length + width)average depth + length × width

Using these formulas as a basis, write a C++ program that accepts the length, width, and average depth measurements, and then calculates the pool's perimeter, volume, and underground surface area. In writing your program, make these two calculations immediately after entering the input data: *length × width* and *length + width*. The results of these two calculations should be used, as needed, in the assignment statements for determining the perimeter, volume, and underground surface area without recalculating them for each equation. Verify your program's results by doing a hand calculation, using the following test data: *length* = 25 feet, *width* = 15 feet, and *average depth* = 5.5 feet. After verifying that your program is working, use it to complete the following chart:

Length	Width	Depth	Perimeter	Volume	Underground Surface Area
25	10	5.0			
25	10	5.5			
25	10	6.0			
25	10	6.5			
30	12	5.0			
30	12	5.5			
30	12	6.0			
30	12	6.5			

7. **(Heat Transfer)** Radiation is the transfer of heat via electromagnetic wave propagation. Examples of heat transfer are the heat radiated from the sun, the heat radiated from Earth, and the heat given off in the evening by objects, such as cars and brick walls, warmed by the sun during the day. The heat radiated by an object can be calculated by using Stephan-Boltzmann's Law:

$$E = e\ \sigma\ T^4$$

E is the energy radiated per second per square meter of its surface.

e is the emissivity of the substance (a number between 0 and 1).

σ is Stephan-Boltzmann's constant (5.6697×10^{-8} Watts/m^{2}K^4).

T is the surface temperature in degrees Kelvin ($^\circ$K = $^\circ$C + 273).

An ideal radiator, such as the sun, has an emissivity of 1, and the heat generated from the sun, with a surface temperature of approximately 6000°K, is as follows:

$$E = 5.6697 \times 10^{-8} \text{ Watts/m}^2\text{K}^4 \ (6 \times 10^3\text{K}^4)$$

$$= 5.6697 \times 10^{-8} \text{ Watts/m}^2\text{K}^4 \ (1296 \times 10^{12}\text{K}^4) = 7.3 \times 10^7 \text{ Watts/m}^2$$

$$= 73{,}000{,}000 \text{ Watts/m}^2$$

Using the formula and this information, write a C++ program that accepts a planet's temperature (assuming an emissivity of 1) and provides the heat generated from the planet as its output. After determining that your program is working correctly (make sure it produces the correct radiation for the sun), use it to complete the following chart (make sure to use correct units):

Planet	Average Surface Temperature (°Celsius)	Heat Radiated (Watts/m²)
Mercury	270	
Venus	462	
Earth	14	
Mars	-46	
Jupiter	-108	
Saturn	-139	
Uranus	-197	
Neptune	-201	

8. **(Heat Transfer)** During the day, heat is absorbed by many objects, such as cars, roofs, and brick walls. This heat is then radiated back into the environment during the cooler evening hours. Using Stephan-Boltzmann's Law, $E = e\ \sigma\ T^4$ (see Exercise 7), write a C++ program that determines the amount of radiation for the objects listed in the following table. Your program should request the object's average surface temperature and emissivity, and then calculate and display the heat radiated. Complete the following chart, making three runs of the program:

Substance	Average Surface Temperature (°Celsius)	Emissivity	Heat Radiated (Watts/m²)
Automobile	47	.3	
Brick	45	.9	
Commercial roof	48	.05	

9. **(Electrical Eng.) a.** Write, compile, and execute a C++ program that calculates and displays the voltage gain of a three-stage amplifier at a frequency of 1000 Hertz. The voltage gains of the stages are as follows:

Stage 1 gain: $23/[2.32 + (0.044f)^2]^{1/2}$
Stage 2 gain: $12/[6.72 + (0.34f)^2]^{1/2}$
Stage 3 gain: $17/[1.92 + (0.45f)^2]^{1/2}$

f is the frequency in Hertz. The voltage gain of the amplifier is the product of the gains of each stage.

b. Redo Exercise 9a, assuming the frequency will be entered when the program runs.

3.7   A Closer Look: Programming Errors

The ideal in programming is to produce readable, error-free programs that work correctly and can be modified or changed with a minimum of testing. To achieve this ideal, keep in mind the different types of errors that can occur, when they're usually detected, and how to correct them.
You can detect an error at any of the following times:

- Before a program is compiled
- While the program is being compiled
- While the program is running
- After the program has been executed and the output is being examined

The method for detecting errors before a program is compiled is called **desk checking** because you're usually sitting at a desk with the code in front of you. It refers to the process of examining the source code for mistakes immediately after you type it.
Errors detected while the program is being compiled are called **compile-time errors**, and errors that occur while the program is running are called **runtime errors**. Other names for compile-time errors are **syntax errors** and **parse errors**, terms that emphasize the type of error the compiler detects.
By now, you have probably encountered numerous compile-time errors. Beginning programmers tend to be frustrated by them, but experienced programmers understand the compiler is doing a lot of valuable checking, and correcting errors the compiler does detect is usually easy. Because these errors occur while the program is being developed, not while a user is performing an important task, no one but the programmer ever knows they occurred. You fix them, and they go away.
Runtime errors are more troubling because they occur while a user is running the program; in most commercial systems, the user isn't the programmer. Many error types can cause a runtime error, such as a hardware failure. From a programming standpoint, however, most runtime errors are referred to as logic errors or faulty logic, which encompasses not analyzing what the program should do or not anticipating how users can make the program fail. For example, if a user enters data that results in an attempt to divide a number by zero, a runtime error occurs.
As a programmer, the only way to protect against runtime errors is to anticipate everything a person might do to cause errors and submit your program to rigorous testing. Beginning programmers tend to blame users for an error caused by entering incorrect data,

but professionals don't. They understand that a runtime error is a flaw that can damage the reputation of the program and programmer.

To prevent compile-time and runtime errors, it's more fruitful to determine what causes them. As mentioned, compile-time errors are also called syntax errors: mistakes in the structure or spelling of a statement. For example, examine the following statements:

```
cout << "There are four syntax errors here\n
cot " Can you find tem";
```

They contain the following syntax errors:

1. A closing quotation mark is missing in line 1.
2. A terminating semicolon (;) is missing in line 1.
3. The keyword cout is misspelled in line 2.
4. The insertion operator, <<, is missing in line 2.

When the program is compiled, the compiler detects all these errors because they're syntax errors that violate the basic rules of C++. If they aren't discovered by desk checking, the compiler detects them and displays an error message.[11] Sometimes the error message is clear and the error is obvious; at other times, understanding the compiler's error message takes a little detective work. Because syntax errors are the only error type that can be detected at compile time, the terms "compile-time errors" and "syntax errors" are used interchangeably. Strictly speaking, however, compile-time refers to when the error is detected, and syntax refers to the type of error detected.

The misspelling of "them" in the second statement isn't a syntax error. Although this spelling error results in displaying an undesirable output line, it's not a violation of C++'s syntax rules. It's a **typographical error**, commonly referred to as a "typo." The compiler doesn't catch this type of typographical error.[12]

Another error the compiler doesn't catch is a logic error, which can cause a runtime error or produce incorrect results. These errors are characterized by erroneous, unexpected, or unintentional output that's a direct result of some flaw in the program's logic. These errors can be detected by desk checking, by program testing, by accident when a user gets erroneous output while the program is executing, or not at all. If the error is detected while the program is executing, a runtime error can occur that generates an error message, causes premature program termination, or both.

The most serious logic error is caused by not fully understanding the program's requirements because the logic in a program reflects the logic on which it's coded. For example, if a program's purpose is to calculate the load-bearing strength of a steel beam and the programmer doesn't fully understand how to make the calculation, what inputs are needed to perform the calculation, or what special conditions exist (such as how temperature affects the beam), a logic error occurs. Because the compiler doesn't detect these errors and they often go undetected at runtime, they are always more difficult to detect than syntax errors.

---

[11]They might not, however, be detected at the same time. Frequently, one syntax error masks another error, and the second error is detected after the first error is corrected.

[12]The misspelling of a C++ keyword or a declared variable name that results in an undeclared name *is* caught, however, because it results in a syntax error or an undeclared variable.

If logic errors *are* detected, typically they're revealed in one of two main ways. First, the program executes to completion but produces incorrect results, such as the following:

- *No output*—This result is caused by omitting an output statement or using a sequence of statements that inadvertently bypasses an output statement.
- *Unappealing or misaligned output*—This result is caused by an error in an output statement.
- *Incorrect numerical results*—This result is caused by assigning incorrect values to variables in an expression, using an incorrect arithmetic expression, omitting a statement, making a round-off error, or using an improper sequence of statements.

Second, a runtime error occurs. Examples of logic errors that cause this result are attempts to divide by zero or take the square root of a negative number.

Plan your program testing carefully to maximize the possibility of locating errors. In addition, remember that although a single test can reveal the presence of an error, it *does not* verify that another error isn't lurking somewhere else in the program. Furthermore, the fact that one test revealed no errors *does not* mean there are no errors.

After you discover an error, however, you must locate where it occurs and fix it. In computer jargon, a program error is referred to as a **bug**, and the process of isolating, correcting, and verifying the correction is called **debugging**.

Although no hard-and-fast rules exist for isolating the cause of an error, some useful techniques can be applied. The first is preventive. Often programmers introduce errors in the rush to code and run a program before understanding what's required and how to achieve the result, as you learned in Chapter 2. Many errors can be eliminated by desk checking the program before entering or compiling it.

A second useful technique is imitating the computer by executing each statement by hand as the computer would. This technique, called **program tracing**, involves writing down each variable, as it's encountered in the program, and listing the value that should be stored in the variable as each input and assignment statement is encountered. Doing this sharpens your programming skills because it helps you understand what each statement in your program causes to happen.

A third useful technique is including some temporary code in your program that displays the values of selected variables. If the displayed values are incorrect, you can determine what part of your program generated them and make the necessary corrections. You could also add temporary code that displays the values of all input data. This technique, called **echo printing**, is useful in establishing that the program is receiving and interpreting input data correctly.

The most powerful technique is using a special program called a **debugger**. A debugger program can control the execution of a C++ program, interrupt the C++ program at any point in its execution, and display the values of all variables at the point of interruption.

Finally, no discussion of debugging is complete without mentioning the main ingredient needed for isolating and correcting errors successfully: the attitude you bring to the task. After you write a program, you naturally assume it's correct. Taking a step back to be objective about testing and finding errors in your own software is difficult. As a programmer, you must remind yourself that just because you think your program is correct doesn't make it so. Finding errors in your own programs is a sobering experience but one that helps you become a better programmer. The process can be exciting and fun if you approach it as a detection problem, with you as the master detective.

3.8   Common Programming Errors

When using the material in this chapter, be aware of the following possible errors:

1. Forgetting to assign or initialize values for all variables before using them in an expression. Values can be assigned by assignment statements, initialized in a declaration statement, or assigned interactively by entering values with a `cin` statement.

2. Using a mathematical library function without including the preprocessor statement `#include <cmath>` (and on a UNIX-based system, forgetting to include the `-lm` argument on the `cc` command line).

3. Using a library function without providing the correct number of arguments of the proper data type.

4. Applying the increment or decrement operator to an expression. For example, the expression `(count + n)++` is incorrect. The increment and decrement operators can be applied only to variables.

5. Forgetting to use the extraction operator, `>>`, to separate variables in a `cin` statement.

6. A more unusual error occurs when increment and decrement operators are used with variables appearing more than once in the same expression. This error occurs because C++ doesn't specify the order in which operands are accessed in an expression. For example, the value assigned to `result` in the following statement depends on the compiler:

   ```
   result = i + i++;
   ```

   If your compiler accesses the first operand (`i`) first, the preceding statement is equivalent to

   ```
   result = 2 * i;
   i++;
   ```

   However, if your compiler accesses the second operand (`i++`) first, the value of the first operand is altered before it's used the second time, and the value 2i + 1 is assigned to result. As a general rule, don't use the increment or decrement operator in an expression when the variable it operates on appears more than once in the expression.

7. Being unwilling to test a program in depth. Being objective about testing your own software is difficult, but as a programmer, you must remind yourself that just because you think your program is correct doesn't make it so.

3.9   Chapter Summary

1. An expression is a sequence of one or more operands separated by operators. An operand is a constant, a variable, or another expression. A value is associated with an expression.

2. Expressions are evaluated according to the precedence and associativity of the operators used in the expression.

3. The assignment operator is the = symbol. Expressions using this operator assign a value to a variable, and the expression also takes on a value. Because assignment is a C++ operation, the assignment operator can be used more than once in the same expression.

4. The increment operator, ++, adds one to a variable, and the decrement operator, --, subtracts one from a variable. Both operators can be used as prefixes or postfixes. In a prefix operation, the variable is incremented (or decremented) before its value is used. In a postfix operation, the variable is incremented (or decremented) after its value is used.

5. C++ provides library functions for calculating square root, logarithmic, and other mathematical computations. Programs using a mathematical function must include the statement #include <cmath> or have a function declaration before calling the mathematical function.

6. Every mathematical library function operates on its arguments to calculate a single value. To use a library function effectively, you must know the function name, what the function does, the number and data types of arguments the function expects, and the data type of the returned value.

7. Values passed to a function are called arguments of the function. Arguments are passed to a library function by including each argument, separated by commas, in the parentheses following the function's name. Each function has its own requirements for the number and data types of the arguments that must be provided.

8. Functions can be included in larger expressions.

9. A cin statement is used for data input. cin accepts a stream of data from the keyboard and assigns the data to variables. This is the general form of a statement using cin:

```
cin >> var1 >> var2 . . . >> varn;
```

The extraction operator, >>, must be used to separate variable names in a cin statement.

10. When a cin statement is encountered, the computer temporarily suspends further execution until enough data has been entered for the number of variables in the cin statement.

11. It's a good programming practice to display a message before a cin statement that alerts users to the type and number of data items to be entered. This message is called a prompt. It's even a better programming practice to permit only one input variable for each cin statement.

12. Values can be equated to a single constant by using the const keyword. This keyword creates a named constant that is read-only after it's initialized in the declaration statement. This declaration has the syntax

```
const dataType SymbolicName = initialValue;
```

and permits using the constant instead of the *initialValue* anywhere in the program after the declaration.

Programming Projects for Chapter 3

1. **(General Math) a.** Write a C++ program to calculate and display the value of the slope of the line connecting two points with the coordinates (3,7) and (8,12). Use the fact that the slope between two points with the coordinates (x_1,y_1) and (x_2,y_2) is $(y_2 - y_1) / (x_2 - x_1)$.

   b. How do you know the result your program produced is correct?

   c. After verifying the output your program produces, modify it to determine the slope of the line connecting the points (2,10) and (12,6).

   d. What do you think will happen if you use the points (2,3) and (2,4), which results in a division by zero? How do you think this situation can be handled?

   e. If your program doesn't already do so, change its output to this:

   ```
   The value of the slope is xxx.xx
   ```

   The xxx.xx denotes placing the calculated value in a field wide enough for three places to the left of the decimal point and two places to the right of it.

2. **(General Math) a.** Write a C++ program to calculate and display the midpoint coordinates of the line segment connecting the two endpoints given in Exercise 1a. Use the fact that the coordinates of the midpoint between two points with the coordinates (x_1,y_1) and (x_2,y_2) are $((x_1+x_2)/2, (y_1+y_2)/2)$. Your program should produce the following display (replacing the underscores with values your program calculates):

   ```
   The x midpoint coordinate is _____
   The y midpoint coordinate is _____
   ```

   b. How do you know the midpoint values your program calculates are correct?

   c. After verifying the output your program produces, modify it to determine the midpoint coordinates of the line connecting the points (2,10) and (12,6).

   d. If your program doesn't already do so, change its output to this:

   ```
   The x coordinate of the midpoint is xxx.xx
   The y coordinate of the midpoint is xxx.xx
   ```

   The xxx.xx denotes placing the calculated value in a field wide enough for three places to the left of the decimal point and two places to the right of it.

3. **(General Math)** Modify the program written for Exercise 2 so that it accepts the x and y coordinates of two points. Have your program determine and display the midpoints of the two points (use the formula given in Exercise 2). Verify your program by using the following test data:

   > Test data set 1: Point 1 = (0,0) and Point 2 = (16,0)
   > Test data set 2: Point 1 = (0,0) and Point 2 = (0,16)
   > Test data set 3: Point 1 = (0,0) and Point 2 = (-16,0)
   > Test data set 4: Point 1 = (0,0) and Point 2 = (0,-16)
   > Test data set 5: Point 1 = (-5,-5) and Point 2 = (5,5)

When you have finished your verification, use your program to complete the following chart:

First Point	Second Point	Midpoint
(4, 6)	(16, 18)	
(22, 3)	(8, 12)	
(-10, 8)	(14, 4)	
(-12, 2)	(14, 3.1)	
(3.1,-6)	(20, 16)	
(3.1, -6)	(-16, -18)	

4. **(Biology)** The number of bacteria, B, in a culture that's subject to refrigeration can be approximated by this formula:

$$B = 300000 \; e^{-0.032t}$$

e is Euler's number 2.71828 (rounded to five decimal places).

t is the time in hours the culture has been refrigerated.

Using this formula, write, compile, and execute a single C++ program that prompts the user for a value of time, calculates the number of bacteria in the culture, and displays the result. For testing purposes, check your program by using a test input of 10 hours. After verifying your program, use it to determine the number of bacteria in the culture after 12, 18, 24, 36, 48, and 72 hours.

5. **(Heat Transfer)** The time it takes for a spherical object to cool from an initial temperature of T_{init} to a final temperature of T_{fin}, caused entirely by radiation, is provided by Kelvin's cooling equation:

$$t = \frac{Nk}{2e\sigma A}\left[\frac{1}{T_{fin}^3} - \frac{1}{T_{init}^3}\right]$$

t is the cooling time in years.
N is the number of atoms.
k is Boltzmann's constant = 1.38×10^{-23} m²kg/s²K (note that 1 Joule = 1 m²kg/s²).
e is emissivity of the object.
σ is Stephan-Boltzmann's constant = 5.6703×10^{-8} Watts/m²K⁴.
A is the surface area.
T_{fin} is the final temperature.
T_{init} is the initial temperature.

Assuming an infinitely hot initial temperature, this formula reduces to

$$t = \frac{Nk}{2e\sigma A T_{fin}^3}$$

Using this second formula, write a C++ program to determine the time it took Earth to cool to its current surface temperature of 300°K from its initial infinitely hot state, assuming the cooling is caused only by radiation. Use the information that the area of the Earth's surface is $5.15 \times 10^{14} \text{m}^2$, its emissivity is 1, the number of atoms contained in the Earth is 1.1×10^{50}, and the radius of the Earth is 6.4×10^6 meters. Additionally, use the relationship that a sphere's surface area is given by this formula:

Surface area of a sphere = 4 π r²

6. **(Heat Transfer)** The formula developed in Exercise 5 can be used to determine the cooling time, *t*, caused only by radiation, of each planet in the solar system. For convenience, this formula is repeated here (see Exercise 5 for a definition of each symbol):

$$t = \frac{Nk}{2e\sigma A T_{fin}^3}$$

A = surface area of a sphere = $4 \pi r^2$

N = number of atoms = $\frac{\text{volume of the sphere}}{\text{volume of an atom}}$

Volume of a sphere = $\frac{4}{3}$ π radius³

The volume of a single atom is approximately $1 \times 10^{-29} \text{m}^3$. Using this information and the current temperatures and radii listed in the following chart, determine the time it took each planet to cool to its current temperature, caused only by radiation.

Planet	Current Average Surface Temperature (°Celsius)	Radius (km)	Cooling Time (years)
Mercury	270	2439	
Venus	462	6051	
Earth	14	6371	
Mars	-46	3396	
Jupiter	-108	7.1492×10^4	
Saturn	-139	6.0268×10^4	
Uranus	-197	2.5559×10^4	
Neptune	-201	2.4764×10^4	

7. **(Physics)** When a particular rubber ball is dropped from a given height (in meters), its impact speed (in meters/second) when it hits the ground is given by the formula

$$speed = \sqrt{2gh}$$

where *g* is the acceleration caused by gravity and *h* is the height. The ball then rebounds to 2/3 the height from which it last fell. Using this information, write, test, and run a C++ program that calculates and displays the impact speed of the first three bounces and the rebound height of each bounce. Test your program by using an initial height of 2.0 meters. Run the program twice, and compare the results for dropping the ball on Earth ($g = 9.81$ meters/sec^2) and on the moon ($g = 1.67$ meters/sec^2).

8. **(Electrical Eng.) a.** The voltage gain of an amplifier is given by this formula:

$$voltage\ gain = \left[\frac{275}{\sqrt{23^2 + 0.5 f^2}} \right]^n$$

f is the frequency in Hz.
n is the number of stages in the amplifier.

Using this formula, write, compile, and execute a C++ program to determine the value of the voltage gain for a four-stage amplifier operating at a frequency of 120 Hz. Your program should produce the following display:

```
At a frequency of xxxxx Hertz, the voltage gain is yyyyy
```

Your program should replace xxxxx with the frequency and yyyyy with the voltage gain.

b. Manually check the value your program produces. After verifying that your program is working correctly, modify it to determine the voltage gain of a 12-stage amplifier operating at a frequency of 9500 Hz.

9. **(Electrical Eng.)** Write, compile, and execute a C++ program that calculates and displays the value of the current flowing through an RC circuit (see Figure 3.18). The circuit consists of a battery connected in a series to a switch, a resistor, and a capacitor. When the switch is closed, the current, i, flowing through the circuit is given by this formula:

$$i = (E/R)\ e^{-t/RC}$$

E is the voltage of the battery in volts.
R is the value of the resistor in ohms.
C is the value of the capacitor in farads.
t is the time in seconds after the switch is closed.
e is Euler's number, which is 2.71828 (rounded to five decimal places).

Using this formula, write, compile, and run a C++ program to determine the voltage across the capacitor shown in Figure 3.18 when t is 0.31 seconds. (*Note*: The value of RC is referred to as the system's **time constant**.)

The program should prompt the user to enter appropriate values and use input statements to accept the data. In constructing the prompts, use statements such as

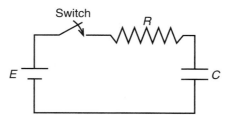

Figure 3.18 A series RC circuit

"Enter the voltage of the battery." Verify your program's operation by calculating by hand the current for the following test data:

Test data set 1: Voltage = 20 volts, R = 10 ohms, RC = 0.044, t = 0.023 seconds.
Test data set 2: Voltage = 35, R = 10 ohms, RC = 0.16, t = 0.067 seconds.

b. Check the value computed by your program by hand. After verifying that your program is working correctly, use your program to complete the following chart:

Voltage V (volts)	Resistance R (ohms)	RC (Time Constant)	Time t (sec)	Current i (amps)
35	10	0.16	0.11	
35	10	0.16	0.44	
35	10	0.16	0.83	
15	10	0.55	0.11	
15	10	0.55	0.44	
15	10	0.55	0.067	
6	1000	2.6	12.4	

10. **(Electrical Eng.)** The amplification of electronic circuits is measured in units of decibels, which is calculated as

10 LOG (P$_o$/P$_i$)

where P_o is the power of the output signal and P_i is the power of the input signal. Using this formula, write, compile, and execute a C++ program to calculate and display the decibel amplification, in which the output power is 50 times the input power. Verify your program's result by using a hand calculation. After verifying that your program is working correctly, use it to determine the amplification of a circuit, where output power is 4.639 Watts and input power is 1 Watt.

11. **(Acoustics)** The loudness of a sound is measured in units of decibels and is calculated as shown:

10 LOG (SL/RL)

　　SL is the intensity of the sound being measured.
　　RL is a reference sound-intensity level.

Using this formula, write a C++ program that calculates and displays the decibel loudness of a busy street having a sound intensity of 10,000,000 RL. Verify your program's result by using a hand calculation. After verifying that your program is working correctly, use it to determine the sound level in decibels of the following sounds:

a. A whisper at sound intensity 200 *RL*

b. A rock band playing at sound intensity 1,000,000,000,000 *RL*

c. An airplane taking off at sound intensity 100,000,000,000,000 *RL*

12. **(General Math) a.** A balance has the following size weights: 100 lb, 50 lb, 10 lb, 5 lb, and 1 lb. The number of 100 lb and 50 lb weights required to weigh an object weighing WEIGHT pounds can be calculated by using the following C++ statements:

```
// Determine the number of 100 lb weights
    w100 = int(WEIGHT/100)
// Determine the number of 50 lb weights
    w50 = int((WEIGHT - w100 * 100)/50)
```

Using these statements as a starting point, write a C++ program that calculates the number of each type of weight needed to weigh a 789 lb object.

b. Without compiling or executing your program, manually check the effect of each statement in the program and determine what's stored in each variable as each statement is encountered.

c. After verifying that your algorithm works correctly, compile and execute your program. Verify that the results your program produces are correct. After verifying that your program is working correctly, use it to determine the weights required to weigh a 626 lb object.

Engineering and Scientific Disciplines

Electrical Engineering

Electrical engineering, the largest engineering field, deals with applying the principles of electricity and electromagnetism to the manufacture of all forms of machines and devices that use electricity or produce electrical energy. In the mid-1800s, this field was concerned solely with generating electrical energy, but it has evolved into a broad field encompassing the following areas, among others:

- Power: This area involves generation of electrical energy in large fossil-fuel, nuclear, solar, and hydroelectric plants as well as efficient use of electrical energy by means of motors or illumination devices. Also important are transmitting and distributing electrical energy through overhead lines, microwaves, light pipes, and superconducting lines.
- Solid-state electronics: Through modern physics and materials science, semiconducting materials are developed and used to construct microcircuitry for monitoring and controlling the operations of all kinds of devices, from video games to assembly-line robots. The improved reliability, rapidly shrinking size, and reduced power requirements of modern miniaturized electrical components have created limitless opportunities for applications.
- Communications: This area involves designing and constructing equipment used to transmit information via electricity or electromagnetic waves (radio, light, microwaves, and so on). This field used to include antenna characteristics and radar, but using laser for communication is the current topic.
- Computers and robotics: Although electronics deals with principles associated with the functions of components, computer engineers are concerned with designing the complex circuitry that interweaves components into a computer. Microprocessors, or small computers, are designed to constantly monitor and control the operations of a piece of equipment, such as a lathe or an autopilot.

Chapter 4

Selection Structures

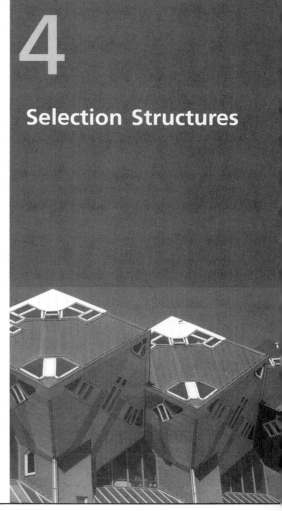

The term "flow of control" refers to the order in which a program's statements are executed. Unless directed otherwise, the normal, default flow of control for all programs is sequential. This term means statements are executed in sequence, one after another, in the order in which they're placed in a program.

In addition to sequential execution, all high-level languages provide three other control structures to alter the sequential flow of control in precisely defined ways. Here, the term "control structure" simply means a construction that specifies the order in which statements are to be executed. The three additional control structures are called selection, repetition, and invocation.

As you might have guessed by its name, a selection structure is used to select statements to be performed next, and a repetition structure is used to force a repeat execution of a set of statements. Invocation is a means of invoking, or forcing, a set of statements, which have previously been combined into a separate function, to be executed at a particular point in a program.

As any algorithm, no matter how complex, can be programmed by using one or more of the four standardized flow of control structures (sequential, selection, repetition, and invocation), understanding how each of these structures is constructed and operates is a primary requirement for all programmers. This chapter discusses C++'s selection control structures, and Chapters 5 and 6 cover repetition and invocation control structures.

4.1   Selection Criteria

In solving many problems, different actions must be taken, depending on the data's value. Examples of simple situations include calculating an area *only if* the measurements are positive, performing a division *only if* the divisor isn't zero, printing different messages *depending on* the value of a grade received, and so on.

The `if-else` statement in C++ is used to implement such a decision structure in its simplest form—choosing between two alternatives. The most commonly used pseudocode syntax of this statement is as follows:

```
if (condition)
    statement executed if the condition is true;
else
    statement executed if the condition is false;
```

When a running program encounters the `if` statement, the condition is evaluated to determine its numerical value, which is then interpreted as `true` or `false`. If the condition evaluates to any positive or negative non-zero numerical value, the condition is considered a "true" condition and the statement following the `if` is executed. If the condition evaluates to a zero numerical value, the condition is considered a "false" condition and the statement following the `else` is executed. The `else` part of the statement is optional and can be omitted.

Relational Operators

The condition used in an `if` statement can be any valid C++ expression (including, as you'll see, even an assignment expression). The most commonly used conditions, however, are simple relational expressions. A **simple relational expression** consists of a relational operator that compares two operands, as shown in Figure 4.1.

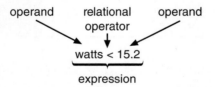

Figure 4.1   A simple relational expression

Although each operand in a relational expression can be a variable or a constant, relational operators must be one of those listed in Table 4.1. These relational operators can be used with integer, float, double, or character operands but must be typed exactly as shown in Table 4.1. For example, although the following examples are all valid,

```
age > 40    length <= 50    temp > 98.6
3 < 4       flag == done    idNum == 682
day != 5    2.0 > 3.3       hours > 40
```

the following are invalid:

```
length =< 50      // operator out of order
2.0 >> 3.3        // invalid operator
flag = = done     // spaces are not allowed
```

Table 4.1 C++'s Relational Operators

Relational Operator	Meaning	Example
<	Less than	age < 30
>	Greater than	height > 6.2
<=	Less than or equal to	taxable <= 20000
>=	Greater than or equal to	temp >= 98.6
==	Equal to	grade == 100
!=	Not equal to	number != 250

The terms relational expression and **condition** are frequently used as synonyms, and both terms are used interchangeably in this book. Like all C++ expressions, relational expressions are evaluated to yield a numerical result.[1] In a relational expression, the value of the expression can be only the integer value 1 or 0. These values are interpreted as true and false, respectively. Conversely, a *relational expression that's true always evaluates to an integer value of 1, and a relational expression that's false always evaluates to an integer value of 0.*

For example, because the relationship 3 < 4 is always true, this expression has a value of 1, and because the relationship 2.0 > 3.0 is always false, the value of the expression itself is 0. This rule can be verified by the following statements,

```
cout << "The value of 3 < 4 is " << (3 < 4) << endl;
cout << "The value of 2.0 > 3.0 is " << (2.0 > 3.0) << endl;
cout << "The value of true is " << true << endl;
cout << "The value of false is " << false << endl;
```

which result in this display:

```
The value of 3 < 4 is 1
The value of 2.0 > 3.0 is 0
The value of true is 1
The value of false is 0
```

The value of a relational expression such as hours > 40 depends on the value stored in the variable hours. In a C++ program, a relational expression's value isn't as important as the interpretation C++ places on the value when the expression is used as part of a selection statement. In these statements, which are explained in the next section, you'll see that C++ uses a zero value to represent a false condition and any non-zero value to represent a true condition. The selection of which statement to execute next is then based on the value.

In addition to numerical operands, character data can be compared by using relational operators. For these comparisons, the char values are coerced to int values automatically for the comparison. For example, in Unicode, the letter 'A' is stored by using a code with a lower numerical value than the letter 'B', the code for 'B' has a lower value than the

---

[1]In this regard, C++ differs from other high-level languages, which yield a Boolean (true or false) result.

code for `'C'`, and so on. For character sets coded in this manner, the following conditions are evaluated as shown:

Expression	Value	Interpretation
`'A' > 'C'`	0	`false`
`'D' <= 'Z'`	1	`true`
`'E' == 'F'`	0	`false`
`'g' >= 'm'`	0	`false`
`'b' != 'c'`	1	`true`
`'a' == 'A'`	0	`false`
`'B' < 'a'`	1	`true`
`'b' > 'Z'`	1	`true`

Comparing letters is essential in alphabetizing names or using characters to select a choice in decision-making situations. Strings of characters can also be compared, and two string expressions can be compared by using relational operators or the `string` class's comparison methods (discussed in Section 9.3). In the ASCII character set, a blank precedes (and is considered "less than") all letters and numbers; the letters of the alphabet are stored in order from A to Z; and digits are stored in order from 0 to 9. In this sequence, lowercase letters come after (are considered "greater than") uppercase letters, and letter codes come after (are "greater than") digit codes (see Appendix B).

When two strings are compared, their characters are compared one pair at a time (both first characters, then both second characters, and so on). If no differences are found, the strings are equal; if a difference is found, the string with the first lower character is considered the smaller string. Following are examples of string comparisons:

Expression	Value	Interpretation	Comment
`"Hello" > "Good-bye"`	1	`true`	The first H in Hello is greater than the first G in Good-bye.
`"SMITH" > "JONES"`	1	`true`	The first S in SMITH is greater than the first J in JONES.
`"123" > "1227"`	1	`true`	The third character in 123, the 3, is greater than the third character in 1227, the 2.
`"Behop" > "Beehive"`	1	`true`	The third character in Behop, the h, is greater than the third character in Beehive, the second e.
`"He" == "She"`	0	`false`	The first H in He is not equal to the first S in She.
`"plant" < "planet"`	0	`false`	The t in plant is greater than the e in planet.

Logical Operators

In addition to using simple relational expressions as conditions, more complex conditions can be created by using the **logical operators** AND, OR, and NOT. These operators are represented by the symbols &&, ||, and !, respectively.

When the AND operator, &&, is used with two simple expressions, the condition is true only if both expressions are true by themselves. Therefore, the logical condition

```
(voltage > 48) && (milliamp < 10)
```

is true only if voltage is greater than 48 and milliamp is less than 10. Because relational operators have a higher precedence than logical operators, the parentheses in this logical expression could have been omitted.

The logical OR operator, ||, is also used with two expressions. When using the OR operator, the condition is satisfied if one or both of the two expressions are true. Therefore, the condition

```
(voltage > 48) || (milliamp < 10)
```

is true if voltage is greater than 48, milliamp is less than 10, or both conditions are true. Again, the parentheses surrounding the relational expressions are included to make the statement easier to read. Because relational operators have a higher precedence than logical operators, the same evaluation is made even if the parentheses are omitted.

For the declarations

```
int i, j;
double a, b, complete;
```

the following are valid conditions:

```
a > b
(i == j) || (a < b) || complete
(a/b > 5) && (i <= 20)
```

Before these conditions can be evaluated, the values of a, b, i, j, and complete must be known. Assuming a = 12.0, b = 2.0, i = 15, j = 30, and complete = 0.0, the previous expressions yield the following results:

Expression	Value	Interpretation
a > b	1	true
(i == j) || (a < b) || complete	0	false
(a/b > 5) && (i <= 20)	1	true

The NOT operator, !, is used to change an expression to its opposite state; that is, if the expression has a non-zero value (true), the statement !expression produces a zero value (false). If an expression is false to begin with (has a zero value), !expression is true and evaluates to 1. For example, if the number 26 is stored in the variable age, the expression age > 40 has a value of 0 (false), and the expression !(age > 40) has a value of 1 (true). Because the NOT operator is used with only one expression, it's a unary operator.

Relational and logical operators have a hierarchy of execution similar to arithmetic operators. Table 4.2 lists the precedence of these operators in relation to the other operators you have used.

Table 4.2 Operator Precedence and Associativity

Operator	Associativity
`! unary - ++ --`	Right to left
`* / %`	Left to right
`+ -`	Left to right
`< <= > >=`	Left to right
`== !=`	Left to right
`&&`	Left to right
`||`	Left to right
`= += -= *= /=`	Right to left

The following chart illustrates using an operator's precedence and associativity to evaluate relational expressions, assuming the following declarations:

```
char key = 'm';
int i = 5, j = 7, k = 12;
double x = 22.5;
```

Expression	Equivalent Expression	Value	Interpretation
`i + 2 == k - 1`	`(i + 2) == (k - 1)`	0	false
`3 * i - j < 22`	`(3 * i) - j < 22`	1	true
`i + 2 * j > k`	`(i + (2 * j)) > k`	1	true
`k + 3 <= -j + 3 * i`	`(k + 3) <= ((-j) + (3*i))`	0	false
`'a' + 1 == 'b'`	`('a' + 1) == 'b'`	1	true
`key - 1 > 'p'`	`(key - 1) > 'p'`	0	false
`key + 1 == 'n'`	`(key + 1) == 'n'`	1	true
`25 >= x + 1.0`	`25 >= (x + 1.0)`	1	true

As with all expressions, parentheses can be used to alter the assigned operator priority and improve the readability of relational expressions. By evaluating the expressions in parentheses first, the following compound condition is evaluated as shown:

```
(6 * 3 == 36 / 2) || (13 < 3 * 3 + 4) && !(6 - 2 < 5)
    (18 == 18)  ||   (13 < 9 + 4)   && !(4 < 5)
         1      ||   (13 < 13)      && !1
         1      ||        0         && 0
         1      ||        0
                     1
```

A Numerical Accuracy Problem

In C++'s relational expressions, a subtle numerical accuracy problem related to single-precision and double-precision numbers can occur. Because of the way computers store these numbers, you should avoid testing for equality of single-precision and double-precision values and variables by using the relational operator ==.

The reason is that many decimal numbers, such as 0.1, can't be represented in binary with a finite number of bits, so testing for exact equality for these numbers can fail. When you want equality of noninteger values, it's better to require that the absolute value of the difference between operands be less than some extremely small value. Therefore, for single-precision and double-precision operands, the general expression

```
operandOne == operandTwo
```

should be replaced by the condition

```
abs(operandOne - operandTwo) < 0.000001
```

where the value 0.000001 can be altered to any other acceptably small value. Therefore, if the difference between the two operands is less than 0.000001 (or another user-selected amount), the two operands are considered essentially equal. For example, if x and y are single-precision variables, a condition such as

```
x/y == 0.35
```

should be programmed as the following:

```
abs(x/y - 0.35) < EPSILON
```

EPSILON can be a constant set to any acceptably small value, such as 0.000001.[2] Not requiring exact equivalence to zero ensures that slight inaccuracies in representing noninteger numbers in binary don't affect evaluation of the tested condition. Because all computers have an exact binary representation of 0, comparisons for exact equality to 0 don't have this numerical accuracy problem.

EXERCISES 4.1

1. **(Practice)** Determine the value of the following expressions, assuming a = 5, b = 2, c = 4, d = 6, and e = 3:

   a. a > b

   b. a != b

   c. d % b == c % b

   d. a * c != d * b

   e. d * b == c * e

---

[2]Using the abs() function requires including the cmath header file by placing the preprocessor command #include<cmath> before or after #include<iostream>. UNIX-based systems also require including the math library with the -lm command-line argument.

    f. `!(a * b)`

    g. `!(a % b * c)`

    h. `!(c % b * a)`

    i. `b % c * a`

2. **(Practice)** Using parentheses, rewrite the following expressions to indicate their order of evaluation correctly. Then evaluate each expression, assuming a = 5, b = 2, and c = 4.

    a. `a % b * c && c % b * a`

    b. `a % b * c || c % b * a`

    c. `b % c * a && a % c * b`

    d. `b % c * a || a % c * b`

3. **(Practice)** Write relational expressions to express the following conditions (using variable names of your choosing):

    a. The distance is equal to 30 feet.

    b. The ambient temperature is 86.4 degrees.

    c. A speed is 55 mph.

    d. The current month is 12 (December).

    e. The letter input is K.

    f. A length is greater than 2 feet and less than 3 feet.

    g. The current day is the 15th day of the 1st month.

    h. The automobile's speed is 35 mph and its acceleration is greater than 4 mph per second.

    i. An automobile's speed is greater than 50 mph and it has been moving for at least 5 hours.

    j. The code is less than 500 characters and takes more than 2 microseconds to transmit.

4. **(Practice)** Determine the value of the following expressions, assuming a = 5, b = 2, c = 4, and d = 5:

    a. `a == 5`

    b. `b * d == c * c`

    c. `d % b * c > 5 || c % b * d < 7`

4.2   The `if-else` Statement

The `if-else` structure directs the computer to select between two statements based on the result of a comparison. For example, suppose you need to calculate the area of a circle, given the radius as an input value. If the input is a negative number, you want to print a message, using one `cout` statement, that the radius can't be a negative value; otherwise, you calculate and print the circle's area, using a second `cout` statement. The `if-else` structure can be used in this situation to select the correct operation based on whether the radius is negative. This is the general syntax of the `if-else` statement:

```
if (expression) statement1;

else statement2;
```

The *expression* is evaluated first. If its value is non-zero, *statement1* is executed. If its value is zero, the statement after the keyword `else` is executed. Therefore, one of the two statements (*statement1* or *statement2*, but not both) is always executed, depending on the expression's value. Notice that the tested expression must be enclosed by parentheses and a semicolon is placed after each statement.

For clarity, the `if-else` statement is typically written on four lines in this form:

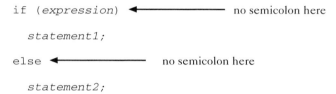

```
if (expression)              no semicolon here

  statement1;

else                         no semicolon here

  statement2;
```

The form of the `if-else` statement that's used typically depends on the length of *statement1* and *statement2*. However, when using this four-line form, don't put a semicolon after the parentheses or the `else` keyword. The semicolons are placed only at the ends of statements. Figure 4.2 shows the flowchart for the `if-else` statement.

As a specific example of an `if-else` structure, take a look at constructing a C++ program for determining a circle's area by examining the value of the radius first. The condition to be tested is whether the radius is less than 0, so the following is an appropriate `if-else` statement for this situation:

```
if (radius < 0.0)
    cout << "A negative radius is invalid" << endl;
else
    cout << "The area of this circle is " << 3.1416 * pow(radius,2) << endl;
```

The relational operator `<` is used to represent the condition "less than." If the value of radius is less than 0, the condition is true (has a value of 1) and the statement `cout << "A negative radius is invalid";` is executed. If the condition is not true, the value of the expression is 0, and the statement after the `else` keyword is executed. Program 4.1 shows using this statement in a complete program.

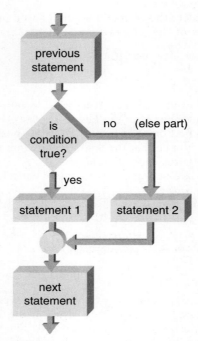

Figure 4.2   The if-else flowchart

Program 4.1

```cpp
#include <iostream>
#include <cmath>
using namespace std;
int main()
{
  double radius;
    cout << "Please type in the radius: ";
  cin  >> radius;

  if (radius < 0.0)
    cout << "A negative radius is invalid" << endl;
  else

    cout << "The area of this circle is " << 3.1416 * pow(radius,2) << endl;
  return 0;
}
```

A blank line is inserted before and after the `if-else` statement to highlight it in the program. This format is used throughout the book to emphasize the statement being discussed.

To illustrate selection in action, Program 4.1 is run twice with different input data. These are the results:

```
Please type in the radius: -2.5
A negative radius is invalid
```

and

```
Please type in the radius: 2.5
The area of this circle is 19.635
```

In reviewing this output, observe that the radius in the first run is less than 0, and the `if` part of the `if-else` structure executes the `cout` statement correctly, telling the user that a negative radius is invalid. In the second run, the radius isn't negative, and the `else` part of the `if-else` structure is used to yield this correct area computation:

$$3.1416 * (2.5)^2 = 19.635$$

Although any expression can be tested by an `if-else` statement, relational expressions are used most often. However, statements such as the following are valid:

```
if (num)
  cout << "Bingo!";
else
  cout << "You lose!";
```

Because num is a valid expression by itself, the message `Bingo!` is displayed if num has any non-zero value, and the message `You lose!` is displayed if num has a value of zero.

Compound Statements

Although only a single statement is permitted in the `if` and `else` parts of the `if-else` statement, each single statement can be a compound statement. A **compound statement** is a sequence of single statements between braces, as shown in this example:

```
{
  statement1;
  statement2;
  statement3;
     .
     .
     .
  last statement;
}
```

Using braces to enclose a set of statements creates a single block of statements, which can be used anywhere in a C++ program in place of a single statement. The next example shows using a compound statement in the general form of an `if-else` statement:

```
if (expression)
{
  statement1;      // as many statements as necessary
  statement2;      // can be put inside the braces
  statement3;      // each statement must end with a ;
}
else
{
  statement4;
  statement5;
       .
       .
  last statement;
}
```

Program 4.2 shows using a compound statement in an actual program.

Program 4.2 checks whether the value in `tempType` is `f`. If so, the compound statement corresponding to the `if` part of the `if-else` statement is executed. Any other letter in `tempType` results in execution of the compound statement corresponding to the `else` part. A sample run of Program 4.2 follows:

```
Enter the temperature to be converted: 212
Enter an f if the temperature is in Fahrenheit
 or a c if the temperature is in Celsius: f
The equivalent Celsius temperature is 100.00
```

Program 4.2

```cpp
#include <iostream>
#include <iomanip>
using namespace std;

// a temperature conversion program
int main()
{
  char tempType;
  double temp, fahren, celsius;

  cout << "Enter the temperature to be converted: ";
  cin  >> temp;
  cout << "Enter an f if the temperature is in Fahrenheit";
  cout << "\n or a c if the temperature is in Celsius: ";
  cin  >> tempType;
    // set output formats
  cout << setiosflags(ios::fixed)
       << setiosflags(ios::showpoint)
       << setprecision(2);

  if (tempType == 'f')
  {
    celsius = (5.0 / 9.0) * (temp - 32.0);
    cout << "\nThe equivalent Celsius temperature is "
         << celsius << endl;
  }
  else
  {
    fahren =  (9.0 / 5.0) * temp + 32.0;
    cout << "\nThe equivalent Fahrenheit temperature is "
         << fahren << endl;
  }

  return 0;
}
```

Block Scope

All statements contained in a compound statement constitute a single block of code, and any variable declared in this block has meaning only between its declaration and the closing braces defining the block. For example, take a look at the following example, which consists of two blocks of code:

```
{    // start of outer block
   int a = 25;
   int b = 17;

   cout << "The value of a is " << a
        <<" and b is " << b << endl;

   {     // start of inner block
     double a = 46.25;

     int c = 10;
     cout << "a is now " << a
          << " b is now " << b
          << " and c is " << c << endl;
   }    // end of inner block

   cout << "a is now " << a
        << " and b is " << b << endl;

}    // end of outer block
```

This section of code produces the following output:

```
The value of a is 25 and b is 17
a is now 46.25 b is now 17 and c is 10
a is now 25 and b is 17
```

This output is produced as follows: The first block of code defines two variables named a and b, which can be used anywhere in this block after their declaration, including any block inside this outer block. In the inner block, two new variables have been declared, named a and c. The a defined in the inner block is stored in a different memory location than the a defined in the outer block. Therefore, at this stage, four different variables have been created, two with the same name. When a variable is referenced, the compiler attempts to first access a variable with the correct name that has been declared in the block containing the reference. If the referenced variable hasn't been defined in the block, the compiler attempts to access the variable declared in the next outer block, until a valid access results.

Point of Information

Placement of Braces in a Compound Statement

A common practice for some C++ programmers is placing the opening brace of a compound statement on the same line as the `if` and `else` statements. Using this convention, the `if` statement in Program 4.2 would look like the following example. (This placement is a matter of style only—both styles are used, and both are acceptable.)

```
if (tempType == 'f') {
  celsius = (5.0 / 9.0) * (temp - 32.0);
  cout << "\nThe equivalent Celsius temperature is "
      << celsius << endl;
}
else {
  fahren =  (9.0 / 5.0) * temp + 32.0;
  cout << "\nThe equivalent Fahrenheit temperature is "
      << fahren << endl;
}
```

Therefore, the values of the variables a and c referenced in the inner block use the values of the variables a and c declared in that block. Because no variable named b was declared in the inner block, the value of b displayed from within the inner block is obtained from the outer block. Finally, the last cout statement, which is outside the inner block, displays the value of the variable a declared in the outer block. If an attempt is made to display the value of c anywhere in the outer block, the compiler issues an error message stating that c is an undefined symbol.

The area in a program where a variable can be used is formally referred to as the **scope of the variable**, and you delve into this subject in Chapter 6.

One-Way Selection

A useful modification of the if-else statement involves omitting the else part of the statement and has this shortened and often useful form:

```
if   (expression)
    statement;
```

The statement following if (*expression*) is executed only if the expression has a non-zero value (a true condition). As before, the *statement* can be a compound statement. Figure 4.3 shows the flowchart for this statement.

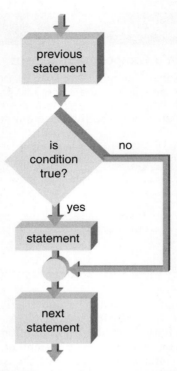

Figure 4.3   A one-way `if` statement

This modified form of the `if` statement is called a **one-way `if` statement**. Program 4.3 uses this statement to display a message only for cars that have been driven more than 3000.0 miles.

To see its one-way selection criteria in action, Program 4.3 was run twice, each time with different input data. Only the input data for the first run causes the message `Car 256 is over the limit` to be displayed.

```
Please type in car number and mileage: 256 3562.8
    Car 256 is over the limit.
End of program output.
```

and

```
Please type in car number and mileage: 23 2562.3
End of program output.
```

Program 4.3

```
#include <iostream>
using namespace std;

int main()
{
  const double LIMIT = 3000.0;
  int idNum;
  double miles;

  cout << "Please type in car number and mileage: ";
  cin  >> idNum >> miles;

  if(miles > LIMIT)
    cout << "  Car " << idNum << " is over the limit.\n";

  cout << "End of program output.\n";

  return 0;
}
```

Problems Associated with the if-else Statement

Two of the most common problems encountered in using C++'s if-else statement are the following:

- Misunderstanding the full implications of what an expression is
- Using the assignment operator, =, in place of the relational operator ==

Recall that an expression is any combination of operands and operators that yields a result. This definition is much broader and more encompassing than is apparent at first. For example, all the following are valid C++ expressions:

```
age + 5
age = 30
age == 40
```

Assuming the variables are declared correctly, each of the preceding expressions yields a result. Program 4.4 uses cout statements to display the value of these expressions when age = 18.

Program 4.4

```cpp
#include <iostream>
using namespace std;

int main()
{
  int age = 18;

  cout << "The value of the first expression is " << (age + 5) << endl;
  cout << "The value of the second expression is " << (age = 30) << endl;
  cout << "The value of the third expression is " << (age == 40) << endl;

  return 0;
}
```

The display Program 4.4 produces is as follows:

```
The value of the first expression is 23
The value of the second expression is 30
The value of the third expression is 0
```

As the output of Program 4.4 shows, each expression has a value associated with it. The value of the first expression is the sum of the variable age plus 5, which is 23. The value of the second expression is 30, which is also assigned to the variable age. The value of the third expression is 0 because age is not equal to 40, and a false condition is represented in C++ with a value of 0. If the value in age had been 40, the relational expression a == 40 would be true and have a value of 1.

Now assume that the relational expression age == 40 was intended to be used in this if statement,

```cpp
if (age == 40)
    cout << "Happy Birthday!";
```

but was mistyped as age = 40, resulting in the following:

```cpp
if (age = 40)
     cout << "Happy Birthday!";
```

Because the mistake results in a valid C++ expression, and any C++ expression can be tested by an if statement, the resulting if statement is valid and causes the message Happy Birthday! to be displayed regardless of what value was previously assigned to age. Can you see why?

The condition tested by the if statement doesn't compare the value in age to the number 40. It assigns the number 40 to age. That is, the expression age = 40 is not a relational expression at all; it's an assignment expression. At the completion of the assignment, the expression itself has a value of 40. Because C++ treats any non-zero value as true,

Point of Information

The Boolean Data Type

Before the current ANSI/ISO C++ standard, C++ didn't have a built-in Boolean data type with its two Boolean values, `true` and `false`. Because this data type wasn't originally part of the language, a tested expression could not evaluate to a Boolean value. Therefore, the syntax

> if(Boolean expression is true)
>   execute this statement;

also wasn't built into C or C++. Instead, both C and C++ use the more encompassing syntax,
> if(expression)
>   execute this statement;

where expression is any expression that evaluates to a numeric value. If the value of the tested expression is a non-zero value, it's considered true, and only a zero value is considered false.

As the ANSI/ISO C++ standard specifies, C++ has a built-in Boolean data type containing the values `true` and `false`. As you learned in Chapter 2, Boolean variables are declared with the `bool` keyword. As currently implemented, the actual values that the Boolean values `true` and `false` represent are the integer values 1 and 0, respectively. For example, examine the following program, which declares two Boolean variables:

```
#include <iostream>
using namespace std;
int main()
{
  bool t1, t2;

  t1 = true;
  t2 = false;
  cout <<"The value of t1 is " << t1
       << "\nand the value of t2 is " << t2 << endl;

  return 0;
}
```

This program produces the following output:

```
The value of t1 is 1
and the value of t2 is 0
```

continued...

Point of Information

The Boolean Data Type (continued)

As shown by this output, the Boolean values `true` and `false` are represented by the integer values 1 and 0 and have the following relationships:

```
!true= is false
!false= is true
```

Additionally, applying a postfix or prefix `++` operator to a variable of type `bool` sets the Boolean value to `true`. The postfix and prefix `--` operators can't be applied to Boolean variables.

Boolean values can also be compared, as shown in the following code:

```
if (t1 == t2)
  cout << "The values are equal" << endl;
else
  cout << "The values are not equal" << endl;
```

Last, assigning any non-zero value to a Boolean variable results in the variable being set to `true` (a value of 1), and assigning a zero value to a Boolean results in the variable being set to `false` (a value of 0).

---

the `cout` statement is executed. Another way of looking at it is to realize that the `if` statement is equivalent to the following two statements:

```
age = 40;      // assign 40 to age
if (age)       // test the value of age
    cout << "Happy Birthday!";
```

Because a C++ compiler has no means of knowing that the expression being tested isn't the one you want, you must be especially careful when writing conditions.

EXERCISES 4.2

1. **(Practice)** Write appropriate `if` statements for the following conditions:

   a. If an angle is equal to 90 degrees, print the message "The angle is a right angle"; else, print the message "The angle is not a right angle."

   b. If the temperature is above 100 degrees, display the message "above the boiling point of water"; else, display the message "below the boiling point of water."

   c. If the number is positive, add the number to the variable `positivesum`; else, add the number to the variable `negativesum`.

   d. If the slope is less than 0.5, set the variable `flag` to zero; else, set `flag` to one.

e. If the difference between `volts1` and `volts2` is less than 0.001, set the variable `approx` to zero; else, calculate `approx` as the quantity (`volts1 - volts2`) / `2.0`.

f. If the frequency is above 60, display the message "The frequency is too high."

g. If the difference between `temp1` and `temp2` exceeds 2.3, calculate the variable `error` as (`temp1 - temp2`) * `factor`.

h. If `x` is greater than `y` and `z` is less than 20, request that the user input a value for the variable `p`.

i. If distance is greater than 20 and less than 35, request that the user input a value for the variable `time`.

2. **(Practice)** Write `if` statements corresponding to the conditions illustrated in the following flowcharts:

a.

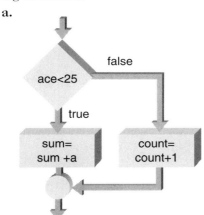

b.

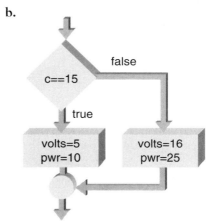

c.

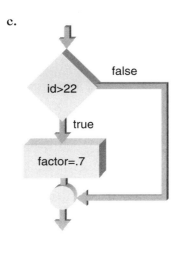

d.

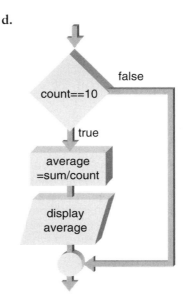

3. **(Practice)** Write a C++ program that asks the user to input two numbers. If the first number entered is greater than the second number, the program should print the message "The first number is greater"; else, it should print the message "The first number is smaller." Test your program by entering the numbers 5 and 8 and then using the numbers 11 and 2. What do you think your program will display if the two numbers entered are equal? Test this case.

4. **(Practice) a.** A certain waveform is 0 volts for time less than 2 seconds and 3 volts for time equal to or greater than 2 seconds. (These waveforms are referred to as step functions.) Write a C++ program that accepts time in the variable named `time` and displays the appropriate voltage, depending on the input value.

   b. How many runs should you make for the program written in Exercise 4a to verify that it's operating correctly? What data should you input in each program run?

5. **(Practice)** An insulation test for a wire requires that the insulation withstand at least 600 volts. Write a C++ program that accepts a test voltage and displays the message "PASSED VOLTAGE TEST" or the message "FAILED VOLTAGE TEST," as appropriate.

6. **(Practice) a.** Write a C++ program to compute the value of pressure in pounds per square inch (psi) of a waveform described as follows: For time, t, equal to or less than 35 seconds, the pressure is $0.46t$ psi, and for time greater than 35 seconds, the pressure is $0.19t + 9.45$ psi. The program should request the time as input and display the pressure as output.

   b. How many runs should you make for the program written in Exercise 6a to verify that it's operating correctly? What data should you input in each program run?

7. **(Practice) a.** Write a C++ program to display the message "PROCEED WITH TAKEOFF" or "ABORT TAKEOFF," depending on the input. If the character g is entered in the variable `code`, the first message should be displayed; otherwise, the second message should be displayed.

   b. How many runs should you make for the program written in Exercise 7a to verify that it's operating correctly? What data should you input in each program run?

8. **(Fluid Mechanics)** A fluid particle flowing through a pipe can flow in a smooth, constant manner, called laminar flow; in a chaotic manner, called turbulent flow; or in an intermediate transitional stage between smooth and turbulent flow. As a practical design parameter, the Reynolds number can be used to determine the type of flow. For a Reynolds number below 2000, the flow is laminar, and for a Reynolds number above 3000, the flow is turbulent. For a Reynolds number between 2000 and 3000, the flow is in transition from laminar to turbulent. Using this information, write and execute a C++ program that accepts a Reynolds number as user input; determines whether the flow is laminar, turbulent, or in transition; and displays a message indicating the type of flow based on the input Reynolds number.

9. **(Electrical Eng.)** A small factory generates its own power with a 20-kilowatt generator and a 50-kilowatt generator. The plant manager indicates which generator is required by typing a character code. Write a C++ program that accepts this code as input. If code s is typed, a message directing the plant foreman to use the smaller generator should be displayed; otherwise, a message directing the use of the larger generator should be displayed.

4.3   Nested `if` Statements

As you have seen, an `if-else` statement can contain any valid C++ simple or compound statements, including another `if-else` statement. Therefore, one or more `if-else` statements can be included in either part of an `if-else` statement. Including one or more `if` statements inside an existing `if` statement is called a **nested `if` statement**. For example, substituting the one-way `if` statement

```
if (distance > 500)
  cout << "snap";
```

for `statement1` in the following `if` statement

```
if (hours < 9)
  statement1;
else
  cout << "pop";
```

results in this nested `if` statement:

```
if (hours < 9)
{
  if (distance > 500)
    cout << "snap";
}
else
  cout << "pop";
```

The braces around the inner one-way `if` statement are essential because in their absence, C++ associates an `else` with the closest unpaired `if`. Therefore, without the braces, the preceding statement is equivalent to the following:

```
if (hours < 9)
  if (distance > 500)
    cout << "snap";
  else
    cout << "pop";
```

In this example, the `else` is paired with the inner `if`, which destroys the meaning of the original `if-else` statement. Notice also that the indentation is irrelevant, as far as the compiler is concerned. Whether the indentation exists or not, *the statement is compiled by associating the last* `else` *with the closest unpaired* `if`, *unless braces are used to alter the default pairing.* The process of nesting `if` statements can be extended indefinitely, so the `cout << "snap";` statement could be replaced by a complete `if-else` statement or another one-way `if` statement.

Figures 4.4a and 4.4b illustrate the general form of a nested `if-else` statement when a second `if-else` statement is nested within a) the `if` part of an `if-else` statement and b) the `else` part of an `if-else` statement.

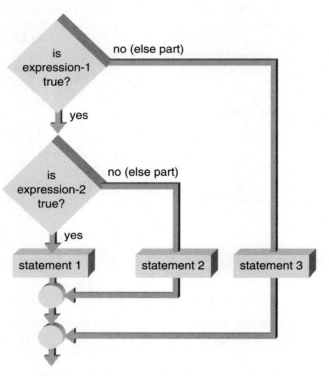

Figure 4.4a   Nested within the `if` part

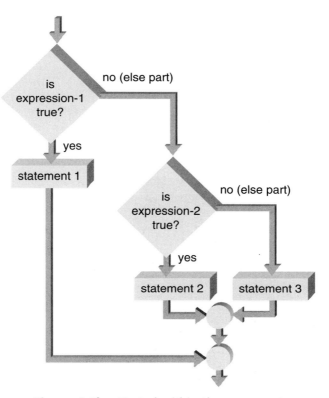

Figure 4.4b   Nested within the `else` part

The `if-else` Chain

In general, the nesting shown in Figure 4.4a tends to be confusing and is best avoided in practice. However, a useful construction for the nesting in Figure 4.4b has this form:

```
if (expression_1)
  statement1;
else
  if (expression_2)
    statement2;
  else
    statement3;
```

As with all C++ programs, because white space is ignored, this indentation isn't required. Typically, the preceding construction is written in the following arrangement:

```
if (expression_1)
  statement1;
else if (expression_2)
  statement2;
else
  statement3;
```

This useful form of a nested `if` statement is called an **if-else chain**. Each condition is evaluated in order, and if any condition is true, the corresponding statement is executed and the remainder of the chain is terminated. The statement associated with the final `else` is executed only if no previous condition is satisfied. This final `else` serves as a default or catch-all case that's useful for detecting an error condition or processing a condition that's not handled specifically by the previous conditions.

The chain can be continued indefinitely by repeatedly making the last statement another `if-else` statement. Therefore, the general form of an `if-else` chain is as follows:

```
if (expression_1)
  statement1;
else if (expression_2)
  statement2;
else if (expression_3)
  statement3;
      .
      .
      .
else if (expression_n)
  statement_n;
else
  last_statement;
```

Each condition is evaluated in the order it appears in the statement. For the first condition that's true, the corresponding statement is executed, and the remainder of the statements in the chain aren't executed. Therefore, if expression_1 is true, only statement1 is executed; otherwise, expression_2 is tested. If expression_2 is true, only statement2 is executed; otherwise, expression_3 is tested, and so on. The final else and its associated statement(s) in the chain are optional, and last_statement is executed only if no previous expressions are true.

To illustrate using an `if-else` chain, Program 4.5 displays an item's specification status corresponding to a letter input. The following input codes are used:

Specification Status	Input Code
Space exploration	S
Military grade	M
Commercial grade	C
Toy grade	T

Program 4.5

```cpp
#include <iostream>
using namespace std;

int main()
{
  char code;

  cout << "Enter a specification code: ";
  cin  >> code;

  if (code == 'S')
     cout << "The item is space exploration grade.";
  else if (code == 'M')
    cout << "The item is military grade.";
  else if (code == 'C')
    cout << "The item is commercial grade.";
  else if (code == 'T')
     cout << "The item is toy grade.";
  else
     cout << "An invalid code was entered.";

  cout << endl;

  return 0;
}
```

As another example of an if-else chain, take a look at determining the output of a digital converter unit by using the following input/output relationship:

Input Weight	Output Reading
Greater than or equal to 90 lbs	1111
Less than 90 lbs but greater than or equal to 80 lbs	1110
Less than 80 lbs but greater than or equal to 70 lbs	1101
Less than 70 lbs but greater than or equal to 60 lbs	1100
Less than 60 lbs	1011

The following statements can be used to determine the correct output corresponding to the value input for the variable inlbs:

```cpp
if (inlbs >= 90)
  digout = 1111;
else if (inlbs >= 80)
```

```
   digout = 1110;
 else if (inlbs >= 70)
   digout = 1101;
 else if (inlbs >= 60)
   digout = 1100;
 else
   digout = 1011;
```

Notice that this example makes use of the chain stopping after a true condition is found by checking for the highest input weight first. If the input value is less than 90, the if-else chain continues checking for the next highest weight, and so on, until the correct weight category is obtained. Program 4.6 uses an if-else chain to calculate and display the correct output corresponding to the weight input in the cin statement.

Program 4.6

```cpp
#include <iostream>
using namespace std;

int main()
{
  int digout;
  double inlbs;

  cout << "Enter the input weight: ";
  cin  >> inlbs;

  if (inlbs >= 90)
    digout = 1111;
  else if (inlbs >= 80)
    digout = 1110;
  else if (inlbs >= 70)
    digout = 1101;
  else if (inlbs >= 60)
    digout = 1100;
  else
    digout = 1011;

  cout << "The digital output is " << digout << endl;

  return 0;
}
```

The following is a sample run of Program 4.6:

```
Enter the input weight: 72.5
The digital output is 1101
```

As with all C++ statements, each statement in an if-else chain can be replaced by a compound statement bounded by braces.

EXERCISES 4.3

1. **(Practice)** Modify Program 4.5 to accept both lower and uppercase letters as codes. For example, if a user enters an m or an M, the program should display the message "The item is military grade."

2. **(Practice)** Write nested if statements corresponding to the conditions illustrated in the following flowcharts:

a.

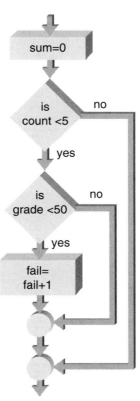

b.

3. **(Practice)** An acute angle is less than 90 degrees, an obtuse angle is greater than 90 degrees, and a right angle is equal to 90 degrees. Using this information, write a C++ program that accepts an angle, in degrees, and displays the type of angle corresponding to the degrees entered.

4. **(Data Processing)** The grade level of undergraduate college students is typically determined according to the following schedule:

Number of Credits Completed	Grade Level
Less than 32	Freshman
32 to 63	Sophomore
64 to 95	Junior
96 or more	Senior

Using this information, write a C++ program that accepts the number of credits a student has completed, determines the student's grade level, and displays the grade level.

5. **(Data Processing)** A student's letter grade is calculated according to the following schedule:

Numerical Grade	Letter Grade
Greater than or equal to 90	A
Less than 90 but greater than or equal to 80	B
Less than 80 but greater than or equal to 70	C
Less than 70 but greater than or equal to 60	D
Less than 60	F

Using this information, write a C++ program that accepts a student's numerical grade, converts the numerical grade to an equivalent letter grade, and displays the letter grade.

6. **(Measurement)** The tolerance of critical components in a system is determined according to the following schedule:

Specification Status	Tolerance
Space exploration	Less than 0.1%
Military grade	Greater than or equal to 0.1% and less than 1%
Commercial grade	Greater than or equal to 1% and less than 10%
Toy grade	Greater than or equal to 10%

Using this information, write a C++ program that accepts a component's tolerance reading and determines the specification that should be assigned to it.

7. **(General Math)** Write a C++ program that accepts a number followed by one space and then a letter. If the letter following the number is f, the program is to treat the number entered as a temperature in degrees Fahrenheit, convert the number to the equivalent degrees Celsius, and display a suitable message. If the letter following the number is c, the

program is to treat the number entered as a temperature in degrees Celsius, convert the
number to the equivalent degrees Fahrenheit, and display a suitable message. If the letter is
neither f nor c, the program is to display a message that the data entered is incorrect and
terminate. Use an if-else chain in your program and make use of these conversion
formulas:

Celsius = (5.0 / 9.0) × (Fahrenheit - 32.0)

Fahrenheit = (9.0 / 5.0) × Celsius + 32.0

8. **(Debugging)** Using the relationships in Program 4.6, the following program calculates the
digital output:

```
int main()
{
  int digout;
  double inlbs;

  cout << "Enter the input weight: ";
  cin  >> inlbs;

  if (inlbs >= 90) digout = 1111;
  if (inlbs >= 80) && (inlbs <= 90) digout = 1110;
  if (inlbs >= 70) && (inlbs <= 80) digout = 1101;
  if (inlbs >= 60) && (inlbs <= 70) digout = 1100;
  if (inlbs < 1000) digout = 1011;

  cout << "The digital output is " << digout << endl;

  return 0;
}
```

a. Will this program produce the same output as Program 4.6?

b. Which program is better and why?

9. **(Debugging)** The following program was written to produce the same result as Program 4.6:

```
int main()
{
  int digout;
  double inlbs;

   cout << "Enter the input weight: ";
   cin  >> inlbs;

  if (inlbs < 60)
    digout = 1011;
  else if (inlbs >= 60)
    digout = 1100;
  else if (inlbs >= 70)
    digout = 1101;
  else if (inlbs >= 80)
    digout = 1110;
  else if (inlbs >= 90)
    digout = 1111;
```

```
    cout << "The digital output is " << digout << endl;

    return 0;
}
```

a. Will this program run?

b. What does this program do?

c. For what values of input pounds does this program calculate the correct digital output?

4.4 The `switch` Statement

An `if-else` chain is used in programming applications when one set of instructions must be selected from many possible alternatives. A **switch statement** is an alternative to the `if-else` chain for situations when the condition involves comparing an integer expression with a specific value. It has this general form:

```
switch (expression)
{     // start of compound statement
  case value_1:   // terminated with a colon
     statement1;
     statement2;
          .
          .
     break;
  case value_2:  // terminated with a colon
     statementm;
     statementn;
          .
          .
     break;
      .
      .
  case value_n:  // terminated with a colon
     statementw;
     statementx;
          .
          .
     break;
  default:  // terminated with a colon
     statementaa;
     statementbb;
          .
          .
}     // end of switch and compound statement
```

The `switch` statement uses four new keywords: `switch`, `case`, `break`, and `default`. The following discussion explains what each of these keywords does.

The `switch` keyword identifies the start of the `switch` statement. The expression in parentheses after `switch` is then evaluated, and this expression must evaluate to an integer result, or a compilation error results.

In the switch statement, the case keyword identifies values that are compared with the switch expression's value. The case values are compared in the order in which they're listed until a match is found, and then execution begins with the statement following the match. As illustrated in Figure 4.5, the switch expression's value determines where execution actually begins.

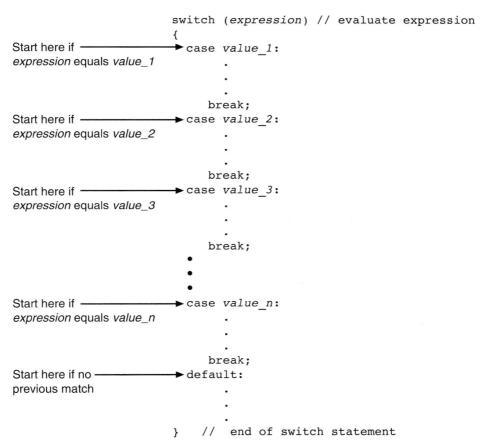

Figure 4.5   The expression determines an entry point for execution

A switch statement can contain any number of case labels in any order. If the value of the expression doesn't match any of the case values, however, no statement is executed unless the default keyword is encountered. (The default keyword is optional and operates the same as the last else in an if-else chain.) If the value of the expression doesn't match any case value, program execution begins with the statement following the default keyword.

After the switch statement has located an entry point, all further case value evaluations are ignored. Execution continues through the end of the compound statement unless the break keyword is encountered, which identifies the end of a case and causes an immediate exit from the switch statement. Just as the case keyword identifies possible entry points in the compound statement, the break keyword determines terminating points.

If break statements are omitted, all cases following the matching case value, including the default case, are executed.

When writing a switch statement, you can use multiple case values to refer to the same set of statements; the default keyword is optional. For example, take a look at the following:

```
switch (number)
{
  case 1:
    cout << "Have a Good Morning\n";
    break;
  case 2:
    cout << "Have a Happy Day\n";
    break;
  case 3:
  case 4:
  case 5:
    cout << "Have a Nice Evening\n";
}
```

If the value stored in the variable number is 1, the message Have a Good Morning is displayed. Similarly, if the value of number is 2, the second message is displayed. Finally, if the value of number is 3, 4, or 5, the last message is displayed. Because the statement to be executed for the last three cases is the same, the case statements for these values can be "stacked together," as shown in the example. Also, because there's no default keyword, no message is printed if the value of number isn't one of the listed case values. Although listing case values in increasing order is a good programming practice, it's not required by the switch statement. A switch statement can have any number of case values, in any order; only the values you're testing for must be listed.

Program 4.7 uses a switch statement to select the arithmetic operation (addition, multiplication, or division) to perform on two numbers, depending on the value of the opselect variable.

In the following two sample runs, the resulting display clearly identifies the case that was selected:

```
Please type in two numbers: 12 3
Enter a select code:
        1 for addition
        2 for multiplication
        3 for division : 2
The product of the numbers entered is 36
```

and

```
Please type in two numbers: 12 3
Enter a select code:
        1 for addition
        2 for multiplication
        3 for division : 3
The first number divided by the second is 4
```

Program 4.7

```cpp
#include <iostream>
using namespace std;

int main()
{
  int opselect;
  double fnum, snum;

  cout << "Please type in two numbers: ";
  cin  >> fnum >> snum;
  cout << "Enter a select code: ";
  cout << "\n        1 for addition";
  cout << "\n        2 for multiplication";
  cout << "\n        3 for division : ";
  cin  >> opselect;

  switch (opselect)
  {
    case 1:
      cout << "The sum of the numbers entered is " << fnum+snum;
      break;
    case 2:
      cout << "The product of the numbers entered is " << fnum*snum;
      break;
    case 3:
      cout << "The first number divided by the second is " << fnum/snum;
      break;
  }     // end of switch

  cout << endl;

  return 0;
}
```

In reviewing Program 4.7, notice the break statement in the last case. Although it's not necessary, terminating the last case in a switch statement with a break is a good programming practice. It prevents a possible program error later if another case is added to the switch statement. With the addition of a new case, the break keyword between cases ensures that you won't forget to include the break at the time of the addition.

Because character data types are always converted to integers in an expression, a `switch` statement can also be used to "switch" based on the value of a character expression. For example, assuming `choice` is a character variable, the following `switch` statement is valid:

```
switch(choice)
{
  case 'a':
  case 'e':
  case 'i':
  case 'o':
  case 'u':
    cout << "The character in choice is a vowel\n";
    break;
  default:
    cout << "The character in choice is not a vowel\n";
    break;      // this break is optional
}      // end of switch statement
```

EXERCISES 4.4

1. **(Practice)** Rewrite the following `if-else` chain by using a `switch` statement:

```
if (letterGrade == 'A')
  cout << "The numerical grade is between 90 and 100\n";
else if (letterGrade == 'B')
  cout << "The numerical grade is between 80 and 89.9\n";
else if (letterGrade == 'C')
  cout << "The numerical grade is between 70 and 79.9\n";
else if (letterGrade == 'D')
  cout << "How are you going to explain this one?\n";
else
{
  cout << "Of course I had nothing to do with my grade.\n";
  cout << "It must have been the professor's fault.\n";
}
```

2. **(Practice)** Rewrite the following `if-else` chain by using a `switch` statement:

```
if (factor == 1)
  pressure = 25.0;
else if (factor == 2)
  pressure = 36.0;
else if (factor == 3)
  pressure = 45.0;
else if (factor == 4) || (factor == 5) || (factor == 6)
  pressure = 49.0;
```

3. (**Data Processing**) Each disk drive in a shipment is stamped with a code from 1 through 4 to indicate the manufacturer, as follows:

Code	Disk Drive Manufacturer
1	3M Corporation
2	Maxell Corporation
3	Sony Corporation
4	Verbatim Corporation

Write a C++ program that accepts the code number as input and, based on the value entered, displays the correct disk drive manufacturer.

4. (**Practice**) Rewrite Program 4.5 by using a `switch` statement.

5. (**Debugging**) Explain why the `if-else` chain in Program 4.6 can't be replaced with a `switch` statement.

6. (**Debugging**) Rewrite Program 4.7 by using a character variable for the select code.

4.5 A Case Study: Solving Quadratic Equations

An important use of C++'s `if` statements is to validate data by checking for clearly invalid cases. For example, a date such as 5/33/06 contains an obviously invalid day. Similarly, the division of any number by zero in a program, such as 14/0, shouldn't be allowed. Both examples illustrate the need for a technique called **defensive programming**, in which the program includes code to check for improper data before an attempt is made to process it further. The defensive programming technique of checking user input data for erroneous or unreasonable data is referred to as **input data validation**.

A second major use of selection statements is to determine the type of calculation to be made based on the data. Both uses are shown in this case study, which illustrates a C++ program that determines the roots of a quadratic equation. A **quadratic equation** has the form $ax^2 + bx + c = 0$ or can be algebraically manipulated into this form. In this equation, x is the unknown variable, and a, b, and c are known constants. Although the constants b and c can be any numbers, including 0, the value of the constant a can't be 0. (If a is 0, the equation would become a linear equation in x.) Here are examples of quadratic equations:

$$5x^2 + 6x + 2 = 0$$
$$x^2 - 7x + 20 = 0$$
$$34x^2 + 16 = 0$$

In the first equation, $a = 5$, $b = 6$, and $c = 2$; in the second equation, $a = 1$, $b = -7$, and $c = 20$; and in the third equation, $a = 34$, $b = 0$, and $c = 16$.

The real roots of a quadratic equation can be calculated by using these quadratic formulas:

$$x = \frac{-b + \sqrt{b^2 - 4ac}}{2a}$$

and

$$x = \frac{-b - \sqrt{b^2 - 4ac}}{2a}$$

Using these formulas, you'll write a C++ program, following the software development procedure, to solve for the roots of a quadratic equation.

Step 1   Analyze the Problem

The problem requires accepting three inputs—the coefficients a, b, and c of a quadratic equation. The outputs are the roots of the equation, found by using the given formulas.

Step 2   Develop a Solution

A first attempt at a solution is using the user-entered values of a, b, and c to calculate a value for each root, as described by the following pseudocode:

Display a program purpose message
Accept user-input values for a, b, and c
Calculate the two roots
Display the values of the calculated roots

However, this solution must be refined to account for possible input conditions. For example, if a user enters a value of 0 for both a and b, the equation is neither quadratic nor linear and has no solution (referred to as a "degenerate case"). Another possibility is that the user enters a zero for a and a non-zero value for b. In this case, the equation becomes linear with a single solution of $-c/b$. A third possibility is that the value of the term $b^2 - 4ac$, which is called the **discriminant**, is negative. Because the square root of a negative number can't be taken, the equation has no real roots (referred to as the "imaginary roots case"). Finally, when the discriminant is 0, both roots are the same (referred to as the "repeated roots case").

Taking into account all four limiting cases, the following pseudocode shows a refined solution for determining the roots of a quadratic equation correctly:

Display a program purpose message
Accept user-input values for a, b, and c
If a = 0 and b = 0 then
        display a message saying that the equation has no solution
Else if a = zero then
        calculate the single root equal to -c/b
        display the single root
Else
   {
        calculate the discriminant
        If the discriminant > 0 then
            solve for both roots using the given formulas
            display the two roots
        Else if the discriminant < 0 then
            display a message that there are no real roots
        Else
            calculate the repeated root equal to -b/(2a)
            display the repeated root
        Endif
   }
Endif

Notice that nested `if-else` statements are used. The outer `if-else` statement validates the entered coefficients and determines whether you have a valid quadratic equation. The inner `if-else` statement then determines whether the equation has two real roots (`discriminant > 0`), two imaginary roots (`discriminant < 0`), or repeated roots (`discriminant = 0`).

Step 3   Code the Solution

Program 4.8 lists the equivalent C++ code for the pseudocode solution.

Program 4.8

```cpp
#include <iostream>
#include <cmath>
using namespace std;

// this program solves for the roots of a quadratic equation
int main()
{
  double a, b, c, disc, root1, root2;

  cout << "This program calculates the roots of a\n";
  cout << "   quadratic equation of the form\n";
  cout << "              2\n";
  cout << "           ax + bx + c = 0\n\n";

  cout << "Please enter values for a, b, and c: ";
  cin >>  a >>  b >> c;

  if ( a == 0.0 && b == 0.0)
    cout << "The equation is degenerate and has no roots.\n";
  else if (a == 0.0)
    cout << "The equation has the single root x = "
         << -c/b << endl;
  else
  { //Start of compound statement for the outer else
    disc = pow(b,2.0) - 4 * a * c;     // calculate discriminant
    if (disc > 0.0)
    {
      disc = sqrt(disc);
      root1 = (-b + disc) / (2 * a);
      root2 = (-b - disc) / (2 * a);
      cout << "The two real roots are "
           << root1 << " and " << root2 << endl;
    }
    else if (disc < 0.0)
      cout << "Both roots are imaginary.\n";
    else
      cout << "Both roots are equal to " << -b / (2 * a) << endl;
  } //end of compound statement for the outer else

  return 0;
}
```

Step 4 Test and Correct the Program

Test values should include values for *a*, *b*, and *c* that result in two real roots, plus limiting values for *a* and *b* that result in a linear equation ($a = 0$, $b \neq 0$), a degenerate equation ($a = 0$, $b = 0$), and a negative and a zero discriminant. Two test runs of Program 4.8 follow:

```
This program calculates the roots of a
   quadratic equation of the form
            2
         ax + bx + c = 0
Please enter values for a, b, and c: 1 2 -35
The two real roots are 5 and -7
```

and

```
This program calculates the roots of a
   quadratic equation of the form
            2u
         ax + bx + c = 0
Please enter values for a, b, and c: 0 0 16
The equation is degenerate and has no roots.
```

The first run solves the quadratic equation $x^2 + 2x - 35 = 0$, which has the real roots $x = 5$ and $x = -7$. The input data for the second run results in the equation $0x^2 + 0x + 16 = 0$. Because it degenerates into the mathematical impossibility of $16 = 0$, the program identifies it correctly as a degenerate equation. As an exercise, you could create test data for the other limiting cases the program checks for.

EXERCISES 4.5

1. **(Data Processing)** Write, compile, and execute a C++ program that accepts a user-entered number and calculates the values of the following:

$$\frac{1}{\sqrt{\text{user-entered number}}} \quad \text{and} \quad \frac{1}{\text{user-entered number}}$$

Before calculating the square root, validate that the number is not negative, and before calculating the reciprocal, check that the number is not zero. If either condition occurs, display a message stating that the operation can't be calculated.

2. **(Data Processing) a.** Write a program that accepts two real numbers and a select code from a user. If the entered select code is 1, have the program add the two previously entered numbers and display the result; if the select code is 2, the numbers should be multiplied, and if the select code is 3, the first number should be divided by the second number.

   b. Determine what the program written in Exercise 2a does when the entered numbers are 3 and 0 and the select code is 3.

c. Modify the program written in Exercise 2a so that division by 0 is not allowed, and a message is displayed when this division is attempted.

3. **(Data Processing) a.** Write a program to display the following two prompts:

```
Enter a month (use a 1 for Jan, etc.):
Enter a day of the month:
```

Have your program accept and store a number in the variable `month` in response to the first prompt and accept and store a number in the variable `day` in response to the second prompt. If the month entered is not between 1 and 12, print a message informing the user that an invalid month has been entered. If the day entered is not between 1 and 31, print a message informing the user that an invalid day has been entered.

b. What will your program do if the user enters a number with a decimal point for the month? How can you make sure your `if` statements check for an integer number?

c. In a non-leap year, February has 28 days; the months January, March, May, July, August, October, and December have 31 days; and all other months have 30 days. Using this information, modify the program written in Exercise 3a to display a message when an invalid day is entered for a user-entered month. For this program, ignore leap years.

4. **(General Math)** The quadrant in which a line drawn from the origin resides is determined by the angle the line makes with the positive x-axis, as follows:

Angle from the Positive X-Axis	Quadrant
Between 0 and 90 degrees	I
Between 90 and 180 degrees	II
Between 180 and 270 degrees	III
Between 270 and 360 degrees	IV

a. Using this information, write a C++ program that accepts the angle of the line as user input and determines and displays the correct quadrant for the input data. (*Note*: If the angle is exactly 0, 90, 180, or 270 degrees, the corresponding line doesn't reside in any quadrant but lies on an axis.)

b. Modify the program written for Exercise 4a to display a message that identifies an angle of 0 degrees as the positive x-axis, an angle of 90 degrees as the positive y-axis, an angle of 180 degrees as the negative x-axis, and an angle of 270 degrees as the negative y-axis.

5. **(Data Processing)** Years that are evenly divisible by 400 or are evenly divisible by 4 but not by 100 are leap years. For example, because 1600 is evenly divisible by 400, 1600 was a leap year. Similarly, because 1988 is evenly divisible by 4 but not by 100, it was also a leap year. Using this information, write a C++ program that accepts the year as user input, determines whether the year is a leap year, and displays a message telling the user whether the entered year is or is not a leap year.

6. **(Data Processing)** Based on an automobile's model year and weight, the state of New Jersey determines the weight class and registration fee by using the following schedule:

Model Year	Weight	Weight Class	Registration Fee
1970 or earlier	Less than 2700 lbs	1	$16.50
	2700 to 3800 lbs	2	25.50
	More than 3800 lbs	3	46.50
1971 to 1979	Less than 2700 lbs	4	27.00
	2700 to 3800 lbs	5	30.50
	More than 3800 lbs	6	52.50
1980 or later	Less than 3500 lbs	7	19.50
	3500 or more lbs	8	52.50

Using this information, write a C++ program that accepts an automobile's year and weight and determines and displays its weight class and registration fee.

7. **(Data Processing)** Modify Program 4.8 so that the imaginary roots are calculated and displayed when the discriminant is negative. For this case, the two roots of the equation are the following:

$$x_1 = \frac{-b + \sqrt{-(b^2 - 4ac)}}{2a} \, i$$

and

$$x_2 = \frac{-b - \sqrt{-(b^2 - 4ac)}}{2a} \, i$$

where i is the imaginary number symbol for the square root of -1. (*Hint*: Calculate the real and imaginary parts of each root separately.)

8. **(Heat Transfer)** The transfer of heat by the movement (currents) of a gas or liquid is referred to as **heat convection**. The heat transferred per unit area of a substance is given by this formula:

$q = hA(T_s - T_a)$

q is the heat transfer rate (Watts or Joules/sec).
h is the convective heat transfer coefficient (BTU/hrft°F or Watts/m²°C).
A is the surface area (ft² or m²).
T_s is the surface temperature (°F or °C).
T_a is the ambient (surrounding) temperature (°F or °C).

a. Write, compile, and execute a C++ program that accepts a substance's surface area, a substance's surface temperature, and the ambient air temperature as inputs and displays the heat transfer rate through air. Users should have three choices for entering the surface area:

1. A rectangular area
2. An elliptical area
3. Other

If the user selects 1, the program should ask the user to enter the surface's length and width, and the program calculates surface area as length times width. If the user selects 2, the program should ask the user to enter the surface's major and minor axii, and the program calculates the surface area as π*(major axis)(minor axis)*. If the user selects 3 (Other), the program should ask the user to enter the surface area. The heat transfer rate should then be calculated and displayed, using the convective heat transfer coefficient of 8.7 Watts/m^2°C, which should be defined as the symbolic constant AIRCONV.

b. After verifying that your program is working correctly, determine the heat transfer rate away from a chip in a computer's console. The chip has a surface temperature of 44°C, and the ambient temperature maintained by the console's fan is 40°C. The rectangular chip has a length of 2 cm and a width of 2 cm.

4.6   A Closer Look: Program Testing[3]

In theory, a comprehensive set of test runs would reveal all possible program errors and ensure that a program works correctly for any combination of input and computed data. In practice, this level of testing requires checking all possible combinations of statement execution. Because of the time and effort required, this goal is usually impossible except for extremely simple programs. To see why this is so, take a look at Program 4.9.

---

[3]This topic can be omitted on first reading without loss of subject continuity.

Program 4.9

```cpp
#include <iostream>
using namespace std;

int main()
{
  int num;

  cout << "Enter a number: ";
  cin  >> num;

  if (num == 5)
    cout << "Bingo!\n";
  else
    cout << "Bongo!\n";

  return 0;
}
```

Program 4.9 has two paths that can be traversed as the program progresses from its opening brace to its closing brace. The first path, which is executed when the input number is 5, is in this sequence:

```cpp
cout << "Enter a number";
cin  >> num;
cout << "Bingo!\n";
```

The second path, which is executed when any number except 5 is input, includes this sequence of instructions:

```cpp
cout << "Enter a number";
cin  >> num;
cout << "Bongo!\n";
```

Testing each possible path through Program 4.9 requires two runs with a judicious selection of test input data to make sure both paths of the `if` statement are exercised. Adding one more `if` statement in the program increases the number of possible execution paths by a factor of two and requires four (that is, 2^2) runs for complete testing. Similarly, two additional `if` statements increase the number of paths by a factor of four and require eight (that is, 2^3) runs for complete testing, and three additional `if` statements produce a program that requires 16 (that is, 2^4) test runs.

Now consider an application program consisting of only 10 modules, with each module containing five `if` statements. Assuming the modules are always called in the same sequence, there are 32 possible paths through each module (2^5) and more than 1,000,000,000,000,000 (2^{50}, representing the number of modules multiplied by the number of `if` statements per module) possible paths through the complete program (all modules executed in sequence). The time needed to create test data to exercise each path and the actual computer runtime required to check each path make complete testing of this program impossible.

The inability to test all combinations of statement execution sequences fully has led to the programming proverb "There is no error-free program." Any testing should be well thought out to maximize the possibility of locating errors. At a minimum, test data should include appropriate input values, illegal input values the program should reject, and limiting values checked by selection statements in the program.

4.7   Common Programming Errors

Four programming errors are common with C++'s selection statements:

1. Using the assignment operator, =, in place of the relational operator ==. This error can cause frustration because any expression can be tested by an `if-else` statement, so it is not immediately obvious that an error is being made. For example, the statement

    ```
    if (opselect = 2)
       cout << "Happy Birthday";
    else
       cout << "Good Day";
    ```

    always results in the message `Happy Birthday` being displayed, regardless of the initial value in the `opselect` variable. The reason is that the assignment expression `opselect = 2` has a value of 2, which is considered a true value in C++. The correct expression to determine the value in `opselect` is `opselect == 2`.

2. Placing a semicolon immediately after the condition, as in this example:

    ```
    if (condition);
       statement;
    ```

    The semicolon after *(condition)* is an error. It creates a null statement, which causes the statement following the semicolon to be a stand-alone statement that's no longer part of the `if` statement. This stand-alone statement is always executed, regardless of the condition tested by the `if` statement.

3. Letting the `if-else` statement appear to select an incorrect choice. In this typical debugging problem, the programmer mistakenly concentrates on the tested condition as the source of the problem. For example, assume the following `if-else` statement is part of your program:

    ```
    if (key == 'F')
    {
       contemp = (5.0/9.0) * (intemp - 32.0);
       cout << "Conversion to Celsius was done";
    }
    else
    {
    ```

```
    contemp = (9.0/5.0) * intemp + 32.0;
    cout << "Conversion to Fahrenheit was done";
}
```

This statement always displays Conversion to Celsius was done when the variable key contains an F. Therefore, if this message is displayed when you believe key doesn't contain F, you should investigate key's value. As a general rule, whenever a selection statement doesn't act as you think it should, test your assumptions about the values assigned to the tested variables by displaying their values. If an unanticipated value is displayed, you have at least isolated the source of the problem to the variables rather than the structure of the if-else statement. From there, you have to determine where and how the incorrect value was produced.

4. Using nested if statements without including braces to indicate the structure. Without braces, the compiler defaults to pairing elses with the closest unpaired ifs, which sometimes destroys the selection statement's original intent. To avoid this problem and create code that's adaptable to change, writing all if-else statements as compound statements in this form is useful:

```
if (expression)
{
// one or more statements in here
}
else
{
// one or more statements in here
}
```

No matter how many statements are added later, this form maintains the if statement's original intent.

4.8   Chapter Summary

1. Relational expressions, also called conditions, are used to compare operands. If a relational expression is true, the value of the expression is the integer 1. If the relational expression is false, it has an integer value of 0. Relational expressions are created by using the following relational operators:

Relational Operator	Meaning	Example
<	Less than	age < 30
>	Greater than	height > 6.2
<=	Less than or equal to	taxable <= 20000
>=	Greater than or equal to	temp >= 98.6
==	Equal to	grade == 100
!=	Not equal to	number != 250

2. More complex conditions can be constructed from relational expressions by using C++'s logical operators, `&&` (AND), `||` (OR), and `!` (NOT).

3. An `if-else` statement is used to select between two alternative statements based on an expression's value. Although relational expressions are usually used for the tested expression, any valid expression can be used. In testing an expression, `if-else` statements interpret a non-zero value as true and a zero value as false. The general form of an `if-else` statement is as follows:

```
if (expression)
   statement1;
else
   statement2;
```

This form is a two-way selection statement. If the expression has a non-zero value, it's considered true and `statement1` is executed; otherwise, `statement2` is executed.

4. An `if-else` statement can contain other `if-else` statements. In the absence of braces, each `else` is associated with the closest preceding unpaired `if`.

5. The `if-else` chain is a multiway selection statement with this general form:

```
if (expression_1)
   statement_1;
else if (expression_2)
   statement_2;
else if (expression_3)
   statement_3;
      .
      .
      .
else if (expression_m)
   statement_m;
else
   statement_n;
```

Each expression is evaluated in the order in which it appears in the chain. If an expression is true (has a non-zero value), only the statement between this expression and the next `else if` or `else` is executed, and no further expressions are tested. The final `else` is optional, and the statement corresponding to the final `else` is executed only if no previous expressions are true.

6. A compound statement consists of any number of single statements enclosed by the brace pair { and }. Compound statements are treated as a single unit and can be used anywhere a single statement is used.

7. The `switch` statement is a multiway selection statement with this general form:

```
switch (expression)
{      // start of compound statement
  case value_1:   // terminated with a colon
     statement1;
     statement2;
        .
        .
     break;
  case value_2:   // terminated with a colon
```

```
      statementm;
      statementn;
         .
         .
         .
      break;
      .
      .
   case value_n:   // terminated with a colon
      statementw;
      statementx;
         .
         .
      break;
   default:   // terminated with a colon
      statementaa;
      statementbb;
         .
         .
         .
}     // end of switch and compound statement
```

For this statement, the value of an integer expression is compared with integer or character constants or constant expressions. Program execution is transferred to the first matching case and continues through the end of the switch statement, unless an optional break statement is encountered. The case values in a switch statement can appear in any order, and an optional default case can be included. The default case is executed if no other cases are matched.

Programming Projects for Chapter 4

1. (Data Processing) Write C++ code sections to make the following decisions:

   a. Ask for two integer temperatures. If their values are equal, display the temperature; otherwise, do nothing.

   b. Ask for character values letter1 and letter2, representing uppercase letters of the alphabet, and display them in alphabetical order.

   c. Ask for three integer values, num1, num2, and num3, and display them in decreasing order.

2. (Data Processing) a. Write a program that displays the message I FEEL GREAT TODAY! or I FEEL DOWN TODAY #$*!, depending on the input. If the character u is entered in the variable code, the first message should be displayed; otherwise, the second message should be displayed.

   b. How many runs should you make for the program written in Exercise 2a to verify that it's operating correctly? What data should you input in each program run?

3. (Data Processing) a. A senior engineer is paid $1700 a week, and a junior engineer, $900 a week. Write a C++ program that accepts as input an engineer's status in the character variable status. If status equals S, the senior engineer's salary should be displayed; otherwise, the junior engineer's salary should be displayed.

b. How many runs should you make for the program written in Exercise 3a to verify that it is operating correctly? What data should you input in each program run?

4. (**Data Processing**) **a.** Write a C++ program to compute and display a person's weekly salary as determined by the following conditions: If the hours worked are less than or equal to 40, the person receives $8.00 per hour; otherwise, the person receives $320.00 plus $12.00 for each hour worked over 40 hours. The program should request the hours worked as input and display the salary as output.

b. How many runs should you make for the program written in Exercise 4a to verify that it's operating correctly? What data should you input in each program run?

5. (**Structural Eng.**) Three of the most commonly used beams in structural engineering are the I-beam, rectangular beam, and cylindrical beam, shown in Figures 4.6 through 4.8. In determining the stress a given weight places on a symmetrical beam, an important design parameter is the beam's rectangular moment of inertia, I, which is typically given in units of in^4. The computation of I depends on the beam's geometry, and for the three beam types shown, the values of I are calculated as follows:

For an I-beam: $I = \dfrac{BH^3 - bh^3}{12}$ where all measurements are in inches

For a rectangular beam: $I = \dfrac{bh^3}{12}$

For a cylindrical beam: $I = \dfrac{\pi r^4}{4}$

Figures 4.6 through 4.8 show the variables b, h, B, H, and r. Using this information, design, write, compile, and execute a C++ program that prompts the user for the type of beam and the necessary data (based on the input), and then computes and displays the beam's rectangular moment of inertia.

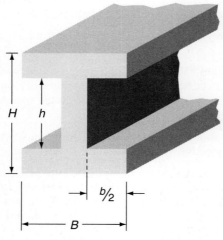

Figure 4.6   An I-beam

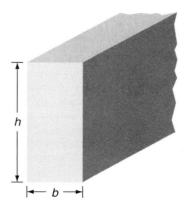

Figure 4.7 A rectangular beam

Figure 4.8 A cylindrical beam

6. **(Fluid Mechanics)** A key parameter used to determine the type of fluid flow through a pipe is the Reynolds number, which is given by this formula:

$$Re = \frac{V\,d}{v}$$

   Re is the Reynolds number (a dimensionless value).

   V is the velocity (m/s or ft/sec).

   d is the diameter of the pipe (m or ft).

   v is the kinematic viscosity of the fluid (m/s^2 or ft/sec^2).

The viscosity, *v*, is a measure of the fluid's resistance to flow and stress. Except at extremely high pressures, a liquid fluid's kinematic viscosity is dependent on temperature and independent of pressure. The following chart provides the viscosity of water at three different temperatures:

Temperature (°C)	Kinematic Viscosity (m/s^2)
5	1.49×10^{-6}
10	1.31×10^{-6}
15	1.15×10^{-6}

Using this information, write, compile, and execute a program that requests the velocity of water flowing through a pipe, the pipe's diameter, the water's temperature, and the water's kinematic viscosity. Based on the input values, your program should calculate the Reynolds number. When you have verified that your program is working, use it to complete the following chart:

Velocity (m/s)	Pipe Diameter (mm)	Temperature (°C)	Reynolds Number
.01	10	5	
.03	10	5	
.04	10	5	
.01	20	10	
.03	20	10	
.04	20	10	
.01	30	15	
.03	30	15	
.04	30	15	

7. **(Data Processing)** Write a C++ program that accepts a character as input data and determines whether the character is an uppercase letter. An uppercase letter is any character that's greater than or equal to "A" and less than or equal to "Z." If the entered character is an uppercase letter, display the message The character just entered is an uppercase letter. If the entered letter isn't uppercase, display the message The character just entered is not an uppercase letter.

8. **(Data Processing)** Repeat Exercise 7 to determine whether the character entered is a lowercase letter. A lowercase letter is any character greater than or equal to "a" and less than or equal to "z."

9. **(General Math) a.** Write, run, and test a C++ program that accepts a user-input integer number and determines whether it's even or odd. Display the entered number and the message Even or Odd.

   b. Modify the program written for Exercise 9a to determine whether the entered number is evenly divisible by a user-specified value, with no remainder. That is, is it evenly divisible by 3, 7, 13, or any other user-specified value?

10. **(Data Processing)** As a part-time student, you took two courses last term. Write, run, and test a C++ program that calculates and displays your grade point average (GPA) for the term. Your program should prompt the user to enter the grade and credit hours for each course. This information should then be displayed with the lowest grade first, and the GPA for the term should be calculated and displayed. A warning message should be printed if the GPA is less than 2.0 and a congratulatory message if the GPA is 3.5 or above.

11. **(Debugging)** The following program displays the message `Hello there!` regardless of the letter input. Determine where the error is.

```
#include <iostream.h>
using namespace std;

int main()
{
  char letter;

  cout << "Enter a letter: ";
  cin >> letter;

  if (letter = 'm')
    cout << "Hello there!\n";

  return 0;
i}
```

12. **(Data Processing)** Write, execute, and verify a C++ program that accepts three numbers as input, and then sorts the three numbers and displays them in ascending order, from lowest to highest. For example, if the input values are 7 5 1, the program should display them in the numerical order 1 5 7.

13. **(Heat Transfer)** The transfer of heat energy through matter, referred to as heat conduction, is always from a region of higher temperature to one of lower temperature. It occurs by transferring energy from atom to atom within a substance. With uniform temperatures on either side of equal-sized surfaces, the rate of heat flow through a substance is provided by Fourier's law of heat conduction, which becomes the following formula:

$$Q = \frac{k(T_2 - T_1)}{w}$$

Q is heat per unit time per unit area (Watts/m^2 or BTU/hrft^2).

k is the thermal conductivity, which is a property of a substance that indicates its capability to conduct heat (Watts/m°K or BTU/hrft°F).

T_2 is the hotter temperature (°F or °K).

T_1 is the cooler temperature (°F or °K).

w is the width of the substance (ft or m).

a. Write, compile, and execute a C++ program that calculates and displays the heat transfer through a substance. The inputs should be the substance's thermal conductivity, its width, and temperatures on either side of it. Your program should determine which unit system is used, item by item, and then convert units as necessary so that a consistent unit system (SI or English Engineering) is used in the final determination of Q. The output should display the value of Q in both unit systems.

b. Verify that your program is working by hand-calculating the heat transfer through a cement wall with a thermal conductivity of .29 Watts/m°K and a thickness of 15 cm. One side of the wall is at a constant temperature of 32°C, and the other side is -7°C.

c. After verifying that your program is working correctly, use the following chart of thermal conductivities to determine the heat transfer rate for the following:

i. A pane of glass that's ½ cm thick and has an inside temperature of 24°C and an outside temperature of 15°C.

ii. A column of air 10 cm thick that's held between two walls, one with a temperature of 23°C and the other of 14°C.

Substance	Thermal Conductivity (Watts/m°K)	Thermal Conductivity (BTU/hrft°F)
Air	.025	.0015
Cement	.29	.17
Glass	1.1	.645
Soil	1.5	.88
Wood, oak	.17	.096
Wood, pine	.12	.065

14. **(General Math)** In the game of blackjack, the cards 2 through 10 are counted as their face values, regardless of suit; all face cards (jack, queen, and king) are counted as 10; and an ace is counted as a 1 or an 11, depending on the total count of all cards in a player's hand. The ace is counted as 11 only if the resulting total value of all cards in a player's hand doesn't exceed 21; otherwise, it's counted as 1. Using this information, write a C++ program that accepts three card values as inputs (a 1 corresponding to an ace, a 2 corresponding to a two, and so on), calculates the total value of the hand, and displays the value of the three cards.

Engineering and Scientific Disciplines

Civil Engineering

The field of civil engineering is concerned primarily with large-scale structures and systems used by a community. A civil engineer designs, constructs, and operates bridges, dams, tunnels, buildings, airports, roads, and other large-scale public works. Civil engineers are also responsible for the effects these large-scale systems have on society and the environment, so they are involved in water resources, flood control, waste disposal, and overall urban planning. The field can be subdivided into three categories:

- Structures: Design, construction, and operation of large-scale public works, such as dams, buildings, and roads. The properties of materials, geology, soil mechanics, and statics and dynamics are important elements of background training. For example, determining a building's maximum height before it buckles under its own weight is a question involving all these subjects.
- Urban planning: Planning, designing, and constructing transportation systems (roads, railroads, river development, airports) and general land use. Surveying and mapmaking are necessary skills.
- Sanitation: Waste treatment, water supply, and sewage systems. Fluid mechanics, hydrology, pollution control, irrigation, and economics are important areas of study.

Chapter 5

Repetition Statements

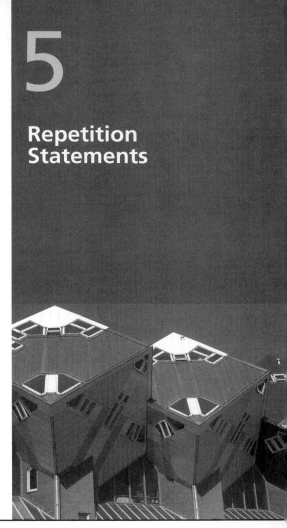

The programs you've examined so far have illustrated the programming concepts involved in input, output, assignment, and selection capabilities. By this time, you should have gained enough experience to be comfortable with these concepts and the mechanics of implementing them in C++. Many problems, however, require a repetition capability, in which the same calculation or sequence of instructions is repeated, over and over, using different sets of data. Examples of this type of repetition include continual checking of user data entries until an acceptable entry, such as a valid password, is entered; counting and accumulating running totals; and constant acceptance of input data and recalculation of output values that stop only at entry of a sentinel value.

This chapter explores the different methods used by programmers in constructing repeating sections of code and explains how they can be implemented in C++. More commonly, a section of code that's repeated is referred to as a **loop** *because after the last statement in the code is executed, the program branches, or loops, back to the first statement and starts another repetition through the code. Each repetition is also referred to as an* **iteration** *or a* **pass through the loop***.*

5.1   Basic Loop Structures

The real power of a program is realized when the same type of operation must be made over and over. For example, in some programs the same set of instructions is repeated multiple times. Retyping the same set of instructions in a program is tedious, time consuming, and subject to error. It certainly would be convenient if you could type repeating instructions only once, and then have a method of informing the program to repeat execution of these instructions three times. This method is available by using repeating sections of code.

Constructing a repeating section of code requires using four elements. The first necessary element is a repetition statement. A **repetition statement** both defines the boundaries of the repeating section of code and controls whether the code will be executed. In general, three different forms of repetition statements are provided in C++:

- `while`
- `for`
- `do while`

Each of these statements must include a condition to be evaluated, which is the second required element for constructing repeating sections of code. Valid conditions are identical to those used in selection statements. If the condition is true, the code is executed; otherwise, it's not.

The third required element is a statement that initially sets the condition. This statement must always be placed before the condition is first evaluated to ensure correct loop execution the first time the condition is evaluated.

Finally, there must be a statement in the repeating section of code that allows the condition to become false. This statement is necessary to ensure that, at some point, the repetitions stop.

Pretest and Posttest Loops

The condition being tested can be evaluated at the beginning or end of the repeating section of code. Figure 5.1 illustrates the test occurring at the beginning of the loop. This type of loop is referred to as a **pretest loop** because the condition is tested before any statements in the loop are executed. If the condition is true, the executable statements in the loop are executed. If the initial value of the condition is false, the executable statements in the loop are never executed at all, and control transfers to the first statement after the loop. To avoid infinite repetitions, the condition must be updated within the loop. Pretest loops are also referred to as **entrance-controlled loops**. Both the `while` and `for` loop structures are examples of these loops.

A loop that evaluates a condition at end of the repeating section of code, as illustrated in Figure 5.2, is referred to as a **posttest** or **exit-controlled loop**. These loops always execute the loop statements at least once before the condition is tested. Because the executable statements in the loop are executed continuously until the condition becomes false, there must always be a statement in the loop that updates the condition and permits it to become false. The `do while` construct is an example of a posttest loop.

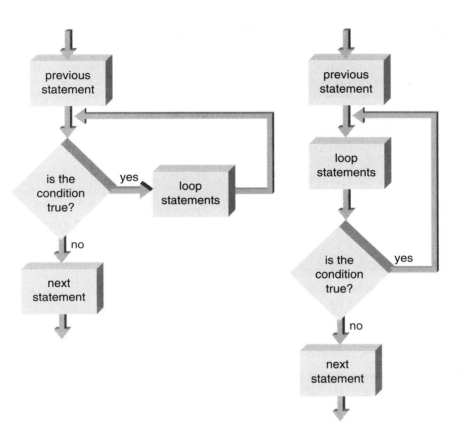

Figure 5.1 A pretest loop   **Figure 5.2** A posttest loop

Fixed-Count Versus Variable-Condition Loops

In addition to classifying repeating sections of code according to where the condition is tested (pretest or posttest), they are also classified by the type of condition being tested. In a **fixed-count loop**, the condition is used to keep track of how many repetitions have occurred. For example, you might want to produce a table of 10 numbers, including the numbers' squares and cubes, or a fixed design, such as the following:

```
* * * * * * * * * * * * * * * * * * * * * * * *
* * * * * * * * * * * * * * * * * * * * * * * *
* * * * * * * * * * * * * * * * * * * * * * * *
* * * * * * * * * * * * * * * * * * * * * * * *
```

In these cases, a fixed number of calculations are performed or a fixed number of lines are printed, at which point the repeating section of code is exited. All of C++'s repetition statements can be used to produce fixed-count loops.

In many situations, the exact number of repetitions isn't known in advance, or the items are too numerous to count beforehand. For example, when entering a large amount of experimental data, you might not want to take the time to count the number of actual data items to be entered. In these cases, a variable-condition loop is used. In a **variable-condition loop**, the tested condition doesn't depend on a count being reached, but on a variable that can change interactively with each pass through the loop. When a specified value is encountered, regardless of how many iterations have occurred, repetitions stop. All of C++'s repetition statements can be used to create variable-condition loops.[1] In this chapter, you encounter examples of both fixed-count and variable-condition loops.

EXERCISES 5.1

1. **(For Review)** List the three repetition statements provided in C++.

2. **(For Review)** List the four elements that must be present in a repetition statement.

3. **(For Review)** **a.** What is an entrance-controlled loop?

   b. Which of C++'s repetition statements produce entrance-controlled loops?

4. **(For Review)** **a.** What is an exit-controlled loop?

   b. Which of C++'s repetition statements produce exit-controlled loops?

5. **(For Review)** **a.** What is the difference between a pretest and posttest loop?

   b. If the condition being tested in a pretest loop is false, how many times are statements in the loop executed?

   c. If the condition being tested in a posttest loop is false, how many times are statements in the loop executed?

6. **(For Review)** What is the difference between a fixed-count and variable-condition loop?

5.2   `while` Loops

In C++, a **while loop** is constructed by using a `while` statement in the following syntax:

while *(expression)*
    statement;

The *expression* in parentheses is the condition tested to determine whether the *statement* following the parentheses is executed. The expression is evaluated in exactly the same manner as one in an `if-else` statement; the difference is in how the expression is used. As you have seen, when the expression in an `if-else` statement is true (has a non-zero value), the statement following the expression is executed once. In a `while` statement, the

---

[1]In loop creation, both C and C++ differ from earlier high-level languages, in which the `for` statement could be used only to produce fixed-count loops. C++'s `for` statement, as you see in Section 5.4, is virtually interchangeable with its `while` statement.

statement following the expression is executed repeatedly as long as the expression evaluates to a non-zero value. Considering just the expression and the statement following the parentheses, the computer uses this process in evaluating a while statement:

1. Test the expression
2. If the expression has a non-zero (true) value
      a. execute the statement following the parentheses
      b. go back to Step 1
    else
      exit the while statement and execute the next executable statement following the
      while statement

Notice that Step 2b forces program control to be transferred back to Step 1. This transfer of control back to the start of a while statement to reevaluate the expression is what forms the program loop. The while statement literally loops back on itself to recheck the expression until it evaluates to zero (becomes false). Naturally, this rechecking means that somewhere in the loop must be a provision that permits altering the value of the tested expression. As you'll see, this provision is indeed made.

Figure 5.3 shows the looping process a while statement produces. A diamond shape is used to show the two entry and two exit points required in the decision part of the while statement.

To make this looping process more tangible, consider the relational expression count <= 10 and the statement cout << count;. Using these elements, you can write the following valid while statement:

```
while (count <= 10)
  cout << count;
```

Although this statement is valid, the alert reader will realize that it creates a situation in which the cout statement is either executed forever (or until you stop the program) or not executed at all. Here's why this happens: If count has a value less than or equal to 10 when the expression is first evaluated, the cout statement is executed. The while statement then automatically loops back on itself and retests the expression. Because you haven't changed the value stored in count, the expression is still true, and another execution of the cout statement is made. This process continues forever, or until the program containing this statement is stopped prematurely by the user. However, if count starts with a value greater than 10, the expression is false to begin with, and the cout statement is never executed.

How do you set an initial value in count to control what the while statement does the first time the expression is evaluated? The answer, of course, is to assign values to each variable in the tested expression before the while statement is encountered. For example, the following sequence of instructions is valid:

```
count = 1;
while (count <= 10)
  cout << count;
```

Using this sequence of instructions ensures that count starts with a value of 1. You could assign any value to count in the assignment statement. What's important is to assign some value. In practice, the assigned value depends on the application.

You must still change the value of count so that you can finally exit the while statement. Doing this requires an expression such as count = count + 1 to increment the value of count each time the while statement is executed. The fact that a while

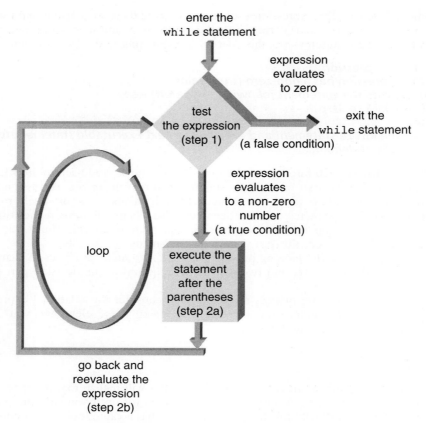

enter the
`while` statement

expression
evaluates
to zero

test
the expression
(step 1)

exit the
`while` statement

(a false condition)

expression
evaluates
to a non-zero
number
(a true condition)

loop

execute the
statement
after the
parentheses
(step 2a)

go back and
reevaluate the
expression
(step 2b)

Figure 5.3   Anatomy of a `while` loop

statement provides for repetition of a single statement doesn't prevent including an additional statement to change the value of count. All you have to do is replace the single statement with a compound statement, as in this example:

```
count = 1;          // initialize count
while (count <= 10)
{
  cout << count;
  count++;          // increment count
}
```

Note that, for clarity, each statement in the compound statement is placed on a different line. This format is consistent with the convention adopted for compound statements in Chapter 4.

Now analyze the preceding sequence of instructions. The first assignment statement sets count equal to 1. The `while` statement is then entered, and the expression is evaluated for the first time. Because the value of count is less than or equal to 10, the expression is true, and the compound statement is executed. The first statement in the compound statement uses the cout object to display the value of count. The next statement adds 1 to the value currently stored in count, making this value equal to 2. The `while` statement then loops back to retest the expression. Because count is still less than or equal to 10, the compound statement is executed again. This process continues until the value of count reaches 11. Program 5.1 illustrates these statements in an actual program.

 Program 5.1

```cpp
#include <iostream>
using namespace std;

int main()
{
  int count;

  count = 1;                 // initialize count
  while (count <= 10)
  {
    cout << count << "   ";
    count++;                 // increment count
  }

  return 0;
}
```

This is the output for Program 5.1:

```
1  2  3  4  5  6  7  8  9  10
```

Note that there's nothing special about the name count used in Program 5.1. Any valid integer variable could have been used.

Before you look at other examples of the while statement, two comments on Program 5.1 are in order. First, the statement count++ can be replaced with any statement that changes the value of count. A statement such as count = count + 2, for example, causes every second integer to be displayed. Second, it's the programmer's responsibility to ensure that count is changed in a way that leads to a normal exit from the while. For example, if you replace the expression count++ with the expression count--, the value of count never exceeds 10 and an infinite loop is created. An **infinite loop** is a loop that never ends; the program just keeps displaying numbers until you realize it isn't working as you expected.

Now that you have some familiarity with the while statement, see whether you can read and determine the output of Program 5.2.

Program 5.2

```cpp
#include <iostream>
using namespace std;

int main()
{
  int i;

  i = 10;

  while (i >= 1)
  {
    cout << i << "  ";
    i--;                  // subtract 1 from i
  }

  return 0;
}
```

The assignment statement in Program 5.2 initially sets the int variable i to 10. The while statement then checks to see whether the value of i is greater than or equal to 1. While the expression is true, the value of i is displayed by the cout statement, and the value of i is decremented by 1. When i finally reaches zero, the expression is false, and the program exits the while statement. Therefore, Program 5.2 produces the following display when it runs:

```
10  9  8  7  6  5  4  3  2  1
```

To illustrate the power of the while statement, consider the task of printing a table of numbers from 1 to 10 with the numbers' squares and cubes. You can do this with a simple while statement, as shown in Program 5.3.

When Program 5.3 runs, the following display is produced:

NUMBER	SQUARE	CUBE
1	1	1
2	4	8
3	9	27
4	16	64
5	25	125
6	36	216
7	49	343
8	64	512
9	81	729
10	100	1000

Program 5.3

```cpp
#include <iostream>
#include <iomanip>
using namespace std;

int main()
{

  int num;

  cout << "NUMBER    SQUARE    CUBE\n"
       << "------    ------    ----\n";

  num = 1;
  while (num < 11)
  {
    cout << setw(3) << num << "          "
         << setw(3) << num * num << "       "
         << setw(4) << num * num * num << endl;
    num++;          // increment num
  }

  return 0;
}
```

Note that the expression used in Program 5.3 is num < 11. For the integer variable num, this expression is exactly equivalent to the expression num <= 10. The choice of which to use is entirely up to you.

If you want to use Program 5.3 to produce a table of 1000 numbers, all you do is change the expression in the while statement from num < 11 to num < 1001. Changing the 11 to 1001 produces a table of 1000 lines—not bad for a simple five-line while statement.

All the program examples of the `while` statement use fixed-count loops because the tested condition is a counter that checks for a fixed number of repetitions. In a variation on the fixed-count loop, the counter is not incremented by one each time through the loop but by some other value. For example, suppose you have the task of producing a Celsius-to-Fahrenheit temperature conversion table. Fahrenheit temperatures corresponding to Celsius temperatures from 5 to 50 degrees are to be displayed in increments of 5 degrees, which can be done with this series of statements:

```
celsius = 5;      // starting Celsius value
while (celsius <= 50)
{
  fahren = (9.0/5.0) * celsius + 32.0;
  cout << celsius << "        "
       << fahren;
  celsius = celsius + 5;
}
```

As before, the `while` statement consists of everything from the word `while` through the compound statement's closing brace. Before the program enters the `while` loop, you must make sure a value is assigned to the counter being evaluated, and there's a statement to alter the value of the counter in the loop (in increments of 5 degrees Celsius) to ensure an exit from the `while` loop. Program 5.4 illustrates using similar code in a complete program.

This is the display produced when Program 5.4 is executed:

```
DEGREES    DEGREES
CELSIUS    FAHRENHEIT
-------    ----------
   5          41.00
  10          50.00
  15          59.00
  20          68.00
  25          77.00
  30          86.00
  35          95.00
  40         104.00
  45         113.00
  50         122.00
```

Program 5.4

```cpp
#include <iostream>
#include <iomanip>
using namespace std;

// a program to convert Celsius to Fahrenheit
int main()
{
  const int MAX_CELSIUS = 50;
  const int START_VAL = 5;
  const int STEP_SIZE = 5;
  int celsius;
  double fahren;

  cout << "DEGREES    DEGREES\n"
       << "CELSIUS  FAHRENHEIT\n"
       << "-------   ----------\n";

  celsius = START_VAL;

    // set output formats for floating point numbers only
  cout << setiosflags(ios::showpoint)
       << setprecision(2);

  while (celsius <= MAX_CELSIUS)
  {
    fahren = (9.0/5.0) * celsius + 32.0;
    cout << setw(4)  << celsius << fixed
         << setw(13) << fahren << endl;
    celsius = celsius + STEP_SIZE;
  }

  return 0;
}
```

Technical Note

Fluid Mechanics

The field of **fluid mechanics** deals with fluids at rest and in motion. Fluids include both liquids and gases and are defined as substances that conform to the shape of their holding containers. These are the primary differences between gases and liquids:

- Gases are expandable and contractible and always expand or contract to fill all space in the container holding them.
- Liquids occupy a definite volume and have a free surface if they don't fill the container holding them.

Fluid statics is the science of fluids at rest, a major subdiscipline of fluid mechanics. The most important property for fluids at rest is their weight. **Fluid dynamics** is the science of fluids in motion, which is the second major subdiscipline of fluid mechanics and includes aerodynamics, the study of gases in motion, and hydrodynamics, the study of liquids in motion.

For flowing fluids, the two most important properties are density and viscosity. **Density** is the measure of how tightly packed the fluid is (*density = mass/volume*). **Viscosity** is the measure of a liquid's resistance to shear stress. A fluid begins to flow when an applied force, known as a shear stress, is large enough to overcome the fluid's weight and internal friction, assuming the fluid isn't totally constrained in the direction of the force. The three types of fluid flow patterns through a pipe or conduit are as follows:

- Laminar—All fluid particles flow in smooth, straight lines parallel to the pipe's wall.
- Turbulent—Fluid particle paths are irregular, but the average motion is in the direction of the flow.
- In transition—The fluid is between laminar and turbulent flow.

Laminar flow generally occurs only when the fluid's viscosity is very high, as in lubricating oils. Most flows, such as water flowing through pipes, are faster and turbulent.

The Reynolds number provides a quick means of determining flow patterns and can be calculated by using this formula:

$$Re = \frac{\rho V d}{\mu}$$

Re = the Reynolds number
ρ = the fluid's density (kg/m^3)
V = the fluid's average speed (m/s)
d = the pipe's diameter (m)
μ = the fluid's viscosity (kg/ms)

continued...

Technical Note

Fluid Mechanics (continued)

Essentially, the Reynolds number is equal to the ratio of

$$\frac{\textit{fluid speed}}{\textit{viscous forces}}$$

A higher Reynolds number correlates with a higher fluid speed. However, when viscous forces predominate (they are retarding forces), the Reynolds number is lower, and the fluid flow is slower. In a highly viscous fluid, such as heavy oil, all the fluid's particles tend to be kept in line, which is referred to as laminar flow. Critical Reynolds number values for determining flow type are as follows:

- Re < 2000: Fluid flow is laminar (least common type of water flow).
- 2000 ≤ Re ≥ 3000: Fluid flow is in transition.
- Re > 3000: Fluid flow is turbulent (most common type of fluid flow).

EXERCISES 5.2

1. **(Practice)** Rewrite Program 5.1 to print the numbers 2 to 10 in increments of two. The output of your program should be the following:

   2   4   6   8   10

2. **(Practice)** Rewrite Program 5.4 to produce a table starting at a Celsius value of -10 and ending with a Celsius value of 60, in increments of 10 degrees.

3. **(Desk Checking)** **a.** For the following program, determine the total number of items displayed as well as the first and last numbers printed:

```cpp
#include <iostream>
using namespace std;

int main()
{
  int num = 0;
  while (num <= 20)
  {
    num++;
    cout << num << " ";
  }

  return 0;
}
```

   b. Enter and run the program from Exercise 3a on a computer to verify your answers to the exercise.

   c. How would the output be affected if the two statements in the compound statement were reversed (that is, if the cout statement came before the num++ statement)?

4. (Conversions) Write a C++ program that converts gallons to liters. The program should display gallons from 10 to 20 in one-gallon increments and the corresponding liter equivalents. Use the relationship that 1 gallon = 3.785 liters.

5. (Conversions) Write a C++ program that converts feet to meters. The program should display feet from 3 to 30 in 3-foot increments and the corresponding meter equivalents. Use the relationship that 1 meter = 3.28 feet.

6. (Practice) An automobile travels at an average speed of 55 mph for four hours. Write a C++ program that displays the distance, in miles, the car has traveled after 1, 2, and so on hours until the end of the trip.

7. (Fluid Mechanics) The maximum laminar flow speed is the speed at which a fluid begins to change from a smooth, straight flow to turbulent flow within a pipe. It can be determined by using this formula:

Maximum laminar flow speed = (2000 × pipe diameter × density)/viscosity

Using this formula, write a C++ program that used a fixed-count repetition loop of four. For each pass through the loop, the program should accept a fluid's density, its viscosity, and a pipe diameter as input, and then calculate and output the maximum laminar flow rate through the pipe. Use the results your program outputs to complete the last column in this chart:

Fluid	Viscosity at 40°C = 77°F (kg/ms)	Density (kg/m³)	Pipe Diameter (m)	Maximum Laminar Flow Speed (m/s)
Gasoline	$.4466 \times 10^{-3}$	$.7186 \times 10^3$	0.4	
Medium fuel oil	2.9922×10^{-3}	$.8496 \times 10^3$	0.4	
Medium lubricating oil	87.0736×10^{-3}	$.8865 \times 10^3$	0.4	
Water	$.8975 \times 10^{-3}$	$.9973 \times 10^3$	0.4	

8. (Numerical Analysis) a. The following is an approximate conversion formula for converting Fahrenheit to Celsius temperatures:

Celsius = (Fahrenheit - 30) / 2

Using this formula, and starting with a Fahrenheit temperature of 0 degrees, write a C++ program that determines when the approximate equivalent Celsius temperature differs from the exact equivalent value by more than four degrees. (*Hint:* Use a while loop that terminates when the difference between approximate and exact Celsius equivalents exceeds 4 degrees.)

b. Using the approximate Celsius conversion formula given in Exercise 8a, write a C++ program that produces a table of Fahrenheit temperatures, exact Celsius equivalent temperatures, approximate Celsius equivalent temperatures, and the difference between the exact and approximate equivalent Celsius values. The table should begin at 0 degrees Fahrenheit, use 2-degree Fahrenheit increments, and terminate when the difference between exact and approximate values is more than 4 degrees.

9. (**Numerical Analysis**) The value of Euler's number, e, can be approximated by using this formula:

$$e = 1 + \frac{1}{1!} + \frac{1}{2!} + \frac{1}{3!} + \frac{1}{4!} + \frac{1}{5!} + \ldots$$

Using this formula, write a C++ program that approximates the value of e, using a while loop that terminates when the difference between two successive approximations is less than 10e-9.

10. (**Numerical Analysis**) The value of sin x can be approximated by using this formula:

$$\sin(x) = x - \frac{x^3}{3!} + \frac{x^5}{5!} - \frac{x^7}{7!} + \frac{x^9}{9!} \ldots$$

Using this formula, determine how many terms are needed to approximate the value returned by the intrinsic sin() function with an error less than 1e-6, when $x = 30$ degrees. (*Hints*: Use a while loop that terminates when the difference between the value returned by the intrinsic sin() function and the approximation is less than 1e-6. Also, note that x must first be converted to radian measure, and the alternating sign in the approximating series can be determined as $(-1) \times (n + 1)$, where n is the number of terms used in the approximation.)

5.3 Interactive while Loops

Combining interactive data entry with the repetition capabilities of the while statement produces adaptable and powerful programs. To understand the concept, take a look at Program 5.5, where a while statement is used to accept and then display four user-entered numbers, one at a time. Although the program uses a simple idea, it highlights the flow of control concepts needed to produce more useful programs.

The following is a sample run of Program 5.5:

```
This program will ask you to enter 4 numbers.

Enter a number: 26.2
The number entered is 26.2
Enter a number: 5
The number entered is 5
Enter a number: 103.456
The number entered is 103.456
Enter a number: 1267.89
The number entered is 1267.89
```

Program 5.5

```cpp
#include <iostream>
#include <iomanip>
using namespace std;

int main()
{
  const int MAXNUMS = 4;
  int count;
  double num;

  cout << "\nThis program will ask you to enter "
       << MAXNUMS << " numbers.\n";

  count = 1;
  while (count <= MAXNUMS)
  {
    cout << "\nEnter a number: ";
    cin  >> num;
    cout << "The number entered is " << num;
    count++;
  }
  cout << endl;

  return 0;
}
```

Review the program so that you understand clearly how the output was produced. The first message displayed is caused by execution of the first `cout` statement. This statement is outside and before the `while` statement, so it's executed once before any statement in the `while` loop.

After the `while` loop is entered, the statements in the compound statement are executed while the tested condition is true. The first time through the compound statement, the message `Enter a number:` is displayed. The program then executes the `cin` statement, which forces the computer to wait for a number to be entered at the keyboard. After a number is typed and the Enter key is pressed, the `cout` statement displays the number. The variable `count` is then incremented by one. This process continues until four passes through the loop have been made and the value of `count` is 5. Each pass causes the message `Enter a number:` to be displayed, causes one `cin` statement to be executed, and causes the message `The number entered is` to be displayed. Figure 5.4 illustrates this flow of control.

Instead of simply displaying the entered numbers, Program 5.5 can be modified to use the entered data. For example, you can add the numbers entered and display the total. To do this, you must be careful about how you add the numbers because the same variable, `num`, is used for each number entered. For this reason, the entry of a new number in Program 5.5

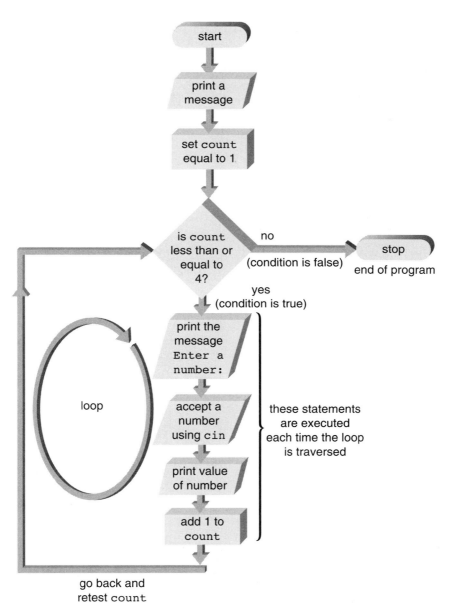

Figure 5.4 Flow of control diagram for Program 5.5

automatically causes the previous number stored in num to be lost. Therefore, each number entered must be added to the total before another number is entered. This is the required sequence:

Enter a number
Add the number to the total

How do you add a single number to a total? A statement such as `total = total + num` does the job perfectly. It's the accumulation statement introduced in Section 3.1. After each number is entered, the accumulating statement adds the number to the total, as shown in Figure 5.5.

The complete flow of control for adding the numbers is illustrated in Figure 5.6. In reviewing Figure 5.6, observe that a provision has been made for initially setting the total to zero before the `while` loop is entered. If you cleared the total inside the `while` loop, it would be set to zero each time the loop was executed, and any value stored previously would be erased.

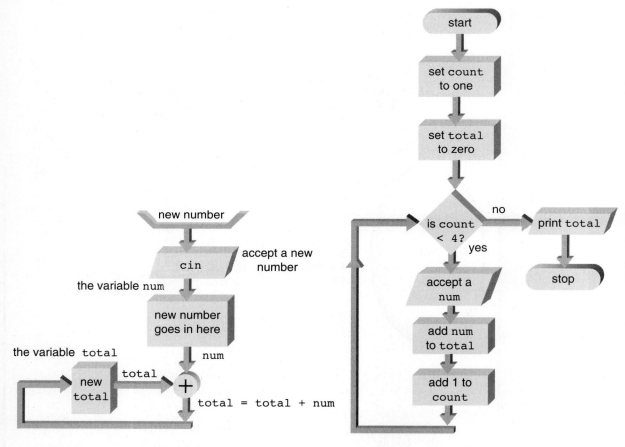

Figure 5.5 Accepting and adding a number to a total

Figure 5.6 Accumulation flow of control

Program 5.6 incorporates the necessary modifications to Program 5.5 to total the numbers entered. As shown, the statement `total = total + num;` is placed immediately after the `cin` statement. Putting the accumulating statement at this point in the program ensures that the entered number is "captured" immediately into the total.

Program 5.6

```cpp
#include <iostream>
#include <iomanip>
using namespace std;

int main()
{
  const int MAXNUMS = 4;
  int count;
  double num, total;

  cout << "\nThis program will ask you to enter "
       << MAXNUMS << " numbers.\n";
  count = 1;

  total = 0;
  while (count <= MAXNUMS)
  {
    cout << "\nEnter a number: ";
    cin  >> num;
    total = total + num;
    cout << "The total is now " << setprecision(7) << total;
    count++;
  }
  cout << "\nThe final total is " << setprecision(7) << total << endl;

  return 0;
}
```

To make sure you understand, review Program 5.6. The variable total was created to store the total of the numbers entered. Before entering the while statement, the value of total is set to zero to make sure any previous value in the storage location(s) assigned to the variable total is erased. Inside the while loop, the statement total = total + num; is used to add the value of the entered number to total. As each value is entered, it's added to the existing total to create a new total. Therefore, total becomes a running subtotal of all the values entered. Only after all numbers are entered does total contain the final sum of all the numbers. After the while loop is finished, a cout statement is used to display this sum.

Using the same data entered in the sample run for Program 5.5, the following sample run of Program 5.6 was made:

```
This program will ask you to enter 4 numbers.

Enter a number: 26.2
The total is now 26.2
Enter a number: 5
The total is now 31.2
Enter a number: 103.456
The total is now 134.656
Enter a number: 1267.89
The total is now 1402.546
The final total is 1402.546
```

Having used an accumulating assignment statement to add the numbers entered, you can go further and calculate the average of the numbers. Where do you calculate the average—inside the `while` loop or outside it?

In the case at hand, calculating an average requires that both a final sum and the number of items in that sum be available. The average is then computed by dividing the final sum by the number of items. At this point, you must ask, "At what point in the program is the correct sum available, and at what point is the number of items available?"

In reviewing Program 5.6, you can see that the correct sum needed for calculating the average is available after the `while` loop is finished. In fact, the whole purpose of the `while` loop is to ensure that the numbers are entered and added correctly to produce a correct sum. After the loop is finished, you also have a count of the number of items used in the sum. However, because of the way the `while` loop was constructed, the number in `count` (5) when the loop is finished is one more than the number of items (four) used to obtain the total. Knowing this, you simply subtract one from `count` before using it to determine the average. With this information as background, take a look at Program 5.7.

Program 5.7 is almost identical to Program 5.6, except for the calculation of the average. The constant display of the total inside and after the `while` loop has also been removed. The loop in Program 5.7 is used to enter and add four numbers. Immediately after the loop is exited, the average is computed and displayed. A sample run of Program 5.7 follows:

```
This program will ask you to enter 4 numbers.
Enter a number: 26.2
Enter a number: 5
Enter a number: 103.456
Enter a number: 1267.89

The average of the numbers is 350.637
```

Program 5.7

```cpp
#include <iostream>
#include <iomanip>
using namespace std;

int main()
{
  const int MAXNUMS = 4;
  int count;
  double num, total, average;

  cout << "\nThis program will ask you to enter "
       << MAXNUMS << " numbers.\n";

  count = 1;
  total = 0;
  while (count <= MAXNUMS)
  {
    cout << "Enter a number: ";
    cin  >> num;
    total = total + num;
    count++;
  }

  count--;
  average = total / count;
  cout << "\nThe average of the numbers is " << average << endl;

  return 0;
}
```

Sentinels

All the loops created so far have been examples of fixed-count loops, in which a counter is used to control the number of loop iterations. By means of a while statement, variable-condition loops can also be constructed. For example, when entering grades, you might not want to count the number of grades that will be entered. Instead, you prefer to enter the grades continuously, and at the end, type in a special data value to signal the end of data input.

In computer programming, data values used to signal the start or end of a data series are called **sentinels**. Sentinel values must, of course, be selected so as not to conflict with legitimate data values. For example, if you're constructing a program to process a student's grades, and assuming no extra credit is given that could produce a grade higher than 100, you could use any grade higher than 100 as a sentinel value. Program 5.8 illustrates this concept: Data is requested and accepted continuously until a number larger than 100 is entered. Entry of a number higher than 100 alerts the program to exit the `while` loop and display the sum of the numbers entered.

Program 5.8

```cpp
#include <iostream>
using namespace std;

int main()
{
  const int HIGHGRADE = 100;
  double grade, total;

  grade = 0;
  total = 0;
  cout << "\nTo stop entering grades, type in any number";
  cout << "\n greater than 100.\n\n";

  while (grade <= HIGHGRADE)
  {
    total = total + grade;
    cout << "Enter a grade: ";
    cin  >> grade;
  }

  cout << "\nThe total of the grades is " << total << endl;
  return 0;
}
```

The following lines show a sample run of Program 5.8. As long as grades less than or equal to 100 are entered, the program continues to request and accept additional data. When a number less than or equal to 100 is entered, the program adds this number to the total. When a number greater than 100 is entered, the loop is exited, and the sum of the grades that were entered is displayed.

```
To stop entering grades, type in any number
 greater than 100.

Enter a grade: 95
Enter a grade: 100
Enter a grade: 82
Enter a grade: 101

The total of the grades is 277
```

break and continue Statements

Two useful statements in connection with repetition statements are the **break** and **continue statements**. You encountered the break statement in Section 4.4 when learning about the switch statement. This is the format of the break statement:

```
break;
```

A break statement, as its name implies, forces an immediate break, or exit, from the switch, while, for, and do-while statements (discussed in the next sections). For example, execution of the following while loop is terminated immediately if a number greater than 76 is entered:

```
while(count <= 10)
{
  cout << "Enter a number: ";
  cin  >> num;
  if (num > 76)
  {
    cout << "You lose!\n";
    break;         // break out of the loop
  }
  else
    cout << "Keep on trucking!\n";
  count++
}
// break jumps to here
```

The break statement violates structured programming principles because it provides a second, nonstandard exit from a loop. Nevertheless, the break statement is extremely useful for breaking out of loops when an unusual condition is detected. The break statement is also used to exit from a switch statement when the matching case value has been detected and processed.

The continue statement is similar to the break statement but applies only to loops created with while, do-while, and for statements. This is the general format of a continue statement:

```
continue;
```

When continue is encountered in a loop, the next iteration of the loop begins immediately. For while loops, this means execution is transferred automatically to the top of the loop, and reevaluation of the tested expression is initiated. Although the continue statement has no direct effect on a switch statement, it can be included in a switch statement, which is contained in a loop. The effect of continue is the same: The next loop iteration begins.

As a general rule, the continue statement is less useful than the break statement, but it's convenient for skipping over data that shouldn't be processed while remaining in a loop.

For example, invalid grades are simply ignored in the following section of code, and only valid grades are added to the total:[2]

```
while (count < 30)
{
  cout << "Enter a grade: ";
  cin  >> grade
  if(grade < 0 || grade > 100)
    continue;
  total = total + grade;
  count++;
}
```

The Null Statement

All statements must be terminated by a semicolon. A semicolon with nothing preceding it is also a valid statement, called the **null statement**, as shown:

```
;
```

It's a do-nothing statement used where a statement is required syntactically, but no action is called for. Typically, null statements are used with `while` or `for` statements. Program 5.10c in Section 5.4 shows an example of a `for` statement using a null statement.

EXERCISES 5.3

1. **(Practice)** Rewrite Program 5.6 to compute the total of eight numbers.

2. **(Practice)** Rewrite Program 5.6 to display this prompt:

```
Please type in the total number of data values to be added:
```

In response to this prompt, the program should accept a user-entered number, and then use this number to control the number of times the `while` loop is executed. So if the user enters 5 in response to the prompt, the program should request the input of five numbers and display the total after five numbers have been entered.

3. **(Practice)** Rewrite Program 5.7 to compute the average of 10 numbers.

4. **(Practice)** Rewrite Program 5.7 to display the following prompt:

```
Please type in the total number of data values to be averaged:
```

---

[2]The continue statement is not essential, however, and the selection could have been written as follows:
```
  if (grade≥ 0 && grade ≤ 100)
  {
    total = total + grade;
    count++;
  }
```

In response to this prompt, the program should accept a user-entered number, and then use this number to control the number of times the while loop is executed. So if the user enters 6 in response to the prompt, the program should request an input of six numbers and display the average of the next six numbers entered.

5. **(Debugging)** By mistake, a programmer puts the statement average = total / count; in the while loop immediately after the statement total = total + num; in Program 5.7. As a result, the while loop becomes the following:

```
while (count <= MAXNUMS)
{
   cout << "Enter a number: ";
   cin  >> num;
   total = total + num;
   average = total / count;
   count++;
}
```

a. Will the program yield the correct result with this while loop?

b. From a programming perspective, which while loop is better to use and why?

6. **(Conversions) a.** Write a C++ program to convert meters to feet. The program should request the starting meter value, the number of conversions to be made, and the increment between metric values. The display should have appropriate headings and list the meters and the corresponding feet value. If the number of iterations is greater than 10, have your program substitute a default increment of 10. Use the relationship that 1 meter = 3.281 feet.

b. Run the program written in Exercise 6a on a computer. Verify that your program begins at the correct starting meter value and contains the exact number of conversions specified in your input data.

7. **(Conversions) a.** Modify the program written in Exercise 6a to request the starting meter value, the ending meter value, and the increment. Instead of the condition checking for a fixed count, the condition checks for the ending meter value. If the number of iterations is greater than 20, have your program substitute a default increment of *(ending value - starting value) / 19*.

b. Run the program written in Exercise 7a on a computer. Verify that your output starts at the correct beginning value and ends at the correct ending value.

8. **(Numerical Analysis)** An arithmetic series is defined by the following:

$$a + (a + d) + (a + 2d) + (a + 3d) + \cdots + [(a + (n - 1)d)]$$

    a is the first term.
    d is the "common difference."
    n is the number of terms to be added.

Using this information, write a C++ program that uses a while loop to display each term and determine the sum of the arithmetic series having $a = 1$, $d = 3$, and $n = 100$. Make sure your program displays the value it has calculated.

9. **(Numerical Analysis)** A geometric series is defined by the following:

$$a + ar + ar^2 + ar^3 + \cdots + ar^{n-1}$$

a is the first term.

r is the "common ratio."

n is the number of terms in the series.

Using this information, write a C++ program that uses a while loop to both display each term and determine the sum of a geometric series having *a* = 1, *r* = .5, and *n* = 10. Make sure your program displays the value it has calculated.

10. **(Misc. Application)** **a.** The data in the following chart was collected on a recent automobile trip:

Mileage	Gallons
22,495	Full tank
22,841	12.2
23,185	11.3
23,400	10.5
23,772	11.0
24,055	12.2
24,434	14.7
24,804	14.3
25,276	15.2

Write a C++ program that accepts a mileage and gallons value and calculates the miles per gallon (mpg) for that segment of the trip. The mpg is obtained as the difference in mileage between fill-ups divided by the number of gallons of gasoline used in the fill-up.

b. Modify the program written for Exercise 10a to also compute and display the cumulative mpg after each fill-up. The cumulative mpg is calculated as the difference between the mileage at each fill-up and the mileage at the start of the trip divided by the sum of gallons used to that point in the trip.

5.4   **for** Loops

In C++, a **for loop** is constructed by using a for statement. This statement performs the same functions as the while statement but uses a different form. In many situations, especially those using a fixed-count condition, the for statement format is easier to use than its while statement equivalent. This is the syntax of the for statement:

for *(initializing list; expression; altering list)*
    statement;

Although the for statement looks a little complicated, it's really quite simple if you consider each part separately. Inside the parentheses of the for statement are three items, separated by semicolons. Each item is optional and can be described separately, but the semicolons must always be present, even if you don't use the items. In the for statement's most common form, the *initializing list* consists of a single statement used to set the starting (initial) value of a counter, the *expression* (also called the "condition") contains the maximum or minimum value the counter can have and determines when the loop is finished, and the *altering list* provides the increment value that's added to or subtracted from the counter each time the loop is executed. Here are two examples of simple for statements having this form:

```
for (count = 1; count < 10; count = count + 1)
  cout << count;
```

and

```
for (i = 5; i <= 15; i = i + 2)
  cout << i;
```

In the first for statement, the counter variable is named count, the initial value assigned to count is 1, the loop continues as long as the value in count is less than 10, and the value of count is incremented by 1 each time through the loop.

In the next for statement, the counter variable is named i, the initial value assigned to i is 5, the loop continues as long as i's value is less than or equal to 15, and the value of i is incremented by 2 each time through the loop. In both examples, a cout statement is used to display the value of the counter. Program 5.9 shows another example of a for loop.

Program 5.9

```
#include <iostream>
#include <iomanip>
#include <cmath>
using namespace std;

int main()
{
  const int MAXCOUNT = 5;
  int count;

  cout << "NUMBER     SQUARE ROOT\n";
  cout << "------     -----------\n";

  cout << setiosflags(ios::showpoint);
  for (count = 1; count <= MAXCOUNT; count++)
    cout << setw(4) << count
         << setw(15) << sqrt(double(count)) << endl;

  return 0;
}
```

When Program 5.9 is executed, the following display is produced:

```
NUMBER      SQUARE ROOT
------      -----------
   1          1.00000
   2          1.41421
   3          1.73205
   4          2.00000
   5          2.23607
```

The first two lines of this output are produced by the two `cout` statements placed before the `for` statement. The remaining output is produced by the `for` loop, which begins with the `for` statement and is executed as follows: The initial value assigned to the counter variable `count` is 1. Because the value in `count` doesn't exceed the final value of 5, the execution of the `cout` statement in the loop produces this display:

```
   1          1.00000
```

Control is then transferred back to the `for` statement, which increments the value in `count` to 2, and the loop is repeated, producing this display:

```
   2          1.41421
```

This process continues until the value in `count` exceeds the final value of 5, producing the complete output table.

For comparison purposes, a `while` loop equivalent to the `for` loop in Program 5.9 is as follows:

```
count = 1
while (count <= MAXCOUNT)
{
  cout << setw(4) << count
       << setw(15) << sqrt(count) << endl;
  count++;
}
```

As you can see in this example, the difference between the `for` and `while` loops is the placement of the initialization, condition being tested, and incrementing items. Grouping these items in the `for` statement is convenient when you must construct fixed-count loops. See whether you can determine the output Program 5.10 produces.

Program 5.10

```cpp
#include <iostream>
using namespace std;

int main()
{
  int count;

  for (count = 2; count <= 20; count = count + 2)
    cout << count << "  ";

  return 0;
}
```

Did you figure it out? The loop starts with count initialized to 2, stops when count exceeds 20, and increments count in steps of 2. This is the output of Program 5.10:

            2   4   6   8   10   12   14   16   18   20

As mentioned, the for statement doesn't require having an initializing or altering list inside for's parentheses; however, the two semicolons must be included in these parentheses. For example, the construction for (; count <= 20 ;) is valid.

If the initializing list is missing, the initialization step is omitted when the for statement is executed. Therefore, the programmer must provide the required initializations before the for statement is encountered. Similarly, if the altering list is missing, any expressions needed to alter the evaluation of the tested expression must be included in the statement part of the loop. The for statement only ensures that all expressions in the initializing list are executed once, before evaluation of the tested expression, and all expressions in the altering list are executed at the end of the loop, before the tested expression is rechecked. Program 5.10 can be rewritten in any of the three ways shown in Programs 5.10a, 5.10b, and 5.10c.

Program 5.10a

```cpp
#include <iostream>
using namespace std;
int main()
{
  int count;
  count = 2;      // initializer outside the for statement
  for ( ; count <= 20; count = count + 2)
    cout << count << "  ";
  return 0;
}
```

Program 5.10b

```cpp
#include <iostream>
using namespace std;
int main()
{
  int count;

  count = 2;     // initializer outside the for loop
  for( ; count <= 20; )
  {
    cout << count << "  ";
    count = count + 2;      // alteration statement
  }
  return 0;
}
```

Program 5.10c

```cpp
#include <iostream>
using namespace std;
int main()    // all expressions inside for's parentheses
{
  int count;

  for (count = 2; count <= 20; cout << count << "  ", count = count + 2);
  return 0;
}
```

In Program 5.10a, count is initialized outside the for statement, and the first list inside the parentheses is left blank. In Program 5.10b, both the initializing list and the altering list are outside the parentheses. Program 5.10b also uses a compound statement in the for loop, with the expression-altering statement included in the compound statement. Finally, Program 5.10c has included all items inside the parentheses, so there's no need for any useful statement following the parentheses. In this example, the null statement satisfies the syntactical requirement of one statement to follow for's parentheses.

Also, observe in Program 5.10c that the altering list (the last set of items in parentheses) consists of two items, and a comma has been used to separate these items. Using commas to separate items in both the initializing and altering lists is required if either of these lists contains more than one item.

Point of Information

Where to Place the Opening Braces

When the for loop contains a compound statement, professional C++ programmers use two styles of writing for loops. The style used in this book takes the following form:

for *(expression)*
{
 compound statement in here
}

An equally acceptable style places the compound statement's opening brace on the first line. Using this style, a for loop looks like the following:

for *(expression) {*
 compound statement in here
}

The advantage of the first style is that the braces line up under one another, making it easier to locate brace pairs. The advantage of the second style is that it makes the code more compact and saves a line, so more code can be viewed in the same display area. Both styles are used but are almost never intermixed. Select whichever style appeals to you and be consistent in its use. As always, the indentation you use in the compound statement (two or four spaces or a tab) should also be consistent throughout all your programs. The combination of styles you select becomes a "signature" for your programming work.

Last, note that Programs 5.10a, 5.10b, and 5.10c are all inferior to Program 5.10, and although you might encounter them in your programming career, you shouldn't use them. Adding items other than loop control variables and their updating conditions in the for statement tends to make it confusing to read and can result in unwanted effects. Keeping the loop control structure "clean," as in Program 5.10, is important and a good programming practice.

Although the initializing and altering lists can be omitted from a for statement, omitting the tested expression results in an infinite loop. For example, this statement creates an infinite loop:

```
for (count = 2; ; count = count + 1)
  cout << count;
```

As with the while statement, both break and continue statements can be used in a for loop. A break forces an immediate exit from the for loop, as it does in the while loop. A continue, however, forces control to be passed to the altering list in a for statement, after which the tested expression is reevaluated. This action differs from continue's action in a while statement, where control is passed directly to reevaluation of the tested expression.

Figure 5.7 illustrates the internal workings of a for loop. As shown, when the for loop is completed, control is transferred to the first executable statement following the loop. To avoid having to illustrate every step, you can use a simplified set of flowchart symbols to describe for loops. If you use the following flowchart symbol to represent a for statement,

for
statement

you can then illustrate a complete for loop, as shown in Figure 5.8.

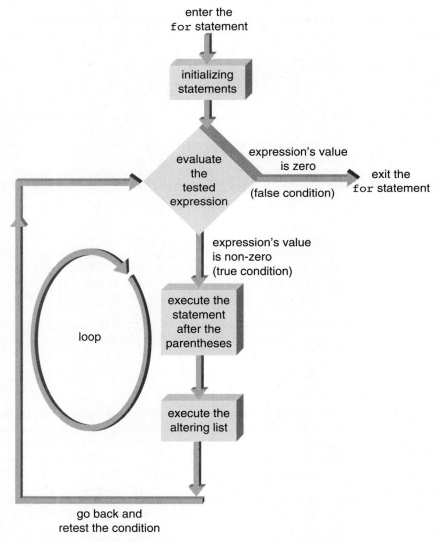

Figure 5.7 A for loop flowchart

Point of Information

Do You Use a for or while Loop?

Beginning programmers often ask which loop structure they should use—a for or while loop. It's a good question because both loop structures are pretest loops that, in C++, can be used to construct fixed-count and variable-condition loops.

In most other computer languages, including Visual Basic and Pascal, the answer is straightforward because the for statement can be used only to construct fixed-count loops. In these languages, then, for statements are used to construct fixed-count loops, and while statements are generally used only for variable-condition loops.

In C++, this easy distinction doesn't hold because both statements can be used to create both types of loops. The answer is more a matter of style. Because a for and while loop are interchangeable in C++, either loop is appropriate. Some professional programmers always use a for statement for pretest loops and almost never use a while statement; others always use a while statement and rarely use a for statement. Still a third group tends to retain the convention used in other languages—a for loop is generally used to create fixed-count loops, and a while loop is used to create variable-condition loops. In C++, it's a matter of style, and you'll encounter all three styles in your programming career.

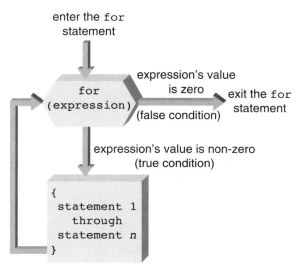

Figure 5.8   A simplified for loop flowchart

To understand the enormous power of for loops, consider the task of printing a table of numbers from 1 to 10, including their squares and cubes, by using a for statement. This table was produced previously by using a while loop in Program 5.3. You might want to review Program 5.3 and compare it to Program 5.11 to get a better sense of the equivalence between for and while loops.

Program 5.11

```cpp
#include <iostream>
#include <iomanip>
using namespace std;

int main()
{
  const int MAXNUMS = 10;
  int num;

  cout << "NUMBER     SQUARE     CUBE\n"
       << "------     ------     ----\n";

  for (num = 1; num <= MAXNUMS; num++)
    cout << setw(3) << num << "        "
         << setw(3) << num * num << "        "
         << setw(4) << num * num * num << endl;

  return 0;
}
```

When Program 5.11 runs, this is the display produced:

NUMBER	SQUARE	CUBE
------	------	----
1	1	1
2	4	8
3	9	27
4	16	64
5	25	125
6	36	216
7	49	343
8	64	512
9	81	729
10	100	1000

Simply changing the number 10 in the `for` statement of Program 5.11 to 1000 creates a loop that's executed 1000 times and produces a table of numbers from 1 to 1000. As with the `while` statement, this small change produces an immense increase in the program's processing and output. Notice also that the expression num++ was used in the altering list in place of the usual num = num + 1.

EXERCISES 5.4

1. **(Practice)** Write a `for` statement for each of the following cases:

   a. Use a counter named `i` that has an initial value of 1, a final value of 20, and an increment of 1.

   b. Use a counter named `icount` that has an initial value of 1, a final value of 20, and an increment of 2.

   c. Use a counter named `j` that has an initial value of 1, a final value of 100, and an increment of 5.

   d. Use a counter named `icount` that has an initial value of 20, a final value of 1, and an increment of -1.

   e. Use a counter named `icount` that has an initial value of 20, a final value of 1, and an increment of -2.

   f. Use a counter named `count` that has an initial value of 1.0, a final value of 16.2, and an increment of 0.2.

   g. Use a counter named `xcnt` that has an initial value of 20.0, a final value of 10.0, and an increment of -0.5.

2. **(Desk Checking)** Determine the number of times each `for` loop is executed for the `for` statements written for Exercise 1.

3. **(Desk Checking)** Determine the value in `total` after each of the following loops is executed:

   a.
   ```
   total = 0;
   for (i = 1; i <= 10; i = i + 1)
      total = total + 1;
   ```

   b.
   ```
   total = 1;
   for (count = 1; count <= 10; count = count + 1)
      total = total * 2;
   ```

   c.
   ```
   total = 0
   for (i = 10; i <= 15; i = i + 1)
      total = total + i;
   ```

   d.
   ```
   total = 50
   for (i = 1; i <=10; i = i + 1)
      total = total - i;
   ```

   e.
   ```
   total = 1
   for (icnt = 1; icnt <= 8; ++icnt)
      total = total * icnt;
   ```

   f.
   ```
   total = 1.0
   for (j = 1; j <= 5; ++j)
      total = total / 2.0;
   ```

4. **(Desk Checking)** Determine the output of the following program:

```cpp
#include <iostream>
using namespace std;

int main()
{
  int i;

  for (i = 20; i >= 0; i = i - 4)
    cout << i << " ";

  return 0;
}
```

5. **(Modify)** Modify Program 5.11 to produce a table of the numbers 0 through 20 in increments of 2, with their squares and cubes.

6. **(Modify)** Modify Program 5.11 to produce a table of numbers from 10 to 1, instead of 1 to 10, as it currently does.

7. **(Conversions)** Write a C++ program to convert kilometers/hr to miles/hr. The program should produce a table of 10 conversions, starting at 60 km/hr and incremented by 5 km/hr. The display should have appropriate headings and list each km/hr and its equivalent miles/hr value. Use the relationship that 1 kilometer = 0.6241 miles.

8. **(Practice)** Write sections of C++ code to do the following:

   a. Display the multiples of 3 backward from 33 to 3, inclusive.

   b. Display the uppercase letters of the alphabet backward from Z to A.

9. **(Practice)** Write, run, and test a C++ program to find the value of 2^n by using a `for` loop, where n is an integer value the user enters at the keyboard. (*Hint*: Initialize result = 1. Accumulate result = 2 * result.)

10. **(Fluid Dynamics)** Write a C++ program that uses a fixed-count loop of four. For each pass through the loop, enter a fluid's viscosity and density from the following chart. Your program should then determine the kinematic viscosity for each fluid, using the following formula (see the Technical Note in Section 5.2 for a description of density and viscosity):

Kinematic viscosity = viscosity / density

Use the results output by your program to complete the last column in this chart:

Fluid	Viscosity at 40°C = 77°F (kg/ms)	Density (kg/m^3)	Kinematic Viscosity (m^2/s)
Gasoline	$.4466 \times 10^{-3}$	$.7186 \times 10^3$	
Medium fuel oil	2.9922×10^{-3}	$.8496 \times 10^3$	
Medium lubricating oil	87.0736×10^{-3}	$.8865 \times 10^3$	
Water	$.8975 \times 10^{-3}$	$.9973 \times 10^3$	

11. **(Fluid Dynamics)** Write a C++ program that calculates the Reynolds number for a pipe having a diameter of 0.1 meters, in which fluid flows at an average rate of .09 m/s. Your program should have a fixed-count loop of four and display both the calculated Reynolds number and the type of fluid flow—laminar, in-transition, or turbulent—for each fluid listed in the following chart, using the information provided after the chart. Use the results your program outputs to fill in the last two columns of this chart:

Fluid	Kinematic Viscosity (m^2/s) at 40°C	Pipe Diameter (m)	Avg. Fluid Speed (m/s)	Reynolds Number	Type of Flow
Gasoline	6.215×10^{-7}	0.1	.09		
Medium fuel oil	3.523×10^{-6}	0.1	.09		
Medium lubricating oil	9.822×10^{-5}	0.1	.09		
Water	8.999×10^{-5}	0.1	.09		

The Reynolds number can be calculated by using this formula:

$$Re = \frac{V\,d}{v}$$

Re is the Reynolds number.
V is the average speed of the fluid (ft/sec or m/s).
d is the pipe diameter (ft or m).
v is the kinematic viscosity (ft^2/sec or m^2/sec).

For the determination of flow type, use these facts:

$Re < 2000$: Fluid flow is smooth (laminar).
$2000 \leq Re \geq 3000$: Fluid flow is in transition.
$Re > 3000$: Fluid flow is turbulent.

12. **(Structural Eng.)** The expansion of a steel bridge as it's heated to a final Celsius temperature, T_F, from an initial Celsius temperature, T_0, can be approximated by using this formula:

Increase in length = $a \times L \times (T_F - T_0)$

a is the coefficient of expansion (which for steel is 11.7×10^{-6}).
L is the length of the bridge at temperature T_0.

Using this formula, write a C++ program that displays a table of expansion lengths for a steel bridge that's 7365 meters long at 0 degrees Celsius, as the temperature increases to 40 degrees in 5-degree increments.

5.5   A Closer Look: Loop Programming Techniques

This section discusses four common programming techniques associated with pretest (`for` and `while`) loops. All these techniques are common knowledge to experienced programmers.

Technique 1: Interactive Input in a Loop

In Section 5.2, you saw the effect of including a `cin` statement in a `while` loop. Entering data interactively in a loop is a general technique that's equally applicable to `for` loops. For example, in Program 5.12, a `cin` statement is used to allow a user to interactively input a set of numbers. As each number is input, it's added to a total. When the `for` loop is exited, the average is calculated and displayed.

The `for` statement in Program 5.12 creates a loop that's executed four times. The user is prompted to enter a number each time through the loop. After each number is entered, it's added to the total immediately. Notice that `total` is initialized to 0 before the initializing list of the `for` statement is executed. The loop in Program 5.12 is executed as long as the value in `count` is less than 4 and is terminated when `count` becomes 4. (The increment to 4, in fact, is what causes the loop to end.) The output produced by Program 5.12 is essentially the same as Program 5.7.

Program 5.12

```cpp
#include <iostream>
using namespace std;
// This program calculates the average of MAXCOUNT user-entered numbers
int main()
{
  const int MAXCOUNT = 4;
  int count;
  double num, total, average;
  total = 0.0;
  for (count = 0; count < MAXCOUNT; count++)
  {
    cout << "Enter a number: ";
    cin  >> num;
    total = total + num;
  }
  average = total / MAXCOUNT;
  cout << "The average of the data entered is "
       << average << endl;
  return 0;
}
```

Technique 2: Selection in a Loop

Another common programming technique is to use a `for` or `while` loop to cycle through a set of numbers and select numbers meeting one or more criteria. For example, assume you want to find both the positive and negative sum of a set of numbers. The criterion is whether the number is positive or negative, and the logic for implementing this program is given by this pseudocode:

> *While the loop condition is true*
>   *Enter a number*
>   *If the number is greater than zero*
>   *add the number to the positive sum*
>   *Else*
>   *add the number to the negative sum*
>   *Endif*
> *Endwhile*

    Program 5.13 describes this algorithm in C++ for a fixed-count loop in which five numbers are to be entered.

 Program 5.13

```cpp
#include <iostream>
using namespace std;

// This program computes the positive and negative sums of a set
// of MAXNUMS user-entered numbers
int main()
{
  const int MAXNUMS = 5;
  int i;
  double usenum, positiveSum, negativeSum;

  positiveSum = 0; // this initialization can be done in the declaration
  negativeSum = 0; // this initialization can be done in the declaration

  for (i = 1; i <= MAXNUMS; i++)
  {
    cout << "Enter a number (positive or negative) : ";
    cin  >> usenum;
    if (usenum > 0)
      positiveSum = positiveSum + usenum;
    else
      negativeSum = negativeSum + usenum;
  }
```

☞

```
  cout << "The positive total is " << positiveSum << endl;
  cout << "The negative total is " << negativeSum << endl;
  return 0;
}
```

The following is a sample run of Program 5.13:

```
Enter a number (positive or negative) : 10
Enter a number (positive or negative) : -10
Enter a number (positive or negative) : 5
Enter a number (positive or negative) : -7
Enter a number (positive or negative) : 11
The positive total is 26
The negative total is -17
```

Technique 3: Evaluating Functions of One Variable

Loops can be constructed to give you a way to determine and display the values of a single variable mathematical function for a set of values over any specified interval. For example, you want to know the values of the following function for x between 2 and 6:

$$y = 10x^2 + 3x - 2$$

Assuming x has been declared as an integer variable, the following for loop can be used to calculate the required values:

```
for (x = 2; x <= 6; x++)
{
  y = 10 * pow(x,2.0) + 3 * x - 2;
  cout << setw(4) << x
       << setw(11) << y << endl;
}
```

In this loop, the variable x is used as both the counter variable and the unknown (independent variable) in the function. For each value of x from 2 to 6, a new value of y is calculated and displayed. This for loop is used in Program 5.14, which also prints headings for the displayed values.

Program 5.14

```cpp
#include <iostream>
#include <iomanip>
#include <cmath>
using namespace std;

int main()
{
  int x, y;

  cout << "x value    y value\n"
       << "-------    --------\n";

  for (x = 2; x <= 6; x++)
  {
    y = 10 * pow(x,2.0) + 3 * x - 2;
    cout << setw(4) << x
         << setw(11) << y << endl;
  }

  return 0;
}
```

The following is displayed when Program 5.14 is executed:

```
x value   y value
-------   --------
      2        44
      3        97
      4       170
      5       263
      6       376
```

Two items are important here. First, any equation with one unknown can be evaluated by using a single `for` or an equivalent `while` loop. This method requires substituting your equation in the loop in place of the equation used in Program 5.14 and adjusting the counter values to match the solution range you want.

Second, you're not constrained to using integer values for the counter variable. For example, by specifying a non-integer increment, solutions for fractional values can be obtained. This technique is shown in Program 5.15, where the equation $y = 10x^2 + 3x - 2$ is evaluated in the range $x = 2$ to $x = 6$ in increments of 0.5.

Program 5.15

```cpp
#include <iostream>
#include <iomanip>
#include <cmath>
using namespace std;

int main()
{
  double x, y;

  cout << "x value      y value\n";
       << "-------      ---------\n"
  cout << setiosflags(ios::fixed)
       << setiosflags(ios::showpoint)
       << setprecision(5);

  for (x = 2.0; x <= 6.0; x = x + 0.5)
  {
    y = 10.0 * pow(x,2.0) + 3.0 * x - 2.0;
    cout << setw(7) <<  x
         << setw(14) << y << endl;
  }

  return 0;
}
```

Notice that *x* and *y* have been declared as floating-point variables in Program 5.15 to allow these variables to take on fractional values. The following is the output this program produces:

```
    x value       y value
    -------       ---------
    2.00000       44.00000
    2.50000       68.00000
    3.00000       97.00000
    3.50000      131.00000
    4.00000      170.00000
    4.50000      214.00000
    5.00000      263.00000
    5.50000      317.00000
    6.00000      376.00000
```

Technique 4: Interactive Loop Control

Values used to control a loop can be set by using variables rather than constant values. For example, these four statements

```
i = 5;
j = 10;
k = 1;
for (count = i; count <= j; count = count + k)
```

produce the same effect as this single statement:

```
for (count = 5; count <= 10; count++)
```

Similarly, these statements

```
i = 5;
j = 10;
k = 1;
count = i;
while (count <= j)
  count = count + k;
```

produce the same effect as the following while loop:

```
count = 5;
while (count <= 10)
  count++;
```

The advantage of using variables in the initialization, condition, and altering expressions is that it allows you to assign values for these expressions outside the for or while statement. This method is especially useful when a cin statement is used to set the actual values. To make this technique a little more tangible, take a look at Program 5.16.

Program 5.16

```cpp
#include <iostream>
#include <iomanip>
using namespace std;

// this program displays a table of numbers with their squares and cubes,
// starting from the number 1. The final number in the table is
// input by the user.

int main()
{
  int num, final;

  cout << "Enter the final number for the table: ";
  cin  >> final;

  cout << "NUMBER SQUARE CUBE\n";
  cout << "------ ------ ----\n";

  for (num = 1; num <= final; num++)
    cout << setw(3) << num
         << setw(8) << num*num
         << setw(7) << num*num*num << endl;

  return 0;
}
```

In Program 5.16, a variable is used in the `for` statement to control the condition (middle) expression. A `cin` statement has been placed before the loop to allow the user to decide what the `final` value should be. Notice that this arrangement permits the user to set the table's size at runtime, instead of having the programmer set the table size at compile time. This arrangement also makes the program more general because it can be used to create a variety of tables without the need for reprogramming and recompiling.

EXERCISES 5.5

1. (**cin** within a loop) Write and run a C++ program that accepts six Fahrenheit temperatures, one at a time, and converts each value entered to its Celsius equivalent before the next value is requested. Use a `for` loop in your program. The conversion required is *Celsius = (5.0/9.0) × (Fahrenheit - 32).*

2. (**cin** within a loop) Write and run a C++ program that accepts 10 values of gallons, one at a time, and converts each value entered to its liter equivalent before the next value is requested. Use a for loop in your program. Use the fact that 1 gallon = 3.785 liters.

3. (**Interactive Loop Control**) Modify the program written for Exercise 2 to initially request the number of data items to be entered and converted.

4. (**Interactive Loop Control**) Modify Program 5.13 so that the number of entries to be input is specified by the user when the program is executed.

5. (**Selection**) Modify Program 5.13 so that it displays the average of the positive and negative numbers. (*Hint*: Be careful not to count the number 0 as a negative number.) Test your program by entering the numbers 17, -10, 19, 0, and -4. The positive average your program displays should be 18, and the negative average should be -7.

6. (**Selection**) **a.** Write a C++ program that selects and displays the maximum value of five numbers to be entered when the program is executed. (*Hint*: Use a for loop with both a cin and if statement inside the loop.)

   b. Modify the program written for Exercise 6a so that it displays both the maximum value and the position in the input set of numbers where the maximum occurs.

7. (**Selection**) Write a C++ program that selects and displays the first 20 integer numbers that are evenly divisible by 3. (*Hint:* Use the modulus operator, %.)

8. (**Selection**) A child's parents promised to give the child $10 on her 12th birthday and double the gift on every subsequent birthday until the annual gift exceeded $1000. Write a C++ program to determine how old the child will be when the last amount is given and the total amount the child will have received.

9. (**Mathematical Functions**) Modify Program 5.15 to produce a table of y values for the following:

   a. $y = 3x^5 - 2x^3 + x$ for x between 5 and 10 in increments of 0.2

   b. $y = 1 + x + \dfrac{x^2}{2} + \dfrac{x^3}{3} + \dfrac{x^4}{24}$ for x between 1 and 3 in increments of 0.1

   c. $y = 2e^{0.8t}$ for t between 4 and 10 in increments of 0.2

10. (**Mathematical Functions**) A model of worldwide population, in billions of people, is given by this formula

    Population = $6.0e^{0.02t}$

    where t is the time in years ($t = 0$ represents January 2000 and $t = 1$ represents January 2001). Using this formula, write a C++ program that displays a yearly population table for the years January 2005 though January 2010.

11. (**Mathematical Functions**) The x and y coordinates, as a function of time, t, of a projectile fired with an initial velocity, v, at an angle of θ with respect to the ground, are given by these formulas:

    $x = v\,t\,\cos(\theta)$

    $y = v\,t\,\sin(\theta)$

Using these formulas, write a C++ program that displays a table of *x* and *y* values for a projectile fired with an initial velocity of 500 ft/sec at an angle of 22.8 degrees. (*Hint:* Remember to convert to radian measure.) The table should contain values corresponding to the time interval 0 to 10 seconds in increments of ½ seconds.

5.6 Nested Loops

In many situations, using a loop within another loop, called a **nested loop**, is convenient. Here's a simple example of a nested loop:

```
for(i = 1; i <= 5; i++)          // start of outer loop
{
  cout << "\ni is now " << i << endl;

  for(j = 1; j <= 4; j++)        // start of inner loop
    cout << "  j = " << j;       // end of inner loop
}                                // end of outer loop
```

The first loop, controlled by the value of i, is called the **outer loop**. The second loop, controlled by the value of j, is called the **inner loop**. Notice that all statements in the inner loop are contained in the boundaries of the outer loop, and a different variable is used to control each loop. For each trip through the outer loop, the inner loop runs through its entire sequence. Therefore, each time the i counter increases by one, the inner for loop executes completely, and goes through four values (j takes on the values 1 to 4), as shown in Figure 5.9. Program 5.17 includes this type of loop in a working program.

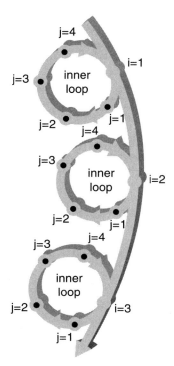

Figure 5.9 For each i, j loops

This is the output of a sample run of Program 5.17:

```
i is now 1
  j = 1  j = 2  j = 3  j = 4
i is now 2
  j = 1  j = 2  j = 3  j = 4
i is now 3
  j = 1  j = 2  j = 3  j = 4
i is now 4
  j = 1  j = 2  j = 3  j = 4
i is now 5
  j = 1  j = 2  j = 3  j = 4
```

Program 5.17

```cpp
#include <iostream>
using namespace std;

int main()
{
  const int MAXI = 5;
  const int MAXJ = 4;
  int i, j;

  for(i = 1; i <= MAXI; i++)      // start of outer loop <----+
  {                               //                          |
    cout << "\ni is now " << i << endl;   //                  |
                                  //                          |
    for(j = 1; j <= MAXJ; j++)    // start of inner loop      |
      cout << "   j = " << j;     // end of inner loop        |
  }                               // end of outer loop   <-----+

  cout << endl;

  return 0;
}
```

To understand the usefulness of a nested loop, take a look at using one to compute the average grade for each student in a class of 20 students. Each student has taken four exams during the semester. The final grade is calculated as the average of these exam grades. The pseudocode describing how to compute this average is as follows:

for 20 times
   set the student grade total to zero
   for 4 times
      input a grade
      add the grade to the total
   endfor // end of inner for loop
   calculate student's average grade
   print the student's average grade
endfor // end of outer for loop

As described by the pseudocode, an outer loop consisting of 20 passes is used to compute the average grade for each student. The inner loop consists of four passes, and one examination grade is entered in each inner loop pass. As each grade is entered, it's added to the total for the student, and at the end of the loop, the average is calculated and displayed. Because both the outer and inner loops are fixed-count loops of 20 and 4, respectively, for statements are used to create these loops. Program 5.18 shows the C++ code corresponding to the pseudocode.

Program 5.18

```cpp
#include <iostream>
using namespace std;

int main()
{
  const int NUMGRADES = 4;
  const int NUMSTUDENTS = 20;
  int i, j;
  double grade, total, average;

  for (i = 1; i <= NUMSTUDENTS; i++) // start of outer loop
  {
    total = 0;                       // clear the total for this student
    for (j = 1; j <= NUMGRADES; j++) // start of inner loop
    {
      cout << "Enter an examination grade for this student: ";
      cin  >> grade;
      total = total + grade;         // add the grade to the total
    }                                // end of the inner for loop
    average = total / NUMGRADES;     // calculate the average
    cout << "\nThe average for student " << i
         << " is " << average << "\n\n";
  }                                  // end of the outer for loop

  return 0;
}
```

In reviewing Program 5.18, pay particular attention to the initialization of `total` in the outer loop, before the inner loop is entered: `total` is initialized 20 times, once for each student. Also, notice that the average is calculated and displayed immediately after the inner loop is finished. Because the statements that compute and display the average are also in the outer loop, 20 averages are calculated and displayed. The entry and addition of each grade in the inner loop uses techniques you have seen before and should be familiar with now.

EXERCISES 5.6

1. **(Misc. Application)** Four experiments are performed, and each experiment has six test results. The results for each experiment are given in the following list. Write a program using a nested loop to compute and display the average of the test results for each experiment.

        1st experiment results: 23.2 31 16.9 27 25.4 28.6

        2nd experiment results: 34.8 45.2 27.9 36.8 33.4 39.4

        3rd experiment results: 19.4 16.8 10.2 20.8 18.9 13.4

        4th experiment results: 36.9 39 49.2 45.1 42.7 50.6

2. **(Modify)** **a.** Modify the program written for Exercise 1 so that the number of test results for each experiment is entered by the user. Write your program so that a different number of test results can be entered for each experiment.

   b. Rewrite the program written for Exercise 2a to eliminate the inner loop.

3. **(Electrical Eng.)** **a.** An electrical manufacturer tests five generators by measuring their output voltages at three different times. Write a C++ program that uses a nested loop to enter each generator's test results, and then computes and displays the average voltage for each generator. Assume the following generator test results:

        1st generator: 122.5 122.7 123.0

        2nd generator: 120.2 127.0 125.1

        3rd generator: 121.7 124.9 126.0

        4th generator: 122.9 123.8 126.7

        5th generator: 121.5 124.7 122.6

   b. Modify the program written for Exercise 3a to calculate and display the average voltage for all the generators. (*Hint:* Use a second variable to store the total of all the generator's voltages.)

4. **(Modify)** Rewrite the program written for Exercise 3a to eliminate the inner loop. To do this, you have to input three voltages for each generator instead of entering one at a time. Each voltage must be stored in its own variable before the average is calculated.

5. **(Mathematical Functions)** Write a program that calculates and displays values for y when

$$y = xz \ / \ (x - z)$$

Your program should calculate y for values of x ranging between 1 and 5 and values of z ranging between 2 and 6. The x variable should control the outer loop and be incremented in steps of 1, and z should be incremented in steps of 1. Your program should also display the message `Function Undefined` when the x and z values are equal.

6. **(Numerical Analysis)** Assembly languages for some microprocessors don't have a multiply operation. Although there are sophisticated algorithms for performing multiplication in these languages, a simple method multiplies by repeated addition. In this case, the algorithm's efficiency can be increased by using nested loops. For example, to multiply a number by 12, first add the number three times, and then add the result four times. This calculation requires only 7 additions as opposed to 12. Using this information, write a C++ program that multiplies 33, 47, and 83 by 1001, using three loops, and then displays the result. (*Hint:* 1001 = 7 × 11 × 13.)

5.7 **do while Loops**

Both while and for statements evaluate an expression at the start of the repetition loop, so they are always used to create pretest loops. Posttest loops, also referred to as exit-controlled loops, can also be constructed in C++. Figure 5.10 shows the basic structure of a posttest loop, which is referred to as a do while loop. Notice that a do while loop continues iterations through the loop while the condition is true and exits the loop when the condition is false.

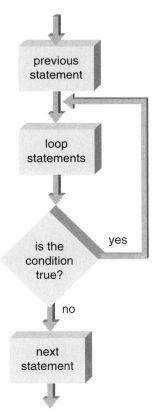

Figure 5.10   The do while loop structure

In C++, a posttest do while loop is created by using a do statement. As its name implies, this statement allows you to perform some statements before an expression is evaluated at the end of the loop. It has this general form in C++:

do
    statement;
while *(expression);* ⟵——————— *don't forget the final semicolon, which is required here*

As with all C++ programs, the single statement in the do can be replaced with a compound statement. Figure 5.11 shows a flow-control diagram illustrating the operation of the do statement.

As shown, all statements within the do statement are executed at least once before the expression is evaluated. Then, if the expression has a non-zero value, the statements are

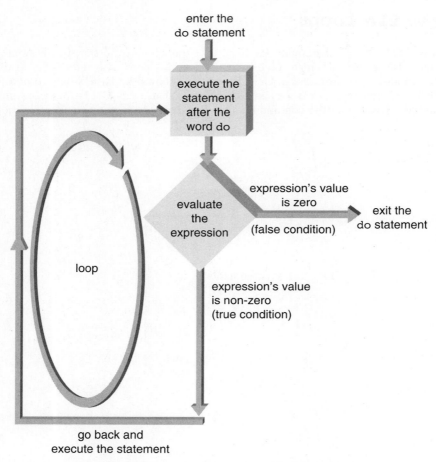

enter the
do statement

execute the
statement
after the
word do

loop

evaluate
the
expression

expression's value
is zero

(false condition)

exit the
do statement

expression's value
is non-zero
(true condition)

go back and
execute the statement

Figure 5.11   The do statement's flow of control

executed again. This process continues until the expression evaluates to zero (becomes false). For example, take a look at the following do statement:

```
do
{
  cout << "\nEnter a price: ";
  cin  >> price;
  if (abs(price - SENTINEL) < 0.0001)
    break;
  salestax = RATE * price;
  cout << setiosflags(ios::showpoint)
       << setprecision(2)
       << "The sales tax is $ " << salestax;
}
while (price != SENTINEL);
```

Observe that the prompt and cin statement are included in the loop because the tested expression is evaluated at the end of the loop.

As with all repetition statements, the do statement can always replace or be replaced by an equivalent while or for statement. The choice of which statement to use depends on the application and the programmer's preferred style. In general, while and for statements are preferred because anyone reading the program can clearly see what's being tested up front, at the top of the program loop.

Validity Checks

The do statement is particularly useful in filtering user-entered input and providing data validation checks. For example, an operator is required to enter a valid customer identification number between 1000 and 1999. A number outside this range is to be rejected, and a new request for a valid number is made. The following section of code provides the necessary data filter to verify the entry of a valid identification number:

```
do
{
  cout << "\nEnter an identification number: ";
  cin  >> id_num;
}
while (id_num < 1000 || id_num > 1999);
```

In this code, a request for an identification number is repeated until a valid number is entered. This section of code is "bare bones," in that it doesn't alert the operator to the cause of the new request for data or allow premature exit from the loop if a valid identification number can't be found. The following code is an alternative for removing the first drawback:

```
do
{
  cout << "\nEnter an identification number: ";
  cin  >> id_num;
  if (id_num < 1000 || id_num > 1999)
  {
    cout << "An invalid number was just entered\n";
    cout << "Please check the ID number and reenter\n";
  }
  else
    break;    // break if a valid id_num was entered
} while(1);  // this expression is always true
```

A break statement is used to exit from the loop. Because the expression the do statement is evaluating is always 1 (true), an infinite loop has been created that's exited only when the break statement is encountered.

EXERCISES 5.7

1. **(Practice)** **a.** Using a do statement, write a program to accept a grade. The program should request a grade continuously as long as an invalid grade is entered. An invalid

grade is any grade less than 0 or greater than 100. After a valid grade has been entered, your program should display the value of the grade entered.

b. Modify the program written for Exercise 1a so that the user is alerted when an invalid grade has been entered.

c. Modify the program written for Exercise 1b so that it allows the user to exit the program by entering the number 999.

d. Modify the program written for Exercise 1b so that it automatically terminates after five invalid grades are entered.

2. **(Misc. Application)** **a.** Write a program that continuously requests a grade to be entered. If the grade is less than 0 or greater than 100, your program should print an appropriate message informing the user that an invalid grade has been entered; else, the grade should be added to a total. When a grade of 999 is entered, the program should exit the repetition loop and compute and display the average of the valid grades entered.

b. Run the program written in Exercise 2a on a computer and verify the program by using appropriate test data.

3. **(Misc. Application)** **a.** Write a program to reverse the digits of a positive integer number. For example, if the number 8735 is entered, the number displayed should be 5378. (*Hint*: Use a do statement and continuously strip off and display the number's units digit. If the variable num initially contains the number entered, the units digit is obtained as (num % 10). After a units digit is displayed, dividing the number by 10 sets up the number for the next iteration. Therefore, (8735 % 10) is 5 and (8735 / 10) is 873. The do statement should continue as long as the remaining number is not zero.

b. Run the program written in Exercise 3a on a computer and verify the program by using appropriate test data.

4. **(Practice)** Repeat any of the exercises in Section 5.3, using a do statement rather than a for statement.

5. **(Numerical Analysis)** Given a number, n, and an approximation for its square root, a closer approximation of the actual square root can be obtained by using this formula:

$$new\ approximation = \frac{(n\ /\ previous\ approximation) + previous\ approximation}{2}$$

Using this information, write a C++ program that prompts the user for a number and an initial guess at its square root. Using this input data, your program should calculate an approximation of the square root that's accurate to 0.00001. (*Hint*: Stop the loop when the difference between the two approximations is less than 0.00001.)

6. **(Numerical Analysis)** Here's a challenging problem for those who know a little calculus. The Newton-Raphson method can be used to find the roots of any equation $y(x) = 0$. In this method, the $(i + 1)$st approximation, x_{i+1}, to a root of $y(x) = 0$ is given in terms of the ith approximation, x_i, by the following formula, where y' denotes the derivative of $y(x)$ with respect to x:

$$x_{i+1} = x_i - y(x_i)\ /\ y'(x_i)$$

For example, if $y(x) = 3x^2 + 2x - 2$, then $y'(x) = 6x + 2$, and the roots are found by making a reasonable guess for a first approximation x_1 and iterating by using this equation:

$x_{i+1} = x_i - (3x_i^2 + 2x_i - 2) / (6x_i + 2)$

a. Using the Newton-Raphson method, find the two roots of the equation $3x^2 + 2x - 2 = 0$. (*Hint*: There's one positive root and one negative root.)

b. Extend the program written for Exercise 6a so that it finds the roots of any function $y(x) = 0$, when the function for $y(x)$ and the derivative of $y(x)$ are placed in the code.

5.8 Common Programming Errors

When using repetition statements, beginning C++ programmers are prone to making the following seven errors:

1. The most troublesome error for new programmers is the "off by one" error, in which the loop executes one too many or one too few times than was intended. For example, the loop created by the statement `for(i = 1; i < 11; i++)` executes 10 times, not 11, even though the number 11 is used in the statement. An equivalent loop can be constructed by using the statement `for(i = 1; i <= 10; i ++)`.

   However, if the loop is started with an initial value of `i = 0`, using the statement `for(i = 0; i < 11; i++)`, the loop is traversed 11 times, as is a loop constructed with the statement `for(i = 0; i <= 10; i++)`. In constructing loops, you must pay particular attention to both the initial and final conditions used to control the loop to make sure the number of loop traversals isn't off by one too many or one too few executions.

   The next two errors pertain to the tested expression, and you have already encountered them with the `if` and `switch` statements:

2. Inadvertently using the assignment operator, =, in place of the equality operator, ==, in the tested expression—for example, typing the assignment expression `a = 5` instead of the correct relational expression `a==5`. Because the tested expression can be any valid C++ expression, including arithmetic and assignment expressions, the compiler doesn't detect this error.

3. Using the equality operator, ==, when testing floating-point or double-precision operands. For example, the expression `fnum == 0.01` should be replaced by a test requiring that the absolute value of `fnum - 0.01` be less than an acceptable amount. The reason is that all numbers are stored in binary form. Using a finite number of bits, decimal numbers such as 0.01 have no exact binary equivalent, so tests requiring equality with these numbers can fail. (See Section 4.1 for a more complete description of this numerical accuracy problem.)

   The next three errors are particular to the `for` statement:

4. Placing a semicolon at the end of `for`'s parentheses, which frequently produces a do-nothing loop. For example, take a look at these statements:

```
for(count = 0; count < 10; count++);
    total = total + num;
```

The semicolon at the end of the first line of code is a null statement. It has the effect of creating a loop that's executed 10 times with nothing done except incrementing and testing count. This error tends to occur because C++ programmers are used to ending most lines with a semicolon.

5. Using commas are used to separate items in a `for` statement instead of the required semicolons, as in this example:

```
for (count = 1, count < 10, count++)
```

Commas must be used to separate items in the initializing and altering lists, but semicolons must be used to separate these lists from the tested expression.

6. Changing the value of the control variable used in the tested condition both inside the body of a `for` loop and in its altering list. For example, take a look at this `for` loop:

```
for(int i=0; i<10; i++)
    cout << i++;
```

In this code, the value of the variable being tested (in this case, `i`) is changed in two places, which is a serious logic error.

7. The final common programming error is omitting the final semicolon from the `do` statement. This error is usually made by programmers who have learned to omit the semicolon after the parentheses of a `while` statement and carry over this habit when encountering the reserved word `while` at the end of a `do` statement.

5.9   Chapter Summary

1. A section of repeating code is referred to as a loop. A loop is controlled by a repetition statement that tests a condition to determine whether the code will be executed. Each pass through the loop is referred to as a repetition or an iteration. The tested condition must always be set explicitly before its first evaluation by the repetition statement. Within the loop, there must always be a statement that permits altering the condition so that the loop, after it's entered, can be exited.

2. There are three basic type of loops: `while`, `for`, and `do while`. The `while` and `for` loops are pretest or entrance-controlled loops. In this type of loop, the tested condition is evaluated at the beginning of the loop, which requires setting the tested condition explicitly before loop entry. If the condition is true, loop repetitions begin; otherwise, the loop is not entered. Iterations continue as long as the condition remains true. In C++, `while` and `for` loops are constructed by using `while` and `for` statements.

   The `do while` loop is a posttest or exit-controlled loop, in which the tested condition is evaluated at the end of the loop. This type of loop is always executed at least once. As long as the tested condition remains true, `do while` loops continue to execute.

3. Loops are also classified according to the type of tested condition. In a fixed-count loop, the condition is used to keep track of how many repetitions have occurred. In a variable-condition loop, the tested condition is based on a variable that can change interactively with each pass through the loop.

4. In C++, a while loop is constructed by using a `while` statement. This is the most commonly used form of this statement:

```
while (expression)
{
   statements;
}
```

The *expression* in parentheses is the condition that's tested to determine whether the statement following the parentheses, which is generally a compound statement, is executed. The expression is evaluated in exactly the same manner as one in an `if-else` statement; the difference is how the expression is used. In a `while` statement, the statement following the expression is executed repeatedly as long as the expression retains a non-zero value, instead of just once, as in an `if-else` statement. An example of a `while` loop follows:

```
count = 1;                // initialize count
while (count <= 10)
{
   cout << count << "   ";
   count++;               // increment count
}
```

The first assignment statement sets `count` equal to 1. The `while` statement is then entered, and the expression is evaluated for the first time. Because the value of `count` is less than or equal to 10, the expression is true, and the compound statement is executed. The first statement in the compound statement uses the `cout` statement to display the value of `count`.

The next statement adds 1 to the value currently stored in `count`, making this value equal to 2. The `while` statement then loops back to retest the expression. Because `count` is still less than or equal to 10, the compound statement is executed again. This process continues until the value of `count` reaches 11.

Because the `while` statement always checks its expression at the top of the loop, any variables in the tested expression must have values assigned before the `while` is encountered. In addition, the `while` loop must contain a statement that alters the tested expression's value.

5. In C++, a `for` loop is constructed by using a `for` statement. This statement performs the same functions as the `while` statement but uses a different form. In many situations, especially those using a fixed-count condition, the `for` statement format is easier to use than its `while` statement equivalent. This is the most commonly used form of the `for` statement:

```
for (initializing list; expression; altering list)
{
   statements;
}
```

Inside the parentheses of the `for` statement are three items, separated by semicolons. Each of these items is optional, but the semicolons must be present.

The *initializing list* is used to set any initial values before the loop is entered; generally, it's used to initialize a counter. Statements in the initializing list are executed only once. The *expression* in the `for` statement is the condition being tested: It's tested at the start of the loop and before each iteration. The *altering list* contains loop statements that aren't within the compound statement; generally, it's used to increment or decrement a counter each time the loop is executed. Multiple statements in both an initializing and altering list are separated by commas. Here's an example of a `for` loop:

```
for (total = 0, count = 1; count < 10; count++)
{
    cout << "Enter a grade: ";
    total = total + grade;
}
```

In this `for` statement, the initializing list is used to initialize both `total` and `count`. The expression determines that the loop executes as long as the value in `count` is less than 10, and the altering list specifies that the value of `count` is incremented by one each time through the loop.

6. The `for` statement is extremely useful in creating fixed-count loops because you can include initializing statements, the tested expression, and statements affecting the tested expression in parentheses at the top of a `for` loop for easy inspection and modification.

7. The `do` statement is used to create posttest loops because it checks its expression at the end of the loop. Checking at the end of the loop ensures that the body of a `do` loop is executed at least once. A `do` loop must contain at least one statement that alters the tested expression's value.

Programming Projects for Chapter 5

1. **(Probability)** The probability that a telephone call will last less than *t* minutes can be approximated by the exponential probability function:

   Probability that a call lasts less than t minutes = 1 - $e^{-t/a}$

   > *a* is the average call length.
   > *e* is Euler's number (2.71828).

   For example, assuming the average call length is 2 minutes, the probability that a call will last less than 1 minute is calculated as $1 - e^{-1/2} = 0.3297$. Using this probability equation, write a C++ program that calculates and displays a list of probabilities of a call lasting less than 1 minute to less than 10 minutes, in 1-minute increments.

2. **(Probability)** **a.** The arrival rate of customers in a busy New York bank can be estimated by using the Poisson probability function:

   $$P(x) = \frac{\lambda^x e^{-\lambda}}{x!}$$

x is the number of customer arrivals per minute.

λ is the average number of arrivals per minute.

e is Euler's number (2.71828).

For example, if the average number of customers entering the bank is three customers per minute, then λ is equal to three. Therefore, the probability of one customer arriving in any one minute is

$$P(x=1) = \frac{3^1 e^{-3}}{1!} = 0.149561$$

and the probability of two customers arriving in any one minute is the following:

$$P(x=2) = \frac{3^2 e^{-3}}{2!} = 0.224454$$

Using the Poisson probability function, write a C++ program that calculates and displays the probability of 1 to 10 customer arrivals in any one minute when the average arrival rate is 3 customers per minute.

b. The formula given in Exercise 2a is also applicable for estimating the arrival rate of planes at a busy airport. (In this situation, an arriving "customer" is an incoming plane.) Using this same formula, modify the program written in Exercise 2a to accept the average arrival rate as an input data item. Then run the modified program to determine the probability of 0 to 10 planes attempting to land at an airport in any one-minute period during peak arrival times. Assume that the average arrival rate for peak arrival times is two planes per minute.

3. (Physics) A golf ball is dropped from an airplane. The distance, *d*, the ball falls in *t* seconds is given by the formula $d = \frac{1}{2} g t^2$, where *g* is the acceleration caused by gravity and is equal to 32 ft/sec². Using this information, write and run a C++ program that displays the distance fallen in each one-second interval for 10 seconds and the total distance the golf ball falls at the end of each interval. The output should complete the following chart:

Time (sec)	Distance in the Current Time Interval (ft)	Total Distance (ft)
0	0.0	
1	16.0	
. . .		
10		

4. (Physics) Assume the airplane in Exercise 3 is flying at a height of 50,000 feet. Modify the program written for Exercise 3 to determine how long it will take the ball to reach the ground. To increase the accuracy of your result without an undue number of calculations, decrease the time interval from 1 second to 0.1 second as the ball nears the ground.

5. (Numerical Analysis) The Fibonacci sequence is 0, 1, 1, 2, 3, 5, 8, 13, . . . ; the first two terms are 0 and 1, and each term thereafter is the sum of the two preceding terms—that is, $Fib[n] = Fib[n-1] + Fib[n-2]$. Using this information, write a C++ program that calculates the *n*th number in a Fibonacci sequence, where the user enters *n* into the program interactively. For example, if *n* = 6, the program should display the value 5.

6. (**Numerical Analysis**) Develop, test, and execute a C++ program that uses a `while` loop to determine the smallest integer power of 3 that exceeds 30,000. That is, find the smallest value of *n* so that $3^n > 30,000$. (*Hint*: Initialize `PowerOfThree = 1`, and then accumulate the expression `PowerOfThree = 3 * PowerOfThree`.)

7. (**Numerical Analysis**) A prime integer number is one that has exactly two different divisors, namely 1 and the number itself. Write, run, and test a C++ program that finds and prints all the prime numbers less than 100. (*Hint*: 1 is a prime number. For each number from 2 to 100, find `Remainder = Number % n`, where n ranges from 2 to `sqrt(number)`. If n is greater than `sqrt(number)`, the number is not equally divisible by n. Why? If any `Remainder` equals 0, the number is not a prime number.)

8. (**Numerical Analysis**) The quotient in long division is the number of times the divisor can be subtracted from the dividend. The remainder is what's left over after the last subtraction. Write a C++ program that performs division by using this method.

9. (**Conversion**) Print the decimal, octal, and hexadecimal values of all characters between the start and stop characters entered by a user. For example, if the user enters an `'a'` and a `'z'`, the program should print all the characters between a and z and their respective values. Make sure the second character the user enters occurs later in the alphabet than the first character. If it doesn't, write a loop that asks the user repeatedly for a valid second character.

10. (**Misc. Application**) **a.** An old Arabian legend has it that a fabulously wealthy but unthinking king agreed to give a beggar one cent and double the amount for 64 days. Using this information, write, run, and test a C++ program that displays how much the king must pay the beggar on each day. The output of your program should appear as follows:

```
Day     Amount Owed
---     -----------
 1          0.01
 2          0.02
 3          0.04
 .           .
 .           .
 .           .
64           .
```

b. Modify the program you wrote for Exercise 10a to determine on which day the king will have paid the beggar a total of one million dollars.

11. (**Misc. Application**) According to legend, the island of Manhattan was purchased from the native Indian population in 1626 for $24. Assuming this money was invested in a Dutch bank paying 5% simple interest per year, construct a table showing how much money the native population would have at the end of each 50-year period, starting in 1626 and ending 400 years later.

Engineering and Scientific Disciplines

Industrial Engineering

Each of the traditional engineering disciplines (civil, mechanical, electrical, chemical, and metallurgical/mining) relies on a particular area of natural science for its foundation. Industrial engineering, however, incorporates knowledge of the social sciences into designing improvements in human-machine systems. Industrial engineers are responsible for designing, installing, and evaluating machines and systems and for monitoring their interface with people to improve overall productivity. This job can also involve understanding human behavioral characteristics and their effects on the design of machines or the workplace. Industrial engineers draw heavily on knowledge in economics, business management, and finance as well as in the natural sciences. The areas of specialization for industrial engineers can be divided into four categories:

- Operations research: This area involves applying analytical techniques and mathematical models to phenomena such as inventory control, simulation, decision theory, and queuing theory to optimize the total systems necessary for the production of goods.
- Management or administrative engineering: The increasingly complex interplay of management and production skills in modern industrial operations has resulted in a need for technically trained managers. These managers evaluate and plan corporate ventures and interact with labor, engineering departments, and subcontractors. A management engineer can also participate in a company's financial operations, drawing on knowledge in economics, business management, and law.
- Manufacturing and production engineering: Before a product is produced, the complete manufacturing process must be designed and set up to optimize the economics involved and the product's final quality. This task requires a broad knowledge of process design, plant layouts, tool design, robotics, and human-machine interactions.
- Information systems: This area involves using computers to gather and analyze data for decision making and planning and to improve human-machine interaction.

The following list includes the most common responsibilities of industrial engineers who responded to a recent survey by the American Institute of Industrial Engineers:

Facilities planning and design	Cost control
Methods engineering	Inventory control
Work systems design	Energy conservation
Production engineering	Computerized process control
Management information and control systems	Product packaging, handling, and testing
Organization analysis and design	Tool and equipment selection
Work measurement	Production control
Wage administration	Product improvement study
Quality control	Preventive maintenance
Project management	Safety programs
	Training programs

Chapter 6

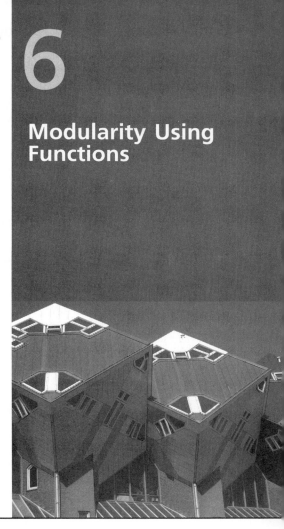

Modularity Using Functions

Professional programs are designed, coded, and tested much like hardware: as a set of modules integrated to perform a completed whole. A good analogy is an automobile; one major module is the engine, another is the transmission, a third the braking system, a fourth the body, and so on. All these modules are linked together and placed under the driver's control, which can be compared to a supervisor or main program module. The whole now operates as a complete unit, able to do useful work, such as driving to the store. During the assembly process, each module is constructed, tested, and found to be free of defects (bugs) before it's installed in the final product.

Now think of what you might do if you wanted to improve your car's performance. You might alter the existing engine or remove it and replace it with a new engine, or you might replace the transmission. You can make each modification separately as your time and budget allow. The majority of the other modules can stay the same, but the car operates differently after your changes are made.

In this analogy, each major car component can be compared to a function. For example, the driver calls on the engine when the gas pedal is pressed. The engine accepts inputs of fuel, air, and electricity to turn the driver's request into a useful product—power—and then sends this output to the transmission for further processing. The transmission receives the engine's output and converts it to a form the drive axle can use.

The engine, transmission, and other modules "know" only the universe bounded by their inputs and outputs. The driver doesn't need to know the internal operation of the modules being controlled. All that's required is understanding what each unit does and how to use it. The driver simply "calls" on a module, such as the brakes, when that module's output is required. Communication between modules is restricted to passing inputs to each module as it's called on to perform its task, and each module operates in a fairly independent manner. Programmers use this same modular approach to create and maintain reliable C++ programs by using functions.

As you have seen, each C++ program must contain a main() *function. In addition to this required function, C++ programs can also contain any number of other functions. In this chapter, you learn how to write these functions, pass data to them, process the passed data, and return a result.*

6.1 Function and Parameter Declarations

In creating C++ functions, you must be concerned with the function itself and how it interacts with other functions, such as main(). Interaction with a function includes passing data to a function correctly when it's called and returning values from a function when it ceases operation. This section describes the first part of the interface, passing data to a function and having the function receive, store, and process the transmitted data correctly.

As you have already seen with mathematical functions, a function is called, or used, by giving the function's name and passing any data to it, as arguments, in the parentheses following the function name (see Figure 6.1). The called function must be able to accept the data passed to it by the function doing the calling. Only after the called function receives the data successfully can the data be manipulated to produce a useful result.

function-name (*data passed to function*);

This identifies the   This passes data
called function   to the function

Figure 6.1   Calling and passing data to a function

To clarify the process of sending and receiving data, take a look at Program 6.1, which calls a function named findMax(). The program, as shown, is not yet complete. After the function findMax() is written and included in Program 6.1, the completed program, consisting of the functions main() and findMax(), can be compiled and executed.

Program 6.1

```cpp
#include <iostream>
using namespace std;

void findMax(int, int);  // the function declaration (prototype)

int main()
{
  int firstnum, secnum;

  cout << "\nEnter a number: ";
  cin  >> firstnum;
  cout << "Great! Please enter a second number: ";
  cin  >> secnum;

  findMax(firstnum, secnum); // the function is called here

  return 0;
}
```

First, examine the declaration and calling of the findMax() function from main(). You then see how to write findMax() to accept data passed to it and determine the largest or maximum value of the two passed values.

The function findMax() is referred to as the **called function** because it's called or summoned into action by its reference in main(). The function that does the calling, in this case main(), is referred to as the **calling function**. The terms "called" and "calling" come from standard telephone usage, in which one party calls the other. The person initiating the call is referred to as the calling party, and the person receiving the call is referred to as the called party. The same terms describe function calls. The called function, in this case findMax(), is declared as a function that expects to receive two integer numbers and to return no value (a void) to main(). This declaration is formally referred to as a function prototype. The function is then called by the last statement in the program.

Function Prototypes

Before a function can be called, it must be declared to the function that will do the calling. The declaration statement for a function is referred to as a **function prototype**. The function prototype tells the calling function the type of value that will be formally returned, if any, and the data type and order of the values the calling function should transmit to the called function. For example, the function prototype previously used in Program 6.1

```cpp
void findMax(int, int);
```

declares that the function findMax() expects two integer values to be sent to it and that this function formally returns no value (void).

Function prototypes can be placed with the variable declaration statements of the calling function, above the calling function name (as in Program 6.1), or in a separate header file specified with an #include preprocessor statement. The function prototype for findMax() could have been placed before or after the statement #include <iostream>, before main(), or within main(). (The reasons for the choice of placement are explained in Section 6.3.) The general form of function prototype statements is as follows:

returnDataType functionName(list of argument data types);

The *DataType* refers to the type of value the function returns. Here are some examples of function prototypes:

```
int fmax(int, int);
double swap(int, char, char, double);
void display(double, double);
```

The function prototype for fmax() declares that this function expects to receive two integer arguments and returns an integer value. The function prototype for swap() declares that this function requires four arguments—consisting of an integer, two characters, and a double-precision argument, in that order—and returns a double-precision number. Finally, the function prototype for display() declares that this function requires two double-precision arguments and doesn't return any value. This function might be used to display the results of a computation without returning any value to the called function.

The use of function prototypes permits the compiler to error-check data types. If the function prototype doesn't agree with data types defined when the function is written, a compiler warning occurs. The prototype also serves another task: It ensures that all arguments passed to the function are converted to the declared data type when the function is called.

Calling a Function

Calling a function is rather easy. The only requirements are using the name of the function and enclosing any data passed to the function in the parentheses following the function name, using the same order and type declared in the function prototype. The items enclosed in parentheses are called **arguments** of the called function (see Figure 6.2).

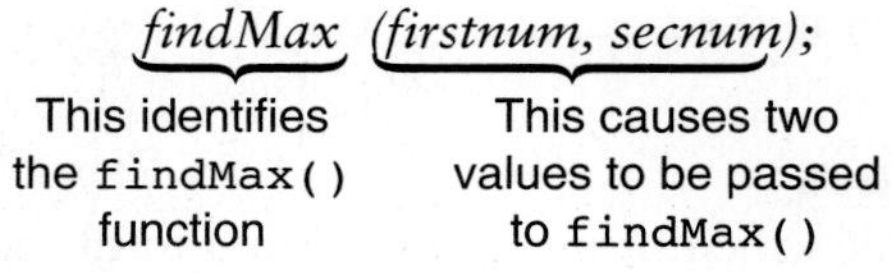

findMax *(firstnum, secnum);*

This identifies	This causes two
the findMax()	values to be passed
function	to findMax()

Figure 6.2 Calling and passing two values to findMax()

If a variable is one of the arguments in a function call, the called function receives a copy of the value stored in the variable. For example, the statement findMax(firstnum, secnum); calls the findMax() function and causes the values stored in the variables firstnum and secnum to be passed to findMax(). The variable names in parentheses are arguments that provide values to the called function. After values are passed, control is transferred to the called function.

As illustrated in Figure 6.3, the findMax() function *does not* receive the variables named firstnum and secnum and has *no* knowledge of these variable names.[1] The function simply receives the values in these variables and must then determine where to store these values before it does anything else. Although this procedure for passing data to a function might seem surprising, it's actually a safety procedure for ensuring that a called function doesn't inadvertently change data stored in a variable. The function gets a copy of the data to use. It can change its copy and, of course, change any variables declared within it. However, unless specific steps to do so are taken, a function isn't allowed to change the contents of variables declared in other functions.

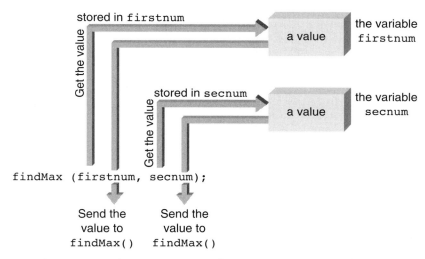

Figure 6.3 The findMax() function receives actual values

Next, you begin writing the findMax() function to process the values passed to it.

Defining a Function

A function is defined when it's written. Each function is defined once (that is, written once) in a program and can then be used by any other function in the program that declares it suitably.

Like the main() function, every C++ function consists of two parts, a **function header** and a **function body**, as illustrated in Figure 6.4. The function header's purpose is to identify the data type of the value the function returns, provide the function with a name, and specify the number, order, and type of arguments the function expects. The function body's purpose is to operate on the passed data and return, at most, one value directly back to the calling function. (In Section 6.3, you see how a function can be made to return multiple values indirectly.)

---

[1]In Section 6.3, you see how C++ also permits direct access to the calling function's variables with reference variables.

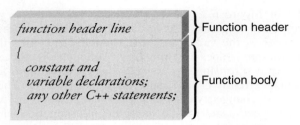

Figure 6.4   The general format of a function

The function header is always the first line of a function and contains the function's returned value type, its name, and the names and data types of its parameters. Because findMax() doesn't formally return any value and receives two integer values, the following function header can be used:

void findMax(int x, int y) ◀─────────── no semicolon

The names in parentheses in the header are called the **formal parameters** of the function (or parameters, for short).[2] Therefore, the parameter x is used to store the first value passed to findMax(), and the parameter y is used to store the second value passed at the time of the function call. The function doesn't know where the values come from when the call is made from main(). The first part of the call procedure the computer executes involves going to the variables firstnum and secnum and retrieving the stored values. These values are then passed to findMax() and stored in the parameters x and y (see Figure 6.5).

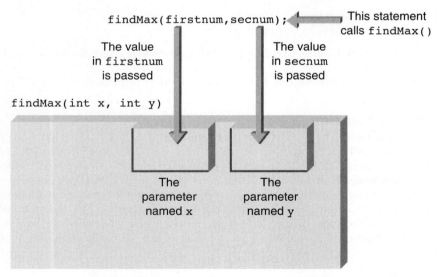

Figure 6.5   Storing values in parameters

---

[2]The portion of the function header containing function names and parameters is formally referred to as a "function declarator." The items enclosed in parentheses, the parameters, are specifications for the arguments. The arguments are the values provided when the function is called.

Point of Information

Function Definitions and Function Prototypes

When you write a function, you're formally creating a function definition. Each definition begins with a function header that includes a parameter list, if any, enclosed in parentheses and ends with the closing brace that terminates the function's body. The parentheses are required whether or not the function uses any parameters. The following is a commonly used syntax for a function definition:

```
returnDataType functionName(parameter list)
{
  constant declarations
  variable declarations

  other C++ statements

  return value
}
```

A function prototype declares a function. The syntax for a function prototype, which provides the function's return data type, the function's name, and the function's parameter list, is as follows:

```
returnDataType functionName(list of parameter data types);
```

The prototype, along with pre- and postcondition comments (see the next Point of Information box), should give users all the programming information needed to call the function successfully.

Generally, all function prototypes are placed at the top of the program, and all definitions are placed after the `main()` function. However, this placement can be changed. The only requirement in C++ is that a function can't be called before it has been declared or defined.

The function name and all parameter names in the header—in this case, `findMax`, `x`, and `y`—are chosen by the programmer. Any names selected according to the rules for choosing variable names can be used. All parameters listed in the function header must be separated by commas and have their data types declared separately.

Now that the function header for `findMax()` has been written, you can construct its body. The function has been written to select and display the larger of the two numbers passed to it.

A function body begins with an opening brace, {, contains any necessary declarations and other C++ statements, and ends with a closing brace, }. This structure should be familiar because it's the same one used in all the `main()` functions you've seen so far. This required structure shouldn't be a surprise because `main()` is a function and must adhere to the rules for constructing all legitimate functions, as shown here:

```
{
  symbolic constant declarations,
  variable declarations, and
  other C++ statements
}
```

Point of Information

Preconditions and Postconditions

Preconditions are any set of conditions a function requires to be true if it's to operate correctly. For example, if a function uses the symbolic constant MAXCHARS, which must have a positive value, a precondition is that MAXCHARS must be declared with a positive value before the function is called. Similarly, a **postcondition** is a condition that will be true after the function is executed, assuming the preconditions are met.

Pre- and postconditions are typically documented as user comments. For example, examine the following declaration and comments:

```
bool leapyr(int)
// Precondition: the integers must represent a year in a four-digit
//               form, such as 2009
// Postcondition: a value of true is returned if the year is a leap year;
//                otherwise, false is returned
```

Pre- and postcondition comments should be included with function prototypes and function definitions whenever clarification is needed.

In the body of the findMax() function, one variable is declared to store the maximum of the two numbers passed to it. An if-else statement is then used to find the maximum of the two numbers. Finally, a cout statement is used to display the maximum. The following shows the complete function definition for findMax():

```
void findMax(int x, int y)
{                       // start of function body
  int maxnum;           // variable declaration

  if (x >= y)           // find the maximum number
    maxnum = x;
  else
    maxnum = y;

  cout << "\nThe maximum of the two numbers is "
       << maxnum << endl;

  return;
}  // end of function body and end of function
```

Notice that the parameter declarations are made in the function header, and the variable declaration is made immediately after the function body's opening brace. This placement is in keeping with the concept that parameter values are passed to a function from outside the function, and variables are declared and assigned values from within the function body. Program 6.2 includes the findMax() function in the program code previously listed in Program 6.1.

Program 6.2

```cpp
#include <iostream>
using namespace std;

void findMax(int, int);   // the function prototype

int main()
{
  int firstnum, secnum;

  cout << "\nEnter a number: ";
  cin  >> firstnum;
  cout << "Great! Please enter a second number: ";
  cin  >> secnum;

  findMax(firstnum, secnum); // the function is called here

  return 0;
}

// following is the function FindMax()

void findMax(int x, int y)
{                       // start of function body
  int maxnum;           // variable declaration

  if (x >= y)           // find the maximum number
    maxnum = x;
  else
    maxnum = y;

  cout << "\nThe maximum of the two numbers is "
       << maxnum << endl;

  return;
}  // end of function body and end of function
```

Program 6.2 can be used to select and print the maximum of any two integer numbers the user enters. A sample run of Program 6.2 follows:

```
Enter a number: 25
Great! Please enter a second number: 5

The maximum of the two numbers is 25
```

The placement of the `findMax()` function after the `main()` function in Program 6.2 is a matter of choice. Usually, `main()` is listed first because it's the driver function that gives anyone reading the program an idea of what the complete program is about before encountering the details of each function. In no case, however, can the definition of `findMax()` be placed inside `main()`. This rule applies to all C++ functions, which must be defined by themselves outside any other function. Each C++ function is a separate and independent entity with its own parameters and variables; nesting functions is *never* permitted.

Placement of Statements

C++ doesn't impose a rigid statement-ordering structure on programmers. The general rule for placing statements in a C++ program is simply that all preprocessor directives, named constants, variables, and functions must be declared or defined before they can be used. As noted previously, although this rule permits placing both preprocessor directives and declaration statements throughout a program, doing so results in poor program structure.

As a matter of good programming form, the following statement ordering should form the basic structure around which all C++ programs are constructed:

```
preprocessor directives

function prototypes

  int main()
  {
    // symbolic constants
    // variable declarations

    // other executable statements

    // return statement
  }

// function definitions
```

As always, comment statements can be intermixed anywhere in this basic structure.

Function Stubs

An alternative to completing each function required in a complete program is writing the `main()` function first and then adding the remaining functions as they're developed.

The problem with this approach, however, is the same one that occurred with Program 6.1: The program can't be run until all the functions are included. For convenience, the code for Program 6.1 has been reproduced here:

```cpp
#include <iostream>
using namespace std;

void findMax(int, int);   // the function declaration (prototype)

int main()
{
  int firstnum, secnum;

  cout << "\nEnter a number: ";
  cin  >> firstnum;
  cout << "Great! Please enter a second number: ";
  cin  >> secnum;

  findMax(firstnum, secnum); // the function is called here

  return 0;
}
```

This program would be complete if there were a function definition for findMax(). However, you really don't need a *correct* findMax() function to test and run what has been written; you just need a function that acts like it is. A "fake" findMax() that accepts the correct number and types of parameters and returns values of the proper form for the function call is all you need for initial testing. This fake function, called a **stub**, is the beginning of a final function and can be used as a placeholder for the final unit until the unit is completed. A stub for findMax() is as follows:

```cpp
void findMax(int x, int y)
{
  cout << "In findMax()\n";
  cout << "The value of x is " << x << endl;
  cout << "The value of x is " << y << endl;
}
```

This stub function can now be compiled and linked with the previously completed code to produce an executable program. The code for the function can then be further developed with the "real" code when it's completed, replacing the stub portion.

The minimum requirement of a stub function is that it compiles and links with its calling module. In practice, it's a good idea to have a stub display a message that it has been entered successfully and display the values of its received parameters, as in the stub for findMax(). As the function is refined, you let it do more, perhaps allowing it to return intermediate or incomplete results. This incremental, or stepwise, refinement is an important concept in efficient program development that gives you the means to run a program that doesn't yet meet all its final requirements.

Functions with Empty Parameter Lists

Although useful functions having an empty parameter list are extremely limited, they can occur. (You see one such function in Exercise 11 at the end of this section.) The function

Point of Information

Isolation Testing

One of the most successful software testing methods is to embed the code being tested in an environment of working code. For example, you have two untested functions called in the following order, and the result the second function returns is incorrect:

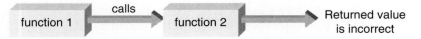

From the information shown in this figure, one or possibly both of the functions could be operating incorrectly. The first order of business is to isolate the problem to a specific function.

One powerful method of performing this code isolation is to decouple the functions. You do this by testing each function separately or by testing one function first and, only after you know it's operating correctly, reconnecting it to the second function. Then, if an error occurs, you have isolated the error to the transfer of data between functions or the internal operation of the second function.

This procedure is an example of the basic rule of testing, which states that each function should be tested only in a program in which all other functions are known to be correct. This rule means one function must first be tested by itself, using stubs if necessary for any called functions, and a second tested function should be tested by itself or with a previously tested function, and so on. This testing procedure ensures that each new function is isolated in a test bed of correct functions, with the final program built from tested function code.

prototype for such a function requires writing the keyword void or nothing at all between the parentheses following the function's name. For example, both these prototypes

```
int display();
```

and

```
int display(void);
```

indicate that the `display()` function takes no parameters and returns an integer. A function with an empty parameter list is called by its name with nothing written inside the required parentheses following the function's name. For example, the statement `display();` correctly calls the `display()` function, whose prototype is shown in the preceding example.

Default Arguments[3]

C++ provides **default arguments** in a function call for added flexibility. The primary use of default arguments is to extend the parameter list of existing functions without requiring any change in the calling parameter lists already used in a program.

Default argument values are listed in the function prototype and transmitted automatically to the called function when the corresponding arguments are omitted from the function call. For example, the function prototype

```
void example(int, int = 5, double = 6.78);
```

provides default values for the last two arguments. If any argument is omitted when the function is actually called, the C++ compiler supplies the default values. Therefore, all the following function calls are valid:

```
example(7, 2, 9.3)   // no defaults used
example(7, 2)        // same as example(7, 2, 6.78)
example(7)           // same as example(7, 5, 6.78)
```

Four rules must be followed when using default arguments. First, default values should be assigned in the function prototype.[4] Second, if any parameter is given a default value in the function prototype, all parameters following it must also be supplied with default values. Third, if one argument is omitted in the actual function call, all arguments to its right must also be omitted. The second and third rules make it clear to the C++ compiler which arguments are being omitted and permits the compiler to supply correct default values for the missing arguments, starting with the rightmost argument and working in toward the left. Fourth, the default value used in the function prototype can be an expression consisting of both constants and previously declared variables. If this kind of expression is used, it must pass the compiler's check for validly declared variables, even though the expression's actual value is evaluated and assigned at runtime.

Default arguments are extremely useful when extending an existing function to include more features that require additional arguments. Adding new arguments to the right of the existing arguments and giving each new argument a default value permits all existing function calls to remain as they are. In this way, the effect of the changes are conveniently isolated from existing code in the program.

Reusing Function Names (Overloading)[5]

C++ provides the capability of using the same function name for more than one function, referred to as **function overloading**. The only requirement for creating more than one function with the same name is that the compiler must be able to determine which function to use based on the parameters' data types (not the data type of the return value, if any). For example, take a look at the three following functions, all named cdabs():

```
void cdabs(int x)   //
 compute and display the absolute value of an integer
{
  if ( x < 0 )
    x = -x;
```

☞

---

[3]This topic can be omitted on first reading without loss of subject continuity.
[4]Some compilers accept default assignments in the function definition.
[5]This topic can be omitted on first reading without loss of subject continuity.

```
  cout << "The absolute value of the integer is " << x << endl;
}

void cdabs(float x)  // compute and display the absolute value of a float
{
  if ( x < 0 )
    x = -x;
  cout << "The absolute value of the float is " << x << endl;
}

void cdabs(double x)  //
 compute and display the absolute value of a double
{
  if ( x < 0 )
    x = -x;
  cout << "The absolute value of the double is " << x << endl;
}
```

Which of the three functions named cdabs() is actually called depends on the argument type supplied at the time of the call. Therefore, the function call cdabs(10); causes the compiler to use the function named cdabs() that expects an integer argument, and the function call cdabs(6.28f); causes the compiler to use the function named cdabs() that uses a single-precision argument.[6]

Notice that overloading a function's name simply means using the same name for more than one function. Each function that uses the name must still be written and exists as a separate entity. The use of the same function name doesn't require code in the functions to be similar, although good programming practice dictates that functions with the same name should perform essentially the same operations. All that's required to use the same function name is that the compiler can distinguish which function to select, based on the data types of the arguments when the function is called. However, if the only difference in the overloaded functions is the argument types, a better programming solution is to create a function template, discussed next. The use of overloaded functions, however, is extremely useful with constructor functions, explained in Section 10.2.

Function Templates[7]

In most high-level languages, including C++'s immediate predecessor, C, each function requires its own unique name. In theory, using unique names makes sense, but in practice, it can lead to a profusion of function names, even for functions that perform essentially the same operations. For example, consider determining and displaying a number's absolute value. If the number passed to the function can be an integer, a single-precision value, or a double-precision value, three distinct functions must be written to handle each case correctly.

---

[6]Selection of the correct function is accomplished by a process called "name mangling." Using this process, the function name the C++ compiler actually generates differs from the function name used in the source code. The compiler appends information to the source code function, depending on the type of data being passed, and the resulting name is said to be a "mangled" version of the source code name.
[7]This topic can be omitted on first reading without loss of subject continuity.

Certainly, you could give each function a unique name, such as `abs()`, `fabs()`, and `dabs()`, having the following function prototypes:

```
void abs(int);
void fabs(float);
void dabs(double);
```

Each of these functions performs essentially the same operation but on different parameter data types. A much cleaner solution is writing a general function that handles all cases, but the compiler can set parameters, variables, and even return type based on the actual function call. You can write this type of function in C++ by using function templates. A **function template** is a single, complete function that serves as a model for a family of functions. The function from the family that's actually created depends on subsequent function calls. To make this concept more concrete, take a look at a function template that computes and displays the absolute value of a passed argument:

```
template <class T>
void showabs(T number)
{
  if (number < 0)
    number = -number;
  cout << "The absolute value of the number "
       << " is " << number << endl;

  return;
}
```

For the moment, ignore the first line, `template <class T>`, and look at the second line, which consists of the function header `void showabs(T number)`. Notice that this function header has the same syntax used for all function definitions, except the T where a data type is usually placed. For example, if the function header were `void showabs(int number)`, you should recognize it as a function named `showabs()` that expects one integer argument to be passed to it and returns no value. Similarly, if the function header were `void showabs(double number)`, you should recognize it as a function that expects one double-precision argument to be passed to it when the function is called.

The advantage of using the `T` in the function template header is that it represents a general data type that's replaced by an actual data type, such as `int`, `float`, `double`, and so forth, when the compiler encounters an actual function call. For example, if a function call with an integer argument is encountered, the compiler uses the function template to construct a function that expects an integer parameter. Similarly, if a call is made with a double-precision argument, the compiler constructs a function that expects a double-precision parameter. As a specific example, take a look at Program 6.3.

Program 6.3

```cpp
#include <iostream>
using namespace std;

template <class T>
void showabs(T number)
{
  if (number < 0)
    number = -number;
  cout << "The absolute value of the number is "
       << number << endl;
  return;
}

int main()
{
  int num1 = -4;
  float num2 = -4.23f;
  double num3 = -4.23456;

  showabs(num1);
  showabs(num2);
  showabs(num3);

  return 0;
}
```

Notice the three function calls made in the main() function; they call the function showabs() with an integer, float, and double value. Now review the function template for showabs() and look at the first line, template <class T>. This line, called a **template prefix**, is used to inform the compiler that the function immediately following is a template using a data type named T. In the function template, the T is used in the same manner as any other data type, such as int, float, and double. When the compiler encounters an actual function call for showabs(), the data type of the argument passed in the call is substituted for T throughout the function. In effect, the compiler creates a specific function, using the template, that expects the argument type in the call.

Because Program 6.3 makes three calls to showabs(), each with a different argument data type, the compiler creates three separate showabs() functions. The compiler knows which function to use based on the arguments passed at the time of the call. This is the output displayed when Program 6.3 runs:

```
The absolute value of the number is 4
The absolute value of the number is 4.23
The absolute value of the number is 4.23456
```

The letter T used in the template prefix template <class T> is simply a placeholder for a data type that's defined when the function is actually called. Any letter or non-keyword identifier can be used instead, so the showabs() function template could just as well have been defined as follows:

```
template <class DTYPE>
void abs(DTYPE number)
{
  if (number < 0)
    number = -number;
  cout << "The absolute value of the number is "
       << number << endl;
  return;
}
```

In this regard, sometimes it's simpler and clearer to read the word *class* in the template prefix as the words *data type*. With this substitution, you can read the template prefix template <class T> as "I'm defining a function template that has a data type named T." Then, in the defined function's header and body, the data type T (or any other letter or identifier defined in the prefix) is used in the same manner as any built-in data type, such as int, float, and double.

Now suppose you want to create a function template to include both a return type and an internally declared variable. For example, take a look the following function template:

```
template <class T> // template prefix
T abs(T value)      // function header line
{
  T absnum;   // variable declaration

  if (value < 0)
    absnum = -value;
  else
    absnum = value;

  return absnum;
}
```

In this template definition, the date type T is used to declare three items: the return type of the function, the data type of a single function parameter named value, and one variable declared in the function. Program 6.4 shows how this function template could be used in the context of a complete program.

Program 6.4

```cpp
#include <iostream>
using namespace std;

template <class T> // template prefix
T abs(T value)     // header line
{
  T absnum;  // variable declaration

  if (value < 0)
    absnum = -value;
  else
    absnum = value;

  return absnum;
}

int main()
{
  int num1 = -4;
  float num2 = -4.23f;
  double num3 = -4.23456;

  cout << "The absolute value of " << num1
       << " is " << abs(num1) << endl;
  cout << "The absolute value of " << num2
       << " is " << abs(num2) << endl;
  cout << "The absolute value of " << num3
       << " is " << abs(num3) << endl;

  return 0;
}
```

In the first call to abs() made within main(), an integer value is passed as an argument. In this case, the compiler substitutes an int data type for the T data type in the function template and creates the following function:

```cpp
int abs(int value) // header line
{
  int absnum;  // variable declaration
  if (value < 0)
    absnum = -value;
  else
    absnum = value;
  return absnum;
}
```

Similarly, in the second and third function calls, the compiler creates two more functions: one in which the data type `T` is replaced by the keyword `float`, and one in which the data type `T` is replaced by the keyword `double`. This is the output produced by Program 6.4:

```
The absolute value of -4 is 4
The absolute value of -4.23 is 4.23
The absolute value of -4.23456 is 4.23456
```

The value of using a function template is that one function definition has been used to create three different functions, each of which uses the same logic and operations but operates on different data types.

Finally, although both Programs 6.3 and 6.4 define a function template using a single placeholder data type, function templates with more than one data type can be defined. For example, the template prefix

```
template <class DTYPE1, class DTYPE2, class DTYPE3>
```

can be used to create a function template requiring three different data types. As before, in the function template's header and body, the data types `DTYPE1`, `DTYPE2`, and `DTYPE3` are used in the same manner as any built-in data type, such as `int`, `float`, and `double`. Also, as noted previously, the names `DTYPE1`, `DTYPE2`, and `DTYPE3` can be any non-keyword identifier. Conventionally, the letter T followed by zero or more digits is used, such as T, T1, T2, T3, and so forth.

EXERCISES 6.1

1. **(Practice)** For the following function headers, determine the number, type, and order (sequence) of the values that must be passed to the function:
   a. `void factorial(int n)`
   b. `void volts(int res, double induct, double cap)`
   c. `void power(int type, double induct, double cap)`
   d. `void flag(char type, double current, double time)`
   e. `void total(double amount, double rate)`
   f. `void roi(int a, int b, char c, char d, double e, double f)`
   g. `void getVal(int item, int iter, char decflag, char delim)`

2. **(Practice) a.** Write a function named `check()` that has three parameters. The first parameter should accept an integer number, and the second and third parameters should accept a double-precision number. The function body should just display the values of data passed to the function when it's called. (*Note*: When tracing errors in functions, having the function display values it has been passed is helpful. Quite often, the error isn't in what the function body does with data, but in the data received and stored.)

   b. Include the function written in Exercise 2a in a working program. Make sure your function is called from `main()`. Test the function by passing various data to it.

3. **(Practice) a.** Write a function named `findAbs()` that accepts a double-precision number passed to it, computes its absolute value, and displays the absolute value. A number's absolute value is the number itself if the number is positive and the negative of the number if the number is negative.

   b. Include the function written in Exercise 3a in a working program. Make sure your function is called from `main()`. Test the function by passing various data to it.

4. **(Practice) a.** Write a function called `mult()` that accepts two floating-point numbers as parameters, multiplies these two numbers, and displays the result.

   b. Include the function written in Exercise 4a in a working program. Make sure your function is called from `main()`. Test the function by passing various data to it.

5. **(Practice) a.** Write a function named `sqrIt()` that computes the square of the value passed to it and displays the result. The function should be capable of squaring numbers with decimal points.

   b. Include the function written in Exercise 5a in a working program. Make sure your function is called from `main()`. Test the function by passing various data to it.

6. **(Practice) a.** Write a function named `powfun()` that raises an integer number passed to it to a positive integer power and displays the result. The positive integer should be the second value passed to the function. Declare the variable used to store the result as a long-integer data type to ensure enough storage for the result.

   b. Include the function written in Exercise 6a in a working program. Make sure your function is called from `main()`. Test the function by passing various data to it.

7. **(Numerical) a.** Write a C++ program that computes and displays the fractional part of any user-entered number. For example, if the number 256.879 is entered, the number 0.879 should be displayed. (*Hint*: Use an int cast.)

   b. Enter, compile, and execute the program written for Exercise 7a.

8. **(Numerical) a.** Write a C++ program that accepts an integer argument and determines whether the passed integer is even or odd. (*Hint*: Use the % operator.)

   b. Enter, compile, and execute the program written for Exercise 8a.

9. **(Practice) a.** Write a function that produces a table of the numbers from 1 to 10, their squares, and their cubes. The function should produce the same display as Program 5.11.

   b. Include the function written in Exercise 9a in a working program. Make sure your function is called from `main()`. Test the function by passing various data to it.

10. **(Modify) a.** Modify the function written for Exercise 9a to accept the starting value of the table, the number of values to be displayed, and the increment between values. If the increment isn't sent explicitly, the function should use a default value of 1. Name your function `selTab()`. A call to `selTab(6,5,2);` should produce a table of five lines, the first line starting with the number 6 and each succeeding number increasing by 2.

   b. Include the function written in Exercise 10a in a working program. Make sure your function is called from `main()`. Test the function by passing various data to it.

11. **(Numerical)** A useful function using no parameters can be constructed to return a value for π that's accurate to the maximum number of decimal places your computer allows. This value is obtained by taking the arcsine of 1.0, which is $\pi / 2$, and multiplying the result by 2. In C++, the required expression is `2.0 * asin(1.0)`; the `asin()` function is provided in the standard C++ mathematics library. (Remember to include `cmath` in your preprocessor directives.) Using this expression, write a C++ function named `pi()` that calculates and displays the value of π. (In the next section, you see how to return this value to the calling function.)

12. **(Practice) a.** Write a function template named `display()` that displays the value of the single argument passed to it when the function is called.

   b. Include the function template created in Exercise 12a in a complete C++ program that calls the function three times: once with a character argument, once with an integer argument, and once with a double-precision argument.

13. **(Numerical) a.** Write a function template named `whole()` that returns the integer value of any argument passed to it when the function is called.

   b. Include the function template created in Exercise 13a in a complete C++ program that calls the function three times: once with a character argument, once with an integer argument, and once with a double-precision argument.

14. **(Numerical) a.** Write a function template named `maximum()` that returns the maximum value of three arguments passed to the function when it's called. Assume that all three arguments are the same data type.

   b. Include the function template created for Exercise 14a in a complete C++ program that calls the function with three integers and then with three double-precision numbers.

15. **(Numerical) a.** Write a function template named `square()` that computes and returns the square of the single argument passed to the function when it's called.

   b. Include the function template created for Exercise 15a in a complete C++ program.

6.2   Returning a Single Value

Using the method of passing data to a function explained in the previous section, the called function receives only copies of the values contained in arguments at the time of the call. (Review Figure 6.3 if it's unclear to you.) When a value is passed to a called function in this manner, the passed argument is referred to as a **passed by value** and is a distinct advantage of C++.[8] Because the called function doesn't have direct access to the variables used as arguments by the calling function, it can't inadvertently alter the value stored in one of these variables.

   The function receiving the passed by value arguments can process the values sent to it in any fashion and return one, and only one, "legitimate" value directly to the calling function (see Figure 6.6). In this section, you see how this value is returned to the calling function. As you

---

[8]This argument is also referred to as a "call by value." These terms, however, don't refer to the function call as a whole, but to how the calling function passes values to the called function.

might expect, given C++'s flexibility, there's a way of returning more than a single value, but that's the topic of the next section.

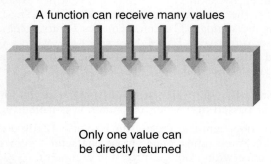

A function can receive many values

Only one value can
be directly returned

Figure 6.6   A function directly returns at most one value

As with calling a function, returning a value directly requires handling the interface between the called and calling functions correctly. From its side of the return transaction, the called function must provide the following items:

- The data type of the returned value
- The actual value being returned

A function returning a value must specify, in its header, the data type of the value to be returned. Recall that the function header includes both the function name and a parameter list. For example, the `findMax()` function written previously determines the maximum value of two numbers passed to it. For convenience, the `findMax()` code is listed again:

```
void findMax(int x, int y)
{                       // start of function body
  int maxnum;           // variable declaration

  if (x >= y)           // find the maximum number
    maxnum = x;
  else
    maxnum = y;

  cout << "\nThe maximum of the two numbers is "
       << maxnum << endl;

  return;
}  // end of function body and end of function
```

In this function header, x and y are the names chosen for the function's parameters:

```
void findMax(int x, int y)
```

If `findMax()` is to return a value, its function header must be amended to include the data type of the value being returned. For example, if an integer value is to be returned, this is the correct function header:

```
int findMax(int x, int y)
```

Similarly, if the function is to receive two single-precision parameters and return a single-precision value, this is the correct function header:

```
float findMax(float x, float y)
```

If the function is to receive two double-precision parameters and return a double-precision value, the function header would be the following:[9]

```
double findMax(double x, double y)
```

Now see how to modify the `findMax()` function to return the maximum value of the two numbers passed to it. To do this, you must first determine the data type of the value to be returned and include this data type in the function header. Because the maximum value determined by `findMax()` is stored in the integer variable `maxnum`, the function should return this variable's value. Returning an integer value from `findMax()` requires the following function declaration:

```
int findMax(int x, int y)
```

Observe that it's the same as the original function header for `findMax()`, with the keyword `int` substituted for the keyword `void`.

Having declared the data type that `findMax()` will return, all that remains is including a statement in the function to cause the return of the correct value. To return a value, a function must use a `return` statement, which has this form:[10]

```
return expression;
```

When the `return` statement is encountered, the expression is evaluated first. The value of the expression is then automatically converted to the data type declared in the function header before being sent back to the calling function. After the value is returned, program control reverts to the calling function. Therefore, to return the value stored in `maxnum`, all you need to do is include the statement `return maxnum;` before the closing brace of the `findMax()` function. The complete function code is as follows:

```
These should ──┬──►int findMax(int x, int y)    // function header
be the same    │   {                            // start of function body
data type      │      int maxnum;               // variable declaration
               │       if (x >= y)
               │          maxnum = x;
               │       else
               │          maxnum = y;
               │
               │       return maxnum;            // return statement
               │   }
               └──────────────────▲
```

---

[9]The return data type is related to the parameter data types only as much as the returned value is typically determined by the parameter values. In this case, because the function is used to return the maximum value of its parameters, it would make little sense to return a data type that doesn't match the function's parameter data types.

[10]Many programmers place the expression in parentheses, as in `return (expression);`. Although either form (with or without parentheses) can be used, choose one and stay with it for consistency.

In this new code for the `findMax()` function, note that the data type of the expression in the `return` statement matches the data type in the function header. It's up to the programmer to ensure this match for every function returning a value. Failure to match the return value with the function's declared data type exactly might not result in an error when your program is compiled, but it could lead to undesired results because the return value is always converted to the data type declared in the function declaration. Usually, this is a problem only when the fractional part of a returned floating-point or double-precision number is truncated because the function was declared to return an integer value.

Having taken care of the sending side of the return transaction, you must now prepare the calling function to receive the value sent by the called function. On the calling (receiving) side, the calling function must

- Be alerted to the type of value to expect back from the called function
- Use the returned value correctly

Alerting the calling function to the type of return value to expect is taken care of by the function prototype. For example, including the function prototype

```
int findMax(int, int);
```

before the `main()` function is enough to alert `main()` that `findMax()` is a function that returns an integer value.

To actually use a returned value, you must provide a variable to store the value or use the value in an expression. To store the returned value in a variable, you use a standard assignment statement. For example, the following assignment statement can be used to store the value returned by `findMax()` in the variable `max`:

```
max = findMax(firstnum, secnum);
```

This assignment statement does two things. First, the right side of the assignment statement calls `findMax()`, and then the result returned by `findMax()` is stored in the variable `max`. Because the value returned by `findMax()` is an integer, the variable `max` should also be declared as an integer variable in the calling function's variable declarations.

The value a function returns need not be stored in a variable, but it can be used wherever an expression is valid. For example, the expression `2 * findMax(firstnum, secnum)` multiplies the value returned by `findMax()` by 2, and the following statement displays the returned value:

```
cout << findMax(firstnum, secnum);
```

Program 6.5 illustrates including prototype and assignment statements for `main()` to declare, call, and store a returned value from `findMax()` correctly. As before, and in keeping with the convention of placing the `main()` function first, the `findMax()` function is placed after `main()`.

Program 6.5

```cpp
#include <iostream>
using namespace std;

int findMax(int, int);   // the function prototype

int main()
{
  int firstnum, secnum, max;

  cout << "\nEnter a number: ";
  cin  >> firstnum;
  cout << "Great! Please enter a second number: ";
  cin  >> secnum;

  max = findMax(firstnum, secnum); // the function is called here

  cout << "\nThe maximum of the two numbers is " << max << endl;

  return 0;
}

int findMax(int x, int y)
{                       // start of function body
  int maxnum;           // variable declaration

  if (x >= y)           // find the maximum number
    maxnum = x;
  else
    maxnum = y;

  return maxnum;        // return statement
}
```

In reviewing Program 6.5, note the four items introduced in this section. First, the function prototype for findMax() is a statement ending with a semicolon, as all declaration statements do; it alerts main() and any subsequent functions using findMax() to the data type that findMax() returns. Second, an assignment statement is used in main() to store the returned value from the findMax() call in the variable max. In Program 6.5, max is declared correctly as an integer in main()'s variable declarations so that it matches the returned value's data type.

The third and fourth items concern coding the findMax() function: The first line of findMax() declares that the function returns an integer value, and the expression in the return statement evaluates to a matching data type. Therefore, findMax() is internally consistent in sending an integer value back to main(), and main() has been alerted to receive and use the returned integer.

In writing your own functions, always keep these four items in mind. For another example, see whether you can identify these four items in Program 6.6.

Program 6.6

```cpp
#include <iostream>
using namespace std;

double tempvert(double);   // function prototype

int main()
{
  const int CONVERTS = 4;   // number of conversions to be made
  int count;
  double fahren;

  for(count = 1; count <= CONVERTS; count++)
  {
    cout << "\nEnter a Fahrenheit temperature: ";
    cin  >> fahren;
    cout << "The Celsius equivalent is "
         << tempvert(fahren) << endl;
  }

  return 0;
}

// convert fahrenheit to celsius
double tempvert(double inTemp)
{
  return (5.0/9.0) * (inTemp - 32.0);
}
```

In reviewing Program 6.6, first analyze the tempvert() function. The function's definition begins with the function header and ends with the closing brace after the return statement. The function is declared as a double, meaning the expression in the function's return statement must evaluate to a double-precision number, which it does. Because a function header is not a statement but the start of the code defining the function, it doesn't end with a semicolon.

On the receiving side, main() has a prototype for the tempvert() function that agrees with tempvert()'s function definition. No variable is declared in main() to store the returned value from `tempvert()` because the returned value is passed immediately to `cout` for display.

Finally, one purpose of declarations, as you learned in Chapter 2, is to alert the computer to the amount of internal storage reserved for data. The prototype for `tempvert()` performs this task and alerts the compiler to the type of storage needed for the returned value. Because `main()` is always the first function in a program, you must include function prototypes for all functions called by `main()` and any subsequent functions.

Inline Functions[11]

Calling a function places a certain amount of overhead on a computer. This overhead consists of the following steps:

1. Placing argument values in a reserved memory region (called the **stack**) that the function has access to
2. Passing control to the function
3. Providing a reserved memory location for any returned value (again, using the stack for this purpose)
4. Returning to the correct point in the calling program

Paying this overhead is justified when a function is called many times because it can reduce a program's size substantially. Instead of the same code being repeated each time it's needed, the code is written once, as a function, and called whenever it's needed.

For small functions that aren't called many times, however, the overhead of passing and returning values might not be warranted. It would still be convenient to group repeating lines of code together under a common function name and have the compiler place this code in the program wherever the function is called. **Inline functions** provide this capability.

Telling the C++ compiler that a function is inline causes a copy of the function code to be placed in the program at the point the function is called. For example, because the `tempvert()` function in Program 6.6 is fairly short, it's an ideal candidate to be an inline function. To make it, or any other function, an inline one simply requires placing the reserved keyword `inline` before the function name and defining the function before any calls are made to it. Program 6.7 makes `tempvert()` an inline function.

Observe in Program 6.7 that the inline function is placed ahead of any calls to it. This placement is a requirement of all inline functions, so a function prototype isn't needed before subsequent calling functions. Because the function is now inline, its code is expanded into the program wherever it's called.

---

[11]This section is optional and can be omitted on first reading without loss of subject continuity.

Program 6.7

```cpp
#include <iostream>
using namespace std;

inline double tempvert(double inTemp)   // an inline function
{
  return (5.0/9.0) * (inTemp - 32.0);
}

int main()
{
  const CONVERTS = 4;    // number of conversions to be made
  int count;
  double fahren;

  for(count = 1; count <= CONVERTS; count++)
  {
    cout << "\nEnter a Fahrenheit temperature: ";
    cin  >> fahren;
    cout << "The Celsius equivalent is "
         << tempvert(fahren) << endl;
  }

  return 0;
}
```

The advantage of using an inline function is an increase in execution speed. Because the inline function is expanded and included in every expression or statement calling it, no execution time is lost because of the call and return overhead a non-inline function requires. The disadvantage is the increase in program size when an inline function is called repeatedly. Each time an inline function is referenced, the complete function code is reproduced and stored as an integral part of the program. A non-inline function, however, is stored in memory only once. No matter how many times the function is called, the same code is used. Therefore, inline functions should be used only for small functions that aren't called extensively in a program.

EXERCISES 6.2

1. **(Modify)** Rewrite Program 6.5 so that the `findMax()` function accepts two double-precision arguments and returns a double-precision value to `main()`. Make sure to modify `main()` to pass two double-precision values to `findMax()` and to accept and store the double-precision value returned by `findMax()`.

2. **(Practice)** For the following function headers, determine the number, type, and order (sequence) of values that should be passed to the function when it's called and the data type of the value the function returns:

   a. `int factorial(int n)`

   b. `double volts(int res, double induct, double cap)`

   c. `double power(int type, double induct, double cap)`

   d. `char flag(char type, float current, float time)`

   e. `int total(float amount, float rate)`

   f. `float roi(int a, int b, char c, char d, float e, float f)`

   g. `void getVal(int item, int iter, char decflag, char delim)`

3. **(Practice)** Write function headers for the following:

   a. A function named `check()` that has three parameters. The first parameter should accept an integer number, and the second and third parameters should accept a double-precision number. The function returns no value.

   b. A function named `findAbs()` that accepts a double-precision number passed to it and returns its absolute value.

   c. A function named `mult()` that accepts two floating-point numbers as parameters, multiplies these two numbers, and returns the result.

   d. A function named `sqrIt()` that computes and returns the square of the integer value passed to it.

   e. A function named `powfun()` that raises an integer number passed to it to a positive integer (as an argument) power and returns the result as an integer.

   f. A function that produces a table of the numbers from 1 to 10, their squares, and their cubes. No arguments are to be passed to the function, and the function returns no value.

4. **(General Math) a.** Write a function named `rightTriangle()` that accepts the lengths of two sides of a right triangle as the arguments a and b. The subroutine should determine and return the hypotenuse, c, of the triangle. (*Hint*: Use Pythagoras' theorem, $c^2 = a^2 + b^2$.)

   b. Include the function written for Exercise 4a in a working program. The `main()` function should call `rightTriangle()` correctly and display the value the function returns.

5. **(General Math) a.** Write a C++ function named `findAbs()` that accepts a double-precision number passed to it, computes its absolute value, and returns the absolute value to the calling function. A number's absolute value is the number itself if the number is positive and the negative of the number if the number is negative.

b. Include the function written in Exercise 5a in a working program. Make sure your function is called from `main()` and returns a value to `main()` correctly. Have `main()` use a `cout` statement to display the returned value. Test the function by passing various data to it.

6. **(General Math) a.** The volume, V, of a cylinder is given by the formula

$V = \pi r^2 L$

where r is the cylinder's radius and L is its length. Using this formula, write a C++ function named `cylvol()` that accepts a cylinder's radius and length and returns its volume.

b. Include the function written in Exercise 6a in a working program. Make sure your function is called from `main()` and returns a value to `main()` correctly. Have `main()` use a `cout` statement to display the returned value. Test the function by passing various data to it.

7. **(General Math) a.** The side surface area, S, of a cylinder is given by the formula

$S = 2\pi r l$

where r is the cylinder's radius, and l is the length of the cylinder. Using this formula, write a C++ function named `surfarea()` that accepts a cylinder's radius and length and returns its side surface area.

b. Include the function written in Exercise 7a in a working program. Make sure your function is called from `main()` and returns a value to `main()` correctly. Have `main()` use a `cout` statement to display the returned value. Test the function by passing various data to it.

8. **(Numerical)** A second-degree polynomial in x is given by the expression $ax^2 + bx + c$, where a, b, and c are known numbers and a is not equal to 0. Write a C++ function named `polyTwo(a,b,c,x)` that computes and returns the value of a second-degree polynomial for any passed values of a, b, c, and x.

9. **(Structural Eng.) a.** The maximum allowable deflection of a beam depends on its function. For a floor, the typical maximum allowable deflection, in inches, is *Dmax = L / 240*, and for a roof beam, *Dmax = L / 180*, where L is the length of the beam in inches. Using these formulas, write and test a function named `maxDeflect()` that accepts the length of a beam, in feet, and the type of beam (floor or roof) as a character code and returns the maximum allowable deflection.

b. Include the function written in Exercise 9a in a working program. Make sure your function is called from `main()` and returns a value to `main()` correctly. Have `main()` use a `cout` statement to display the returned value. Test the function by passing various data to it.

10. **(Structural Eng.) a.** The load, *Pcr*, in units of kips, applied to a column that causes the column to buckle is referred to as the critical buckling load. This load can be determined by using this formula:

Pcr $= \pi^2 E A / (L / r)^2$

E is the modulus of elasticity of the column's material.

A is the cross-sectional area.

L is the length of the column.

r is the column's radius of gyration.

Using this formula, write a C++ function named cLoad() that accepts values of E, A, L, and r and returns the critical buckling load.

b. Include the function written in Exercise 10a in a working program. Make sure your function is called from main() and returns a value to main() correctly. Have main() use a cout statement to display the returned value. Test the function by passing various data to it.

11. **(Numerical) a.** The following is an extremely useful programming algorithm for rounding a real number to n decimal places:

Step 1: Multiply the number by 10^n

Step 2: Add 0.5

Step 3: Delete the fractional part of the result

Step 4: Divide by 10^n

For example, using this algorithm to round the number 78.374625 to three decimal places yields:

Step 1: $78.374625 \times 10^3 = 78374.625$

Step 2: $78374.625 + 0.5 = 78375.125$

Step 3: Retaining the integer part = 78375

Step 4: 78375 divided by $10^3 = 78.375$

Using this algorithm, write a C++ function that accepts a user-entered value and returns the result rounded to two decimal places.

b. Enter, compile, and execute the program written for Exercise 11a.

12. **(Numerical) a.** Write a C++ function named whole() that returns the integer part of any number passed to the function. (*Hint*: Assign the passed argument to an integer variable.)

b. Include the function written in Exercise 12a in a working program. Make sure your function is called from main() and returns a value to main() correctly. Have main() use a cout statement to display the returned value. Test the function by passing various data to it.

13. **(Numerical) a.** Write a C++ function named fracpart() that returns the fractional part of any number passed to it. For example, if the number 256.879 is passed to fracpart(), the number 0.879 should be returned. Have fracpart() call the whole() function you wrote in Exercise 12. The number returned can then be determined as the number passed to fracpart() less the returned value when the same argument is passed to whole(). The completed program should consist of main() followed by fracpart() followed by whole().

b. Include the function written in Exercise 13a in a working program. Make sure your function is called from main() and returns a value to main() correctly. Have main() use a cout statement to display the returned value. Test the function by passing various data to it.

14. **(Numerical)** Years that are evenly divisible by 400 or are evenly divisible by 4 but not by 100 are leap years. For example, because 1600 is evenly divisible by 400, 1600 was a leap year. Similarly, because 1988 is evenly divisible by 4 but not by 100, it was also a leap year. Using this information, write a C++ function that accepts the year as user input and returns a 1 if the passed year is a leap year or a 0 if it isn't.

6.3   Returning Multiple Values

In a typical function invocation, the called function receives values from its calling function, stores and manipulates the passed values, and directly returns at most one value. When data is passed in this manner, it's referred to as a **pass by value**.

Calling a function and passing arguments by value is a distinct advantage of C++. It allows functions to be written as independent entities that can use any variable or parameter name without concern that other functions might be using the same name. It also alleviates any concern that altering a parameter or variable in one function could inadvertently alter a parameter or variable's value in another function. In this approach, parameters can be considered initialized variables, or variables assigned values when the function is executed. At no time, however, does the called function have direct access to any variable defined in the calling function, even if the variable is used as an argument in the function call.

At times, however, you need to modify this approach by giving a called function direct access to its calling function's variables. This approach allows one function—the called function—to use and change the value of variables that have been defined in the calling function. Doing this requires passing the variable's address to the called function. After the called function has the variable's address, it "knows where the variable lives," so to speak, and can access and change the value stored there.

Passing addresses is referred to as a function **pass by reference**[12] because the called function can reference, or access, the variable whose address has been passed. C++ provides two types of address parameters: references and pointers. This section describes the method that uses reference parameters.

Passing and Using Reference Parameters

As always, when exchanging data between two functions, you must be concerned with both the sending and receiving sides. From the sending side, calling a function and passing an address as an argument that's accepted as a reference parameter is the same as calling a function and passing a value; the called function is summoned into action by giving its name and a list of arguments. For example, the statement `newval(firstnum, secnum);` calls the function named `newval()` and passes two arguments to it. Whether a value or an address is actually passed depends on the parameter types declared for `newval()`. Now take a look at writing the `newval()` function and prototype so that it receives the addresses rather than the values of the variables `firstnum` and `secnum`, which are assumed to be double-precision variables.

---

[12]It's also referred to as a "call by reference," and again, both terms refer only to the argument whose address has been passed.

One of the first requirements in writing newval() is to declare two reference parameters for accepting passed addresses. In C++, a reference parameter is declared with this syntax:

dataType& referenceName

For example, the reference declaration

double& num1;

declares that num1 is a reference parameter used to store the address of a double. Similarly, int& secnum; declares that secnum is a reference to an integer, and char& key; declares that key is a reference to a character.

Recall from Section 2.4 that the ampersand, &, in C++ means "the address of." Additionally, when & is used in a declaration, it refers to "the address of" the preceding data type. Using this information, declarations such as double& num1 and int& secnum are sometimes more clearly understood if they are read backward. Reading the declaration double& num1 in this manner yields the information "num1 is the address of a double-precision value."

Because you need to accept two addresses in the parameter list for newval(), the declarations double& num1 and double& num2 can be used. Including these declarations in the parameter list for newval(), and assuming the function returns no value (void), the function header for newval() becomes the following:

void newval(double& num1, double& num2)

For this function header, the following is an appropriate function prototype:

void newval(double&, double&);

This prototype and function header are included in Program 6.8, which uses a newval() function body that displays and alters the values stored in these reference variables from within the called function.

In calling the newval() function in Program 6.8, you need to understand the connection between the arguments, firstnum and secnum, used in the function call and the parameters, xnum and ynum, used in the function header. Both refer to the same data items. The significance is that the values in the arguments (firstnum and secnum) can now be altered from within newval() by using the parameter names (xnum and ynum). Therefore, the parameters xnum and ynum don't store copies of the values in firstnum and secnum; instead, they access the locations in memory set aside for these two arguments.

Program 6.8

```cpp
#include <iostream>
using namespace std;

void newval(double&, double&);  // prototype with two reference parameters

int main()
{
  double firstnum, secnum;

  cout << "Enter two numbers: ";
  cin  >> firstnum >> secnum;
  cout << "\nThe value in firstnum is: " << firstnum << endl;
  cout << "The value in secnum is: " << secnum << "\n\n";
  newval(firstnum, secnum);   // call the function
  cout << "The value in firstnum is now: " << firstnum << endl;
  cout << "The value in secnum is now: " << secnum << endl;

  return 0;
}

void newval(double& xnum, double& ynum)
{
  cout << "The value in xnum is: " << xnum << endl;
  cout << "The value in ynum is: " << ynum << "\n\n";
  xnum = 89.5;
  ynum = 99.5;

  return;
}
```

The equivalence of argument names in Program 6.8, which is the essence of a pass by reference, is illustrated in Figure 6.7. As shown in this figure, the argument names and their matching parameter names are simply different names referring to the same memory storage areas. In main(), these memory locations are referenced by the argument names firstnum and secnum, and in newval(), the same locations are referenced by the parameter names xnum and ynum.

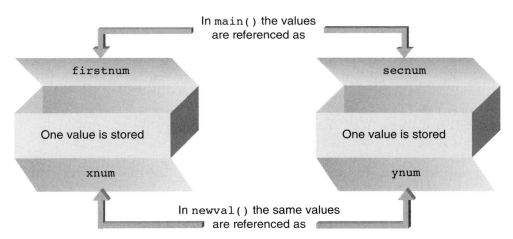

In main() the values
are referenced as

firstnum

One value is stored

xnum

secnum

One value is stored

ynum

In newval() the same values
are referenced as

Figure 6.7 The equivalence of arguments and parameters in Program 6.8

The following is a sample run of Program 6.8:

```
Enter two numbers: 22.5 33.0

The value in firstnum is: 22.5
The value in secnum is:    33

The value in xnum is: 22.5
The value in ynum is: 33

The value in firstnum is now: 89.5
The value in secnum is now: 99.5
```

In reviewing this output, notice that the values initially displayed for the parameters xnum and ynum are the same as those displayed for the arguments firstnum and secnum. Because xnum and ynum are reference parameters, however, newval() now has direct access to the arguments firstnum and secnum. Therefore, any change to xnum in newval() alters the value of firstnum in main(), and any change to ynum changes secnum's value. As the final displayed values show, the assignment of values to xnum and ynum in newval() is reflected in main() as the altering of firstnum's and secnum's values.

The equivalence between actual calling arguments and function parameters shown in Program 6.8 provides the basis for returning multiple values from within a function. For example, say you want to write a function that's required to accept three values, compute these values' sum and product, and return these computed results to the calling routine. By naming the function `calc()` and providing five parameters (three for input data and two references for returned values), the following function can be used:

```
void calc(double num1, double num2, double num3, double& total, double&
product)
{
   total = num1 + num2 + num3;
   product = num1 * num2 * num3;
   return;
}
```

This function has five parameters named num1, num2, num3, total, and product. Only the last two are declared as references, so the first three arguments are passed by value and the last two arguments are passed by reference. In this function, only the last two parameters are altered. The value of the fourth parameter, total, is calculated as the sum of the first three parameters, and the last parameter, product, is computed as the product of the parameters num1, num2, and num3. Program 6.9 includes this function in a complete program.

Program 6.9

```
#include <iostream>
using namespace std;

void calc(double, double, double, double&, double&);   // prototype

int main()
{
   double firstnum, secnum, thirdnum, sum, product;

   cout << "Enter three numbers: ";
   cin  >> firstnum >> secnum >> thirdnum;
   calc(firstnum, secnum, thirdnum, sum, product);   // function call
   cout << "\nThe sum of the numbers is: " << sum << endl;
   cout << "The product of the numbers is: " << product << endl;

   return 0;
}

void calc(double num1, double num2, double num3, double& total, double& product)
{
   total = num1 + num2 + num3;
   product = num1 * num2 * num3;
   return;
}
```

In main(), the function calc() is called with the five arguments firstnum, secnum, thirdnum, sum, and product. As required, these arguments agree in number and data type with the parameters declared by calc(). Of the five arguments passed, only firstnum, secnum, and thirdnum have been assigned values when the call to calc() is made. The remaining two arguments haven't been initialized and are used to receive values back from calc(). Depending on the compiler used, these arguments initially contain zeros or "garbage" values. Figure 6.8 shows the relationship between actual and parameter names and the values they contain after the return from calc().

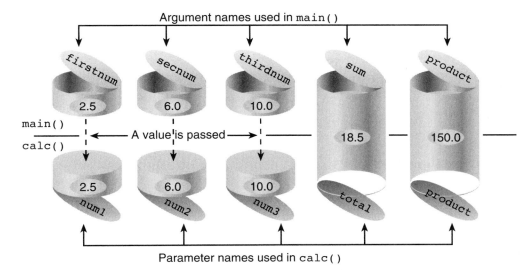

Figure 6.8 The relationship between argument and parameter names

After calc() is called, it uses its first three parameters to calculate values for total and product and then returns control to main(). Because of the order of its actual calling arguments, main() knows the values calculated by calc() as sum and product, which are then displayed. Following is a sample run of Program 6.9:

```
Enter three numbers: 2.5 6.0 10.0

The sum of the entered numbers is: 18.5
The product of the entered numbers is: 150
```

As a final example of the usefulness of passing references to a called function, take a look at constructing a function named swap() that exchanges the values of two of main()'s double-precision variables. This type of function is useful when sorting a list of numbers.

Because the value of more than one variable is affected, swap() can't be written as a pass by value function that returns a single value. The exchange of main()'s variables by swap() can be accomplished only by giving swap() access to main()'s variables. One way of doing this is using reference parameters.

You have already seen how to pass references to two variables in Program 6.8. Now you see how to construct a function to exchange the values in the passed reference parameters.

Exchanging values in two variables is accomplished by using the three-step exchange algorithm:

1. Save the first parameter's value in a temporary location (see Figure 6.9a).
2. Store the second parameter's value in the first variable (see Figure 6.9b).
3. Store the temporary value in the second parameter (see Figure 6.9c).

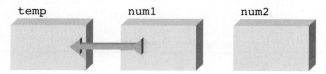

Figure 6.9a   Save the first value

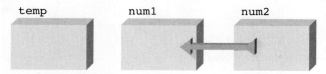

Figure 6.9b   Replace the first value with the second value

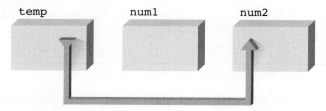

Figure 6.9c   Change the second value

Following is the swap() function written according to these specifications:

```
void swap(double& num1, double& num2)
{
  double temp;

  temp = num1;      // save num1's value
  num1 = num2;      // store num2's value in num1
  num2 = temp;      // change num2's value

  return;
}
```

Notice that the use of references in swap()'s function header gives swap() access to equivalent arguments in the calling function. Therefore, any changes to the two reference parameters in swap() change the values in the calling function's arguments automatically. Program 6.10 contains swap() in a complete program.

Program 6.10

```cpp
#include <iostream>
using namespace std;

void swap(double&, double&);    // function receives two references
int main()
{
  double firstnum = 20.5, secnum = 6.25;

  cout << "The value stored in firstnum is: " << firstnum << endl;
  cout << "The value stored in secnum is: "<< secnum << "\n\n";

  swap(firstnum, secnum);       // call the function with references

  cout << "The value stored in firstnum is now: "
       << firstnum << endl;
  cout << "The value stored in secnum is now: "
       << secnum << endl;

  return 0;
}

void swap(double& num1, double& num2)
{
  double temp;

  temp = num1;      // save num1's value
  num1 = num2;      // store num2's value in num1
  num2 = temp;      // change num2's value

  return;
}
```

The following is a sample run of Program 6.10:

```
The value stored in firstnum is: 20.5
The value stored in secnum is: 6.25

The value stored in firstnum is now: 6.25
The value stored in secnum is now: 20.5
```

As shown by Program 6.10's output, the values stored in main()'s variables have been modified from within swap(), which was made possible by using reference parameters. If a pass by value had been used instead, the exchange in swap() would affect only swap()'s parameters and accomplish nothing with main()'s variables. A function such as swap() can be written only by using a reference or some other means that provides access to main()'s variables. (This other means is with pointers, the topic of Chapter 12.)

In using reference parameters, two cautions need to be mentioned. First, reference parameters must be variables (that is, they can't be used to change constants). For example, calling swap() with two literals, as in the call swap(20.5, 6.5), passes two constants to the function. Although swap() can execute, it doesn't change the values of these constants.[13]

Second, a function call gives no indication that the called function will be using reference parameters. The default in C++ is to make passes by value rather than passes by reference, specifically to limit a called function's ability to alter variables in the calling function. This calling procedure should be adhered to whenever possible, which means reference parameters should be used only in restricted situations that require multiple return values, as in the swap() function in Program 6.10. The calc() function included in Program 6.9, although useful for illustration purposes, could also be written as two separate functions, each returning a single value.

EXERCISES 6.3

1. **(Practice)** Write parameter declarations for the following:
   a. A parameter named slope that will be a reference to a double-precision value
   b. A parameter named energy that will be a reference to a double-precision number
   c. A parameter named minutes that will be a reference to an integer number
   d. A parameter named key that will be a reference to a character
   e. A parameter named yield that will be a reference to a double-precision number

2. **(Practice)** Three integer arguments are to be used in a call to a function named time(). Write a suitable function header for time(), assuming that time() accepts these variables as the reference parameters sec, min, and hours and returns no value to its calling function.

3. **(Modify)** Rewrite the findMax() function in Program 6.5 so that the variable max, declared in main(), is used to store the maximum value of the two passed numbers. The value of max should be set from within findMax(). (*Hint:* A reference to max has to be accepted by findMax().)

4. **(Practice)** Write a function named change() that has an integer parameter and six integer reference parameters named hundreds, fifties, twenties, tens, fives, and ones. The function is to consider the passed integer value as a dollar amount and convert the value into the fewest number of equivalent bills. Using the reference parameters, the function should alter the arguments in the calling function.

5. **(Practice)** Write a function named time() that has an integer parameter named seconds and three integer reference parameters named hours, mins, and secs. The

---
[13]Most compilers catch this error.

function is to convert the passed number of seconds into an equivalent number of hours, minutes, and seconds. Using the reference parameters, the function should alter the arguments in the calling function.

6. **(Practice)** Write a function named yearCalc() that has an integer parameter representing the total number of days from the date 1/1/2000 and reference parameters named year, month, and day. The function is to calculate the current year, month, and day given the number of days passed to it. Using the reference parameters, the function should alter the arguments in the calling function. For this problem, assume each year has 365 days, and each month has 30 days.

7. **(Desk Check)** The following program uses the same argument and parameter names in both the calling and called functions. Determine whether doing so causes any problem for the compiler.

```cpp
#include <iostream>
using namespace std;

void time(int&, int&);   // function prototype

int main()
{
  int min, hour;

  cout << "Enter two numbers :";
  cin  >> min >> hour;
  time(min, hour);

  return 0;
}

void time(int& min, int& hour)    // accept two references
{
  int sec;

  sec = (hour * 60 + min) * 60;
  cout << "The total number of seconds is " << sec << endl;

  return;
```

6.4 A Case Study: Rectangular to Polar Coordinate Conversion

Preparing a well-designed computer program is much like preparing a well-designed term paper, in that both should start with an outline. This outline can be written down or, for very small programs, simply kept in mind as the program is being developed. As with a term-paper outline that lists the main topics, a computer program's initial outline lists the primary tasks the program is to accomplish.

In written form, a computer program's initial outline is typically a pseudocode description or a first-level structure diagram. (Both were described in Section 1.3.) This initial outline begins the process of defining a more complicated problem as a set of smaller, more manageable tasks. Each of these tasks can be further subdivided or refined into even smaller tasks, if required. After the tasks are well defined, the actual work of coding can begin, starting with any task, in any order. If there are more tasks than one programmer can handle, they can be distributed among as many programmers as necessary. This workload distribution is equivalent to having many people work on a large research project, with each person responsible for a topic or project component. A general outline applicable to many engineering and scientific tasks is the following algorithm:

Get the inputs to the problem
Calculate the desired result
Report the results of the calculation

These three tasks are the primary responsibilities of every program, and this algorithm is referred to as the **problem-solver algorithm**. Figure 6.10 shows a first-level structure diagram of this algorithm.

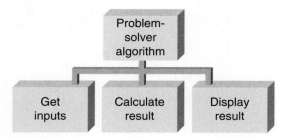

Figure 6.10   The problem-solver algorithm

Each task in the problem-solver algorithm can be worked on independently as a function—a sort of "mini" C++ program that's easier to complete than a whole program. Each function task can be refined and coded in any order, although completing the input section first usually makes testing and development easier. Next, you apply this development procedure to the programming problem of converting rectangular coordinates to their polar equivalents.

Step 1   Problem Definition

A program is to be written to convert a point's rectangular (x,y) coordinates into polar form. That is, given an x and y position on a Cartesian coordinate system, shown in Figure 6.11, you must calculate the distance from the origin, r, and the angle from the x-axis, θ, specified by the point. The values of r and θ are referred to as the point's polar coordinates.

When the x and y coordinates of a point are known, the equivalent r and θ coordinates can be calculated by using these formulas:

$$r = \sqrt{x^2 + y^2}$$

$$\theta = \tan^{-1}(y/x) \quad x \neq 0$$

You begin developing your program with an outline of what the program is to accomplish. You can construct an initial pseudocode description by applying the problem-solver algorithm

A Case Study: Rectangular to Polar
Coordinate Conversion

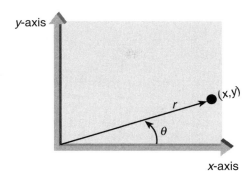

Figure 6.11   The correspondence between polar (distance and angle) and Cartesian (*x* and *y*)
coordinates

to the specifics of the program. The required inputs are *x* and *y* coordinates, the calculation
is to convert the input values to their polar coordinate form, and the display is the calculated
polar coordinates. The initial pseudocode description is as follows:

Get the x and y coordinate values
Calculate the polar (r and θ) coordinate values
Display the polar coordinate values

Figure 6.12 shows the equivalent first- or top-level structure diagram for this algorithm.

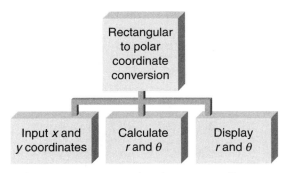

Figure 6.12   A top-level structure diagram

As this program is rather simple and each task described by the algorithm is well defined, you
can begin coding each task. To show that any task can be coded independently of any other task,
you start by coding the function that calculates polar coordinates, although you could start with
any function. As an added feature, this function will return the angle θ in degrees rather than
the radian measure the atan() function returns. Because this function must receive two inputs,
the *x* and *y* coordinates, and return two outputs, the *r* and θ coordinates, you provide four
parameters: two for the inputs and two for the outputs. Using the parameter names x, y, r, and

theta and the function name `polar()`, the following code performs the required calculation of polar coordinates:

```
void polar(double x, double y, double& r, double& theta)
{
  const double TODEGREES = 180.0/3.141593;

  r = sqrt(x * x + y * y);
  theta = atan(y/x) * TODEGREES;

  return;
}
```

The `polar()` function is straightforward. The function header declares that the function returns no value, and each of its parameters is declared as a floating-point data type. The first two parameters are used to accept x and y values, and the last two parameters, which are reference parameters, are used to pass the converted distance and angle values back to the calling function.

In the function body, a constant named TODEGREES is defined as the factor 180.0 / 3.142593. The next two assignment statements use the parameters x and y to assign values to the r and theta parameters. The TODEGREES named constant is used to convert the radian value returned from the `atan()` function into degrees. As written, the `polar()` function can be compiled to check for any compile-time errors.

To understand how the return values are passed, it's helpful to think of the reference parameters r and theta as containers (or variables) through which values can be passed in either direction. This situation is shown in Figure 6.13, which illustrates the fundamental characteristics of reference parameters: *They simply make it possible for both called functions and calling functions to access the same storage area with different names*. As shown in Figure 6.13, the calling function can access the values assigned to r and theta in `polar()` with the argument names `distance` and `angle` or any other programmer-selected argument names.

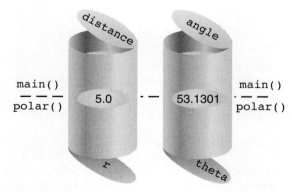

Figure 6.13   Parameter values when `polar()` is called

Step 2   Testing the Function

After `polar()` is written, it can be tested independently of any other function. For this testing, you write a dedicated driver function that calls only `polar()`, as shown in Program 6.11.

Program 6.11

```cpp
#include <iostream>
#include <cmath>
using namespace std;

void polar(double, double, double&, double&); // function prototype

int main()
{
   double distance, angle;
   polar(3.0, 4.0, distance, angle);

   cout << "r = " << distance << endl;
   cout << "angle = " << angle << endl;

   return 0;
}

void polar(double x, double y, double& r, double& theta)
{
   const double TODEGREES = 180.0/3.141593;

   r = sqrt(x * x + y * y);
   theta = atan(y/x) * TODEGREES;

   return;
}
```

Notice that in `main()`, the literals 3.0 and 4.0 are passed to `polar()`. The function accepts these inputs as the parameters x and y and uses these parameters in calculating values for the parameters r and `theta`. In `main()`, these last two parameters are known as `distance` and `angle`, and their values are displayed immediately after the call to `polar()` is made. This is the output produced when Program 6.11 runs:

```
r = 5
angle = 53.1301
```

These results are the same as those you would get from a hand calculation. As the function performs only two calculations, and the results displayed by the test program agree with those from a hand calculation, the function has been completely tested. It still remains to be group tested with the other two functions required for the complete program to make sure correct argument values are exchanged between each function.

Step 3   Completing the Program

The structure diagram for the complete program (shown previously in Figure 6.12) also requires writing functions for accepting two rectangular coordinates and displaying the calculated polar coordinates. The following function, getrec(), can be used to accept the input data:

```
void getrec(double& x, double& y)
{
  cout << "Rectangular to Polar Coordinate"
       << " Conversion Program\n" << endl;
  cout << "Enter the x coordinate: ";
  cin  >> x;
  cout << "Enter the y coordinate: ";
  cin  >> y;

  return;
}
```

In this function, the reference parameters x and y are used to return the values entered in response to the two cin prompts. As with the polar() function, this function can be tested by using a small dedicated driver program. Program 6.12 shows the function with its driver program.

Notice that the dedicated driver program, also referred to as a "front-end driver," has been used to call getrec() and display the values this function returns. The following output produced by Program 6.12 verifies the correct operation of the getrec() function:

```
Rectangular to Polar Coordinate Conversion Program

Enter the x coordinate: 3
Enter the y coordinate: 4
The entered value for x is 3
The entered value for y is 4
```

Program 6.12

```
#include <iostream>
using namespace std;

void getrec(double&, double&); // function prototype

int main()
{
  double xcoord, ycoord;

  getrec(xcoord, ycoord);

  cout << "The entered value for x is " << xcoord << endl;
  cout << "The entered value for y is " << ycoord << endl;

  return 0;
}

void getrec(double& x, double& y)
{
  cout << "Rectangular to Polar Coordinate"
       << " Conversion Program\n" << endl;
  cout << "Enter the x coordinate: ";
  cin  >> x;
  cout << "Enter the y coordinate: ";
  cin  >> y;

  return;
}
```

The function for displaying polar coordinates is constructed in a similar manner. Program 6.13 contains both the function, named `showit()`, and a front-end driver for testing the function. Notice that the parameter names used in the function header for `showit()` need not be the same as those used in any other function. `showit()` is constructed to simply display the values in its two parameters, which in this case have been named `radius` and `angle`.

The following output of Program 6.13 verifies that `showit()` displays the values passed to it correctly:

```
The polar coordinates are:
  Distance from origin: 5
  Angle (in degrees) from x-axis: 53.1301
```

Program 6.13

```cpp
#include <iostream>
using namespace std;

void showit(double, double); // function prototype

int main()
{
  showit(5.0, 53.1301);

  return 0;
}

void showit(double radius, double angle)
{
  cout << "\nThe polar coordinates are: " << endl;
  cout << "  Distance from origin: " << radius << endl;
  cout << "  Angle (in degrees) from x-axis: " << angle << endl;

  return;
}
```

It now remains to create one `main()` program that calls each of the developed functions in the correct order. This is done in Program 6.14, which also includes the functions `getrec()`, `polar()`, and `showit()`.

Program 6.14

```cpp
// This program converts rectangular coordinates to polar coordinates
// Functions used: getrec() - obtain the rectangular coordinates
//                : polar() - calculate the polar coordinates
//                : showit() - display the polar coordinates
#include <iostream>
#include <cmath>
using namespace std;

void getrec(double&, double&);                // function prototype
void polar(double, double, double&, double&); // function prototype
void showit(double, double);                  // function prototype
```

☞

```cpp
int main()
{
  double x, y, distance, angle;

  getrec(x, y);
  polar(x, y, distance, angle);
  showit(distance, angle);

  return 0;
}

void getrec(double& x, double& y)
{
  cout << "Rectangular to Polar Coordinate"
       << " Conversion Program\n" << endl;
  cout << "Enter the x coordinate: ";
  cin  >> x;
  cout << "Enter the y coordinate: ";
  cin  >> y;

  return;
}

void polar(double x, double y, double& r, double& theta)
{
  const double TODEGREES = 180.0/3.141593;

  r = sqrt(x * x + y * y);
  theta = atan(y/x) * TODEGREES;
  return;
}

void showit(double radius, double angle)
{
  cout << "\nThe polar coordinates are: " << endl;
  cout << "   Distance from origin: " << radius << endl;
  cout << "   Angle (in degrees) from x-axis: " << angle << endl;

  return;
}
```

The following output was produced from one run of Program 6.14:

```
Rectangular to Polar Coordinate Conversion Program

Enter the x coordinate: 3
Enter the y coordinate: 4

The polar coordinates are:
   Distance from origin: 5
   Angle (in degrees) from x-axis: 53.1301
```

Before leaving Program 6.14, note that an alternative to writing driver programs for each function during program development is writing a `main()` program first and adding the functions later as they're developed. To do this, you use stubs for each function (see Section 6.1) and then replace each stub, one at a time, with the completed function.

EXERCISES 6.4

1. **(Practice)** The volume, v, and side surface area, s, of a cylinder are given by the formulas

   $v = \pi r^2 l$

   $s = 2\pi r l$

   where r is the cylinder's radius, and l is its length. Using these formulas, write and test a function named `cylinder()` that accepts a cylinder's radius and length and returns its volume and side surface area.

2. **(Practice)** Write a C++ program that accepts the rectangular coordinates of two points (x_1, y_1) and (x_2, y_2), calculates the distance of each point from the origin, and calculates the distance between the two points. The distance, d, between two points is given by this formula:

   $$d = \sqrt{\left(x_2 - x_1\right)^2 + \left(y_2 - y_1\right)^2}$$

3. **(Fluid Mechanics)** Fluid flowing in a pipe flows in a smooth pattern, known as laminar flow, or a turbulent pattern, known as turbulent flow. The velocity, V, that produces each type of flow in the pipe can be determined by using these formulas:

   $V_{laminar} = (2100 \; \mu) / (\rho \, d)$

   $V_{turbulent} = (4000 \; \mu) / (\rho \, d)$

   $V_{laminar}$ is the velocity of the fluid, in ft/sec, that produces a definite laminar flow.
   $V_{turbulent}$ is the velocity of the fluid, in ft/sec, that produces a definite turbulent flow.
   μ is the fluid's viscosity in lbf-sec/ft^2.
   ρ is the fluid's density in slug/ft^3.
   d is the pipe's inside diameter in feet.

Using these formulas, write and test a C++ function named `flow()` that returns both the laminar flow velocity, $V_{laminar}$, and the turbulent flow velocity, $V_{turbulent}$, using reference parameters. The function should calculate these velocities for water, which has a viscosity, μ, of 1.9×10^5 lbf-sec/ft^2 and a density, ρ, of 1.94 slug/ft^3. The pipe diameter should be passed by value to the `flow()` function.

4. **(Fluid Mechanics)** The viscosity and density of three common fluids are listed in the following chart:

Fluid	Viscosity (lbf-sec/ft^2)	Density (slug/ft^3)
Ethyl alcohol	2.29×10^5	1.527
Methyl alcohol	1.17×10^5	1.531
Propyl alcohol	4.01×10^5	1.556

Using this data, write and test a C++ function named `viscDen()` that returns the viscosity and density of the selected fluid by using reference parameters. The type of fluid should be input to the function as a character that's passed by value.

5. **(Numerical)** Many algorithms have been developed for generating pseudorandom numbers. Some use a counting scheme, such as counting bits beginning at an arbitrary location in a changing memory. Another scheme, which creates pseudorandom numbers by performing a calculation, is the power residue method.

The **power residue method** begins with an odd n-digit integer, referred to as the "seed" number. The seed is multiplied by the value $(10^{n/2} - 3)$. Using the lowest n digits of the result (the "residue") produces a new seed. Continuing this procedure produces a series of random numbers, with each new number used as the seed for the next number. If the original seed has four or more digits (n equal to or greater than 4) and is not divisible by 2 or 5, this procedure yields $5 \times 10^{(n-2)}$ random numbers before a sequence of numbers repeats itself. For example, starting with a six-digit seed ($n = 6$), such as 654321, a series of $5 \times 10^4 = 50,000$ random numbers can be generated.

As an algorithm, the steps in generating pseudorandom numbers with a power residue method consist of the following:

Step 1: Have a user enter a six-digit integer seed that isn't divisible by 2 or 5—this means the number should be an odd number not ending in 5.

Step 2: Multiply the seed number by 997, which is $10^3 - 3$.

Step 3: Extract the lower six digits of the result produced by Step 2. Use this random number as the next seed.

Step 4: Repeat Steps 2 and 3 for as many random numbers as needed.

Therefore, if the user-entered seed number is 654321 (Step 1), the first random number generated is calculated as follows:

Step 2: 654321 × 997 = 652358037

Step 3: Extract the lower six digits of the number obtained in Step 2, using a standard programming "trick" that involves the following:

Step 3a: Divide the number by 10^6 = 1000000 (for example, 652358037 / 1000000 = 652.358037).

Step 3b: Take the integer part of the result of Step 3a (for example, the integer part of 652.358037 = 652).

Step 3c: Multiply the previous result by 10^6 (for example, 652 × 10^6 = 652000000).

Step 3d: Subtract this result from the original number (for example, 652358037 - 652000000 = 358037).

The integer part of a floating-point number can be determined by assigning the floating-point number to an integer variable or using a C++ cast (see Section 3.3). In this procedure, you'll use the cast mechanism. The algorithm for producing a random number can be accomplished with the following code:

```
i = int(997.0 * x / 1.e6);    // take the integer part
x = 997.0 * x - i * 1.e6;
```

Using this information, do the following:

a. Create a function named `randnum()` that accepts a floating-point "seed" as a parameter and returns a floating-point random number between 0 and 1.e6.

b. Incorporate the `randnum()` function created in Exercise 5a into a working C++ program that produces 10 random numbers between 0 and 1.e6.

c. Test the randomness of the `randnum()` function created in Exercise 5a by using the method described in Exercise 9. Try some even seed values and odd seed values ending in 5 to determine whether they affect the randomness of the numbers.

6. **(Mathematical)** Write a C++ function that determines in which quadrant a line drawn from the origin resides. The determination of the quadrant is made by using the angle the line makes with the positive x-axis, as follows:

Angle from the Positive X-Axis	Quadrant
Between 0 and 90 degrees	1
Between 90 and 180 degrees	2
Between 180 and 270 degrees	3
Between 270 and 360 degrees	4

Note: If the angle is exactly 0, 90, 180, or 270 degrees, the corresponding line doesn't reside in any quadrant; it lies on an axis. For this case, your function should return a 0.

7. **(Simulation)** Write a program to simulate the roll of two dice. If the total of the two dice is 7 or 11, you win; otherwise, you lose. Embellish this program as much as you like, with betting, different odds, different combinations for win or lose, stopping play when you have no money left or reach the house limit, displaying the dice, and so forth. (*Hint*: Calculate the dots showing on each die with the expression dots = int(6.0 * random number + 1), where the random number is between 0 and 1.)

8. **(Desk Check)** The following program uses the same variable names in both the calling and called functions. Determine whether doing so causes any problem for the compiler.

```
#include <iostream.h>

int time(int, int);   // function prototype

int main()
{
  int min, hour, sec;

  cout << "Enter two numbers: ";
  cin  >> min, hour;
  sec = time(min, hour);
  cout << "The total number of seconds is " << sec << endl;

  return 0;
}

int time(int min, int hour)
{
  int sec;

  sec = (hour * 60 + min) * 60;

  return sec;
}
```

9. **(Numerical)** Write a program that tests the effectiveness of the rand() library function. Start by initializing 10 counters to 0. Then generate a large number of pseudorandom integers between 0 and 9. Each time a 0 occurs, increment the variable you have designated as the zero counter; when a 1 occurs, increment the counter variable that's keeping count of the 1s that occur; and so on. Finally, display the number of 0s, 1s, 2s, and so on that occurred and the percentage of the time they occurred.

6.5   Variable Scope

Now that you have begun to write programs containing more than one function, you can look more closely at the variables declared in each function and their relationship to variables in other functions. By their nature, C++ functions are constructed to be independent modules. As you have seen, values are passed to a function by using the function's parameter list, and a value is returned from a function by using a `return` statement. Seen in this light, a function can be thought of as a closed box, with slots at the top to receive values and a single slot at the bottom to return a value (see Figure 6.14).

Values passed to the function

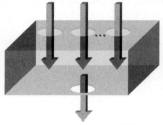

A single value directly
returned by the function

Figure 6.14   A function can be considered a closed box

The metaphor of a closed box is useful because it emphasizes that what goes on inside the function, including all variable declarations in the function body, is hidden from the view of all other functions. Because the variables created in a function are conventionally available only to the function, they are said to be local to the function, or **local variables**. This term refers to the scope of an identifier; **scope** is the section of the program where the identifier, such as a variable, is valid or "known." This section of the program is also referred to as where the variable is "visible."

A variable can have a local scope or a global scope. A variable with a **local scope** is simply one with storage locations set aside for it by a declaration statement in a function body. Local variables are meaningful only when used in expressions or statements inside the function that declared them. This means the same variable name can be declared and used in more than one function. For each function that declares the variable, a separate and distinct variable is created.

All the variables you have used until now have been local variables, a result of placing declaration statements inside functions and using them as definition statements that cause the computer to reserve storage for the declared variable. As you'll see in the next section, declaration statements can be placed outside functions and also need not act as definitions that reserve new storage areas for the declared variable.

A variable with **global scope**, more commonly termed a **global variable**, has storage created for it by a declaration statement located outside any function. These variables can be used by all functions that are placed after the global variable declaration. Program 6.15 shows using a global variable, and the same variable name has been used on purpose inside both functions in the program.

Program 6.15

```cpp
#include <iostream>
using namespace std;

int firstnum;      // create a global variable named firstnum

void valfun();    // function prototype (declaration)

int main()
{
  int secnum;        // create a local variable named secnum

  firstnum = 10;    // store a value in the global variable
  secnum = 20;       // store a value in the local variable

  cout << "From main(): firstnum = " << firstnum << endl;
  cout << "From main(): secnum =  " << secnum << endl;

  valfun();         // call the function valfun

  cout << "\nFrom main() again: firstnum = " << firstnum << endl;
  cout << "From main() again: secnum = " << secnum << endl;
  return 0;
}

void valfun()    // no values are passed to this function
{
  int secnum;     // create a second local variable named secnum

  secnum = 30;    // affects only this local variable's value

  cout << "\nFrom valfun(): firstnum = " << firstnum << endl;
  cout << "From valfun(): secnum = " << secnum << endl;

  firstnum = 40;      // changes firstnum for both functions

  return;
}
```

The variable `firstnum` in Program 6.15 is a global variable because its storage is created by a definition statement located outside a function. Because both `main()` and `valfun()` follow the definition of `firstnum`, both functions can use this global variable with no further declaration needed.

Program 6.15 also contains two separate local variables, both named `secnum`. Storage for the `secnum` variable named in `main()` is created by the definition statement in `main()`. A different storage area for the `secnum` variable in `valfun()` is created by the definition statement in the `valfun()` function. Figure 6.15 shows the three distinct storage areas reserved by the three definition statements in Program 6.15.

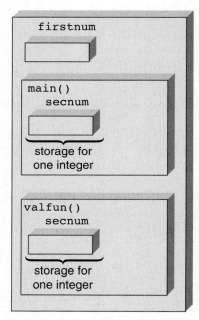

Figure 6.15   The three storage areas reserved by Program 6.15

Each variable named `secnum` is local to the function in which its storage is created, and each variable can be used only from within its corresponding function. Therefore, when `secnum` is used in `main()`, the storage area `main()` reserves for its `secnum` variable is accessed, and when `secnum` is used in `valfun()`, the storage area `valfun()` reserves for its `secnum` variable is accessed. The following output is produced when Program 6.15 runs:

```
From main(): firstnum = 10
From main(): secnum = 20

From valfun(): firstnum = 10
From valfun(): secnum = 30

From main() again: firstnum = 40
From main() again: secnum = 20
```

Now analyze this output to see how local and global variables work. Because `firstnum` is a global variable, both `main()` and `valfun()` can use and change its value. Initially, both functions print the value of 10 that `main()` stored in `firstnum`. Before returning, `valfun()` changes the value of `firstnum` to 40, which is the value displayed when the `firstnum` is next displayed from within `main()`.

Because each function "knows" only its own local variables, `main()` can send only the value of its `secnum` to `cout`, and `valfun()` can send only the value of its `secnum` to `cout`. Therefore, whenever `secnum` is obtained from `main()`, the value of 20 is displayed, and whenever `secnum` is obtained from `valfun()`, the value 30 is displayed.

C++ doesn't confuse the two `secnum` variables because only one function can execute at a time. While a function is executing, only variables and parameters that are "in scope" for that function (global and local) can be accessed.

The scope of a variable in no way influences or restricts its data type. Just as a local variable can be a character, an integer, a Boolean, a double, or any other data type that's been introduced, global variables can be all these data types, as illustrated in Figure 6.16. A variable's scope is determined by the placement of the definition statement that reserves storage for it and optionally by a declaration statement that makes it visible, whereas a variable's data type is determined by using a keyword (`char`, `int`, `bool`, `double`, and so on) before the variable's name in a declaration statement.

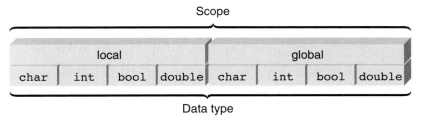

Figure 6.16   Relating the scope and type of a variable

Scope Resolution Operator

When a local variable has the same name as a global variable, all references to the variable name made within the local variable's scope refer to the local variable. This situation is illustrated in Program 6.16, where the variable name `number` is defined as both a global and local variable.

When Program 6.16 is run, the following output is displayed:

```
The value of number is 26.4
```

Program 6.16

```cpp
#include <iostream>
using namespace std;

double number = 42.8;      // a global variable named number

int main()
{
  double number = 26.4;    // a local variable named number

  cout << "The value of number is " << number << endl;

  return 0;
}
```

As shown by the program's output, the local variable name takes precedence over the global variable. In these cases, you can still access the global variable by using C++'s scope resolution operator, which has the symbol ::. This operator must be placed immediately before the variable name, as in ::number. When used in this manner, the :: tells the compiler to use the global variable. As an example, the scope resolution operator is used in Program 6.16a.

Program 6.16a

```cpp
#include <iostream>
using namespace std;

double number = 42.5;      // a global variable named number

int main()
{
  double number = 26.4;    // a local variable named number

  cout << "The value of number is " << ::number << endl;

  return 0;
}
```

This is the output produced by Program 6.16a:

```
The value of number is 42.5
```

As indicated by this output, the scope resolution operator causes the global, rather than the local, variable to be accessed.

Misuse of Globals

Global variables allow programmers to "jump around" the normal safeguards provided by functions. Instead of passing variables to a function, it's possible to make all variables global. *Do not do this.* By indiscriminately making all variables global, you destroy the safeguards C++ provides to make functions independent and insulated from each other, including carefully designating the type of arguments a function needs, the variables used in the function, and the value returned.

Using only global variables can be especially disastrous in large programs with many user-created functions. Because all variables in a function must be declared, creating functions that use global variables requires remembering to write the appropriate global declarations at the top of each program using the function—they no longer come along with the function. More devastating, however, is trying to track down an error in a large program with global variables. Because a global variable can be accessed and changed by any function following the global declaration, locating the origin of an erroneous value is a time-consuming and frustrating task.

Global definitions, however, are sometimes useful in creating variables and constants that must be shared between many functions. Instead of passing the same variable to each function, defining the variable once as global is easier. Doing so also alerts anyone reading the program that many functions use the variable. Most large programs almost always make use of a few global variables or constants. Smaller programs containing a few functions, however, should almost never contain global variables.

The misuse of globals doesn't apply to function prototypes, which typically are global. All the function prototypes you have used have been of global scope, which declares the prototype to all subsequent functions. Placing a function prototype in a function makes the prototype a local declaration, which makes it available only to the function it's declared within.

EXERCISES 6.5

1. **(Practice) a.** For the following section of code, determine the data type and scope of all declared variables on a separate sheet of paper, using the column headings shown in the following chart. (The entries for the first variable have been filled in.)

Variable Name	Data Type	Scope
volts	int	global to main(), roi(), and step()

```
#include <iostream>
using namespace std;

int volts;
long int resistance;
double current;

int main()
{
  int power;
  double factor, time;
     .
       .
  return 0;
}

double roi(int mat1, int mat2)
{
  int count;
  double weight;
     .
       .
  return weight;
}

int step(double first, double last)
{
  int hours;
  double fracpart;
     .
       .
  return 10*hours;
}
```

    b. Draw boxes around the appropriate section of the preceding code to enclose each variable's scope.

    c. Determine the data type of parameters that the `roi()` and `step()` functions expect and the data type of the value these functions return.

2. (Practice) a. For the following section of code, determine the data type and scope of all declared variables on a separate sheet of paper, using the column headings shown in the following chart. (The entries for the first variable have been filled in.)

Variable Name	Data Type	Scope
key	char	global to `main()`, `func1()`, and `func2()`

```
#include <iostream>
using namespace std;

char key;
long int number;
```

```
int main()
{
  int a,b,c;
  double x,y;
    .
    .
  return 0;
}

double secnum;

int func1(int num1, int num2)
{
  int o,p;
  float q;
    .
    .
  return p;
}

double func2(double first, double last)
{
  int a,b,c,o,p;
  double r;
  double s,t,x;
    .
    .
  return s * t;
}
```

   b. Draw a box around the appropriate section of the preceding code to enclose the scope of the variables key, secnum, y, and r.

   c. Determine the data type of the arguments that the func1() and func2() functions expect and the data type of the value these functions return.

3. **(Practice)** The term "scope" can also apply to a function's parameters. What do you think is the scope of all function parameters?

4. **(Practice)** Define the scope of the parameter p2 and the variables a, b, c, d, m, n, p, d, q, and r in the following program structure:

```
#include <iostream>
using namespace std;

int a, b;
double One(float);
void Two(void);

int main()
{
  int c, d;
  double e, f;
    .
    .
  return 0;
}
```

```
double One(double p2)
{
  char m, n;
     .
     .
     .
}

void Two(void)
{
  int p, d;
  double q, r;
     .
     .
     .
}
```

5. **(Desk Check)** Determine the values displayed by each cout statement in the following program:

```
#include <iostream>
using namespace std;

int firstnum = 10;   // declare and initialize a global variable
void display();       // function prototype

int main()
{
  int firstnum = 20;    // declare and initialize a local variable

  cout << "\nThe value of firstnum is " << firstnum << endl;

  display();

  return 0;
}

void display(void)
{
  cout << "The value of firstnum is now " << firstnum << endl;

  return;
}
```

6.6   Variable Storage Categories

The scope of a variable defines the location in a program where that variable can be used. If you draw a box around the section of program code where each variable is valid, the space inside the box would represent the variable's scope. From this viewpoint, a variable's scope can be thought of as the space in the program where the variable is valid.

In addition to the space dimension represented by scope, variables have a time dimension that refers to the length of time storage locations are reserved for a variable. This time dimension is referred to as the variable's **lifetime**. For example, all variable storage locations are released back to the computer when a program is finished running. However, while a program is still executing, interim variable storage locations are reserved and subsequently released back to the computer. Where and how long a variable's storage locations are kept before they're released can be determined by the variable's **storage category**.

Besides having a data type and scope, every variable has a storage category. The four available storage categories are `auto`, `static`, `extern`, and `register`. If one of these category names is used, it must be placed before the variable's data type in a declaration statement. The following are examples of declaration statements that include a storage category designation:

```
auto int num;        // auto storage category and int data type
static int miles;    // static storage category and int data type
register int dist;   // register storage category and int data type
extern int volts;    // extern storage category and int data type
auto float coupon;   // auto storage category and float data type
static double yrs;   // static storage category and double data type
extern float yld;    // extern storage category and float data type
auto char inKey;     // auto storage category and char variable type
```

To understand what a variable's storage category means, next you examine local variables (created inside a function) and then global variables (created outside a function).

Local Variable Storage Categories

Local variables can be members only of the `auto`, `static`, or `register` storage categories. If no category description is included in the declaration statement, the variable is assigned to the `auto` category automatically, so `auto` is the default category C++ uses. All the local variables you have used have been `auto` variables because the storage category designation was omitted.

The term `auto` is short for "automatic." Storage for automatic local variables is reserved or created automatically each time a function declaring automatic variables is called. As long as the function hasn't returned control to its calling function, all automatic variables local to the function are "alive"—meaning storage for the variables is available. When the function returns control to its calling function, its local automatic variables "die"—meaning storage for the variables is released back to the computer. This process repeats each time a function is called. For example, in Program 6.17, the `testauto()` function is called three times from `main()`.

This is the output produced by Program 6.17:

```
The value of the automatic variable num is 0
The value of the automatic variable num is 0
The value of the automatic variable num is 0
```

Program 6.17

```cpp
#include <iostream>
using namespace std;

void testauto();      // function prototype

int main()
{
  int count;          // count is a local auto variable

  for(count = 1; count <= 3; count++)
    testauto();

  return 0;
}

void testauto()
{
  int num = 0;        // num is a local auto variable
                      // initialized to 0
  cout << "The value of the automatic variable num is "
       << num << endl;
  num++;

  return;
}
```

Each time `testauto()` is called, the automatic variable `num` is created and initialized to 0. When the function returns control to `main()`, the variable `num` is destroyed along with any value stored in `num`. Therefore, the effect of incrementing `num` in `testauto()`, before the function's `return` statement, is lost when control is returned to `main()`.

For most applications, the use of automatic variables works just fine. In some cases, however, you want a function to remember values between function calls, which is the purpose of the `static` storage category. A local variable declared as `static` causes the program to keep the variable and its latest value even when the function that declared it has finished executing. The following are examples of `static` variable declarations:

```cpp
static int rate;
static double resistance;
static char inKey;
```

A local static variable isn't created and destroyed each time the function declaring it is called. After they're created, local static variables remain in existence for the program's lifetime. This means the last value stored in the variable when the function finishes executing is available to the function the next time it's called.

Because local static variables retain their values, they aren't initialized in a declaration statement in the same way as automatic variables. To understand why, consider the automatic declaration int num = 0;, which causes the automatic variable num to be created and set to 0 each time the declaration is encountered. This procedure is called a **runtime initialization** because initialization occurs each time the declaration statement is encountered. This type of initialization would be disastrous for a static variable because resetting the variable's value to 0 each time the function is called destroys the very value you're trying to save.

Initialization of static variables (both local and global) is done only once, when the program is first compiled. At compile time, the variable is created and any initialization value is placed in it.[14] Thereafter, the value in the variable is kept without further initialization. To see how this process works, examine Program 6.18.

Program 6.18

```
#include <iostream>
using namespace std;

void teststat();     // function prototypeint main()
{
  int count;         // count is a local auto variable

  for(count = 1; count <= 3; count++)
    teststat();

  return 0;
}

void teststat()
{
  static int num = 0;     // num is a local static variable
  cout << "The value of the static variable num is now "
      << num << endl;
  num++;

  return;
}
```

[14]Some compilers initialize static local variables the first time the definition statement is executed rather than when the program is compiled.

This is the output produced by Program 6.18:

```
The value of the static variable num is now 0
The value of the static variable num is now 1
The value of the static variable num is now 2
```

As this output shows, the static variable num is set to 0 only once. The teststat() function then increments this variable just before returning control to main(). The value num has when leaving the teststat() function is retained and displayed when the function is next called.

Unlike automatic variables that can be initialized by constants or expressions using both constants and previously initialized variables, static variables can be initialized only by using constants or constant expressions, such as 3.2 + 8.0. Also, unlike automatic variables, all static variables are set to 0 when no explicit initialization is given. Therefore, the specific initialization of num to 0 in Program 6.17 isn't required.

The remaining storage category available to local variables, register, isn't used as extensively as auto or static variables. The following are examples of register variable declarations:

```
register int time;
register double diffren;
register float coupon;
```

The register variables have the same time duration as auto variables; that is, a local register variable is created when the function declaring it is entered and is destroyed when the function finishes running. The only difference between register and auto variables is where storage for the variable is located.

Storage for all variables (local and global), except register variables, is reserved in the computer's memory. Most computers also have a few high-speed storage areas, called **registers**, located in the CPU that can also be used for variable storage. Because registers are located in the CPU, they can be accessed faster than the normal memory storage areas located in the computer's memory unit. Also, computer instructions referencing registers typically require less space than instructions referencing memory locations because there are fewer registers than memory locations that can be accessed. When the compiler substitutes a register's location for a variable during program compilation, the instruction needs less space than address memory having millions of locations.

Besides decreasing a compiled C++ program's size, using register variables can increase the program's execution speed if your computer supports this data type. Application programs intended to be executed on different types of computers shouldn't use registers, however. Generally, the compiler foils attempts to do so by switching variables declared with the register storage category to the auto storage category automatically. The only restriction in using the register storage category is that a register variable's address can't be taken by using the address operator, &. This concept is easier to understand when you realize that registers don't have standard memory addresses.

Global Variable Storage Categories

Global variables are created by definition statements external to a function. By their nature, these externally defined variables don't come and go with the calling of a function. After a global variable is created, it exists until the program in which it's declared has finished executing. Therefore, global variables can't be declared as auto or register variables that are created and destroyed as the program is running. Global variables can be declared with the `static` or `extern` storage category (but not both). The following are examples of declaration statements including these two category descriptions:

```
extern int sum;
extern double volts;
static double current;
```

The `static` and `extern` storage categories affect only the scope, not the lifetime, of global variables. As with `static` local variables, all global variables are initialized to 0 at compile time. The purpose of the `extern` storage category is to extend a global variable's scope beyond its normal boundaries. To understand this concept, first note that all the programs written so far have been contained in one file. Therefore, when you have saved or retrieved programs, you have needed to give the computer only a single name for your program. C++ doesn't require doing this, however.

Large programs typically consist of many functions stored in multiple files. For example, Figure 6.17 shows the three functions `main()`, `func1()`, and `func2()` stored in one file and the two functions `func3()` and `func4()` stored in a second file.

file1

```
int volts;
double current;
static double power;

       .
       .
       .
int main()
{
   func1();
   func2();
   func3();
   func4();
}
int func1()
{

       .
       .
       .

}
int func2()
{

       .
       .
       .

}
```

file2

```
double factor;
int func3()
{

       .
       .
       .

}
int func4()

       .
       .
       .

}
```

Figure 6.17 A program can extend beyond one file

For the files shown in Figure 6.17, the global variables `volts`, `current`, and `power` declared in `file1` can be used only by the functions `main()`, `func1()`, and `func2()` in this file. The single global variable, `factor`, declared in `file2` can be used only by the functions `func3()` and `func4()` in `file2`.

Although the variable `volts` has been created in `file1`, you might want to use it in `file2`. To do this, you place the declaration statement `extern int volts;` in `file2`, as shown in Figure 6.18. Putting this statement at the top of `file2` extends the scope of `volts` into `file2` so that it can be used by both `func3()` and `func4()`. The `extern` designation simply declares a global variable that's defined in another file. So placing the statement `extern double current;` in `func4()` extends the scope of this global variable, created in `file1`, into `func4()`. Additionally, the scope of the global variable `factor`, created in `file2`, is extended into `func1()` and `func2()` by the declaration statement `extern double factor;` placed before `func1()`. Notice that `factor` is not available to `main()`.

file1

file2

```
int volts;
double current;
static double power;
         .
         .
         .
int main()
{
   func1();
   func2();
   func3();
   func4();
}
extern double factor;
int func1()
{
         .
         .
         .
}
int func2()
{
         .
         .
         .
}
```

```
double factor;
extern int volts;
int func3()
{
         .
         .
         .
}
int func4()
{
   extern double current;
         .
         .
         .
}
```

Figure 6.18   Extending the scope of global variables

A declaration statement containing the word `extern` is different from other declaration statements, in that it doesn't cause a new variable to be created by reserving new storage for the variable. An `extern` declaration statement simply informs the computer that a global

> ## Point of Information
>
> ### Storage Categories
>
> Variables of type `auto` and `register` are always local variables. Only non-`static` global variables can be declared by using the `extern` keyword. Doing so extends the variable's scope into another file or function.
>
> Making a global variable `static` makes the variable private to the file in which it's declared. Therefore, `static` variables can't use the `extern` keyword. Except for `static` variables, all variables are initialized each time they come into scope; `static` variables are initialized only once, when they're defined.

variable already exists and can now be used. The actual storage for the variable must be created somewhere else in the program by using one, and only one, global declaration statement in which the word `extern` hasn't been used. The global variable can, of course, be initialized in its original declaration. Initialization in an `extern` declaration statement is not allowed, however, and causes a compilation error.

The existence of the `extern` storage category is the reason for carefully distinguishing between the creation and declaration of a variable. Declaration statements containing the word `extern` don't create new storage areas; they only extend the scope of existing global variables.

The last global storage category, `static`, is used to prevent extending a global variable into a second file. Global `static` variables are declared in the same way as local `static` variables, except the declaration statement is placed outside any function.

The scope of a global `static` variable can't be extended beyond the file in which it's declared. This rule provides a degree of privacy for global `static` variables. Because they are "known" and can be used only in the file where they're declared, other files can't access or change their values. Therefore, global `static` variables can't subsequently be extended to a second file by using an `extern` declaration statement. Trying to do so results in a compilation error.

EXERCISES 6.6

1. **(Practice) a.** List the storage categories available to local variables.

   b. List the storage categories available to global variables.

2. **(Practice)** Describe the difference between a local `auto` variable and a local `static` variable.

3. **(Practice)** What is the difference between the following functions?

```
void init1()
{
  static int yrs = 1;
```

☞

```
    cout << "The value of yrs is " << yrs << endl;
    yrs = yrs + 2;

    return;
}

void init2()
{
  static int yrs;

  yrs = 1;
  cout << "The value of yrs is " << yrs << endl;
  yrs = yrs + 2;

  return;
}
```

4. **(Practice) a.** Describe the difference between a global `static` variable and a global `extern` variable.

   b. If a variable is declared with an `extern` storage category, what other declaration statement must be present somewhere in the program?

5. **(Practice)** The declaration statement `static double resistance;` can be used to create a local or global `static` variable. What determines the scope of the variable `resistance`?

6. **(Practice)** For the function and variable declarations shown in Figure 6.19, place an `extern` declaration to accomplish each of the following:

   a. Extend the scope of the global variable `choice` into `file2`.

   b. Extend the scope of the global variable `flag` into the `average()` function only.

   c. Extend the scope of the global variable `date` into `average()` and `variance()`.

   d. Extend the scope of the global variable `date` into `roi()` only.

   e. Extend the scope of the global variable `factor` into `roi()` only.

   f. Extend the scope of the global variable `bondtype` into `file1`.

   g. Extend the scope of the global variable `resistance` into both `watts()` and `thrust()`.

6.7 Common Programming Errors

The following programming errors are common when constructing and using functions:

  1. An extremely common error related to functions is passing incorrect data types. The values passed to a function must correspond to the data types of parameters declared for the function. One way to verify that correct values have been received is to

file1

```
char choice;
int flag;
long date, time;
int main()
{
    .
    .
    .
}
double factor;
double watts()
{
    .
    .
    .
}
double thrust()
{
    .
    .
    .

}
```

file2

```
char bondtype;
double resistance;
double roi()
{
    .
    .
    .
}
double average()
{
    .
    .
    .
}
double variance
{
    .
    .
    .
}
```

Figure 6.19 Files for Exercise 6

display all passed values in the function body before any calculations are made. After this verification has taken place, you can dispense with the display.[15]

2. Another common error can occur when the same variable is declared locally in both the calling and called functions. Even though the variable name is the same, a change to one local variable *does not* alter the value in the other local variable.

3. A related error is one that can occur when a local variable has the same name as a global variable. Inside the function declaring it, the use of the variable's name affects only the local variable's contents unless the scope resolution operator, : :, is used.

4. Another common error is omitting the called function's prototype before or within the calling function. The called function must be alerted to the type of value to be returned, and the function prototype provides this information. The prototype can be omitted if the called function is placed in a program before its calling function. Although omitting the prototype and return type for functions returning an integer is permitted, doing so is poor documenting practice. The actual value a function returns can be verified by displaying it both before and after it's returned.

5. The last two common errors are terminating a function header with a semicolon and forgetting to include the data type of a function's parameters in the function header.

---

[15]In practice, a good debugger program should be used.

6.8   Chapter Summary

1. A function is called by giving its name and passing any data to it in the parentheses following the name. If a variable is one of the arguments in a function call, the called function receives a copy of the variable's value.

2. The common form of a user-written function is as follows:

```
returnDataType functionName(parameter list)
{
  // declarations and other C++ statements;

  // return expression;
}
```

The first line of the function is called the function header. The opening and closing braces of the function and all statements between these braces constitute the function body. The returned data type is, by default, an integer when no returned data type is specified. The parameter list is a comma-separated list of parameter declarations.

3. A function's return type is the data type of the value the function returns. If no type is declared, the function is assumed to return an integer value. If the function doesn't return a value, it should be declared as a void type.

4. Functions can return at most a single data type value to their calling functions. This value is the value of the expression in the return statement.

5. Arguments passed to a function, when it's called, must conform to the parameters specified by the function header in terms of order, number of arguments, and specified data type.

6. Using reference parameters, a variable's address is passed to a function. If a called function is passed an address, it has the capability to access the calling function's variable. Using passed addresses permits a called function to return multiple values.

7. Functions can be declared to all calling functions by means of a function prototype. The prototype provides a declaration for a function that specifies the data type the function returns, the function's name, and the data types of the arguments the function expects. As with all declarations, a function prototype is terminated with a semicolon and can be included in local variable declarations or as a global declaration. This is the most common form of a function prototype:

dataType functionName(parameter data type list);

If the called function is placed above the calling function in the program, no further declaration is required because the function's definition serves as a global declaration to all subsequent functions.

8. Every variable in a program has a scope, which determines where in the program the variable can be used. A variable's scope is local or global and is determined by where the variable's definition statement is placed. A local variable is defined in a function and can be used only in its defining function or block. A global variable is defined outside a function and can be used in any function following the variable's definition. All global variables that aren't specifically initialized by the user are initialized to 0 by the compiler, and global variables not declared as static can be shared between files by using the keyword extern.

9. Every variable also has a storage category, which determines how long the value in the variable is retained, also known as the variable's lifetime. auto variables are local variables that exist only while their defining function is executing; register variables are similar to auto variables but are stored in a computer's registers rather than in memory; and static variables can be global or local and retain their values while the program is running. All static variables are set to 0 when they're defined if the user doesn't initialize them explicitly.

Programming Projects for Chapter 6

1. **(Practice)** The volume, *V*, of a right circular cylinder is given by the formula

$$V = \pi\, r^2\, h$$

where *r* is the cylinder's radius and *h* is the cylinder's height. Write a function that accepts two double-precision arguments—a cylinder's radius and height—and returns the cylinder's volume.

2. **(Practice) a.** Write a function that calculates the area, *a*, of a circle when its circumference, *c*, is given. This function should call a second function that returns the radius, *r*, of the circle, given *c*. The relevant formulas are $r = c/2\pi$ and $a = \pi r^2$.

   b. Write a C++ program that accepts the value of the circumference from the user, calculates the radius and area, and displays the calculated values. Your program should use the functions written for Exercise 2a.

3. **(Practice)** Write a function named pass() that returns a reject or accept code depending on whether the mean tolerance of a group of parts is less than or greater than 1.0%. If the average is less than 1.0%, the function should return an A for accept; otherwise, it should return an R for reject.

4. **(Practice)** A function is defined by the following code:

```
double FractionToDecimal(double numerator, double denominator)
{
  return (numerator/denominator);
}
```

   a. Write the shortest front-end driver you can to test this function and check the passing of parameters.

   b. Complete the FractionToDecimal() function so that it correctly calculates and returns the decimal value of values passed to it when it's called.

5. **(Data Processing) a.** The time in hours, minutes, and seconds is to be passed to a function named totsec(). Write totsec() to accept these values, determine the total number of seconds in the passed data, and display the calculated value.

   b. Include the totsec() function written for Exercise 5a in a working program. The main() function should correctly call totsec() and display the value the function returns. Use the following test data to verify your program's operation: hours = 10, minutes = 36, and seconds = 54. Make sure to do a hand calculation to verify the result your program displays.

6. (**Data Processing**) **a.** Write a function named `daycount()` that accepts a month, day, and year as its input arguments; calculates an integer representing the total number of days from the turn of the century to the date that's passed; and returns the calculated integer to the calling function. For this problem, assume each year has 365 days and each month has 30 days. Test your function by verifying that the date 1/1/00 returns a day count of 1.

   b. Include the `daycount()` function written for Exercise 6a in a working program. The `main()` function should correctly call `daycount()` and display the integer returned by the function.

7. (**Data Processing**) **a.** A clever and simple method of preparing to sort dates into ascending (increasing) or descending (decreasing) order is to convert a date in the form month/day/year into an integer number with the formula *date = year × 10000 + month × 100 + day*. For example, using this formula, the date 12/6/1988 converts to the integer 19881206, and the date 2/28/2010 converts to the integer 20100228. Sorting the resulting integer numbers puts dates into the correct order automatically. Using this formula, write a function named `convertdays()` that accepts a month, day, and year; converts the passed data into a single date integer; and returns the integer to the calling function.

   b. Include the `convertdays()` function written for Exercise 7a in a working program. The `main()` function should call `convertdays()` correctly and display the integer the function returns.

8. (**Data Processing**) Write a program that reads a key pressed on the keyboard and displays its code on the screen. Use the program to determine the code for the Enter key. Then write a function named `ReadOneChar()` that reads a character and ignores any succeeding characters until the Enter key is pressed. The entered character should be returned by `ReadOneChar()`.

9. (**Conversion**) **a.** Write and test a C++ function named `MakeMilesKmTable()` to display a table of miles converted to kilometers. The arguments to the function should be the starting and stopping values of miles and the increment. The output should be a table of miles and their equivalent kilometer values. Use the relationship that 1 mile = 1.61 kilometers.

   b. Modify the function written for Exercise 9a so that two columns are printed. For example, if the starting value is 1 mile, the ending value is 20 miles, and the increment is 1, the display should look like the following:

Miles	=	Kilometers	Miles	=	Kilometers
1		1.61	11		17.70
2		3.22	12		19.31
.		.	.		.
.		.	.		.
10		16.09	20		32.18

   (*Hint*: Find *split = (start + stop)/2*. Let a loop execute from *miles = start* to *split*, and calculate and print across one line the values of miles and kilometers for both *miles* and (*miles - start + split + 1*).)

10. **(Conversion)** Your company will soon open a new office in France. So that it can do business there, your manager has asked you to prepare a comprehensive package that performs the following American-to-metric conversions on demand:

Measure	American	Metric	Formula
distance	inch	centimeter	2.54 cm/in
	foot	meter	0.305 m/ft
	yard	meter	0.9144 m/yd
	mile	kilometer	1.6109 km/mi
temperature	Fahrenheit	Celsius	C = (5/9)(F - 32)
weight	pound	kilogram	0.454 kg/lb
	ounce	gram	28.35 gm/oz
currency	dollar	franc	entered by the user, about 5 francs/$
capacity	quart	liter	0.946 liter/qt
	teaspoon	milliliter	4.9 ml/tsp
math	degree	radian	rad = (π/180)(degree)
	degree	grad	grad = (200/180)(degree)

11. **(Numerical)** Heron's formula for the area, A, of a triangle with sides of length a, b, and c is

$$A = \sqrt{\left[s\left(s - a\right)\left(s - b\right)\left(s - c\right) \right]}$$

where

$$s = \frac{\left(a + b + c\right)}{2}$$

Write, test, and execute a function that accepts the values of a, b, and c as parameters from a calling function, and then calculates the values of s and *[s(s - a)(s - b)(s - c)]*. If this quantity is positive, the function calculates A. If the quantity is negative, a, b, and c do not form a triangle, and the function should set $A = -1$. The value of A should be returned by the function.

12. **(Numerical)** A formula to raise a real number, a, to the real power, b, is given by the formula

$$a^b = e^{\left[b \times \ln(a) \right]}$$

where a must be positive and b must be positive or 0. Using this formula, write a function named `power()` that accepts a and b as real values and returns a^b.

13. **(Numerical)** A fraction-handling program contains this menu:

```
A. Add two fractions
B. Convert a fraction to decimal
C. Multiply two fractions
Q. Quit
```

a. Write C++ code for the program with stub functions for the choices.

    b. Insert the `FractionToDecimal()` function from Exercise 4b into the code with commands to pass and display the parameters.

    c. Complete the program by replacing the stub functions with functions that perform appropriate operations.

14. (Numerical) A value that's sometimes useful is the greatest common divisor of two integers, *n1* and *n2*. Euclid discovered an efficient method to do this more than 2000 years ago. For this exercise, however, a stub is enough. Write the integer function stub `gcd(n1, n2)`. Simply have it return a value that suggests it received its arguments correctly. (*Hint: N1 + N2* is a good choice of return values. Why isn't *N1 / N2* a good choice?)

15. (Numerical) a. Euclid's method for finding the greatest common divisor (GCD) of two positive integers consists of the following steps:

    Step 1: Divide the larger number by the smaller and retain the remainder.

    Step 2: Divide the smaller number by the remainder, again retaining the remainder.

    Step 3: Continue dividing the previous remainder by the current remainder until the remainder is zero, at which point the last non-zero remainder is the GCD.

For example, if the two positive integers are 84 and 49, you have the following:

    Step 1: 84/49 yields a remainder of 35.

    Step 2: 49/35 yields a remainder of 14.

    Step 3: 35/14 yields a remainder of 7.

    Step 3: 14/7 yields a remainder of 0.

Therefore, the last non-zero remainder, which is 7, is the GCD of 84 and 49.

Using Euclid's algorithm, replace the stub function written for Exercise 14 with an actual function that determines and returns the GCD of its two integer arguments.

16. (Data Processing) a. Write a function named `date()` that accepts a long integer of the form `yyyymmdd`, such as 19980412; determines the corresponding month, day, and year; and returns these three values to the calling function. For example, if `date` is called by using the statement

```
date(20110412, &month, &day, &year)
```

the number 4 should be returned in `month`, the number 12 in `day`, and the number 2011 in `year`.

    b. Include the `date()` function written for Exercise 16a in a working program. The `main()` function should call `date()` and display the three values returned by the function.

17. **(Numerical)** The determinant of the 2 by 2 matrix

$$\begin{vmatrix} a_{11} & a_{12} \\ a_{21} & a_{22} \end{vmatrix}$$

is defined as the scalar value $a_{11}a_{22} - a_{21}a_{12}$. Similarly, the determinant of a 3 by 3 matrix, defined as

$$\begin{vmatrix} a_{11} & a_{12} & a_{13} \\ a_{21} & a_{22} & a_{23} \\ a_{31} & a_{32} & a_{33} \end{vmatrix}$$

is determined as

$$a_{11} \begin{vmatrix} a_{22} & a_{23} \\ a_{32} & a_{33} \end{vmatrix} - a_{21} \begin{vmatrix} a_{12} & a_{13} \\ a_{32} & a_{33} \end{vmatrix} + a_{31} \begin{vmatrix} a_{12} & a_{13} \\ a_{22} & a_{23} \end{vmatrix}$$

a. Using this information, write and test two functions named `det2()` and `det3()`. The `det2()` function should accept the four coefficients of a 2 by 2 matrix and return its determinant. The `det3()` function should accept the nine coefficients of a 3 by 3 matrix and return its determinant by calling `det2()` to calculate the required 2 by 2 determinants.

b. Write and run a C++ program that accepts the nine coefficients of a 3 by 3 matrix in one function, passes these coefficients to `det3()`, and uses a third function to display the calculated determinant.

Engineering and Scientific Disciplines

Chemical Engineering

Chemical engineering is the application of the knowledge or techniques of science, particularly chemistry, to industry. Chemical engineers are responsible for designing and operating large-scale manufacturing plants for materials that undergo chemical changes in their production. These materials include all the new and improved products that have so profoundly affected society, such as petrochemicals, rubbers and polymers, new metal alloys, industrial and fine chemicals, foods, paints, detergents, cements, pesticides, industrial gases, and medicines.

Chemical engineers also play an important role in pollution abatement and management of existing energy resources. Because the field of chemical engineering has become so broad, classifying the activities of chemical engineers is difficult. They can be subdivided roughly into large-scale production systems (chemical processing) and smaller scale (molecular) systems.

Chemical Processing

Chemical processing concerns all aspects of designing and operating large chemical-processing plants. It includes the following areas:

- Petrochemicals: Distilling and refining fuels, such as gasoline, synthetic natural gas, and coal liquefaction and gasification, and producing an infinite variety of petroleum products, from cosmetics to pharmaceuticals.
- Synthetic materials: The process of polymerization, joining simple molecules into large complex molecules, is responsible for many modern materials, such as nylon, synthetic rubbers, polystyrene, and a wide variety of plastics and synthetic fibers.
- Food and biochemical engineering: The manufacture of packaged food, improvement of food additives, sterilization, and use of industrial bacteria, fungi, and yeasts in processes such as fermentation.
- Unit operations: Analyzing the transport of heat or fluid, such as pumping chemicals through a pipeline or transferring heat between substances. This area also includes the effect of heat transfer on chemical reactions, such as oxidation, chlorination, and so on.
- Cryogenic engineering: The design of plants operating at temperatures near absolute zero.
- Electrochemical engineering: Using electricity to alter chemical reactions, such as electroplating, or designing batteries and energy cells.
- Pollution control: Monitoring and reducing the harmful effects of chemical processing on the environment. Topics of concern are wastewater control, air pollution abatement, and the economics of pollution control.

continued...

Engineering and Scientific Disciplines

Molecular Systems

This field involves applying laboratory techniques to large-scale processes and includes the following areas:

- Biochemical engineering: Application of enzymes, bacteria, and so on to improve large-scale chemical processes.
- Polymer synthesis: Molecular basis for polymer properties and the chemical synthesis of new polymers adapted for large-scale production.
- Research and development in all areas of chemical processing.

Preparation for a career in chemical engineering requires a thorough background in physics, chemistry, and mathematics and a knowledge of thermodynamics and physical, analytic, and organic chemistry. Although extensively trained in chemistry, chemical engineers differ from chemists, in that their main concern is adapting laboratory techniques to large-scale manufacturing plants.

Chapter 7

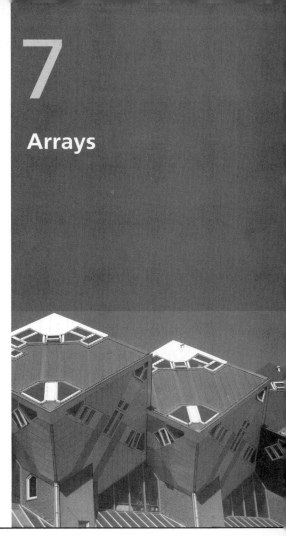

7

Arrays

All the variables you have used so far have a common characteristic: Each variable can be used to store only a single value at a time. For example, although the variables key, count, *and* grade *declared in the statements*

```
char key;
int count;
double grade;
```

are of different data types, each variable can store only one value of the declared data type. These types of variables are called **atomic variables** *(also referred to as* **scalar variables***), which means their values can't be further subdivided or separated into a legitimate data type.*

Often you have a set of values, all the same data type, that form a logical group. For example, the following lists show three groups of items: 1) a list of five double-precision temperatures, 2) a list of four character codes, and 3) a list of six integer voltages:

Temperatures	Codes	Voltages
95.75	Z	98
83.0	C	87
97.625	K	92
72.5	L	79
86.25		85
		72

A simple list containing items of the same data type is called a one-dimensional array. This chapter describes how one-dimensional arrays are declared, initialized, stored in a computer, and used. You also explore the use of one-dimensional arrays with sample programs and see the procedures for declaring and using multidimensional arrays.

7.1   One-Dimensional Arrays

A **one-dimensional array**, also referred to as a **single-dimensional array**, is a list of related values, all having the same data type, that's stored with a single group name.[1] In C++, as in other computer languages, the group name is referred to as the **array name**. For example, consider this list of temperatures:

95.75
83.0
97.625
72.5
86.25

All the temperatures in the list are double-precision numbers and must be declared as such. However, each item in the list doesn't have to be declared separately. The items in the list can be declared as a single unit and stored under a common variable name called the array name. For example, `temp` is used as the name for this list, and the declaration statement `double temp[5];` specifies that `temp` is to store five double-precision values. Notice that this declaration statement gives the array (or list) name, the data type of items in the array, and the number of items in the array. It's a specific example of the general syntax of an array declaration statement:

```
dataType arrayName[number-of-items]
```

---

[1]Lists can be implemented in a variety of ways. An array is simply one list implementation in which all list elements are of the same type, and each element is stored consecutively in a set of contiguous memory locations.

Good programming practice requires defining *number-of-items* in the array as a constant before declaring the array. So in practice, the previous array declaration for temp would be declared with two statements, as in these examples:

```
const int NUMELS = 5; // define a constant for the number of items
double temp[NUMELS];   // declare the array
```

The following are other examples of array declarations using this two-line syntax:

```
const int NUMELS = 6;
int volts[NUMELS];

const int ARRAYSIZE = 4;
char code[ARRAYSIZE];

const int SIZE = 100;
double amount[SIZE];
```

In these declaration statements, each array is allocated enough memory to hold the number of data items specified in the declaration statement. For example, the array named volts has storage reserved for six integers, the array named code has storage reserved for four characters, and the array named amount has storage reserved for 100 double-precision numbers. The constant identifiers, NUMELS, ARRAYSIZE, and SIZE, are programmer-selected names. Figure 7.1 illustrates the storage reserved for the volts and code arrays.

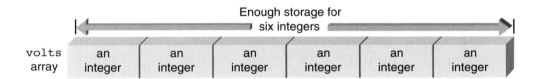

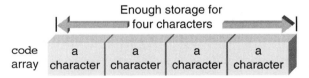

Figure 7.1 The volts and code arrays in memory

Each item in an array is called an **element** or a **component** of the array. The elements in the arrays shown in Figure 7.1 are stored sequentially, with the first element stored in the first reserved location, the second element stored in the second reserved location, and so on until the last element is stored in the last reserved location. This contiguous storage allocation is a key feature of arrays because it provides a simple mechanism for locating any element in the list easily.

Because elements in the array are stored sequentially, any single element can be accessed by giving the array's name and the element's position. This position is called the element's

index or **subscript** value. (The two terms are synonymous.) For a one-dimensional array, the first element has an index of 0, the second element has an index of 1, and so on. In C++, the array name and element index are combined by listing the index in brackets after the array name. For example, the declaration `double temp[5];` creates five elements, with the following correspondences:

`temp[0]` refers to the first temperature stored in the `temp` array
`temp[1]` refers to the second temperature stored in the `temp` array
`temp[2]` refers to the third temperature stored in the `temp` array
`temp[3]` refers to the fourth temperature stored in the `temp` array
`temp[4]` refers to the fifth temperature stored in the `temp` array

Figure 7.2 illustrates the `temp` array in memory with the correct designation for each array element. Each element is referred to as an **indexed variable** or a **subscripted variable** because both a variable name (the array name, in this case) and an index or a subscript value must be used to reference the element. Remember that the index or subscript value gives the element's position in the array.

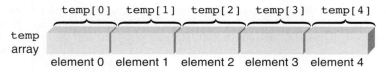

Figure 7.2   Identifying array elements

The subscripted variable, `temp[0]`, is read as "temp sub zero" or "temp zero." This is a shortened way of saying "the `temp` array subscripted by zero." Similarly, `temp[1]` is read as "temp sub one" or "temp one," `temp[2]` as "temp sub two" or "temp two," and so on.

Although referencing the first element with an index of 0 might seem unusual, doing so increases the computer's speed when it accesses array elements. Internally, unseen by the programmer, the computer uses the index as an offset from the array's starting position. As illustrated in Figure 7.3, the index tells the computer how many elements to skip, starting from the beginning of the array, to get to the desired element.

Subscripted variables can be used anywhere that scalar (atomic) variables are valid. Here are examples of using the elements of the `temp` array:

```
temp[0] = 95.75;
temp[1] = temp[0] - 11.0;
temp[2] = 5.0 * temp[0];
temp[3] = 79.0;
temp[4] = (temp[1] + temp[2] - 3.1) / 2.2;
sum = temp[0] + temp[1] + temp[2] + temp[3] + temp[4];
```

The subscript in brackets need not be an integer constant; any expression that evaluates to an integer can be used as a subscript.[2] In each case, of course, the value of the expression

---

[2]Some compilers permit floating-point variables as subscripts; in these cases, the floating-point value is truncated to an integer value.

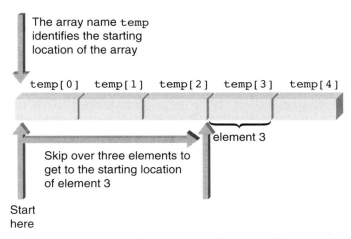

The array name `temp` identifies the starting location of the array

temp[0] temp[1] temp[2] temp[3] temp[4]

element 3

Skip over three elements to get to the starting location of element 3

Start here

Figure 7.3 Accessing an array element—element 3

must be within the valid subscript range defined when the array is declared. For example, assuming i and j are int variables, the following subscripted variables are valid:

```
temp[i]
temp[2*i]
temp[j-i]
```

An important advantage of using integer expressions as subscripts is that it allows sequencing through an array by using a loop. This makes statements such as the following unnecessary:

```
sum = temp[0] + temp[1] + temp[2] + temp[3] + temp[4];
```

The subscript values in this statement can be replaced by a for loop counter to access each element in the array sequentially. For example, the code

```
sum = 0;                 // initialize the sum to zero
for (i = 0; i < 5; i++)
   sum = sum + temp[i];  // add in a value
```

retrieves each array element sequentially and adds the element to sum. The variable i is used as both the counter in the for loop and a subscript. As i increases by one each time through the loop, the next element in the array is referenced. The procedure for adding array elements in the for loop is similar to the accumulation procedure you have used before.

The advantage of using a for loop to sequence through an array becomes apparent when working with larger arrays. For example, if the temp array contains 100 values rather than just 5, simply changing the number 5 to 100 in the for statement is enough to sequence through the 100 elements and add each temperature to the sum.

As another example of using a for loop to sequence through an array, say you want to locate the maximum value in an array of 1000 elements named volts. The procedure to locate the maximum value is to assume initially that the first element in the array is the largest number. Then, as you sequence through the array, the maximum is compared to each

> ## Point of Information
>
> ### Aggregate Data Types
>
> In contrast to atomic types, such as integer and floating-point data, there are aggregate types. An **aggregate type**, also referred to as both a structured type and a data structure, is any type whose values can be decomposed and are related by some defined structure. Additionally, operations must be available for retrieving and updating values in the data structure.
>
> One-dimensional arrays are examples of a structured type. In a one-dimensional array, such as an array of integers, the array is composed of integer values, with the integers related by their position in the list. Indexed variables provide the means of accessing and modifying values in the array.

element. When an element with a higher value is located, that element becomes the new maximum. The following code does the job:

```
const int NUMELS = 1000;

maximum = volts[0];             // set the maximum to element 0
for (i = 1; i < NUMELS; i++)    // cycle through the rest of the array
   if (volts[i] > maximum)      // compare each element to the maximum
      maximum = volts[i];       // capture the new high value
```

In this code, the `for` statement consists of one `if` statement. The search for a new maximum value starts with element 1 of the array and continues through the last element. Each element is compared to the current maximum, and when a higher value is encountered, it becomes the new maximum.

Input and Output of Array Values

An array element can be assigned a value interactively by using a `cin` statement, as shown in these examples of data entry statements:

```
cin >> temp[0];
cin >> temp[1] >> temp[2] >> temp[3];
cin >> temp[4] >> volts[6];
```

In the first statement, a single value is read and stored in the variable `temp[0]`. The second statement causes three values to be read and stored in the variables `temp[1]`, `temp[2]`, and `temp[3]`. Finally, the last `cin` statement is used to read values into the variables `temp[4]` and `volts[6]`.

Alternatively, a `for` loop can be used to cycle through the array for interactive data input. For example, the following code prompts the user for five temperatures:

```
const int NUMELS = 5;
for(i = 0; i < NUMELS; i++)
{
   cout << "Enter a temperature: ";
   cin  >> temp[i];
}
```

The first temperature entered is stored in temp[0], the second temperature entered is stored in temp[1], and so on until five temperatures have been entered.

One caution about storing data in an array: C++ doesn't check the value of the index being used (called a **bounds check**). If an array has been declared as consisting of 10 elements, for example, and you use an index of 12, which is outside the bounds of the array, C++ doesn't notify you of the error when the program is compiled. The program attempts to access element 12 by skipping over the appropriate number of bytes from the start of the array. Usually, this attempt results in a program crash, but not always. If the referenced location contains a value of the correct data type, the new value simply overwrites the value in the referenced memory locations. This leads to more errors, which are troublesome to locate when the variable legitimately assigned to the storage location is used at a different point in the program.

During output, an array element can be displayed by using a cout statement, or complete sections of the array can be displayed by including a cout statement in a for loop. Examples of both methods are shown:

```
cout << volts[6];
```

and

```
cout << "The value of element " << i << " is " << temp[i];
```

and

```
const int NUMELS = 20;
for (k = 5; k < NUMELS; k++)
  cout <<  k << "   " << amount[k] << endl;
```

The first statement displays the value of the subscripted variable volts[6]. The second statement displays the values of subscript i and of temp[i]. Before this statement can be executed, i must have an assigned value. Finally, the last example includes a cout statement in a for loop that displays both the value of the index and the value of elements 5 to 20.

Program 7.1 illustrates these input and output techniques, using an array named temp that's defined to store five integer numbers. The program includes two for loops. The first for loop is used to cycle through each array element and allows the user to input array values. After five values have been entered, the second for loop is used to display the stored values.

 ## Program 7.1

```
#include <iostream>
using namespace std;

int main()
{
  const int MAXTEMPS = 5;
  int i, temp[MAXTEMPS];
```

```
for (i = 0; i < MAXTEMPS; i++)      // Enter the temperatures
{
   cout << "Enter a temperature: ";
   cin  >> temp[i];
}

cout << endl;

for (i = 0; i < MAXTEMPS; i++)      // Print the temperatures
   cout << "temperature " << i << " is " << temp[i] << endl;

return 0;
}
```

A sample run of Program 7.1 follows:

```
Enter a temperature: 85
Enter a temperature: 90
Enter a temperature: 78
Enter a temperature: 75
Enter a temperature: 92

temperature 0 is 85
temperature 1 is 90
temperature 2 is 78
temperature 3 is 75
temperature 4 is 92
```

In reviewing the output of Program 7.1, pay attention to the difference between the index value displayed and the numerical value stored in the corresponding array element. The index value refers to the element's location in the array, and the subscripted variable refers to the value stored in the designated location.

In addition to simply displaying the values stored in each array element, the elements can also be processed by referencing the desired element. For example, in Program 7.2, the value of each element is accumulated in a total, which is displayed after all array elements have been displayed.

Program 7.2

```cpp
#include <iostream>
using namespace std;

int main()
{
  const int MAXTEMPS = 5;
  int i, temp[MAXTEMPS], total = 0;

  for (i = 0; i < MAXTEMPS; i++)      // Enter the temperatures
  {
    cout << "Enter a temperature: ";
    cin  >> temp[i];
  }

  cout << "\nThe total of the temperatures";

  for (i = 0; i < MAXTEMPS; i++)      // Display and total the temperatures
  {
    cout << "  " << temp[i];
    total =  total + temp[i];
  }

  cout << " is " << total << endl;

  return 0;
}
```

A sample run of Program 7.2 follows:

```
Enter a temperature: 85
Enter a temperature: 90
Enter a temperature: 78
Enter a temperature: 75
Enter a temperature: 92
The total of the temperatures  85  90  78  75  92 is 420
```

Notice that in Program 7.2, unlike Program 7.1, only the values stored in each array element, not the index numbers, are displayed. Although the second for loop is used to accumulate the total of each element, the accumulation could also have been accomplished in the first `for` loop by placing the statement `total = total + temp[i];` after the `cin` statement used to enter a value. Also, the `cout` statement used to display the total is placed outside the second `for` loop so that the total is displayed only once, after all values have been added to the total. If this `cout` statement were placed inside the `for` loop, five totals would be displayed, with only the last displayed total containing the sum of all array values.

EXERCISES 7.1

1. (**Practice**) Write array declarations for the following:
   a. A list of 100 double-precision voltages
   b. A list of 50 double-precision temperatures
   c. A list of 30 characters, each representing a code
   d. A list of 100 integer years
   e. A list of 32 double-precision velocities
   f. A list of 1000 double-precision distances
   g. A list of 6 integer code numbers

2. (**Practice**) Write correct notation for the first, third, and seventh elements of the following arrays:
   a. `int grades[20]`
   b. `double volts[10]`
   c. `double amps[16]`
   d. `int dist[15]`
   e. `double velocity[25]`
   f. `double time[100]`

3. (**Practice**) a. Write input statements using `cin` that can be used to enter values in the first, third, and seventh elements of each array declared in Exercise 2.
   b. Write a `for` loop that can be used to enter values for each array declared in Exercise 2.

4. (**Practice**) a. Write output statements using `cout` that can be used to display values from the first, third, and seventh elements of each array declared in Exercise 2.
   b. Write a `for` loop that can be used to display values for the complete array declared in Exercise 2.

5. (**Desk Check**) List the elements displayed by the following sections of code:
   a. `for (m = 1; m <= 5; m++)`

   `cout << a[m] << " ";`
   b. `for (k = 1; k <= 5; k = k + 2)`

   `cout << a[k] << " ";`

c. for (j = 3; j <= 10; j++)

cout << b[j] << " ";

d. for (k = 3; k <= 12; k = k + 3)

cout << b[k] << " ";

e. for (i = 2; i < 11; i = i + 2)

cout << c[i] << " ";

6. **(Practice) a.** Write a program to input the following values in an array named `volts`: 11.95, 16.32, 12.15, 8.22, 15.98, 26.22, 13.54, 6.45, and 17.59. After the data has been entered, have your program display the values.

   b. Repeat Exercise 6a, but after the data has been entered, have your program display it in the following form:

   ```
   11.95    16.32    12.15
    8.22    15.98    26.22
   13.54     6.45    17.59
   ```

7. **(Practice)** Write a program to input eight integer numbers in an array named `temp`. As each number is input, add the numbers to a total. After all numbers are input, display the numbers and their average.

8. **(Data Processing) a.** Write a program to input 10 integer numbers in an array named `fmax` and determine the maximum value entered. Your program should contain only one loop, and the maximum should be determined as array element values are being input. (*Hint*: Set the maximum equal to the first array element, which should be input before the loop used to input the remaining array values.)

   b. Repeat Exercise 8a, keeping track of both the maximum element in the array and the index number for the maximum. After displaying the numbers, print these two messages (replacing the underlines with the correct values):

   ```
   The maximum value is: ___
   This is element number ____ in the list of numbers
   ```

   c. Repeat Exercise 8b, but have your program locate the minimum of the data entered.

9. **(Data Processing) a.** Write a program to input the following integer numbers in an array named `grades`: 89, 95, 72, 83, 99, 54, 86, 75, 92, 73, 79, 75, 82, and 73. As each number is input, add the numbers to a total. After all numbers are input and the total is obtained, calculate the average of the numbers, and use the average to determine the deviation of each value from the average. Store each deviation in an array named `deviation`. Each deviation is obtained as the element value less the average of all the data. Have your program display each deviation with its corresponding element from the `grades` array.

   b. Calculate the variance of the data used in Exercise 9a. The variance is obtained by squaring each deviation and dividing the sum of the squared deviations by the number of deviations.

10. **(Electrical Eng.)** Write a program that specifies three one-dimensional arrays named `current`, `resistance`, and `volts`. Each array should be capable of holding 10 elements.

Using a `for` loop, input values for the `current` and `resistance` arrays. The entries in the `volts` array should be the product of the corresponding values in the `current` and `resistance` arrays (so `volts[i] = current [i] * resistance[i]`). After all the data has been entered, display the following output, with the appropriate value under each column heading:

```
Current    Resistance    Volts
```

7.2   Array Initialization

Array elements can be initialized in their declaration statements in the same manner as scalar variables, except the initializing elements must be included in braces, as shown in these examples:

```
int temp[5] = {98, 87, 92, 79, 85};
char codes[6] = {'s', 'a', 'm', 'p', 'l', 'e'};
double slopes[7] = {11.96, 6.43, 2.58, .86, 5.89, 7.56, 8.22};
```

Initializers are applied in the order they are written, with the first value used to initialize element 0, the second value used to initialize element 1, and so on, until all values have been used. For example, in the declaration

```
int temp[5] = {98, 87, 92, 79, 85};
```

`temp[0]` is initialized to 98, `temp[1]` is initialized to 87, `temp[2]` is initialized to 92, `temp[3]` is initialized to 79, and `temp[4]` is initialized to 85.

Because white space is ignored in C++, initializations can be continued across multiple lines. For example, the following declaration uses four lines to initialize all the array elements:

```
int gallons[20] = {19, 16, 14, 19, 20, 18,  // initializing values
                   12, 10, 22, 15, 18, 17,  // can extend across
                   16, 14, 23, 19, 15, 18,  // multiple lines
                   21, 5};
```

If the number of initializers is less than the declared number of elements listed in square brackets, the initializers are applied starting with array element 0. Therefore, in the declaration

```
double length[7] = {7.8, 6.4, 4.9, 11.2};
```

only `length[0]`, `length[1]`, `length[2]`, and `length[3]` are initialized with the listed values. The other array elements are initialized to 0.

Unfortunately, there's no method of indicating repetition of an initialization value or of initializing later array elements without first specifying values for earlier elements.

A unique feature of initializers is that the array size can be omitted when initializing values are included in the declaration statement. For example, the following declaration reserves enough storage room for five elements:

```
int gallons[] = {16, 12, 10, 14, 11};
```

Similarly, the following two declarations are equivalent:

```
char codes[6] = {'s', 'a', 'm', 'p', 'l', 'e'};
char codes[] = {'s', 'a', 'm', 'p', 'l', 'e'};
```

Both these declarations set aside six character locations for an array named `codes`. An interesting and useful simplification can also be used when initializing character arrays. For example, the following declaration uses the string `"sample"` to initialize the `codes` array:

```
char codes[] = "sample";   // no braces or commas
```

Recall that a string is any sequence of characters enclosed in quotation marks. The preceding declaration creates an array named `codes` with seven elements and fills the array with the seven characters shown in Figure 7.4. The first six characters, as expected, consist of the letters s, a, m, p, l, and e. The last character, the escape sequence \0, is called the **null character**. The null character is appended automatically to all strings used to initialize a character array. It's what distinguishes a C-string from a `string` class string. This character has an internal storage code numerically equal to zero. (The storage code for the 0 character has a numerical value of decimal 48, so the computer can't confuse the two.) The null character is used as a sentinel to mark the end of a string.

codes[0]   codes[1]   codes[2]   codes[3]   codes[4]   codes[5]   codes[6]

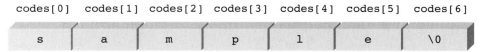

Figure 7.4   Initializing a character array with a string adds a terminating \0 character

After values have been assigned to array elements, through initialization in the declaration statement or with interactive input, array elements can be processed as described in the previous section. For example, Program 7.3 shows the initialization of array elements in the array declaration statement, and then uses a `for` loop to locate the maximum value stored in the array. The following output is produced by Program 7.3:

```
The maximum value is 27
```

Program 7.3

```cpp
#include <iostream>
using namespace std;

int main()
{
  const int MAXELS = 5;

  int i, max, nums[MAXELS] = {2, 18, 1, 27, 16};

  max = nums[0];

  for (i = 1; i < MAXELS; i++)
    if (max < nums[i])
      max = nums[i];

  cout << "The maximum value is " << max << endl;

  return 0;
}
```

EXERCISES 7.2

1. **(Practice)** Write array declarations, including initializers, for the following:
   a. A list of 10 integer voltages: 89, 75, 82, 93, 78, 95, 81, 88, 77, and 82.
   b. A list of five double-precision slopes: 11.62, 13.98, 18.45, 12.68, and 14.76.
   c. A list of 100 double-precision distances; the first six distances are 6.29, 6.95, 7.25, 7.35, 7.40, and 7.42.
   d. A list of 64 double-precision temperatures; the first 10 temperatures are 78.2, 69.6, 68.5, 83.9, 55.4, 67.0, 49.8, 58.3, 62.5, and 71.6.
   e. A list of 15 character codes; the first seven codes are f, j, m, q, t, w, and z.

2. **(Data Processing)** Write an array declaration statement that stores the following values in an array named `volts`: 16.24, 18.98, 23.75, 16.29, 19.54, 14.22, 11.13, and 15.39. Include these statements in a program that displays the values in the array.

3. **(Data Processing)** Write a program that uses an array declaration statement to initialize the following numbers in an array named `slopes`: 17.24, 25.63, 5.94, 33.92, 3.71, 32.84, 35.93, 18.24, and 6.92. Your program should locate and display the maximum and minimum values in the array.

4. **(Electrical Eng.)** Write a program that stores the following resistance values in an array named `resistance`: 16, 27, 39, 56, and 81. Your program should also create two arrays named `current` and `power`, each capable of storing five double-precision numbers. Using a `for` loop and a `cin` statement, have your program accept five user-input numbers in the `current` array when the program is run. Your program should store the product of the values of the squares of the `current` array and the `resistance` array in the `power` array. For example, use `power[1]` = `resistance[1]` * `pow(current[1],2)`. Your program should then display the following output (fill in the chart):

Resistance	Current	Power
16		
27		
39		
56		
81		
Total:		

5. **(Practice) a.** Write a declaration to store the string `"This is a test"` in an array named `strtest`. Include the declaration in a program to display the message, using the following loop:

```
for (i = 0; i < NUMDISPLAY; i++)
    cout << strtest[i];
```

`NUMDISPLAY` is a named constant for the number 14.

   b. Modify the `for` statement in Exercise 5a to display only the array characters t, e, s, and t.

   c. Include the array declaration written in Exercise 5a in a program that uses a `cout` statement to display characters in the array. For example, the statement `cout << strtest;` causes the string stored in the `strtest` array to be displayed. Using this statement requires having the end-of-string marker, `\0`, as the last character in the array.

   d. Repeat Exercise 5a, using a `while` loop. (*Hint:* Stop the loop when the `\0` escape sequence is detected. The expression `while (strtest[i] != '\0')` can be used.)

7.3   Declaring and Processing Two-Dimensional Arrays

A **two-dimensional array**, sometimes referred to as a table, consists of both rows and columns of elements. For example, the following array of numbers is called a two-dimensional array of integers:

```
 8   16    9   52
 3   15   27    6
14   25    2   10
```

This array consists of three rows and four columns. To reserve storage for this array, both the number of rows and the number of columns must be included in the array's declaration. Calling the array `val`, the following is the correct specification for this two-dimensional array:

```
int val[3][4];
```

Similarly, the declarations

```
double volts[10][5];
char code[6][26];
```

specify that the array `volts` consists of 10 rows and 5 columns of floating-point numbers, and the array `code` consists of 6 rows and 26 columns, with each element capable of holding one character.

To locate each element in a two-dimensional array, you use its position in the array. As shown in Figure 7.5, the term `val[1][3]` uniquely identifies the element in row 1, column 3. As with one-dimensional array variables, two-dimensional array variables can be used anywhere that scalar variables are valid, as shown in these examples using elements of the `val` array:

```
watts = val[2][3];
val[0][0] = 62;
newnum = 4 * (val[1][0] - 5);
sumRow0 = val[0][0] + val[0][1] + val[0][2] + val[0][3];
```

The last statement causes the values of the four elements in row 0 to be added and the sum to be stored in the scalar variable `sumRow0`.

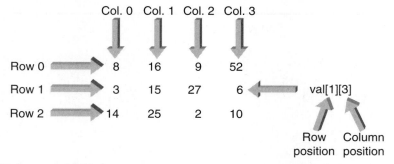

Figure 7.5   Each array element is identified by its row and column position

Declaring and Processing Two-
Dimensional Arrays

As with one-dimensional arrays, two-dimensional arrays can be initialized in their declaration statements by listing the initial values inside braces and separating them with commas. Additionally, braces can be used to separate rows. For example, the declaration

```
int val[3][4] = { {8,16,9,52},
                  {3,15,27,6},
                  {14,25,2,10} };
```

declares val as an array of integers with three rows and four columns, with the initial values given in the declaration. The first set of internal braces contains values for row 0 of the array, the second set of internal braces contains values for row 1, and the third set of braces contains values for row 2.

Although the commas in the initialization braces are always required, the inner braces can be omitted. Without them, the initialization for val can be written as follows:

```
int val[3][4] = {8,16,9,52,
                 3,15,27,6,
                 14,25,2,10};
```

Separating initial values into rows in the declaration statement isn't necessary because the compiler assigns values beginning with the [0][0] element and proceeds row by row to fill in the remaining values. Therefore, the initialization

```
int val[3][4] = {8,16,9,52,3,15,27,6,14,25,2,10};
```

is equally valid but doesn't clearly indicate to another programmer where one row ends and another begins.

As shown in Figure 7.6, a two-dimensional array is initialized in row order. The elements of row 0 are initialized, then the elements of row 1 are initialized, and so on, until the initializations are completed. This row ordering is the same ordering used to store two-dimensional arrays. That is, array element [0][0] is stored first, followed by element [0][1], then element [0][2], and so on. Following row 1's elements are row 2's elements, and so on for all rows in the array.

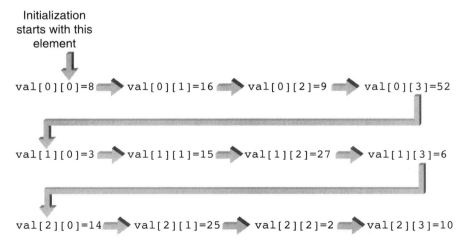

Figure 7.6 Storage and initialization of the val array

As with one-dimensional arrays, two-dimensional arrays can be displayed with element notation or by using loops (while or for). Program 7.4, which displays all elements of a 3-by-4 two-dimensional array, shows these two techniques. Notice that constants are used to define the array's rows and columns.

 ## Program 7.4

```cpp
#include <iostream>
#include <iomanip>
using namespace std;
int main()
{
  const int NUMROWS = 3;
  const int NUMCOLS = 4;
  int i, j;
  int val[NUMROWS][NUMCOLS] = {8,16,9,52,3,15,27,6,14,25,2,10};

  cout << "\nDisplay of val array by explicit element"
       << endl << setw(4) << val[0][0] << setw(4) << val[0][1]
       << setw(4) << val[0][2] << setw(4) << val[0][3]
       << endl << setw(4) << val[1][0] << setw(4) << val[1][1]
       << setw(4) << val[1][2] << setw(4) << val[1][3]
       << endl << setw(4) << val[2][0] << setw(4) << val[2][1]
       << setw(4) << val[2][2] << setw(4) << val[2][3];
  cout << "\n\nDisplay of val array using a nested for loop";

  for (i = 0; i < NUMROWS; i++)
  {
    cout << endl;       // print a new line for each row
    for (j = 0; j < NUMCOLS; j++)
      cout << setw(4) <<  val[i][j];
  }

  cout << endl;
  return 0;
}
```

This is the display produced by Program 7.4:

```
Display of val array by explicit element
    8   16    9   52
    3   15   27    6
   14   25    2   10
```

```
Display of val array using a nested for loop
    8   16    9   52
    3   15   27    6
   14   25    2   10
```

The first display of the val array produced by Program 7.4 is constructed by designating each array element. The second display of array element values, which is identical to the first, is produced by using a nested for loop. Nested loops are especially useful when dealing with two-dimensional arrays because they allow the programmer to designate and cycle through each element easily. In Program 7.4, the variable i controls the outer loop, and the variable j controls the inner loop. Each pass through the outer loop corresponds to a single row, with the inner loop supplying the column elements. After a complete row is printed, a new line is started for the next row. The result is a display of the array in a row-by-row fashion.

After two-dimensional array elements have been assigned, array processing can begin. Typically, for loops are used to process two-dimensional arrays because, as noted previously, they allow the programmer to designate and cycle through each array element easily. For example, the nested for loop in Program 7.5 is used to multiply each element in the val array by the scalar number 10 and display the resulting value.

 ## Program 7.5

```cpp
#include <iostream>
#include <iomanip>
using namespace std;
int main()
{
  const int NUMROWS = 3;
  const int NUMCOLS = 4;
  int i, j;
  int val[NUMROWS][NUMCOLS] = {8,16,9,52,
                               3,15,27,6,
                               14,25,2,10};
// multiply each element by 10 and display it
  cout << "\nDisplay of multiplied elements";
  for (i = 0; i < NUMROWS; i++)
  {
    cout << endl;    // start each row on a new line
    for (j = 0; j < NUMCOLS; j++)
    {
      val[i][j] = val[i][j] * 10;
      cout << setw(5) << val[i][j];
    }   // end of inner loop
  }     // end of outer loop
  cout << endl;
  return 0;
}
```

Following is the output produced by Program 7.5:

```
Display of multiplied elements
   80   160    90   520
   30   150   270    60
  140   250    20   100
```

Larger Dimensional Arrays

Although arrays with more than two dimensions aren't commonly used, C++ does allow declaring any number of dimensions by listing the maximum size of all dimensions for the array. For example, the declaration int response [4][10][6]; declares a three-dimensional array. The first element in the array is designated as response[0][0][0] and the last element as response[3][9][5].

As shown in Figure 7.7, you can think of a three-dimensional array as a book of data tables. Using this analogy, think of the first index as the location of the desired row in a table, the second index value as the desired column, and the third index value, often called the "rank," as the page number of the selected table.

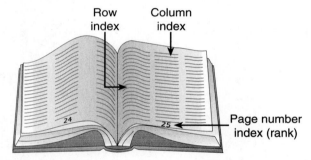

Figure 7.7   Representation of a three-dimensional array

Similarly, arrays of any dimension can be declared. Conceptually, a four-dimensional array can be represented as a shelf of books, with the fourth dimension used to declare a selected book on the shelf, and a five-dimensional array can be viewed as a bookcase filled with books, with the fifth dimension referring to a selected shelf in the bookcase. Using the same analogy, a six-dimensional array can be thought of as a single row of bookcases, with the sixth dimension referring to the desired bookcase in the row; a seven-dimensional array can be thought of as multiple rows of bookcases, with the seventh dimension referring to the desired row, and so on. Alternatively, arrays of three, four, five, six, and so on dimensional arrays can be viewed as mathematical *n*-tuples of order three, four, five, six, and so forth.

EXERCISES 7.3

1. **(Practice)** Write specification statements for the following:
   a. An array of integers with 6 rows and 10 columns
   b. An array of integers with 2 rows and 5 columns
   c. An array of characters with 7 rows and 12 columns
   d. An array of characters with 15 rows and 7 columns
   e. An array of double-precision numbers with 10 rows and 25 columns
   f. An array of double-precision numbers with 16 rows and 8 columns

2. **(Desk Check)** Determine the output produced by the following program:

```
#include <iostream>
using namespace std;

int main()
{
   int i, j, val[3][4] = {8,16,9,52,3,15,27,6,14,25,2,10};

   for (i = 0; i < 3; ++i)
     for (j = 0; j < 4; ++j)
       cout << "   " << val[i][j];

   return 0;
}
```

3. **(Practice) a.** Write a C++ program that adds the values of all elements in the `val` array used in Exercise 2 and displays the total.

   b. Modify the program written for Exercise 3a to display the total of each row separately.

4. **(Practice)** Write a C++ program that adds equivalent elements of the two-dimensional arrays named `first` and `second`. Both arrays should have two rows and three columns. For example, element `[1][2]` of the resulting array should be the sum of `first[1][2]` and `second[1][2]`. The first and second arrays should be initialized as follows:

   ```
        first                second
   16    18    23        24    52    77
   54    91    11        16    19    59
   ```

5. **(Data Processing) a.** Write a C++ program that finds and displays the maximum value in a two-dimensional array of integers. The array should be declared as a 4-by-5 array of integers and initialized with the data 16, 22, 99, 4, 18, -258, 4, 101, 5, 98, 105, 6, 15, 2, 45, 33, 88, 72, 16, and 3.

   b. Modify the program written in Exercise 5a so that it also displays the maximum value's row and column subscript numbers.

6. **(Data Processing)** Write a C++ program that selects the values in a 4-by-5 array of positive integers in increasing order and stores the selected values in the one-dimensional array named `sort`. Use the data statement in Exercise 5a to initialize the two-dimensional array.

7. **(Electrical Eng.)** **a.** An engineer has constructed a two-dimensional array of real numbers with three rows and five columns. This array currently contains test voltages of an amplifier. Write a C++ program that interactively inputs 15 array values, and then determines the total number of voltages in these ranges: less than 60, greater than or equal to 60 and less than 70, greater than or equal to 70 and less than 80, greater than or equal to 80 and less than 90, and greater than or equal to 90.

 b. Entering 15 voltages each time the program written for Exercise 7a runs is cumbersome. What method could be used for initializing the array during the testing phase?

 c. How might the program you wrote for Exercise 7a be modified to include the case of no voltage being present? That is, what voltage could be used to indicate an invalid voltage, and how would your program have to be modified to exclude counting such a voltage?

7.4   Arrays as Arguments

Array elements are passed to a called function in the same manner as scalar variables; they are simply included as subscripted variables when the function call is made. For example, the following function call passes the values of the elements `volts[2]` and `volts[6]` to the function `findMin()`:

```
findMin(volts[2], volts[6]);
```

Passing a complete array of values to a function is, in many respects, easier than passing each element. The called function receives access to the actual array rather than a copy of values in the array. For example, if `volts` is an array, the function call `findMax(volts);` makes the complete `volts` array available to the `findMax()` function. This function call is different from passing a single variable to a function.

Recall that when a single scalar argument is passed to a function (see Section 6.1), the called function receives only a copy of the passed value, which is stored in one of the function's parameters. If arrays were passed in this manner, a copy of the complete array would have to be created. For large arrays, making copies for each function call would waste computer storage and frustrate the effort to return multiple-element changes made by the called program. (Remember that a function returns at most one direct value.)

To avoid these problems, the called function is given direct access to the original array.[3] In this way, any changes the called function makes are made directly to the array. For the following specific examples of function calls, the arrays `nums`, `keys`, `volts`, and `current` are declared as shown:

```
int nums[5];                        // an array of five integers
char keys[256];                     // an array of 256 characters
double volts[500], current[500];   // two arrays of 500 doubles
```

---

[3]The called function has access to the original array because the array's starting address is actually passed as an argument. The formal parameter receiving this address argument is a pointer. Chapter 12 explains the intimate relationship between array names and pointers.

For these arrays, the following function calls can be made; note that in each case, the called function receives direct access to the named array:

```
findMax(nums);
findCh(keys);
calcTot(nums, volts, current);
```

On the receiving side, the called function must be alerted that an array is being made available. For example, the following are suitable function headers for the previous functions:

```
int findMax(int vals[5])
char findCh(char in_keys[256])
void calcTot(int arr1[5], double arr2[500], double arr3[500])
```

In each function header, the programmer chooses the names in the parameter list. However, the parameter names used by the functions still refer to the original array created outside the function, as Program 7.6 makes clear.

Program 7.6

```cpp
#include <iostream>
using namespace std;

const int MAXELS = 5;
int findMax(int [MAXELS]);          // function prototype

int main()
{
  int nums[MAXELS] = {2, 18, 1, 27, 16};

  cout << "The maximum value is " << findMax(nums) << endl;

  return 0;
}

// find the maximum value
int findMax(int vals[MAXELS])
{
  int i, max = vals[0];

  for (i = 1; i < MAXELS; i++)
    if (max < vals[i]) max = vals[i];

  return max;
}
```

Notice that the function prototype for findMax() declares that findMax returns an integer and expects an array of five integers as an actual argument. It's also important to know that only one array is created in Program 7.6. In main(), this array is known as nums, and in findMax(), the array is known as vals. As illustrated in Figure 7.8, both names refer to the same array, so vals[3] is the same element as nums[3].

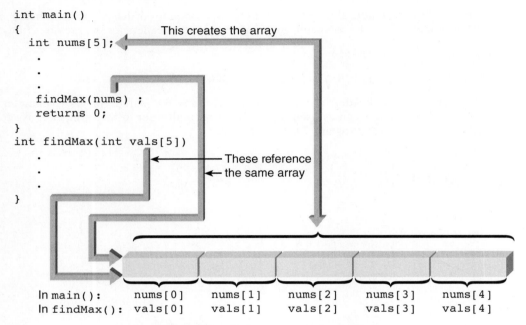

Figure 7.8　Only one array is created

The parameter declaration in the findMax() header actually contains extra information not required by the function. All that findMax() must know is that the parameter vals references an array of integers. Because the array has been created in main() and no additional storage space is needed in findMax(), the declaration for vals can omit the array size. Therefore, the following is an alternative function header:

```
int findMax(int vals[])
```

This form of the function header makes more sense when you realize that only one item is actually passed to findMax() when the function is called: the starting address of the num array, as shown in Figure 7.9.

Because only the starting address of vals is passed to findMax(), the number of elements in the array need not be included in the declaration for vals.[4] In fact, generally

---

[4]An important consequence of passing the starting address is that findMax() has direct access to the passed array. This access means any change to an element of the vals array is a change to the nums array. This result is much different from the situation with scalar variables, where the called function doesn't receive direct access to the passed variable.

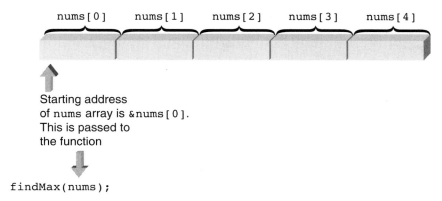

```
findMax(nums);
```

Figure 7.9 The array's starting address is passed

it's advisable to omit the array size from the function header. For example, the more general form of findMax() can be used to find the maximum value of an integer array of arbitrary size:

```
int findMax(int vals[], int numels)    //find the maximum value
{
  int i, max = vals[0];

  for (i = 1; i < numels; i++)
   if (max < vals[i])
     max = vals[i];

  return max;
}
```

The more general form of findMax() declares that the function returns an integer value. The function expects the starting address of an integer array and the number of elements in the array as arguments. Then, using the number of elements as the boundary for its search, the function's for loop causes each array element to be examined in sequential order to locate the maximum value. Program 7.7 shows using findMax() in a complete program.

 ## Program 7.7

```
#include <iostream>
using namespace std;

int findMax(int [], int);    // function prototype

int main()
{
```

☞

```
   const int MAXELS = 5;
   int nums[MAXELS] = {2, 18, 1, 27, 16};

   cout << "The maximum value is "
        << findMax(nums, MAXELS) << endl;

   return 0;
}

// find the maximum value
int findMax(int vals[], int numels)
{
   int i, max = vals[0];

   for (i = 1; i < numels; i++)
     if (max < vals[i]) max = vals[i];

   return max;
}
```

The following is the output displayed by Programs 7.6 and 7.7:

```
    The maximum value is 27
```

Passing two-dimensional arrays to a function is identical to passing one-dimensional arrays. The called function receives access to the entire array. For example, if `val` is a two-dimensional array, the function call `display(val);` makes the complete `val` array available to the function `display()`. Consequently, any changes `display()` makes are made directly to the `val` array. As further examples, if the following two-dimensional arrays named `test`, `factors`, and `thrusts` are declared as

```
int test[7][9];
float factors[26][10];
double thrusts[256][52];
```

then the following function calls are valid:

```
findMax(test);
obtain(factors);
average(thrusts);
```

On the receiving side, the called function must be alerted that a two-dimensional array is being made available. For example, assuming the previous functions return an integer, the following are suitable function headers:

```
int findMax(int nums[7][9])
int obtain(float values[26][10])
int average(double vals[256][52])
```

The parameter names chosen are used inside the function body. However, the parameter names still refer to the original array created outside the function. Program 7.8 shows passing a two-dimensional array to a function that displays the array's values.

Program 7.8

```
#include <iostream>
#include <iomanip>
using namespace std;
const int ROWS = 3;
const int COLS = 4;
void display(int [ROWS][COLS]);     // function prototype
int main()
{
  int val[ROWS][COLS] = {8,16,9,52,
                         3,15,27,6,
                        14,25,2,10};
  display(val);
  return 0;
}
void display(int nums[ROWS][COLS])
{
  int rownum, colnum;
  for (rownum = 0; rownum < ROWS; rownum++)
  {
    for(colnum = 0; colnum < COLS; colnum++)
      cout << setw(4) <<nums[rownum][colnum];
    cout << endl;
  }
  return;
}
```

Only one array is created in Program 7.8. This array is known as val in main() and as nums in display(). Therefore, val[0][2] refers to the same element as nums[0][2].

Notice the use of the nested for loop in Program 7.8 for cycling through each array element. The variable rownum controls the outer loop, and the variable colnum controls the inner loop. For each pass through the outer loop, which corresponds to a single row, the innerloop makes one pass through the column elements. After a complete row is printed, a new line is started for the next row. The result is a display of the array in a row-by-row fashion:

```
 8   16    9   52
 3   15   27    6
14   25    2   10
```

The parameter declaration for nums in display() contains extra information not required by the function. The declaration for nums can omit the row size of the array, so the following is an alternative function prototype:

```
display(int nums[][4]);
```

The reason the column size must be included but the row size is optional becomes obvious when you see how array elements are stored in memory. Starting with element val[0][0], each succeeding element is stored consecutively, row by row, as val[0][0], val[0][1], val[0][2], val[0][3], val[1][0], val[1][1], and so on, as illustrated in Figure 7.10.

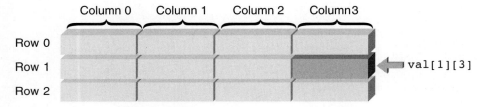

Figure 7.10   Storage of the val array

As with all array accesses, a single element of the val array is obtained by adding an offset to the array's starting location. For example, element val[1][3] of the val array in Figure 7.10 is located at an offset of 28 bytes from the start of the array. Internally, the compiler uses the row index, column index, and column size to determine this offset, using the following calculation (assuming 4 bytes for an int):

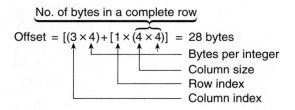

The column size is necessary in the offset calculation so that the compiler can determine the number of positions to skip over to get to the correct row.

Internal Array Element Location Algorithm[5]

Internally, each element in an array is obtained by adding an offset to the starting address of the array. Therefore, the memory address of each array element is calculated internally as follows:

Address of element i = starting array address + the offset

For one-dimensional arrays, the offset to the element with index i is calculated as follows:

*Offset = i * the size of an element*

For two-dimensional arrays, the same address calculation is made, except that the offset is determined as

*Offset = column index value * the size of an element*
*+ row index value * number of bytes in a complete row*

where the number of bytes in a complete row is calculated as follows:

number of bytes in a complete row =
*maximum column specification * the size of an element*

For example, as illustrated in Figure 7.11, for a one-dimensional array of integers in which each integer is stored with 4 bytes, the offset to the element with an index value of 5 is 5 * 4 = 20. Using the address operator, &, you can check this address algorithm, as shown in Program 7.9.

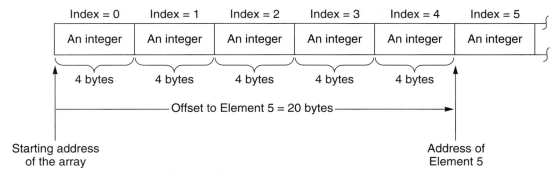

Figure 7.11 The offset to the element with an index value of 5

Program 7.9

```cpp
#include <iostream>
using namespace std;

int main()
{
const int NUMELS = 20;

int arr[NUMELS];

cout << "The starting address of the arr array is: "
     << int (&arr[0]) << endl;
cout << "The storage size of each array element is: "
     << sizeof(int) << endl;
cout << "The address of element number 5 is: "
     << int (&arr[5]) << endl;
cout << "The starting address of the array, "

<< "\ndisplayed using the notation arr, is: "

<< int (arr) << endl;

return 0;
}
```

Here is a sample output produced by Program 7.9:

```
The starting address of the arr array is: 1244796
The storage size of each array element is: 4
The address of element number 5 is: 1244816
The starting address of the array,
displayed using the notation arr, is: 1244796
```

Notice that the addresses have been displayed in decimal form, and element 5 is 20 bytes beyond the array's starting address. Also, the array's starting address is the same as the address of element 0, which is coded as &arr[0]. Alternatively, as shown by the displayed line, the starting array address can also be obtained as arr, which is the array name, because an array name is a pointer constant, which is an address. (Chapter 12 explains the close association of array names and pointers.)

EXERCISES 7.4

1. **(Practice)** The following declaration was used to create the volts array:

   ```
   int volts[500];
   ```

   Write two different function headers for a function named sortArray() that accepts the volts array as a parameter named inArray.

2. **(Practice)** The following declaration was used to create the factors array:

   ```
   double factors[256];
   ```

   Write two different function headers for a function named findKey() that accepts the factors array as a parameter named select.

3. **(Practice)** The following declaration was used to create the power array:

   ```
   double power[256];
   ```

   Write two different function headers for a function named prime() that accepts the power array as an argument named watts.

4. **(Modify) a.** Modify the findMax() function in Program 7.6 to locate the minimum value of the passed array.

   b. Include the function written in Exercise 4a in a complete program and run the program.

5. **(Practice)** Write a program that has a declaration in main() to store the following numbers in an array named temps: 6.5, 7.2, 7.5, 8.3, 8.6, 9.4, 9.6, 9.8, and 10.0. There should be a function call to show() that accepts the temps array as a parameter named temps and then displays the numbers in the array.

6. **(Electrical Eng.)** Write a program that declares three one-dimensional arrays named volts, current, and resistance. Each array should be declared in main() and be capable of holding 10 double-precision numbers. The numbers to store in current are 10.62, 14.89, 13.21, 16.55, 18.62, 9.47, 6.58, 18.32, 12.15, and 3.98. The numbers to store in resistance are 4, 8.5, 6, 7.35, 9, 15.3, 3, 5.4, 2.9, and 4.8. Your program should pass these three arrays to a function named calc_volts(), which should calculate elements in the volts array as the product of the corresponding elements in the current and resistance arrays (for example, volts[1] = current[1] * resistance[1]). After calc_volts() has passed values to the volts array, the values in the array should be displayed from within main().

7. **(Statistics)** Write a program that includes two functions named calcavg() and variance(). The calcavg() function should calculate and return the average of values stored in an array named testvals. The array should be declared in main() and include the values 89, 95, 72, 83, 99, 54, 86, 75, 92, 73, 79, 75, 82, and 73. The variance() function should calculate and return the variance of the data. The variance is obtained by subtracting the average from each value in testvals, squaring the values

obtained, adding them, and dividing by the number of elements in testvals. The values returned from calcavg() and variance() should be displayed by using cout statements in main().

7.5   A Case Study: Statistical Analysis

Arrays are extremely useful in applications that require multiple passes through the same set of data elements. This section uses one such application that's a statistical data analysis requiring two passes through the data. The first pass is used to input the list and determine the average of the data. The second pass uses the average to determine a standard deviation. This application illustrates one-dimensional array processing and helps you understand passing an array to a function.

Step 1   Analyze the Problem

The statement of the problem indicates that two output values are required: an average and a standard deviation. The input item defined in the problem statement is a list of integer numbers. Because the problem statement doesn't specify the list size, and to make the application's functions as general as possible, both functions will be designed to handle any size list passed to them. This design also requires passing the exact number of elements in the array to each function at the time of the function call. This capability means each function must be capable of receiving at least two input items as parameters: an array of arbitrary size and an integer number corresponding to the number of elements in the passed array.

Step 2   Develop a Solution

The I/O specifications determined from the problem analysis imply that the each function's parameter list must be capable of receiving at least two items: one parameter to accommodate the integer array and the second parameter to accept an integer. The first function returns the average of the numbers in the passed array, and the second function returns the standard deviation. These items are determined as follows:

Calculate the average by adding the grades and dividing by the number of grades that was added.
Determine the standard deviation by:
> *Subtracting the average from each grade. (This results in a set of new numbers, each of which is called a deviation.)*
> *Squaring each deviation found in the previous step.*
> *Adding the squared deviations and dividing the sum by the number of deviations.*
> *The square root of the number found in the previous step is the standard deviation.*

The standard deviation can be calculated only after the average has been computed. Therefore, in addition to requiring the array of integers and the number of values in the array, the standard deviation function also requires that the average be passed to it. Specifying the algorithm in detail, before any coding is done, ensures that all necessary inputs and requirements are discovered early in the program development process.

To make sure you understand the required processing, do a hand calculation, assuming the average and standard deviation of the following 10 grades are to be determined: 98, 82, 67, 54, 78, 83, 95, 76, 68, and 63. Here's the average of these grades:

$$\text{Average} = (98 + 82 + 67 + 54 + 78 + 83 + 95 + 76 + 68 + 63)/10 = 76.4$$

The standard deviation is calculated by first determining the sum of the squared deviations, and then dividing the resulting sum by 10 and taking its square root, as shown:

$$\text{Sum of squared deviations} = (98\text{-}76.4)^2 + (82\text{-}76.4)^2$$
$$+ (67\text{-}76.4)^2 + (54\text{-}76.4)^2$$
$$+ (78\text{-}76.4)^2 + (83\text{-}76.4)^2$$
$$+ (95\text{-}76.4)^2 + (76\text{-}76.4)^2$$
$$+ (68\text{-}76.3)^2 + (63\text{-}76.4)^2 = 1730.400700$$

$$\text{Standard deviation} = \sqrt{1730.4007/10} = \sqrt{173.04007} = 13.154470$$

Having specified the algorithm for both functions, you're now in a position to code them.

Step 3 Code the Solution

When writing functions, concentrating on the function header first is helpful. You can then write the function body to process the input parameters correctly to produce the desired results. Naming the averaging function findAvg() and selecting the parameter names nums for the passed array and numel for the number of elements, the function header becomes the following:

```
double findAvg(int nums[], int numel)
```

This function header begins the definition of the averaging function and allows the function to accept an array of integer values and an integer number. As shown by the hand calculation, the average of a set of integer numbers can be a floating-point number; therefore, the function is defined as returning a floating-point value. The function body calculates the average as described by the algorithm developed earlier. The completed findAvg() function is as follows:

```
double findAvg(int nums[], int numel)
{
  int i;
  double sumnums = 0.0;

  for (i = 0; i < numel; i++) // calculate the sum of the grades
    sumnums = sumnums + nums[i];

  return (sumnums / numel);   // calculate and return the average
}
```

The function body contains a for loop to sum the numbers. Notice also that the termination value of the loop counter in the for loop is numel, the number of integers in the array passed to the function through the parameter list. Using this parameter gives the function its generality and allows it to be used for input arrays of any size. For example, calling the function with the statement

```
findAvg(values,10)
```

tells the function that numel is 10 and the values array consists of 10 values, whereas the statement

```
findAvg(values,1000)
```

tells findAvg() that numel is 1000 and the values array consists of 1000 numbers. In both calls, the actual argument named values corresponds to the parameter named nums in the findAvg() function.

Using similar reasoning as for the averaging function, the function header for the standard deviation function, named stdDev(), is as follows:

```
double stdDev(int nums[], int numel, double av)
```

This header begins the definition of the stdDev() function. It defines the function as returning a double-precision value and accepting an array of integers, an integer value, and a double-precision value as inputs to the function. The body of the stdDev() function must calculate the standard deviation as described in the algorithm. This is the complete standard deviation function:

```
double stdDev(int nums[], int numel, double av)
{
  int i;
  double sumdevs = 0.0;

  for (i = 0; i < numel; i++)
    sumdevs = sumdevs + pow((nums[i] - av),2.0);

 return(sqrt(sumdevs/numel));
}
```

Step 4   Test and Correct the Program

Testing a program's function requires writing a main() function to call the function you're testing and display the returned results. Program 7.10 uses a main() function to set up a grade array with the data previously used in the hand calculation and to call the findAvg() and stdDev() functions.

Program 7.10

```cpp
#include <iostream>
#include <iomanip>
#include <cmath>
using namespace std;

double findAvg(int [], int);           // function prototype
double stdDev(int [], int, double); // function prototype

int main()
{
  const int NUMELS = 10;

  int values[NUMELS] = {98, 82, 67, 54, 78, 83, 95, 76, 68, 63};
  double average, sDev;
  average = findAvg(values, NUMELS);          // call the function
  sDev = stdDev(values, NUMELS, average); // call the function
  cout << "The average of the numbers is "
       << setw(5) << setiosflags(ios::showpoint)
       << setprecision(2) << average << endl;

  cout << "The standard deviation of the numbers is "
       << setw(5) << setiosflags(ios::showpoint)
       << setprecision(2) << sDev << endl;
  return 0;
}

double findAvg(int nums[], int numel)
{
  int i;
  double sumnums = 0.0;

  for (i = 0; i < numel; i++) // calculate the sum of the grades
    sumnums = sumnums + nums[i];

  return (sumnums / numel);   // calculate and return the average
}
```

☞

```
double stdDev(int nums[], int numel, double av)
{
 int i;
 double sumdevs = 0.0;

 for (i = 0; i < numel; i++)
  sumdevs = sumdevs + pow((nums[i] - av),2);

 return(sqrt(sumdevs/numel));
}
```

A test run of Program 7.10 produced the following display:

```
The average of the numbers is 76.40
The standard deviation of the numbers is 13.15
```

Although this result agrees with the previous hand calculation, testing isn't complete without verifying the calculation at the boundary points. For this program, the test consists of checking the calculation with all the same values, such as all 0s and all 100s. Another simple test is to use five 0s and five 100s. You can try these tests on your own as an exercise.

 EXERCISES 7.5

1. **(Practice)** Enter and run Program 7.10 on your computer.

2. **(Practice)** Run Program 7.10 to determine the average and standard deviation of the following list of 15 grades: 68, 72, 78, 69, 85, 98, 95, 75, 77, 82, 84, 91, 89, 65, and 74.

3. **(List Maintenance)** A common programming problem is maintaining a list in numerical or alphabetical order. For example, inventory part numbers are typically kept in numerical order, but telephone lists are kept in alphabetical order.

   For this exercise, write a function that inserts a three-digit part number in a list of part numbers. The list is maintained in increasing numerical order, and duplicate part numbers aren't allowed. Allocate a maximum list size of 100 values, and use a sentinel value of 9999 to indicate the end of the list. For example, if the current list contains nine part numbers, the 10th position in the list contains the sentinel value. Figure 7.12 shows the insertion process for an original list of nine part numbers, using the following processing algorithm:

Determine where in the list the new part number should be placed
This is done by comparing the new part number to each value in the current list
until a match is found, a part number larger than the new part number is
located, or the end of the list is encountered
If the new part number matches an existing part number,
display a message that the part number exists
Else
To make room for the new element in the array, move each element down one
position. This is done by starting from the sentinel value and coping each
item to the next position down until the desired position in the list is vacated.
Insert the new part number in the vacated position
Endif

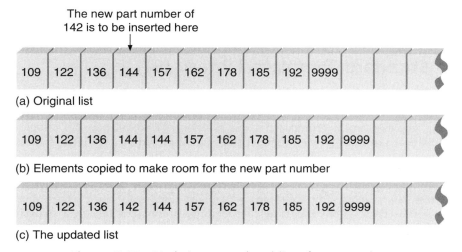

The new part number of
142 is to be inserted here

| 109 | 122 | 136 | 144 | 157 | 162 | 178 | 185 | 192 | 9999 | | | |

(a) Original list

| 109 | 122 | 136 | 144 | 144 | 157 | 162 | 178 | 185 | 192 | 9999 | | |

(b) Elements copied to make room for the new part number

| 109 | 122 | 136 | 142 | 144 | 157 | 162 | 178 | 185 | 192 | 9999 | | |

(c) The updated list

Figure 7.12 Updating an ordered list of part numbers

4. **(List Maintenance) a.** Write a complete C++ program that can be used to update an ordered list of numbers. Use the list of numbers shown in Figure 7.12 to test that your program is working correctly.

   b. Test the program you wrote for Exercise 4a, using a new part number of 86 with the list of numbers shown in Figure 7.12. This test should place this new part number at the beginning of the existing list.

   c. Test the program you wrote for Exercise 4a, using a part number of 200 with the list of numbers shown in Figure 7.12. This test should place this new part number at the end of the existing list.

5. **(List Maintenance) a.** Determine an algorithm for deleting an entry from an ordered list of numbers.

   b. Write a function named delete(), which uses the algorithm determined in Exercise 5a, to delete a part number from the list shown in Figure 7.12.

6. **(List Maintenance)** The following letters are stored in an alphabet array: B, J, K, M, S, and Z. Write and test a function named `adlet()`, which accepts the alphabet array and a new letter as arguments, and then inserts the new letter in the correct alphabetical order in the alphabet array.

7. **(File Creation)** Write a C++ program that creates an array containing the integer numbers 60, 40, 80, 90, 120, 150, 130, 160, 170, and 200. Your program should then write the data in the array to a text file. (Alternatively, you can create the file with a text editor.)

8. **(File Update)** **a.** Develop, write, and execute a C++ program that reads in the list of 10 integer numbers from the data file created in Exercise 7.

   b. Modify the program you wrote for Exercise 8a so that the program does the following:
   - Deletes the first number input from the file
   - Accepts a new integer value that will be placed at the end of the list of numbers
   - Computes and displays the average of all numbers (not including the deleted value)
   - Overwrites the old file with the new list of numbers

7.6   The Standard Template Library (STL)[6]

Many programming applications require expanding and contracting lists as list items are added and removed. Although expanding and contracting an array can be accomplished by creating, copying, and deleting arrays, this solution is costly in terms of initial programming, maintenance, and testing time. To meet the need of providing a tested and generic set of data structures that can be modified, expanded, and contracted, C++ includes a useful set of classes in its **Standard Template Library (STL)**.

Additionally, the functions included in the STL provide useful ways of sorting and searching lists of data. For example, you might need to arrange experimental results in increasing (ascending) or decreasing (descending) order for a statistical analysis. Perhaps an array of names, as string data, must be sorted in alphabetical order, or an array of part names needs to be searched to find a particular part.

Each STL class is coded as a template (see Section 6.1) that permits constructing a generic data structure, referred to as a **container**. The terms **list** and **collection** are synonyms for a container, and both these terms refer to a set of data items that form a natural unit or group. Using this definition, an array can also be considered a container, but not in the technical sense that it's created by using the STL; rather, it's provided as a built-in data type. Figure 7.13 shows the container types in the STL.

This section discusses the vector container class, along with the most commonly used algorithms for this class and the arguments, known as iterators, these algorithms require. A **vector** is similar to an array, in that it stores elements that can be accessed by using an integer index starting at 0. However, a vector is different from an array, in that a vector expands automatically as needed and is provided by several extremely useful class functions[7] for

---

[6]This topic can be omitted on first reading without loss of subject continuity.
[7]In general computer terminology, functions defined in a class (discussed in Part Two) are referred to as "methods." In C++, the terms "class functions" and "class methods" are used interchangeably.

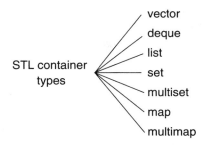

Figure 7.13 The collection of STL container types

operating on the vector. Table 7.1 lists these vector class functions, with shading to identify the functions used in the demonstration program.

Table 7.1 Summary of Vector Class Functions and Operations

Class Functions and Operations	Description
`vector<DataType> name`	Creates an empty vector with compiler-dependent initial size
`vector<DataType> name(source)`	Creates a copy of the source `vector`
`vector<DataType> name(n)`	Creates a `vector` of size n
`vector<DataType> name (n, elem)`	Creates a `vector` of size n with each element initialized as `elem`
`vector<DataType> name(src.beg, src.end)`	Creates a `vector` initialized with elements from a source container beginning at `src.beg` and ending at `src.end`
`~vector(DataType>()`	Destroys the `vector` and all elements it contains
`name[index]`	Returns the element at the designated `index`, with no bounds checking
`name.at(index)`	Returns the element at the specified `index` argument, with bounds checking on the `index` value
`name.front()`	Returns the first element in the `vector`
`name.back()`	Returns the last element in the `vector`
`dest = src`	Assigns all elements of `src vector` to `dest vector`
`name.assign(n, elem)`	Assigns n copies of `elem`
`name.assign (src.begin, src.end)`	Assigns the elements of the `src` container (need not be between the range `src.begin` and `src.end`) to the `name` vector

Table 7.1   Summary of Vector Class Functions and Operations (continued)

Class Functions and Operations	Description
`insert(pos, elem)`	Inserts `elem` at position `pos`
`name.insert` `(pos, n, elem)`	Inserts *n* copies of `elem` starting at position `pos`
`name.insert(pos, src.begin, src.end)`	Inserts elements from `src.begin` to `src.end`, starting at position `pos`
`name.push_back(elem)`	Appends `elem` at the end of the `vector`
`name.erase(pos)`	Removes the element at the specified position `pos`
`name.erase(begin, end)`	Removes elements within the specified range
`name.resize(value)`	Resizes the `vector` to a larger size, with new elements created by using the default constructor
`name.resize(value, elem)`	Resizes the `vector` to a larger size, with new elements created as `elem`
`name.clear()`	Removes all elements from the `vector`
`name.swap(nameB)`	Swaps the elements of `nameA` and `nameB` vectors; can be performed by using the `swap` algorithm
`nameA == nameB`	Returns a Boolean `true` if `nameA` elements equal `nameB` elements; otherwise, returns `false`
`nameA != nameB`	Returns a Boolean `false` if `nameA` elements equal `nameB` elements; otherwise, returns `true`; same as `!(nameA == nameB)`
`nameA < nameB`	Returns a Boolean `true` if `nameA` is less than `nameB`; otherwise, returns `false`
`nameA > nameB`	Returns a Boolean `true` if `nameA` is greater than `nameB`; otherwise, returns `false`; same as `nameB < nameA`
`nameA <= nameB`	Returns a Boolean `true` if `nameA` is less than or equal to `nameB`
`nameA >= nameB`	Returns a Boolean `true` if `nameA` is greater than or equal to `nameB`
`name.size()`	Returns the size of the `vector`
`name.empty()`	Returns a Boolean `true` if the `vector` is empty; otherwise, returns `false`
`name.max_size()`	Returns the maximum possible elements as an integer
`name.capacity()`	Returns the maximum possible elements as an integer without relocating the `vector`

In addition to the vector class functions listed in Table 7.1, vectors have access to the complete set of generic STL functions, referred to in the STL as algorithms. Table 7.2 summarizes the most commonly used STL algorithms.

Table 7.2 Commonly Used STL Algorithms

Algorithm Name	Description
accumulate	Returns the sum of the numbers in a specified range
binary_search	Returns a Boolean value of true if the specified value exists within the specified range; otherwise, returns false. Can be used only on a sorted set of values.
copy	Copies elements from a source range to a destination range
copy_backward	Copies elements from a source range to a destination range in a reverse direction
count	Returns the number of elements in a specified range that match a specified value
equal	Compares the elements in one range of elements, element by element, to the elements in a second range
fill	Assigns every element in a specified range to a specified value
find	Returns the position of an element's first occurrence in a specified range having a specified value if the value exists. Performs a linear search, starting with the first element in a specified range, and proceeds one element at a time until the complete range has been searched or the specified element has been found.
max_element	Returns the maximum value of elements in the specified range
min_element	Returns the minimum value of elements in the specified range
random_shuffle	Randomly shuffles element values in a specified range
remove	Removes a specified value in a specified range without changing the order of the remaining elements
replace	Replaces each element in a specified range having a specified value with a newly specified value
reverse	Reverses elements in a specified range
search	Finds the first occurrence of a specified value or sequence of values within a specified range
sort	Sorts elements in a specified range into ascending order
swap	Exchanges element values between two objects
unique	Removes duplicate adjacent elements in a specified range

Point of Information

When to Use an Array or a Vector

An array is the data structure of first choice when you have a list of primitive data types or objects that don't have to be expanded or contracted. A vector is the data structure of first choice when you have a list of primitive data types or objects that can be grouped as an array but must be expanded or contracted.

Whenever possible, use STL's algorithms to operate on arrays and vectors. STL classes and algorithms provide verified and reliable code that can shorten program development time.

Notice that there's both a swap algorithm (Table 7.2) and a swap() vector function (Table 7.1). Because a function is targeted to work specifically with its container type and generally executes faster when a container class provides a function with the same name as an algorithm, you should use the class functions.

Finally, the STL provides additional items referred to as **iterators**, used to specify which elements in a container are to be operated on when an algorithm is called. Two of the most useful iterators are returned by the STL iterator functions begin() and end(). These general-purpose functions return the positions of the first and last elements in a container.

To better understand using an STL container class, in this section you see how to use the vector container class to create a vector for holding a list of part numbers. As you'll see, a vector is similar to a C++ array, except it can automatically expand as needed.

Program 7.11 constructs a vector and initializes it with integers stored in an integer array. After it's initialized, various vector functions and STL algorithms are used to operate on the vector. Specifically, one function is used to change an existing value, a second is used to insert a value into the vector, and a third is used to add a value to the end of the list. After each function and algorithm are applied, a cout statement is used to display the results.

In reviewing Program 7.11, notice these four header files that precede the using namespace std; statement:

- The <iostream> header is required to create and use cout.
- The <string> header is required for constructing strings.
- The <vector> header is required to create one or more vector objects.
- The <algorithm> header is required for the sort algorithm that's applied after vector elements have been added and replaced.

Program 7.11

```cpp
#include <iostream>
#include <string>
#include <vector>
#include <algorithm>
using namespace std;

int main()
{
  const int NUMELS = 4;

  int n[] ={136, 122, 109, 146};
  int i;

  // create a vector of strings using the n[] array
  vector<int> partnums(n, n + NUMELS);

  cout << "\nThe vector initially has a size of "
       << int(partnums.size()) << ",\n and contains the elements:\n";
  for (i = 0; i < int(partnums.size()); i++)
    cout << partnums[i] << "   ";

  // modify the element at position 4 (i.e. index = 3) in the vector
  partnums[3] = 144;

  cout << "\n\nAfter replacing the fourth element, the vector has a size of "
       << int(partnums.size()) << ",\n and contains the elements:\n";
  for (i = 0; i < int(partnums.size()); i++)
    cout << partnums[i] << "   ";

  // insert an element into the vector at position 2 (i.e. index = 1)
  partnums.insert(partnums.begin()+1, 142);

  cout << "\n\nAfter inserting an element into the second position,"
       << "\n the vector has a size of " << int(partnums.size()) << ","
       << " and contains the elements:\n";
  for (i = 0; i < int(partnums.size()); i++)
    cout << partnums[i] << "   ";

  // add an element to the end of the vector
  partnums.push_back(157);
```

☞

```
cout << "\n\nAfter adding an element to the end of the list,"
     << "\n  the vector has a size of " << int(partnums.size()) << ","
     << " and contains the elements:\n";
for (i = 0; i < int(partnums.size()); i++)
  cout << partnums[i] << "   ";

// sort the vector
sort(partnums.begin(), partnums.end());

cout << "\n\nAfter sorting, the vector's elements are:\n";
for (i = 0; i < int(partnums.size()); i++)
  cout << partnums[i] << "   ";

cout << endl;

return 0;
}
```

The following statement in Program 7.11 is used to create and initialize the vector named partnums:

```
vector<int> partnums(n, n + NUMELS);
```

The vector partnums is declared as a vector of type int and initialized with elements from the n array, starting with the first array element (element n[0]) and ending with the last array element, located at position n + NUMELS. Therefore, the vector size is large enough for four integer values and has been initialized with the integers 136, 122, 109, and 146.

The next set of statements in Program 7.11 displays the initial values in the vector by using standard subscripted vector notation that's identical to the notation for accessing array elements. Displaying vector values in this manner, however, requires knowing how many elements each vector contains. As you insert and remove elements, you would like the vector to track the first and last elements' locations. This capability is provided automatically by the two STL iterator functions mentioned previously: begin() and end().

The next major set of statements consists of the following:

```
// modify the element at position 4 (i.e. index = 3) in the vector
partnums[3] = 144;

// insert an element into the vector at position 2 (i.e. index = 1)
partnums.insert(partnums.begin()+1, 142);
```

These statements are used to modify an existing vector value and insert a new value into the vector. Specifically, the partnums[3] notation uses standard indexing, and the insert() function uses an iterator argument, which is constructed as an offset by using the begin() or end() function. Additionally, you have to specify the value to be inserted at the designated position. Therefore, partnums[3] specifies changing the fourth element in the vector. (Vectors, like arrays, begin at index position 0.) The insert() function is used to insert the integer value 142 in the vector's second position. Because the begin() function returns a value corresponding to the start of the vector, adding 1 to it designates the vector's second position.[8] At this position, the new value is inserted. All subsequent values are moved up by one position in the vector, and the vector expands automatically to accept the inserted value. At this point in the program, the vector partnums now contains the following elements:

136   142   122   109   144

This arrangement of values was obtained by replacing the original value 146 with 144 and inserting the 142 into the second position, which moves all subsequent elements up automatically by one position and increases the total vector size to five integers.

Next, the statement partnums.push_back(157); is used to append the integer 157 to the end of the vector, which results in the following elements:

136   142   122   109   144   157

Finally, the last section of code in Program 7.11 uses the sort() algorithm to sort elements in the vector. After the algorithm is applied, the vector's values are displayed again. Following is the complete output Program 7.11 produces:

```
The vector initially has a size of 4,
 and contains the elements:
136    122    109    146

After replacing the fourth element, the vector has a size of 4,
 and contains the elements:
136  122  109  144

After inserting an element into the second position,
 the vector has a size of 5, and contains the elements:
136  142  122  109  144

After adding an element to the end of the list,
  the vector has a size of 6, and contains the elements:
136  142  122  109  144  157

After sorting, the vector's elements are:
109  122  136  142  144  157
```

---

[8]More precisely, begin() requires an iterator argument, not an integer index argument. The begin() and end() functions return iterators, to which offsets can be applied. In this behavior, they are similar to pointers (covered in Chapter 12).

EXERCISES 7.6

1. **(For Review)** Define the terms "container" and "Standard Template Library."

2. **(For Review)** What include statements should be included with programs using the Standard Template Library?

3. **(Practice)** Enter and execute Program 7.11.

4. **(Modify)** Modify Program 7.11 so that the user inputs the initial set of numbers when the program executes. Have the program request the number of initial numbers to be entered.

5. **(Modify)** Modify Program 7.11 to use and display the results reported by the vector class's capacity() and max_size() functions.

6. **(Modify)** Modify Program 7.11 to use the random_shuffle algorithm.

7. **(Modify)** Modify Program 7.11 to use the binary_search and find algorithms. Have your program request the number to be found.

8. **(Modify)** Using Program 7.11 as a starting point, create an equivalent program that uses a vector of strings. Initialize the vector by using the array string names[] = {"Donavan", "Michaels", "Smith", "Jones"};.

9. **(Practice)** Use the max_element and min_element algorithms to determine the maximum and minimum values in the vector created for Exercise 8. (*Hint:* Use the expression max_element(vectorName.begin(), vectorName.end()) to determine the maximum value stored in the vector. Then use the same arguments for the min_element algorithm.)

7.7 A Closer Look: Searching and Sorting[9]

Most programmers encounter the need to both sort and search a list of data items at some time in their programming careers. For example, you might have to sort a list of names in alphabetical order and search this list to find a particular name. Similarly, you might have to arrange a list of dates in ascending order and search this list to locate a certain date. This section introduces the fundamentals of sorting and searching lists. Note that sorting a list before searching it isn't necessary, although much faster searches are possible if the list is in sorted order, as you'll see.

Search Algorithms

A common requirement of many programs is searching a list for a certain element. For example, in a list of names and telephone numbers, you might search for a specific name so

---

[9]This topic can be omitted on first reading without loss of subject continuity.

that the corresponding telephone number can be printed, or you might need to search the list simply to determine whether a name is there. The two most common methods of performing these searches are the linear and binary search algorithms.

Linear Search   In a **linear search**, also known as a **sequential search**, each item in the list is examined in the order in which it occurs until the desired item is found or the end of the list is reached. This search method is analogous to looking at every name in the phone directory, beginning with Aardvark, Aaron, until you find the one you want or until you reach Zzxgy, Zora. Obviously, it's not the most efficient way to search a long alphabetized list. However, a linear search has these advantages:

- The algorithm is simple.
- The list need not be in any particular order.

In a linear search, the search begins at the first item in the list and continues sequentially, item by item, through the list. The pseudocode for a function performing a linear search is as follows:

For all items in the list
    Compare the item with the desired item
    If the item is found
        Return the index value of the current item
    Endif
EndFor
Return -1 if the item is not found

Notice that the function's return value indicates whether the item was found. If the return value is -1, the item isn't in the list; otherwise, the return value in the for loop provides the index of where the item is located in the list. The linearSearch() function illustrates this procedure as a C++ function:

```
// this function returns the location of key in the list
// a -1 is returned if the value is not found
int linearSearch(int list[], int size, int key)
{
  int i;

  for (i = 0; i < size; i++)
  {
    if (list[i] == key)
      return i;
  }

  return -1;
}
```

In reviewing linearSearch(), notice that the for loop is simply used to access each element in the list, from first element to last, until a match with the desired item is found. If the item is located, the index value of the current item is returned, which causes the loop to terminate; otherwise, the search continues until the end of the list is encountered.

To test this function, a main() driver function has been written to call linearSearch() and display the results it returns. Program 7.12 shows the complete test program.

Program 7.12

```cpp
#include <iostream>
using namespace std;

int linearSearch(int [], int, int);   //function prototype

int main()
{
  const int NUMEL = 10;

  int nums[NUMEL] = {5,10,22,32,45,67,73,98,99,101};
  int item, location;


  cout << "Enter the item you are searching for: ";
  cin  >> item;

  location = linearSearch(nums, NUMEL, item);

  if (location > -1)
    cout << "The item was found at index location " << location
         << endl;
  else
    cout << "The item was not found in the list\n";

  return 0;
}

// this function returns the location of key in the list
// a -1 is returned if the value is not found
int linearSearch(int list[], int size, int key)
{
  int i;

  for (i = 0; i < size; i++)
  {
    if (list[i] == key)
      return i;
  }

  return -1;
}
```

Sample runs of Program 7.12 follow:

```
Enter the item you are searching for: 101
The item was found at index location 9
```

and

```
Enter the item you are searching for: 65
The item was not found in the list
```

As noted previously, an advantage of linear searches is that the list doesn't have to be in sorted order to perform the search. Another advantage is that if the desired item is toward the front of the list, only a small number of comparisons are made. The worst case, of course, occurs when the desired item is at the end of the list. On average, however, and assuming the item is equally likely to be anywhere in the list, the number of required comparisons is $n/2$, where n is the list's size. Therefore, for a 10-element list, the average number of comparisons needed for a linear search is 5, and for a 10,000-element list, the average number of comparisons needed is 5000. As you see next, this number can be reduced significantly by using a binary search algorithm.

Binary Search   In a **binary search**, the list must be in sorted order. Starting with an ordered list, the desired item is first compared to the element in the middle of the list. (For lists with an even number of elements, either of the two middle elements can be used.) There are three possibilities after the comparison is made: The desired item might be equal to the middle element, it might be greater than the middle element, or it might be less than the middle element.

In the first case, the search has been successful, and no further searches are required. In the second case, because the desired item is greater than the middle element, it must be in the second half of the list, if it's found at all. This means the first part of the list, consisting of all elements from the first to the midpoint, can be discarded from any further search. In the third case, because the desired item is less than the middle element, it must be in the first part of the list, if it's found at all. For this case, the second half of the list, containing all elements from the midpoint to the last element, can be discarded from any further search.

The algorithm for this search strategy is shown in Figure 7.14 and defined by the following pseudocode:

Set the lower index to 0
Set the upper index to one less than the size of the list
Begin with the first item in the list
While the lower index is less than or equal to the upper index
    Set the midpoint index to the integer average of the lower and upper index values
    Compare the desired item to the midpoint element
        If the desired item equals the midpoint element
            Return the index value of the current item
        Else If the desired item is greater than the midpoint element
            Set the lower index value to the midpoint value plus 1
        Else If the desired item is less than the midpoint element
            Set the upper index value to the midpoint value less 1
    Endif
EndWhile
Return -1 if the item is not found

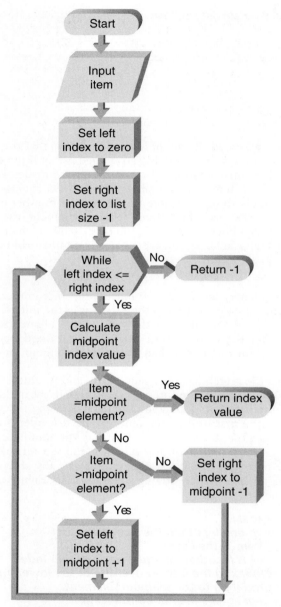

Figure 7.14   The binary search algorithm

In both the pseudocode and Figure 7.14's flowchart, a `while` loop is used to control the search. The initial list is defined by setting the left index value to 0 and the right index value to one less than the number of elements in the list. The midpoint element is then taken as the integerized average of the left and right values.

After the comparison to the midpoint element is made, the search is subsequently restricted by moving the left index to one integer value above the midpoint or by moving the right index one integer value below the midpoint. This process is continued until the desired element is found or the left and right index values become equal. The `binarySearch()` function presents the C++ version of this algorithm:

```cpp
// this function returns the location of key in the list
// a -1 is returned if the value is not found
int binarySearch(int list[], int size, int key)
{
  int left, right, midpt;

  left = 0;
  right = size -1;

  while (left <= right)
  {
    midpt = (int) ((left + right) / 2);
    if (key == list[midpt])
    {
      return midpt;
    }
    else if (key > list[midpt])
      left = midpt + 1;
    else
      right = midpt - 1;
  }

  return -1;
}
```

For purposes of testing this function, Program 7.13 is used. A sample run of Program 7.13 yielded the following:

```
Enter the item you are searching for: 101
The item was found at index location 9
```

Program 7.13

```cpp
#include <iostream>
using namespace std;

int binarySearch(int [], int, int);   //function prototype

int main()
{
  const int NUMEL = 10;
```

```cpp
   int nums[NUMEL] = {5,10,22,32,45,67,73,98,99,101};
   int item, location;

   cout << "Enter the item you are searching for: ";
   cin  >> item;

   location = binarySearch(nums, NUMEL, item);

   if (location > -1)
     cout << "The item was found at index location "
        << location << endl;
   else
     cout << "The item was not found in the array\n";

   return 0;
}

// this function returns the location of key in the list
// a -1 is returned if the value is not found
int binarySearch(int list[], int size, int key)
{
  int left, right, midpt;

  left = 0;
  right = size -1;

  while (left <= right)
  {
    midpt = (int) ((left + right) / 2);
    if (key == list[midpt])
    {
      return midpt;
    }
    else if (key > list[midpt])
      left = midpt + 1;
    else
      right = midpt - 1;
  }

  return -1;
}
```

The value of using a binary search algorithm is that the number of elements that must be searched is cut in half each time through the while loop. So the first time through the loop, n elements must be searched; the second time through the loop, $n/2$ of the elements has been eliminated and only $n/2$ remain. The third time through the loop, another half of the remaining elements has been eliminated, and so on.

In general, after p passes through the loop, the number of values remaining to be searched is $n/(2^p)$. In the worst case, the search can continue until less than or equal to one element remains to be searched. Mathematically, this procedure can be expressed as $n/(2^p) \leq 1$. Alternatively, it can be rephrased as p is the smallest integer so that $2^p > n$. For example, for a 1000-element array, n is 1000 and the maximum number of passes, p, required for a binary search is 10. Table 7.3 compares the number of loop passes needed for a linear and binary search for different list sizes.

Table 7.3 A Comparison of while Loop Passes for Linear and Binary Searches

Array size	10	50	500	5000	50,000	500,000	5,000,000	50,000,000
Average linear search passes	5	25	250	2500	25,000	250,000	2,500,000	25,000,000
Maximum linear search passes	10	50	500	5000	50,000	500,000	5,000,000	50,000,000
Maximum binary search passes	4	6	9	13	16	19	23	26

As shown, the maximum number of loop passes for a 50-item list is almost 10 times more for a linear search than for binary search, and even more spectacular for larger lists. As a rule of thumb, 50 elements are usually taken as the switch-over point: For lists smaller than 50 elements, linear searches are acceptable; for larger lists, a binary search algorithm should be used.

Big O Notation

On average, over a large number of linear searches with n items in a list, you would expect to examine half ($n/2$) of the items before locating the desired item. In a binary search, the maximum number of passes, p, occurs when $n/(2)^p = 1$. This relationship can be manipulated algebraically to $2^p = n$, which yields $p = \log_2 n$, which approximately equals $3.33 \log_{10} n$.

For example, finding a particular name in an alphabetical directory with $n = 1000$ names requires an average of 500 ($=n/2$) comparisons using a linear search. With a binary search, only about 10 ($\approx 3.33 * \log_{10} 1000$) comparisons are required.

A common way to express the number of comparisons required in any search algorithm using a list of n items is to give the order of magnitude of the number of comparisons required, on average, to locate a desired item. Therefore, the linear search is said to be of order n and the binary search of order $\log_2 n$. Notationally, they're expressed as $O(n)$ and $O(\log_2 n)$, where the O is read as "the order of."

Sort Algorithms

Two major categories of sorting techniques, called internal and external sorts, are available for sorting data. **Internal sorts** are used when the data list isn't too large and the complete list can be stored in the computer's memory, usually in an array. **External sorts** are used for much larger data sets that are stored in external disk or tape files and can't be accommodated in the computer's memory as a complete unit. Next, you learn about two internal sort algorithms that can be used when sorting lists with fewer than approximately 50 elements. For larger lists, more sophisticated sorting algorithms are typically used.

Selection Sort   One of the simplest sorting techniques is the **selection sort**, in which the smallest value is selected from the complete list of data and exchanged with the first element in the list. After this first selection and exchange, the next smallest element in the revised list is selected and exchanged with the second element in the list. Because the smallest element is already in the first position in the list, this second pass needs to consider only the second through last elements. For a list consisting of *n* elements, this process is repeated *n* - 1 times, with each pass through the list requiring one less comparison than the previous pass.

For example, take a look at the list of numbers shown in Figure 7.15. The first pass through the initial list results in the number 32 being selected and exchanged with the first element in the list. The second pass, made on the reordered list, results in the number 155 being selected from the second through fifth elements. This value is then exchanged with the second element in the list. The third pass selects the number 307 from the third through fifth elements in the list and exchanges this value with the third element. Finally, the fourth and last pass through the list selects the remaining minimum value and exchanges it with the fourth list element. Although each pass in this example resulted in an exchange, no exchange would have been made in a pass if the smallest value were already in the correct location.

Initial list	Pass 1	Pass 2	Pass 3	Pass 4
690	32	32	32	32
307	307	155	144	144
32	690	690	307	307
155	155	307	690	426
426	426	426	426	690

Figure 7.15   A sample selection sort

In pseudocode, the selection sort is described as follows:

Set exchange count to zero (not required, but done to keep track of the exchanges)
For each element in the list, from the first to the next to last
  Find the smallest element from the current element being referenced to the last
    element by:
  Setting the minimum value equal to the current element
  Saving (storing) the index of the current element
  For each element in the list, from the current element + 1 to the last element in the list
    If element[inner loop index] < minimum value
      Set the minimum value = element[inner loop index]
      Save the index value corresponding to the newfound minimum value
    Endif
  EndFor
  Swap the current value with the new minimum value
  Increment the exchange count
EndFor
Return the exchange count

The selection Sort() function incorporates this procedure into a C++ function:

```cpp
int selectionSort(int num[], int numel)
{
   int i, j, min, minidx, temp, moves = 0;

   for ( i = 0; i < (numel - 1); i++)
   {
     min = num[i];    // assume minimum is the first array element
     minidx = i;      // index of minimum element
     for(j = i + 1; j < numel; j++)
     {
        if (num[j] < min)   // if you've located a lower value
        {                    // capture it
        min = num[j];
        minidx = j;
        }
     }
     if (min < num[i])   // check whether you have a new minimum
     {                    // and if you do, swap values
        temp = num[i];
        num[i] = min;
        num[minidx] = temp;
        moves++;
     }
   }

   return moves;
}
```

The `selectionSort()` function expects two arguments: the list to be sorted and the number of elements in the list. As the pseudocode specifies, a nested set of `for` loops performs the sort. The outer `for` loop causes one less pass through the list than the total number of items in the list. For each pass, the variable `min` is initially assigned the value `num[i]`, where `i` is the outer `for` loop's counter variable. Because `i` begins at 0 and ends at one less than `numel`, each element in the list, except the last, is successively designated as the current element.

The inner loop cycles through the elements below the current element and is used to select the next smallest value. Therefore, this loop begins at the index value `i + 1` and continues through the end of the list. When a new minimum is found, its value and position in the list are stored in the variables `min` and `minidx`. At completion of the inner loop, an exchange is made only if a value less than that in the current position is found.

Program 7.14 was constructed to test `selectionSort()`. This program implements a selection sort for the same list of 10 numbers used to test the search algorithms. For later comparison to other sorting algorithms, the number of actual moves the program makes to get data into sorted order is counted and displayed.

The output Program 7.14 produces is as follows:

```
The sorted list, in ascending order, is:
  5   10   22   32   45   67   73   98   99   101
8 moves were made to sort this list
```

Clearly, the number of moves displayed depends on the initial order of values in the list. An advantage of the selection sort is that the maximum number of moves that must be made is $n - 1$, where n is the number of items in the list. Further, each move is a final move that results in an element residing in its final location in the sorted list.

A disadvantage of the selection sort is that $n(n - 1)/2$ comparisons are always required, regardless of the initial arrangement of data. This number of comparisons is obtained as follows: The last pass always requires one comparison, the next-to-last pass requires two comparisons, and so on, to the first pass, which requires $n - 1$ comparisons. Therefore, the total number of comparisons is the following:

$$1 + 2 + 3 + \ldots + n - 1 = n(n - 1)/2 = n^2/2 - n/2$$

For large values of n, the n^2 term dominates, and the order of the selection sort is $O(n^2)$.

Program 7.14

```cpp
#include <iostream>
using namespace std;

int selectionSort(int [], int);

int main()
{
  const int NUMEL = 10;
  int nums[NUMEL] = {22,5,67,98,45,32,101,99,73,10};
  int i, moves;

  moves = selectionSort(nums, NUMEL);

  cout << "The sorted list, in ascending order, is:\n";
  for (i = 0; i < NUMEL; i++)
    cout << "   " <<nums[i];

  cout << endl << moves << " moves were made to sort this list\n";

  return 0;
}

int selectionSort(int num[], int numel)
{
  int i, j, min, minidx, temp, moves = 0;

  for ( i = 0; i < (numel - 1); i++)
  {
    min = num[i];    // assume minimum is the first array element
    minidx = i;      // index of minimum element
    for(j = i + 1; j < numel; j++)
    {
      if (num[j] < min)    // if you've located a lower value
      {                    // capture it
      min = num[j];
      minidx = j;
      }
    }
    if (min < num[i])  // check whether you have a new minimum
    {                  // and if you do, swap values
```

☞

```
        temp = num[i];
        num[i] = min;
        num[minidx] = temp;
        moves++;
    }
}

return moves;
}
```

Exchange (Bubble) Sort   In an **exchange sort**, adjacent elements of the list are exchanged with one another so that the list becomes sorted. One example of this sequence of exchanges is the **bubble sort**, in which successive values in the list are compared, beginning with the first two elements. If the list is to be sorted in ascending (from smallest to largest) order, the smaller value of the two being compared is always placed before the larger value. For lists sorted in descending (from largest to smallest) order, the smaller of the two values being compared is always placed after the larger value.

For example, a list of values is to be sorted in ascending order. If the first element in the list is larger than the second, the two elements are exchanged. Then the second and third elements are compared. Again, if the second element is larger than the third, these two elements are exchanged. This process continues until the last two elements have been compared and exchanged, if necessary. If no exchanges were made during this initial pass through the data, the data is in the correct order and the process is finished; otherwise, a second pass is made through the data, starting from the first element and stopping at the next-to-last element. The reason for stopping at the next-to-last element on the second pass is that the first pass always results in the most positive value "sinking" to the bottom of the list.

To see a specific example, examine the list of numbers in Figure 7.16. The first comparison results in exchanging the first two element values, 690 and 307. The next comparison, between elements two and three in the revised list, results in exchanging values between the second and third elements, 690 and 32. This comparison and possible switching of adjacent values is continued until the last two elements have been compared and possibly exchanged. This process completes the first pass through the data and results in the largest number moving to the bottom of the list. As the largest value sinks to the bottom of the list, the smaller elements slowly rise, or "bubble," to the top of the list. This bubbling effect of the smaller elements is what gives rise to the name "bubble sort" for this sorting algorithm.

690	307	307	307	307
307	690	32	32	32
32	32	690	155	155
155	155	155	690	426
426	426	426	426	690

Figure 7.16   The first pass of an exchange sort

Because the first pass through the list ensures that the largest value always moves to the bottom of the list, the second pass stops at the next-to-last element. This process continues with each pass stopping at one higher element than the previous pass, until n - 1 passes through the list have been completed or no exchanges are necessary in any single pass. In both cases, the resulting list is in sorted order. The pseudocode describing this sort is as follows:

Set exchange count to zero (not required, but done to keep track of the exchanges)
For the first element in the list to one less than the last element (i index)
  For the second element in the list to the last element (j index)
    If num[j] < num[j - 1]
    {
      Swap num[j] with num[j - 1]
      Increment exchange count
    }
  EndFor
EndFor
Return exchange count

This sort algorithm is coded in C++ as the bubbleSort() function, which is included in Program 7.15 for testing purposes. This program tests bubbleSort() with the same list of 10 numbers used in Program 7.14 to test selectionSort(). For comparison to the earlier selection sort, the number of adjacent moves (exchanges) bubbleSort() makes is also counted and displayed.

 ## Program 7.15

```cpp
#include <iostream>
using namespace std;

int bubbleSort(int [], int);   // function prototype

int main()
{
  const int NUMEL = 10;
  int nums[NUMEL] = {22,5,67,98,45,32,101,99,73,10};
  int i, moves;

  moves = bubbleSort(nums, NUMEL);

  cout << "The sorted list, in ascending order, is:\n";
  for (i = 0; i < NUMEL; ++i)
    cout << "   " <<nums[i];

  cout << endl << moves << " moves were made to sort this list\n";

  return 0;
}
```

```
int bubbleSort(int num[], int numel)
{
  int i, j, temp, moves = 0;

  for ( i = 0; i < (numel - 1); i++)
  {
    for(j = 1; j < numel; j++)
    {
      if (num[j] < num[j-1])
      {
        temp = num[j];
        num[j] = num[j-1];
        num[j-1] = temp;
        moves++;
      }
    }
  }

  return moves;
}
```

Here's the output produced by Program 7.15:

```
The sorted list, in ascending order, is:
  5  10  22  32  45  67  73  98  99  101
18 moves were made to sort this list
```

As with the selection sort, the number of comparisons in a bubble sort is $O(n^2)$, and the number of required moves depends on the initial order of values in the list. In the worst case, when the data is in reverse sorted order, the selection sort performs better than the bubble sort. Both sorts require $n(n - 1)/2$ comparisons, but the selection sort needs only $n - 1$ moves, and the bubble sort needs $n(n - 1)/2$ moves. The additional moves the bubble sort requires result from the intermediate exchanges between adjacent elements to "settle" each element into its final position. In this regard, the selection sort is superior because no intermediate moves are necessary. For random data, such as that used in Programs 7.14 and 7.15, the selection sort generally performs equal to or better than the bubble sort.

7.8 Common Programming Errors

Four common errors are associated with using arrays:

1. Forgetting to declare the array. This error results in a compiler error message such as "invalid indirection" each time a subscripted variable is encountered in a program.

Chapter 12 explains the exact meaning of this error message when establishing the relationship between arrays and pointers.

2. Using a subscript that references a nonexistent array element, such as declaring the array as size 20 and using a subscript value of 25. Most C++ compilers don't detect this error. However, it results in a runtime error that causes a program crash or results in a value with no relation to the intended element being accessed from memory. In either case, this error is usually difficult to locate. The only solution is to make sure, by specific programming statements or by careful coding, that each subscript references a valid array element.

3. Not using a large enough counter value in a `for` loop counter to cycle through all the array elements. This error usually occurs when an array is initially specified as size *n* and there's a `for` loop in the program of the form `for(i = 0; i < n; i++)`. The array size is then expanded, but the programmer forgets to change the interior `for` loop parameters. Declaring an array's size with a named constant and consistently using the named constant throughout the function in place of the variable n eliminates this problem.

4. Forgetting to initialize the array. Although many compilers set all elements of integer and real value arrays to 0 automatically, and all elements of character arrays to blanks, it's up to the programmer to make sure each array is initialized correctly before processing of array elements begins.

7.9   Chapter Summary

1. A one-dimensional array is a data structure that can be used to store a list of values of the same data type. These arrays must be declared by giving the data type of values stored in the array and the array size. For example, the declaration

```
int num[100];
```

creates an array of 100 integers. A preferable approach is first using a named constant to set the array size, and then using this constant in the array definition, as shown in these examples:

```
const int MAXSIZE = 100;
```

and

```
int num[MAXSIZE];
```

2. Array elements are stored in contiguous locations in memory and referenced by using the array name and a subscript (or index), such as `num[22]`. Any non-negative integer value expression can be used as a subscript, and the subscript 0 always refers to the first element in an array.

3. A two-dimensional array is declared by listing a row and a column size with the data type and array name. For example, the following declaration creates a two-dimensional array consisting of five rows and seven columns of integer values:

```
int mat[5][7];
```

4. Arrays can be initialized when they are declared. For two-dimensional arrays, you list the initial values, row by row, inside braces and separate them with commas. For example, the declaration

```
int vals[3][2] = { {1, 2},
                   {3, 4},
                   {5, 6} };
```

produces the following three-row-by-two-column array:

```
1   2
3   4
5   6
```

As C++ uses the convention that initialization proceeds in row order, the inner braces can be omitted. Therefore, the following statement is an equivalent initialization:

```
int vals[3][2] = { 1, 2, 3, 4,  5, 6};
```

5. Arrays are passed to a function by passing the array name as an argument. The value actually passed is the address of the first array storage location. Therefore, the called function receives direct access to the original array, not a copy of the array elements. A formal argument must be declared in the called function to receive the passed array name. The declaration of the formal argument can omit the array's row size.

Programming Projects for Chapter 7

1. **(Statistics)** **a.** Write a C++ program that reads a list of double-precision grades from the keyboard into an array named grade. The grades are to be counted as they're read, and entry is to be terminated when a negative value has been entered. After all grades have been input, your program should find and display the sum and average of the grades. The grades should then be listed with an asterisk (*) placed in front of each grade that's below the average.

   b. Extend the program written for Exercise 1a to display each grade and its letter equivalent, using the following scale:

   Between 90 and 100 = A.
   Greater than or equal to 80 and less than 90 = B.
   Greater than or equal to 70 and less than 80 = C.
   Greater than or equal to 60 and less than 70 = D.
   Less than 60 = F.

2. **(Practice)** Define an array named peopleTypes that can store a maximum of 50 integer values entered at the keyboard. Enter a series of 1s, 2s, 3s, and 4s into the array to represent people at a local school function; 1 represents an infant, 2 represents a child, 3 represents a teenager, and 4 represents an adult. No other integer value should be accepted as valid input, and data entry should stop when a negative value is entered. Your program should count the number of each 1, 2, 3, and 4 in the array and display a list of how many infants, children, teenagers, and adults were at the school function.

3. **(Numerical)** Given a one-dimensional array of integer numbers, write and test a function that prints the array elements in reverse order.

4. **(Numerical)** Write and test a function that returns the position of the largest and smallest values in an array of double-precision numbers.

5. **(Sorting)** Read a set of numerical grades from the keyboard into an array. The maximum number of grades to be entered is 50, and data entry should be terminated when a negative number is entered. Have your program sort and print the grades in descending order.

6. **(Numerical) a.** Define an array with a maximum of 20 integer values, and fill the array with numbers input from the keyboard or assigned by the program. Then write a function named `split()` that reads the array and places all zeros or positive numbers in an array named `positive` and all negative numbers in an array named `negative`. Finally, have your program call a function that displays the values in both the `positive` and `negative` arrays.

   b. Extend the program written for Exercise 6a to sort the `positive` and `negative` arrays into ascending order before they are displayed.

7. **(Numerical)** Using the `srand()` and `rand()` C++ library functions, fill an array of 1000 floating-point numbers with random numbers that have been scaled to the range 1 to 100. Then determine and display the number of random numbers having values between 1 and 50 and the number having values greater than 50. What do you expect the output counts to be?

8. **(Statistical)** In many statistical analysis programs, data values considerably outside the range of the majority of values are simply dropped from consideration. Using this information, write a C++ program that accepts up to 10 floating-point values from a user and determines and displays the average and standard deviation of the input values. All values more than four standard deviations away from the computed average are to be displayed and dropped from any further calculation, and a new average and standard deviation should be computed and displayed.

9. **(Data Processing)** Your professor has asked you to write a C++ program that determines grades at the end of the semester. For each student, identified by an integer number between 1 and 60, four exam grades must be kept, and two final grade averages must be computed. The first grade average is simply the average of all four grades. The second grade average is computed by weighting the four grades as follows: The first grade gets a weight of 0.2, the second grade gets a weight of 0.3, the third grade gets a weight of 0.3, and the fourth grade gets a weight of 0.2. That is, the final grade is computed as follows:

   ```
   0.2 * grade1 + 0.3 * grade2 + 0.3 * grade3 + 0.2 * grade4
   ```

   Using this information, construct a 60-by-7 two-dimensional array, in which the first column is used for the student number, the next four columns for the grades, and the last two columns for the computed final grades. The program's output should be a display of the data in the completed array. For testing purposes, the professor has provided the following data:

Student	Grade 1	Grade 2	Grade 3	Grade 4
1	100	100	100	100
2	100	0	100	0
3	82	94	73	86
4	64	74	84	94
5	94	84	74	64

10. **(Modify)** Modify the program written for Exercise 9 by adding an eighth column to the array. The grade in the eighth column should be calculated by computing the average of the top three grades only.

11. **(Data Processing) a.** Create a two-dimensional list of integer part numbers and quantities of each part in stock, and write a function that displays data in the array in *decreasing* quantity order. No more than 100 different parts are being kept track of. Test your program with the following data:

Part No.	Quantity
1001	62
949	85
1050	33
867	125
346	59
1025	105

b. Modify the function written in Exercise 11a to display the data in part number order.

12. **(Data Processing)** The answers to a true-false test are as follows: T T F F T. Given a two-dimensional answer array, in which each row corresponds to the answers provided on one test, write a function that accepts the two-dimensional array and number of tests as parameters and returns a one-dimensional array containing the grades for each test. (Each question is worth 5 points so that the maximum possible grade is 25.) Test your function with the following data:

Test 1:	T	F	T	T	T
Test 2:	T	T	T	T	T
Test 3:	T	T	F	F	T
Test 4:	F	T	F	F	F
Test 5:	F	F	F	F	F
Test 6:	T	T	F	T	F

13. **(Modify)** Modify the function you wrote for Exercise 12 so that each test is stored in column order rather than row order.

14. **(Data Processing)** A three-dimensional weather array for the months July and August 2008 has planes labeled by the month numbers 7 and 8. In each plane, there are rows numbered 1 through 31, representing the days, and two columns labeled H and L, representing the day's high and low temperatures. Use this information to write a C++ program that assigns the high and low temperatures for each element of the arrays. Then allow the user to request the following:

- Any day's high and low temperatures

- Average high and low temperatures for a given month

- Month and day with the highest temperature

- Month and day with the lowest temperature

15. **(Computational)** A magic square is a square of numbers with N rows and N columns, in which each integer value from 1 to ($N * N$) appears exactly once, and the sum of each column, each row, and each diagonal is the same value. For example, Figure 7.17 shows a magic square in which $N = 3$, and the sum of the rows, columns, and diagonal is 15. Write a program that constructs and displays a magic square for any given odd number N. This is the algorithm:

    Insert the value 1 in the middle of the first row (element [0][N%2]).
    After a value, x, has been placed, move up one row and to the right one column.
    Place the next number, x + 1, there, unless:
    > *(1) You move off the top (row = -1) in any column. Then move to the bottom row and place the next number, x + 1, in the bottom row of that column.*
    > *(2) You move off the right end (column = N) of a row. Then place the next number, x + 1, in the first column of that row.*
    > *(3) You move to a position that is already filled or out of the upper-right corner. Then place the next number, x + 1, immediately below x.*
    Stop when you have placed as many elements as there are in the array.

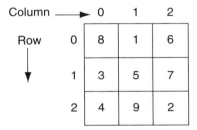

Figure 7.17   A magic square

16. **(Computational)** Among other applications, Pascal's triangle (see Figure 7.18) provides a means of determining the number of possible combinations of n things taken r at a time. For example, the number of possible combinations of five people ($n = 5$) taken two at a time ($r = 2$) is 10.

    Each row of the triangle begins and ends with 1. Every other element in a row is the sum of the element directly above it with the element to the left of the one above it. That is,

    ```
    element[n][r] = element[n-1][r] + element[n-1][r-1]
    ```

    Using this information, write and test a C++ program to create the first 11 rows of a two-dimensional array representing Pascal's triangle. For any given value of n less than 11 and r less than or equal to n, the program should display the correct element. Use your program to determine in how many ways a committee of 8 can be selected from a group of 10 people.

n \ r	0	1	2	3	4	5 •••
0	1					
1	1	1				
2	1	2	1			
3	1	3	3	1		
4	1	4	6	4	1	
5	1	5	10	10	5	1

Figure 7.18 Pascal's triangle

Engineering and Scientific Disciplines

Mechanical Engineering

Generally speaking, mechanical engineers are concerned with machines or systems that produce or apply energy. The range of technological activities considered part of mechanical engineering is probably broader than in any other engineering field. The field can be roughly subdivided into four categories:

- Power: Designing power-generating machines and systems, such as boiler-turbine engines for generating electricity, solar power, heating systems, and heat exchanges.
- Design: Innovative design of machine parts or components, from the most intricate and small to the gigantic. For example, mechanical engineers work alongside electrical engineers to design automatic control systems, such as robots.
- Automotive: Designing and testing transportation vehicles and the machines used to manufacture them.
- Heating, ventilation, air conditioning, and refrigeration: Designing systems to control the environment, both indoors and outside, and to control pollution.

Mechanical engineers usually have a thorough background in subjects such as thermodynamics, heat transfer, statics and dynamics, and fluid mechanics.

Chapter 8

I/O Streams and Data Files

The data for the programs you have used so far has been assigned internally in the programs or entered by the user during program execution. As such, data used in these programs is stored in the computer's main memory and ceases to exist after the program using it has finished executing. This type of data entry is fine for small amounts of data. However, imagine a company having to pay someone to type in the names and addresses of hundreds or thousands of customers every month when bills are prepared and sent.

As you learn in this chapter, storing large amounts of data outside a program on a convenient storage medium is more sensible. Data stored together under a common name on a storage medium other than the computer's main memory is called a data file. Typically, data files are stored on disks, USB drives, or CD/DVDs. Besides providing permanent storage for data, data files can be shared between programs, so the data one program outputs can be input in another program. In this chapter, you learn how data files are created and maintained in C++.

8.1   I/O File Stream Objects and Methods

To store and retrieve data outside a C++ program, you need two things:

- A file
- A file stream object

You learn about these important topics in this section.

Files

A **file** is a collection of data stored together under a common name, usually on a disk, magnetic tape, USB drive, or CD/DVD. For example, the C++ programs you store on disk are examples of files. The stored data in a program file is the code that becomes input data to the C++ compiler. In the context of data processing, however, a C++ program isn't usually considered data, and the term "file" or "data file" typically refers only to external files containing the data used in a C++ program.

A file is physically stored on an external medium, such as a disk. Each file has a unique filename, referred to as the file's **external name**. The external name is how the operating system (OS) knows the file. When you review the contents of a directory or folder (for example, in Windows Explorer), you see files listed by their external names. Each computer OS has its own specification for the maximum number of characters permitted for an external filename. Table 8.1 lists these specifications for commonly used OSs.

Table 8.1   Maximum Allowable Filename Characters

OS	Maximum Filename Length
DOS	8 characters plus an optional period and 3-character extension
Windows 98, 2000, XP, Vista	255 characters
UNIX Early versions Current versions	 14 characters 255 characters

To make sure examples in this book are compatible with all the OSs listed in Table 8.1, the more restrictive DOS specification has been adhered to generally (but not always). If you're using one of the other OSs, however, you can take advantage of the increased length specification to create descriptive filenames, but avoid using extremely long filenames because they take more time to type and can result in typing errors. A manageable length for a filename is usually 12 to 14 characters, with a maximum of 25 characters.

Using the DOS convention, all the following are valid data filenames:

```
prices.dat      records        info.txt
exper1.dat      scores.dat     math.mem
```

Choose filenames that indicate the type of data in the file and the application for which it's used. Typically, the first eight characters describe the data, and an extension (the characters after the decimal point) describes the application used to create the file. For example, the Excel program adds the `.xls` or `.xlsx` extension automatically to all spreadsheet files, Microsoft Word and WordPerfect use the extensions `.doc` (or `.docx`) and

---

Point of Information

Functions and Methods

C++ programmers can make full use of the many functions C++ classes provide without knowing the internal details of how the function is constructed or even how to construct a class. Functions provided as part of a class are formally referred to as **class methods** (or **methods**, for short). Therefore, a method can be referred to as a function, although the term "method" provides more information in telling you the function is available as part of a class.

Part Two (Chapters 10 and 11) explains classes and their construction in detail. As you'll see, a class is constructed from C++ code that includes both data and functions (although the functions are more accurately referred to as methods). An object is simply a specific item constructed from a class. For example, a specific car is an object, which is a specific item from the class of all cars, or the book you're reading now is an object, which is a specific item from the class of all third editions of the book C++ *For Engineers and Scientists*.

.wpx (x refers to the version number), and C++ compilers require a program file with the extension .cpp. When creating your own filenames, you should adhere to this practice. For example, using the DOS convention, the name exper1.dat is suitable for describing a file of data corresponding to experiment number 1.

Two basic types of files exist: **text files**, also known as **character-based files**, and **binary-based files**. Both file types store data by using a binary code; the difference is in what the codes represent. Briefly, text files store each character, such as a letter, digit, dollar sign, decimal point, and so on, by using a character code (typically ASCII or Unicode). With a character code, a word processing program or text editor can display the files so that a person can read them.

Binary-based files use the same code the C++ compiler uses for primitive data types. This means numbers appear in their true binary form, and strings retain their ASCII or Unicode form. The advantage of binary-based files is compactness; storing numbers with their binary code usually takes less space than with character values. In general, programmers use text files more often because the file's data can be displayed by word processing programs and simple text editors. The default file type in C++ is always a text file and is the file type discussed in this chapter.

File Stream Objects

A **file stream** is a one-way transmission path used to connect a file stored on a physical device, such as a disk or CD, to a program. Each file stream has its own mode that determines the direction of data on the transmission path—that is, whether the path moves data from a file to a program *or* from a program to a file. A file stream that receives or reads data from a file to a program is an **input file stream**. A file stream that sends or writes data to a file is an **output file stream**. The direction, or mode, is defined in relation to the program, not the file; data going into a program is considered input data, and data sent out from a program is considered output data. Figure 8.1 illustrates the data flow from and to a file, using input and output file streams.

For each file your program uses, regardless of the file's type (text or binary), a distinct file stream object must be created. If you want your program to read from and write to a file, both input and output file stream objects are required. Input file stream objects are declared to be

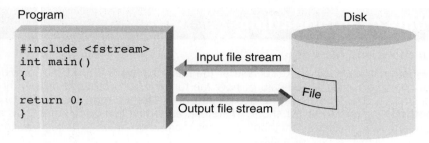

Figure 8.1   Input and output file streams

of type `ifstream`, and output file stream objects are declared to be of type `ofstream`. For example, the following declaration statement declares an input file stream object named `inFile` to be an object of the `ifstream` class:

```
ifstream inFile;
```

Similarly, the following declaration statement declares an output file stream object named `outFile` to be an object of the `ofstream` class:

```
ofstream outFile;
```

In a C++ program, a file stream is accessed by its stream object name: one name for reading the file and one name for writing to the file. Object names, such as `inFile` and `outFile`, can be any programmer-selected name that conforms to C++'s identifier rules.

File Stream Methods

Each file stream object has access to the methods defined for its `ifstream` or `ofstream` class. These methods include connecting a stream object name to an external filename (called **opening a file**), determining whether a successful connection has been made, closing a connection (called **closing a file**), getting the next data item into the program from an input stream, putting a new data item from the program onto an output stream, and detecting when the end of a file has been reached.

Opening a file connects a file stream object to a specific external filename by using a file stream's `open()` method, which accomplishes two purposes. First, opening a file establishes the physical connecting link between a program and a file. Because details of this link are handled by the computer's OS and are not visible to the program, normally the programmer doesn't need to consider them.

From a coding perspective, the second purpose of opening a file is more relevant. Besides establishing the actual physical connection between a program and a data file, opening a file connects the file's external name to the stream object name that the program uses internally. The method that performs this task, `open()`, is provided by the `ifstream` and `ofstream` classes.

Point of Information

Input and Output Streams

A **stream** is a one-way transmission path between a source and a destination. In data transmission, a stream of bytes is sent down this transmission path, similar to a stream of water providing a one-way path for water to travel from a source to a destination.

Stream objects are created from stream classes. You have already used two stream objects extensively: the input stream object named `cin` and the output stream object named `cout`. The `cin` object, created from the `istream` stream class, provides a transmission path from keyboard to program. The `cout` object, created from the `ostream` stream class, provides a transmission path from program to screen. The `istream` and `ostream` stream classes are parent classes to the `iostream` class. When the `iostream` header file is included in a program with the `#include <iostream>` directive, the `cin` and `cout` stream objects are declared automatically and opened by the C++ compiler.

File stream objects provide the same capabilities as the `cin` and `cout` objects, except they connect a program to a file rather than the keyboard or screen. File stream objects must be declared explicitly as objects of the `ifstream` class (for input) or objects of the `ofstream` class (for output). The `ifstream` and `ofstream` classes are made available by including the `fstream` header file with the directive `#include <fstream>`. The `fstream` class is derived from the `ifstream` and `ofstream` classes.

In using the `open()` method to connect the file's external name to its internal object stream name, only one argument is required: the external filename. For example, the following statement connects the external file named `prices.dat` to the internal file stream object named `inFile`:

```
inFile.open("prices.dat");
```

This statement assumes, of course, that `inFile` has been declared as an `ifstream` or `ofstream` object. If a file has been opened with the preceding statement, the program accesses the file by using the internal object name `inFile`, and the computer saves the file under the external name `prices.dat`. The external filename argument passed to `open()` is a string enclosed in double quotation marks. Calling the `open()` method requires standard object notation, in which the method name, in this case `open()`, is preceded by an object name (`inFile`, in this example) followed by a period.

When an existing file is connecting to an input file stream, the file's data is made available for input, starting at the first data item in the file. Similarly, a file connected to an output file stream creates a new file, said to be in **output mode**, and makes the file available for output. If a file exists with the same name as a file opened in output mode, the old file is erased (overwritten) and all its data is lost.

When opening a file for input or output, good programming practice requires checking that the connection has been established before attempting to use the file. You can do this with the `fail()` method, which returns a true value if the file was opened unsuccessfully (that is, it's true the open failed) or a false value if the open succeeded. Typically, the `fail()` method is used in code similar to the following, which attempts to open a file named `prices.dat` for input, checks that a valid connection was made, and reports an error message if the file wasn't opened for input successfully:

```
ifstream inFile;  // any object name can be used here
inFile.open("prices.dat");  // open the file
// check that the connection was successfully opened
if (inFile.fail())
{
  cout << "\nThe file was not successfully opened"
       << "\n Please check that the file currently exists."
       << endl;
  exit(1);
}
```

If the `fail()` method returns a true, indicating the open failed, this code displays an error message. In addition, the `exit()` function, which is a request to the OS to end program execution immediately, is called. The `cstdlib` header function must be included in any program using `exit()`, and `exit()`'s single-integer argument is passed directly to the OS for any further program action or user inspection. Throughout the remainder of the book, this type of error checking is included whenever a file is opened. (Section 9.2 shows how to use exception handling for the same type of error checking.) In addition to the `fail()` method, C++ provides three other methods, listed in Table 8.2, for detecting a file's status.

Table 8.2 File Status Methods

Prototype	Description
`fail()`	Returns a Boolean `true` if the file hasn't been opened successfully; otherwise, returns a Boolean `false` value.
`eof()`	Returns a Boolean `true` if a read has been attempted past the end-of-file; otherwise, returns a Boolean `false` value. The value becomes `true` only when the first character after the last valid file character is read.
`good()`	Returns a Boolean `true` value while the file is available for program use. Returns a Boolean `false` value if a read has been attempted past the end-of-file. The value becomes `false` only when the first character after the last valid file character is read.
`bad()`	Returns a Boolean `true` value if a read has been attempted past the end-of-file; otherwise, returns a `false`. The value becomes `true` only when the first character after the last valid file character is read.

Program 8.1 shows the statements required to open a file for input, including an error-checking routine to ensure that the open was successful. A file opened for input is said to be in **read mode** or **input mode**. (These two terms are synonymous.)

Program 8.1

```cpp
#include <iostream>
#include <fstream>
#include <cstdlib>    // needed for exit()
using namespace std;

int main()
{
  ifstream inFile;

  inFile.open("prices.dat");  // open the file with the
                              // external name prices.dat
  if (inFile.fail())  // check for a successful open
  {
    cout << "\nThe file was not successfully opened"
         << "\n Please check that the file currently exists."
         << endl;
    exit(1);
  }

  cout << "\nThe file has been successfully opened for reading."
       << endl;
  // statements to read data from the file would be placed here

  return 0;
}
```

A sample run of Program 8.1 produces the following output:

```
The file has been successfully opened for reading.
```

A different check is required for output files (files that are written to) because if a file exists with the same name as the file to be opened in output mode, the existing file is erased and all its data is lost. To avoid this situation, the file is first opened in input mode to see whether it exists. If it does, the user is given the choice of permitting it to be overwritten when it's opened later in output mode. The code to accomplish this check is shaded in Program 8.2.

Program 8.2

```cpp
#include <iostream>
#include <fstream>
#include <cstdlib>    // needed for exit()
using namespace std;

int main()
{
  ifstream inFile;
  ofstream outFile;

  inFile.open("prices.dat");   // attempt to open the file for input

  char response;

  if (!inFile.fail())  // if it doesn't fail, the file exists
  {
    cout << "A file by the name prices.dat exists.\n"
         << "Do you want to continue and overwrite it\n"
         << " with the new data (y or n): ";
    cin >> response;
    if (tolower(response) == 'n')
    {
      cout << "The existing file will not be overwritten." << endl;
      exit(1);   //terminate program execution
    }
  }

  outFile.open("prices.dat"); // now open the file for writing

  if (inFile.fail())  // check for a successful open
  {
    cout << "\nThe file was not successfully opened"
         << endl;
    exit(1);
  }

  cout << "The file has been successfully opened for output."
       << endl;


  // statements to write to the file would be placed here

  return 0;
}
```

The following two runs were made with Program 8.2:

```
A file by the name prices.dat exists.
Do you want to continue and overwrite it
  with the new data (y or n): n
The existing file will not be overwritten.
```

and

```
A file by the name prices.dat exists.
Do you want to continue and overwrite it
  with the new data (y or n): y
The file has been successfully opened for output.
```

Although Programs 8.1 and 8.2 can be used to open an existing file for reading and writing, both programs lack statements to perform a read or write and close the file. These topics are discussed shortly. Before moving on, however, it's possible to combine the declaration of an `ifstream` or `ofstream` object and its associated open statement into one statement. For example, examine the following two statements in Program 8.1:

```
ifstream inFile;
inFile.open("prices.dat");
```

They can be combined into a single statement:

```
ifstream inFile("prices.dat");
```

Embedded and Interactive Filenames   Programs 8.1 and 8.2 have two problems:

- The external filename is embedded in the program code.
- There's no provision for a user to enter the filename while the program is running.

As both programs are written, if the filename is to change, a programmer must modify the external filename in the call to `open()` and recompile the program. Both these problems can be avoided by assigning the filename to a string variable.

A string variable, as used in this book, is a variable that can hold a string value, which is any sequence of zero or more characters enclosed in quotation marks, such as `"Hello World"` and `""`. Remember that the quotation marks delimit the beginning and end of a string but aren't stored as part of the string.

In declaring and initializing a string variable for use in an `open()` method, the string is considered a C-string. (See the Point of Information "Using C-Strings as Filenames" for precautions when using a C-string.) A safer alternative, and one used throughout this book, is to use a `string` class object and convert it to a C-string by using the `c_str()` method.

Point of Information

Using C-Strings as Filenames

If you use a C-string (which is simply a one-dimensional array of characters) to store an external filename, you must specify the C-string's maximum length in brackets immediately after it's declared. For example, examine the following declaration:

```
char filename[21] = "prices.dat";
```

The number in brackets (21) is one more than the maximum number of characters that can be assigned to the variable `filename` because the compiler adds an end-of-string character to terminate the string. Therefore, the string value `"prices.dat"`, which consists of 10 characters, is actually stored as 11 characters. In this example, the maximum value that can be assigned to the string variable `filename` is a string value consisting of 20 characters.

After a string variable is declared to store a filename, it can be used in one of two ways. First, as shown in Program 8.3a, it can be placed at the top of a program to clearly identify a file's external name, instead of embedding it in an `open()` method call.

Program 8.3a

```cpp
#include <iostream>
#include <fstream>
#include <cstdlib>    // needed for exit()
#include <string>
using namespace std;
int main()
{
  string filename = "prices.dat"; // place the filename up front
  ifstream inFile;
  inFile.open(filename.c_str());  // open the file
  if (inFile.fail())  // check for successful open
  {
    cout << "\nThe file named " << filename
         << " was not successfully opened"
         << "\n Please check that the file currently exists."
         << endl;
    exit(1);
  }
  cout << "\nThe file has been successfully opened for reading.\n";
  return 0;
}
```

In Program 8.3a, the string object is declared and initialized with the name `filename`. This name is placed at the top of `main()` for easy file identification. When a string object is used, as opposed to a string literal, the variable name isn't enclosed in quotation marks in the `open()` method call. In the `open()` call, the value of the string object, which is a C-string, is provided by the expression `filename.c_str()`.

Finally, in the `fail()` method, the file's external name is displayed by inserting the string object's name in the `cout` output stream. External names of files are identified in this manner in this book.

Another useful role string objects play is to permit users to enter the filename as the program is executing. For example, the code

```
string filename;

cout << "Please enter the name of the file you wish to open: ";
cin  >> filename;
```

allows a user to enter a file's external name at runtime. The only restriction in this code is that the user must not enclose the entered string value in quotation marks, and the entered string value can't contain any blanks. The reason no blanks can be included is that when `cin` is used, the compiler terminates the string when it encounters a blank. Program 8.3b uses this code in the context of a complete program.

Program 8.3b

```cpp
#include <iostream>
#include <fstream>
#include <cstdlib>    // needed for exit()
#include <string>
using namespace std;
int main()
{
  string filename;
  ifstream inFile;
  cout << "Please enter the name of the file you wish to open: ";
  cin  >> filename;
  inFile.open(filename.c_str());  // open the file
  if (inFile.fail())  // check for successful open
  {
    cout << "\nThe file named " << filename
         << " was not successfully opened"
         << "\n Please check that the file currently exists."
         << endl;
    exit(1);
  }
  cout << "\nThe file has been successfully opened for reading.\n";
  return 0;
}
```

Point of Information

Using `fstream` Objects

In using `ifstream` and `ofstream` objects, the input or output mode is indicated by the object. Therefore, `ifstream` objects must be used for input, and `ofstream` objects must be used for output. Another means of creating file streams is to use `fstream` objects that can be used for input or output, but this method requires an explicit mode designation. An `fstream` object is declared by using the following syntax:

```
fstream objectName;
```

When using the `fstream` class's `open()` method, two arguments are required: a file's external name and a mode indicator. Here are the permissible mode indicators:

Indicator	Description
`ios::in`	Open a text file in input mode
`ios::out`	Open a text file in output mode
`ios::app`	Open a text file in append mode
`ios::ate`	Go to the end of the opened file
`ios::binary`	Open a binary file in input mode (default is text file)
`ios::trunc`	Delete file contents if it exists
`ios::nocreate`	If file doesn't exist, open fails
`ios::noreplace`	If file exists, open for output fails

As with `ofstream` objects, an `fstream` object in output mode creates a new file and makes the file available for writing. If a file exists with the same name as a file opened for output, the old file is erased. For example, the following statement declares `file1` as an object of type `fstream`:

```
fstream file1;
```

The following statement attempts to open the text file `prices.dat` for output:

```
file1.open("prices.dat",ios::out);
```

After this file has been opened, the program accesses the file by using the internal object name `file1`, and the computer saves the file under the external name `prices.dat`.

An `fstream` file object opened in **append mode** means an existing file is available for data to be added to the end of the file. If the file opened for appending doesn't exist, a new file with the designated name is created and made available to receive output from the program. For example, the following statement declares `file1` to be of type `fstream` and attempts to open a text file named `prices.dat` and make it available for data to be added to the end of the file:

```
file1.open("prices.dat",ios::app);
```

continued...

> ## Point of Information
>
> ### Using `fstream` Objects (continued)
>
> Finally, an `fstream` object opened in input mode means an existing external file has been connected and its data is available as input. For example, the following statement declares `file1` to be of type `fstream` and attempts to open a text file named `prices.dat` for input:
>
> ```
> file1.open("prices.dat",ios::in);
> ```
>
> The mode indicators can be combined by the bitwise OR operator, `|` (see Section 15.2). For example, the following statement opens the `file1` stream, which can be an `fstream` or `ifstream`, as an input binary stream:
>
> ```
> file1.open("prices.dat", ios::in | ios::binary)
> ```
>
> If the mode indicator is omitted as the second argument for an `ifstream` object, the stream is opened as a text input file by default; if the mode indicator is omitted for an `ofstream` object, the stream is opened as a text output file by default.

The following is a sample output of Program 8.3b:

```
Please enter the name of the file you wish to open: foobar

The file named foobar was not successfully opened
   Please check that the file currently exists.
```

Closing a File A file is closed by using the `close()` method. This method breaks the connection between the file's external name and the file stream object, which can be used for another file. Examine the following statement, which closes the `inFile` stream's connection to its current file:

```
inFile.close();
```

As indicated, the `close()` method takes no argument.

Because all computers have a limit on the maximum number of files that can be open at one time, closing files that are no longer needed makes good sense. Any open files existing at the end of normal program execution are closed automatically by the OS.

EXERCISES 8.1

1. **(Practice)** Write declaration and open statements that link the following external filenames to their corresponding internal object names. All files are text-based.

External Filename	Internal Object Name	Mode
coba.mem	memo	output
book.let	letter	output
coupons.bnd	coups	append
yield.bnd	yield	append
prices.dat	priFile	input
rates.dat	rates	input

2. **(Practice)** **a.** Write a set of two statements that declares the following objects as ifstream objects, and then opens them as text input files: inData.txt, prices.txt, coupons.dat, and exper.dat.

   b. Rewrite the two statements for Exercise 2a, using a single statement.

3. **(Practice)** **a.** Write a set of two statements that declares the following objects as ofstream objects, and then opens them as text output files: outDate.txt, rates.txt, distance.txt, and file2.txt.

   b. Rewrite the two statements for Exercise 3a, using a single statement.

4. **(Practice)** Enter and execute Program 8.1 on your computer.

5. **(Practice)** Enter and execute Program 8.2 on your computer.

6. **(Practice)** **a.** Enter and execute Program 8.3a on your computer.

   b. Add a close() method to Program 8.3a, and then execute the program.

7. **(Practice)** **a.** Enter and execute Program 8.3b on your computer.

   b. Add a close() method to Program 8.3b, and then execute the program.

8. **(Practice)** Using the reference manuals provided with your computer's OS, determine the following:

   a. The maximum number of characters the computer can use to name a file for storage

   b. The maximum number of data files that can be open at the same time

9. **(Practice)** Would it be appropriate to call a saved C++ program a file? Why or why not?

10. **(Practice)** **a.** Write declaration and open statements to link the following external file-names to their corresponding internal object names. Use only ifstream and ofstream objects.

External Name	Internal Object Name	Mode
coba.mem	memo	binary and output
coupons.bnd	coups	binary and append
prices.dat	priFile	binary and input

   b. Redo Exercise 10a, using only fstream objects.

   c. Write close statements for each file opened in Exercise 10a.

Point of Information

Checking for a Successful Connection

You must check that the `open()` method established a connection between a file stream and an external file successfully because the `open()` call is a request to the OS that can fail for various reasons. Chief among these reasons is a request to open an existing file for reading that the OS can't locate or a request to open a file for output in a nonexistent folder. If the OS can't satisfy the open request, you need to know about it and terminate your program. Failure to do so can result in abnormal program behavior or a program crash.

There are two styles of coding for checking the return value. The most common method for checking that a fail didn't occur when attempting to use a file for input is the one coded in Program 8.1. It's used to distinguish the `open()` request from the check made via the `fail()` call and is repeated here for convenience:

```
inFile.open("prices.dat");  // request to open the file
if (inFile.fail())   // check for a failed connection
{
    cout << "\nThe file was not successfully opened"
         << "\n Please check that the file currently exists."
         << endl;
    exit(1);
}
```

Similarly, the check made in Program 8.2 is typically included when a file is being opened in output mode. Alternatively, you might encounter programs that use `fstream` objects in place of `ifstream` and `ofstream` objects (see the previous Point of Information box). When using `fstream`'s `open()` method, two arguments are required: a file's external name and an explicit mode indication. Using an `fstream` object, the open request and check for an input file typically appear as follows:

```
fstream inFile;

inFile.open("external name", ios::in);
if (inFile.fail())
{
    cout << "\nThe file was not successfully opened"
         << "\n Please check that the file currently exists."
         << endl;
    exit(1);
}
```

Many times, the conditional expression `inFile.fail()` is replaced by the equivalent expression `!inFile`. Although `ifstream` and `ofstream` objects are always used in this book, be prepared to encounter styles that use `fstream` objects.

8.2 Reading and Writing Character-Based Files

Reading or writing character-based files involves almost the identical operations for reading input from the keyboard and writing data to the screen. For writing to a file, the cout object is replaced by the ofstream object name declared in the program. For example, if outFile is declared as an object of type ofstream, the following output statements are valid:

```
outFile << 'a';
outFile << "Hello World!";
outFile << descrip << ' ' << price;
```

The filename in each of these statements, in place of cout, directs the output stream to a specific file instead of to the standard display device (the screen). Program 8.4 shows using the insertion operator, <<, to write a list of descriptions and prices to a file.

Program 8.4

```
#include <iostream>
#include <fstream>
#include <cstdlib>   // needed for exit()
#include <string>
#include <iomanip>  // needed for formatting
using namespace std;

int main()
{
  string filename = "prices.dat";  // put the filename up front
  ofstream outFile;

  outfile.open(filename.c_str());

  if (outFile.fail())
  {
    cout << "The file was not successfully opened" << endl;
    exit(1);
  }

  // set the output file stream formats
  outFile << setiosflags(ios::fixed)
          << setiosflags(ios::showpoint)
          << setprecision(2);
```

☞

```
// send data to the file
outFile << "Mats " << 39.95 << endl
        << "Bulbs "  << 3.22 << endl
        << "Fuses " << 1.08 << endl;

outFile.close();
cout << "The file " << filename
     << " has been successfully written." << endl;

return 0;
}
```

When Program 8.4 runs, the, `prices.dat` file is created and saved by the computer as a text file. It's a sequential file consisting of the following data:

```
Mats 39.95
Bulbs 3.22
Fuses 1.08
```

The actual storage of characters in the file depends on the character codes the computer uses. Although only 30 characters appear to be stored in the file—corresponding to the descriptions, blanks, and prices written to the file—the file contains 36 characters.

The extra characters consist of the newline escape sequence at the end of each line created by the `endl` manipulator, which is created as a carriage return character (`cr`) and linefeed (`lf`). Assuming characters are stored with the ASCII code, the `prices.dat` file is physically stored as shown in Figure 8.2. For convenience, the character corresponding to each hexadecimal code is listed below the code. A code of 20 represents the blank character. Additionally, C and C++ append the low-value hexadecimal byte 0x00 as the end-of-file (`EOF`) sentinel when the file is closed. This `EOF` sentinel is never counted as part of the file.

```
4D 61 74 73 20 33 39 2E 39 35 0D 0A 42 75 6C 62 73 20

 M  a  t  s     3  9  .  9  5 cr 1f  B  u  l  b  s


33 2E 32 32 0D 0A 46 75 73 65 73 20 31 2E 30 38 0D 0A

 3  .  2  2 cr 1f  F  u  s  e  s     1  .  0  8 cr 1f
```

Figure 8.2 The `prices.dat` file as stored by the computer

Point of Information

Formatting Text File Output Stream Data

Output file streams can be formatted in the same manner as the `cout` standard output stream. For example, if an output stream named `fileOut` has been declared, the following statement formats all data inserted in the `fileOut` stream in the same way these parameterized manipulators work for the `cout` stream:

```
fileOut << setiosflags(ios::fixed)
        << setiosflags(ios::showpoint)
        << setprecision(2);
```

The first manipulator parameter, `ios::fixed`, causes the stream to output all numbers as though they were floating-point values. The next parameter, `ios::showpoint`, tells the stream to provide a decimal point. Therefore, a value such as 1.0 appears as 1.0, not 1. Finally, the `setprecision()` manipulator tells the stream to display two decimal values after the decimal point. Therefore, the number 1.0, for example, appears as 1.00.

Instead of using manipulators, you can use the stream methods `setf()` and `precision()`. For example, the previous formatting can be accomplished with the following code:

```
fileOut.setf(ios::fixed);
fileOut.setf(ios::showpoint);
fileOut.precision(2);
```

Which style you select is a matter of preference. In both cases, the formats need be specified only once and remain in effect for every number subsequently inserted in the file stream.

Reading from a Text File

Reading data from a character-based file is almost identical to reading data from a standard keyboard, except the `cin` object is replaced by the `ifstream` object declared in the program. For example, if inFile is declared as an object of type `ifstream` that's opened for input, the following statement reads the next two items in the file and stores them in the variables `descrip` and `price`:

```
inFile >> descrip >> price;
```

The file stream name in this statement, in place of `cin`, directs the input to come from the file stream rather than the standard input device stream. Table 8.3 lists other methods that can be used for stream input. These methods must be preceded by a stream object name. All these methods, except `getline()`, are defined in the `iostream` class. The `getline()` method is defined in the `string` class.

Point of Information

The `put()` Method

All output streams have access to the `fstream` class's `put()` method, which permits character-by-character output to a stream. This method works in the same manner as the character insertion operator, `<<`. The syntax of this method call is the following:

```
ofstreamName.put(characterExpression);
```

The `characterExpression` can be a character variable or literal value. For example, the following code can be used to output an `'a'` to the standard output stream:

```
cin.put('a');
```

In a similar manner, if `outFile` is an `ofstream` object file that has been opened, the following code outputs the character value in the character variable named `keycode` to this output:

```
char keycode;
  .
  .
  .
outFile.put(keycode);
```

Table 8.3 Stream Input Class Methods

Method Name	Description
`get()`	Returns the next character extracted from the input stream as an `int`.
`get(charVar)`	Overloaded version of `get()` that extracts the next character from the input stream and assigns it to the specified character variable, `charVar`.
`getline(fileObject, strObj, termChar)`	Extracts characters from the specified input stream, `fileObject`, until the terminating character, `termChar`, is encountered. Assigns the characters to the specified string class object, `strObj`.
`peek()`	Returns the next character in the input stream without extracting it from the stream.
`ignore(int n)`	Skips over the next *n* characters. If n is omitted, the default is to skip over the next single character.

Program 8.5 shows how the `prices.dat` file created in Program 8.4 can be read. This program illustrates one way of detecting the EOF marker by using the `good()` method (see Table 8.2). Because this method returns a Boolean `true` value before the EOF marker has been read or passed over, it can be used to verify that the data read is valid file data. Only after the EOF marker has been read or passed over does this method return a Boolean `false`. Therefore, the notation `while(inFile.good())` used in Program 8.5 ensures that the data is read from the file before the EOF has been read.

Program 8.5

```cpp
#include <iostream>
#include <fstream>
#include <cstdlib>    // needed for exit()
#include <string>
using namespace std;

int main()
{
  string filename = "prices.dat";  // put the filename up front
  string descrip;
  double price;

  ifstream inFile;

  inFile.open(filename.c_str());

  if (inFile.fail())  // check for successful open
  {
    cout << "\nThe file was not successfully opened"
         << "\n Please check that the file currently exists."
         << endl;
    exit(1);
  }

  // read and display the file's contents
  inFile >> descrip >> price;
  while (inFile.good()) // check next character
  {
    cout << descrip << ' ' << price << endl;
    inFile >> descrip >> price;
  }

  inFile.close();

  return 0;
}
```

Program 8.5 produces the following display:

```
Mats 39.95
Bulbs 3.22
Fuses 1.08
```

Point of Information

A Way to Identify a File's Name and Location

During program development, test files are usually placed in the same directory as the program. Therefore, a method call such as `inFile.open("exper.dat")` causes no problems to the OS. In production systems, however, it's not uncommon for data files to reside in one directory and program files to reside in another. For this reason, including the full pathname of any file that's opened is always a good idea.

For example, if the `exper.dat` file resides in the `C:\test\files` directory, the `open()` call should include the full pathname: `inFile.open("C:\\test\\files\\exper.dat")`. Then, no matter where the program is run from, the OS knows where to locate the file. Note the use of double backslashes, which is required.

Another important convention is to list all filenames at the top of a program instead of embedding the names deep in the code. You can do this easily by using string variables to store each filename. For example, if the statement

```
string filename = "c:\\test\\files\\exper.dat";
```

is placed at the top of a program file, the declaration statement clearly lists both the name of the file and its location. Then, if some other file is to be tested, all that's required is a simple one-line change at the top of the program.

Using a string variable for the file's name is also useful for the `fail()` method check. For example, take a look at the following code:

```
string filename;
ifstream infile;

inFile.open(filename.c_str());
if (inFile.fail())
{
  cout << "\n The file named " << filename
       << " was not successfully opened"
       <<"\n Please check that this file currently exists.";
  exit(1);
}
```

In this code, the name of the file that failed to open is displayed in the error message without the name being embedded as a string value.

Examine the expression inFile.good() used in the while statement. This expression is true as long as the EOF marker hasn't been read. Therefore, as long as the item read is good, the loop continues to read the file. Within the loop, the items just read are displayed, and then a new string and a double-precision number are input to the program. When the EOF has been detected, the expression returns a Boolean value of false and the loop terminates. This termination ensures that data is read and displayed up to, but not including, the EOF marker.

A replacement for the statement while(inFile.good()) is while(!inFile.eof()), which is read as "while the end of file has not been reached." This replacement works because the eof() method returns a true only after the EOF marker has been read or passed over. In effect, the relational expression checks that the EOF hasn't been read—hence, the use of the NOT operator, !.

Another means of detecting the EOF is to use the fact that the extraction operation, >>, returns a Boolean value of true if data is extracted from a stream; otherwise, it returns a Boolean false value. Using this return value, the following code can be used in Program 8.5 to read the file:

```
// read and display the file's contents
while (inFile >> descrip >> price) // check next character
  cout << descrip << ' ' << price << endl;
```

Although this code seems a bit cryptic at first glance, it makes perfect sense when you understand that the expression being tested extracts data from the file and returns a Boolean value to indicate whether the extraction was successful.

Finally, in the previous while statement or in Program 8.5, the expression inFile >> descrip >> price can be replaced by a getline() method (see Table 8.3). For file input, this method has the following syntax:

```
getline(fileObject, strObj, terminatingChar)
```

fileObject is the name of the ifstream file, *strObj* is a string class object, and *terminatingChar* is an optional character constant or variable specifying the terminating character. If this optional third argument is omitted, the default terminating character is the newline ('\n') character. Program 8.6 shows using getline() in the context of a complete program.

Program 8.6 is a line-by-line text-copying program, which reads a line of text from the file and then displays it on the screen. The output of Program 8.6 is the following:

```
Mats 39.95
Bulbs 3.22
Fuses 1.08
```

If obtaining the description and price as separate variables were necessary, either Program 8.5 should be used, or the string returned by getline() in Program 8.6 must be processed further to extract the separate data items. (See Section 8.6 for parsing procedures.)

Program 8.6

```cpp
#include <iostream>
#include <fstream>
#include <cstdlib>    // needed for exit()
#include <string>
using namespace std;

int main()
{
  string filename = "prices.dat";  // put the filename up front
  string line;
  ifstream inFile;

  inFile.open(filename.c_str());

  if (inFile.fail())  // check for successful open
  {
    cout << "\nThe file was not successfully opened"
         << "\n Please check that the file currently exists."
         << endl;
    exit(1);
  }

  // read and display the file's contents
  while (getline(inFile,line))
    cout << line << endl;

  inFile.close();

  return 0;
}
```

Standard Device Files

The file stream objects you have seen so far have been logical file objects. A **logical file object** is a stream that connects a file of logically related data, such as a data file, to a program. In addition to logical file objects, C++ supports physical file objects. A **physical file object** is a stream that connects to a hardware device, such as a keyboard, screen, or printer.

The actual physical device assigned to your program for data entry is formally called the **standard input file**. Usually, it's the keyboard. When a cin object method call is encountered in a C++ program, it's a request to the OS to go to this standard input file for the expected input. Similarly, when a cout object method call is encountered, the output is automatically displayed or "written to" a device that has been assigned as the **standard output file**. For most systems, it's a computer screen, although it can also be a printer.

Point of Information

The `get()` and `putback()` Methods

All input streams have access to the `fstream` class's `get()` method, used for character-by-character input from an input stream. This method works similarly to character extraction, using the `>>` operator, with two important differences: If a newline character, `'\n'`, or a blank character, `' '`, is encountered, these characters are read in the same manner as any other alphanumeric character. The syntax of this method call is the following:

```
istreamName.get(characterVariable);
```

For example, the following code can be used to read the next character from the standard input stream and store the character in the variable `ch`:

```
char ch;
cin.get(ch);
```

Similarly, if `inFile` is an `ifstream` object that has been opened to a file, the following code reads the next character in the stream and assigns it to the character variable `keycode`:

```
char keycode;
inFile.get(keycode);
```

In addition to the `get()` method, all input streams have a `putback()` method for putting the last character read from an input stream back on the stream. This method has the following syntax (with `characterExpression` representing any character variable or character value):

```
ifstreamName.putback(characterExpression);
```

The `putback()` method provides output capability to an input stream. The putback character need not be the last character read; it can be any character. All putback characters, however, have no effect on the data file. They affect only the open input stream. Therefore, the data file characters remain unchanged, although the characters subsequently read from the input stream can change.

When a program is executed, the standard input stream `cin` is connected to the standard input device. Similarly, the standard output stream `cout` is connected to the standard output device. These two object streams are available for programmer use, as are the standard error stream, `cerr`, and the standard log stream, `clog`. Both these streams connect to the screen.

Other Devices

The keyboard, display, error, and log streams are connected automatically to the stream objects `cin`, `cout`, `cerr`, and `clog` when the `iostream` header file is included in a program. Other devices can be used for input or output if the name assigned by the system is known. For example, most IBM or IBM-compatible PCs assign the name `prn` to the printer connected to the computer. For these computers, a statement such as `outFile.open("prn")` connects the printer to the `ofstream` object named `outFile`. A subsequent statement, such as `outFile << "Hello World!";`, would cause the string `Hello World!` to be output directly to the printer. As the name of an actual file, `prn` must be enclosed in quotation marks in the `open()` method call.

EXERCISES 8.2

1. **(Practice and Modify) a.** Enter and execute Program 8.5.

   b. Modify Program 8.5 to use the expression `!inFile.eof()` in place of the expression `inFile.good()`, and execute the program to see whether it operates correctly.

2. **(Practice and Modify) a.** Enter and execute Program 8.6.

   b. Modify Program 8.6 by replacing `cout` with `cerr`, and verify that the output for the standard error stream is the screen.

   c. Modify Program 8.6 by replacing `cout` with `clog`, and verify that the output for the standard log stream is the screen.

3. **(Practice and Modify) a.** Write a C++ program that accepts lines of text from the keyboard and writes each line to a file named `text.dat` until an empty line is entered. An empty line is a line with no text that's created by pressing the Enter (or Return) key.

   b. Modify Program 8.6 to read and display the data stored in the `text.dat` file created in Exercise 3a.

4. **(Practice)** Determine the OS command or procedure your computer provides to display the contents of a saved file.

5. **(Data Processing) a.** Create a text file named `employee.dat` containing the following data:

Anthony	A	10031	7.82	12/18/2008
Burrows	W	10067	9.14	06/9/2006
Fain	B	10083	8.79	05/18/2007
Janney	P	10095	10.57	09/28/2008
Smith	G	10105	8.50	12/20/2007

   b. Write a C++ program to read the `employee.dat` file created in Exercise 5a and produce a duplicate copy of the file named `employee.bak`.

   c. Modify the program written in Exercise 5b to accept the names of the original and duplicate files as user input.

   d. The program written for Exercise 5c always copies data from an original file to a duplicate file. What's a better method of accepting the original and duplicate filenames, other than prompting the user for them each time the program runs?

6. **(Data Processing) a.** Write a C++ program that opens a file and displays its contents with line numbers. That is, the program should print the number 1 before displaying the first line, print the number 2 before displaying the second line, and so on for each line in the file.

   b. Modify the program written in Exercise 6a to list the file's contents on the printer assigned to your computer.

7. **(Data Processing) a.** Create a text file containing the following data (without the headings):

Name	Social Security Number	Hourly Rate	Hours Worked
B Caldwell	555-88-2222	7.32	37
D Memcheck	555-77-4444	8.32	40
R Potter	555-77-6666	6.54	40
W Rosen	555-99-8888	9.80	35

   b. Write a C++ program that reads the data file created in Exercise 7a and computes and displays a payroll schedule. The output should list the Social Security number, name, and gross pay for each person, calculating gross pay as *Hourly Rate × Hours Worked*.

8. **(Data Processing) a.** Create a text file containing the following data (without the headings):

Car Number	Miles Driven	Gallons of Gas Used
54	250	19
62	525	38
71	123	6
85	1322	86
97	235	14

   b. Write a C++ program that reads the data in the file created in Exercise 8a and displays the car number, miles driven, gallons of gas used, and miles per gallon (mpg) for each car. The output should contain the total miles driven, total gallons of gas used, and average mpg for all cars. These totals should be displayed at the end of the output report.

9. **(Data Processing) a.** Create a text file with the following data (without the headings):

Part Number	Initial Amount	Quantity Sold	Minimum Amount
QA310	95	47	50
CM145	320	162	200
MS514	34	20	25
EN212	163	150	160

b. Write a C++ program to create an inventory report based on the data in the file created in Exercise 9a. The display should consist of the part number, current balance, and the amount needed to bring the inventory to the minimum level. The current balance is the initial amount minus the quantity sold.

8.3   Random File Access

The term **file access** refers to the process of retrieving data from a file. There are two types of file access: sequential access and random access. To understand file access types, first you need to understand how data is organized in a file.

The term **file organization** refers to the way data is stored in a file. The files you have used, and will continue to use, have a **sequential organization**, meaning characters in the file are stored in a sequential manner. In addition, each open file has been read in a sequential manner, meaning characters are accessed one after another, which is called **sequential access**. Although characters are stored sequentially, they don't have to be accessed the same way. In fact, you can skip over characters and read a sequentially organized file in a nonsequential manner.

In **random access**, any character in the opened file can be read without having to sequentially read all characters stored ahead of it first. To provide random access to files, each `ifstream` object creates a file position marker automatically. This marker is a long integer representing an offset from the beginning of the file and keeps track of where the next character is to be read from or written to. Table 8.4 lists the methods used to access and change the file position marker. The suffixes g and p in these method names denote `get` and `put`; `get` refers to an input (get from) file, and `put` refers to an output (put to) file.

Table 8.4   File Position Marker Methods

Name	Description
`seekg(offset, mode)`	For input files, move to the offset position indicated by the mode.
`seekp(offset, mode)`	For output files, move to the offset position indicated by the mode.
`tellg(void)`	For input files, return the current value of the file position marker.
`tellp(void)`	For output files, return the current value of the file position marker.

The `seek()` methods allow the programmer to move to any position in the file. To understand these methods, you must understand how data is referenced in the file by using the file position marker.

Each character in a data file is located by its position in the file. The first character in the file is located at position 0, the next character at position 1, and so forth. A character's position is referred to as its **offset** from the start of the file. Therefore, the first character has a 0 offset, the second character has an offset of 1, and so on, for each character in the file.

The `seek()` methods require two arguments: the offset, as a long integer, in the file and where the offset is to be calculated from, determined by the mode. The three alternatives for the mode are `ios::beg`, `ios::cur`, and `ios::end`, which denote the beginning of the file, current position, and end of the file. Therefore, the mode ios::beg means the offset is the true offset from the start of the file. The mode ios::cur means the offset is relative to the current position in the file, and the mode ios::end means the offset is relative to the end of the file. A positive offset means move forward in the file, and a negative offset means move backward.

Examples of seek() method calls are shown in the following code. In these examples, inFile has been opened as an input file and outFile as an output file. The offset passed to seekg() and seekp() must be a long integer, hence the uppercase L appended to each number in the method calls.

```
inFile.seekg(4L,ios::beg);    // go to the fifth character in the input file
outFile.seekp(4L,ios::beg);   // go to the fifth character in the output file
inFile.seekg(4L,ios::cur);    // move ahead five characters in the input file
outFile.seekp(4L,ios::cur);   // move ahead five characters in the output file
inFile.seekg(-4L,ios::cur);   // move back five characters in the input file
outFile.seekp(-4L,ios::cur);  // move back five characters in the output file
inFile.seekg(0L,ios::beg);    // go to start of the input file
outfile.seekp(0L,ios::beg);   // go to start of the output file
inFile.seekg(0L,ios::end);    // go to end of the input file
outFile.seekp(0L,ios::end);   // go to end of the output file
inFile.seekg(-10L,ios::end);  // go to 10 characters before the input file's end
outFile.seekp(-10L,ios::end); // go to 10 characters before the output file's end
```

As opposed to seek() methods that move the file position marker, the tell() methods return the file position marker's offset value. For example, if 10 characters have been read from an input file named inFile, the method call returns the long integer 10:

```
inFile.tellg();
```

This means the next character to be read is offset 10 byte positions from the start of the file and is the 11th character in the file.

Program 8.7 shows using seekg() and tellg() to read a file in reverse order, from last character to first. As each character is read, it's also displayed.

Assume the test.dat file contains the following characters:

```
The grade was 92.5
```

The output of Program 8.7 is the following:

```
5 : . : 2 : 9 :   : s : a : w :   : e : d : a : r : g :   : e : h : T :
```

Program 8.7

```cpp
#include <iostream>
#include <fstream>
#include <string>
#include <cstdlib>
using namespace std;

int main()
{
  string filename = "test.dat";
  char ch;
  long offset, last;

  ifstream inFile(filename.c_str());

  if (inFile.fail())   // check for successful open
  {
    cout << "\nThe file was not successfully opened"
         << "\n Please check that the file currently exists"
         << endl;
    exit(1);
  }

  inFile.seekg(0L,ios::end);   // move to the end of the file
  last = inFile.tellg();       // save the offset of the last character

  for(offset = 1L; offset <= last; offset++)
  {
    inFile.seekg(-offset, ios::end);
    ch = inFile.get();
    cout << ch << " : ";
  }

  inFile.close();

  cout << endl;

  return 0;
}
```

Program 8.7 initially goes to the last character in the file. The offset of this character, the EOF character, is saved in the variable `last`. Because `tellg()` returns a long integer, `last` has been declared as a long integer.

Starting from the end of the file, `seekg()` is used to position the next character to be read, referenced from the end of the file. As each character is read, the character is displayed, and the offset is adjusted to access the next character. The first offset used is -1, which represents the character immediately preceding the EOF marker.

EXERCISES 8.3

1. **(Practice)** a. Create a file named `test.dat` containing the data in the `test.dat` file used in Program 8.7. (You can use a text editor or copy the `test.dat` file from this book's Web site.)

   b. Enter and execute Program 8.7 on your computer.

2. **(Modify)** Rewrite Program 8.7 so that the origin for the `seekg()` method used in the `for` loop is the start of the file rather than the end.

3. **(Modify)** Modify Program 8.7 to display an error message if `seekg()` attempts to reference a position beyond the end of the file.

4. **(Practice)** Write a program that reads and displays every second character in a file named `test.dat`.

5. **(Practice)** Using the `seek()` and `tell()` methods, write a function named `fileChars()` that returns the total number of characters in a file.

6. **(Practice)** a. Write a function named `readBytes()` that reads and displays *n* characters starting from any position in a file. The function should accept three arguments: a file object name, the offset of the first character to be read, and the number of characters to be read. (*Note*: The prototype for `readBytes()` should be `void readBytes(fstream&, long, int)`.)

   b. Modify the `readBytes()` function written in Exercise 6a to store the characters read into a string or an array. The function should accept the storage address as a fourth argument.

8.4   File Streams as Function Arguments

A file stream object can be used as a function argument. The only requirement is that the function's formal parameter be a reference (see Section 6.3) to the appropriate stream, either `ifstream&` or `ofstream&`. For example, in Program 8.8, an `ofstream` object named `outFile` is opened in `main()`, and this stream object is passed to the `inOut()` function. The function prototype and header for `inOut()` declare the formal parameter as a reference to an `ostream` object type. The `inOut()` function is then used to write five lines of user-entered text to the file.

Program 8.8

```cpp
#include <iostream>
#include <fstream>
#include <cstdlib>
#include <string>
using namespace std;

int main()
{
  string fname = "list.dat";  // here is the file you are working with
  void inOut(ofstream&);    // function prototype
  ofstream outFile;

  outFile.open(fname.c_str());

  if (outFile.fail())   // check for a successful open
  {
    cout << "\nThe output file " << fname << " was not successfully opened"
         << endl;
    exit(1);
  }

  inOut(outFile);  // call the function

  return 0;
}

void inOut(ofstream& fileOut)
{
  const int NUMLINES = 5;  // number of lines of text
  string line;
  int count;

  cout << "Please enter five lines of text:" << endl;
  for (count = 0; count < NUMLINES; count++)
  {
    getline(cin,line);
    fileOut << line << endl;
  }

  cout << "\nThe file has been successfully written." << endl;

  return;
}
```

In main(), the file is an ofstream object named outFile. This object is passed to the inOut() function and accepted as the formal parameter fileOut, which is declared to be a reference to an ofstream object type. The inOut() function then uses its reference parameter outFile as an output file stream name in the same manner that main() would use the fileOut stream object. Program 8.8 uses the getline() method introduced in Section 8.2 (see Table 8.3).

Program 8.9 expands on Program 8.8 by adding a getOpen() function to perform the open. Like inOut(), getOpen() accepts a reference argument to an ofstream object. After the getOpen() function finishes executing, this reference is passed to inOut(), as in Program 8.8. Although you might be tempted to write getOpen() to return a reference to an ofstream, it won't work because it results in an attempt to assign a returned reference to an existing one.

Program 8.9

```
#include <iostream>
#include <fstream>
#include <cstdlib>
#include <string>
using namespace std;

int getOpen(ofstream&);   // function prototype - pass a reference to an fstream
void inOut(ofstream&);    // function prototype - pass a reference to an fstream

int main()
{
  ofstream outFile;    // filename is an fstream object

  getOpen(outFile);    // open the file
  inOut(outFile);      // write to it

  return 0;
}
```

☞

```cpp
int getOpen(ofstream& fileOut)
{
  string name;

  cout << "\nEnter a file name: ";
  getline(cin,name);

  fileOut.open(name.c_str());        // open the file

  if (fileOut.fail())        // check for successful open
  {
    cout << "Cannot open the file" << endl;
    exit(1);
  }
  else
    return 1;
}

void inOut(ofstream& fileOut)
{
  const int NUMLINES = 5;   // number of lines
  int count;
  string line;

  cout << "Please enter five lines of text:" << endl;
  for (count = 0; count < NUMLINES; ++count)
  {
    getline(cin,line);
    fileOut << line << endl;
  }
  cout << "\nThe file has been successfully written.";

  return;
}
```

Program 8.9 allows the user to enter a filename from the standard input device and then opens the `ofstream` connection to the external file. If an existing data file's name is entered, the file is destroyed when it's opened for output. A useful trick for preventing this mishap is to open the entered file by using an input file stream. If the file exists, the `fail()` method indicates a successful open (that is, the open doesn't fail), which indicates the file is available for input. This technique can be used to alert the user that a file with the entered name exists in the system and to request confirmation that data in the file can be destroyed and the file opened for output. Before the file is reopened for output, the input file stream should be closed. Implementing this trick is left for you to try in Exercise 4.

EXERCISES 8.4

1. **(Practice)** A function named pFile() is to receive a filename as a reference to an ifstream object. What declarations are required to pass a filename to pFile()?

2. **(Practice)** Write a function named fcheck() that checks whether a file exists. The function should accept an ifstream object as a formal reference parameter. If the file exists, the function should return a value of 1; otherwise, the function should return a value of 0.

3. **(Practice)** A data file consisting of a group of lines has been created. Write a function named printLine() that reads and displays any line of the file. For example, the function called printLine(fstream& fName,5); should display the fifth line of the passed object stream.

4. **(Modify)** Rewrite the getOpen() function used in Program 8.9 to incorporate the file-checking procedures described in this section. Specifically, if the entered filename exists, an appropriate message should be displayed. The user should be presented with the option of entering a new filename or allowing the program to overwrite the existing file. Use the function written for Exercise 2 in your program.

8.5   A Case Study: Pollen Count File Update

After a data file has been created, application programs are typically written to read and update the file with current data. In this case study, a file is used as a database for storing the 10 most recent pollen counts, which are used in the summer as allergy "irritability" measures. As a new reading is obtained, it's added to the file, and the oldest stored reading is deleted.

Step 1   Analyze the Problem

Pollen count readings, which are taken from August through September in the northeastern United States, measure the number of ragweed pollen grains in the air. Pollen counts in the range of 10 to 200 grains per cubic meter of air are normal during this time of year. Typically, pollen counts above 10 begin affecting a small percentage of hay fever sufferers, counts in the range of 30 to 40 noticeably bother approximately 30% of hay fever sufferers, and counts between 40 and 50 adversely affect more than 60% of all hay fever sufferers.

A program is to be written that updates a file containing the 10 most recent pollen counts. As a new count is obtained, it's added to the end of the file, and the oldest count is deleted from the file.[1] Additionally, the average of the new file's data is calculated and displayed. The existing file, named pollen.in, contains the data shown in Figure 8.3.

The input data for this problem consist of a file of 10 integer numbers and a user-input value of the most recent integer value pollen count. There are two required outputs:

- A file of the 10 most recent integer values
- The average of the data in the updated file

---

[1]This type of data storage is formally referred to as a first-in/first-out (FIFO) list, also called a "queue." If the list is maintained in last-in/first-out order (LIFO), it's called a "stack."

A Case Study: Pollen Count File
Update

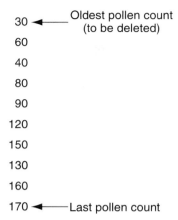

30 ⟵ ── Oldest pollen count
(to be deleted)
60
40
80
90
120
150
130
160
170 ⟵───── Last pollen count

Figure 8.3 Data currently in the `pollen.in` file

Step 2   Develop a Solution

The algorithm for solving this problem is straightforward and is described by the following pseudocode:

main() function
  Display a message indicating what the program does.
  Call the Input stream function.
  Call the Output stream function.
  Call the Update function.
  Display the new 10-week average.
Input stream function
  Request the name of the input data file.
  Open an input file stream and validate a successful connection.
Output stream function
  Request the name of the output data file.
  Open an output file stream and validate a successful connection.
Update function
  Request a new pollen count reading.
  Read the oldest pollen count from the input data file.
  For the remaining input file pollen counts:
    Read an input value.
    Add the value to a total.
    Write the input value to the output file stream.
  Endfor
  Write the new pollen count to the output file stream.
  Add the new pollen count to the total.
  Calculate the average as total / (number of pollen counts).
  Return the new 10-week average.
  Close all files.

In reviewing this algorithm, notice that the oldest pollen count is read but never used in any computation. The remaining pollen counts are read, "captured" in a total, and written to the output data file. The last pollen count is then added to the total and also written to the output data file. Finally, the average of the most recent pollen counts is computed and displayed, and all file streams are closed.

Step 3   Code the Solution

Program 8.10 presents a C++ representation of the selected design; the algorithm has been coded as the pollenUpdate() function.

Program 8.10

```cpp
#include <iostream>
#include <fstream>
#include <cstdlib>
#include <string>
using namespace std;

void openInput(ifstream&);   // pass a reference to an ifstream
void openOutput(ofstream&);  // pass a reference to an ofstream
double pollenUpdate(ifstream&, ofstream&); // pass two references

int main()

{
   ifstream inFile;         // inFile is an istream object
   ofstream outFile;        // outFile is an ofstream object
   double average;

  // display a user message

  cout << "\n\nThis program reads the old pollen count file, "
       << "creates a current pollen"
       << "\n count file, and calculates and displays "
       << "the latest 10-week average.";

  openInput(inFile);
  openOutput(outFile);

  average = pollenUpdate(inFile, outFile);

  cout << "\nThe new 10-week average is: " << average << endl;

  return 0;
}
```

☞

```cpp
// this function gets an external filename and opens the file for input
void openInput(ifstream& fname)
{

  string filename;

  cout << "\n\nEnter the input pollen count filename: ";
  cin >> filename;
  fname.open(filename.c_str());

  if (fname.fail()) // check for a successful open
  {
    cout << "\nFailed to open the file named " << filename << "for input"
         << "\n Please check that this file exists"
         << endl;

    exit(1);
  }

  return;
}

// this function gets an external filename and opens the file for output
void openOutput(ofstream& fname)
{

  string filename;

  cout << "Enter the output pollen count filename: ";
  cin >> filename;

  fname.open(filename.c_str());

  if (fname.fail()) // check for a successful open
  {
    cout << "\nFailed to open the file named " << filename << "for output"
         << endl;
    exit(1);
  }

  return;
}
```

☞

```cpp
// the following function reads the pollen file,
// writes a new file,
// and returns the new weekly average
double pollenUpdate(ifstream& inFile, ofstream& outFile)
{

  const int POLNUMS = 10; // maximum number of pollen counts
  int i, polreading;
  int oldreading, newcount;
  double sum = 0;
  double average;
  // get the latest pollen count
  cout << "Enter the latest pollen count reading: ";
  cin >> newcount;

  // read the oldest pollen count
  inFile >> oldreading;

  // read, sum, and write out the rest of the pollen counts
  for(i = 0; i < POLNUMS; i++)
  {
    inFile >> polreading;
    sum  += polreading;
    outFile << polreading << endl;

  }

  // write out the latest reading
  outFile << newcount << endl;

  // compute and display the new average
  average = (sum + newcount) / double(POLNUMS);

  inFile.close();
  outFile.close();

  cout << "\nThe output file has been written.\n";

  return average;
}
```

Step 4 Test and Correct the Program

Testing Program 8.10 requires providing both valid and invalid input data for the program. Invalid data consists of a nonexistent input data filename and a data file containing fewer than 10 items. Valid data consists of a file containing 10 integers. A sample run of Program 8.10 follows with a valid input file:

```
This program reads the old pollen count file, creates a current
pollen count file, and calculates and displays the latest
10-week average.

Enter the input pollen count filename: pollen.in
Enter the output pollen count filename: pollen.out
Enter the latest pollen count reading: 200

The output file has been written.
The new 10-week average is: 120
```

The updated file Program 8.10 creates is shown in Figure 8.4. In reviewing this file's contents, notice that the most current reading has been added to the end of the file, and other pollen readings from the original file shown in Figure 8.3 have been moved up one position in the new file. Also, notice that the output of the sample run calculates the new 10-week average correctly.

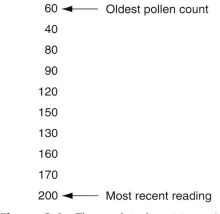

60 ◄——— Oldest pollen count
40
80
90
120
150
130
160
170
200 ◄——— Most recent reading

Figure 8.4 The updated `pollen.in` file

EXERCISES 8.5

1. **(Practice)** Write a C++ program to create the `pollen.in` file shown in Figure 8.3.

2. **(Practice)** Using the file created in Exercise 1 or the `pollen.in` file provided on this book's Web site, enter and run Program 8.10 on your computer.

3. (Conversion) a. A file named `polar.dat` contains the polar coordinates needed in a graphics program. Currently, this file contains the following data:

Distance (Inches)	Angle (Degrees)
2.0	45.0
6.0	30.0
10.0	45.0
4.0	60.0
12.0	55.0
8.0	15.0

Write a C++ program to create this file on your computer.

b. Using the `polar.dat` file created in Exercise 3a, write a C++ program that accepts distance and angle data from the user and adds the data to the end of the file.

c. Using the `polar.dat` file created in Exercise 3a, write a C++ program that reads this file and creates a second file named `xycord.dat`. The entries in the new file should contain the rectangular coordinates corresponding to the polar coordinates in the `polar.dat` file. Polar coordinates are converted to rectangular coordinates by using these formulas:

$$x = r\ (cos\ \theta)$$
$$y = r\ (sin\ \theta)$$

The r is the distance coordinate and θ is the radian equivalent of the angle coordinate in the `polar.dat` file.

4. (Data Processing) a. Write a C++ program to create a data file containing the following information:

Student ID Number	Student Name	Course Code	Course Credits	Course Grade
2333021	BOKOW, R.	NS201	3	A
2333021	BOKOW, R.	MG342	3	A
2333021	BOKOW, R.	FA302	1	A
2574063	FALLIN, D.	MK106	3	C
2574063	FALLIN, D.	MA208	3	B
2574063	FALLIN, D.	CM201	3	C
2574063	FALLIN, D.	CP101	2	B
2663628	KINGSLEY, M.	QA140	3	A
2663628	KINGSLEY, M.	CM245	3	B
2663628	KINGSLEY, M.	EQ521	3	A
2663628	KINGSLEY, M.	MK341	3	A
2663628	KINGSLEY, M.	CP101	2	B

b. Using the file created in Exercise 4a, write a C++ program that creates student grade reports. The grade report for each student should contain the student's name and ID number, a list of courses taken, the credits and grade for each course, and a semester grade point average (GPA). For example, this is the grade report for the first student:

```
Student Name: BOKOW, R.
Student ID Number: 2333021

Course Code      Course Credits   Course Grade
NS201                 3                A
MG342                 3                A
FA302                 1                A

Total Semester Course Credits Completed: 7
Semester GPA: 4.0
```

The semester GPA is computed in two steps. First, each course grade is assigned a numerical value (A = 4, B = 3, C = 2, D = 1, F = 0), and the sum of each course's grade value times the credits for each course is computed. This sum is then divided by the total number of credits taken during the semester.

5. (File Update) a. Write a C++ program to create a data file containing the following information:

Student ID Number	Student Name	Course Credits	Course GPA
2333021	BOKOW, R.	48	4.0
2574063	FALLIN, D.	12	1.8
2663628	KINGSLEY, M.	36	3.5

b. Write a C++ program to update the file created in Exercise 5a with the data from the file created in Exercise 4a.

8.6   A Closer Look: The iostream Class Library[2]

As you have seen, the classes in the iostream class library access files by using entities called streams. For most systems, the data bytes transferred on a stream represent ASCII characters or binary numbers. The mechanism for reading a byte stream from a file or writing a byte stream to a file is hidden when using a high-level language, such as C++. Nevertheless, understanding this mechanism is useful so that you can place the services provided by the iostream class library in context.

File Stream Transfer Mechanism
Figure 8.5 illustrates the mechanism for transferring data between a program and a file. As shown, this transfer involves an intermediate file buffer contained in the computer's memory.

---

[2]This topic can be omitted on first reading without loss of subject continuity.

Each opened file is assigned its own file buffer, which is a storage area used by the data transferred between the program and the file.

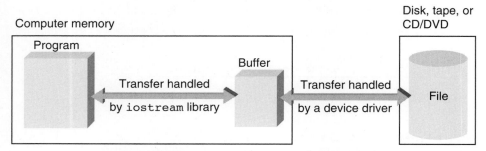

Figure 8.5   The data transfer mechanism

The program either writes a set of data bytes to the file buffer or reads a set of data bytes from the file buffer by using a stream object. The data transfer between the device storing the data file (usually a disk or CD/DVD) and the file buffer is handled by special OS programs. These programs, called device drivers, aren't stand-alone programs; they're an integral part of the OS. A **device driver** is a section of OS code that accesses a hardware device, such as a disk, and handles the data transfer between the device and the computer's memory. Because the computer's internal data transfer rate is generally much faster than any device connected to it, the device driver must correctly synchronize the data transfer speed between the computer and the device sending or receiving data.

Typically, a disk device driver transfers data between the disk and file buffer only in fixed sizes, such as 1024 bytes at a time. Therefore, the file buffer is a convenient means of permitting a device driver to transfer data in blocks of one size, and the program can access them by using a different size (typically, as separate characters or as a fixed number of characters per line).

Components of the `iostream` Class Library

The `iostream` class library consists of two primary base classes: `streambuf` and `ios`. The `streambuf` class provides the file buffer, illustrated in Figure 8.5, and general routines for transferring binary data. The `ios` class contains a pointer to the file buffers provided by the `streambuf` class and general routines for transferring text data. From these two base classes, several other classes are derived and included in the `iostream` class library.

Figure 8.6 is an inheritance diagram for the `ios` family of classes as it relates to the `ifstream`, `ofstream`, and `fstream` classes. Figure 8.7 is an inheritance diagram for the `streambuf` family of classes. In these diagrams, the arrows point from a derived class to a base class.

Table 8.5 lists the correspondence between the classes shown in Figures 8.6 and 8.7, including the header files defining these classes.

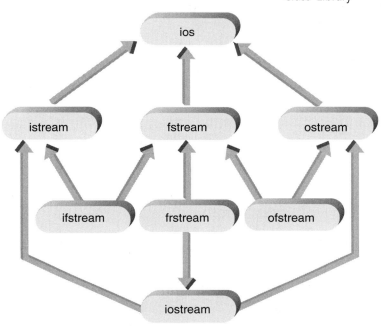

Figure 8.6 The base class `ios` and its derived classes

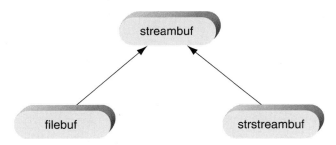

Figure 8.7 The base class `streambuf` and its derived classes

Table 8.5 Correspondence Between Classes in Figures 8.6 and 8.7

ios Class	streambuf Class	Header File
istream ostream iostream	streambuf	iostream or fstream
ifstream ofstream fstream	filebuf	fstream

Therefore, the `ifstream`, `ofstream`, and `fstream` classes you have used for file access use a buffer provided by the `filebuf` class and defined in the `fstream` header file. Similarly, the `cin`, `cout`, `cerr`, and `clog` iostream objects use a buffer provided by the `streambuf` class and defined in the `iostream` header file.

In-Memory Formatting

In addition to the classes shown in Figure 8.7, a class named `strstream` is derived from the `ios` class. This class uses the `strstreambuf` class shown in Figure 8.7, requires the `strstream` header file, and provides capabilities for writing and reading strings to and from in-memory defined streams.

As an output stream, these streams are typically used to "assemble" a string from smaller pieces until a complete line of characters is ready to be written to `cout` or to a file. Attaching a `strstream` object to a buffer for this purpose is similar to attaching an `fstream` object to an output file. For example, the statement

```
strstream inmem(buf, 72, ios::out);
```

attaches a `strstream` object to an existing buffer of 72 bytes in output mode. Program 8.11 shows how this statement is used in the context of a complete program.

 Program 8.11

```cpp
#include <iostream>
#include <strstream>
#include <iomanip>
using namespace std;

int main()
{
  const int MAXCHARS = 81;   // one more than the maximum characters in a line
  int units = 10;
  double price = 36.85;
  char buf[MAXCHARS];

  strstream inmem(buf, MAXCHARS, ios::out);   // open an in-memory stream

  // write to the buffer through the stream
  inmem << "No. of units = "
        << setw(3) << units
        << "  Price per unit = $"
        << setw(6) << setprecision(2) << fixed << price << '\0';

  cout << '|' << buf << '|';

  cout << endl;

  return 0;
}
```

Program 8.11 produces the following output:

```
|No. of units =  10   Price per unit = $  36.85|
```

This output illustrates that the character buffer has been filled in correctly by insertions to the inmem stream. (Note that the end-of-string NULL, '\0', which is the last insertion to the stream, is required to close off the C-string correctly.) After the character array has been filled, it's written to a file as a single string.

In a similar manner, a strstream object can be opened in input mode. This stream would be used as a working storage area, or buffer, for storing a complete line of text from a file or standard input. After the buffer has been filled, the extraction operator would be used to "disassemble" the string into component parts and convert each data item into its designated data type. Doing this permits inputting data from a file on a line-by-line basis before assigning data items to their respective variables.

8.7   Common Programming Errors

The common programming errors with files are as follows:

1. Forgetting to open a file before attempting to read from it or write to it.
2. Using a file's external name in place of the internal file stream object name when accessing the file. The only stream method that uses the data file's external name is the open() method. As always, all stream methods discussed in this chapter must be preceded by a stream object name followed by a period (the dot operator).
3. Opening a file for output without first checking that a file with the same name already exists. If it does and you didn't check for a preexisting filename, the file is overwritten.
4. Not understanding that the end of a file is detected only after the EOF marker has been read or passed over.
5. Attempting to detect the end of a file by using character variables for the EOF marker. Any variable used to accept the EOF must be declared as an integer variable. For example, if ch is declared as a character variable, the following expression produces an infinite loop:[3]

   ```
   while ( (ch = in.file.peek()) != EOF )
   ```

   This problem occurs because a character variable can never take on an EOF code. EOF is an integer value (usually -1) with no character representation, which ensures that the EOF code can't be confused with a legitimate character encountered as normal data in the file. To terminate the loop created by the preceding expression, the variable ch must be declared as an integer variable.
6. Using an integer argument with the seekg() and seekp() functions. This offset must be a long integer constant or variable. Any other value passed to these functions can have unpredictable results.

---

[3]This infinite loop doesn't occur on UNIX systems, where characters are stored as signed integers.

8.8   Chapter Summary

1. A data file is any collection of data stored together in an external storage medium under a common name.

2. A data file is connected to a file stream by using `fstream`'s `open()` method. This method connects a file's external name with an internal object name. After the file is opened, all subsequent accesses to the file require the internal object name.

3. A file can be opened in input or output mode. An opened output file stream creates a new data file or erases the data in an existing opened file. An opened input file stream makes an existing file's data available for input. An error condition results if the file doesn't exist and can be detected by using the `fail()` method.

4. All file streams must be declared as objects of the `ifstream` or `ofstream` class. Therefore, a declaration similar to either of the following must be included with the declaration to open the file:

   ```
   ifstream inFile;
   ofstream outfile;
   ```

   The stream object names `inFile` and `outfile` can be replaced with any user-selected object name.

5. In addition to any files opened in a function, the standard stream objects `cin`, `cout`, and `cerr` are declared and opened automatically when a program runs. `cin` is an input file stream object used for data entry (usually from the keyboard), `cout` is an output file stream object used for data display (usually on screen), and `cerr` is an output file stream object used for displaying system error messages (usually on screen).

6. Data files can be accessed randomly by using the `seekg()`, `seekp()`, `tellg()`, and `tellp()` methods. The g versions of these methods are used to alter and query the file position marker for input file streams, and the p versions do the same for output file streams.

7. Table 8.6 lists class-supplied methods for file manipulation. The `getline()` method is defined in the `string` class, and all other methods are defined in the `fstream` class.

Table 8.6   File Manipulation Methods

Method Name	Description
`get()`	Extract the next character from the input stream and return it as an `int`.
`get(chrVar)`	Extract the next character from the input stream and assign it to `chrVar`.
`getline(fileObject, strObj, termChar)`	Extract the next string of characters from the input file stream object and assign them to `strObj` until the specified terminating character is detected. If omitted, the default terminating character is a newline.

Table 8.6 File Manipulation Methods (continued)

Method Name	Description
`getline(C-stringVar,int n,'\n')`	Extract and return characters from the input stream until `n-1` characters are read or a newline is encountered (terminates the input with a `'\0'`).
`peek()`	Return the next character in the input stream without extracting it from the stream.
`put(chrExp)`	Put the character specified by `chrExp` on the output stream.
`putback(chrExp)`	Push the character specified by `chrExp` back onto the input stream. Does not alter the data in the file.
`ignore(int n)`	Skip over the next `n` characters; if `n` is omitted, the default is to skip over the next single character.
`eof()`	Returns a Boolean `true` value if a read has been attempted past the end of file; otherwise, it returns a Boolean `false` value. The value becomes `true` only when the first character after the last valid file character is read.
`good()`	Returns a Boolean `true` value while the file is available for program use. Returns a Boolean `false` value if a read has been attempted past the end of file. The value becomes `false` only when the first character after the last valid file character is read.
`bad()`	Returns a Boolean `true` value if a read has been attempted past the end of file; otherwise, it returns a `false`. The value becomes `true` only when the first character after the last valid file character is read.
`fail()`	Returns a Boolean `true` if the file hasn't been opened successfully; otherwise, it returns a Boolean `false` value.

Programming Projects for Chapter 8

1. (**Data Processing**) **a.** Create a text file containing the following data (without the headings):

Name	Rate	Hours
Callaway, G.	6.00	40
Hanson, P.	5.00	48
Lasard, D.	6.50	35
Stillman, W.	8.00	50

   b. Write a C++ program that uses the information in the file created in Exercise 1a to produce the following pay report for each employee:

   ```
   Name    Pay Rate    Hours    Regular Pay    Overtime Pay    Gross Pay
   ```

   Compute regular pay as any hours worked up to and including 40 hours multiplied by the pay rate. Compute overtime pay as any hours worked above 40 hours times a pay rate of 1.5 multiplied by the regular rate. The gross pay is the sum of regular and overtime pay. At the end of the report, the program should display the totals of the regular, overtime, and gross pay columns.

2. (**Data Processing**) **a.** Store the following data in a file:

   ```
   5  96  87  78  93  21  4  92  82  85  87  6  72  69  85  75  81  73
   ```

   b. Write a C++ program to calculate and display the average of each group of numbers in the file created in Exercise 2a. The data is arranged in the file so that each group of numbers is preceded by the number of data items in the group. Therefore, the first number in the file, 5, indicates that the next five numbers should be grouped together. The number 4 indicates that the following four numbers are a group, and the 6 indicates that the last six numbers are a group. (*Hint*: Use a nested loop. The outer loop should terminate when the end of file has been encountered.)

3. (**Data Processing**) Write a C++ program that allows the user to enter the following information from the keyboard for each student in a class (up to 20 students):

   ```
   Name    Exam 1 Grade    Exam 2 Grade    Homework Grade    Final Exam Grade
   ```

   For each student, your program should first calculate a final grade, using this formula:

   Final Grade = 0.20 × Exam 1 + 0.20 × Exam 2 + 0.35 × Homework + 0.25 × Final Exam

   Then assign a letter grade on the basis of 90–100 = A, 80–89 = B, 70–79 = C, 60–69 = D, and less than 60 = F. All the information, including the final grade and the letter grade, should then be displayed and written to a file.

4. (**Data Processing**) Write a C++ program that permits users to enter the following information about your small company's 10 employees, sorts the information in ascending ID number, and then writes the sorted information to a file:

   ```
   ID No.    Sex(M/F)    Hourly Wage    Years with the Company
   ```

5. (**Data Processing**) Write a C++ program that reads the file created in Exercise 4, changes the hourly wage or years for each employee, and creates a new updated file.

6. **(Data Processing)** Write a C++ program that reads the file created in Exercise 4 one record at a time, asks for the number of hours each employee worked each month, and calculates and displays each employee's total pay for the month.

7. **(Data Processing)** **a.** You have collected information about cities in your state. You decide to store each city's name, population, and mayor in a file. Write a C++ program to accept the data for a number of cities from the keyboard and store the data in a file in the order in which they're entered.

 b. Read the file created in Exercise 7a, sort the data alphabetically by city name, and display the data.

8. **(Data Processing)** A bank's customer records are to be stored in a file and read into a set of arrays so that a customer's record can be accessed randomly by account number. Create the file by entering five customer records, with each record consisting of an integer account number (starting with account number 1000), a first name (maximum of 10 characters), a last name (maximum of 15 characters), and a double-precision number for the account balance.

 After the file is created, write a C++ program that requests a user-input account number and displays the corresponding name and account balance from the file.

9. **(Inventory)** Create an ASCII file with the following data or use the `shipped.txt` file provided on this book's Web site. The headings are not part of the file but indicate what the data represents.

Shipped Date	Tracking Number	Part Number	First Name	Last Name	Company
04/12/97	D50625	74444	James	Lehoff	Rotech
04/12/97	D60752	75255	Janet	Lezar	Rotech
04/12/97	D40295	74477	Bill	McHenry	Rotech
04/12/97	D23745	74470	Diane	Kaiser	Rotech
04/12/97	D50892	75155	Helen	Richardson	NapTime

The format of each line in the file is identical, with fixed-length fields defined as follows:

Field Position	Field Name	Starting Col. No.	Ending Col. No.	Field Length
1	Shipped Date	1	8	8
2	Tracking Number	12	17	6
3	Part Number	22	26	5
4	First Name	31	35	5
5	Last Name	39	48	10
6	Company	51	64	14

Using this data file, write a C++ program that reads the file and produces a report listing the shipped date, part number, first name, last name, and company name.

Engineering and Scientific Disciplines

Environmental Science and Technology

Two of the newest areas of science and engineering are the related fields of environmental science and technology. Environmental science began as an extension of ecology, a biological field that gained prominence in the 1960s. Ecology studies the interrelationships between specific biological organisms and their environment.

In the 1970s, the study of the larger interplay among physical, chemical, and biological components of the environment, both locally and globally, began and became the field known as environmental science. This field now includes study of the following areas, among others:

- Climate change
- Ozone depletion
- Weather pattern changes
- Water quality
- Air pollution
- Noise pollution
- Conservation of natural resources
- Disposal of toxic substances

The impact of human activities on these environmental areas is a chief concern of environmental science. Typically, many different scientific and engineering experts are needed to work as a team in analyzing and solving environmental issues.

Applying engineering and scientific expertise to solving environmental problems falls within the purview of environmental technology. This field is concerned with preserving the natural environment and its resources by providing solutions in areas such as water purification, human waste management, renewable energy, and recycling, among others.

Chapter 9

Completing the Basics

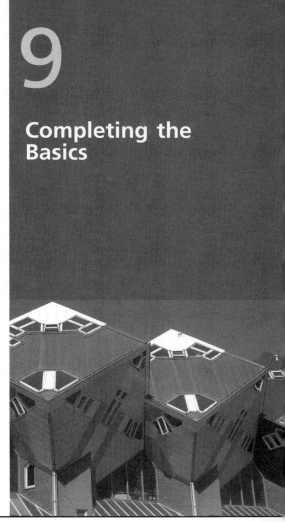

The current ANSI/ISO C++ standard introduces two new features that weren't part of the original C++ specification: exception handling and the string *class. This chapter covers both these new features.*

Exception handling is a means of error detection and processing, which has gained increasing acceptance in programming technology. It permits detecting an error at the point in the code where the error has occurred and provides a means of processing the error and returning control to the line that generated the error. Although error detection and code correction are possible by using if *statements and functions, exception handling gives you another useful programming tool targeted at error detection and processing.*

With the new ANSI/ISO C++ standard, the string *class is now part of the standard C++ library. This class provides an expanded set of class functions, including easy insertion and removal of characters from a string, automatic string expansion when a string's original capacity is exceeded, string contraction when characters are removed from a string, and range checking to detect invalid character positions.*

In addition to discussing these two new C++ features, this chapter shows how exception handling, when applied to strings, is a useful means of validating user input.

9.1   Exception Handling

The traditional C++ approach to error handling uses a function to return a specific value to indicate specific operations. Typically, a return value of 0 or 1 is used to indicate successful completion of the function's task, whereas a negative value indicates an error condition. For example, with a function used to divide two numbers, a return value of -1 could indicate that the denominator is zero, and the division can't be performed. When multiple error conditions can occur, different return values can be used to indicate specific errors.

Although this approach is still available and often used, a number of problems can occur. First, the programmer must check the return value to detect whether an error did occur. Next, the error-handling code that checks the return value frequently becomes intermixed with normal processing code, so sometimes it's difficult to determine which part of the code is handling errors. Finally, returning an error condition from a function means the condition must be the same data type as a valid returned value; hence, the error code must be a specified value that can be identified as an error alert. This means the error code is embedded as one of the possible nonerror values the function might require and is available only at the point where the function returns a value. In addition, a function returning a Boolean value has no additional values for reporting an error condition.

None of these problems are insurmountable, and many times this approach is simple and effective. However, the latest C++ compilers have added a technique designed for error detection and handling referred to as **exception handling**. With this technique, when an error occurs while a function is executing, an exception is created. An **exception** is a value, a variable, or an object containing information about the error at the point the error occurs. This exception is immediately passed, at the point it was generated, to code called the **exception handler**, which is designed to deal with the exception. The process of generating and passing the exception is referred to as **throwing an exception**. The exception is thrown from within the function while it's still executing, which permits handling the error and then returning control back to the function so that it can complete its assigned task.

In general, two fundamental types of errors can cause C++ exceptions: those resulting from a program's inability to obtain a required resource and those resulting from flawed data. Examples of the first error type are attempts to obtain a system resource, such as locating and finding a file for input. These errors are the result of external resources over which the programmer has no control.

The second type of error can occur when a program prompts the user to enter an integer, and the user enters a string, such as e234, that can't be converted to a numerical value. Another example is the attempt to divide two numbers when the denominator has a 0 value, a condition referred to as a "division by zero error." These errors can always be checked and handled in a manner that doesn't result in a program crash. Before seeing how to use exception handling, review Table 9.1 to familiarize yourself with the terminology used with processing exceptions.

Table 9.1   Exception-Handling Terminology

Terminology	Description
Exception	A value, a variable, or an object that identifies a specific error that has occurred while a program is executing
Throw an exception	Send the exception to a section of code that processes the detected error

Table 9.1 Exception-Handling Terminology (continued)

Terminology	Description
Catch or handle an exception	Receive a thrown exception and process it
Catch clause	The section of code that processes the error
Exception handler	The code that throws and catches an exception

The general syntax of the code required to throw and catch an exception is the following:

```
try
{
  // one or more statements,
  // at least one of which should
  // be capable of throwing an exception
}
catch(exceptionDataType parameterName)
{
  // one or more statements
}
```

This example uses two new keywords: `try` and `catch`. The `try` keyword identifies the start of an exception-handling block of code. At least one of the statements inside the braces defining this block of code should be capable of throwing an exception. As an example, examine the `try` block in the following section of code:

```
try
{
  cout << "Enter the numerator (whole numbers only): ";
  cin >> numerator;
  cout << "Enter the denominator (whole numbers only):";
  cin >> denominator;
  result = numerator/denominator;
}
```

The `try` block contains five statements, three of which might result in an error you want to catch. In particular, a professionally written program would make sure valid integers are entered in response to both prompts and the second entered value is not a zero. For this example, you just check that the second value entered isn't zero.

From the standpoint of the `try` block, only the value of the second number matters. The `try` block is altered to say "Try all the statements within me to see whether an exception, which in this case is a zero second value, occurs." To check that the second value isn't zero, you add a `throw` statement in the `try` block, as follows:

```
try
{
  cout << "Enter the numerator: (whole number only): ";
  cin >> numerator;
  cout << "Enter the denominator: (whole number only): ";
  cin >> denominator;
  if (denominator == 0)
    throw denominator;
  else
    result = numerator/denominator;
}
```

In this `try` block, the thrown item is an integer value. A string literal, a variable, or an object could have been used, but only one of these items can be thrown by any single `throw` statement. The first four statements in the `try` block don't have to be included in the code; however, doing so keeps all the relevant statements together. Keeping related statements together makes it easier to add `throw` statements in the same `try` block to ensure that both input values are integer values.

A `try` block must be followed by one or more `catch` blocks, which serve as exception handlers for any exceptions thrown by statements in the `try` block. Here's a `catch` block that handles the thrown exception, which is an integer:

```
catch(int e)
  {
    cout << "A denominator value of " << e << " is invalid." << endl;
    exit (1);
  }
```

The exception handling this `catch` block provides is an output statement that identifies the caught exception and then terminates program execution. Notice the parentheses following the `catch` keyword. Inside the parentheses are the data type of the exception that's thrown and a parameter name used to receive the exception. This parameter, which is a programmer-selected identifier but conventionally uses the letter e for exception, is used to hold the exception value generated when an exception is thrown.

Multiple `catch` blocks can be used as long as each block catches a unique data type. The only requirement is providing at least one `catch` block for each `try` block. The more exceptions that can be caught with the same `try` block, the better. Program 9.1 provides a complete program that includes a `try` block and a `catch` block to detect a division by zero error.

Following are two sample runs of Program 9.1. Note that the second output indicates that an attempt to divide by a zero denominator has been detected successfully before the operation is performed.

```
Enter the numerator (whole number only): 12
Enter the denominator(whole number only): 3
12/3 = 4
```

and

```
Enter the numerator (whole number only): 12
Enter the denominator(whole number only): 0
A denominator value of 0 is invalid.
```

Program 9.1

```cpp
#include <iostream>
using namespace std;

int main()
{
  int numerator, denominator;

  try
  {
    cout << "Enter the numerator (whole number only): ";
    cin  >> numerator;
    cout << "Enter the denominator(whole number only): ";
    cin  >> denominator;

    if (denominator == 0)
        throw denominator;  // an integer value is thrown
    else
        cout << numerator <<'/' << denominator
            << " = " << double(numerator)/ double(denominator) << endl;
  }
  catch(int e)
  {
    cout << "A denominator value of " << e << " is invalid." << endl;
    exit (1);
  }

  return 0;
}
```

Instead of terminating program execution when a zero denominator is detected, a more robust program can give the user the opportunity to reenter a non-zero value. To do this, the try block is included in a while statement, and then the catch block returns program control to the while statement after informing the user that a zero value has been entered. Program 9.2 accomplishes this task.

Program 9.2

```cpp
#include <iostream>
using namespace std;

int main()
{
  int numerator, denominator;
  bool needDenominator = true;

  cout << "Enter a numerator (whole number only): ";
  cin  >> numerator;

  cout << "Enter a denominator (whole number only): ";

  while(needDenominator)
  {
    cin  >> denominator;
    try
    {
      if (denominator == 0)
        throw denominator;  // an integer value is thrown
    }
    catch(int e)
    {
      cout << "A denominator value of " << e << " is invalid." << endl;
      cout << "Please reenter the denominator (whole number only): ";
      continue;  // this sends control back to the while statement
    }
    cout << numerator <<'/' << denominator
         << " = " << double(numerator)/ double(denominator) << endl;
    needDenominator = false;
  }

  return 0;
}
```

In reviewing this code, notice that it's the `continue` statement in the `catch` block that returns control to the top of the `while` statement. (See Section 5.3 for a review of the `continue` statement.) Following is a sample run of Program 9.2:

```
Enter a numerator (whole number only): 12
Enter a denominator (whole number only): 0
A denominator value of 0 is invalid.
Please reenter the denominator (whole number only): 5
12/5 = 2.4
```

One caution should be mentioned when throwing string literals as opposed to numeric values. When a string literal is thrown, it's a C-string, not a `string` class object, that is thrown. This means the `catch` statement must declare the received argument as a C-string (which is a character array) rather than a string. As an example, take a look at using the following statement instead of throwing the value of the `denominator` variable in Programs 9.1 and 9.2:

```
throw "***Invalid input - A denominator value of zero is not
   permitted***";
```

Here's a correct `catch` statement for the preceding `throw` statement:

```
catch(char e[])
```

An attempt to declare the exception as a `string` class variable results in a compiler error.

EXERCISES 9.1

1. **(Practice)** Define the following terms:
   a. exception
   b. `try` block
   c. `catch` block
   d. exception handler
   e. throw an exception
   f. catch an exception

2. **(Practice)** Enter and execute Program 9.1.

3. **(Practice)** Replace the following statement in Program 9.1

   ```
   cout << numerator <<'/' << denominator
        << " = " << double (numerator)/ double (denominator) << endl;
   ```

   with the statement

   ```
   cout << numerator <<'/' << denominator
        << " = " << numerator/denominator << endl;
   ```

   and execute the modified program. Enter the values 12 and 5, and explain why the result is incorrect from the user's viewpoint.

4. **(Modify)** Modify Program 9.1 so that it throws and catches the message `***Invalid input -A denominator value of zero is not permitted***`. (*Hint*: Review the caution at the end of this section.)

5. **(Practice)** Enter and execute Program 9.2.

6. **(Modify)** Modify Program 9.2 so that it continues to divide two numbers until the user enters the character q (as a numerator or denominator) to terminate program execution.

7. **(Validation)** Include the exception-handling code provided in this section in Program 9.1 to ensure that the user enters a valid integer value for both the numerator and denominator.

9.2   Exceptions and File Checking

Error detection and processing with exception handling is used extensively in C++ programs that use one or more files. For example, if a user deletes or renames a file by using an OS command, this action causes a C++ program to fail when an `open()` method call attempts to open the file with its original name. Exception handling is typically used when opening a data file to ensure that the file opens successfully before attempting any processing of data in the file.

Recall from Section 9.1 that the code for general exception handling looks like this:

```
try
{
    // one or more statements,
    // at least one of which should
    // throw an exception
}
catch(exceptionDataType parameterName)
{
    // one or more statements
}
```

In this code, the `try` block statements are executed. If no error occurs, the `catch` block statements are omitted, and processing continues with the statement following the `catch` block. However, if any statement in the `try` block throws an exception, the `catch` block with the exception data type matching the exception is executed. If no `catch` block is defined for a `try` block, a compiler error occurs. If no `catch` block exists that catches a thrown data type, a program crash occurs if the exception is thrown. Most times, the `catch` block displays an error message and terminates processing with a call to the `exit()` function. Program 9.3 shows the statements required to open a file in read mode and includes exception handling.

Program 9.3

```
#include <iostream>
#include <fstream>
#include <cstdlib>    // needed for exit()
#include <string>
using namespace std;
```

☞

```
int main()
{
   string filename = "prices.dat";   // put the filename up front
   string descrip;
   double price;

   ifstream inFile;

   try  // this block tries to open the file, read it,
        // and display the file's data
   {
     inFile.open(filename.c_str());

     if (inFile.fail()) throw filename; // this is the exception being checked

     // read and display the file's contents
     inFile >> descrip >> price;
     while (inFile.good()) // check next character
     {
       cout << descrip << ' ' << price << endl;
       inFile >> descrip >> price;
     }
     inFile.close();

     return 0;
   }
   catch (string e)
   {
     cout << "\nThe file "<< e << " was not successfully opened."
          << "\n Please check that the file currently exists."
          << endl;
     exit(1);
   }
}
```

This is the exception message Program 9.3 displays when the prices.dat file isn't found:

```
The file prices.dat was not successfully opened.
 Please check that the file currently exists.
```

Point of Information

Checking That a File Was Opened Successfully

Using exception handling, the most common method for checking that the operating system located the designated file is the one coded in Program 9.3. The key coding points are repeated here for convenience:

```
try // this block tries to open the file, read it,
    // and display the file's data
{
  // open the file, throwing an exception if the open fails
  // perform all required file processing
  // close the file
}
catch (string e)
{
  cout << "\nThe file "<< e << " was not successfully opened."
       << "\n Please check that the file currently exists."
       << endl;
  exit(1);
}
```

Although the exception-handling code in Program 9.3 can be used to check for a successful file open for input and output, a more rigorous check is usually required for an output file because a file opened for output is almost guaranteed to be found. If it exists, the file will be found; if it doesn't exist, the operating system creates it (unless append mode is specified and the file exists, or the operating system can't find the indicated folder). Knowing that the file has been found and opened, however, isn't enough for output purposes when an existing output file must not be overwritten. In these cases, the file can be opened for input, and, if the file is found, a further check can be made to ensure that the user explicitly approves overwriting it. The shaded code in Program 9.4 shows how to make this check.

Program 9.4

```
#include <iostream>
#include <fstream>
#include <cstdlib>    // needed for exit()
#include <string>
#include <iomanip>    // needed for formatting
using namespace std;

int main()
{
  char response;
  string filename = "prices.dat";  // put the filename up front
  ifstream inFile;
  ofstream outfile;
```

☞

```
try // open a basic input stream simply to check whether the file exists
{
  inFile.open(filename.c_str());

  if (inFile.fail()) throw 1; // this means the file doesn't exist
    // only get here if the file is found;
    // otherwise, the catch block takes control
  cout << "A file by the name " << filename << " currently exists.\n"
       << "Do you want to overwrite it with the new data (y or n): ";
  cin >> response;

  if (tolower(response) == 'n')
  {
    inFile.close();
    cout << "The existing file has not been overwritten." << endl;
    exit(1);
  }

}
catch(int e) {};  // a do-nothing block that permits
                  // processing to continue
try
{
  // open the file in write mode and continue with file writes
  outfile.open(filename.c_str());

  if (outfile.fail()) throw filename;
  // set the output file stream formats
  outfile << setiosflags(ios::fixed)
          << setiosflags(ios::showpoint)
          << setprecision(2);
  // write the data to the file
  outfile << "Mats " << 39.95 << endl
          << "Bulbs "  << 3.22 << endl
          << "Fuses " << 1.08 << endl;
  outfile.close();
  cout << "The file " << filename
       << " has been successfully written." << endl;
    return 0;
}
catch(string e)
{
  cout << "The file " << filename
       << " was not opened for output and has not been written."
       << endl;
}
}
```

In Program 9.4, the `try` blocks are separate. Because a `catch` block is affiliated with the closest previous `try` block, there's no ambiguity about unmatched `try` and `catch` blocks.

Opening Multiple Files

To understand how to apply exception handling to opening two files at the same time, assume you want to read data from a character-based file named `info.txt`, one character at a time, and write this data to a file named `info.bak`. Essentially, this application is a file-copying program that reads data from one file in a character-by-character manner and writes the data to a second file. Figure 9.1 shows the characters stored in the input file.

```
Now is the time for all good people
    to come to the aid of their party.
Please call (555) 888-6666 for
    further information.
```

Figure 9.1   The data stored in the `info.txt` file

Figure 9.2 illustrates the structure of the streams needed to produce the file copy. In this figure, an input stream object referenced by the variable `inFile` reads data from the `info.txt` file, and an output stream object referenced by the variable `outfile` writes data to the `info.bak` file.

Now examine Program 9.5, which creates the `info.bak` file as a duplicate of the `info.txt` file, using the procedure shown in Figure 9.2.

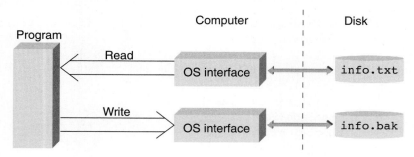

Figure 9.2   The file copy stream structure

Program 9.5

```cpp
#include <iostream>
#include <fstream>
#include <cstdlib>    // needed for exit()
#include <string>
using namespace std;
```

☞

```cpp
int main()
{
  string fileOne = "info.txt";  // put the filename up front
  string fileTwo = "info.bak";
  char ch;
  ifstream inFile;
  ofstream outfile;

  try  //this block tries to open the input file
  {
    // open a basic input stream
    inFile.open(fileOne.c_str());
    if (inFile.fail()) throw fileOne;
  } // end of outer try block
  catch (string in)  // catch for outer try block
  {
    cout << "The input file " << in
         << " was not successfully opened." << endl
         << " No backup was made." << endl;
    exit(1);
  }

  try  // this block tries to open the output file and
  {    // perform all file processing
    outfile.open(fileTwo.c_str());

    if (outfile.fail())throw fileTwo;

    while ((ch = inFile.get())!= EOF)
       outfile.put(ch);

    inFile.close();
    outfile.close();
  }
  catch (string out)  // catch for inner try block
  {
    cout << "The backup file " << out
         << " was not successfully opened." << endl;
    exit(1);
  }

    cout << "A successful backup of " << fileOne
         << " named " << fileTwo << " was successfully made." << endl;

    return 0;
}
```

Point of Information

Nesting `try` Blocks

When more than one file stream is involved, opening each file stream in its own `try` block permits isolating and identifying exactly which file caused an exception, if one occurs. The `try` blocks can be nested. For example, Program 9.5 has been rewritten with nested `try` blocks. Notice that the `catch` block for the inner `try` block must be nested in the same block scope as the `try` block:

```
#include <iostream>
#include <fstream>
#include <cstdlib>    // needed for exit()
#include <string>
using namespace std;

int main()
{
  string fileOne = "info.txt";  // put the filename up front
  string fileTwo = "info.bak";
  char ch;
  ifstream inFile;
  ofstream outfile;

  try  //this block tries to open the input file
  {
    // open a basic input stream
    inFile.open(fileOne.c_str());
    if (inFile.fail()) throw fileOne;
    try  // this block tries to open the output file and
```

continued...

For simplicity, Program 9.5 attempts to open the input and output files in separate and unnested `try` blocks. More generally, the second file is opened in a nested inner `try` block, so the attempt to open this second file wouldn't be made if opening the first file threw an exception. (The Point of Information box explains how to nest `try` blocks.)

In reviewing Program 9.5, pay particular attention to this statement:

```
while((ch = inFile.get())!= EOF)
```

This statement reads a value from the input stream continuously until the EOF value is detected. As long as the returned value doesn't equal the EOF value, the value is written to the output object stream. The parentheses surrounding the expression (ch = inFile. get()) are necessary to make sure a value is read and assigned to the variable ch before the retrieved value is compared to the EOF value. Without parentheses, the complete expression would be ch = inFile.get()!= EOF. Given the precedence of operations, the relational expression inFile.get()!= EOF would be executed first. Because it's a relational expression, its result is a Boolean `true` or `false` value based on the data the get() method retrieves. Attempting to assign this Boolean result to the character variable ch is an invalid conversion across an assignment operator.

Point of Information

Nesting `try` Blocks (continued)

```
{       // perform all file processing
        // open a basic output stream
   outfile.open(fileTwo.c_str());
   if (outfile.fail())throw fileTwo;
   while ((ch = inFile.get()) != EOF)
      outfile.put(ch);

   inFile.close();
   outfile.close();
}   // end of inner try block
catch (string out)   // catch for inner try block
{
   cout << "The backup file " << out
        << " was not successfully opened." << endl;
   exit(1);
}
}   // end of outer try block
catch (string in)   // catch for outer try block
{
   cout << "The input file " << in
        << " was not successfully opened." << endl
        << " No backup was made." << endl;
   exit(1);
}

cout << "A successful backup of " << fileOne
     << " named " << fileTwo << "was successfully made." << endl;

return 0;
}
```

The important point to notice is nesting the `try` blocks. If the two `try` blocks aren't nested and the input stream declaration, `ifstream inFile;`, is placed in the first block, it can't be used in the second `try` block without producing a compiler error. The reason is that all variables declared in a block of code (defined by an opening and closing brace pair) are local to the block in which they're declared.

EXERCISES 9.2

1. **(For Review)** List two conditions that cause a fail condition when a file is opened for input.

2. **(For Review)** List two conditions that cause a fail condition when a file is opened for output.

3. **(For Review)** If a file that exists is opened for output in write mode, what happens to the data currently in the file?

4. **(Modify)** Modify Program 9.3 to use an identifier of your choice, in place of the letter e, for the `catch` block's exception parameter name.

5. **(Practice)** Enter and execute Program 9.4.

6. **(Debug)** Determine why the two `try` blocks in Program 9.4, which are not nested, cause no problems in compilation or execution. (*Hint*: Place the declaration for the filename in the first `try` block and compile the program.)

7. **(Debug)** **a.** If the nested `try` blocks in the Point of Information on nested `try` blocks are separated into unnested blocks, the program won't compile. Determine why this is so.

   b. What additional changes have to be made to the program in Exercise 7a that would allow it to be written with unnested blocks? (*Hint*: See Exercise 6.)

9.3 The `string` Class

The programs in this book have used the `istream` class's `cout` object extensively, but you haven't investigated this class in detail or learned how the `cout` object is created. However, an advantage of object-oriented program design is that you can use thoroughly tested classes without knowing how the class is constructed. In this section, you use another class provided by C++'s standard library: the `string` class. However, you're going to create objects from the class before using them instead of using an existing object, such as `cout`.

A class is a user-created data type. Like built-in data types, a class defines a valid set of data values and a set of operations that can be used on them. The difference between a user-created class and a built-in data type is how the class is constructed. A built-in data type is provided as an integral part of the compiler, and a class is constructed by a programmer using C++ code. Other than that and the terminology, the two data types are used in much the same manner. The key difference in terminology is that storage areas for built-in data types are referred to as variables, whereas storage areas declared for a class are referred to as objects.

The values the `string` class permits are referred to as string literals. A **string literal** is any sequence of characters enclosed in quotation marks. A string literal is also referred to as a string value, a string constant, and, more conventionally, a string. Examples of strings are `"This is a string"`, `"Hello World!"`, and `"xyz 123 *!#@&"`. The quotation marks indicate the beginning and ending points of the string and are never stored with the string.

Figure 9.3 shows the programming representation of the string `Hello` when it's created as an object of the `string` class. By convention, the first character in a string is always designated as position 0. This position value is also referred to as both the character's **index value** and its **offset value**.

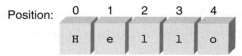

Figure 9.3 The storage of a string as a sequence of characters

string Class Functions

The string class provides a number of functions for declaring, creating, and initializing a string. In earlier versions of C++, the process of creating a new object is referred to as **instantiating an object**, which in this case becomes instantiating a string object, or creating a string, for short. Table 9.2 lists the functions the string class provides for creating and initializing a string object. In class terminology, functions are formally referred to as methods, and the methods that perform the tasks of creating and initializing are called **constructor methods**, or **constructors**, for short.

Table 9.2 string Class Constructors (Require the Header File string)

Constructor	Description	Examples

string objectName = value	Creates and initializes a string object to a value that can be a string literal, a previously declared string object, or an expression containing string literals and string objects	string str1 = "Good Morning";
		 string str2 = str1;
		 string str3 = str1 + str2;

string objectName(stringValue)	Produces the same initialization as the preceding item	string str1("Hot"); string str1(str1 + "Dog");
string objectName(str, n)	Creates and initializes a string object with a substring of string object str, starting at index position n of str	string str1(str2, 5) If str2 contains the string Good Morning, then str1 becomes the string Morning
string objectName(str, n, p)	Creates and initializes a string object with a substring of string object str, starting at index position n of str and containing p characters	string str1(str2, 5,2) If str2 contains the string Good Morning, then str1 becomes the string Mo
string objectName(n, char)	Creates and initializes a string object with n copies of char	string str1(5,'*') This makes str1 = "*****"

Table 9.2   string Class Constructors (Require the Header File string) (continued)

Constructor	Description	Examples
`string objectName`	Creates and initializes a string object to represent an empty character sequence (same as string `objectName = "";`, so the length of the string is 0)	`string message;`

Program 9.6 shows examples of each constructor the string class provides.

 ## Program 9.6

```
#include <iostream>
#include <string>
using namespace std;

int main()
{
  string str1; // an empty string
  string str2("Good Morning");
  string str3 = "Hot Dog";
  string str4(str3);
  string str5(str4, 4);
  string str6 = "linear";
  string str7(str6, 3, 3);

  cout << "str1 is: " << str1 << endl;
  cout << "str2 is: " << str2 << endl;
  cout << "str3 is: " << str3 << endl;
  cout << "str4 is: " << str4 << endl;
  cout << "str5 is: " << str5 << endl;
  cout << "str6 is: " << str6 << endl;
  cout << "str7 is: " << str7 << endl;

  return 0;
}
```

Here is the output created by Program 9.6:

```
str1 is:
str2 is: Good Morning
str3 is: Hot Dog
str4 is: Hot Dog
str5 is: Dog
str6 is: linear
str7 is: ear
```

Although this output is straightforward, `str1` is an empty string consisting of no characters; because the first character in a string is designated as position 0, not 1, the character position of the D in the string `Hot Dog` is position 4, which is shown in Figure 9.4.

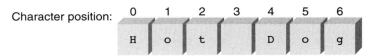

Character position:

Figure 9.4 The character positions of the string `Hot Dog`

String Input and Output

In addition to a string being initialized with the constructors listed in Table 9.2, strings can be input from the keyboard and displayed on screen. Table 9.3 lists the basic functions and objects for input and output of string values.

Table 9.3 string Class Input and Output

C++ Object or Function	Description
cout	General-purpose screen output object
cin	General-purpose keyboard input object that stops reading string input when white space is encountered
getline(cin, strObj)	General-purpose keyboard input function that inputs all characters entered, stores them in the string strObj, and stops accepting characters when it receives a newline character (\n)

In addition to the standard `cout` and `cin` objects you have been using throughout the book, the `string` class provides the `getline()` function for string input. For example, the expression `getline(cin, message)` accepts and stores characters typed at the terminal continuously until the Enter key is pressed. Pressing the Enter key generates a newline character, `'\n'`, which `getline()` interprets as the end-of-line entry. All the characters encountered by `getline()`, except the newline character, are stored in the string `message`, as illustrated in Figure 9.5.

Program 9.7 shows using the `getline()` function and `cout` statement to input and output a string that's entered at the user's terminal. Although `cout` is used in Program 9.7 for string output, `cin` generally can't be used in place of `getline()` for string input because `cin` reads a set of characters up to a blank space or a newline character. Therefore, attempting to enter the characters This is a string by using the statement `cin >> message;` results in only the

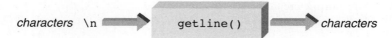

Figure 9.5 Inputting a string with `getline()`

word `This` being assigned to `message`. Because a blank terminates a `cin` extraction operation, `cin`'s usefulness for entering string data is restricted; therefore, `getline()` is used.

Program 9.7

```
#include <iostream>
#include <string>
using namespace std;

int main()
{
  string message;       // declare a string object

  cout << "Enter a string:\n";

  getline(cin, message);

  cout << "The string just entered is:\n"
       << message << endl;

  return 0;
}
```

The following is a sample run of Program 9.7:

```
Enter a string:
This is a test input of a string of characters.
The string just entered is:
This is a test input of a string of characters.
```

In its most general form, the `getline()` function has the syntax

```
getline(cin, strObj, terminatingChar)
```

where *strObj* is a string variable name and *terminatingChar* is an optional character constant, or variable, specifying the terminating character. For example, the expression `getline(cin, message, '!')` accepts all characters entered at the keyboard, including a newline character, until an exclamation point is entered. The exclamation point isn't stored as part of the string.

If the optional third argument, *terminatingChar*, is omitted when getline() is called, the default terminating character is the newline ('\n') character. Therefore, the statement getline(cin,message,'\n'); can be used in place of the statement getline(cin, message);. Both these statements stop reading characters when the Enter key is pressed. In all the programs used from this point forward, input is terminated by pressing the Enter key, which generates a newline character. For this reason, the optional third argument passed to getline(), which is the terminating character, is omitted.

Caution: The Phantom Newline Character   Seemingly strange results can happen when the cin input stream object and getline() function are used together to accept data or when cin is used by itself to accept characters. To see how this result can occur, take a look at Program 9.8, which uses cin to accept an integer entered at the keyboard. The integer is then stored in the variable value, and a getline() function call follows.

Program 9.8

```
#include <iostream>
#include <string>
using namespace std;

int main()
{
    int value;
    string message;

    cout << "Enter a number: ";
    cin  >> value;
    cout << "The number entered is:\n"
         << value << endl;

    cout << "Enter text:\n";
    getline(cin, message);
    cout << "The text entered is:\n"
         << message << endl;
    cout << int(message.length());

    return 0;
}
```

When Program 9.8 runs, the number entered in response to the prompt Enter a number: is stored in the variable value. At this point, everything seems to be working fine. Notice, however, that in entering a number, you enter the number and press the Enter key. On almost all computer systems, this entered data is stored in a temporary holding area called a buffer immediately after the characters are entered, as shown in Figure 9.6.

Point of Information

The `string` and `char` Data Types

A string can consist of zero, one, or more characters. When the string has no characters, it's said to be an empty string with a length of zero. A string with a single character, such as `"a"`, is a string of length one and is stored differently from a `char` data type, such as `'a'`.

However, for many practical purposes, a string of length one and a `char` respond in the same manner; for example, both `cout >> "\n"` and `cout >> '\n'` produce a new line on the screen. It's important to understand that they are different data types; for example, both these declarations

```
string s1 = 'a';   // INVALID INITIALIZATION
char key = "\n";   // INVALID INITIALIZATION
```

produce a compiler error because they attempt to initialize one data type with literal values of another type.

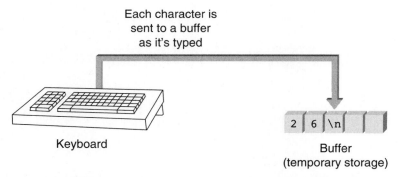

Figure 9.6   Typed characters are first stored in a buffer

The `cin` input stream in Program 9.8 first accepts the number entered but leaves the `'\n'` in the buffer. The next input statement, which is a call to `getline()`, picks up thecode for the Enter key as the next character and terminates any further input. Following is a sample run of Program 9.8:

```
Enter a number: 26
The number entered is 26
Enter text:
The text entered is
```

In this output, no text is accepted in response to the prompt `Enter text:`. No text occurs because, after the program accepts the number 26, the code for the Enter key, which is a newline escape sequence, remains in the buffer and is picked up and interpreted by the `getline()` function as the end of its input. This result occurs whether an integer (as in

Program 9.8), a string, or any other input is accepted by cin and then followed by a getline() function call. There are three solutions to this "phantom" Enter key problem:

- Don't mix cin with getline() inputs in the same program.
- Follow the cin input with the call to cin.ignore().
- Accept the Enter key in a character variable and then ignore it.

The preferred solution is the first one. All solutions, however, center on the fact that the Enter key is a legitimate character input and must be recognized as such. You encounter this problem again when you learn about accepting char data types in Section 9.4.

String Processing

Strings can be manipulated by using string class functions or the character-at-a-time functions described in Section 9.4. Table 9.4 lists the most commonly used string class functions plus the standard arithmetic and comparison operators that can also be used with strings.

Table 9.4 The string Class Processing Functions (Require the Header File string)

Function/Operation	Description	Example
int length()	Returns the length of the string	string.length()
int size()	Same as the preceding item	string.size()
at(int index)	Returns the character at the specified index and throws an exception if the index is nonexistent	string.at(4)
int compare(str)	Compares the given string to str; returns a negative value if the given string is less than str, a 0 if they are equal, and a positive value if the given string is greater than str	string1.compare(string2)
c_str()	Returns the string as a null-terminated C-string	string1.c_str()
bool empty	Returns true if the string is empty; otherwise, returns false	string1.empty()

Table 9.4 The `string` Class Processing Functions (Require the Header File `string`) (continued)

Function/Operation	Description	Example
`erase(ind,n)`	Removes `n` characters from the string, starting at index `ind`	`string1.erase(2,3)`
`erase(ind)`	Removes all characters from the string, starting from index `ind` until the end of the string, and the length of the remaining string becomes `ind`	`string1.erase(4)`
`int find(str)`	Returns the index of the first occurrence of `str` in the complete string	`string1.find("the")`
`int find(str, ind)`	Returns the index of the first occurrence of `str` in the complete string, with the search beginning at index `ind`	`string1.find("the",5)`
`int find_first_of(str, ind)`	Returns the index of the first occurrence of any character in `str` in the complete string, with the search starting at index `ind`	`string1.find_first_of("lt",6)`
`int find_first_not_of(str, ind)`	Returns the index of the first occurrence of any character not in `str` in the complete string, with the search starting at index `ind`	`string1.find_first_not_of("lt",6)`

Table 9.4 The string Class Processing Functions (Require the Header File string) (continued)

Function/Operation	Description	Example
`void insert(ind, str)`	Inserts the string `str` into the complete string, starting at index `ind`	`string.insert(4, "there")`
`void replace(ind, n, str)`	Removes `n` characters in the string object, starting at index position `ind`, and inserts the string `str` at index position `ind`	`string1.replace(2,4,"okay")`
`string substr(ind,n)`	Returns a string consisting of `n` characters extracted from the string, starting at index `ind`; if `n` is greater than the remaining number of characters, the rest of the string is used	`string2 = string1.substr(0,10)`
`void swap(str)`	Swaps characters in `str` with those in the first string	`string1.swap(string2)`
`[ind]`	Returns the character at index x, without checking whether `ind` is a valid index	`string1[5]`
`=`	Assignment (also converts a C-string to a string)	`string1 = string`
`+`	Concatenates two strings	`string1 + string2`

Table 9.4 The `string` Class Processing Functions (Require the Header File `string`) (continued)

Function/Operation	Description	Example
`+=`	Concatenation and assignment	`string2 += string1`

`== !=`
`< <=`
`> >=`
	Relational operators Return `true` if the relation is satisfied; otherwise, return `false`	`string1 == string2`
		`string1 <= string2`
		`string1 > string2`

The most commonly used function in Table 9.4 is `length()`. It returns the number of characters in the string, which is referred to as the string's length. For example, the value returned by the function call `"Hello World!".length()` is 12. As always, the quotation marks surrounding a string value aren't considered part of the string. Similarly, if the string referenced by `string1` contains the value `"Have a good day."`, the value returned by the call `string1.length()` is 16.

Two string expressions can be compared for equality by using the standard relational operators. Each character in a string is stored in binary with the ASCII or Unicode code. Although these codes are different, they have some characteristics in common. In both, a blank precedes (is less than) all letters and numbers; letters of the alphabet are stored in order from A to Z; and digits are stored in order from 0 to 9. In addition, digits come before (are less than) uppercase characters, which are followed by lowercase characters. Therefore, uppercase characters are mathematically less than lowercase characters.

When two strings are compared, their characters are compared a pair at a time (both first characters, then both second characters, and so on). If no differences are found, the strings are equal; if a difference is found, the string with the first lower character is considered the smaller string, as shown in these examples:

- `"Hello"` is greater than `"Good Bye"` because the first H in `Hello` is greater than the first G in `Good Bye`.
- `"Hello"` is less than `"hello"` because the first H in `Hello` is less than the first h in `hello`.
- `"SMITH"` is greater than `"JONES"` because the first S in `SMITH` is greater than the first J in `JONES`.
- `"123"` is greater than `"1227"` because the third character in `123`, the 3, is greater than the third character in `1227`, the 2.
- `"Behop"` is greater than `"Beehive"` because the third character in `Behop`, the h, is greater than the third character in `Beehive`, the e.

Program 9.9 uses `length()` and several relational expressions in the context of a complete program.

Program 9.9

```cpp
#include <iostream>
#include <string>
using namespace std;

int main()
{
  string string1 = "Hello";
  string string2 = "Hello there";

  cout << "string1 is the string: " <<  string1 << endl;
  cout << "The number of characters in string1 is " <<  int(string1.length())
       << endl << endl;

  cout << "string2 is the string: " <<  string2 << endl;
  cout << "The number of characters in string2 is " <<  int(string2.length())
       << endl << endl;

  if (string1 < string2)
    cout << string1 <<  " is less than " <<  string2 << endl << endl;
  else if (string1 == string2)
    cout << string1 <<  " is equal to " <<  string2 << endl << endl;
  else
    cout << string1 <<  " is greater than " <<  string2 << endl << endl;

  string1 = string1 + " there world!";
  cout << "After concatenation, string1 contains the characters:
" << string1 << endl;
  cout << "The length of this string is " <<  int(string1.length()) << endl;

  return 0;
}
```

Following is a sample output produced by Program 9.9:

```
string1 is the string: Hello
The number of characters in string1 is 5

string2 is the string: Hello there
The number of characters in string2 is 11

Hello is less than Hello there
```

☞

```
After concatenation, string1 contains the characters:
 Hello there world!
The length of this string is 18
```

When reviewing this program's output, refer to Figure 9.7, which shows how the characters in `string1` and `string2` are stored in memory. The length of each string refers to the total number of characters in the string, and the first character in each string is located at index position 0. Therefore, the length of a string is always one more than the index number of the last character's position in the string.

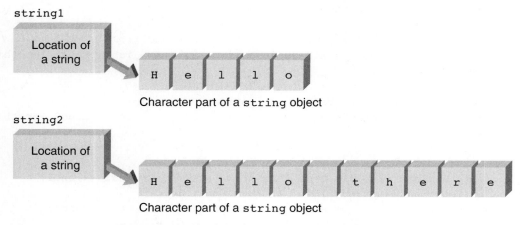

Figure 9.7   The initial strings used in Program 9.9

Although you use the concatenation operator and `length()` function most often, at times you'll find the other string functions in Table 9.4 useful. One of the most useful is the `at()` function, which enables you to retrieve separate characters in a string. Program 9.10 uses this function to select one character at a time from the string, starting at string position 0 and ending at the index of the last character in the string. This last index value is always one less than the number of characters (that is, the string's length) in the string.

The expression `str.at(i)` in the `switch` statement retrieves the character at position i in the string. This character is then compared to five different character values. The `switch` statement uses the fact that selected cases "drop through" in the absence of `break` statements. Therefore, all selected cases result in an increment to `vowelCount`. Program 9.10 displays the following output:

```
The string: Counting the number of vowels
has 9 vowels.
```

Program 9.10

```cpp
#include <iostream>
#include <string>
using namespace std;

int main()
{

  string str = "Counting the number of vowels";
  int i, numChars;
  int vowelCount = 0;

  cout << "The string: " <<  str << endl;

  numChars = int(str.length());
  for (i = 0; i < numChars; i++)
  {
    switch(str.at(i))    // here is where a character is retrieved
    {
      case 'a':
      case 'e':
      case 'i':
      case 'o':
      case 'u':
         vowelCount++;
    }
  }
  cout << "has " <<  vowelCount <<  " vowels." << endl;

  return 0;
}
```

As an example of inserting and replacing characters in a string with the functions listed in Table 9.4, assume you start with a string created by the following statement:

```cpp
string str = "This cannot be";
```

Figure 9.8 illustrates how this string is stored in the buffer created for it. As indicated, the length of the string is 14 characters.

Now assume the following statement is executed:

```cpp
str.insert(4," I know");
```

Character position:

Figure 9.8 Initial storage of a `string` object

This statement inserts the designated seven characters in " I know", beginning with a blank, in the existing string starting at index position 4. Figure 9.9 shows the string after the insertion.

Character position:

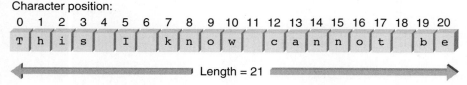

Figure 9.9 The string after the insertion

If the statement `str.replace(12, 6, "to");` is executed next, the existing characters in index positions 12 through 17 are deleted, and the two characters contained in `to` are inserted starting at index position 12. Figure 9.10 shows the net effect of this replacement. The number of replacement characters (in this case, two) can be fewer than, equal to, or greater than the number of characters being replaced, which in this case is six.

Character position:

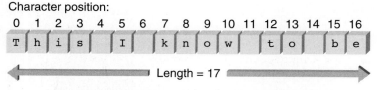

Figure 9.10 The string after the replacement

Finally, if you append the string `"correct"` to the string shown in Figure 9.10 by using the concatenation operator, +, you get the string shown in Figure 9.11. Program 9.11 uses these statements in a complete program.

Character position:

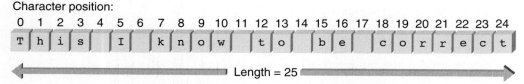

Figure 9.11 The string after the append

Program 9.11

```cpp
#include <iostream>
#include <string>
using namespace std;

int main()
{
  string str = "This cannot be";

  cout << "The original string is: " << str << endl
       << "  and has " << int(str.length()) << " characters." << endl;

  // insert characters
  str.insert(4," I know");
  cout << "The string, after insertion, is: " << str << endl
       << "  and has " << int(str.length()) << " characters." << endl;

  // replace characters
  str.replace(12, 6, "to");
  cout << "The string, after replacement, is: " << str << endl
       << "  and has " << int(str.length()) << " characters." << endl;

  // append characters
  str = str + " correct";
  cout << "The string, after appending, is: " << str << endl
       << "  and has " << int(str.length()) << " characters." << endl;

    return 0;
}
```

The following output produced by Program 9.11 matches the strings shown in Figures 9.8 to 9.11:

```
The original string is: This cannot be
   and has 14 characters.
The string, after insertion, is: This I know cannot be
   and has 21 characters.
The string, after replacement, is: This I know to be
   and has 17 characters.
The string, after appending, is: This I know to be correct
   and has 25 characters.
```

Of the remaining string functions listed in Table 9.4, the most commonly used are those that locate specific characters in a string and create substrings. Program 9.12 shows how some of these other functions are used.

Program 9.12

```
#include <iostream>
#include <string>
using namespace std;

int main()
{

  string string1 = "LINEAR PROGRAMMING THEORY";
  string s1, s2, s3;
  int j, k;

  cout << "The original string is " <<  string1 << endl;

  j = int(string1.find('I'));
  cout << "  The first position of an 'I' is " <<  j << endl;

  k = int(string1.find('I', (j+1)));
  cout << "  The next position of an 'I' is " <<  k << endl;

  j = int(string1.find("THEORY"));
  cout << "  The first location of \"THEORY\" is " <<  j << endl;

  k = int(string1.find("ING"));
  cout << "  The first index of \"ING\" is " <<  k << endl;

  // now extract three substrings
  s1 = string1.substr(2,5);
  s2 = string1.substr(19,3);
  s3 = string1.substr(6,8);

  cout << "The substrings extracted are:" << endl
       << "   " << s1 + s2 + s3 << endl;


  return 0;
}
```

Here is the output produced by Program 9.12:

```
The original string is LINEAR PROGRAMMING THEORY
   The first position of an 'I' is 1
   The next position of an 'I' is 15
   The first location of "THEORY" is 19
   The first index of "ING" is 15
The substrings extracted are:
   NEAR THE PROGRAM
```

The main point shown in Program 9.12 is that characters and sequences of characters can be located and extracted from a string.

EXERCISES 9.3

1. **(Practice)** Enter and execute Program 9.7.

2. **(Practice)** Determine the value of `text.at(0)`, `text.at(3)`, and `text.at(10)`, assuming for each one that `text` is each of the following strings:

   a. Now is the time

   b. Rocky raccoon welcomes you

   c. Happy Holidays

   d. The good ship

3. **(Practice)** Enter and execute Program 9.10.

4. **(Modify)** Modify Program 9.10 to count and display the numbers of each vowel contained in the string.

5. **(Modify)** Modify Program 9.10 to display the number of vowels in a user-entered string.

6. **(Program)** Using the `at()` function, write a C++ program that reads in a string by using `getline()` and then displays the string in reverse order. (*Hint*: After the string has been entered and saved, retrieve and display characters, starting from the end of the string.)

7. **(Program)** Write a C++ program that accepts both a string and a single character from the user. The program should determine how many times the character is contained in the string. (*Hint*: Search the string by using the `find(str, ind)` function. This function should be used in a loop that starts the index value at 0 and then changes the index value to one past the index of where the `char` was last found.)

8. **(Practice)** Enter and execute Program 9.11.

9. **(Practice)** Enter and execute Program 9.12.

9.4 Character Manipulation Functions

In addition to the string functions provided by the `string` class, the C++ language provides several useful `character` class functions, listed in Table 9.5. The function declaration (prototype) for each function is contained in the header file `string` or `cctype`, which must be included in any program using these functions.

Table 9.5 Character Library Functions (Require the Header File `string` or `cctype`)

Function Prototype	Description	Example
`int isalpha(charExp)`	Returns a `true` (non-zero integer) if `charExp` evaluates to a letter; otherwise, it returns a `false` (zero integer)	`isalpha('a')`
`int isalnum(charExp)`	Returns a `true` (non-zero integer) if `charExp` evaluates to a letter or a digit; otherwise, it returns a `false` (zero integer)	`char key;` `cin >> key;` `isalnum(key);`
`int isupper(charExp)`	Returns a `true` (non-zero integer) if `charExp` evaluates to an uppercase letter; otherwise, it returns a `false` (zero integer)	`isupper('a')`
`int islower(charExp)`	Returns a `true` (non-zero integer) if `charExp` evaluates to a lowercase letter; otherwise, it returns a `false` (zero integer)	`islower('a')`
`int isdigit(charExp)`	Returns a `true` (non-zero integer) if `charExp` evaluates to a digit (0 through 9); otherwise, it returns a `false` (zero integer)	`isdigit('a')`
`int isascii(charExp)`	Returns a `true` (non-zero integer) if `charExp` evaluates to an ASCII character; otherwise, returns a `false` (zero integer)	`isascii('a')`
`int isspace(charExp)`	Returns a `true` (non-zero integer) if `charExp` evaluates to a space; otherwise, returns a `false` (zero integer)	`isspace(' ')`
`int isprint(charExp)`	Returns a `true` (non-zero integer) if `charExp` evaluates to a printable character; otherwise, returns a `false` (zero integer)	`isprint('a')`
`int isctrl(charExp)`	Returns a `true` (non-zero integer) if `charExp` evaluates to a control character; otherwise, it returns a `false` (zero integer)	`isctrl('a')`

Table 9.5   Character Library Functions (Require the Header File `string` or `cctype`) (continued)

Function Prototype	Description	Example
`int ispunct(charExp)`	Returns a `true` (non-zero integer) if `charExp` evaluates to a punctuation character; otherwise, returns a `false` (zero integer)	`ispunct('!')`
`int isgraph(charExp)`	Returns a `true` (non-zero integer) if `charExp` evaluates to a printable character other than white space; otherwise, returns a `false` (zero integer)	`isgraph(' ')`
`int toupper(charExp)`	Returns the uppercase equivalent if `charExp` evaluates to an lowercase character; otherwise, it returns the character code without modification	`toupper('a')`
`int tolower(charExp)`	Returns the lowercase equivalent if `charExp` evaluates to an uppercase character; otherwise, it returns the character code without modification	`tolower('A')`

Because all the `istype()` functions listed in Table 9.5 return a non-zero integer (a Boolean `true` value) when the character meets the condition and a zero integer (a Boolean `false` value) when the condition is not met, these functions are typically used in an `if` statement. For example, the following code segment assumes `ch` is a character variable:

```
if(isdigit(ch))
  cout << "The character just entered is a digit" << endl;
else if(ispunct(ch))
  cout << "The character just entered is a punctuation mark" << endl;
```

In this example, if `ch` contains a digit character, the first `cout` statement is executed; if the character is a letter, the second `cout` statement is executed. In both cases, however, the character to be checked is included as an argument to the function. Program 9.13 illustrates this type of code in a program that counts the number of letters, digits, and other characters in a string. The characters to be checked are obtained by using the `string` class's `at()` function. In Program 9.13, this function is used in a `for` loop that cycles through the string from the first character to the last.

The output produced by Program 9.13 is the following:

```
The original string is: This -123/ is 567 A ?<6245> Test!
This string contains 33 characters, which consist of
      11 letters
      10 digits
      12 other characters.
```

As indicated by this output, each of the 33 characters in the string has been categorized correctly as a letter, a digit, or other character.

Program 9.13

```cpp
#include <iostream>
#include <string>
#include <cctype>
using namespace std;

int main()
{
    string str = "This -123/ is 567 A ?<6245> Test!";
    char nextChar;
    int i;
    int numLetters = 0, numDigits = 0, numOthers = 0;

    cout << "The original string is: " <<  str
         << "\nThis string contains " <<  int(str.length())
            <<  " characters," <<  " which consist of" << endl;

    // check each character in the string
    for (i = 0; i < int(str.length()); i++)
    {
      nextChar = str.at(i);  // get a character
      if (isalpha(nextChar))
        numLetters++;
      else if (isdigit(nextChar))
        numDigits++;
      else
        numOthers++;
    }

    cout << "      " <<  numLetters <<  " letters" << endl;
    cout << "      " <<  numDigits <<  " digits" << endl;
    cout << "      " <<  numOthers <<  " other characters." << endl;

    cin.ignore();
    return 0;
}
```

Typically, as in Program 9.13, the functions in Table 9.5 are used in a character-by-character manner on each character in a string. You see this again in Program 9.14, where each lowercase string character is converted to its uppercase equivalent by using the `toupper()` function. This function converts only lowercase letters, leaving all other characters unaffected.

In Program 9.14, pay particular attention to the statement `for (i = 0; i < int(str.length()); i++)` used to cycle through each character in the string. Typically, this cycling through the string, a character at a time, is how each element in a string is accessed, using the `length()` function to determine when the end of the string has been reached. (Review Program 9.13 to see that it's used in the same way.) The only real difference is that in Program 9.14, each element is accessed by using the subscript notation `str[i]`; in Program 9.13, the `at()` function is used. Although these two notations are interchangeable—and which one you use is a matter of choice—for consistency, the two notations shouldn't be mixed in the same program.

Program 9.14

```cpp
#include <iostream>
#include <string>
using namespace std;

int main()
{
  int i;
  string str;

  cout << "Type in any sequence of characters: ";
  getline(cin,str);

  // cycle through all elements of the string
  for (i = 0; i < int(str.length()); i++)
    str[i] = toupper(str[i]);

  cout << "The characters just entered, in uppercase, are: "
       << str << endl;

  cin.ignore();
  return 0;
}
```

A sample run of Program 9.14 produced the following output:

```
Type in any sequence of characters: this is a test of 12345.
The characters just entered, in uppercase, are: THIS IS A TEST OF 12345.
```

Character I/O

Although you have used `cin` and `getline()` to accept data entered from the keyboard in a more or less "cookbook" manner, you need to understand what data is being sent to the program and how the program must react to process the data. At a fundamental level, all input (as well as output) is done on a character-by-character basis, as illustrated in Figure 9.12.

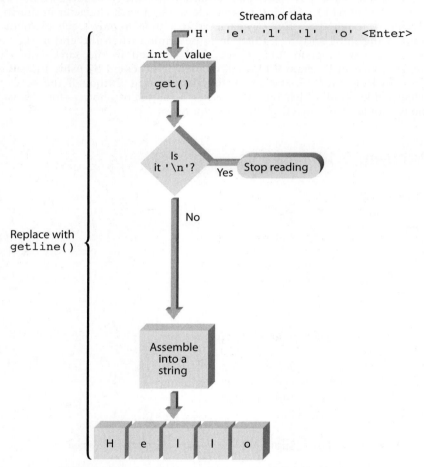

Figure 9.12 Accepting keyboard-entered characters

As Figure 9.12 shows, the entry of every piece of data, whether it's a string or a number, consists of typing characters. For example, entry of the string `Hello` consists of pressing and releasing the five character keys H, e, l, l, o, and the Enter key. Similarly, output of the number `26.95` consists of displaying the five characters 2, 6, ., 9, and 5. Although programmers typically don't think of data in this manner, programs are restricted to this character-by-character I/O, and all of C++'s higher-level I/O functions and stream objects are based on lower-level character I/O functions. These more elemental character functions, which can be used by a programmer, are listed in Table 9.6.

Point of Information

Why the `char` Data Type Uses Integer Values

In C++, a character is stored as an integer value, which is sometimes confusing to beginning programmers. The reason is that, in addition to standard English letters and characters, a program needs to store special characters that have no printable equivalents. One is the end-of-file (EOF) sentinel that all computer systems use to designate the end of a data file. The EOF sentinel can be transmitted from the keyboard. For example, on UNIX-based systems, it's generated by holding down the Ctrl key and pressing the D key; on Windows-based systems, it's generated by holding down Ctrl and pressing Z. On both systems, the EOF sentinel is stored as the integer number -1, which has no equivalent character value. (You can check this by displaying the integer value of each entered character [see Program 9.15] and typing Ctrl+D or Ctrl+Z, depending on the system you're using.)

By using a 16-bit integer value, more than 64,000 different characters can be represented. This number of characters provides enough storage for multiple character sets, including Arabic, Chinese, Hebrew, Japanese, and Russian, and almost all known language symbols. Therefore, storing a character as an integer value has a practical value.

An important consequence of using integer codes for string characters is that characters can be compared easily for alphabetical ordering. For example, as long as each subsequent letter in an alphabet has a higher value than its preceding letter, the comparison of character values is reduced to the comparison of numeric values. Storing characters in sequential numerical order ensures that adding one to a letter produces the next letter in the alphabet.

Table 9.6 Basic Character I/O Functions (Require the Header File `cctype`)

Function	Description	Example
`cout.put(charExp)`	Places the character value of `charExp` on the output stream.	`cout.put('A');`
`cin.get(charVar)`	Extracts the next character from the input stream and assigns it to the variable `charVar`.	`cin.get(key);`
`cin.peek(charVar)`	Assigns the next character from the input stream to the variable `charVar` *without* extracting the character from the stream.	`cin.peek(nextKey);`
`cin.putback(charExp)`	Pushes a character value of `charExp` back onto the input stream.	`cin.putback(cKey);`

Table 9.6   Basic Character I/O Functions (Require the Header File `cctype`) (continued)

Function	Description	Example
`cin.ignore(n, char)`	Ignores a maximum of the next n input characters, up to and including the detection of `char`. If no arguments are specified, ignores the next single character on the input stream.	`cin.ignore(80,'\n');` `cin.ignore();`

The `get()` function reads the next character in the input stream and assigns it to the function's character variable. For example, examine this statement:

`cin.get(nextChar);`

It causes the next character entered at the keyboard to be stored in the character variable `nextChar`. This function is useful for inputting and checking characters before they are assigned to a complete string or C++ data type.

The character output function corresponding to `get()` is `put()`. This function expects a single-character argument and displays the character passed to it on the screen. For example, the statement `cout.put('A')` causes the letter A to be displayed on the screen.

Of the last three functions listed in Table 9.6, the `cin.ignore()` function is the most useful. This function permits skipping over input until a designated character, such as `'\n'`, is encountered. For example, the statement `cin.ignore(80, '\n')` skips up to a maximum of the next 80 characters or stops skipping if the newline character is encountered. This statement can be useful in skipping all further input on a line, up to a maximum of 80 characters, or until the end of the current line is encountered. Input would begin with the next line.

The `peek()` function returns the next character on the stream but doesn't remove it from the stream's buffer (see Table 9.6). For example, the expression `cin.peek(nextChar)` returns the next character input on the keyboard but leaves it in the buffer. This action is sometimes useful for peeking ahead and seeing what the next character is but leaving it in place for the next input.

Finally, the `putback()` function places a character back on the stream so that it's the next character read. The argument passed to `putback()` can be any character expression that evaluates to a legitimate character value; it doesn't have to be the last input character.

The Phantom Newline Character Revisited   As you saw in Section 9.3, sometimes you get seemingly strange results when a `cin` input stream is followed by a `getline()` function call. This same result can occur when characters are inputted by using the `get()` character function. To see how it can occur, take a look at Program 9.15, which uses the `get()` function to accept the next character entered at the keyboard and stores the character in the variable `fkey`.

Point of Information

A Notational Inconsistency

All the character class functions listed in Table 9.6 use the standard object-oriented notation of preceding the function's name with an object name, as in `cin.get()`. However, the `string` class `getline()` function uses the notation `getline(cin, strVar)`. In this notation, the object (`cin`) appears as an argument, which is how procedural-based functions pass variables. For consistency, you would expect `getline()` to be called as `cin.getline()`. Unfortunately, this notation was already in use for a `getline()` function created for C-style strings (which are simply one-dimensional arrays of characters, as discussed in Section 7.2), so a notational inconsistency was created.

Program 9.15

```
#include <iostream>
using namespace std;

int main()
{
  char fkey;

  cout << "Type in a character: ";
  cin.get(fkey);
  cout << "The key just accepted is " << int(fkey) << endl;

  return 0;
}
```

When Program 9.15 runs, the character entered in response to the prompt `Type in a character:` is stored in the character variable `fkey`, and the decimal code for the character is displayed by explicitly casting the character into an integer to force its display as an integer value. The following sample run illustrates this technique:

```
Type in a character: m
The key just accepted is 109
```

At this point, everything seems to be working, although you might be wondering why the decimal value of `m` is displayed instead of the character. In typing `m`, two keys are usually pressed, the `m` key and the Enter key. As in the previous section, these two characters are stored in a buffer after they're pressed (refer back to Figure 9.12). The first key pressed, `m` in this case, is taken from the buffer and stored in `fkey`, but the code for the Enter key is still in the buffer. Therefore, a subsequent call to `get()` for a character input picks up the code for the Enter key as the next character automatically. For example, take a look at Program 9.16.

Program 9.16

```
#include <iostream>
using namespace std;

int main()
{
  char fkey, skey;

  cout << "Type in a character: ";
  cin.get(fkey);
  cout << "The key just accepted is " << int(fkey) << endl;

  cout << "Type in another character: ";
  cin.get(skey);
  cout << "The key just accepted is " << int(skey) << endl;

  return 0;
}
```

The following is a sample run of Program 9.16:

```
Type in a character: m
The key just accepted is 109
Type in another character: The key just accepted is 10
```

After entering the letter m in response to the first prompt, the Enter key is also pressed. From a character standpoint, this input represents the entry of two distinct characters. The first character is m, which is coded and stored as the integer 109. The second character also gets stored in the buffer with the numerical code for the Enter key. The second call to get() picks up this code immediately, without waiting for another key to be pressed. The last cout stream displays the code for this key. The reason for displaying the numerical code rather than the character is that the Enter key has no printable character associated with it that can be displayed.

Remember that every key has a numerical code, including Enter, the spacebar, Esc, and Ctrl. These keys generally have no effect when entering numbers because the input functions ignore them as leading or trailing input with numerical data. These keys also don't affect the entry of a single character requested as the first user data to be inputted, as in Program 9.15. Only when a character is requested after the user has already input other data, as in Program 9.16, does the usually invisible Enter key become noticeable.

In Section 9.1, you learned some ways to prevent the Enter key from being accepted as a legitimate character input when the getline() function is used. You can use the following ways when the get() function is used in a program:

- Follow the cin.get() input with the call cin.ignore().
- Accept the Enter key in a character variable, and then don't use it again.

Program 9.17 applies the first solution to Program 9.16. Ignoring the Enter key after the first character is read and displayed clears the buffer of the Enter key and gets it ready to store the next valid input character as its first character.

Program 9.17

```
#include <iostream>
using namespace std;

int main()
{
  char fkey, skey;

  cout << "Type in a character: ";
  cin.get(fkey);
  cout << "The key just accepted is " << int(fkey) << endl;
  cin.ignore();

  cout << "Type in another character: ";
  cin.get(skey);
  cout << "The key just accepted is " << int(skey) << endl;

  cin.ignore();
  return 0;
}
```

In Program 9.17, observe that when the user types the letter m and presses the Enter key, the m is assigned to fkey and the code for the Enter key is ignored. The next call to get() stores the code for the next key pressed in the variable skey. From the user's standpoint, the Enter key has no effect, except to signal the end of each character input. The following is a sample run of Program 9.17:

```
Type in a character: m
The key just accepted is 109
Type in another character: b
The key just accepted is 98
```

A Second Look at User-Input Validation

As mentioned in the first look at user-input validation (in Section 3.4), programs that respond effectively to unexpected user input are formally referred to as robust programs and informally as "bulletproof" programs. Code that validates user input and ensures that a program doesn't produce unintended results caused by unexpected input is a sign of a well-constructed, robust program. One of your jobs as a programmer is to produce robust programs. To see how unintended results can occur, examine the following two code examples. First, assume your program contains the following statements:

```
cout << "Enter an integer: ";
cin  >> value;
```

By mistake, a user enters the characters e4. In earlier versions of C++, this input would cause the program to terminate unexpectedly, or **crash**. Although a crash can still occur with the current ANSI/ISO standard, it doesn't in this case. Instead, a meaningless integer value is assigned to the variable value. This assignment, of course, invalidates any results obtained by using this variable.

As a second example, take a look at the following code, which causes an infinite loop if the user enters a non-numeric value. (The program can be halted by holding down Ctrl and pressing C.)

```
double value;

  do
  {
    cout << "Enter a number (enter 0 to exit): ";
    cin  >> value;

    cout << "The square root of this number is: " << sqrt(value) << endl;
  }while (value !=0);
```

The basic technique for handling invalid data input and preventing seemingly innocuous code, as in these two examples, from producing unintended results is referred to as **user-input validation**. This term means validating the entered data during or after data entry and giving the user a way of reentering data, if it's invalid. User-input validation is an essential part of any commercially viable program, and if done correctly, it protects a program from attempting to process data types that can cause a program to crash, create infinite loops, or produce more invalid results.

The central element in user-input validation is checking each entered character to verify that it qualifies as a legitimate character for the expected data type. For example, if an integer is required, the only acceptable characters are a leading plus (+) or minus (-) sign and the digits 0 through 9. These characters can be checked as they're being typed, which means the get() function is used to input a character at a time, or after all the characters can be accepted in a string, and then each string character is checked for validity. After all the entered characters have been validated, the entered string can be converted into the correct data type.

Two basic techniques can be used to verify the validity of entered characters. Section 9.5 explains one of these techniques: character-by-character checking. A second technique, which encompasses a broader scope of data-processing tasks using exception handling, is discussed at the end of Section 9.5.

 EXERCISES 9.4

1. **(Practice)** Enter and execute Program 9.13.

2. **(Practice)** Enter and execute Program 9.14.

3. **(Practice)** Write a C++ program that counts the number of words in a string. A word is encountered whenever a transition from a blank space to a nonblank character is encountered. The string contains only words separated by blank spaces.

4. **(Practice)** Generate 10 random numbers in the range 0 to 129. If the number represents a printable character, print the character with an appropriate message that indicates the following:

> The character is a lowercase letter.
> The character is an uppercase letter.
> The character is a digit.
> The character is a space.
> If the character is none of these, display its value in integer format.

5. **(Practice) a.** Write a function named `length()` that determines and returns the length of a string without using the `string` class `length()` function.

   b. Write a simple `main()` function to test the `length()` function written for Exercise 5a.

6. **(Practice) a.** Write a function named `countlets()` that returns the number of letters in a string passed as an argument. Digits, spaces, punctuation, tabs, and newline characters should not be included in the returned count.

   b. Include the `countlets()` function written for Exercise 6a in an executable C++ program, and use the program to test the function.

7. **(Practice)** Write a program that accepts a string from the console and displays the hexadecimal equivalent of each character in the string.

8. **(Practice)** Write a C++ program that accepts a string from the console and displays the string one word per line.

9. **(Debug)** In response to the following code, suppose a user enters the data 12e4:

```
cout << "Enter an integer: ";
cin  >> value;
```

What value will be stored in the integer variable `value`?

9.5 Input Data Validation

One of the major uses of strings in programs is for user-input validation. Validating user input is essential: Even though a program prompts the user to enter a specific type of data, such as an integer, the prompt doesn't ensure that the user will comply. What a user enters is, in fact, totally out of the programmer's control. What *is* in your control is how you deal with the entered data.

It certainly does no good to tell a frustrated user that "The program clearly tells you to enter an integer, and you entered a date." Successful programs anticipate invalid data and prevent it from being accepted and processed. Typically, this is accomplished by first validating that data is of the correct type. If it is, the data is accepted; otherwise, the user is requested to reenter the data, with an explanation of why the entered data was invalid.

A common method of validating numerical input data is accepting all numbers as strings. Each character in the string can then be checked to make sure it complies with the requested data type. After this check is made and data is verified to be the correct type, the string is converted to an integer or double-precision value by using the conversion functions listed in Table 9.7. (For data accepted with `string` class objects, the `c_str()` function must be applied to the string before the conversion function is called.)

As an example, consider inputting an integer number. To be valid, the data entered must adhere to the following conditions:

- The data must contain at least one character.
- If the first character is a + or - sign, the data must contain at least one digit.
- Only digits from 0 to 9 are acceptable following the first character.

Table 9.7 C-String Conversion Functions

Function	Description	Example
`int atoi(stringExp)`	Converts `stringExp` to an integer. Conversion stops at the first non-integer character.	`atoi("1234")`
`double atof(stringExp)`	Converts `stringExp` to a double-precision number. Conversion stops at the first character that can't be interpreted as a `double`.	`atof("12.34")`
`char[] itoa(integerExp)`	Converts `integerExp` to a character array. The space allocated for the returned characters must be large enough for the converted value.	`itoa(1234)`

The following function, `isvalidInt()`, can be used to check that an entered string complies with these conditions. This function returns the Boolean value of `true` if the conditions are satisfied; otherwise, it returns a Boolean `false` value.

```
bool isvalidInt(string str)
{
  int start = 0;
  int i;
  bool valid = true;   // assume a valid
  bool sign = false;   // assume no sign


  // check for an empty string
  if (int(str.length()) == 0)  valid = false;

  // check for a leading sign
  if (str.at(0) == '-'|| str.at(0) == '+')
  {
    sign = true;
    start = 1;  // start checking for digits after the sign
  }
```

☞

```
        // check that there is at least one character after the sign
        if (sign && int(str.length()) == 1) valid = false;

        // now check the string, which you know
        // has at least one non-sign character
        i = start;
        while(valid && i < int(str.length()))
        {
          if(!isdigit(str.at(i))) valid = false;   //found a non-digit character
          i++;   // move to next character
        }

        return valid;
    }
```

In the code for the `isvalidInt()` function, pay attention to the conditions being checked. They are commented in the code and consist of the following:

- The string is not empty.
- A valid sign (+ or -) is present.
- If a sign is present, at least one digit follows it.
- All the remaining characters in the string are digits.

Only if all these conditions are met does the function return a Boolean `true` value. After this value is returned, the string can be converted into an integer safely with the assurance that no unexpected value will result to hamper further data processing. Program 9.18 uses this function in the context of a complete program.

Program 9.18

```
#include <iostream>
#include <string>
using namespace std;

int main()
{
    bool isvalidInt(string);   // function prototype (declaration)
    string value;
    int number;

    cout << "Enter an integer: ";
    getline(cin, value);
```

☞

```cpp
    if (!isvalidInt(value))
      cout << "The number you entered is not a valid integer.";
    else
    {
        number = atoi(value.c_str());
      cout << "The integer you entered is " << number;
    }


    return 0;
}

bool isvalidInt(string str)
{
  int start = 0;
  int i;
  bool valid = true;   // assume a valid
  bool sign = false;   // assume no sign


  // check for an empty string
  if (int(str.length()) == 0)  valid = false;

  // check for a leading sign
  if (str.at(0) == '-'|| str.at(0) == '+')
  {
    sign = true;
    start = 1;   // start checking for digits after the sign
  }

  // check that there is at least one character after the sign
  if (sign && int(str.length()) == 1) valid = false;

  // now check the string, which you know
  // has at least one non-sign character
  i = start;
  while(valid && i < int(str.length()))
  {
    if(!isdigit(str.at(i))) valid = false;   //found a non-digit character
    i++;   // move to next character
  }

  return valid;
}
```

Two sample runs of Program 9.18 produced the following output:

```
Enter an integer: 12e45
The number you entered is not a valid integer.
```

and

```
Enter an integer: -12345
The integer you entered is -12345
```

As shown by this output, the program successfully determines that an invalid character was entered in the first run.

A second line of defense is to provide error-processing code in the context of exception-handling code. This type of code is typically used to permit the user to correct a problem, such as invalid data entry, by reentering a new value. The means of providing this code in C++ is referred to as exception handling.

Using exception handling, you can construct a complete means of ensuring that the user enters an integer number in response to a request for an integer value. The technique involves extending the isvalidInt() function in Program 9.18 to ensure that not only is an invalid integer value detected, but also the program gives the user the option of reentering values until a valid integer is entered. This technique can be applied easily to ensure the entry of a valid double-precision number, which is the other numerical data type often requested as user-entered data.

Using the isvalidInt() function from Program 9.18, a more comprehensive function named getanInt() is developed that uses exception processing to accept user input continuously until a string corresponding to a valid integer is detected. After a valid string is entered, the getanInt() function converts the string to an integer and returns the integer value. This technique ensures that the program requesting an integer actually receives aninteger and prevents any unwarranted effects, such as a program crash caused by an invalid data type being entered. The algorithm used to perform this task is as follows:

Set a Boolean variable named notanint to true
while (notanint is true)
   try
     Accept a string value
     If the string value does not correspond to an integer, throw an exception
   catch the exception
     Display the error message "Invalid integer - Please reenter: "
     Send control back to the while statement
     Set notanint to false (causes the loop to terminate)
End while
Return the integer corresponding to the entered string

The code corresponding to this algorithm is shaded in Program 9.19.

Program 9.19

```cpp
#include <iostream>
#include <string>
using namespace std;

int main()
{
  int getanInt();  // function declaration (prototype)
  int value;

  cout << "Enter an integer value: ";
  value = getanInt();
  cout << "The integer entered is: " << value << endl;

  return 0;
}
```

```cpp
int getanInt()
{
  bool isvalidInt(string);  // function declaration (prototype)
  bool notanint = true;
  string svalue;

  while (notanint)
  {
    try
    {
      cin >> svalue;  // accept a string input
      if (!isvalidInt(svalue)) throw svalue;
    }
    catch (string e)
    {
      cout << "Invalid integer - Please reenter: ";
        continue; // send control to the while statement
    }
    notanint = false;
  }
  return atoi(svalue.c_str());  // convert to an integer
}
```

☞

```
bool isvalidInt(string str)
{
  int start = 0;
  int i;
  bool valid = true;   // assume a valid
  bool sign = false;   // assume no sign

  // check for an empty string
  if (int(str.length()) == 0)  valid = false;

  // check for a leading sign
  if (str.at(0) == '-'|| str.at(0) == '+')
  {
    sign = true;
    start = 1;  // start checking for digits after the sign
  }

  // check that there is at least one character after the sign
  if (sign && int(str.length()) == 1) valid = false;

  // now check the string, which you know
  // has at least one non-sign character
  i = start;
  while(valid && i < int(str.length()))
  {
    if(!isdigit(str.at(i))) valid = false;  // found a non-digit character
    i++;  // move to next character
  }

  return valid;
}
```

Following is a sample output produced by Program 9.19:

```
Enter an integer value: abc
Invalid integer - Please reenter: 12.
Invalid integer - Please reenter: 12e
Invalid integer - Please reenter: 120
The integer entered is: 120
```

As this output shows, the getanInt() function works correctly. It requests input continuously until a valid integer is entered.

EXERCISES 9.5

1. **(Practice)** Write a C++ program that prompts the user to type in an integer. Have your program use `cin` to accept the number as an integer and use `cout` to display the value your program actually accepted from the data entered. Run your program four times. The first time you run the program, enter a valid integer number; the second time, enter a double-precision number; the third time, enter a character; and the fourth time, enter the value 12e34.

2. **(Modify)** Modify the program you wrote for Exercise 1, but have your program use a double-precision variable. Run the program four times: First, enter an integer; second, enter a decimal number; third, enter a decimal number with an f as the last character entered; and fourth, enter a character. Using the output display, keep track of what number your program actually accepted from the data you entered. What happened, if anything, and why?

3. **(For Thought) a.** Why do you think successful application programs contain extensive data input validity checks? (*Hint*: Review Exercises 1 and 2.)

   b. What do you think is the difference between a data-type check and a data-reasonableness check?

   c. A program requests that the user enter a month, day, and year. What are some reasonableness checks that could be made on the data entered?

4. **(Practice) a.** Enter and execute Program 9.18.

   b. Run Program 9.18 four times, using the data referred to in Exercise 1 for each run.

5. **(Modify)** Modify Program 9.18 to display any invalid characters that were entered.

6. **(Modify)** Modify Program 9.18 to request an integer continuously until a valid number is entered.

7. **(Modify)** Modify Program 9.18 to remove all leading and trailing spaces from the entered string before it's checked for validity.

8. **(Useful Utility)** Write a function that checks each digit as it's entered, instead of checking the completed string, as in Program 9.18.

9. **(Practice)** Enter and execute Program 9.19.

10. **(Modify)** Modify the `isvalidInt()` function used in Program 9.19 to remove all leading and trailing blank spaces from its string argument before determining whether the string corresponds to a valid integer.

11. **(Modify)** Modify the `isvalidInt()` function used in Program 9.19 to accept a string that ends in a decimal point. For example, the input 12. should be accepted and converted to the integer number 12.

9.6 A Closer Look: Namespaces and Creating a Personal Library

Until the introduction of PCs in the early 1980s, with their extensive use of integrated circuits and microprocessors, computer speed and available memory were severely restricted. For example, the most advanced computers had speeds measured in milliseconds; current computers have speeds measured in nanoseconds and higher. Similarly, the memory capacity of early desktop computers consisted of 4000 bytes of internal memory, but today's computer memories are in the 512 MB range and higher.

With these early hardware restrictions, programmers had to use every possible trick to save memory space and make programs run more efficiently. Almost every program was hand-crafted and included what was called "clever code" to minimize runtime and maximize use of memory storage. Unfortunately, this individualized code became a liability. New programmers had to spend considerable time to understand existing code; even the original programmer had trouble figuring out code written only months before. This complexity in code made modifications time consuming and costly and precluded cost-effective reuse of existing code for new installations.

The inability to reuse code efficiently, combined with expanded hardware capabilities, prompted the discovery of more efficient programming. This discovery began with structured programming concepts incorporated into procedural languages, such as Pascal, and led to the object-oriented techniques that form the basis of C++. An early criticism of C++, however, was that it didn't have a comprehensive library of classes, but with the current ANSI/ISO standard, an extensive C++ library is available.

No matter how many useful classes and functions the standard library provides, however, each major type of programming application, such as engineering, scientific, and financial, has its own specialized requirements. For example, the `ctime` header file in C++ provides good date and time functions. However, for specialized needs, such as scheduling problems, these functions must be expanded to include finding the number of working days between two dates, taking into account weekends and holidays, among other tasks. These functions could be provided as part of a more complete `Date` class or as non-class functions.

To meet these specialized needs, programmers create and share their own libraries of classes and functions with other programmers working on the same or similar projects. After the classes and functions have been tested, they can be incorporated into any program without further coding time.

At this stage in your programming career, you can begin building your own library of specialized functions and classes. Section 9.5 described how to do this with the input validation functions, `isvalidInt()` and `getanInt()`, which are reproduced here for convenience:

```
bool isvalidInt(string str)
{
    int start = 0;
    int i;
    bool valid = true;   // assume a valid
    bool sign = false;   // assume no sign

    // check for an empty string
    if (int(str.length()) == 0)  valid = false;
```

☞

```
      // check for a leading sign
      if (str.at(0) == '-'|| str.at(0) == '+')
      {
        sign = true;
        start = 1;  // start checking for digits after the sign
      }

      // check that there is at least one character after the sign
      if (sign && int(str.length()) == 1) valid = false;

      // now check the string, which you know
      // has at least one non-sign character
      i = start;
      while(valid && i < int(str.length()))
      {
        if(!isdigit(str.at(i))) valid = false;   // found a
                                                 // non-digit character
        i++;  // move to next character
      }

   return valid;
}
int getanInt()
{
   bool isvalidInt(string);  // function declaration (prototype)
   bool notanint = true;
   string svalue;

   while (notanint)
   {
     try
     {
       cin >> svalue;  // accept a string input
       if (!isvalidInt(svalue)) throw svalue;
     }
     catch (string e)
     {
       cout << "Invalid integer - Please reenter: ";
          continue; // send control to the while statement
     }
     notanint = false;
   }
   return atoi(svalue.c_str());   // convert to an integer
}
```

The first step in creating a library is to encapsulate all the specialized functions and classes into one or more namespaces and then store the complete code (with or without using a namespace) into one or more files. For example, you can create one namespace, dataChecks, and save it in the file named dataChecks.cpp. Note that the namespace's filename need not be the same as the namespace name used in the code.

The syntax for creating a namespace is the following:

```
namespace name
{
   // functions and/or classes in here
}  // end of namespace
```

The following code includes the two functions isvalidInt() and getanInt() in the
namespace dataChecks, adds the appropriate include files, and uses a declaration statement
needed by the new namespace. The syntax required to create the namespace has been shaded:

```cpp
#include <iostream>
#include <string>
using namespace std;

namespace dataChecks
{
    bool isvalidInt(string str)
    {
      int start = 0;
      int i;
      bool valid = true;   // assume a valid
      bool sign = false;   // assume no sign

      // check for an empty string
      if (int(str.length()) == 0)  valid = false;

      // check for a leading sign
      if (str.at(0) == '-'|| str.at(0) == '+')
      {
        sign = true;
        start = 1;  // start checking for digits after the sign
      }

      // check that there is at least one character after the sign
      if (sign && int(str.length()) == 1) valid = false;

      // now check the string, which you know
      // has at least one non-sign character
      i = start;
      while(valid && i < int(str.length()))
      {
        if(!isdigit(str.at(i))) valid = false;  // found a
                                                // non-digit character
        i++;  // move to next character
      }
      return valid;
    }

    int getanInt()
    {
      bool isvalidInt(string);  // function declaration (prototype)
      bool notanint = true;
      string svalue;

      while (notanint)
      {
        try
        {
          cin >> svalue;  // accept a string input
          if (!isvalidInt(svalue)) throw svalue;
        }
```

☞

```
        catch (string e)
        {
          cout << "Invalid integer - Please reenter: ";
          continue; // send control to the while statement
        }
        notanint = false;
      }
      return atoi(svalue.c_str());   // convert to an integer
    }
} // end of dataChecks namespace
```

After the namespace has been created and stored in a file, it can be included in another file by supplying a preprocessor directive to inform the compiler where the namespace is found and by including a using directive that tells the compiler which namespace in the file to use. For the dataChecks namespace, which is stored in a file named dataChecks. cpp, the following statements perform these tasks:

```
#include <c:\\mylibrary\\dataChecks.cpp>
using namespace dataChecks;
```

The first statement provides the full pathname for the source code file. Notice that two backslashes are used to separate items in pathnames. The double backslashes are required when providing a relative or full pathname. The only time backslashes aren't required is when the library code is in the same directory as the program being executed. As indicated, the dataChecks source file is saved in the mylibrary folder. The second statement tells the compiler to use the dataChecks namespace in the designated file. Program 9.20 includes these two statements in an executable program.

 Program 9.20

```
#include <c:\\mylibrary\\dataChecks.cpp>
using namespace dataChecks;

int main()
{
  int value;

  cout << "Enter an integer value: ";
  value = getanInt();
  cout << "The integer entered is: " << value << endl;

  return 0;
}
```

The only requirement for the include statement in Program 9.20 is that the filename and location must correspond to an existing file with the same name in the designated path;

otherwise, a compiler error occurs. If you want to name the source code file with a file extension, any extension can be used as long as these rules are followed:

- The filename under which the code is stored includes the extension.
- The same filename, including extension, is used in the `include` statement.

Therefore, if the filename used to store the functions is `dataLib.cpp`, the `include` statement in Program 9.20 would be the following:

```
#include <c:\\mylibrary\\dataLib.cpp>
```

Additionally, a namespace isn't required in the file. Using a namespace permits you to isolate the data-checking functions in one area and add more namespaces to the file as needed. Designating a namespace in the `using` statement tells the compiler to include only the code in the specified namespace rather than all code in the file. In Program 9.20, if the data-checking functions weren't enclosed in a namespace, the `using` statement for the `dataChecks` namespace would have to be omitted.

Including the previously written and tested data-checking functions in Program 9.20 as a separate file enables you to focus on the program code using these functions instead of being concerned with function code that's already been written and tested. In Program 9.20, the `main()` function exercises the data-checking functions and produces the same output as Program 9.19. In creating the `dataChecks` namespace, you have included source code for the two functions. Including this code isn't required, and a compiled version of the source code can be saved instead. Finally, additions to a namespace defined in one file can be made in another file by using the same namespace name in the new file and including a `using` statement for the first file's namespace.

EXERCISES 9.6

1. **(Practice)** Enter and compile Program 9.20. (*Hint*: The namespace file `dataChecks` and the program file are available with the source code provided on this book's Web site.)

2. **(For Thought)** Why would a programmer supply a namespace file in its compiled form rather than as source code?

3. **(For Thought) a.** What is an advantage of namespaces?

   b. What is a possible disadvantage of namespaces?

4. **(For Thought)** What types of classes and functions would you include in a personal library? Why?

5. **(Useful Utility) a.** Write a C++ function named `whole()` that returns the integer part of any number passed to the function. (*Hint*: Assign the passed argument to an integer variable.)

   b. Include the function written in Exercise 5a in a working program. Make sure your function is called from `main()` and correctly returns a value to `main()`. Have `main()` use a `cout` statement to display the returned value. Test the function by passing various data to it.

c. When you're confident that the whole() function written for Exercise 5a works correctly, save it in a namespace and a personal library of your choice.

6. (Useful Utility) a. Write a C++ function named fracpart() that returns the fractional part of any number passed to the function. For example, if the number 256.879 is passed to fracpart(), the number .879 should be returned. Have the fracpart() function call the whole() function you wrote in Exercise 5a. The number returned can then be determined as the number passed to fracpart() less the returned value when the same argument is passed to whole().

b. Include the function written in Exercise 6a in a working program. Make sure the function is called from main() and correctly returns a value to main(). Have main() use a cout statement to display the returned value. Test the function by passing various data to it.

c. When you're confident the fracpart() function written for Exercise 6a works correctly, save it in the same namespace and personal library selected for Exercise 5c.

9.7   Common Programming Errors

Here are the common errors associated with defining and processing strings:

1. Forgetting to include the string header file when using string class objects.
2. Forgetting that the newline character, '\n', is a valid data input character.
3. Forgetting to convert a string class object by using the c_str() function when converting string class objects to numerical data types.

9.8   Chapter Summary

1. A string literal is any sequence of characters enclosed in quotation marks. It's referred to as a string value, a string constant, and, more conventionally, a string.

2. A string can be constructed as an object of the string class.

3. The string class is commonly used for constructing strings for input and output purposes, such as for prompts and displayed messages. Because of its capabilities, this class is used when strings need to be compared or searched or specific characters in a string need to be examined or extracted as a substring. It's also used in more advanced situations when characters in a string need to be replaced, inserted, or deleted regularly.

4. Strings can be manipulated by using the functions of the class they're objects of or by using the general-purpose string and character functions.

5. The cin object, by itself, tends to be of limited usefulness for string input because it terminates input when a blank is encountered.

6. For string class data input, use the getline() function.

7. The cout object can be used to display string class strings.

Programming Projects for Chapter 9

1. **(Practice)** Enter the data for the info.txt file in Figure 9.1 or download it from this book's Web site. Then enter and execute Program 9.5 and verify that the backup file was written.

2. **(Modify)** Modify Program 9.5 to use a getline() function in place of the get() method currently in the program.

3. **(Useful Utility) a.** Write a C++ function that accepts a string and two character values. The function should return the string with each occurrence of the first character replaced by the second character.

   b. Test the function written for Exercise 3a by writing a program that accepts a string from the user, calls the function written for Exercise 3a to replace all occurrences of the letter e with the letter x from the user-entered string, and then displays the changed string.

4. **(Useful Utility)** Modify the function written for Exercise 3a to search for the first occurrence of a user-entered sequence of characters, and then replace this sequence, when it's found in the string, with a second user-entered sequence. For example, if the entered string is Figure 4-4 illustrates the output of Program 4-2 and the user enters that 4- is to be replaced by 3-, the resulting string is Figure 3-4 illustrates the output of Program 4-2. (Only the first occurrence of the searched for sequence has been changed.)

5. **(Useful Utility)** Modify the program written for Exercise 4 to replace all occurrences of the designated sequence of characters with the new sequence of characters. For example, if the entered string is Figure 4-4 illustrates the output of Program 4-2 and the user enters that 4- is to be replaced by 3-, the resulting string is Figure 3-4 illustrates the output of Program 3-2.

6. **(Data Processing) a.** Write a C++ program that stops reading a line of text when a period is entered and displays the sentence with correct spacing and capitalization. For this program, correct spacing means only one space between words, and all letters should be lowercase, except the first letter. For example, if the user enters the text i am going to Go TO THe moVies., the displayed sentence should be I am going to go to the movies.

   b. Determine what characters, if any, aren't displayed correctly by the program you created for Exercise 6a.

7. **(Data Processing)** Write a C++ program that accepts a name as first name followed by last name, and then displays the name as last name, first name. For example, if the user enters Gary Bronson, the output should be Bronson, Gary.

8. **(Data Processing)** Modify the program written for Exercise 7 to include an array of five names.

9. **(Useful Utility) a.** Write a C++ function named `isvalidReal()` that checks for a valid double-precision number. This kind of number can have an optional + or - sign, at most one decimal point (which can be the first character), and at least one digit between 0 and 9. The function should return a Boolean value of `true` if the entered number is a real number; otherwise, it should return a Boolean value of `false`.

    b. Modify the `isvalidReal()` function written for Exercise 9a to remove all leading and trailing blank spaces from its string argument before determining whether the string corresponds to a valid real number.

10. **(Useful Utility)** Write and execute a C++ function named `getareal()` that uses exception handling to accept an input string continuously until a string that can be converted to a real number is entered. The function should return a `double` value corresponding to the string value the user enters.

Engineering and Scientific Disciplines

Materials Science and Metallurgical Engineering

Advances in many areas of engineering have been made possible by discoveries of new materials and a better understanding of the properties of existing materials. Knowledge of the physical and chemical principles determining the electrical properties of exotic materials called semiconductors have resulted in fantastic progress in the field of solid-state devices, from transistors to integrated-circuit chips to large computers. Better understanding of the origins of metallic properties, such as hardness, strength, ductility, corrosiveness, and others, have led to improved design of automobiles, aircraft, space-craft, and all types of machinery. The field is generally subdivided into metals and non-metals, although interests and activities often overlap considerably.

Materials Science

Materials science concerns the behavior and properties of materials (metals and nonmetals) from both microscopic and macroscopic perspectives. It includes the following areas:
- Ceramics: Noncrystalline materials, such as glass, that are nonmetallic and require high temperatures in processing. Ceramics can be made brittle or flexible, hard or soft, or stronger than steel. They can be made to have a variety of chemical properties.
- Polymers: Structural and physical properties of organic, inorganic, and natural polymers that are useful in engineering applications.
- Materials fabrication, processing, and treatment: All aspects of manufacturing ceramics, metals, and polymer synthesis, from the growth of crystals and fibers to metal forming.
- Corrosion: The reaction mechanism and thermodynamics of metal corrosion in the atmosphere or submerged under water or chemicals, whether standing or under stress.
- Stress-strain and fatigue-fracture of engineering materials: Physical properties governing deformation and fracture of materials and their improvement and use in construction and design.

Metallurgical Engineering

Metallurgical engineering is the branch of engineering responsible for production of metals and metal alloys, from discovering ore deposits to fabricating refined metal into useful products. Metallurgical engineers are important in every step of producing metal from metal ore. Metallurgical engineering includes the following areas:
- Mining engineering: Usually a separate branch of engineering, but the concerns of mining engineers and metallurgists often overlap in the processes of extracting metals from metal ores and refining them into usable products. Extraction metallurgy makes use of physical and chemical reactions to optimize metal production.
- Metals fabrication: Forming metal into products such as cans, wires, and tubes as well as casting and joining metals—for example, by welding.
- Physical metallurgy: Analysis of stress-strain and fatigue-fracture characteristics of metals and metal alloys to prevent engineering component failures.

Part Two

Object-Oriented Programming

Chapter

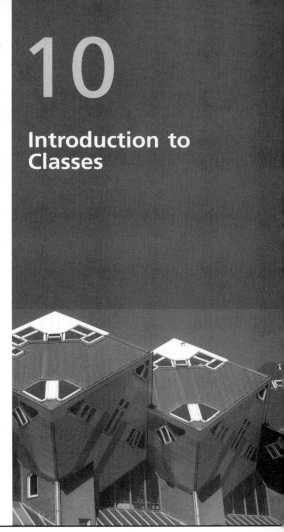

10

Introduction to Classes

Besides being an improved version of C, the distinguishing characteristic of C++ is its support of object-oriented programming. Central to this object orientation is the concept of an abstract data type, which is a programmer-defined data type. This chapter explores the implications of permitting programmers to define their own data types and then explains C++'s mechanism for constructing them. As you'll see, the construction of a data type is based on variables and functions; variables provide the means for creating new data structures, and functions provide the means for performing operations on these structures. What C++ provides is a unique way of combining variables and functions into a self-contained, cohesive unit from which objects can be created.

10.1 Abstract Data Types in C++ (Classes)

A procedural program consists of one or more algorithms that have been written in a computer-readable language. This type of program, as you have seen in Part One of this book, is especially useful for solving engineering and scientific problems, in which inputs

---

Point of Information

Procedural, Hybrid, and Pure Object-Oriented Languages

Most high-level programming languages can be categorized as procedural, object-oriented, or hybrid. FORTRAN, the first commercial high-level programming language, is procedural. This makes sense because FORTRAN was designed to perform mathematical calculations that use standard algebraic formulas. These formulas were described as algorithms, and then the algorithms were coded by using function and subroutine procedures. Subsequent procedural languages included BASIC, COBOL, and Pascal.

Currently, there are only two pure object-oriented languages: Smalltalk and Eiffel. The first requirement of a pure object-oriented language is that it must contain three specific features: classes, inheritance, and polymorphism (described in this chapter and Chapter 11). In addition, however, a "pure" object-oriented language must, as a minimum, always use classes. In a pure object-oriented language, all data types are constructed as classes, all data values are objects, all operators can be overloaded, and every data operation can be executed only by using a class member function. In a pure object-oriented language, it's impossible *not* to use object-oriented features in a program. This isn't the case in a hybrid language.

In a hybrid language, such as C++, it's impossible *not* to use procedural elements in programs because the use of any built-in data type or operation violates the pure object-oriented requirements. Although a hybrid language must be able to define classes, its distinguishing feature is that it's possible to write a complete program with only procedural code. Additionally, hybrid languages need not provide inheritance and polymorphism—but they must provide classes. Languages that use classes but don't provide inheritance and polymorphism are referred to as object-*based* languages rather than object-*oriented* languages.

---

must be processed to produce outputs by using clearly defined steps. In these applications, data is typically entered as character data from a keyboard, and then displayed as character data on a printer or screen. Input and display of program output have always taken a back seat to processing, with a clear emphasis on the formulas and calculations being used.

With the emergence of graphical screens on computer desktops and laptops in the 1980s and 1990s, and the subsequent interest in multicolored, windowed systems, this emphasis has shifted to a more balanced approach between input, output, and processing. Unfortunately, providing a graphical user interface (GUI) is a challenge with procedural code, even an interface that requires only a single window. Programming multiple and overlapping windows increases the complexity enormously when pure procedural code is used.

Unlike a procedural approach, an object-oriented approach fits graphically windowed environments well. Each window can be constructed as a self-contained rectangular object that can be moved and resized in relation to other objects on screen, and other visual objects, such as check boxes, option buttons, labels, and text boxes, can be placed and moved easily.

Central to the creation of objects is the concept of an abstract data type, which is simply a user-defined data type, as opposed to the built-in data types provided by all languages (such as integer and floating-point types). Permitting a programmer to define new data types, such as a rectangular type, out of which specific rectangular objects can be created and displayed on screen, forms the basis of C++'s object orientation.

Abstract Data Types

To gain a clear understanding of what an abstract data type is, take another look at the four built-in data types in C++: integers, doubles, Boolean, and characters. In using these data types, typically you declare one or more variables of the desired type, use them in their accepted ways, and avoid using them in ways that aren't specified. For example, you wouldn't use the modulus operator on two double-precision numbers. Because this operation makes no sense for double-precision numbers, it's never defined, in any programming language, for these numbers. Therefore, each data type consists of both a type of data, such as integer or double, *and* specific operational capabilities.

In computer terminology, the combination of data and associated operations is defined as a **data type**. That is, a data type defines *both* the types of data and the types of operations that can be performed on the data. Seen in this light, the integer data type, the double-precision data type, and the character data type provided in C++ are all examples of **built-in data types** defined by a type of data and specific operational capabilities for initializing and manipulating the type. In a simplified form, this relationship can be described as follows:

Data Type = Allowable Data Values + Operational Capabilities

Therefore, the operations you have been using in C++ are an inherent part of each data type you have been using. For each of these data types, C++ designers had to carefully consider and then implement specific operations.

To understand the importance of the operational capabilities a programming language provides, take a moment to review a list of some capabilities supplied with C++'s built-in data types (int, double, bool, and char). Table 10.1 lists the minimum set of these capabilities.[1]

Table 10.1   C++ Built-In Data Type Capabilities

Capability	Example
Define one or more variables of the data type	`int a, b;`
Initialize a variable at definition	`int a = 5;`
Assign a value to a variable	`a = 10;`
Assign one variable's value to another variable	`a = b;`
Perform mathematical operations	`a + b`
Perform relational operations	`a > b`
Convert from one data type to another	`a = int (7.2);`

Now see how all this information relates to **abstract data types (ADTs)**. By definition, an abstract data type is simply a user-defined type that defines both a type of data and the operations that can be performed on it. User-defined data types are required when you want to create objects that are more complex than simple integers and characters. To create your own data types, you must be aware of both the type of data you're creating and the capabilities you provide to initialize and manipulate the data.

As a specific example, say you're programming an application that uses dates extensively. Clearly, from a data standpoint, a date must be capable of accessing and storing a month, day, and year designation. From an implementation standpoint, there are several means of storing

[1]You might notice the absence of reading and writing operations. In both C and C++, except for primitive operations, input and output are provided by standard library routines and class functions.

a date, but from a user viewpoint, the implementation isn't relevant. For example, a date can be stored as three integers, one each for the month, day, and year. Alternatively, a single long integer in the form *yyyymmdd* can be used, so the date 5/16/08 is stored as the integer 20080516. For sorting dates, the long integer format is attractive because the numerical sequence of dates corresponds to their calendar sequence.

The method of structuring the date internally supplies only a partial answer to your programming effort, unfortunately. You must still supply a set of operations that can be used with dates. These operations could include assigning values to a date, subtracting two dates to determine the number of days between them, comparing two dates to determine which is earlier and which is later, and displaying a date in a form such as 12/03/06 rather than 12/3/6.

Notice that the details of how each operation works depend on how you choose to store a date (called its **data structure**) and are of interest to you only as you develop each operation. For example, the implementation of comparing two dates differs if you store a date as a single long integer instead using separate integers for the month, day, and year.

The combination of the data structure used for dates with a set of available operations appropriate for dates would then define an abstract `Date` data type. After this data type is developed, programmers who want to use it don't need to be concerned with *how* dates are stored or *how* operations are performed. All they need to know is *what* each operation does and *how* to invoke it, much as they use C++'s built-in operations. For example, you don't really care how the addition of two integers is performed—only that it's done correctly.

In C++, an abstract data type is referred to as a **class**. Construction of a class is easy, and you already have all the necessary tools in variables and functions. What C++ provides is a mechanism for packaging these two items together in a self-contained unit. Next, you see how this is done.

Class Construction

A class defines both data and functions. This definition is usually accomplished by constructing a class in two parts: a declaration section and an implementation section. As shown in the following code example, the **declaration section** declares both the data types and functions for the class. The **implementation section** then defines the functions whose prototypes have been declared in the declaration section.[2]

```
// class declaration section
class className
{
  data members // the variables
  function members // prototypes
};
// class implementation section
function definitions
```

Both the variables and functions listed in the class declaration section are collectively referred to as **class members**. Separately, the variables are referred to as both **data members** and **instance variables** (the terms are synonymous), and the functions are referred to as **member functions**. A member function name can't be the same as a data member name. (When a function is part of a class, it's formally referred to as a **method** to denote class membership. By convention, however, the terms "class method" and "class function" are used interchangeably in C++.)

---

[2]This separation into two parts isn't mandatory, as the implementation can be included in the declaration statement (described at the end of Section 10.2).

As a specific example of a class, take a look at the following definition of a class named `Date`. This type of class is important in applications where equipment delivery dates and schedules depend on exact date determinations. To accomplish this task, a number of functions for determining whether a date falls on a weekend or holiday, for example, would still have to be added to this class.

```
//--- class declaration section
class Date
{
  private:          // notice the colon after the word private
     int month;     // a data member
     int day;       // a data member
     int year;      // a data member
  public:           // again, notice the colon here
     Date(int = 7, int = 4, int = 2005); // a member function -
                                         // the constructor
     void setDate(int, int, int);        // a member function
     void showDate();                    // a member function
};  // this is a declaration - don't forget the semicolon
//--- class implementation section
Date::Date(int mm, int dd, int yyyy)
{
  month = mm;
  day = dd;
  year = yyyy;
}
void Date::setDate(int mm, int dd, int yyyy)
{
  month = mm; day = dd; year = yyyy;
  return;
}
void Date::showDate()
{
  cout << "The date is ";
  cout << setfill('0')
       << setw(2) << month << '/'
       << setw(2) << day << '/'
       << setw(2) << year % 100; // extract the last 2 year digits
  cout << endl;
  return;
}
```

Because this definition might look overwhelming, first notice that it does consist of two sections—a declaration section and an implementation section. The declaration section begins with the keyword `class` followed by a class name. Following the class name are the class's variable declarations and function prototypes, enclosed in a brace pair terminated with a semicolon. The general structure of this form is as follows:[3]

```
class Name
{
  private:
    a list of variable declarations
  public:
    a list of function prototypes
};
```

Notice that the Date class follows this format. For convenience, it's listed again with no internal comments:

```
//--- class declaration section
class Date
{
  private:
    int month;
    int day;
    int year;
  public:
    Date(int = 7, int = 4, int = 2005);
    void setDate(int, int, int);
    void showDate();
};
```

The name of this class is Date. Although the initial uppercase letter isn't required, it's used by convention to designate a class. The body of the declaration section, enclosed in braces, consists of variable and function declarations. In this case, the data members month, day, and year are declared as integers, and three functions named Date(), setDate(), and showDate() are declared via prototypes. The keywords private and public are access specifiers that define access rights. The private keyword specifies that the class members following it—in this case, month, day, and year—can be accessed only by using the class functions (or friend functions, as discussed in Section 10.2).[4] The private designation is meant to enforce data security by requiring all access to private data members through the provided member functions. This type of access, which restricts a user from seeing how data is actually stored, is referred to as **data hiding**. After a class category such as private is designated, it remains in force until a new category is listed.

In this Date class, a date is stored by using three integers for the month, day, and year. In addition, the year is always stored as a four-digit number. For example, the year 1998 is stored as 1998, not as 98. Making sure to store all years with their century designation eliminates a multitude of problems that can crop up if only the last two digits are stored. For example, the number of years between 2006 and 1999 can be calculated quickly as 2006 - 1999 = 7 years, but getting this same answer isn't as easy with the year values 06 and 99. Additionally, with four digits, it's clear what the year 2006 refers to, but a two-digit value, such as 06, could refer to either 1906 or 2006.

Following the private class data members, the function prototypes listed in the Date class have been declared as public. This means these class functions *can* be called by any objects

---

[3]Other forms are possible. However, this form is commonly used and easy to understand, so it serves as the standard model in this book.
[4]Note that the default membership category in a class is private, which means this keyword can be omitted. In this book, the private designation is used to reinforce the idea of access restrictions in class memberships.

and functions not in the class (from outside the class, in other words). In general, all class functions should be `public` so that they provide capabilities to manipulate class variables from outside the class.

The `Date` class provides three functions named `Date()`, `setDate()`, and `showDate()`. Notice that one of these member functions has the same name, `Date`, as the class name. This function is referred to as a **constructor function**, and it has a special purpose: It can be used to initialize class data members with values. The default values used for this function are the numbers 7, 4, and 2001, which, as you see shortly, are used as the default `month`, `day`, and `year` values. Note that the default year is represented as a four-digit integer to retain the century designation. Also, notice that the constructor function has no return type, which is a requirement for this special function. The two remaining functions declared in the `Date` class, `setDate()` and `showDate()`, have been declared as returning no value (`void`). (It's in the implementation section that these three member functions are written to permit the initialization, assignment, and display capabilities implied by their names.)

The implementation section is where the member functions declared in the declaration section are written.[5] The following example shows the general form of functions written in the implementation section. This format is correct for all functions except the constructor, which, as stated previously, has no return type:

```
returnType className::functionName(parameter list)
{
    function body
}
```

As this example shows, member functions defined in the implementation section have the same format as all user-written C++ functions, with the addition of the class name and scope resolution operator, `::`, that identifies the function as a member of a particular class. Now take another look at the implementation section of the `Date` class, which is repeated for convenience:

```
//--- class implementation section
Date::Date(int mm, int dd, int yyyy)
{
  month = mm;
  day = dd;
  year = yyyy;
}
void Date::setDate(int mm, int dd, int yyyy)
{
  month = mm;
  day = dd;
  year = yyyy;
  return;
}
void Date::showDate()
{
  cout << "The Date is ";
  cout << setfill('0')
       << setw(2) << month << '/'
       << setw(2) << day << '/'
       << setw(2) << year % 100; // extract the last 2 year digits
  cout << endl;
  return;
}
```

---

[5]You can also define these functions in the declaration section by declaring and writing them as inline functions. Section 10.2 includes examples of inline member functions.

Notice that the first function in this implementation section has the same name as the class, which makes it a constructor function. Therefore, it has no return type. The `Date::` at the beginning of the function header identifies this function as a member of the `Date` class. The rest of the function header

```
Date(int mm, int dd, int yyyy)
```

defines the function as having three integer parameters. The body of this function simply assigns the data members `month`, `day`, and `year` with the values of the parameters `mm`, `dd`, and `yyyy`.

The next function header

```
void Date::setDate(int mm, int dd, int yyyy)
```

defines the `setDate()` function as belonging to the `Date` class (`Date::`). This function returns no value (`void`) and expects three integer parameters: `mm`, `dd`, and `yyyy`. In a manner similar to the `Date()` function, the body of this function assigns the data members `month`, `day`, and `year` with the values of its parameters.

Finally, the last function header in the implementation section

```
void Date::showDate()
```

defines a function named `showDate()`. This function has no parameters, returns no value, and is a member of the `Date` class. The body of this function, however, needs a little more explanation.

Although all years have been stored as four-digit values to retain century information, users are accustomed to seeing dates with the year represented as a two-digit value, such as 12/15/99. To display the last two digits of the `year` value, the expression `year % 100` can be used. For example, if the year is 1999, the expression `1999 % 100` yields the value 99, and if the year is 2006, the expression `2006 % 100` yields the value 6.

If you had used an assignment such as `year = year % 100;`, however, you would actually be altering the stored value of `year` to correspond to the last two digits of the year. Because you want to retain the year as a four-digit number, you must be careful to manipulate only the *displayed* value by using the expression `year % 100` in the `cout` statement. The `setfill` and `setw` manipulators are used to make sure the displayed values correspond to conventionally accepted dates. For example, the date March 9, 2006, should appear as 3/9/06 or 03/09/06. The `setw` manipulator forces each value to be displayed in a field width of 2. Because this manipulator remains in effect only for the next insertion, it's used before the display of each date value. As the `setfill` manipulator, however, remains in effect until the fill character is changed, it must be included only once. The `setfill` manipulator has been used to change the fill character from the default of a blank space to the character 0. Doing this ensures that a date such as December 9, 2006 appears as `12/09/06`, not as `12/ 9/ 6`.

To see how the `Date` class can be used in the context of a complete program, take a look at Program 10.1. To make the program easier to read, the shaded area contains the class declaration and implementation sections. The unshaded area contains the header and `main()` function. This shading convention is used in the remainder of the book for all programs using classes.[6]

---

[6]This shading isn't accidental. In practice, the shaded area containing the class definition is placed in a separate file. A single `#include` statement is then used to include this class declaration in the program. The final program would consist of the shaded and unshaded areas in Program 10.1 with the addition of another `#include` statement in the unshaded area.

Program 10.1

```cpp
#include <iostream>
#include <iomanip>
using namespace std;

// class declaration section
class Date
{
  private:
    int month;
    int day;
    int year;
  public:
    Date(int = 7, int = 4, int = 2005);  // constructor
    void setDate(int, int, int);              // member function to copy a date
    void showDate();                          // member function to display a date
};
// class implementation section
Date::Date(int mm, int dd, int yyyy)
{
  month = mm;
  day = dd;
  year = yyyy;
}
void Date::setDate(int mm, int dd, int yyyy)
{
  month = mm;
  day = dd;
  year = yyyy;
  return;
}
void Date::showDate()
{
    cout << "The date is ";
    cout << setfill('0')
         << setw(2) << month << '/'
         << setw(2) << day << '/'
         << setw(2) << year % 100; // extract the last 2 year digits
    cout << endl;

  return;
}
```

```
int main()
{
   Date a, b, c(4,1,2000);   // declare 3 objects

   b.setDate(12,25,2006);    // assign values to b's data members
   a.showDate();             // display object a's values
   b.showDate();             // display object b's values
   c.showDate();             // display object c's values

   return 0;
}
```

The declaration and implementation sections in the shaded area of Program 10.1 should look familiar. Notice, however, that this area only declares the class; it doesn't create any variables of this class type. This is true of all C++ types, including the built-in types, such as integers and doubles. Just as a variable of an integer type must be defined, variables of a user-declared class must also be defined. Variables defined to be of a user-declared class are referred to as **objects**.

Using this new terminology, the first statement in the Program 10.1 main() function defines three objects—named a, b, and c—to be of the class type Date. In C++, when a new object is defined, memory is allocated for the object, and its data members are initialized automatically by a call to the class constructor function. For example, consider the definition Date a, b, c(4,1,2000); in main(). When the object named a is defined, the constructor function Date() is called automatically. Because no parameters have been assigned to a, the default values of the constructor function are used, resulting in this initialization:

```
a.month = 7
a.day = 4
a.year = 2005
```

Notice the notation used here: an object name and an attribute name separated by a period. This is the standard syntax for referring to an object's attribute:

objectName.attributeName

The *objectName* is the name of a specific object, and *attributeName* is the name of a data member defined for the object's class. Therefore, the notation a.month = 7 indicates that object a's month data member has been set to the value 7. Similarly, the notations a.day = 4 and a.year = 2005 indicate that a's day and year data members have been set to the values 4 and 2005.

In the same manner, when the object named b is defined, the same default parameters are used, resulting in the initialization of b's data members as follows:

```
b.month = 7
b.day = 4
b.year = 2005
```

The object named c, however, is defined with the arguments 4, 1, and 2000. These three arguments are passed to the constructor function when the object is defined, resulting in the following initialization of c's data members:

```
c.month = 4
c.day = 1
c.year = 2000
```

The next statement in main(), b.setDate(12,25,2006), calls b's setDate() function, which assigns the argument values 12, 25, and 2006 to b's data members, resulting in this assignment:

```
b.month = 12
b.day = 25
b.year = 2006
```

Notice the syntax for referring to an object's method:

objectName.methodName(parameters)

The *objectName* is the name of a specific object, and *methodName* is the name of a function defined for the object's class. Because all class functions have been defined as public, a statement such as b.setDate(12,25,2006) is valid inside the main() function and is a call to the class's setDate() function. This statement tells the setDate() function to operate on the b object with the arguments 12, 25, and 2006. It's important to understand that because all class data members were specified as private, a statement such as b.month = 12 would be invalid inside main(). Therefore, you're forced to rely on member functions to access data member values.

The last three statements in main() call the showDate() function to operate on the a, b, and c objects. The first call results in the display of a's data values, the second call in the display of b's data values, and the third call in the display of c's data values. Therefore, the output of Program 10.1 is the following:

```
The date is 07/04/05
The date is 12/25/06
The date is 04/01/00
```

Notice that a statement such as cout << a; is invalid inside main() because cout doesn't know how to handle an object of class Date. Therefore, the Date class is supplied with a function that can be used to access and display an object's internal values.

Terminology

As there's sometimes confusion about the terms classes, objects, and other object-oriented programming terminology, taking a moment to clarify and review the terminology is helpful.

Point of Information

Interfaces, Implementations, and Information Hiding

The terms "interface" and "implementation" are used extensively in object-oriented programming literature and can be equated to specific parts of a class's declaration and implementation sections.

An **interface** consists of a class's public member function declarations and any supporting comments. The **implementation** consists of both the class implementation section (containing private and public member definitions) *and* the class's private data members, which are defined in the class declaration section.

The implementation is the means of providing data hiding, which generally refers to the principal that *how* a class is constructed internally isn't relevant to programmers who want to use the class. The implementation can and should be hidden from all class users to ensure that the class isn't altered or compromised in any way. All that a programmer needs to know to use a class correctly should be provided by the interface.

A **class** is a programmer-defined data type from which objects can be created. **Objects** are created from classes; they have the same relationship to classes as variables do to C++'s built-in data types. For example, in the declaration

```
int a;
```

a is said to be a variable, and in the Program 10.1 declaration

```
Date a;
```

a is said to be an object. If it helps you to think of an object as a variable, do so.

Objects are also referred to as **instances** of a class, and the process of creating a new object is often referred to as an **instantiation** of the object. Each time a new object is instantiated (created), a new set of data members belonging to the object is created.[7] The values contained in these data members determine the object's **state**.

Seen in this way, a class can be thought of as a blueprint for creating particular instances (objects). Each instance (object) of a class has its own set of values for the set of data members specified in the class declaration section.

In addition to the data types allowed for an object, a class also defines **behavior**—that is, the operations permitted to be performed on an object's data members. Users of the object need to know *what* these functions can do and how to activate them through function calls, but unless runtime or space implications are relevant, they don't need to know *how* the operation is done. The actual implementation details of an object's operations are in the class implementation, which can (and should) be hidden from the user. Other names for the operations defined in a class implementation section are procedures, functions, services, and methods. These terms are used interchangeably throughout the remainder of the book.

---

[7]Note that only one set of class functions is created. These functions are shared between objects.

EXERCISES 10.1

1. **(For Review)** Define the following terms:

   a. Class

   b. Object

   c. Declaration section

   d. Implementation section

   e. Instance variable

   f. Member function

   g. Data member

   h. Constructor

   i. Class instance

   j. Services

   k. Methods

   l. Interface

   m. State

   n. Behavior

2. **(For Thought) a.** Instead of specifying a rectangle's location by listing the position of two diagonal corner points, what other attributes could be used?

   b. What other attributes, besides length and width, could be used to describe a rectangle to be drawn on a color monitor?

   c. Describe a set of attributes that could be used to define circles to be drawn on a black-and-white monitor.

   d. What attributes would you add to those selected in Exercise 2c if the circles are to be drawn on a color monitor?

3. **(Practice) a.** The attributes of a class represent how objects of the class appear to the outside world. The behavior represents how an object of a class reacts to an external stimulus. Given this, what do you think is the mechanism by which one object "triggers" the designated behavior in another object?

   b. If behavior in C++ is constructed by defining an appropriate function, how do you think the behavior is activated in C++?

4. **(Practice)** Write a class declaration section for each of the following specifications. In each case, include a prototype for a constructor and a member function named `showdata()` that can be used to display data member values.

   a. A class named `Time` that has integer data members named `secs`, `mins`, and `hours`

   b. A class named `Complex` that has double-precision data members named `real` and `imaginary`

   c. A class named `Circle` that has integer data members named `xcenter` and `ycenter` and a double-precision data member named `radius`

   d. A class named `System` that has character data members named `computer`, `printer`, and `screen`, each capable of holding 30 characters (including the end-of-string NULL), and double-precision data members named `compPrice`, `printPrice`, and `scrnPrice`

5. **(Practice) a.** Construct a class implementation section for the constructor and `showdata()` member functions corresponding to the class declaration created for Exercise 4a.

 b. Construct a class implementation section for the constructor and `showdata()` function members corresponding to the class declaration created for Exercise 4b.

 c. Construct a class implementation section for the constructor and `showdata()` function members corresponding to the class declaration created for Exercise 4c.

 d. Construct a class implementation section for the constructor and `showdata()` function members corresponding to the class declaration created for Exercise 4d.

6. **(Program) a.** Include the class declaration and implementation sections prepared for Exercises 4a and 5a in a complete working program.

 b. Include the class declaration and implementation sections prepared for Exercises 4b and 5b in a complete working program.

 c. Include the class declaration and implementation sections prepared for Exercises 4c and 5c in a complete working program.

 d. Include the class declaration and implementation sections prepared for Exercises 4d and 5d in a complete working program.

7. **(Debug)** Determine the errors in the following class declaration section:

```
class employee
  {
  public:
    int empnum;
    char code;
  private:
    class(int = 0);
    void showemp(int, char);
  };
```

8. **(General Math) a.** Construct a class named `Rectangle` that has double-precision data members named `length` and `width`. The class should have member functions named `perimeter()` and `area()` to calculate a rectangle's perimeter and area, a member function named `setdata()` to set a rectangle's length and width, and a member function named `showdata()` that displays a rectangle's length, width, perimeter, and area.

 b. Include the `Rectangle` class constructed in Exercise 8a in a working C++ program.

9. **(Modify) a.** Modify the `Date` class defined in Program 10.1 to include a `nextDay()` function that increments a date by one day. Test your function to ensure that it increments days into a new month and into a new year correctly.

 b. Modify the `Date` class defined in Program 10.1 to include a `priorDay()` function that decrements a date by one day. Test your function to ensure that it decrements days into a prior month and into a prior year correctly.

10. **(Modify)** Modify the Date class in Program 10.1 to contain a method that compares two Date objects and returns the larger of the two. The method should be written according to the following algorithm:

Comparison function
  Accept two Date values as parameters
  Determine the later date by using the following procedure:
    Convert each date into an integer value having the form yyyymmdd
    *This can be accomplished by using the formula year * 100000 + month * 100 + day*
    Compare the corresponding integers for each date
    The larger integer corresponds to the later date
  Return the later date

11. **(Modify) a.** Add a member function to Program 10.1's class definition that determines the day of the week for any Date object. An algorithm for determining the day of the week, known as Zeller's algorithm, is the following:

For dates in the form of *mm/dd/ccyy*, *mm* is the month, *dd* is the day, *cc* is the century, and *yy* is the year in the century. For example, with 12/28/2006, *mm* = 12, *dd* = 28, *cc* = 20, and *yy* = 06.

If mm is less than 3
  Set mm = mm + 12 and ccyy = ccyy - 1
Endif
Set cc = int(ccyy/100)
Set yy = ccyy % 100
*Set the variable T = dd + int(26 * (mm + 1)/10) + yy + int(yy/4) - 2 * cc*
dayOfWeek = T % 7
If dayOfWeek is less than 0
  dayOfWeek = dayOfWeek + 7
Endif

Using this algorithm, dayOfWeek has a value of 0 if the date is a Saturday, 1 if it's a Sunday, and so forth.

b. Include the class definition constructed for Exercise 11a in a complete C++ program. The main() function should display the name of the day (Sun, Mon, Tue, and so on) for the Date object being tested.

10.2 Constructors

A **constructor function** is any function with the same name as its class. Multiple constructors can be defined for each class, as long as they can be distinguished by the number and types of their parameters.

A constructor's intended purpose is to initialize a new object's data members. Depending on the number and types of supplied arguments, one constructor function is called automatically each time an object is created. If no constructor function is written, the compiler supplies a default constructor. In addition to its initialization role, a constructor function can perform other tasks when it's called and be written in a variety of ways. This section explains possible variations of constructor functions and introduces another function, the destructor, which is called automatically whenever an object goes out of existence.

Point of Information

Constructors

A **constructor** is any function with the same name as its class. Its main purpose is to initialize an object's member variables when an object is created, so a constructor is called automatically when an object is declared.

A class can have multiple constructors if each constructor can be distinguished by having a different formal parameter list. A compiler error results when unique identification of a constructor isn't possible. If no constructor is provided, the compiler supplies a do-nothing default constructor.

Every constructor function must be declared with *no return type* (not even `void`). Because they are functions, constructors can also be called in nondeclarative statements. When used in this manner, the function call requires parentheses following the constructor name, even if no parameters are used. However, when used in a declaration, parentheses *must not* be included for a constructor. For example, the declaration `Date a();` is incorrect. The correct declaration is `Date a;`. When parameters are used, however, they must be enclosed in parentheses in both declarative and nondeclarative statements. Default parameter values should be included in the constructor's prototype.

The following code example shows the general format of a constructor:

```
className::className(parameter list)
{
  // function body
}
```

As this format shows, a constructor must have the following:

- The same name as the class to which it belongs
- No return type (not even `void`)

If you don't include a constructor in your class definition, the compiler supplies a do-nothing default one for you. For example, examine the following class declaration:

```
class Date
{
  private:
    int month, day, year;
  public:
    void setDate(int, int, int);
    void showDate(void);
};
```

Because no user-defined constructor has been declared, the compiler creates a default constructor. For the `Date` class, this default constructor is equivalent to `Date::Date(void){}`—that is, the compiler-supplied default constructor expects no parameters and has an empty body. Clearly, this default constructor isn't very useful, but it does exist if no other constructor is declared.

The term **default constructor** is used often in C++ and refers to any constructor that doesn't require arguments when it's called. The reason it doesn't require arguments is that no arguments are declared, as with the compiler-supplied default, or all arguments have been given default values. For example, Date(int mm = 7, int dd = 4, int yyyy = 2005) is a valid prototype for a default constructor. Each argument has been given a default value, and an object can be declared as type Date without supplying any further arguments. Using this default constructor, the declaration Date a; initializes the a object with the default values 7, 4, and 2005.

To verify that a constructor function is called automatically when a new object is created, examine Program 10.2. Notice that in the implementation section, the constructor function uses cout to display the message Created a new date object with data values. Therefore, whenever the constructor is called, this message is displayed. Because the main() function creates three objects, the constructor is called three times, and the message is displayed three times.

 Program 10.2

```cpp
#include <iostream>
using namespace std;
// class declaration section
class Date
{
  private:
    int month;
    int day;
    int year;
  public:
    Date(int = 7, int = 4, int = 2005);      // constructor
};

// class implementation section
Date::Date(int mm, int dd, int yyyy)
{
  month = mm;
  day = dd;
  year = yyyy;
  cout << "Created a new date object with data values "
       << month << ", " << day << ", " << year << endl;
}
int main()
{
  Date a;                // declare an object
  Date b;                // declare an object
  Date c(4,1,2006);      // declare an object
  return 0;
}
```

The following output is produced when Program 10.2 runs:

```
Created a new date object with data values 7, 4, 2005
Created a new date object with data values 7, 4, 2005
Created a new date object with data values 4, 1, 2006
```

Although any legitimate C++ statement can be used in a constructor function, such as the cout statement in Program 10.2, it's best to keep constructors simple and use them only for initializing purposes. One further point needs to be made about the constructor function in Program 10.2. According to C++ rules, object members are initialized in the order they are declared in the class declaration section, *not* in the order they might appear in the function's definition in the implementation section. Usually, this order isn't an issue, unless one data member is initialized by using another data member's value.

Calling Constructors

As you have seen, constructors are called whenever an object is created. The actual declaration, however, can be made in a variety of ways. For example, the declaration

```
Date c(4,1,2006);
```

used in Program 10.2 could also have been written as

```
Date c = Date(4,1,2006);
```

This second form declares c as being of type Date and then makes a direct call to the constructor function with the arguments 4, 1, and 2006. This second form can be simplified when only one argument is passed to the constructor. For example, if only the month data member of the c object needs to be initialized with the value 8 and the day and year members can use the default values, the object can be created by using this declaration:

```
Date c = 8;
```

Because the form using an equal sign resembles declarations in C, it's referred to as the **C style of initialization**. The declaration form in Program 10.2, referred to as the **C++ style of initialization**, is the form used predominantly in the remainder of this book.

Regardless of which initialization form you use, an object should never be declared with empty parentheses. For example, the declaration Date a(); is not the same as the declaration Date a;. The second declaration uses the default constructor values, and the first declaration results in no object being created.

Overloaded and Inline Constructors

The primary difference between a constructor and other user-written functions is how the constructor is called: Constructors are called automatically each time an object is created, and other functions must be called explicitly by name.[8] As a function, however, a constructor must still follow all the rules for user-written functions discussed in Chapter 6. Therefore, constructors can have default arguments (as in Program 10.1), can be overloaded, and can be written as inline functions.

---

[8]This rule is true for all functions except destructors, described later in this section. A destructor function is called automatically each time an object is destroyed.

Recall from Section 6.1 that function overloading permits using the same function name with different argument lists. Based on the supplied argument types, the compiler determines which function to use when the call is encountered. To see how overloading can be applied to the Date class, take another look at the class declaration repeated here:

```
// class declaration section
class Date
{
  private:
    int month;
    int day;
    int year;
  public:
    Date(int = 7, int = 4, int = 2005);     // constructor
};
```

The constructor prototype specifies three integer parameters, which are used to initialize the month, day, and year data members.

Another method of specifying a date is using a long integer in the form year * 10000 + month * 100 + day. With this form, the date 12/24/1998 is 19981224, and the date 2/5/2006 is 20060205.[9] A suitable prototype for a constructor that uses dates in this form is shown here:

```
Date(long);    // an overloaded constructor
```

The constructor is declared as receiving one long integer argument. The code for this new Date() function must, of course, convert its single argument into a month, day, and year and is included in the class implementation section. The actual code for this constructor is as follows:

```
Date::Date(long yyyymmdd)    // a second constructor
{
  year = int(yyyymmdd/10000.0);     // extract the year
  // extract the month
  month = int( (yyyymmdd - year * 10000.0) / 100.00 );
  // extract   the day
  day = int(yyyymmdd - year * 10000.0 - month * 100.0);
}
```

Don't be overly concerned with the conversion code used in the function body. The important point is the concept of overloading the Date() function to provide two constructors. Program 10.3 contains the complete class definition in the context of a working program. The output of Program 10.3 is as follows:

```
The date is 07/04/05
The date is 04/01/98
The date is 05/15/06
```

---

[9]The reason for specifying dates in this manner is that only one number needs to be used per date, and sorting the numbers puts the corresponding dates into chronological order automatically.

Program 10.3

```cpp
#include <iostream>
#include <iomanip>
using namespace std;

// class declaration section
class Date
{
  private:
    int month;
    int day;
    int year;
  public:
    Date(int = 7, int = 4, int = 2005);    // constructor
    Date(long);                  // another constructor
    void showDate();             // member function to display a date
};

// class implementation section
Date::Date(int mm, int dd, int yyyy)
{
  month = mm;
  day = dd;
  year = yyyy;
}
Date::Date(long yyyymmdd)
{
  year = int(yyyymmdd/10000.0);       // extract the year
  month = int( (yyyymmdd - year * 10000.0)/100.00 ); // extract the month
  day = int(yyyymmdd - year * 10000.0 - month * 100.0); // extract the day
}
void Date::showDate()
{
  cout << "The date is ";
  cout << setfill('0')
       << setw(2) << month << '/'
       << setw(2) << day << '/'
       << setw(2) << year % 100; // extract the last 2 year digits
  cout << endl;
  return;
}
```

☞

```
int main()
{
  Date a, b(4,1,1998), c(20060515L);  // declare three objects
  a.showDate();            // display object a's values
  b.showDate();            // display object b's values
  c.showDate();            // display object c's values

  return 0;
}
```

Three objects are created in the Program 10.3 main() function. The first object, a, is initialized with the default constructor, using its default arguments. Object b is also initialized with the default constructor but uses the arguments 4, 1, and 1998. Finally, object c, which is initialized with a long integer, uses the second constructor in the class implementation section. The compiler knows to use this second constructor because the argument specified, 20060515L, is designated as a long integer by the uppercase L. It's worth pointing out that a compiler error would occur if both Date constructors had default values. For example, a declaration such as Date d; would be ambiguous to the compiler because it couldn't determine which constructor to use. Therefore, in each implementation section, only one constructor can be written as the default.

As mentioned, constructors can also be written as inline functions. Doing so simply means defining the function in the class declaration section. For example, the following declaration section makes both constructors in Program 10.3 inline:

```
// class declaration
class Date
{
  private:
    int month;
    int day;
    int year;
  public:
    Date(int mm = 7, int dd = 4, int yyyy = 2005)
    {
      month = mm;
      day = dd;
      year = yyyy;
    }
    Date(long yyyymmdd)    // here is the overloaded constructor
    {
      year = int(yyyymmdd/10000.0);    // extract the year
      // extract the month
      month = int( (yyyymmdd - year * 10000.0)/100.00 );
      // extract the day
      day = int(yyyymmdd - year * 10000.0 - month * 100.0);
    }
};
```

The keyword inline isn't required in this declaration because member functions defined in the class declaration are inline by default.

Generally, only functions that can be coded on a single line are good candidates for inline functions. This guideline reinforces the convention that inline functions should be small. Therefore, the first constructor is more conventionally written as follows:

```
Date(int mm = 7, int dd = 4, int yyyy = 2005)
  { month = mm; day = dd; year = yyyy; }
```

The second constructor, which extends over three lines, should not be written as an inline function.

Destructors

The counterpart to constructor functions are **destructor functions**. Destructors are functions with the same class name as constructors but are preceded with a tilde (~). Therefore, for the Date class, the destructor name is ~Date(). Like constructors, the C++ compiler provides a default do-nothing destructor in the absence of an explicit destructor. Unlike constructors, however, there can be only one destructor function per class because destructors take no parameters and return no values.

Destructors are called automatically when an object goes out of existence and are meant to "clean up" any undesirable effects the object might leave. Generally, these effects occur only when an object contains a pointer member.

EXERCISES 10.2

1. **(For Review)** Determine whether the following statements are true or false:
   a. A constructor function must have the same name as its class.
   b. A class can have only one constructor function.

Point of Information

Mutator Methods

A **mutator method**, more commonly called a "mutator," is any nonconstructor class method that changes an object's data values. Mutators are used to alter an object's data values after a constructor method has created and initialized the object automatically. A class can contain multiple mutators, as long as each one has a unique name or parameter list. For example, in the Date class, you could have a mutator for changing a Date object's month, day, and year values. Constructors, which have the main purpose of initializing an object's member variables when the object is created, aren't considered mutators.

    c. A class can have only one default constructor function.

    d. A default constructor can be supplied only by the compiler.

    e. A default constructor can have no parameters or all parameters must have default values.

    f. A constructor must be declared for each class.

    g. A constructor must be declared with a return type.

    h. A constructor is called automatically each time an object is created.

    i. A class can have only one destructor function.

    j. A destructor must have the same name as its class, preceded by a tilde (~).

    k. A destructor can have default arguments.

    l. A destructor must be declared for each class.

    m. A destructor must be declared with a return type.

    n. A destructor is called automatically each time an object goes out of existence.

    o. Destructors aren't useful when the class contains a pointer data member.

2. **(Desk Check)** For Program 10.3, what date is initialized for object c if the declaration Date c(15); is used instead of the declaration Date c(20060515L);?

3. **(Modify)** Modify Program 10.3 so that the only data member of the class is a long integer named yyyymmdd. Do this by substituting the declaration long yyyymmdd; for these existing declarations:

```
int month;
int day;
int year;
```

Using the same constructor function prototypes currently declared in the class declaration section, rewrite them so that the Date(long) function becomes the default constructor, and the Date(int, int, int) function converts a month, day, and year into the correct form for the class data members.

4. **(Program) a.** Construct a Time class containing integer data members seconds, minutes, and hours. Have the class contain two constructors: The first should be a default constructor

having the prototype `Time(int, int, int)`, which uses default values of 0 for each data member. The second constructor should accept a long integer representing a total number of seconds and disassemble the long integer into `hours`, `minutes`, and `seconds`. The final member function should display the class data members.

   b. Include the class written for Exercise 4a in the context of a complete program.

5. **(Program) a.** Construct a class named `Student` consisting of an integer student ID number, an array of five double-precision grades, and an integer representing the total number of grades entered. The constructor for this class should initialize all `Student` data members to 0. Included in the class should be member functions to 1) enter a student ID number, 2) enter a single test grade and update the total number of grades entered, and 3) compute an average grade and display the student ID followed by the average grade.

   b. Include the class constructed in Exercise 5a in the context of a complete program. Your program should declare two objects of type `Student` and accept and display data for the two objects to verify operation of the member functions.

6. **(Modify) a.** In Exercise 4, you were asked to construct a `Time` class. For this class, include a `tick()` function that increments the time by one second. Test your function to ensure that it increments time into a new minute and a new hour correctly.

   b. Modify the `Time` class written for Exercise 6a to include a `detick()` function that decrements the time by one second. Test your function to ensure that it decrements time into a prior hour and into a prior minute correctly.

10.3 A Case Study: Constructing a Room Object

Now that you have an understanding of how classes are constructed and the terminology for describing them, you can apply this knowledge to creating a class from which room objects can be constructed. The room's floor area must be calculated for any size room when its length and width are known. For modeling purposes, assume every room is rectangular.

Step 1   Analyze the Problem

In this application, you have one type of object, a rectangular room. Because of the room's shape, the floor can be designated by its length and width. After these attributes have been assigned for a room, its floor area can be calculated as the room's length multiplied by its width.

Step 2   Develop a Solution

For this application, a room's length and width are the only attributes of interest. They can be represented by double-precision variables named `length` and `width`. The services required of the class are a constructor to set a room's length and width attributes, an accessor to display a room's attribute values, a mutator to change a room's attribute values, and a function to determine a room's floor area from its length and width values. Name the class `RoomType`, the accessor function `showRoomValues()`, the mutator function `setNewRoomValues()`, and the area calculation function `calculateRoomArea()`.

Step 3   Code the Solution

Given the selection of attribute and class function names, the following class declaration is
suitable:

```
class RoomType
{
  // class declaration section
  private:
    double length;   // declare length as a double variable
    double width;    // declare width as a double variable

  public:
    RoomType(); // the constructor's declaration statement
    void showRoomValues();
    void setNewRoomValues();
    void calculateRoomArea();
};
```

This code declares two data members, `length` and `width`, and four class functions. The
data members `length` and `width` store a room's length and width. The class functions are
a constructor to create a room object, an accessor to display a room object's length and width
values, a mutator to change a room's length and width values, and a calculation function for
calculating a room's floor area. To accomplish these services, the following class implementation is suitable:

```
// class implementation section
RoomType::RoomType(double l, double w)   // this is a constructor
{
  length = l;
  width = w;
  cout << "Created a new room object using the default constructor.\n\n";
}

void RoomType::showRoomValues()     // this is an accessor
{
  cout << "  length = " << length
       << "\n  width = " << width << endl;
}

void RoomType::setNewRoomValues(double l, double w)     // this is a
                                                        // mutator
{
  length = l;
  width = w;
}

 void RoomType::calculateRoomArea()   // this performs a calculation
{
  cout << (length * width);
}
```

These functions are straightforward. When a room object is declared, it's initialized with
a `length` and `width` of 0, unless specific values are provided in the declaration. The

accessor function displays the values stored in length and width, and the mutator permits reassigning values after a room object has been created. Finally, the calculation function displays a room's area by multiplying its length by its width.

Step 4 Test and Correct the Program

Testing the RoomType class entails testing each class function. To do this, Program 10.4 includes the RoomType class in the context of a working program.

Program 10.4

```
#include <iostream>
using namespace std;
class RoomType
{

    // class declaration section
    private:
      double length;   // declare length as a double variable
      double width;    // declare width as a double variable
    public:
      RoomType(double = 0.0, double = 0.0); // the constructor's declaration
                                            // statement
      void showRoomValues();
      void setNewRoomValues(double, double);
      void calculateRoomArea();
};

// class implementation section
RoomType::RoomType(double l, double w)  // this is a constructor
{
  length = l;
  width = w;
  cout << "Created a new room object using the default constructor.\n\n";
}

void RoomType::showRoomValues()    // this is an accessor
{
  cout << "   length = " << length
       << "\n   width = " << width << endl;
}
```

☞

```
void RoomType::setNewRoomValues(double l, double w)    // this is a mutator
{
  length = l;
  width = w;
}


void RoomType::calculateRoomArea()   // this performs a calculation
{
  cout << (length * width);
}
```

```
int main()
{
  RoomType roomOne(12.5, 18.2);   // declare a variable of type RoomType

  cout << "The values for this room are:\n";
  roomOne.showRoomValues();          // use a class method on this object
  cout << "\nThe floor area of this room is: ";
  roomOne.calculateRoomArea();      // use another class method on this object

  roomOne.setNewRoomValues(5.5, 10.3);    // call the mutator

  cout << "\n\nThe values for this room have been changed to:\n";
  roomOne.showRoomValues();
  cout << "\nThe floor area of this room is: ";
  roomOne.calculateRoomArea();

  cout << endl;
  return 0;
}
```

The shaded portion of Program 10.4 contains the class construction sections. To see how this class is used, concentrate on the unshaded section containing the main() function. This function creates a room object with a length of 12.5 and a width of 18.2. These room dimensions are displayed by using the showRoomValues() function, and the area is calculated and displayed by using the calculateRoomArea() function. The room's dimensions are reset and displayed, and the room's area is recalculated. Program 10.4 produces the following output:

```
Created a new room object using the default constructor.

The values for this room are:
   length = 12.5
    width = 18.2

The floor area of this room is: 227.5
```

Point of Information

Encapsulation

The term **encapsulation** refers to packaging a number of items into a single unit. For example, a function is used to encapsulate the details of an algorithm. Similarly, a class encapsulates variables and functions together in a single package. Although "encapsulation" is sometimes used to refer to the process of data hiding, this usage isn't technically accurate. The correct relationship between terms is that data hiding refers to encapsulating and hiding all implementation details.

```
The values for this room have been changed to:
  length = 5.5
   width = 10.3

The floor area of this room is: 56.65
```

The basic requirements of object-oriented programming are evident even in as simple a program as Program 10.4. Before the main() function can be written, a useful class must be constructed, which is typical of programs using objects. For these programs, the design process is front-loaded with the requirement to give careful consideration to the class—its declaration and implementation. Code in the implementation section effectively removes code that would otherwise be part of main()'s responsibility. Therefore, any program using the object doesn't have to repeat the implementation details in its main() function. Instead, the main() function and any function called by main() are concerned only with sending messages to objects to activate them correctly. How the object responds to the messages and how the object's state is retained are not main()'s concern—these details are hidden in the class construction.

 EXERCISES 10.3

1. **(Practice)** Enter Program 10.4 and execute it.

2. **(Modify)** Modify the main() function in Program 10.4 to create a second room with a length of 9 and a width of 12. Have the program calculate this new room's area.

3. **(Modify) a.** Modify the main() function in Program 10.4 to create four rooms: hall, kitchen, dining room, and living room. The dimensions for these rooms are as follows:

   Hall: length = 12.40, width = 3.5
   Kitchen: length = 14, width = 14
   Living room: length = 12.4, width = 20
   Dining room: length = 14, width = 10.5

Your program should display the area of each room and the total area of all four rooms combined.

b. The total area of all rooms can be calculated and saved by using a class variable. To do this, what type of variable do you think this class variable must be?

4. **(Debug)** Remove the public access from the RoomType function declarations in Program 10.4 and compile the program. Determine why the compiler returns the error messages that it does.

5. **(Program) a.** Complete the following class by adding a constructor, an accessor, and a calculation function. The constructor should initialize all objects with firstNumber = 10 and secondNumber = 15. The calculation function should calculate and display the average of the two numbers.

```
class TwoNumbers
{
// class declaration section
  private
     int firstNumber;
     int secondNumber;
     double average;
};

// class implementation section
```

b. Include the class written for Exercise 5a in the context of a complete program. The program should create a single object and display the object's values and the average of these values.

6. **(Program) a.** Construct a Time class containing the integer instance variables seconds, minutes, and hours. Include a constructor that initializes each data member with a value of 10 and an accessor that displays the value of all data members.

b. Include the class written for Exercise 6a in the context of a complete program.

7. **(Program)** Construct a class named Light that simulates a traffic light. The class's color attribute should change from Green to Yellow to Red and then back to Green by using the class's change() function. When a new Light object is created, its initial color should be Red.

8. **(Program) a.** Construct a class named Student consisting of an integer student ID number and a double-precision grade point average. The constructor for this class should initialize the ID number to 111111 and the grade point average to 0.0. Include an accessor function to display all data values.

b. Include the class constructed in Exercise 8a in the context of a complete program. Your program should declare two objects of type Student and display data for the two objects to verify operation of the class functions.

9. **(Program) a.** Construct a class definition to represent an employee of a company. Each employee is defined by an integer ID number, a floating-point pay rate, and the maximum number of hours the employee should work each week. The services the class provides should be the capability to enter data for a new employee, the capability to change data for a new employee, and the capability to display existing data for a new employee.

b. Include the class definition created for Exercise 9a in a working C++ program that asks the user to enter data for three employees and then displays the entered data.

c. Modify the program written for Exercise 9b to include a menu that offers the user the following choices:

1. Add an employee
2. Modify employee data
3. Delete an employee
4. Exit this menu

In response to the user's choice, the program should initiate an action to implement the choice.

10. **(Program) a.** Construct a class definition to represent types of food. A type of food is classified as basic or prepared. Basic foods are further classified as Dairy, Meat, Fruit, Vegetable, or Grain. The services the class provides should be the capability to enter data for a new food, the capability to change data for a new food, and the capability to display existing data for a new food.

b. Include the class definition created for Exercise 10a in a working C++ program that asks the user to enter data for four food items and then displays the entered data.

c. Modify the program written for Exercise 10b to include a menu that offers the user the following choices:

1. Add a food item
2. Modify a food item
3. Delete a food item
4. Exit this menu

In response to the user's choice, the program should initiate an action to implement the choice.

10.4 A Closer Look: Object Identification and the Unified Modeling Language (UML)[10]

When solving any problem, often it's helpful to start by creating a diagram or map or devising a theoretical analogy for the problem you're trying to solve. In other words, you need to create some kind of model. Creating a model helps you see all parts of the problem and helps you understand what you need to do to solve it.

The first step in constructing an object-based program is developing an object-based model of the problem. For example, the RoomType class developed in Section 10.3 is based on the model of a room as a rectangular object. Each class then becomes a description of the model written in C++. Thinking about a room as an object probably isn't difficult because in a physical sense, a room is an object.

---

[10]This topic can be omitted on first reading without loss of subject continuity.

To become a good object-oriented programmer, however, you need to be able to analyze more complex situations so that you can think of and organize programming problems as the interaction of different objects. In this section, you explore this object-based concept in more detail. You also learn how to develop programs systematically by using object-based models. Figure 10.1 illustrates the concepts discussed in this section.

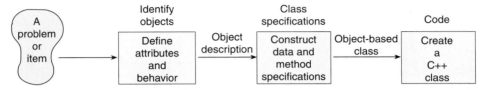

Figure 10.1   A class is a programming-language description of a model

Representing Problems with Models

Formally, a **model** is a representation of a problem. The first step in creating an object-based model is to begin "thinking in objects." For example, if you want to know the result of tossing a coin 100 times, you can certainly do so by tossing a real coin. However, if a coin could be modeled accurately, you could find the result by writing a program to simulate a coin toss. Similarly, a game of solitaire could be simulated if a realistic model of a deck of cards could be created and if methods such as shuffling the deck could be coded.

Objects, such as coins, cards, and more complicated graphical objects, are well suited to a programming representation because they can be modeled by two basic characteristics: attributes and behaviors. **Attributes** define the properties of interest, and **behaviors** define how the object reacts to its environment. When designing and developing an object-oriented program, you need to follow these two steps:

1. Identify the required objects.
2. For each object:
   a. Identify the attributes of interest.
   b. Identify the behaviors (operations) of interest.

To make this process more tangible, think about a coin-tossing experiment. Step 1 tells you to identify the required objects. For this experiment, the object is a coin. Step 2 tells you to identify the relevant attributes and behaviors. In terms of attributes, a coin has a denomination, size, weight, color, condition (tarnished, worn, proof), country of origin, and side (head or tail). If you're purchasing a coin for collectible purposes, you're interested in all these attributes but the side. For a coin toss, however, the only attribute that's of interest is the side; it doesn't matter whether the coin is a penny or a quarter, copper or silver, or tarnished or not. In terms of modeling a coin for a coin-tossing experiment, the only attribute you must consider is what side is visible when the coin is tossed. It's important to understand the significance of the choice of attributes. Very few models include every aspect of the objects they represent; a model should include only attributes that are relevant to the problem.

Having determined the attributes to use in modeling a coin, the next step requires identifying the behavior this object should exhibit. In this case, you must have a means of simulating a toss and determining the side that faces up when the toss is completed.

Figure 10.2 summarizes the initial results of the two steps in developing the object-oriented coin toss program: It identifies the required object and lists its relevant attributes and behaviors. This diagram is called an **object description**. It doesn't tell you everything there is to know about a coin, only what you need to know to create a coin toss program. For programming purposes, this description must be translated into a programming language, whether it's C++ or another object-oriented language.

```
Object: A coin

Attributes: Side (head or tail)

Behavior: Landing with heads up or tails up
```

Figure 10.2   An initial object diagram

As you expand your design for a program, often you have to refine and expand the object description. Refinement, or improving and modifying the model, is almost always required for all but extremely simple problems. As a tool for modifying models, this section introduces the **Unified Modeling Language (UML)**, which is widely accepted as a technique for developing object-oriented programs. UML isn't a programming language, nor is it part of C++. It's a program-modeling language with its own rules and notations for creating an object-oriented design. If used correctly, a UML design can help you understand and clarify a program's requirements. The finished design can serve as a set of detailed specifications (which can be coded easily in an object-oriented programming language, such as C++) and as documentation for the final program.

UML uses diagrams and techniques that are easy to understand and support all the features required to implement an object-oriented design. Additionally, UML is currently the predominant object-oriented design procedure that professional programmers use. At the most fundamental level, designing an object-oriented program requires understanding and specifying the following:

- The objects in the system
- What can happen to these objects
- When something can happen to these objects

In a UML analysis, each item is addressed by separate views and diagrams. This procedure is similar to the plan for a house, which contains several diagrams required for the final construction. For example, there must be blueprints for the physical outlay as well as diagrams for electrical, plumbing, heating and cooling ducts, landscaping, and elevation views. Each diagram presents a different view of the completed house, and provides different information, but all the information is required for the finished product.

The same is true for the diagrams in a UML analysis. UML provides seven diagram types: class, object, state, sequence, activity, use case, component, deployment, and collaboration. Not all these diagram types are required for every analysis; some provide specific details that are needed only in more advanced situations. This book covers the two basic UML diagrams you should be familiar with and the rules for creating them: class and object diagrams. These two diagrams are similar in structure, and both include attributes and operations for classes or objects and the relationship between classes or objects.

Although both diagrams can contain information included in the other diagram types, each diagram type is intended to model and emphasize a different aspect of a system. In other words, each diagram type views the same system from a different angle and highlights a particular characteristic of the system. The most important and useful when you first start developing an object-oriented program are class and object diagrams, described in this section. For many systems, the descriptions that class and object diagrams provide are more than enough for design and implementation purposes.

Class and Object Diagrams

Class diagrams are used to describe classes and their relationships, and **object diagrams** are used to describe objects and their relationships. As you know, a class refers to a type of object, from which many specific objects can be created, and an object refers to a specific single item created from a class. For example, a class of books might be described as fiction or nonfiction, of which many specific instances, or objects, exist. The book *A History of England* is a specific object of the nonfiction class, and *Pride and Prejudice* is a specific object of the fiction class. Therefore, the class is always the basic plan, or recipe, from which real objects are created. It's the class that describes the properties and operations each object must have to be a member of the class.

An attribute, as you have seen, is simply a characteristic each object in the class must have. For example, title and author are attributes of Book objects; name, age, sex, weight, and height are attributes of Person objects. After data values are assigned to attributes, a unique object is created. Every object created from a class must also have an identity to distinguish it from another object of the same class. This rule isn't true of a pure data value, such as the number 5; all occurrences of this number are indistinguishable from one another.

Both classes and objects are represented with a diagram consisting of a box. In class diagrams, the class name is in bold text and centered at the top of the box. In object diagrams, the object's name is also centered at the top of box, but it's underlined. Figure 10.3 shows the representation of a Person class along with a Person object named Janet Smith.

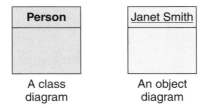

A class diagram   An object diagram

Figure 10.3 Class and object representations

Including the class name in object diagrams is optional, but if you do, simply underline it. You can precede the class name with an object name, but you must use a colon to separate the two names. For example, in Figure 10.3's object diagram, you could use the name <u>Janet Smith:Person</u>. Figure 10.4 shows the basic symbols and notations used in constructing class and object diagrams.

After class attributes have been identified, they are listed in a box below the class name, separated by a line. Objects are shown in a similar manner, with data values included for all attributes. For example, Figure 10.5 shows the attributes associated with the Country class and the values of these attributes for the U.S.A. and Spain objects. As you might expect, the attributes listed in a class diagram become, in C++, the variables declared in the class declaration section.

Attributes have two qualities: type and visibility. An attribute's **type** is either a primitive data type—such as integer, double, Boolean, or character—or a class data type, such as a string. Type is required in a class diagram and is indicated after an attribute name with acolon followed by the data type.

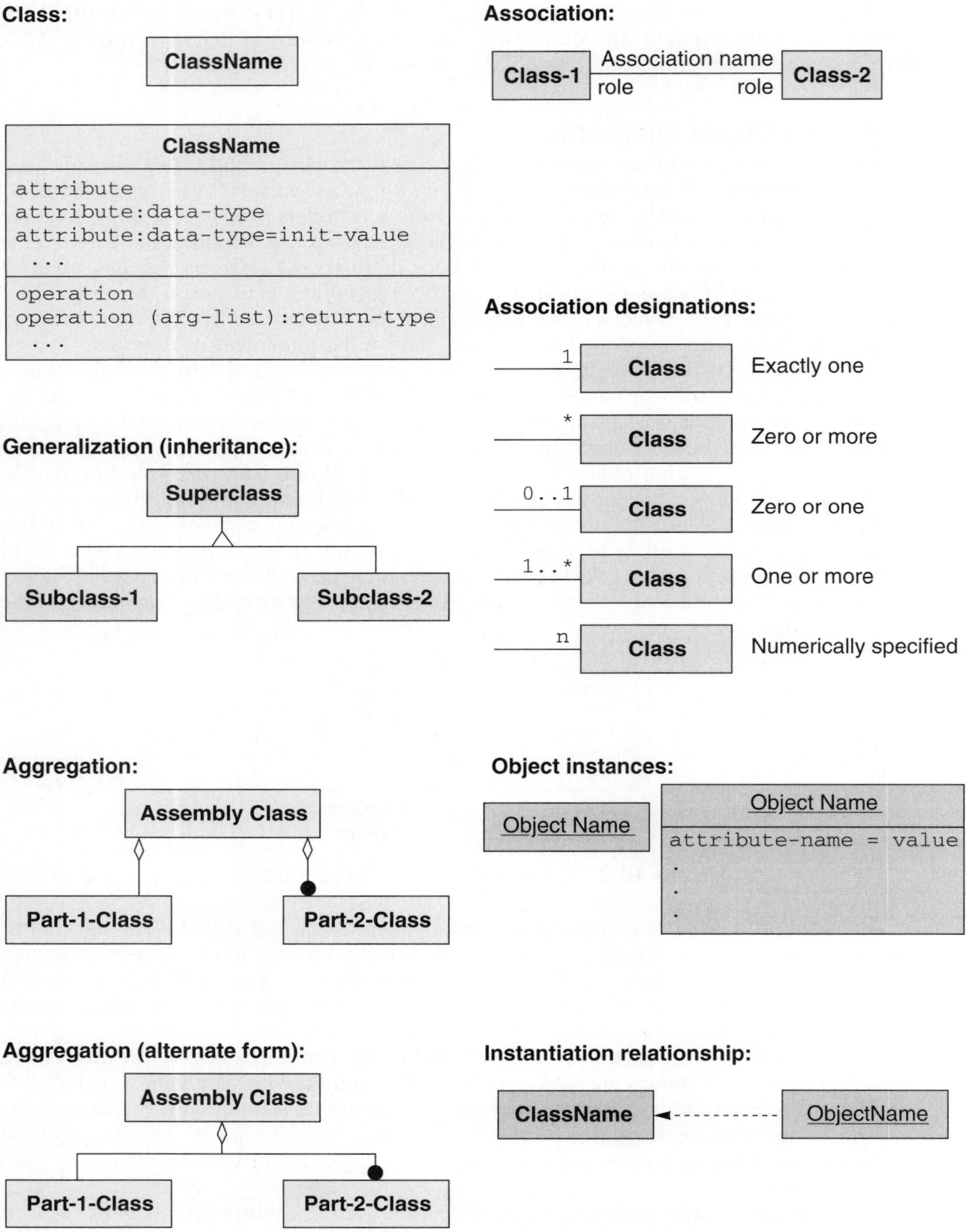

Class:

ClassName

ClassName
attribute attribute:data-type attribute:data-type=init-value   ...
operation operation (arg-list):return-type   ...

Association:

Class-1 — Association name / role — role — Class-2

Association designations:

1 — Class	Exactly one
* — Class	Zero or more
0..1 — Class	Zero or one
1..* — Class	One or more
n — Class	Numerically specified

Generalization (inheritance):

Superclass → Subclass-1, Subclass-2

Aggregation:

Assembly Class → Part-1-Class, Part-2-Class

Object instances:

Object Name

Object Name
attribute-name = value . . .

Aggregation (alternate form):

Assembly Class → Part-1-Class, Part-2-Class

Instantiation relationship:

ClassName ◄------------ ObjectName

Figure 10.4   Basic UML symbols and notation

A Closer Look: Object Identification and
the Unified Modeling Language (UML)

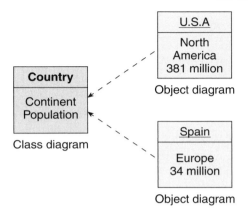

Figure 10.5 Including attributes in UML class and object diagrams

Visibility defines where an attribute can be seen—that is, whether the attribute can be used in other classes or is restricted to the class defining it. The following list explains the types of visibility and the UML notation for indicating visibility:

- *Private*—An attribute with private visibility can be used only in its defining class and can't be accessed by other classes directly. A minus sign (-) in front of the attribute name designates the attribute as private.
- *Public*—An attribute with public visibility can be used in any other class. Public visibility is indicated with a plus sign (+) in front of the attribute name.
- *Protected*—An attribute with protected visibility can be passed along to a derived class; neither a plus sign nor a minus sign is used to indicate protected visibility.

In a class diagram, an attribute's name and type are required; all other information is optional. Figure 10.6 illustrates the class diagram for a class named RoomType containing two private attributes: length and width. Notice that it includes the default values the class is expected to provide to its attributes.

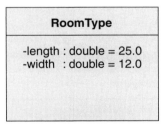

Figure 10.6 A class with attributes

Just as attributes are designated in a class diagram, so are operations. **Operations** are transformations that can be applied to attributes and are coded as C++ functions. Operation names are listed below attributes and separated from them by a line. Figure 10.7 shows two class diagrams that include operations.

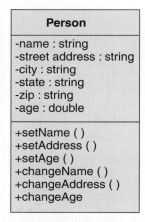

Person
-name : string -street address : string -city : string -state : string -zip : string -age : double
+setName ( ) +setAddress ( ) +setAge ( ) +changeName ( ) +changeAddress ( ) +changeAge

Gas Pump
-gallonsInTank : double -costPerGallon : double
+enablePump ( ) +disablePump ( ) +setPricePerGallon ( )

Figure 10.7   Including operations in class diagrams

Relationships

In addition to describing classes and objects, UML class and object diagrams show the relationships between classes and/or objects. The three basic relationships are association, aggregation, and generalization.

Associations between classes are typically signified by phrases such as "is related to," "is associated with," "has a," "is employed by," "works for," and so forth. This relationship is indicated by a straight line connecting two classes or objects, and the type of association is listed above or below the line. For example, Figure 10.8 shows an association between a Person and a Company. As indicated, a Company "employs" zero or more Persons. The designation of "zero or more," referred to as the **multiplicity** of the relationship, is indicated by the * symbol in the diagram. Table 10.2 lists the symbols for indicating an association's multiplicity. These symbols can be placed above or below the line connecting two classes or objects.

Company	employs ★	Person

Figure 10.8   An association

Table 10.2   UML Association Notation

Symbol	Relationship
1	One and only one
n	Exactly the specified number (n is an integer)
0..1	Zero or one
m..n	From m to n (m and n are integers)
* or 0..*	From zero to any positive integer
1..*	From one to any positive integer

An **aggregation** is a type of association in which one class or object, referred to as the whole element, "consists of" or "is composed of" other classes or objects, which are referred to as parts. For example, a sentence consists of words, which consist of characters. Therefore, characters are parts of words, which are parts of sentences. This relationship is indicated by a diamond symbol attached to the class or object representing the whole element. Figures 10.9, 10.10, and 10.11 illustrate three aggregation associations. Reading these class diagrams is easier if you replace the diamond with the words "consists of" or "is composed of." When the diamond symbol is hollow, as in Figure 10.9, it indicates that the parts can still exist independent of the whole to which they belong. In other words, even if the team is broken up or destroyed, its members can still exist.

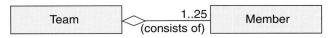

Figure 10.9 Single-level aggregation

A solid diamond symbol, as in Figures 10.10 and 10.11, indicates that the component parts are intrinsic members of the whole. Therefore, if the whole class or object is removed, its aggregate parts are also destroyed. As indicated in Figure 10.10, if a sentence is removed, all its associated words are removed. Similarly, erasing a word erases the characters in the word.

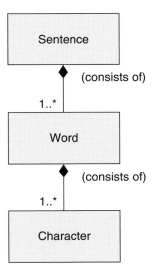

Figure 10.10 Another single-level aggregation

The last type of relationship to consider is generalization, more commonly referred to as inheritance. **Inheritance** is a relationship between a class and a derived version of the class. For example, a derived version of the class `Vehicle` can be `Land`, `Space`, or `Water`. In this case, `Vehicle` is the base class, and `Land`, `Space`, and `Water` are the derived classes. Figure 10.12 shows a class diagram of this inheritance relationship.

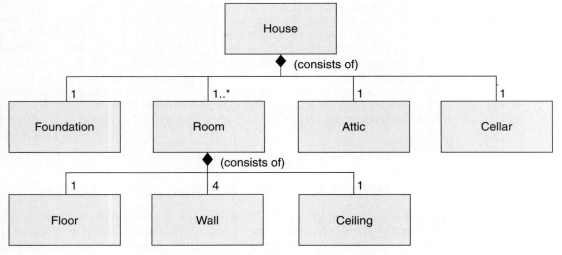

Figure 10.11 Multilevel aggregation

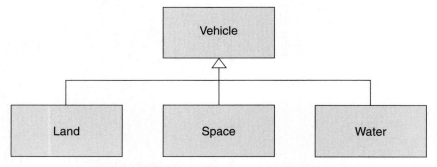

Figure 10.12 An inheritance relationship

 EXERCISES 10.4

1. **(For Review)** Define the following terms:
   a. Attribute
   b. Behavior
   c. Class
   d. Identity
   e. Model
   f. Object
   g. Object diagram
   h. State
   i. Value
   j. Operation

2. (**For Review**) Classify the following as classes or objects:

   a. Maple trees   **f.** Your Ford Taurus

   b. Ford automobiles   **g.** Kitchen tables

   c. My collie dog   **h.** Student desks

   d. The oak tree in your   **i.** The chair you're sitting on
   neighbor's yard

   e. Boeing 767 planes

3. (**Practice**) **a.** For each of the following, determine what attributes might be of interest to someone buying the item:

   i. A book

   ii. A can of soda

   iii. A pen

   iv. A CD/DVD

   v. A CD/DVD player

   vi. An elevator

   vii. A car

   b. Do the attributes you used in Exercise 3a model an object or a class of objects?

4. (**Practice**) For each of the following, what behavior might be of interest to someone buying the item?

   a. A car

   b. A CD/DVD player

   c. An elevator

5. (**Practice**) **a.** List five attributes for a character in a video game.

   b. List five behaviors that a character in a video game should have.

6. (**Practice**) **a.** List attributes and behaviors of interest in a program that simulates dealing a hand of playing cards. For this exercise, use any card game you're familiar with.

   b. What attributes of cards wouldn't be of interest for purposes of the simulation?

7. (**Practice**) **a.** List attributes and behaviors of interest in a program intended to simulate an elevator moving between the 1st to the 15th floors of a building.

   b. What attributes of the elevator wouldn't be of interest for purposes of the simulation?

8. (**Practice**) Construct a class diagram for a `Country` class. Each country has a capital city. The attributes of interest for each country are its population, size, main agricultural product, and main manufactured product.

9. (**Practice**) Construct a class diagram for a book consisting of one or more chapters, each of which consists of one or more sections.

10. **(Practice) a.** Construct a class diagram for a computer that consists of a monitor, keyboard, mouse, printer, and system box.

   b. Modify the class diagram constructed in Exercise 10a to denote that one or more monitors and keyboards might be attached to the system box, and the system might have no mouse or multiple mice.

   c. Extend the class diagram constructed for Exercise 10b to denote that the system box is composed of a CPU chip, a memory board containing zero or more RAM chips, and a case.

11. **(Practice) a.** Construct a class diagram for a single gas tank connected to one or more gas pumps. The attributes of interest for the tank are its capacity, current level, and grade of gas. The attributes of interest for a pump are the number of gallons dispensed and the cost per gallon. Additionally, a pump responds to being enabled and disabled.

   b. Modify the class diagram constructed in Exercise 11a to denote that a gas pump can be associated with more than one gas tank.

12. **(Practice)** Construct a class diagram for a class of circles that's the base class for a class of spheres and a class of cylinders.

13. **(Practice)** Construct a class diagram for a collection of cards consisting of zero or more cards. The collection of cards forms a base class for both a deck of cards and a hand of cards.

14. **(Practice)** Determine a car's major subsystems, such as brakes, steering, and so forth. Considering these subsystems as classes, construct a class diagram for a `Car` class that simply shows the associations between classes (no attributes or operations). Then determine a set of attributes and operations for each subsystem, and modify the original class diagram to include the additional information.

15. **(Practice)** Determine a cell phone's major subsystems, such as keypad, antenna, and so on. Considering these subsystems as classes, construct a class diagram for a `CellPhone` class that simply shows the associations between classes (no attributes or operations). Then determine a set of attributes and operations for each subsystem, and modify the original class diagram to include the additional information.

10.5 Common Programming Errors

Some common programming errors associated with constructing classes are as follows:

1. Failing to terminate the class declaration section with a semicolon.
2. Including a return type with the constructor's prototype or failing to include a return type with the other functions' prototypes.
3. Using the same name for a data member as for a member function.
4. Defining more than one default constructor for a class.
5. Forgetting to include the class name and scope operator, : :, in the function header of all member functions defined in the class implementation section.

All these errors result in a compiler error message.

10.6 Chapter Summary

1. A class is a programmer-defined data type. Objects of a class can be defined and have the same relationship to their class as variables do to C++'s built-in data types.

2. A class definition consists of a declaration and implementation section. The most common form of a class definition is as follows:

```
// class declaration section
class name
{
  private:
    // a list of variable declarations;
  public:
    // a list of function prototypes;
};
// class implementation section
    // class function definitions
```

   The variables and functions declared in the class declaration section are collectively called class members. The variables are referred to as class data members, and the functions are referred to as class member functions. The keywords `private` and `public` are access specifiers. After an access specifier is listed, it remains in force until another access specifier is given. The `private` keyword specifies that class members following it are private to the class and can be accessed only by member functions. The `public` keyword specifies that the class members following it can be accessed from outside the class. Generally, all data members should be specified as `private` and all member functions as `public`.

3. Class functions listed in the declaration section can be written inline, or their definitions can be included in the class implementation section. Except for constructor and destructor functions, all class functions defined in the class implementation section use this form for the function header:

   returnType className::functionName(parameter list);

   Except for the addition of the class name and scope operator, `::`, which are required to identify the function name with the class, this function header is identical to the one used for any user-written function.

4. A constructor function is a special function that's called automatically each time an object is declared. It must have the same name as its class and can't have any return type. Its purpose is to initialize each declared object.

5. If no constructor is declared for a class, the compiler supplies a default constructor. It's a do-nothing function having the definition *className::className(void){}.*

6. The term default constructor refers to any constructor that doesn't require arguments when it's called. The reason it doesn't require arguments is that no parameters are declared (as with the compiler-supplied default constructor) or all arguments have been given default values.

7. Each class can only have one default constructor. If a user-defined constructor is defined, the compiler doesn't create a default constructor.

8. Objects are created by using a C++ or C style of declaration. The C++ style of declaration has the form

   ```
   className list-of-objectNames(list of initializers);
   ```

   where the *list of initializers* is optional. An example of this style of declaration, including initializers, for a class named `Date` is as follows:

   ```
   Date a, b, c(12,25,2006);
   ```

   The objects a and b are declared to be of type `Date` and are initialized by using the default constructor; the object c is initialized with the values 12, 25, and 2006.

   The equivalent C style of declaration, including the optional list of initializers, has this form:

   ```
   className objectName = className(list of initializers);
   ```

   An example of this style of declaration for a class named `Date` is as follows:

   ```
   Date c = Date(12,25,2006);
   ```

   The object c is created and initialized with the values 12, 25, and 2006.

9. Constructors can be overloaded in the same manner as any other user-written C++ function.

10. If a constructor is defined for a class, a user-defined default constructor should also be written, as the compiler doesn't supply it.

11. A destructor function is called each time an object goes out of scope. Destructors must have the same name as their class but are preceded with a tilde (~). There can only be one destructor per class.

12. A destructor function takes no arguments and returns no value. If a user-defined destructor isn't included in a class, the compiler provides a do-nothing destructor.

Programming Projects for Chapter 10

1. (**Numerical**) **a.** Construct a class named `Cartesian` containing two floating-point data members named x and y, used to store a point's x and y values in rectangular coordinates. The member functions should include a constructor that initializes an object's x and y values to 0, functions to input and display an object's x and y values, and an assignment function that performs a memberwise assignment between two `Cartesian` objects.

   b. Include the class written for Exercise 1a in a working C++ program that creates and displays the values of two `Cartesian` objects; the second object is assigned the values of the first object.

2. (**General Math**) **a.** Construct a class named `XY_Coord` containing two floating-point data members named `xval` and `yval`, used to store a point's x and y values in Cartesian coordinates. The member functions should include constructor and display functions and a function named `convToCartesian()`. The `convToCartesian()` function should accept two floating-point numbers representing a point in polar coordinates and convert

them into Cartesian coordinates. For conversion from polar to Cartesian coordinates, use these formulas:

$x = r \cos \theta$
$y = r \sin \theta$

b. Include the program written for Exercise 2a in a working C++ program.

3. **(General Math) a.** Construct a class named `Pol_coord` containing two floating-point data members named `dist` and `theta`, used to store the distance and angle values of a point in polar coordinates. The member functions should include constructor and display functions and a function named `convToPolar()`. The `convToPolar()` function should accept two floating-point numbers representing a point in Cartesian coordinates (x and y) and convert them into polar coordinates (r and θ). For conversion from Cartesian to polar coordinates, use these formulas:

$r = \sqrt{x^2 + y^2}$

$\theta = \tan^{-1}\left(y / x\right)$

b. Include the program written for Exercise 3a in a working C++ program.

4. **(General Math) a.** Construct a class named `Savings` containing three floating-point data members named `balance`, `rate`, and `interest` and a constructor that initializes each data member to 0. Include a member function that inputs a balance and rate and then calculates an interest. The rate should be stored as a percent, such as 6.5 for 6.5%, and the interest is computed as *interest = (balance)(rate/100)*. Add a member function to display all data member values.

b. Include the class written for Exercise 4a in a working C++ program that tests each member function.

5. **(General Math) a.** Create a class named `Fractions` having two integer data members named for a fraction's numerator and denominator. The class's default constructor should provide both data members with default values of 1 if no explicit user initialization is provided. The constructor must also prohibit a 0 denominator value. Include member functions for displaying an object's data values and mathematical functions capable of adding, subtracting, multiplying, and dividing two `Fraction` objects according to the following formulas:

$$\text{Sum of two fractions}: \frac{a}{b} + \frac{c}{d} = \frac{ad + cb}{bd}$$

$$\text{Difference of two fractions}: \frac{a}{b} - \frac{c}{d} = \frac{ad - cb}{bd}$$

$$\text{Product of two fractions}: \frac{a}{b} \times \frac{c}{d} = \frac{ac}{bd}$$

$$\text{Division of two fractions}: \frac{\left(\dfrac{a}{b}\right)}{\left(\dfrac{c}{d}\right)} = \frac{ad}{bc}$$

    b. Include the class written for Exercise 5a in a working C++ program that tests each of the class's member functions.

6. **(Modify) a.** Include a member function named `gcd()` in the `Fraction` class constructed in Exercise 5a that reduces a fraction to its lowest common terms. For example, a fraction such as 2/4 is reduced to 1/2. The way to do this is divide both the numerator and denominator values by their greatest common divisor (GCD). (*Hint*: See Exercise 15 in "Programming Projects for Chapter 6" for a description of finding the greatest common divisor of two numbers.)

    b. Modify the constructor written for Exercise 6a to include a call to `gcd()` so that every initialized fraction is in lowest common terms. Also, make sure each mathematical function also uses `gcd()` to return a fraction in lowest common terms.

Chapter

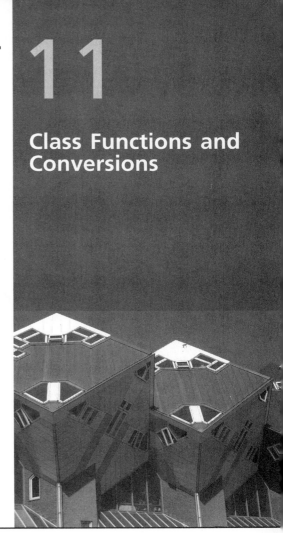

11

Class Functions and Conversions

11.1 Assignment

11.2 Additional Class Features

11.3 Operator Functions

11.4 Data Type Conversions

11.5 A Case Study: Random Numbers and Simulations

11.6 Class Inheritance

11.7 Polymorphism

11.8 Common Programming Errors

11.9 Chapter Summary

Creating a class requires providing the capability to declare, initialize, assign, manipulate, and display data members. In Chapter 10, you learned about declaring, initializing, and displaying objects. In this chapter, you continue constructing classes by providing the ability to create operator and conversion capabilities, similar to those inherent in C++'s built-in types. With these additions, your user-defined types will have all the functionality of built-in types.

11.1 Assignment

In Chapter 3, you saw how C++'s assignment operator, =, performs assignment between variables. In this section, you see how assignment works when it's applied to objects and how to define your own assignment operator to override the default one for user-defined classes. For a specific assignment example, take a look at the main() function in Program 11.1.

Program 11.1

```cpp
#include <iostream>
#include <iomanip>
using namespace std;
// class declaration section
class Date
{
  private:
    int month;
    int day;
    int year;
  public:
    Date(int = 7, int = 4, int = 2005);      // constructor
    void showDate();       // member function to display a Date
};
// class implementation section
Date::Date(int mm, int dd, int yyyy)
{
  month = mm;
  day = dd;
  year = yyyy;
}
void Date::showDate()
{
  cout << setfill('0')
       << setw(2) << month << '/'
       << setw(2) << day << '/'
       << setw(2) << year % 100;
  return;
}

int main()
{
  Date a(4,1,2007), b(12,18,2008); // declare two objects

  cout << "\nThe date stored in a is originally ";
  a.showDate();  // display the original date
  a = b;         // assign b's values to a
  cout << "\nAfter assignment the date stored in a is ";
  a.showDate();  // display a's values
  cout << endl;
  return 0;
}
```

Notice that the class implementation section of the Date class in Program 11.1 contains no assignment function. Nevertheless, you would expect the assignment statement a = b; in main() to assign b's data member values to their counterparts in a. In fact, this assignment does take place and is verified by the output produced when Program 11.1 runs:

```
The date stored in a is originally 04/01/07
After assignment the date stored in a is 12/18/08
```

The type of assignment shown in Program 11.1 is referred to as **memberwise assignment**. In the absence of any specific instructions, the C++ compiler builds this type of default assignment operator for each class. If the class doesn't contain any pointer data members, this default assignment operator is adequate and can be used without further consideration. Before seeing the problems that can occur with pointer data members, see how to construct your own explicit assignment operators.

Assignment operators, like all class members, are declared in the class declaration section and defined in the class implementation section. For the declaration of operators, however, the keyword operator must be included in the declaration. Using this keyword, a simple assignment operator declaration has this form:

```
void operator=(ClassName&);
```

The keyword void indicates that the assignment returns no value, the operator= indicates that you're overloading the assignment operator with your own version, and the class name and ampersand in parentheses indicate that the argument to the operator is a class reference. For example, to declare a simple assignment operator for the Date class, this declaration can be used:

```
void operator=(Date&);
```

The actual implementation of the assignment operator is defined in the class implementation section. For this declaration, the following implementation is suitable:

```
void Date::operator=(Date& newdate)
{
  day = newdate.day;       // assign the day
  month = newdate.month;   // assign the month
  year = newdate.year;     // assign the year
}
```

Using the reference argument in the definition of this operation is not accidental. In fact, one of the primary reasons for adding reference variables to C++ was to facilitate the construction of overloaded operators and make the notation more natural.[1] In this definition, newdate is defined as a reference to a Date class. In the body of the definition, the day

---

[1]Passing a reference is preferable to passing an object by value because it reduces the overhead of making a copy of each object's data members.

member of the object referenced by `newdate` is assigned to the `day` member of the current object, which is then repeated for the `month` and `year` members. Assignments such as `a.operator=(b);` can then be used to call the overloaded assignment operator and assign b's member values to a. For convenience, the expression `a.operator=(b)` can be replaced with `a = b;`.

Program 11.2 contains the new assignment operator in the context of a complete program. Except for the addition of the overloaded assignment operator declaration and definition, Program 11.2 is identical to Program 11.1 and produces the same output. Its usefulness is that it illustrates how you can construct your own assignment definitions. Before moving on, however, two simple modifications to the assignment operator need to be made.

 Program 11.2

```
#include <iostream>
#include <iomanip>
using namespace std;

// class declaration section
class Date
{
  private:
    int month;
    int day;
    int year;
  public:
    Date(int = 7, int = 4, int = 2005);    // constructor
    void operator=(Date&);    // define assignment of a date
    void showDate();        // member function to display a date
};

// class implementation section
Date::Date(int mm, int dd, int yyyy)
{
  month = mm;
  day = dd;
  year = yyyy;
}

void Date::operator=(Date& newdate)
{
  day = newdate.day;        // assign the day
```

☞

```
   month = newdate.month;    // assign the month
   year = newdate.year;      // assign the year
   return;
}


void Date::showDate()
{
  cout << setfill('0')
       << setw(2) << month << '/'
       << setw(2) << day << '/'
       << setw(2) << year % 100;
  return;
}
```

```
int main()
{
  Date a(4,1,2007), b(12,18,2008); // declare two objects

  cout << "\nThe date stored in a is originally ";
  a.showDate();  // display the original date
  a = b;         // assign b's value to a
  cout << "\nAfter assignment the date stored in a is ";
  a.showDate();  // display a's values
  cout << endl;

  return 0;
}
```

First, to preclude any inadvertent alteration to the object on the right-hand side of the assignment, a constant reference argument should be used. For the Date class, it takes this form:

```
void Date::operator=(const Date& newdate)
```

The final modification concerns the operation's return value. As constructed, your simple assignment operator returns no value, which precludes you from using it in multiple assignments, such as a = b = c. The reason is that overloaded operators retain the same precedence and associativity as their built-in versions. Therefore, an expression such as a = b = c is evaluated in the order a = (b = c). As assignment has been defined, unfortunately, the expression b = c returns no value, making subsequent assignment to a an error. To allow multiple assignments, a more complete assignment operation would return a reference to its class type. Because implementing this assignment requires a special class pointer, this more complete assignment operator is discussed in Chapter 12. Until then, the simple assignment operator is more than adequate for your needs.

Copy Constructors

Although assignment looks similar to initialization, it's worth noting that they are entirely different operations. In C++, an initialization occurs every time a new object is created. In an assignment, no new object is created—the value of an existing object is simply changed. Figure 11.1 illustrates this difference.

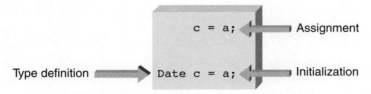

Figure 11.1   Initialization and assignment

One type of initialization that closely resembles assignment occurs in C++ when one object is initialized by using another object of the same class. For example, in the declaration

```
Date b = a;
```

or its equivalent form

```
Date b(a);
```

the b object is initialized to the previously declared a object. The constructor performing this type of initialization is called a **copy constructor**, and if you don't declare one, the compiler constructs it for you. The compiler's default copy constructor performs similarly to the default assignment operator by doing a memberwise assignment between objects. Therefore, for the declaration Date b = a;, the default copy constructor sets b's month, day, and year values to their counterparts in a.

As with default assignment operators, default copy constructors work just fine unless the class contains pointer data members. Before considering the possible complications with pointer data members and how to handle them, seeing how to construct your own copy constructor is helpful.

Copy constructors, like all class functions, are declared in the class declaration section and defined in the class implementation section. The declaration of a copy constructor has this general form:

```
ClassName(const ClassName&);
```

As with all constructors, the function name must be the class name. Also, the argument is a reference to the class, which is a characteristic of all copy constructors.[2] To ensure that the argument isn't altered inadvertently, it's always specified as a constant. Applying this general form to the Date class, a copy constructor can be declared as follows:

```
Date(const Date&);
```

---

[2]A copy constructor is often defined as a constructor whose first argument is a reference to its class type, with any additional arguments being defaults.

The actual implementation of this constructor, if it were to perform the same member-wise assignment as the default copy constructor, would take this form:

```
Date:: Date(const Date& olddate)
{
  month = olddate.month;
  day = olddate.day;
  year = olddate.year;
}
```

As with the assignment operator, using a reference argument for the copy constructor is no accident: The reference argument makes it possible to use a simple notation in the function body. Program 11.3 contains this copy constructor in the context of a complete program.

Program 11.3

```
#include <iostream>
#include <iomanip>
using namespace std;
```

```
// class declaration section
class Date
{
  private:
    int month;
    int day;
    int year;
  public:
    Date(int = 7, int = 4, int = 2005);     // constructor
    Date(const Date&);    // copy constructor
    void showDate();      // member function to display a date
};
// class implementation section
Date::Date(int mm, int dd, int yyyy)
{
  month = mm;
  day = dd;
  year = yyyy;
}
Date::Date(const Date& olddate)
{
  month = olddate.month;
  day = olddate.day;
  year = olddate.year;
}
```

```cpp
void Date::showDate()
{
  cout << setfill('0')
       << setw(2) << month << '/'
       << setw(2) << day << '/'
       << setw(2) << year % 100;
  return;
}
```

```cpp
int main()
{
  Date a(4,1,2007), b(12,18,2008); // use the constructor
  Date c(a);   // use the copy constructor
  Date d = b;  // use the copy constructor

  cout << "\nThe date stored in a is ";
  a.showDate();
  cout << "\nThe date stored in b is ";
  b.showDate();
  cout << "\nThe date stored in c is ";
  c.showDate();
  cout << "\nThe date stored in d is ";
  d.showDate();
  cout << endl;

  return 0;
}
```

Program 11.3 produces the following output:

```
The date stored in a is 04/01/07
The date stored in b is 12/18/08
The date stored in c is 04/01/07
The date stored in d is 12/18/08
```

As this output shows, the copy constructor has initialized c's and d's data members to a's and b's values. Although the copy constructor in Program 11.3 adds nothing to the functionality of the compiler's default copy constructor, it does give you the fundamentals of defining your own copy constructors.

Point of Information

Values and Identities

Apart from object behaviors, a characteristic feature of objects shared with variables is they always have a unique identity. An object's identity is what permits distinguishing one object from another. This feature isn't true of a value, such as the number 5, because all occurrences of 5 are indistinguishable from one another. Therefore, values are not considered objects in object-oriented programming languages, such as C++.

Another difference between an object and a value is that a value can never be a container whose value can change, but an object clearly can. A value is simply an entity that stands for itself.

Now consider a string such as `"Chicago"`. As a string, it's a value. However, because Chicago could also be a specific and identifiable object of the class `City`, the context in which the name is used is important. If the string `"Chicago"` is assigned to an object's `name` attribute, for example, it reverts to being a value.

Base/Member Initialization[3]

Except for the reference names `olddate` and `newdate`, a comparison of Program 11.3's copy constructor to Program 11.2's assignment operator shows them to be essentially the same function. The difference is that the copy constructor first creates an object's data members before using assignment to specify member values. Therefore, the copy constructor doesn't perform a true initialization, but a creation followed by assignment.

A true initialization has no reliance on assignment and is possible in C++ by using a **base/member initialization list**. This list can be applied only to constructor functions and can be written in two ways. The first way is inside a class's declaration section in this form:

```
ClassName(argument list) : list of data members(initializing values) {}
```

Here's an example of a default constructor performing true initialization in this form:

```
// class declaration section
public:
Date(int mo = 4, int da = 1, int yr = 2006) : month(mo), day(da), year(yr) {}
```

The second way is to declare a function prototype with defaults in the class declaration section followed by the initialization list in the class implementation section. For the `Date` constructor, it takes this form:

```
// class declaration section
public:
   Date(int = 4, int = 1, int = 2006);   // prototype with defaults

// class implementation section
Date::Date(int mo, int da, int yr) : month(mo), day(da), year(yr) {}
```

---

[3]The material in this section is presented for completeness only and can be omitted without loss of subject continuity.

Notice that in both forms, the body of the constructor function is empty. This isn't a requirement, and the body can include any subsequent operations you want the constructor to perform. The interesting feature of this type of constructor is that it clearly differentiates between the initialization tasks performed in the member initialization list (between the colon and the braces) and any subsequent assignments in the function's body. Although you won't be using this type of initialization, it's required whenever a `const` class instance variable is used.

EXERCISES 11.1

1. **(For Review)** Describe the difference between assignment and initialization.

2. **(Program) a.** Construct a class named `Time` containing three integer data members named `hours`, `mins`, and `secs` used to store hours, minutes, and seconds. The member functions should include a constructor that provides default values of 0 for each data member, a display function that prints an object's data values, and an assignment operator that performs a memberwise assignment between two `Time` objects.

   b. Include the `Time` class developed in Exercise 2a in a working C++ program that creates and displays two `Time` objects; the second object is assigned the values of the first object.

3. **(General Math) a.** Construct a class named `Complex` containing two double-precision data members named `real` and `imag`, used to store the real and imaginary parts of a complex number. The member functions should include a constructor that provides default values of 0 for each data member, a display function that prints an object's data values, and an assignment operator that performs a memberwise assignment between two `Complex` objects.

   b. Include the class written for Exercise 3a in a working C++ program that creates and displays the values of two `Complex` objects; the second object is assigned the values of the first object.

4. **(Program) a.** Construct a class named `Car` containing the following three data members: a double-precision variable named `engineSize`, a character variable named `bodyStyle`, and an integer variable named `colorCode`. The member functions should include a constructor that provides default values of 0 for each numeric data member and an X for each character variable; a display function that prints the engine size, body style, and color code; and an assignment operator that performs a memberwise assignment between two `Car` objects for each instance variable.

   b. Include the class written for Exercise 4a in a working C++ program that creates and displays two `Car` objects; the second object is assigned the values of the first object.

11.2 Additional Class Features

This section covers additional features of classes, including defining the scope of a class, creating static class members, and granting access privileges to nonmember functions. Each of these topics can be read independently of the others.

Class Scope

You learned about local and global scope in Section 6.5. As you saw, the scope of a variable defines the portion of a program where the variable can be accessed. For local variables, this scope is defined by any block inside a brace pair, {}. This block includes both the function body and any internal subblocks. Additionally, all parameters of a function are considered local function variables.

Global variables can be accessed from their point of declaration throughout the remaining portion of the file containing them, with three exceptions:

- If a local variable has the same name as a global variable, the global variable can be accessed only in the local variable's scope by using the scope resolution operator, ::.
- A global variable's scope can be extended into another file by using the keyword extern.
- The same global name can be reused in another file to define a separate and distinct variable by using the keyword static. Static global variables are unknown outside their files.

In addition to local and global scopes, each class defines an associated **class scope**. That is, names of data and function members are local to the scope of their class. Therefore, if a global variable name is reused in a class, the global variable is hidden by the class data member in the same way that a local function variable hides a global variable of the same name. Similarly, member function names are local to the class they're declared in and can be used only by objects declared for the class. Additionally, local function variables hide the names of class data members having the same name. Figure 11.2 illustrates the scope of variables and functions for the following declarations:

```
double rate;     // global scope
// class declaration section
class Test
{
  private:
    double amount, price, total;    // class scope
  public:
    double extend(double, double);  // class scope
};
```

Static Class Members

As each class object is created, it gets its own block of memory for its data members. In some cases, however, it's convenient for every instantiation of a class to share the same memory location for a specific variable. For example, in a class consisting of employee payment information, each employee is subject to the same social security tax rate. Clearly, you could make the tax rate a global variable, but this method isn't very safe. The data could be

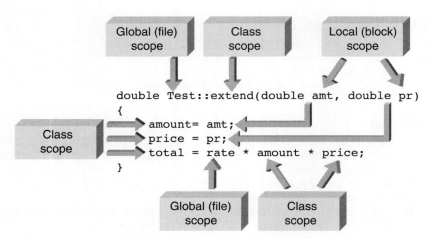

Figure 11.2 Examples of scopes

modified anywhere in the program or could conflict with an identical variable name in a function, and it certainly violates C++'s principle of data hiding.

C++ handles this situation by declaring a class variable to be static. Static class data members share the same storage space for all class objects; in this way, they act as global variables for the class and provide a means of communication between objects.

C++ requires declaring static variables in the class declaration section. To create these variables, the declared static variable must be redeclared, with or without an initial value (which defines the variable, in contrast to a formal declaration statement that doesn't allocate physical storage for the variable) and outside the class declaration section. For example, take a look at this class declaration:

```
//class declaration section
class Employee
{
  private:
    static double taxRate;
    int idNum;
  public:
    Employee(int);    //constructor
    void display();
};
```

The static variable `taxRate` is defined and initialized by using a statement such as the following:

```
double Employee::taxRate = 0.07;  // this defines taxRate
```

In this statement, the scope resolution operator, `::`, is used to identify `taxRate` as a member of the class `Employee`, and the keyword `static` is not included. Program 11.4 uses this definition in the context of a complete program.

Program 11.4

```cpp
#include <iostream>
using namespace std;

// class declaration section
class Employee
{
  private:
    static double taxRate;
    int idNum;
  public:
    Employee(int = 0);     // constructor
    void display();    // access function
};
// static member definition
double Employee::taxRate = 0.07;   // this defines taxRate
// class implementation section
Employee::Employee(int num)
{
  idNum = num;
}
void Employee::display()
{
  cout << "Employee number " << idNum
       << " has a tax rate of " << taxRate << endl;
  return;
}

int main()
{
  Employee emp1(11122), emp2(11133);

  emp1.display();
  emp2.display();

  return 0;
}
```

The output produced by Program 11.4 is as follows:

```
Employee number 11122 has a tax rate of 0.07
Employee number 11133 has a tax rate of 0.07
```

Although it might seem that the initialization of taxRate is global, it is not. After the definition is made, any other definition results in an error. Therefore, the actual definition of a static member remains the responsibility of the class creator, and a compiler error occurs if this definition is omitted.

Figure 11.3 illustrates the storage sharing produced by the static data member and the objects created in Program 11.4.

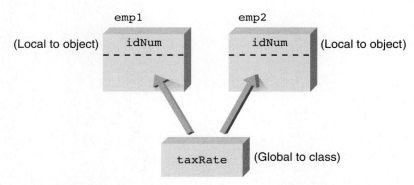

Figure 11.3   Sharing the static data member taxRate

In addition to static data members, static member functions can be created. These functions apply to a class as a whole instead of to class objects and can access only static data members and other static member functions of the class. Program 11.5 includes an example of a static member function.

 ## Program 11.5

```
#include <iostream>
using namespace std;

// class declaration section
class Employee
{
  private:
    static double taxRate;
    int idNum;
```

```
   public:
     Employee(int = 0);      // constructor
     void display();         // access function
     static void disp();     // static function
};
// static member definition
double Employee::taxRate = 0.07;
// class implementation section
Employee::Employee(int num)
{
  idNum = num;
}

void Employee::display()
{
  cout << "Employee number " << idNum
       << " has a tax rate of " << taxRate << endl;
  return;
}

void Employee::disp()
{
  cout << "The static tax rate is " << taxRate << endl;
  return;
}
```

```
int main()
{
  Employee::disp();   // call the static functions
  Employee emp1(11122), emp2(11133);

  emp1.display();
  emp2.display();

  return 0;
}
```

Program 11.5 produces the following output:

```
The static tax rate is 0.07
Employee number 11122 has a tax rate of 0.07
Employee number 11133 has a tax rate of 0.07
```

Friend Functions

The only method you currently have for accessing and manipulating a class's private variables is through the class's member functions. You can view this arrangement as illustrated in Figure 11.4a. At times, however, providing access to selected nonmember functions is useful.

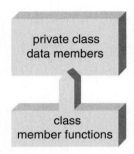

Figure 11.4a   Direct access provided to member functions

The procedure for providing this external access is simple: The class maintains an approved list of nonmember functions that are granted the same privileges as its member functions. The nonmember functions in the list are called **friend functions**, and the list is referred to as a **friends list**.

Figure 11.4b shows using a friends list for nonmember access. Any function attempting access to an object's private variables is first checked against the friends list: If the function is on the list, access is approved; otherwise, access is denied.

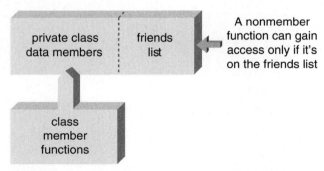

Figure 11.4b   Access provided to nonmember functions

From a coding standpoint, the friends list is simply a series of function prototype declarations preceded with the keyword `friend` and included in the class declaration section. For example, if the `addreal()` and `addimag()` functions are to be allowed access to private members of the `Complex` class, the following prototypes must be included in `Complex`'s class declaration section:

```
friend double addreal(Complex&, Complex&);
friend double addimag(Complex&, Complex&);
```

This friends list consists of two declarations. The prototypes indicate that each function returns a floating-point number and expects two references to objects of type `Complex` as arguments. Program 11.6 includes these two friend declarations in a complete program.

Program 11.6

```cpp
#include <iostream>
#include <cmath>
using namespace std;
```

```cpp
// class declaration section
class Complex
{
  // friends list
  friend double addreal(Complex&, Complex&);
  friend double addimag(Complex&, Complex&);
  private:
    double real;
    double imag;
  public:
    Complex(double = 0, double = 0);  // constructor
    void display();
};

// class implementation section
Complex::Complex(double rl, double im)
{
  real = rl;
  imag = im;
}

void Complex::display()
{
  char sign = '+';

  if(imag < 0) sign = '-';
  cout << real << sign << abs(imag) << 'i';

  return;
}
```

```
// friend implementations
double addreal(Complex &a, Complex &b)
{
  return(a.real + b.real);
}

double addimag(Complex &a, Complex &b)
{
  return(a.imag + b.imag);
}

int main()
{
  Complex a(3.2, 5.6), b(1.1, -8.4);
  double re, im;

  cout << "\nThe first complex number is ";
  a.display();
  cout << "\nThe second complex number is ";
  b.display();

  re = addreal(a,b);
  im = addimag(a,b);
  Complex c(re,im);  // create a new Complex object
  cout << "\n\nThe sum of these two complex numbers is ";
  c.display();

  return 0;
}
```

The output produced by Program 11.6 is the following:

```
The first complex number is 3.2+5.6i
The second complex number is 1.1-8.4i
The sum of these two complex numbers is 4.3-2.8i
```

In reviewing Program 11.6, notice these four points:

- Because friends are not class members, they aren't affected by the access section in which they're declared—they can be declared *anywhere in the declaration section*. The convention Program 11.6 follows is to include all friend declarations immediately following the class header.
- The keyword friend (like the keyword static) is used only in the class declaration, not in the actual function definition.

- Because a friend function is intended to have access to an object's private variables, at least one of the friend's arguments should be a reference to an object of the class that made it a friend.
- As Program 11.6 shows, it's the class that grants friend status to a function, not the other way around. A function can never confer friend status on itself because doing so violates the concepts of data hiding and access provided by a class.

EXERCISES 11.2

1. **(Modify) a.** Rewrite Program 11.5 to include an integer static variable named numemps. This variable should act as a counter that's initialized to 0 and incremented by the class constructor each time a new object is declared. Rewrite the static function disp() to display this counter's value.

   b. Test the program written for Exercise 1a. Have the main() function call disp() after each Employee object is created.

2. **(General Math) a.** Construct a class named Circle containing two integer variables named xCenter and yCenter and a double-precision variable named radius. Additionally, the class should contain a static data member named scaleFactor. The xCenter and yCenter values represent a circle's center point, radius represents the circle's actual radius, and scaleFactor represents a scale factor used to scale the circle to fit on a variety of display devices.

   b. Include the class written for Exercise 2a in a working C++ program.

3. **(Debug) a.** State whether the following three statements in Program 11.6

   ```
   re = addreal(a,b);
   im = addimag(a,b);
   Complex c(re,im);   // create a new complex object
   ```

   could be replaced by this single statement:

   ```
   Complex c(addreal(a,b), addimag(a,b));
   ```

   b. Verify your answer to Exercise 3a by running Program 11.6 with the suggested replacement statement.

4. **(Modify) a.** Rewrite the program written for Exercise 2a, but include a friend function that multiplies an object's radius by a static scaleFactor and then displays the actual radius value and the scaled value.

   b. Test the program written for Exercise 4a.

5. **(Modify)** Rewrite Program 11.6 to have only one friend function named addComplex(). This function should accept two Complex objects and return a Complex object. The real and imaginary parts of the returned object should be the sum of the real and imaginary parts of the two objects passed to addComplex().

6. **(General Math) a.** Construct a class named Coord containing two double-precision variables named xval and yval, used to store the x and y values of a point in rectangular coordinates. The class functions should include constructor and display functions and a friend function named convPol(). The convPol() function should accept two double-precision numbers representing a point in polar coordinates and convert them into rectangular coordinates. For conversion from polar to rectangular coordinates, use these formulas:

$$x = r \cos \theta$$
$$y = r \sin \theta$$

b. Include the class written for Exercise 6a in a working C++ program.

11.3 Operator Functions

You constructed a simple assignment operator in Section 11.1. In this section, you extend this capability and see how to broaden C++'s built-in operators to work with class objects. As you'll discover, class operators are also member or friend functions.

The only symbols permitted for user-defined purposes are the C++ built-in symbols listed in Table 11.1. These symbols can be adopted for class use with no limitation in their meaning by making each operation a function that can be overloaded like any other function.[4] The operation of the symbols in Table 11.1 can be redefined as you see fit for your classes, subject to the following restrictions:

- Symbols not in Table 11.1 can't be redefined. For example, the ., ::, and ?: symbols can't be redefined.
- New operator symbols can't be created. For example, because %% is not an operator in C++, it can't be defined as a class operator.
- Neither the precedence nor the associativity of C++'s operators can be modified. Therefore, you can't give the addition operator a higher precedence than the multiplication operator.
- Operators can't be redefined for C++'s built-in types.
- A unary C++ operator can't be changed to a binary operator, and a binary operator can't be changed to a unary operator.
- The operator must be a member of a class or defined to take at least one class member as an operand.

Table 11.1   Operators Available for Class Use

Operator	Description
()	Function call
[]	Array element
->	Structure member pointer reference
new	Dynamic allocation of memory

---

[4]The only limitation is that the operator's syntax can't be changed. Therefore, a binary operator must remain binary, and a unary operator must remain unary. In this syntax restriction, an operator symbol can be used to produce any operation, whether or not the operation is consistent with the symbol's accepted use. For example, you could redefine the addition symbol to provide multiplication. Clearly, this redefinition violates the intent of making these symbols available, so care has been taken to redefine each symbol in a manner consistent with its accepted use.

Table 11.1 Operators Available for Class Use (continued)

Operator	Description
delete	Dynamic deallocation of memory
++	Increment
--	Decrement
-	Unary minus
!	Logical negation
~	Ones complement
*	Indirection
*	Multiplication
/	Division
%	Modulus (remainder)
+	Addition
-	Subtraction
<<	Left shift
>>	Right shift
<	Less than
<=	Less than or equal to
>	Greater than
>=	Greater than or equal to
==	Equal to
!=	Not equal to
&&	Logical AND
||	Logical OR
&	Bit-by-bit AND
^	Bit-by-bit exclusive OR
|	Bit-by-bit inclusive OR
= += -= *= /= %= &= ^= |= <<= >>=	Assignment
,	Comma

The first step in providing a class with operators from Table 11.1 is to decide which operations make sense for the class and how they should be defined. As an example, you'll continue building on the Date class introduced previously. For this class, a small, meaningful set of class operations is defined.

Clearly, the addition of two dates is not meaningful. The addition of a date and an integer, however, does make sense if the integer is taken as the number of days to be added to the date. Likewise, subtracting an integer from a date makes sense. Also, the subtraction of two dates is meaningful if you define the difference to mean the number of days between the two dates. Similarly, it makes sense to compare two dates and determine whether the dates are equal or one date occurs before or after another date. Now see how these operations can be implemented with C++'s operator symbols.

A user-defined operation is created as a function that redefines C++'s built-in operator symbols for class use. Functions that define operations on class objects and use C++'s built-in operator symbols are referred to as **operator functions**. Operator functions are declared and implemented in the same manner as all member functions, with one exception: It's the function name that connects the operator symbol to the operation defined by the function. An operator function's name is always in the form *operator<symbol>*, where *<symbol>* is one of the operators in Table 11.1. For example, operator+ is the name of the addition function, and operator== is the name of the equal-to comparison function.

After the function name is selected, the process of writing the function simply amounts to having it accept inputs and produce the correct returned value.[5] For example, to compare two Date objects for equality, you select C++'s equality operator, and the function name becomes operator==. You want the comparison operation to accept two Date objects, compare them, and return an integer value indicating the result of the comparison: true for equality and false for inequality. As a member function, a suitable prototype to include in the class declaration section is as follows:

```
bool operator==(Date&);
```

This prototype indicates the function is named operator==, it returns a Boolean value, and it accepts a reference to a Date object.[6] Only one Date object is required because the second Date object is the object that calls the function. Now see how to write the function definition to include in the class implementation section. For the Date class, the following definition is suitable:

```
bool Date::operator==(Date& Date2)
{
  if( day == date2.day && month == date2.month && year == date2.year)
    return true;
  else
    return false;
}
```

After this function has been defined, it can be called by using the same syntax as for C++'s built-in types. For example, if a and b are objects of type Date, the expression if (a == b) is valid. Program 11.7 includes this if statement as well as this operator function's declaration and definition in the context of a complete program.

---

[5] As noted previously, an operator function can be redefined to perform any operation. Good programming practice, however, dictates writing a function to actually perform the operation implied by the function name.
[6] The prototype bool operator==(Date) works, too. Passing a reference, however, is preferable to passing an object because it reduces the function call's overhead. Overhead is reduced because passing an object means a copy of the object must be made for the called function, but passing a reference gives the function access to the object whose address is passed.

Program 11.7

```cpp
#include <iostream>
using namespace std;
// class declaration section
class Date
{
  private:
    int month;
    int day;
    int year;
  public:
    Date(int = 7, int = 4, int = 2005);  // constructor
    bool operator==(Date &);  // declare the operator== function
};
// class implementation section
Date::Date(int mm, int dd, int yyyy)
{
  month = mm;
  day = dd;
  year = yyyy;
}
bool Date::operator==(Date &date2)
{
  if(day == date2.day && month == date2.month && year == date2.year)
    return true;
  else
    return false;
}
int main()
{
  Date a(4,1,2007), b(12,18,2008), c(4,1,2007); // declare 3 objects

  if (a == b)
    cout << "Dates a and b are the same." << endl;
  else
    cout << "Dates a and b are not the same." << endl;
  if (a == c)
    cout << "Dates a and c are the same." << endl;
  else
    cout << "Dates a and c are not the same." << endl;
  return 0;
}
```

The following output is produced by Program 11.7:

```
Dates a and b are not the same.
Dates a and c are the same.
```

The first new feature shown in Program 11.7 is the declaration and implementation of the operator== function. Except for its name, this operator function is constructed in the same manner as any other member function: It's declared in the class declaration section and defined in the class implementation section.

The second new feature is how the function is called. Operator functions can be called by using their associated symbols instead of the way other functions are called. Because operator functions are true functions, however, the traditional method of calling them can also be used—specifying the function name and including appropriate arguments. Therefore, instead of being called by the expression a == b in Program 11.7, the call a.operator==(b) could have been used.

Now see how to create another operator for the Date class—an addition operator. As before, creating this operator requires specifying three items:

- The name of the operator function
- The processing the function is to perform
- The data type, if any, the function is to return

Clearly, for addition you use the operator function named operator+. Having selected the function's name, you must now determine what you want this function to do with Date objects. As noted previously, adding two dates makes no sense. Adding an integer to a date is meaningful, however, when the integer represents the number of days before or after a given date. The sum of an integer and a Date object is simply another Date object, which should be returned by the addition operation. Therefore, the following prototype is suitable for the addition function:

```
Date operator+(int);
```

This prototype, included in the class declaration section, specifies adding an integer to a class object and returning a Date object. Therefore, if a is a Date object, the function call a.operator+(284), or its more common alternative, a + 284, should cause the number 284 to be added to a's date value correctly. Next, you must construct the function to accomplish this task.

Constructing the function requires selecting a date convention first. For simplicity, adopt the financial date convention that considers each month to consist of 30 days and each year to consist of 360 days. Using this convention, the function first adds an integer number of days to the Date object's day value, and then adjusts the resulting day value to lie in the range 1 to 30 and the month value to lie in the range 1 to 12. The following function accomplishes these tasks:

```
Date Date::operator+(int days)
{
  Date temp;  // a temporary Date to store the result

  temp.day = day + days;  // add the days
  temp.month = month;
  temp.year = year;
  while (temp.day > 30)    // now adjust the months
  {
    temp.month++;
    temp.day -= 30;
  }
  while (temp.month > 12)  // adjust the years
  {
    temp.year++;
    temp.month -= 12;
  }
  return temp;      // the values in temp are returned
}
```

The important feature to notice is the use of the `temp` object. Its purpose is to ensure that none of the function's arguments, which become the operator's operands, are altered. To understand this point, consider a statement such as `b = a + 284;` that uses this operator function, where a and b are `Date` objects. This statement should never modify a's value. Rather, the expression `a + 284` should yield a `Date` value that's then assigned to b. The result of the expression is, of course, the `temp Date` object returned by the `operator+()` function. Program 11.8 uses this function in the context of a complete program.

Program 11.8

```
#include <iostream>
#include <iomanip>
using namespace std;
// class declaration section
class Date
{
  private:
    int month;
    int day;
    int year;
  public:
    Date(int = 7, int = 4, int = 2005);   // constructor
    Date operator+(int);      // overload the + operator
    void showDate();      // member function to display a date
};
```

```cpp
// class implementation section
Date::Date(int mm, int dd, int yyyy)
{
  month = mm;
  day = dd;
  year = yyyy;
}

Date Date::operator+(int days)
{
  Date temp;  // a temporary date to store the result

  temp.day = day + days;  // add the days
  temp.month = month;
  temp.year = year;
  while (temp.day > 30)     // now adjust the months
  {
    temp.month++;
    temp.day -= 30;
  }
  while (temp.month > 12)  // adjust the years
  {
    temp.year++;
    temp.month -= 12;
  }
  return temp;      // the values in temp are returned
}

void Date::showDate()
{
  cout << setfill('0')
       << setw(2) << month << '/'
       << setw(2) << day << '/'
       << setw(2) << year % 100;
  return;
}

int main()
{
  Date a(4,1,2007), b; // declare two objects
```

☞

```
cout << "The initial date is ";
a.showDate();
cout << endl;
b = a + 284;    // add in 284 days = 9 months and 14 days
cout << "The new date is ";
b.showDate();
cout << endl;

return 0;
}
```

Program 11.8 produces the following output:

```
The initial date is 04/01/07
The new date is 01/15/08
```

Operator Functions as Friends

The operator functions in Programs 11.7 and 11.8 have been constructed as class members. An interesting feature of operator functions is that, except for the operator functions =, (), [], and ->, they can also be written as friend functions. For example, if the operator+() function used in Program 11.8 is written as a friend, the following is a suitable declaration section prototype:

```
friend Date operator+(Date& , int);
```

Notice that the friend version contains a reference to a Date object that isn't in the member function version. In all cases, the friend version of a member operator function *must* contain an additional class reference that the member function doesn't require.[7] Table 11.2 lists this equivalence for both unary and binary operators.

Table 11.2 Operator Function Argument Requirements

Operator	Member Function	Friend Function
Unary	1 implicit	1 explicit
Binary	1 implicit and 1 explicit	2 explicit

Program 11.8's operator+() function, written as a friend function, is as follows:

```
Date operator+(Date& op1, int days)
{
  Date temp;  // a temporary Date to store the result

  temp.day = op1.day + days;  // add the days
  temp.month = op1.month;
  temp.year = op1.year;
  while (temp.day > 30)     // now adjust the months
```

```
    {
        temp.month++;
        temp.day -= 30;
    }
    while (temp.month > 12)   // adjust the years
    {
        temp.year++;
        temp.month -= 12;
    }
    return temp;      // the values in temp are returned
}
```

The only difference between this version and the member version is the explicit use of a `Date` argument named `op1` (an arbitrary name choice) in the friend version. Therefore, in the friend function's body, the first three assignment statements reference `op1`'s data members as `op1.day`, `op1.month`, and `op1.year`, whereas the member function simply refers to its arguments as `day`, `month`, and `year`.

In determining whether to overload a binary operator as a friend or member operator function, follow this guideline: Friend functions are more appropriate for binary functions that don't modify either of their operands (such as `==`, `+`, `-`, and so forth), and member functions are more appropriate for binary functions that modify operands (such as `=`, `+=`, and `-=`, and so forth).

EXERCISES 11.3

1. **(Program) a.** Define a *greater than* relational operator function named `operator>()` that can be used with the `Date` class declared in Program 11.7.

    b. Define a *less than* operator function named `operator<()` that can be used with the `Date` class declared in Program 11.7.

    c. Include the operator functions written for Exercises 1a and 1b in a working C++ program.

2. **(Program) a.** Define a subtraction operator function named `operator-()` that can be used with the `Date` class defined in Program 11.7. The subtraction should accept a long integer argument representing the number of days to be subtracted from an object's date and return a `Date`. In doing the subtraction, assume all months consist of 30 days and all years consist of 360 days. Additionally, an end-of-month adjustment should be made, if necessary, that converts any resulting day of 31 to a day of 30, except if the month is February. If the resulting month is February and the day is 29, 30, or 31, it should be changed to 28.

    b. Define another subtraction operator function named `operator-()` that can be used with the `Date` class defined in Program 11.7. The subtraction should yield a long integer representing the difference in days between two dates. In calculating the day difference, use the financial date convention that all months have 30 days and all years have 360 days.

    c. Include the overloaded operators written for Exercises 2a and 2b in a working C++ program.

3. **(Debug) a.** Determine whether the following addition operator function produces the same result as the function in Program 11.8:

```
Date Date::operator+(int days)    // return a Date object
{
  Date temp;

  temp.day = day + days;    // add the days in
  temp.month = month + int(day/30);  // determine total months
  temp.day = temp.day % 30;          // determine actual day
  temp.year = year + int(temp.month/12);  // determine total years
  temp.month = temp.month % 12;      // determine actual month
  return temp;
}
```

   b. Verify your answer to Exercise 3a by including the function in a working C++ program.

4. **(Modify) a.** Rewrite the equality relational operator function in Program 11.7 as a friend function.

   b. Verify the operation of the friend operator function written for Exercise 4a by including it in a working C++ program.

5. **(Modify) a.** Construct an addition operator for the `Complex` class declared in Program 11.6. It should be a member function that adds two complex numbers and returns a complex number.

   b. Add a member multiplication operator function to the class used in Exercise 5a that multiplies two complex numbers and returns a complex number.

   c. Verify the operation of the operator functions written for Exercises 5a and 5b by including them in a working C++ program.

6. **(Modify) a.** Rewrite the addition operator function in Program 11.8 to account for the actual days in a month, omitting leap years. (*Note*: This function requires an array to store the days in each month.)

   b. Verify the operation of the operator function written for Exercise 6a by including it in a working C++ program.

11.4 Data Type Conversions

Sections 3.1 and 3.3 described the conversion from one built-in data type to another. With the introduction of user-defined data types, the possibilities for conversion between data types expand to the following:

- Conversion from built-in type to built-in type
- Conversion from built-in type to class type
- Conversion from class type to built-in type
- Conversion from class type to class type

The first conversion is handled by C++'s implicit conversion rules or its explicit cast operator. The second conversion is made by using a type conversion constructor. The third and fourth conversions are made by using a conversion operator function. This section explains how to perform each conversion.

Built-in to Built-in Conversion

Sections 3.1 and 3.3 already explained conversion from one built-in data type to another. To review briefly, this type of conversion is implicit or explicit. An implicit conversion occurs in C++'s operations. For example, when a floating-point value is assigned to an integer variable, only the integer portion of the value is stored. The conversion is implied by the operation and performed automatically by the compiler.

An explicit conversion occurs when a cast is used. In C++, two cast notations exist. The older C notation has the form `(dataType)expression`, and the newer C++ notation has the function-like form `dataType(expression)`. For example, both the expressions `(int)24.32` and `int(24.32)` cause the double-precision value 24.32 to be truncated to the integer value 24.

Built-in to Class Conversion

User-defined casts for converting a built-in type to a class type are created by using constructor functions. A constructor whose first argument is not a member of its class and whose remaining arguments, if any, have default values is a **type conversion constructor**. If the first argument of a type conversion constructor is a built-in data type, the constructor can be used to cast the built-in data type to a class object. Clearly, one restriction of these functions is that, as constructors, they must be member functions.

Although this type of cast occurs when the constructor is invoked to initialize an object, it's actually a more general cast than might be evident at first glance. The reason is that a constructor function can be called explicitly after all objects have been declared, whether or not it was called previously as part of an object's declaration. Before exploring this point further, first see how to construct a type conversion constructor. Then you see how to use it as a cast independent of its initialization purpose.

The cast constructed here converts a long integer into a `Date` object, which consists of dates in the form *month/day/year* and uses the now familiar `Date` class. The long integer is used to represent dates in the form `year * 10000 + month * 100 + day`. For example, the date 12/31/2000 becomes the long integer 20001231. Dates represented in this fashion are useful for two reasons: First, this representation permits storing a date as a single integer, and second, dates are in numerically increasing date order, which makes sorting easy. For example, the date 01/03/2002, which occurs after 12/31/2001, becomes the integer 20020103, which is larger than 20011231. Because integers representing dates can exceed the size of a normal integer, these integers are always declared as `long`s.

A suitable constructor function for converting a long integer date to a date stored as a month, day, and year is as follows:

```
// type conversion constructor from long to Date
Date::Date(long findate)
{
  year = int(findate/10000.0);
  month = int((findate - year * 10000.0)/100.0);
  day = int(findate - year * 10000.0 - month * 100.0);
}
```

Program 11.9 uses this type conversion constructor as an initialization function at declaration time and as an explicit cast later in the program.

Program 11.9

```cpp
#include <iostream>
#include <iomanip>
using namespace std;
// class declaration section
class Date
{
  private:
    int month, day, year;
  public:
    Date(int = 7, int = 4, int = 2005);   // constructor
    Date(long);              // type conversion constructor
    void showDate();
};
// class implementation section
// constructor
Date::Date(int mm, int dd, int yyyy)
{
  month = mm;
  day = dd;
  year = yyyy;
}
// type conversion constructor from long to Date
Date::Date(long findate)
{
  year = int(findate/10000.0);
  month = int((findate - year * 10000.0)/100.0);
  day = int(findate - year * 10000.0 - month * 100.0);
}
// member function to display a date
void Date::showDate()
{
  cout << setfill('0')
       << setw(2) << month << '/'
       << setw(2) << day << '/'
       << setw(2) << year % 100;
  return;
}
```

☞

```
int main()
{
  Date a, b(20061225L), c(4,1,2007);   // declare 3 objects and
                                        // initialize 2 of them

  cout << "Dates a, b, and c are ";
  a.showDate();
  cout << ", ";
  b.showDate();
  cout << ", and ";
  c.showDate();
  cout << ".\n";

  a = Date(20080103L);   // cast a long to a Date

  cout << "Date a is now ";
  a.showDate();
  cout << ".\n";

  return 0;
}
```

The following output is produced by Program 11.9:

```
Dates a, b, and c are 07/04/05, 12/25/06, and 04/01/07.
Date a is now 01/03/08.
```

The change in a's date value is produced by the assignment expression a = Date(20080103L);, which uses a type conversion constructor to perform the cast from long to Date.

Class to Built-in Conversion

Conversion from a user-defined data type to a built-in data type is accomplished by using a **conversion operator function**, which is a member operator function having the name of a built-in data type or class. When the operator function has a built-in data type name, it's used to convert from a class to a built-in data type. For example, a conversion operator function for casting a class object to a long integer has the name operator long(). The operator function's name indicates that a conversion to a long takes place. If this function were part of a Date class, it would be used to cast a Date object to a long integer. This use is shown in Program 11.10.

Program 11.10

```cpp
#include <iostream>
#include <iomanip>
using namespace std;

// class declaration section
class Date
{
  private:
    int month, day, year;
  public:
    Date(int = 7, int = 4, int = 2005);    // constructor
    operator long();          // conversion operator function
    void showDate();
};

// class implementation section
// constructor
Date::Date(int mm, int dd, int yyyy)
{
  month = mm;
  day = dd;
  year = yyyy;
}

// conversion operator function converting from Date to long
Date::operator long()   // must return a long
{
  long yyyymmdd;
  yyyymmdd = year * 10000 + month * 100 + day;
  return(yyyymmdd);
}

// member function to display a date
void Date::showDate()
{
   cout << setfill('0')
        << setw(2) << month << '/'
        << setw(2) << day << '/'
        << setw(2) << year % 100;
   return;
}
```

```
int main()
{
  Date a(4,1,2007);    // declare and initialize one object of type Date
  long b;              // declare an object of type long

  b = a;               // a conversion takes place here

  cout << "a's date is ";
  a.showDate();
  cout << "\nThis date, as a long integer, is " << b << endl;

  return 0;
}
```

Program 11.10 produces the following output:

```
a's date is 04/01/07
This date, as a long integer, is 20070401
```

As this output shows, the change in a's date value to a long integer is produced by the assignment expression b = a. This assignment, which could also have been written as b = long(a), calls the conversion operator function long() to perform the cast from Date to long. In general, because explicit conversion more clearly documents what's happening, its use is preferred to implicit conversion.

Notice that the conversion operator has no explicit argument or return type, which is true of all conversion operators. The implicit argument is always an object of the class being cast from, and the return type is implied by the function's name. Additionally, as stated previously, a conversion operator function must be a member function.

Class to Class Conversion

Converting from a class data type to a class data type is done in the same manner as a conversion from a class to a built-in data type—by using a conversion operator function. In this case, however, the operator function uses the class name being converted to instead of a built-in data name. For example, if you have two classes named Date and Intdate, the operator function operator Intdate() could be placed in the Date class to convert from a Date object to an Intdate object. Similarly, the operator function Date() could be placed in the Intdate class to convert from an Intdate to a Date. Notice that as before, in converting from a class data type to a built-in data type, the operator function's name determines the result of the conversion; the class containing the operator function determines the data type being converted from.

Before seeing an example of a class to class conversion, you should note one additional point. Converting between classes clearly implies having two classes; one is always defined first, and one is defined second. Having a conversion operator function in the second class that has the same name as the first class poses no problem because the compiler knows of the first class's existence. However, including a conversion operator function with the second class's name in the first class *does* pose a problem because the second class hasn't been

defined yet. To remedy this problem, include a declaration for the second class before the
first class's definition. This declaration, formally called a **forward declaration**, is shown in
Program 11.11, which also includes conversion operators between the two defined classes.

Program 11.11

```cpp
#include <iostream>
#include <iomanip>
using namespace std;

// forward declaration of class Intdate
class Intdate;

// class declaration section for Date
class Date
{
  private:
    int month, day, year;
  public:
    Date(int = 7, int = 4, int = 2005);     // constructor
    operator Intdate();      // conversion operator from Date to Intdate
    void showDate();
};

// class declaration section for Intdate
class Intdate
{
  private:
    long yyyymmdd;
  public:
    Intdate(long = 0);      // constructor
    operator Date();   // conversion operator from Intdate to Date
    void showint();
};

// class implementation section for Date
Date::Date(int mm, int dd, int yyyy)   // constructor
{
  month = mm;
  day = dd;
  year = yyyy;
}
```

```cpp
// conversion operator function converting from Date to Intdate class
Date::operator Intdate()    // must return an Intdate object
{
  long temp;
  temp = year * 10000 + month * 100 + day;
  return(Intdate(temp));
}

// member function to display a Date
void Date::showDate()
{
  cout << setfill('0')
       << setw(2) << month << '/'
       << setw(2) << day << '/'
       << setw(2) << year % 100;
  return;
}

// class implementation section for Intdate
Intdate::Intdate(long ymd)   // constructor
{
  yyyymmdd = ymd;
}

// conversion operator function converting from Intdate to Date class
Intdate::operator Date()     // must return a Date object
{
  int mo, da, yr;
  yr = int(yyyymmdd/10000.0);
  mo = int((yyyymmdd - yr * 10000.0)/100.0);
  da = int(yyyymmdd - yr * 10000.0 - mo * 100.0);
  return(Date(mo,da,yr));
}

// member function to display an Intdate
void Intdate::showint()
{
  cout << yyyymmdd;
  return;
}
```

☞

```
int main()
{
  Date a(4,1,2007), b;       // declare two Date objects
  Intdate c(20081215L), d;   // declare two Intdate objects

  b = Date(c);        // cast c into a Date object
  d = Intdate(a);     // cast a into an Intdate object

  cout << " a's date is ";
  a.showDate();
  cout << "\n   as an Intdate object this date is ";
  d.showint();

  cout << "\n c's date is ";
  c.showint();
  cout << "\n   as a Date object this date is ";
  b.showDate();
  cout << endl;

  return 0;
}
```

Program 11.11 produces the following output:

```
a's date is 04/01/07
  as an Intdate object this date is 20070401
c's date is 20081215
  as a Date object this date is 12/15/08
```

As Program 11.11 shows, the cast from `Date` to `Intdate` is produced by the assignment `b = Date(c)`, and the cast from `Intdate` to `Date` is produced by the assignment `d = Intdate(a)`. Alternatively, the assignments `b = c` and `d = a` would produce the same results. Notice, too, the forward declaration of the `Intdate` class before the `Date` class's declaration. This forward declaration is required so that the `Date` class can reference `Intdate` in its conversion operator function.

EXERCISES 11.4

1. **(For Review) a.** Define the four data type conversions in C++ and the method of performing each conversion.

   b. Define the terms type conversion constructor and conversion operator function and describe how they are used in user-defined conversions.

2. **(Program)** Write a C++ program that declares a class named `Time` having integer data members named `hours`, `minutes`, and `seconds`. Include a type conversion constructor that converts a long integer, representing the elapsed seconds from midnight, into an equivalent representation as *hours:minutes:seconds*. For example, the long integer 30336 should convert to the time 8:25:36. Use military time so that 2:30 p.m. is represented as 14:30:00. The relationship between time representations is as follows:

   elapsed seconds = hours × 3600 + minutes × 60 + seconds

3. **(Program)** A Julian date is represented as the number of days from a known base date. The following pseudocode shows one algorithm for converting from a Gregorian date, in the form *month/day/year*, to a Julian date with a base date of 00/00/0000. All calculations in this algorithm use integer arithmetic, which means the fractional part of all divisions must be discarded. In this algorithm, M = month, D = day, and Y = year.

   If M is less than or equal to 2
     Set the variable MP = 0 and YP = Y - 1
   Else
     Set MP = int(0.4 × M + 2.3) and YP = Y
   EndIf
   T = int(YP / 4) - int(YP / 100) + int(YP / 400)
   Julian date = 365 × Y + 31 × (M - 1) + D + T - MP

   Using this algorithm, modify Program 11.10 to cast from a Gregorian `Date` object to its corresponding Julian representation as a long integer. Test your program by using the Gregorian dates 1/31/2005 and 3/16/2006, which correspond to the Julian dates 732342 and 732751.

4. **(Modify)** Modify the program written for Exercise 2 to include a conversion operator function that converts an object of type `Time` into a long integer representing the number of seconds from midnight.

5. **(Program)** Write a C++ program that has a `Date` class and a `Julian` class. The `Date` class should be the same `Date` class used in Program 11.11, and the `Julian` class should represent a date as a long integer. For this program, include a conversion operator function in the `Date` class that converts a `Date` object to a `Julian` object, using the algorithm shown in Exercise 3. Test your program by converting the dates 1/31/2006 and 3/16/2007, which correspond to the Julian dates 732707 and 733116.

6. **(Program)** Write a C++ program that has a `Time` class and an `Ltime` class. The `Time` class should have integer data members named `hours`, `minutes`, and `seconds`, and the `Ltime` class should have a long integer data member named `elsecs`, which represents the number of elapsed seconds since midnight. For the `Time` class, include a conversion operator function named `Ltime()` that converts a `Time` object to an `Ltime` object. For the `Ltime` class, include a conversion operator function named `Time()` that converts an `Ltime` object to a `Time` object.

11.5 A Case Study: Random Numbers and Simulations

There are many scientific and engineering problems in which probability must be considered or statistical sampling techniques must be used. For example, to simulate automobile traffic flow or telephone usage patterns, statistical models are required. In addition, applications such as simple computer games and more involved gaming scenarios can only be described statistically. All these statistical models require generating **random numbers**—a series of numbers whose order can't be predicted.

In practice, finding truly random numbers is hard. Dice are never perfect, cards are never shuffled completely randomly, and digital computers can handle numbers only in a finite range and with limited precision. The best you can do in most cases is generate **pseudorandom numbers**, which are random enough for the type of applications being programmed.

Some computer languages contain a library function that produces random numbers; others do not. All C++ compilers provide a general-purpose function, named rand() and defined in the Math class, for creating random numbers. This function produces a series of double-precision random numbers in the range 0.0 up to, but not including, RAND_MAX, a compiler-defined named constant.

Program 11.12 shows the general procedure for creating a series of N random numbers in C++. It uses the rand() function to generate a series of 10 random numbers.

 Program 11.12

```cpp
#include <iostream>
#include <ctime>
#include <cmath>
using namespace std;

int main()
{
  double randValue;
  int i;
  srand(time(NULL));  // this generates the first "seed" value
  for (i = 1; i <= 10; i++)
  {
    randValue = rand();
    cout << randValue << endl;
  }
  return 0;
}
```

Point of Information

Monte Carlo Techniques

Monte Carlo, a city in Monaco on France's Mediterranean coast, is famous as a gambling resort, so its name was adopted for mathematical functions involving random numbers.

Monte Carlo techniques involve creating random numbers within specified limits and determining what percentage of these numbers meet certain criteria. This technique can be used to calculate the area between curves, to estimate the arrival of airplanes at an airport, to predict the percentage of manufactured parts that will be defective, to project the growth and decline of populations with fixed resources, to specify the needed thickness of nuclear-reactor shielding, and so forth.

Monte Carlo calculations weren't feasible before the development of high-speed computers. In many cases, billions of random numbers must be generated to achieve statistically accurate results. If, on an early PC, one random number selection and test calculation requires a microsecond, a billion calculations would take about 1000 seconds (roughly 17 minutes).

Clearly, then, a computer's speed and capacity are critical for effective application of Monte Carlo techniques. With newer parallel-processing machines, which can handle many operations concurrently, the time required for Monte Carlo calculations using large data samples has been reduced to the point that Monte Carlo simulations are now routine.

The following is the output produced by one run of Program 11.12:

```
25140
17626
21997
657
31803
29419
31873
3263
13106
24521
```

Each time Program 11.12 runs, it creates a different series of 10 random numbers.

Scaling

In practice, typically you need to make one modification to the random numbers produced by the rand() function. The reason is that, in most applications, the random numbers must be integers in a specified range, such as 1 to 100. The procedure for adjusting the random numbers produced by a random-number generator to fall in a specified range is called **scaling**. Scaling random numbers to lie in the range 0.0 to 1.0 is easily done by dividing the returned value of rand() by RAND_MAX.[8] Therefore, the expression double(rand())/RAND_MAX produces a floating-point random number between 0.0 and 1.0.

---

[8]RAND_MAX is the maximum number returned by rand() and is compiler dependent.

> ## Point of Information
>
> ### Program and Class Libraries
>
> The concept of a **program library** began with FORTRAN. The FORTRAN library consisted of a group of tested and debugged mathematical routines provided with the compiler. Since then, every programming language has provided its own library of functions. In C and C++, this library, referred to as the **standard program library**, includes more than 12,000 functions declared in 15 different header files. Examples of standard library functions include `sqrt()`, `pow()`, `abs()`, `rand()`, `srand()`, and `time()`. The advantage of library functions is that they enhance program development and design by providing code known to work without the need for additional testing and debugging.
>
> With the introduction of object-oriented languages, the concept of a program library has been extended to include class libraries. A **class library** is a library of tested and debugged classes. A key practical feature of class libraries is that they help achieve the goal of code reuse. By providing tested and debugged code consisting of data and function members, class libraries furnish large sections of prewritten, reusable code ready for incorporation into new applications. Having this code available shifts the focus in writing application programs from creating new code to using predefined objects and stitching them together in a cohesive and useful way.

Scaling a random number as an integer value between 0 and N - 1 is done with the expression `int(double(rand())/RAND_MAX * N)` or `rand() % N`. For example, `int(double(rand())/RAND_MAX * 100)` produces a random integer between 0 and 99, as does the expression `rand() % 100`.

To produce an integer random number between 1 and N, you can use the expression

```
1 + int(double(rand())/RAND_MAX * N)
```

or

```
1 + rand() % N
```

For example, in simulating the roll of a die, the expression

```
1 + int(double(rand())/RAND_MAX * 6)
```

produces a random integer between 1 and 6, as does `1 + rand()%6`. In general, to produce a random integer between the numbers a and b, you can use the expression

```
a + int(double(rand())/RAND_MAX * (b + 1 - a))
```

or

```
a + rand() % (b + 1 - a)
```

Elevator Simulation

Random numbers are commonly used to simulate events, instead of going through the time and expense of constructing a real-life experiment. The example in this section illustrates the general concepts and techniques often used in constructing simulations.

In this application, you see how to simulate an elevator's operation. The required output is describing the current floor on which the elevator is stationed or passing by. Additionally, you should provide an internal elevator button that's pushed as a request to move to another floor. The elevator can travel between the 1st and 15th floor of the building in which it's situated.

Step 1   Analyze the Problem

For this application, you have one object, an elevator. The only attribute of interest is the elevator's location. The single requested service is the ability to request a change in the elevator's position (its state). Additionally, you must be able to establish the initial floor position when a new elevator is put into service. Figure 11.5 is a class diagram that includes the required attributes and operations.

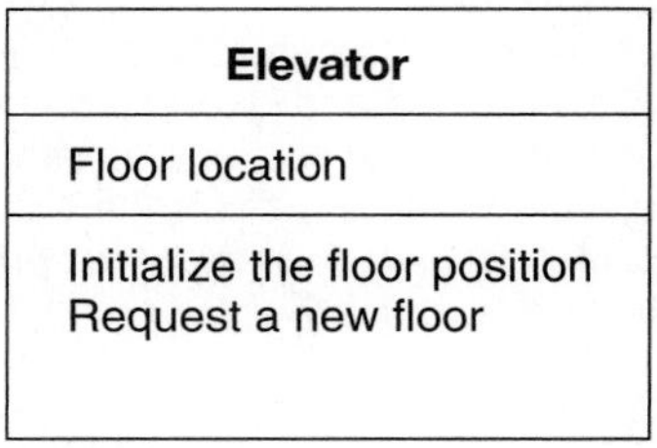

Elevator
Floor location
Initialize the floor position Request a new floor

Figure 11.5   An `Elevator` class diagram

Step 2   Develop a Solution

The elevator's location, which corresponds to its current floor position, can be represented by an integer instance variable whose value ranges between 1 and 15. The value of this variable, named currentFloor, represents the elevator's current state. Each object is also provided with a maximum floor it can travel to, which is useful for simulating multiple elevators in larger buildings. The services for changing the elevator's state are a constructor function to set the initial floor position when a new elevator is put in service and a request function to change the elevator's position (state) to a new floor. Putting an elevator into service is accomplished by declaring a single class instance (declaring an object of the class Elevator), and requesting a new floor position is equivalent to pushing an elevator button.

The response to the elevator button is described by the following algorithm:

If a request is made for a nonexistent floor or the current floor,
*   Do nothing*
ElseIf the request is for a floor above the current floor
*   Display the current floor number*
*   While not at the designated floor*
*   Increment the floor number*
*   Display the new floor number*
*   EndWhile*
*   Display the ending floor number*

☞

Else   // the request must be for a floor below the current floor
   Display the current floor number
   While not at the designated floor
      Decrement the floor number
      Display the new floor number
   EndWhile
   Display the ending floor number
EndIf

This algorithm consists of an `if-else` statement with three parts:

- If an incorrect service is requested, no action is taken.
- If a floor above the current position is selected, the elevator moves up.
- If a floor below the current position is selected, the elevator moves down.

Step 3   Code the Solution

A suitable function for the preceding algorithm can be coded by using a while loop to increment and decrement the elevator's position one floor at a time and using a cout statement to report the elevator's position, as follows:

```
void Elevator::request(int newfloor)
{
  if (newfloor < 1 || newfloor > maxFloor || newfloor == currentFloor)
    ;  // do nothing
  else if ( newfloor > currentFloor)  // move elevator up
  {
    cout << "\nStarting at floor " << currentFloor << endl;
    while (newfloor > currentFloor)
    {
      currentFloor++;    // add one to current floor
      cout << "   Going Up - now at floor " << currentFloor << endl;
    }
    cout << "Stopping at floor " << currentFloor << endl;
  }
  else  // move elevator down
  {
    cout << "\nStarting at floor " << currentFloor << endl;
    while (newfloor < currentFloor)
    {
      currentFloor--;    // subtract one from current floor
      cout << "   Going Down - now at floor " << currentFloor << endl;
    }
    cout << "Stopping at floor " << currentFloor << endl;
  }
}
```

Class 11.1 includes this function in the context of a complete class. The remaining functions in this class are straightforward. When an `Elevator` object is created, it can be initialized to a specified floor by the overloaded constructor or, if no floor is given, a default value of 1 is used. In both constructors, a default value of 15 is provided for the highest floor. This value can be altered by the `setMaxFloor()` function.

Class 11.1

```cpp
#include <iostream>
using namespace std;

class Elevator
{
  // class declaration section
  private:
    int maxFloor;
    int currentFloor;
  // function declaration section
  public:
    Elevator(); // default constructor
    Elevator(int); // overloaded constructor
    void setMaxFloor(int);
    void request(int);
};
  // class implementation section
  Elevator::Elevator()  // default constructor
  {
    currentFloor = 1;
    maxFloor = 15;
  }

  Elevator::Elevator(int cfloor)  // overloaded constructor
  {
    currentFloor = cfloor;
    maxFloor = 15;
  }
```

☞

```
void Elevator::setMaxFloor(int max)
{
  maxFloor = max;
}
void Elevator::request(int newfloor)
{
  if (newfloor < 1 || newfloor > maxFloor || newfloor == currentFloor)
    ;  // do nothing
  else if ( newfloor > currentFloor)  // move elevator up
  {
    cout << "\nStarting at floor " << currentFloor << endl;
    while (newfloor > currentFloor)
    {
      currentFloor++;    // add one to current floor
      cout << "   Going Up - now at floor " << currentFloor << endl;
    }
    cout << "Stopping at floor " << currentFloor << endl;
  }
  else  // move elevator down
  {
    cout << "\nStarting at floor " << currentFloor << endl;
    while (newfloor < currentFloor)
    {
      currentFloor--;    // subtract one from current floor
      cout << "   Going Down - now at floor " << currentFloor << endl;
    }
    cout << "Stopping at floor " << currentFloor << endl;
  }
}
```

Step 4 Test and Correct the Program

Testing the `Elevator` class requires putting an elevator into service, and then requesting various floors and seeing that the elevator responds correctly. Putting an elevator in service is accomplished by creating an object of type `Elevator`, and requesting a new floor position is equivalent to pushing an elevator button. Program 11.13 accomplishes these tasks.

Program 11.13

```
#include <iostream>
using namespace std;
```

☞

```
class Elevator
{
  // class declaration section
  private:
    int maxFloor;
    int currentFloor;
  // function declaration section
  public:
    Elevator(); // default constructor
    Elevator(int); // overloaded constructor
    void setMaxFloor(int);
    void request(int);
};
  // class implementation section
  Elevator::Elevator()  // default constructor
  {
    currentFloor = 1;
    maxFloor = 15;
  }

  Elevator::Elevator(int cfloor)  // overloaded constructor
  {
    currentFloor = cfloor;
    maxFloor = 15;
  }
  void Elevator::setMaxFloor(int max)
  {
    maxFloor = max;
  }
  void Elevator::request(int newfloor)
  {
    if (newfloor < 1 || newfloor > maxFloor || newfloor == currentFloor)
      ;  // do nothing
    else if ( newfloor > currentFloor)  // move elevator up
    {
      cout << "\nStarting at floor " << currentFloor << endl;
      while (newfloor > currentFloor)
      {
        currentFloor++;    // add one to current floor
        cout << "   Going Up - now at floor " << currentFloor << endl;
      }
      cout << "Stopping at floor " << currentFloor << endl;
    }
```

☞

```
      else  // move elevator down
      {
        cout << "\nStarting at floor " << currentFloor << endl;
        while (newfloor < currentFloor)
        {
          currentFloor--;    // subtract one from current floor
          cout << "   Going Down - now at floor " << currentFloor << endl;
        }
        cout << "Stopping at floor " << currentFloor << endl;
      }
    }
```

```
int main()
{
  Elevator a;   // declare 1 object of type Elevator

  a.request(16);      // try to go above the highest floor
  a.setMaxFloor(6);   // set the highest floor for this elevator
  a.request(7);       // try to go above the new maximum floor

  a.request(6);
  a.request(3);

  return 0;

}
```

Program 11.13 produces the following output:

```
Starting at floor 1
   Going Up - now at floor 2
   Going Up - now at floor 3
   Going Up - now at floor 4
   Going Up - now at floor 5
   Going Up - now at floor 6
Stopping at floor 6

Starting at floor 6
   Going Down - now at floor 5
   Going Down - now at floor 4
   Going Down - now at floor 3
Stopping at floor 3
```

The first statement in Program 11.13's main() function creates an object of type Elevator that can be accessed with the reference variable named a. Because no explicit floor has been given, this elevator begins at floor 1, which is provided by the default constructor. A request is then made to move the elevator to floor 16. Because this floor number exceeds the highest floor this elevator can travel to, no elevator movement is displayed. This sequence of no movement is repeated by setting the maximum floor value to 6, and then requesting that the elevator travel to the 7th floor. The next two statements, however, cause the elevator to move by using a request to move to the 6th floor, followed by a request to move to the 3rd floor.

In Program 11.13, notice the control the `main()` function provides. This sequential control, with subsequent calls made to various class functions and using different argument values, is suitable for testing purposes. However, by incorporating calls to `request()` inside a `while` loop and using the random number function `Math.random()` to generate random floor requests, a continuous simulation of the elevator's operation is possible (see Exercise 5).

EXERCISES 11.5

1. **(Practice)** Enter and execute Program 11.13 on your computer.

2. **(Modify) a.** Modify the `main()` function in Program 11.13 to put a second elevator in service starting at the 5th floor. Have this second elevator move to the 1st floor and then move to the 12th floor.

   b. Verify that the constructor function is called by adding a message in the constructor that's displayed each time a new object is created. Run your program to verify its operation.

3. **(Modify)** Modify the `main()` function in Program 11.13 to use a `while` loop that calls the `Elevator`'s `request()` function with a random number between 1 and 15. If the random number is the same as the elevator's current floor, generate another request. The `while` loop should terminate after five valid requests have been made and be satisfied by movement of the elevator.

4. **(Statistics) a.** Construct a class named `Person`. The class should have no attributes, a single constructor function, and two member functions named `arrive()` and `request()`. The constructor function should be an empty, do-nothing function. The `arrive()` function should return a random number between 1 and 10, and the `request()` function should provide a random number between 1 and 15.

   b. Test the `Person` class functions written for Exercise 4a in a complete working program.

   c. Use the `Person` class functions to simulate a random arrival of a person and a random request for a floor to which the elevator should take this person.

5. **(Modify)** Using the `Elevator` class defined in this section and the `Person` class created in Exercise 4, construct a simulation in which a person arrives randomly at any time from 1 to 10 minutes on any floor and calls the elevator. If the elevator isn't on the floor where the person is, it must move to the floor the person is on. After the person is inside the elevator, he or she can select any floor except the current one. Run the simulation for three randomly arriving people and have the simulation display the elevator's movement.

6. **(Statistics)** Create a coin toss simulation that simulates flipping a single coin 1000 times. Knowing that any single toss has a 50% chance of being a head or a tail, designate a "head" as any number equal to or greater than 0.5 and any other result as a "tail." Use the following algorithm, knowing that the final number of tails can be calculated as *1000 - number of heads.*

> **Coin toss algorithm**
> **For 1000 times**
>   **Generate a random number between 0 and 1**
>   **If the random number is equal to or greater than 0.5, increment the heads count**
>   **Increment the tosses count**
> **End For**

After all 1000 flips have been made, the algorithm for the calculating the percentages of heads and tails for the final output your program displays is as follows:

> **Percentage algorithm**
> **If the number of tosses equals zero**
>   **Display a message indicating that no tosses were made**
> **Else**
>   **Calculate the number of tails as the number of tosses minus the number of heads**
>   **Display the number of tosses, number of heads, and number of tails**
>   **Calculate the percentage of heads as the number of heads divided by the number of tosses × 100%**
>   **Calculate the percentage of tails as the number of tails divided by the number of tosses × 100%**
>   **Print the percentage of heads and tails**
> **EndIf**

7. **(Modify)** Modify the program written for Exercise 6 so that it requests the number of tosses from the user. (*Hint:* Make sure to have the program correctly determine the percentages of heads and tails obtained.)

11.6 Class Inheritance

The ability to create new classes from existing ones is the underlying motivation and power behind class- and object-oriented programming techniques. Doing so facilitates reusing existing code in new ways without the need for retesting and validation. It also permits designers of a class to make it available to others for additions and extensions without relinquishing control over existing class features.

Constructing one class from another is accomplished by using **inheritance**, which is the capability of deriving one class from another class. Related to this capability is an equally important feature called **polymorphism** that allows redefining how member functions of related classes operate, based on the class object being referenced. In fact, for a programming language to be classified as an object-oriented language, it must provide the features of classes, inheritance, and polymorphism. This section describes the inheritance and polymorphism features in C++.

The initial class used as the basis for a derived class is referred to as the **base**, **parent**, or **superclass**. The **derived class**, also referred to as the **child class** or **subclass**, is a new class incorporating all the data members and member functions of its base class. However, it can, and usually does, add its own new data members and member functions and can override any base class function.

As an example of inheritance, consider three geometric shapes: a circle, a cylinder, and a sphere. All these shapes share a common characteristic—a radius. Therefore, you can make the circle a base type for the other two shapes, as illustrated in Figure 11.6. By convention, arrows always point from the derived class to the base class. In this example, the circle is the base class, and the cylinder and sphere are the derived classes.

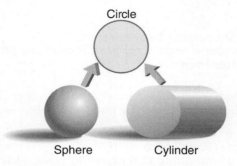

Figure 11.6   Relating object types

The relationships illustrated in Figure 11.6 are examples of **simple inheritance**, in which each derived type has only one base type. The complement to simple inheritance is **multiple inheritance**, in which a derived type has two or more base types. Figure 11.7 illustrates an example of multiple inheritance, but only simple inheritance is discussed in this section.

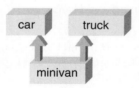

Figure 11.7   An example of multiple inheritance

The class derivations in Figures 11.6 and 11.7 are formally referred to as **class hierarchies** because they illustrate the hierarchy, or order, in which one class is derived from another. With this information as background, now you can see how to derive one class from another.

A derived class has the same form as any other class: It consists of both a declaration and an implementation. The only difference is in the first line of the declaration section. For a derived class, this line is extended to include an access specifier and a base class name in this form:

class derivedClassName : classAccess baseClassName

For example, if `Circle` is the name of an existing class, a new class named `Cylinder` can be derived as follows:

```
class Cylinder : public Circle
{
    // place any additional data members and
    // member functions in here
};  // end of Cylinder class declaration
```

Point of Information

Object-Based Versus Object-Oriented Languages

In an **object-based** language, data and operations can be incorporated together in such a way that data values can be isolated and accessed through the specified class functions. The capability to bind data members with operations in a single unit is referred to as encapsulation. In C++, encapsulation is provided by its class capability.

For a language to be classified as **object-oriented**, it must also provide inheritance and polymorphism. As discussed, inheritance is the capability to derive one class from another. A derived class incorporates all the data members and member functions of the parent class and can add its own data and function members. Polymorphism permits using the same function name to call one operation in a parent class's objects and a different operation in a derived class's objects.

C++, which provides encapsulation, inheritance, and polymorphism, is a true object-oriented language. Because C, which is C++'s predecessor, doesn't provide these features, it's not an object-based or object-oriented language.

Except for the class-access specifier after the colon and the base class name, there's nothing new or complicated about the construction of the Cylinder class. Before providing a description of the Circle class and adding data and function members to the derived Cylinder class, you need to reexamine access specifiers and how they relate to derived classes.

Access Specifications

Until now, you have used only private and public access specifiers in a class. Giving all data members private status ensures that they can be accessed only by class member functions or friends. This restricted access prevents access by any nonclass functions (except friends) but also precludes access by any derived class functions. This restriction is sensible because without it, anyone could bypass the private restriction simply by deriving a class.

To retain restricted access across derived classes, C++ provides a third access specification—protected. A **protected access** behaves the same as private access, in that it permits access only to member or friend functions, but it permits any derived class to inherit this restriction. The derived class then defines the type of inheritance it's willing to take on, subject to the base class's access restrictions. This definition is done by the class-access specifier, which is listed after the colon at the start of the class declaration section. Table 11.3 lists the derived class member access resulting from the base class member specifications and the derived class-access specifier.

The shaded region in Table 11.3 shows that if the base class member has a protected access and the derived class-access specifier is public, the derived class member is protected to its class. Similarly, if the base class has a public access and the derived class-access specifier is public, the derived class member is public. These specifications for base class data members and member functions are the most commonly used, so they are the ones used in this section. So for all classes intended for use as a base class, a protected data member access is used instead of a private designation.

Table 11.3 Inherited Access Restrictions

Base Class Member	Derived Class-Access Specifier	Derived Class Member
private	`: private`	inaccessible
protected	`: private`	private
public	`: private`	private
private	`: public`	inaccessible
protected	`: public`	protected
public	`: public`	public
private	`: protected`	inaccessible
protected	`: protected`	protected
public	`: protected`	protected

An Example To understand the process of deriving one class from another, examine deriving a Cylinder class from a base Circle class. The definition of the Circle class is as follows:

```
// class declaration section
class Circle
{
  protected:
    double radius;
  public:
    Circle(double = 1.0);  // constructor
    double calcval();
};

// class implementation section
Circle::Circle(double r)  // constructor
{
  radius = r;
}

// calculate the area of a circle
double Circle::calcval()
{
  return(PI * radius * radius);
}
```

Except for substituting the access specifier protected in place of the usual private specifier for the data member, this code is a standard class definition. The only variable not defined is PI, which is used in the calcval() function. It's defined as follows:

```
const double PI = 2.0 * asin(1.0);
```

This definition is simply a "trick" that forces the computer to return the value of PI accurate to as many decimal places as your computer allows. This value is obtained by taking the arcsin of 1.0, which is $\pi/2$, and multiplying the result by 2.

Having defined the base class, you can now extend it to a derived class, which has this definition:

```
// class declaration section where Cylinder is derived from Circle
class Cylinder : public Circle
{
  protected:
    double length;   // add one additional data member and
  public:            // two additional member functions
  Cylinder(double r = 1.0, double l = 1.0) : Circle(r), length(l) {}
  double calcval();
};

// class implementation section
double Cylinder::calcval()   // this calculates a volume
{
  return (length * Circle::calcval()); // note the base function call
}
```

This definition encompasses several important concepts related to derived classes. First, as a derived class, Cylinder contains all the data members and member functions of its base class, Circle, plus any of its own members it might add. In this case, the Cylinder class consists of a radius data member, inherited from the Circle class, plus a length data member. Therefore, each Cylinder object contains two data members, as shown in Figure 11.8.

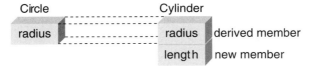

Figure 11.8 Relationship between Circle and Cylinder data members

In addition, the Cylinder class inherits Circle's member functions. This inheritance is shown in the Cylinder constructor, which uses a base/member initialization list (see Section 11.1) that calls the Circle constructor. It's also shown in Cylinder's calcval() function, which makes a call to Circle::calcval().

In both classes, the same function name, calcval(), has been used to illustrate overriding a base function with a derived function. When a Cylinder object calls calcval(), it's a request to use the Cylinder version of the function; a Circle object call to calcval() is a request to use the Circle version. In this case, the Cylinder class can access only the class version of calcval() by using the scope resolution operator, as in the call Circle::calcval(). Program 11.14 uses these two classes in the context of a complete program.

Program 11.14

```cpp
#include <iostream>
#include <cmath>
using namespace std;

const double PI = 2.0 * asin(1.0);

// class declaration section
class Circle
{
  protected:
    double radius;
  public:
    Circle(double = 1.0);   // constructor
    double calcval();
};

// class implementation section for Circle
Circle::Circle(double r)   // constructor
{
  radius = r;
}

// calculate the area of a circle
double Circle::calcval()
{
  return(PI * radius * radius);
}
// class declaration section where Cylinder is derived from Circle
class Cylinder : public Circle
{
  protected:
    double length;  // add one additional data member and
  public:           // two additional member functions
    Cylinder(double r = 1.0, double l = 1.0) : Circle(r), length(l) {}
    double calcval();
};
// class implementation section for Cylinder
double Cylinder::calcval()   // this calculates a volume
{
  return (length * Circle::calcval()); // note the base function call
}
```

☞

```
int main()
{
  Circle circle_1, circle_2(2);  // create two Circle objects
  Cylinder cylinder_1(3,4);       // create one Cylinder object

  cout << "The area of circle_1 is " << circle_1.calcval() << endl;
  cout << "The area of circle_2 is " << circle_2.calcval() << endl;
  cout << "The volume of cylinder_1 is " << cylinder_1.calcval() << endl;

  circle_1 = cylinder_1;  // assign a Cylinder to a Circle

  cout << "\nThe area of circle_1 is now " << circle_1.calcval() << endl;
  return 0;
}
```

Program 11.14 produces the following output:

```
The area of circle_1 is 3.14159
The area of circle_2 is 12.5664
The volume of cylinder_1 is 113.097


The area of circle_1 is now 28.2743
```

The first three output lines are straightforward and are produced by the first three cout statements in the program. As the output shows, a call to calcval() with a Circle object activates the Circle version of this function, and a call to calcval() with a Cylinder object activates the Cylinder version.

The assignment statement circle_1 = cylinder_1; introduces another important relationship between a base and derived class: *A derived class object can be assigned to a base class object.* This relationship shouldn't be surprising because base and derived classes share a common set of data member types. In this type of assignment, only this set of data members, which consists of all the base class data members, is assigned. Therefore, as illustrated in Figure 11.9, the Cylinder to Circle assignment results in the following memberwise assignment:

```
circle_1.radius = cylinder_1.radius;
```

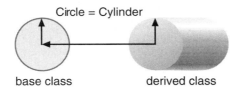

Figure 11.9 An assignment from derived to base class

The `length` data member of the `Cylinder` object isn't used in the assignment because it has no equivalent variable in the `Circle` class. The reverse cast, from base to derived class, isn't as simple and requires a constructor to correctly initialize the derived class members that aren't in the base class.

Before leaving Program 11.14, one other point should be made. Although the `Circle` constructor was called explicitly by using a base/member initialization list for the `Cylinder` constructor, an implicit call could have been made. In the absence of an explicit derived class constructor, the compiler automatically calls the default base class constructor first, before the derived class constructor is called. This order of calling works because the derived class contains all the base class data members. In a similar fashion, destructor functions are called in the reverse order—first derived class and then base class.

EXERCISES 11.6

1. **(For Review)** Define the following terms:

   a. inheritance

   b. base class

   c. derived class

   d. simple inheritance

   e. multiple inheritance

   f. class hierarchy

2. **(For Review)** Describe the difference between a private and a protected class member.

3. **(For Review)** What three features must a programming language provide to be classified as an object-oriented language?

4. **(Modify) a.** Modify Program 11.14 to include a derived class named `Sphere` from the base `Circle` class. The only additional class members of `Sphere` should be a constructor and a `calcval()` function that returns the sphere's volume. (*Note: Volume* = $4/3 \, \pi r^3$.)

   b. Include the class constructed for Exercise 4a in a working C++ program. Have your program call all the member functions in the `Sphere` class.

5. **(General Math) a.** Create a base class named `Point` consisting of x and y data members representing point coordinates. From this class, derive a class named `Circle` with another data member named `radius`. For this derived class, the x and y data members represent a circle's center coordinates. The member functions of the `Point` class should consist of a constructor, an `area()` function that returns 0, and a `distance()` function that returns the distance between two points, (x_1, y_1) and (x_2, y_2), where

$$distance = \sqrt{(x_2 - x_1)^2 + (y_2 - y_1)^2}$$

   Additionally, the derived class should have a constructor and an override function named `area()` that returns a circle's area.

   b. Include the classes constructed for Exercise 5a in a working C++ program. Have your program call all the member functions in each class. In addition, call the base class `distance()` function with two `Circle` objects and explain the result this function returns.

6. **(Modify) a.** Using the classes constructed for Exercise 5a, derive a class named `Cylinder` from the `Circle` class. The `Cylinder` class should have a constructor and a member function named `area()` that determines a cylinder's surface area. For this function, use the algorithm *surface area = 2 π r (l + r)*, where *r* is the radius of the cylinder and *l* is the length.

    b. Include the classes constructed for Exercise 6a in a working C++ program. Have your program call all the member functions in the `Cylinder` class.

    c. What do you think the result might be if the `Point` (base) class's `distance()` function is called with two `Cylinder` objects?

11.7 Polymorphism

Overriding a base member function by using an overloaded derived member function, as shown with the `calcval()` function in Program 11.14, is an example of polymorphism. As defined previously, polymorphism permits using the same function name to invoke one response in a base class's objects and another response in a derived class's objects. In some situations, however, this method of overriding doesn't work the way you might want. To understand why, take a look at Program 11.15.

 ## Program 11.15

```cpp
#include <iostream>
#include <cmath>
using namespace std;
```

```cpp
// class declaration section for the base class
class One
{
  protected:
    double a;
  public:
    One(double = 2.0);    // constructor
    double f1(double);    // a member function
    double f2(double);    // another member function
};
// class implementation section for One
One::One(double val)    // constructor
{
  a = val;
}
```

☞

```cpp
double One::f1(double num)   // a member function
{
  return(num/2);
}

double One::f2(double num)   // another member function
{
  return( pow(f1(num),2) );   // square the result of f1()
}

// class declaration section for the derived class
class Two : public One
{
  public:
    double f1(double);     // this overrides class One's f1()
};

// class implementation section for Two
double Two::f1(double num)
{
  return(num/3);
}
```

```cpp
int main()
{
  One object_1;   // object_1 is an object of the base class
  Two object_2;   // object_2 is an object of the derived class

  // call f2() using a base class object call
  cout << "The computed value using a base class object call is "
       << object_1.f2(12) << endl;

  // call f2() using a derived class object call
  cout << "The computed value using a derived class object call is "
       << object_2.f2(12) << endl;

  return 0;
}
```

The following output is produced by Program 11.15:

```
The computed value using a base class object call is 36
The computed value using a derived class object call is 36
```

As this output shows, the same result is obtained, no matter which object type calls the f2() function, because the derived class doesn't have an override of the base class f2() function. Therefore, both calls to f2() result in the base class f2() function being called.

After the base class f2() function is called, it always calls the base class version of f1() rather than the derived class override version. This behavior is caused by a process referred to as **function binding**. In normal function calls, **static binding** is used, meaning the determination of which function is called is made at compile time. Therefore, when the compiler first encounters the f1() function in the base class, it makes the determination that whenever f2() is called, from either a base or derived class object, it subsequently calls the base class f1() function.

In place of static binding, you would like a binding method capable of determining which function should be called at runtime, based on the object type making the call. This type of binding, referred to as **dynamic binding**, is achieved in C++ with virtual functions. A **virtual function** tells the compiler to create a pointer to a function, but not fill in the pointer's value until the function is actually called. Then at runtime, *based on the object making the call*, the appropriate function address is used.

Creating a virtual function is easy—simply place the keyword virtual before the function's return type in the declaration section. For example, examine Program 11.16, which is identical to Program 11.15, except for the virtual declaration of the f1() function.

 Program 11.16

```cpp
#include <iostream>
#include <cmath>
using namespace std;
```

```cpp
// class declaration section for the base class
class One
{
  protected:
    double a;
    public:
    One(double = 2.0);    // constructor
    virtual double f1(double);   // a member function
    double f2(double);    // another member function
};
```

☞

```cpp
// class implementation section for One
One::One(double val)    // constructor
{
  a = val;
}

double One::f1(double num)   // a member function
{
  return(num/2);
}

double One::f2(double num)   // another member function
{
  return( pow(f1(num),2) );   // square the result of f1()
}

// class declaration section for the derived class
class Two : public One
{
  public:
    virtual double f1(double);    // this overrides class One's f1()
};

// class implementation section for Two
double Two::f1(double num)
{
  return(num/3);
}
```

```cpp
int main()
{
  One object_1;  // object_1 is an object of the base class
  Two object_2;  // object_2 is an object of the derived class

  // call f2() using a base class object call
  cout << "The computed value using a base class object call is "
       << object_1.f2(12) << endl;

  // call f2() using a derived class object call
  cout << "The computed value using a derived class object call is "
       << object_2.f2(12) << endl;

  return 0;
}
```

Program 11.16 produces the following output:

```
The computed value using a base class object call is 36
The computed value using a derived class object call is 16
```

As this output shows, the f2() function now calls different versions of the overloaded f1() function based on the object type making the call. Basing the selection on the object making the call is the classic definition of polymorphic behavior and is caused by the dynamic binding imposed on f1() because it's a virtual function.

After a function is declared as virtual, it remains virtual for the next derived class, with or without a virtual declaration in the derived class. Therefore, the second virtual declaration in the derived class isn't strictly necessary but should be included for clarity and to make sure any subsequently derived classes inherit the function correctly.

In the inheritance diagram in Figure 11.10, class C is derived from class B and class B is derived from class A.[9] In this situation, if the f1() function is virtual in class A but not declared in class B, it isn't virtual in class C. The only other requirement is that after a function has been declared as virtual, the return type and parameter list of all subsequent derived class override versions *must* be the same.

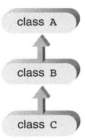

Figure 11.10 An inheritance diagram

EXERCISES 11.7

1. **(Practice)** Enter and execute Programs 11.15 and 11.16 so that you understand the relationship between function calls in each program.

2. **(For Review)** Describe the difference between static binding and dynamic binding.

3. **(For Review)** Describe the difference between a virtual function and a nonvirtual function.

4. **(For Review)** Explain what polymorphism is and provide an example of polymorphic behavior.

5. **(For Review)** Describe the two methods C++ provides for implementing polymorphism.

---

[9]By convention, as noted previously in Section 11.6, arrows always point from the derived class to the base class.

6. **(For Review)** Explain whether the multiplication operator provided for integer and double-precision built-in types is an example of overloading or polymorphism.

11.8 Common Programming Errors

1. Using a user-defined assignment operator in a multiple assignment expression when the operator hasn't been defined to return an object.
2. Using the keyword `static` when defining a static data member or member function. The `static` keyword should be used only in the class declaration section.
3. Using the keyword `friend` when defining a friend function. The `friend` keyword should be used only in the class declaration section.
4. Failing to instantiate static data members before creating class objects that must access these data members.
5. Attempting to redefine an operator's meaning as it applies to C++'s built-in data types.
6. Redefining an overloaded operator to perform a function not indicated by its conventional meaning. Although this method works, it's an example of bad programming practices.
7. Attempting to make a conversion operator function a friend rather than a member function.
8. Attempting to specify a return type for a conversion operator function.
9. Attempting to override a virtual function without using the same type and number of arguments as the original function.
10. Using the keyword `virtual` in the class implementation section. Functions are declared as virtual only in the class declaration section.

11.9 Chapter Summary

1. An assignment operator can be declared for a class with this function prototype:

```
void operator=(className&);
```

The argument is a reference to the class name. The return type of `void` precludes using this operator in multiple assignment expressions, such as a = b = c.

2. A type of initialization that closely resembles assignment occurs in C++ when one object is initialized by using another object of the same class. The constructor performing this type of initialization is called a copy constructor and has this function prototype:

```
className(const className&);
```

It's often represented with the notation `X(X&)`.

3. Each class has an associated class scope, which is defined by the brace pair, { }, containing the class declaration. Data and function members are local to the scope of their class and can be used only by objects declared for the class. If a global variable name is reused in a class, the global variable is hidden by the class variable. Within the scope of the class variable, the global variable can be accessed by using the scope resolution operator, `: :`.

4. For each class object, a separate set of memory locations is reserved for all data members, except those declared as static. A static data member is shared by all class objects and provides a means of communication between objects. Static data members must be declared in the class declaration section and are defined outside the declaration section.

5. Static function members apply to the class as a whole rather than to separate objects. Therefore, a static function member can access only static data members and other static function members. Any static function members must be declared in the class declaration section and are defined outside the declaration section.

6. A nonmember function can access a class's private data members if it's granted friend status by the class. This is done by declaring the function as a friend in the class's declaration section. Therefore, the class always determines which nonmember functions are friends; a function can never confer friend status on itself.

7. User-defined operators can be constructed for classes by using operator functions. An operator function has the form *operator<symbol>*, where *<symbol>* is one of the following:

```
()   []   ->   new   delete   ++   --   !   ~   *   /   %   +   -
<<   >>   <   <=   >   >=   ++   !=   &&   ||   &   ^   |   =   +=
-=   *=   /=   %=   &=   ^=   |=   <<=   >>=   ,
```

For example, the function prototype `Date operator+(int);` declares that the addition operator is defined to accept an integer and return a `Date` object.

8. User-defined operators can be called in one of two ways—as a conventional function with arguments or as an operator function. For example, for an operator function having the function header

```
Date Date::operator+(int)
```

if `dte` is an object of type `Date`, the following two calls produce the same effect:

```
dte.operator+(284)
dte + 284
```

9. Operator functions can also be written as friend functions. The friend version of an operator function always contains an additional class reference that isn't required by the member function.

10. There are four categories of data type conversions:

   - Built-in types to built-in types
   - Built-in types to class types
   - Class types to built-in types
   - Class types to class types

   Built-in to built-in type conversions are done by using C++'s implicit conversion rules or its explicit cast operator. Built-in to class type conversions are done by using type conversion constructors. Conversions from class types to built-in types or from class types to class types are done by using conversion operator functions.

11. A type conversion constructor is a constructor whose first argument is not a member of its class and whose remaining arguments, if any, have default values.

12. A conversion operator function is a member operator function having the name of a class. It has no explicit arguments or return type; rather, the return type is the name of the function.

13. Inheritance is the capability of deriving one class from another class. The initial class used as the basis for the derived class is referred to as the base, parent, or superclass. The derived class is also referred to as the child class or subclass.

14. Base class functions can be overridden by derived class functions with the same name. The override function is simply an overloaded version of the base member function defined in the derived class.

15. Polymorphism is the capability of having the same function name invoke different responses, based on the object making the function call. It can be accomplished with override functions or virtual functions.

16. In static binding, the determination of which function is called is made at compile time. In dynamic binding, the determination is made at runtime.

17. A virtual function designates that dynamic binding should take place. The specification is made in the function's prototype by placing the keyword `virtual` before the function's return type. After a function has been declared as virtual, it remains so for all derived classes, as long as there's a continuous trail of function declarations through the derived chain of classes.

Programming Projects for Chapter 11

1. **(General Math) a.** Construct a class named `Cartesian` containing two double-precision data members named `x` and `y`, used to store the x and y values of a point in rectangular coordinates. The member functions should include a constructor that initializes an object's x and y values to 0 and functions to input and display an object's x and y values. Additionally, include an assignment function that performs a member-wise assignment between two `Cartesian` objects.

   b. Include the class written for Exercise 1a in a working C++ program that creates and displays the values of two `Cartesian` objects; the second object is assigned the values of the first object.

2. **(General Math) a.** Construct a class named `Fractions` containing two integer data members named `num` and `denom`, used to store the numerator and denominator of a fraction having the form num/denom. Your class should include a default constructor that initializes `num` and `denom` to 1 and four operator functions for adding, subtracting, multiplying, and dividing the two fractions, as follows:

   ```
   Addition: a/b + c/d = (a * d + b * c) / (b * d)
   Subtraction: a/b - c/d = (a * d - b * c) / (b * d)
   Multiplication: a/b * c/d = (a* c) / (b * d)
   Division: (a/b) / (c/d) = (a * d) / (b * c)
   ```

   Finally, your class should have a member function that reduces each fraction to its terms (refer to Exercise 15 in Programming Projects for Chapter 6 for how to do this) as well as input and output functions for entering and displaying a fraction.

3. (General Math) a. Create a base class named `Rectangle` containing `length` and `width` data members. From this class, derive a class named `Box` with another data member named `depth`. The member functions of the base `Rectangle` class should consist of a constructor and an `area()` function. The derived `Box` class should have a constructor, a `volume()` function, and an override function named `area()` that returns the surface area of the box.

   b. Include the classes constructed for Exercise 3a in a working C++ program. Have your program call all the member functions in each class and verify the results manually.

4. (General Math) a. Construct two classes named `Rec_coord` and `Pol_coord`. The `Rec_coord` class should contain two double-precision data members named `xval` and `yval`, used to store a point's x and y values in rectangular coordinates. The member functions should include constructor and display functions and a friend function named `conv_pol()`. The `Pol_coord` class should contain two double-precision data members named `dist` and `theta`, used to store a point's distance and angle values in polar coordinates. The member functions should include constructor and display functions and a friend function named `conv_pol()`.

   The friend function should accept an integer argument named `dir`, two double-precision arguments named `val1` and `val2`, and two reference arguments named `recref` and `polref`. The `recref` argument should be a reference to an object of type `Rec_coord`, and the `polref` argument should be a reference to an object of type `Pol_coord`. If the value of `dir` is 1, `val1` and `val2` should be considered x and y rectangular coordinates to be converted to polar coordinates; if the value of `dir` is any other value, `val1` and `val2` should be considered distance and angle values to be converted to rectangular coordinates. For conversion from rectangular to polar coordinates, use the following formulas:

$$r = \sqrt{x^2 + y^2}$$

$$\theta = \tan^{-1}\left(y\,/\,x\right)$$

   For conversion from polar to rectangular coordinates, use the following formulas:

$$x = r\,\cos\theta$$
$$y = r\,\sin\theta$$

   b. Include the program written for Exercise 4a in a working C++ program.

Part Three

Data Structures

Chapter 12

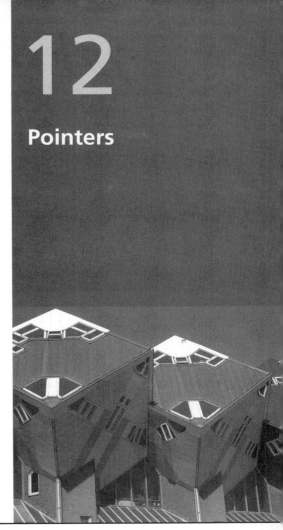

Pointers

One of C++'s advantages is that it allows programmers to access the addresses of variables used in a program. This access gives programmers a view into a computer's basic storage structure, resulting in capabilities and programming power that aren't available in other high-level languages. This is accomplished by using a feature called pointers. Although other languages provide pointers, C++ extends this feature by providing pointer arithmetic; that is, pointer values can be added, subtracted, and compared.

Fundamentally, pointers are simply variables used to store memory addresses. This chapter discusses the basics of declaring pointers, and then explains methods of applying pointer variables to access and use stored addresses in meaningful ways.

12.1 Addresses and Pointers

As you saw in Section 2.5, to display the address of a variable, you can use C++'s address operator, &, which means "the address of." When used in a nondeclarative statement, the address operator placed in front of a variable's name refers to the address of the variable.[1] For example, in a nondeclarative statement, &num means *the address of* num, &miles means *the address of* miles, and &foo means *the address of* foo. Program 12.1, which is a copy of Program 2.10, uses the address operator to display the address of the num variable.

 Program 12.1

```
#include <iostream>
using namespace std;

int main()
{
  int num;

  num = 22;
  cout << "The value stored in num is " << num << endl;
  cout << "The address of num = " << &num << endl;

  return 0;
}
```

The output of Program 12.1 is as follows:

```
The value stored in num is 22
The address of num = 0012FED4
```

Figure 12.1 illustrates the contents and address of the num variable, as shown in Program 12.1's output.

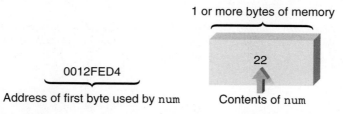

Figure 12.1   A more complete picture of the num variable

---

[1]As you saw in Chapter 6, when used in declaring reference arguments, the ampersand refers to the data type *preceding* it. Therefore, both the declarations double& num and double # are read as "num is the address of a double" or, more commonly, as "num is a reference to a double."

As mentioned in Section 2.5, address information changes, depending on what computer is executing the program and how many other programs are currently loaded into memory.

Storing Addresses

Besides displaying the address of a variable, as in Program 12.1, you can store addresses in suitably declared variables. For example, the statement

```
numAddr = &num;
```

stores the address corresponding to the variable num in the variable numAddr, as illustrated in Figure 12.2.

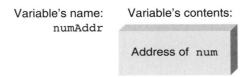

Variable's name: Variable's contents:
       numAddr

                        Address of num

Figure 12.2   Storing num's address in numAddr

Similarly, the statements

```
d = &m;
tabPoint = &list;
chrPoint = &ch;
```

store addresses of the variables m, list, and ch in the variables d, tabPoint, and chrPoint, as illustrated in Figure 12.3.

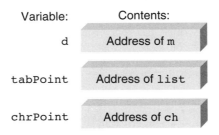

Variable: Contents:

      d   Address of m

 tabPoint   Address of list

 chrPoint   Address of ch

Figure 12.3   Storing more addresses

The variables numAddr, d, tabPoint, and chrPoint are formally called **pointer variables** or **pointers**. Pointers are simply variables used to store the addresses of other variables.

Using Addresses

To use a stored address, C++ provides an **indirection operator**, *. The * symbol, when followed by a pointer (with a space permitted both before and after the *), means "the variable whose address is stored in." Therefore, if numAddr is a pointer (a variable that stores an address), *numAddr means *the variable whose address is stored in* numAddr. Similarly, *tabPoint means *the variable whose address is stored in* tabPoint, and *chrPoint means *the variable whose address is stored in* chrPoint. Figure 12.4 shows the relationship between the address contained in a pointer variable and the variable.

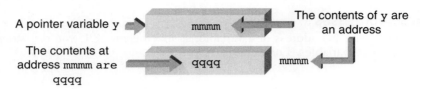

Figure 12.4   Using a pointer variable

Although *d means "the variable whose address is stored in d," it's commonly shortened to the statement "the variable pointed to by d." Similarly, referring to Figure 12.4, *y can be read as "the variable pointed to by y." The value that's finally obtained, as shown in Figure 12.4, is qqqq.

When using a pointer variable, the value that's finally obtained is always found by first going to the pointer for an address. The address contained in the pointer is then used to get the variable's contents. Certainly, this procedure is a rather indirect way of getting to the final value, so the term **indirect addressing** is used to describe it.

Because using a pointer requires the computer to do a double lookup (retrieving the address first, and then using the address to retrieve the actual data), you might wonder why you'd want to store an address in the first place. The answer lies in the intimate relationship between pointers and arrays and the ability of pointers to create and delete variable storage locations dynamically, as a program is running. Both topics are discussed later in this chapter. For now, however, given that each variable has a memory address associated with it, the idea of storing an address shouldn't seem unusual.

Declaring Pointers

Like all variables, pointers must be declared before they can be used to store an address. When you declare a pointer variable, C++ requires also specifying the type of variable that's pointed to. For example, if the address in the pointer numAddr is the address of an integer, this is the correct declaration for the pointer:

```
int *numAddr;
```

This declaration is read as "the variable pointed to by numAddr (from *numAddr in the declaration) is an integer."[2]

Notice that the declaration int *numAddr; specifies two things: First, the variable pointed to by numAddr is an integer, and second, numAddr must be a pointer (because it's used with the indirection operator, *). Similarly, if the pointer tabPoint points to (contains the address of) a double-precision number and chrPoint points to a character variable, the required declarations for these pointers are as follows:

```
double *tabPoint;
char *chrPoint;
```

---

[2]Pointer declarations can also be written in the form *dataType* pointerName, with a space between the indirection operator and the pointer name. This form, however, is error prone when multiple pointers are declared in the same declaration statement and the asterisk is inadvertently omitted after declaring the first pointer name. For example, the declaration int* num1, num2; declares num1 as a pointer variable and num2 as an integer variable. To accommodate multiple pointers in the same declaration and clearly mark a variable as a pointer, the examples in this book adhere to the convention of placing an asterisk in front of each pointer name. This potential error rarely occurs with reference declarations because references are used almost exclusively as formal parameters, and single declarations of parameters are mandatory.

These two declarations can be read as "the variable pointed to by tabPoint is a double" and "the variable pointed to by chrPoint is a char." Because all addresses appear the same, the compiler needs this additional information to know how many storage locations to access when it uses the address stored in the pointer.

Here are other examples of pointer declarations:

```
char *inkey;
int *numPt;
double *nm1Ptr
```

To understand pointer declarations, reading them "backward" is helpful, starting with the indirection operator, *, and translating it as "the variable whose address is stored in" or "the variable pointed to by." Applying this method to pointer declarations, the declaration char *inkey;, for example, can be read as "the variable whose address is stored in inkey is a char" or "the variable pointed to by inkey is a char." Both these statements are often shortened to the simpler "inkey points to a char." All three interpretations of the declaration statement are correct, so you can use the description that makes the most sense to you. Program 12.2 puts this information together to construct a program using pointers.

Program 12.2

```cpp
#include <iostream>
using namespace std;

int main()
{
  int *numAddr;        // declare a pointer to an int
  int miles, dist;     // declare two integer variables

  dist = 158;          // store the number 158 in dist
  miles = 22;          // store the number 22 in miles
  numAddr = &miles;    // store the 'address of miles' in numAddr

  cout << "The address stored in numAddr is " << numAddr << endl;
  cout << "The value pointed to by numAddr is " << *numAddr << "\n\n";

  numAddr = &dist;  // now store the address of dist in numAddr
  cout << "The address now stored in numAddr is " << numAddr << endl;
  cout << "The value now pointed to by numAddr is " << *numAddr << endl;

  return 0;
}
```

The output of Program 12.2 is as follows:

```
The address stored in numAddr is 0012FEC8
The value pointed to by numAddr is 22

The address now stored in numAddr is 0012FEBC
The value now pointed to by numAddr is 158
```

The only use for Program 12.2 is to help you understand what gets stored where, so review the program to see how the output was produced. The declaration statement `int *numAddr;` declares `numAddr` to be a pointer used to store the address of an integer variable. The statement `numAddr = &miles;` stores the address of the variable `miles` in the pointer `numAddr`. The first `cout` statement causes this address to be displayed. The second `cout` statement uses the indirection operator to retrieve and display the value pointed to by `numAddr`, which is, of course, the value stored in `miles`.

Because `numAddr` has been declared as a pointer to an integer variable, you can use this pointer to store the address of any integer variable. The statement `numAddr = &dist` illustrates this use by storing the address of the variable `dist` in `numAddr`. The last two `cout` statements verify the change in `numAddr`'s value and confirm that the new stored address points to the variable `dist`. As shown in Program 12.2, only addresses should be stored in pointers.

It certainly would have been much simpler if the pointer used in Program 12.2 could have been declared as `pointer numAddr;`. This declaration, however, conveys no information about the storage used by the variable whose address is stored in `numAddr`. This information is essential when the pointer is used with the indirection operator, as in the second `cout` statement in Program 12.2. For example, if an integer's address is stored in `numAddr`, typically only 4 bytes of storage are retrieved when the address is used. If a character's address is stored in `numAddr`, only 1 byte of storage is retrieved, and a `double` typically requires retrieving 8 bytes of storage. The declaration of a pointer must, therefore, include the type of variable being pointed to, as illustrated in Figure 12.5.

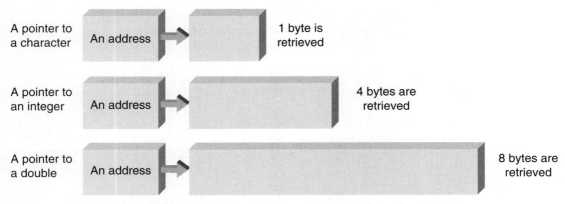

Figure 12.5　Addressing different data types by using pointers

References and Pointers

At this point, you might be asking what the difference is between a pointer and a reference. Essentially, a **reference** is a named constant for an address; therefore, the address named as a reference can't be altered. Because a pointer is a variable, the address in a pointer can be changed. For most applications, using references rather than pointers as arguments to functions is easier and preferred. The reason is the simpler notation for locating a reference parameter, which eliminates the address operator (&) and indirection operator (*) that are required for pointers. Technically, references are said to be **automatically dereferenced** or **implicitly dereferenced** (the two terms are used synonymously), and pointers must be dereferenced explicitly to locate the value being accessed.

For example, in passing a scalar variable's address as a function argument, references provide a simpler notation and are usually preferred. For other situations, such as dynamically allocating new sections of memory for additional variables as a program is running or using alternatives to array notation (both are discussed later in this chapter), pointers are required.

Reference Variables[3]   References are used almost exclusively as formal function parameters and return types. Nevertheless, reference variables are also available in C++. For completeness, you see how to declare and use these variables.

After a variable has been declared, it can be given additional names by using a **reference declaration**, which has this form:

dataType& newName = existingName;

For example, the reference declaration

```
double& sum = total;
```

equates the name sum to the name total. Both now refer to the same variable, as illustrated in Figure 12.6.

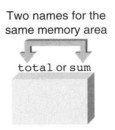

Figure 12.6   sum is an alternative name for total

After establishing another name for a variable by using a reference declaration, the new name, referred to as an **alias**, can be used in place of the original name. For example, take a look at Program 12.3.

---

[3]This section can be omitted with no loss of subject continuity.

Program 12.3

```cpp
#include <iostream>
using namespace std;

int main()
{
  double total = 20.5;      // declare and initialize total
  double& sum = total;      // declare another name for total

  cout << "sum = " << sum << endl;
  sum = 18.6;               // this changes the value in total
  cout << "total = " << total << endl;

  return 0;
}
```

The following output is produced by Program 12.3:

```
    sum = 20.5
    total = 18.6
```

Because the variable sum is simply another reference to the variable total, the first cout statement in Program 12.3 displays the value stored in total. Changing the value in sum then changes the value in total, which the second cout statement in Program 12.3 displays.

When constructing references, keep two points in mind. First, the reference should be of the same data type as the variable it refers to. For example, this sequence of declarations

```cpp
int num = 5;
double& numref = num;   // INVALID - CAUSES A COMPILER ERROR
```

doesn't equate numref to num; rather, it causes a compiler error because the two variables are of different data types.

Second, a compiler error is produced when an attempt is made to equate a reference to a constant. For example, the following declaration is invalid:

```cpp
int& val = 5;   // INVALID - CAUSES A COMPILER ERROR
```

After a reference name has been equated to one variable name correctly, the reference can't be changed to refer to another variable.

As with all declaration statements, multiple references can be declared in a single statement, as long as each reference name is preceded by the ampersand. Therefore, the following declaration creates two reference variables named sum and average:[4]

```cpp
double& sum = total, & average;
```

---

[4]Reference declarations can also be written in the form *dataType &newName=existingName*, with a space between the ampersand and the data type. This form isn't used much, however, probably to distinguish reference variable address notation from the notation used to assign addresses to pointer variables.

Another way of looking at references is to consider them as pointers with restricted capabilities that hide a lot of the dereferencing required with pointers. For example, take a look at these statements:

```
int b;       // b is an integer variable
int& a = b; // a is a reference variable that stores b's address
a = 10;      // this changes b's value to 10
```

Here, a is declared as a reference variable that's effectively a named constant for the address of the b variable. Because the compiler knows from the declaration that a is a reference variable, it automatically assigns b's address (rather than b's contents) to a in the declaration statement. Finally, in the statement a = 10;, the compiler uses the address stored in a to change the value stored in b to 10. The advantage of using the reference is that it accesses b's value automatically without having to use the indirection symbol, *. As noted previously, this type of access is referred to as an automatic dereference.

The following sequence of instructions makes use of this same correspondence between a and b by using pointers:

```
int b;        // b is an integer variable
int *a = &b; // a is a pointer - store b's address in a
*a = 10;      // this changes b's value to 10 by explicit
              // dereference of the address in a
```

Here, a is defined as a pointer initialized to store the address of b. Therefore, *a (which can be read as "the variable whose address is in a" or "the variable pointed to by a") is b, and the expression *a = 10 changes b's value to 10. Notice that with pointers, the stored address can be altered to point to another variable; with references, the reference variable can't be altered to refer to any variable except the one it's initialized to. Also, notice that to dereference a, you must use the indirection operator, *. As you might expect, the * is also called the **dereferencing operator**.

EXERCISES 12.1

1. **(For Review)** If average is a variable, what does &average mean?

2. **(Practice)** For the variables and addresses shown in Figure 12.7, determine the addresses corresponding to the expressions &temp, &dist, &date, and &miles.

3. **(Practice) a.** Write a C++ program that includes the following declaration statements. Have the program use the address operator and a cout statement to display the addresses corresponding to each variable.

```
int num, count;
long date;
float slope;
double power;
```

   b. After running the program written for Exercise 3a, draw a diagram of how your computer has set aside storage for the variables in the program. On your diagram, fill in the addresses the program displays.

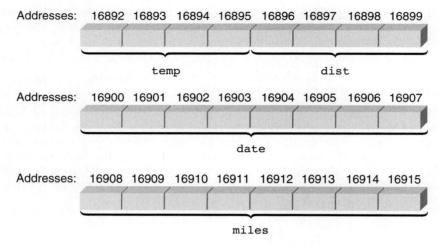

Figure 12.7 Memory bytes for Exercise 2

   c. Modify the program written in Exercise 3a (using the sizeof() operator) to display the amount of storage your computer reserves for each data type. With this information and the address information provided in Exercise 3b, determine whether your computer set aside storage for the variables in the order in which they were declared.

4. (For Review) If a variable is declared as a pointer, what must be stored in the variable?

5. (Practice) Using the indirection operator, write expressions for the following:
   a. The variable pointed to by xAddr
   b. The variable whose address is in yAddr
   c. The variable pointed to by ptYld
   d. The variable pointed to by ptMiles
   e. The variable pointed to by mptr
   f. The variable whose address is in pdate
   g. The variable pointed to by distPtr
   h. The variable pointed to by tabPt
   i. The variable whose address is in hoursPt

6. (Practice) Write declaration statements for the following:
   a. The variable pointed to by yAddr is an integer.
   b. The variable pointed to by chAddr is a character.
   c. The variable pointed to by ptYr is a long integer.
   d. The variable pointed to by amt is a double-precision variable.
   e. The variable pointed to by z is an integer.
   f. The variable pointed to by qp is a single-precision variable.
   g. datePt is a pointer to an integer.
   h. yldAddr is a pointer to a double-precision variable.

    i. `amtPt` is a pointer to a single-precision variable.

    j. `ptChr` is a pointer to a character.

7. (For Review) a. What are the variables `yAddr`, `chAddr`, `ptYr`, `amt`, `z`, `qp`, `datePt`, `yldAddr`, `amtPt`, and `ptChr` used in Exercise 6 called?

    b. Why are the variable names `amt`, `z`, and `qp` used in Exercise 6 not good choices for pointer names?

8. (Practice) Write English sentences that describe what's contained in the following declared variables:

    a. `char *keyAddr;`

    b. `int *m;`

    c. `double *yldAddr;`

    d. `long *yPtr;`

    e. `double *pCou;`

    f. `int *ptDate;`

9. (Practice) Which of the following is a declaration for a pointer?

    a. `long a;`

    b. `char b;`

    c. `char *c;`

    d. `int x;`

    e. `int *p;`

    f. `double w;`

    g. `float *k;`

    h. `float l;`

    i. `double *z;`

10. (Practice) For the following declarations,

```
int *xPt, *yAddr;
long *dtAddr, *ptAddr;
double *ptZ;
int a;
long b;
double c;
```

determine which of the following statements is valid:

a. `yAddr = &a;`	**h.** `dtAddr = &b;`	**o.** `ptAddr = &c;`
b. `yAddr = &b;`	**i.** `dtAddr = &c;`	**p.** `ptAddr = a;`
c. `yAddr = &c;`	**j.** `dtAddr = a;`	**q.** `ptAddr = b;`
d. `yAddr = a;`	**k.** `dtAddr = b;`	**r.** `ptAddr = c;`
e. `yAddr = b;`	**l.** `dtAddr = c;`	**s.** `yAddr = xPt;`
f. `yAddr = c;`	**m.** `ptZ = &a;`	**t.** `yAddr = dtAddr;`
g. `dtAddr = &a;`	**n.** `ptAddr = &b;`	**u.** `yAddr = ptAddr;`

11. **(Practice)** For the variables and addresses illustrated in Figure 12.8, fill in the data determined by the following statements:

   a. ptNum = &m;

   b. amtAddr = &amt;

   c. *zAddr = 25;

   d. k = *numAddr;

   e. ptDay = zAddr;

   f. *ptYr = 1987;

   g. *amtAddr = *numAddr;

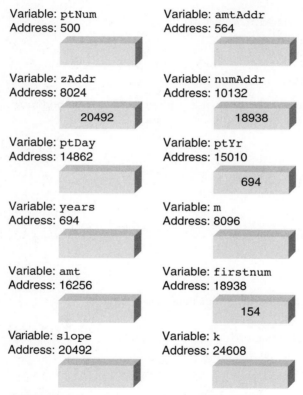

Figure 12.8 Memory locations for Exercise 11

12. **(Practice)** Using the sizeof() operator, determine the number of bytes your computer uses to store the address of an integer, a character, and a double-precision number. (*Hint*: sizeof(*int) can be used to determine the number of memory bytes used for a pointer to an integer.) Would you expect the size of each address to be the same? Why or why not?

12.2 Array Names as Pointers

Although pointers are simply, by definition, variables used to store addresses, there's also a direct and intimate relationship between array names and pointers. This section describes this relationship in detail. Figure 12.9 illustrates the storage of a one-dimensional array named grade, which contains five integers. Each integer requires 4 bytes of storage.

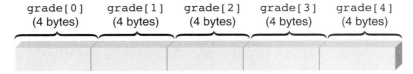

Figure 12.9 The grade array in storage

Using subscripts, the fourth element in the grade array is referred to as grade[3]. The use of a subscript, however, conceals the computer's extensive use of addresses. Internally, the computer immediately uses the subscript to calculate the array element's address based on both the array's starting address and the amount of storage each element uses. Calling the fourth element grade[3] forces the compiler to make this address computation:

```
&grade[3] = &grade[0] + (3 * sizeof(int))
```

Remembering that the address operator, &, means "the address of," this statement is read "the address of grade[3] equals the address of grade[0] plus 12." Figure 12.10 illustrates the address computation used to locate grade[3].

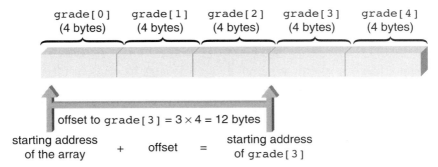

Figure 12.10 Using a subscript to obtain an address

Recall that a pointer is a variable used to store an address. If you create a pointer to store the address of the first element in the grade array, you can mimic the computer's operation to access the array elements. Before you do this, take a look at Program 12.4.

Program 12.4

```cpp
#include <iostream>
using namespace std;

int main()
{
  const int ARRAYSIZE = 5;

  int i, grade[ARRAYSIZE] = {98, 87, 92, 79, 85};

  for (i = 0; i < ARRAYSIZE; i++)
    cout << "\nElement " << i << " is " << grade[i];

  cout << endl;

  return 0;
}
```

When Program 12.4 runs, it produces the following display:

```
Element 0 is 98
Element 1 is 87
Element 2 is 92
Element 3 is 79
Element 4 is 85
```

Program 12.4 displays the values of the grade array by using standard subscript notation. Now store the address of array element 0 in a pointer. Then, using the * operator, you can use the address in the pointer to access each array element. For example, if you store the address of grade[0] in a pointer named gPtr by using the assignment statement gPtr = &grade[0];, the expression *gPtr (which means "the variable pointed to by gPtr") references grade[0], as shown in Figure 12.11.

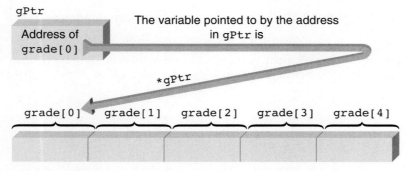

Figure 12.11   The variable pointed to by *gPtr is grade[0]

One unique feature of pointers is that offsets can be included in expressions using pointers. For example, the 1 in the expression `*(gPtr + 1)` is an **offset**. The complete expression references the integer that's one beyond the variable pointed to by gPtr. Similarly, as illustrated in Figure 12.12, the expression `*(gPtr + 3)` references the variable that's three integers beyond the variable pointed to by gPtr: the variable grade[3].

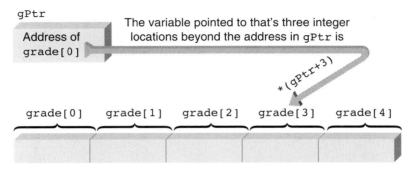

Figure 12.12   An offset of 3 from the address in gPtr

Table 12.1 shows the correspondence between elements referenced by subscripts and by pointers and offsets. Figure 12.13 illustrates the relationships listed in Table 12.1.

Table 12.1   Array Elements Can Be Referenced in Two Ways

Array Element	Subscript Notation	Pointer Notation
Element 0	grade[0]	*gPtr or (gPtr + 0)
Element 1	grade[1]	*(gPtr + 1)
Element 2	grade[2]	*(gPtr + 2)
Element 3	grade[3]	*(gPtr + 3)
Element 4	grade[4]	*(gPtr + 4)

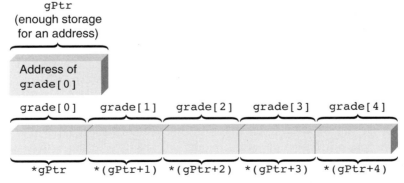

Figure 12.13   The relationship between array elements and pointers

Using the correspondence between pointers and subscripts shown in Figure 12.13, the array elements accessed in Program 12.4 with subscripts can now be accessed with pointers, which is done in Program 12.5.

Program 12.5

```cpp
#include <iostream>
using namespace std;

int main()
{

  const int ARRAYSIZE = 5;

  int *gPtr;             // declare a pointer to an int
  int i, grade[ARRAYSIZE] = {98, 87, 92, 79, 85};

  gPtr = &grade[0];      // store the starting array address
  for (i = 0; i < ARRAYSIZE; i++)
    cout << "\nElement " << i << " is " << *(gPtr + i);

  cout << endl;

  return 0;
}
```

The following display is produced when Program 12.5 runs:

```
Element 0 is 98
Element 1 is 87
Element 2 is 92
Element 3 is 79
Element 4 is 85
```

Notice that this display is the same as Program 12.4's display. The method used in Program 12.5 to access array elements simulates how the compiler references array elements internally. The compiler automatically converts any subscript used by a programmer to an equivalent pointer expression. In this case, because the declaration of gPtr includes the information that integers are pointed to, any offset added to the address in gPtr is scaled automatically by the size of an integer. Therefore, *(gPtr + 3), for example, refers to the address of grade[0] plus an offset of 12 bytes (3 * 4), assuming sizeof(int) = 4. This result is the address of grade[3] shown in Figure 12.13.

The parentheses in the expression * (gPtr + 3) are necessary to reference an array element correctly. Omitting the parentheses results in the expression *gPtr + 3. Because of operator precedence, this expression adds 3 to "the variable pointed to by gPtr." Because gPtr points to grade[0], this expression adds the value of grade[0] and 3 together. Note also that the expression * (gPtr + 3) doesn't change the address stored in gPtr. After the computer uses the offset to locate the correct variable from the starting address in gPtr, the offset is discarded and the address in gPtr remains unchanged.

Although the pointer gPtr used in Program 12.5 was created specifically to store the grade array's starting address, doing so is unnecessary. When an array is created, the compiler creates an internal pointer constant for it automatically and stores the array's starting address in this pointer. In almost all respects, a pointer constant is identical to a programmer-created pointer variable, but as you'll see, there are some differences.

For each array created, the array name becomes the name of the pointer constant the compiler creates for the array, and the starting address of the first location reserved for the array is stored in this pointer. Therefore, declaring the grade array in Programs 12.4 and 12.5 actually reserves enough storage for five integers, creates an internal pointer named grade, and stores the address of grade[0] in the pointer, as shown in Figure 12.14.

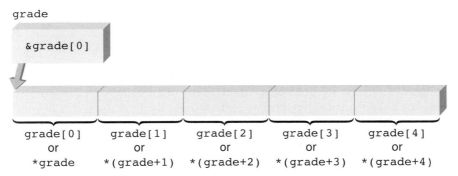

Figure 12.14 Creating an array also creates a pointer

The implication is that every reference to grade made with a subscript can be replaced by a reference using grade as a pointer. Therefore, wherever the expression grade[i] is used, the expression * (grade + i) can also be used. This equivalence is shown in Program 12.6, where grade is used as a pointer to reference all its elements. Program 12.6 produces the same output as Programs 12.4 and 12.5. However, using grade as a pointer makes it unnecessary to declare and initialize the pointer gPtr used in Program 12.5.

Program 12.6

```cpp
#include <iostream>
using namespace std;

int main()
{
  const int ARRAYSIZE = 5;

  int i, grade[ARRAYSIZE] = {98, 87, 92, 79, 85};

  for (i = 0; i < ARRAYSIZE; i++)
    cout << "\nElement " << i << " is " << *(grade + i);
  cout << endl;

  return 0;
}
```

In most respects, an array name and a pointer can be used interchangeably. A true pointer, however, is a variable, and the address stored in it *can* be changed. An array name is a pointer constant, and the address stored in the pointer *can't* be changed by an assignment statement. Therefore, a statement such as grade = &grade[2]; is invalid. This should come as no surprise. Because the purpose of an array name is to locate the beginning of the array correctly, allowing a programmer to change the address stored in the array name defeats this purpose and leads to havoc when array elements are referenced. Also, expressions taking the address of an array name are invalid because the pointer the compiler creates is internal to the computer, not stored in memory, as pointer variables are. Therefore, trying to store the address of grade by using the expression &grade results in a compiler error.

An interesting sidelight to referencing array elements with pointers is that a pointer reference can always be replaced with a subscript reference. For example, if numPtr is declared as a pointer variable, the expression *(numPtr + i) can also be written as numPtr[i], even though numPtr isn't created as an array. As before, when the compiler encounters the subscript notation, it replaces it internally with the pointer notation.

Dynamic Array Allocation[5]

As each variable is defined in a program, sufficient storage for it is assigned from a pool of computer memory locations made available to the compiler. After memory locations have been reserved for a variable, these locations are fixed for the life of that variable, whether or not they're used. For example, if a function requests storage for an array of 500 integers, the storage is allocated and fixed from the point of the array's definition. If the application requires fewer than 500 integers, the unused allocated storage isn't released back to the system until the array goes out of existence. If, on the other hand, the application requires

---

[5]This topic can be omitted on first reading with no loss of subject continuity.

more than 500 integers, the integer array's size must be increased and the function defining the array must be recompiled.

An alternative to this fixed or static allocation of memory storage locations is **dynamic allocation** of memory. Under a dynamic allocation scheme, the amount of storage to be allocated is determined and adjusted at runtime rather than compile time. Dynamic allocation of memory is useful when dealing with lists because it allows expanding the list as new items are added and contracting the list as items are deleted. For example, in constructing a list of grades, you don't need to know the exact number of grades. Instead of creating a fixed array to store grades, having a mechanism for enlarging and shrinking the array as needed is useful. Table 12.2 describes two C++ operators, `new` and `delete`, that provide this capability. (These operators require the `new` header file.)

Table 12.2   The `new` and `delete` Operators (Require the `new` Header File)

Operator Name	Description
`new`	Reserves the number of bytes requested by the declaration. Returns the address of the first reserved location or `NULL` if not enough memory is available.
`delete`	Releases a block of bytes reserved previously. The address of the first reserved location must be passed as an argument to the operator.

Dynamic storage requests for scalar variables or arrays are made as part of a declaration or an assignment statement.[6] For example, the declaration statement `int *num = new int;` reserves an area large enough to hold one integer and places this storage area's address in the pointer num. This same dynamic allocation can be made by first declaring the pointer with the declaration statement `int *num;`, and then assigning the pointer an address with the assignment statement `num = new int;`. In either case, the allocated storage comes from the computer's free storage area.[7]

Dynamic allocation of arrays is similar but more useful. For example, the declaration

```
int *grades = new int[200];
```

reserves an area large enough to store 200 integers and places the first integer's address in the pointer grades. Although the constant 200 has been used in this declaration, a variable dimension can be used. For example, take a look at this sequence of instructions:

```
cout << "Enter the number of grades to be processed: ";
cin  >> numgrades;
int *grades = new int[numgrades];
```

In this sequence, the actual size of the array that's created depends on the number the user inputs. Because pointer and array names are related, each value in the newly created storage area can be accessed by using standard array notation, such as `grades[i]`, instead of the pointer notation `*(grades + i)`. Program 12.7 shows this sequence of code in the context of a complete program.

---

[6]Note that the compiler provides dynamic allocation and deallocation from the stack for all `auto` variables automatically.
[7]A computer's free storage area is formally called the **heap**. It consists of unallocated memory that can be allocated to a program, as requested, while the program is running.

Program 12.7

```cpp
#include <iostream>
#include <new>
using namespace std;

int main()
{
  int numgrades, i;

  cout << "Enter the number of grades to be processed: ";
  cin  >> numgrades;

  int *grades = new int[numgrades];  // create the array

  for(i = 0; i < numgrades; i++)
  {
    cout << "  Enter a grade: ";
    cin  >> grades[i];
  }
  cout << "\nAn array was created for " << numgrades << " integers\n";
  cout << " The values stored in the array are:";
  for (i = 0; i < numgrades; i++)
    cout << "\n    " << grades[i];
  cout << endl;

  delete[] grades;   // return the storage to the heap

  return 0;
}
```

Notice in Program 12.7 that the delete operator is used with braces where the new operator was used previously to create an array. The delete[] statement restores the allocated block of storage back to the free storage area (the heap) while the program is running.[8] The only address delete requires is the starting address of the dynamically allocated storage block. Therefore, any address returned by new can be used subsequently by delete to restore reserved memory back to the computer. The delete operator doesn't

---

[8]The operating system should return allocated storage to the heap automatically when the program has finished running. Because this return doesn't always happen, however, it's crucial to restore dynamically allocated memory explicitly to the heap when the storage is no longer needed. The term **memory leak** describes the condition that occurs when dynamically allocated memory isn't returned explicitly by using the delete operator and the operating system doesn't reclaim allocated memory.

alter the address passed to it, but simply removes the storage the address references. Following is a sample run of Program 12.7:

```
Enter the number of grades to be processed: 4
   Enter a grade: 85
   Enter a grade: 96
   Enter a grade: 77
   Enter a grade: 92

An array was created for 4 integers
 The values stored in the array are:
   85
   96
   77
   92
```

EXERCISES 12.2

1. **(Practice)** Replace each of the following references to a subscripted variable with a pointer reference:

   a. prices[5]   **d.** dist[9]   **g.** celsius[16]

   b. grades[2]   **e.** mile[0]   **h.** num[50]

   c. yield[10]   **f.** temp[20]   **i.** time[12]

2. **(Practice)** Replace each of the following pointer references with a subscript reference:

   a. *(message + 6)   **c.** *(yrs + 10)   **e.** *(rates + 15)

   b. *amount   **d.** *(stocks + 2)   **f.** *(codes + 19)

3. **(For Review) a.** List three things the declaration statement double slopes[5]; causes the compiler to do.

   b. If each double-precision number uses 8 bytes of storage, how much storage is set aside for the slopes array?

   c. Draw a diagram similar to Figure 12.14 for the slopes array.

   d. Determine the byte offset in relation to the start of the slopes array, corresponding to the offset in the expression *(slopes + 3).

4. **(Program)** Write a declaration to store the following values in an array named rates: 12.9, 18.6, 11.4, 13.7, 9.5, 15.2, and 17.6. Include the declaration in a program that displays the values in the array by using pointer notation.

12.3 Pointer Arithmetic

Pointer variables, like all variables, contain values. The value stored in a pointer is, of course, an address. Therefore, by adding and subtracting numbers to pointers, you can obtain different addresses. Additionally, the addresses in pointers can be compared by using any of the relational operators (==, !=, <, >, and so forth) that are valid for comparing other variables. When performing arithmetic on pointers, you must be careful to produce addresses that point to something meaningful. In comparing pointers, you must also make comparisons that make sense. Consider these declarations:

```
int nums[100];
int *nPt;
```

To set the address of nums[0] in nPt, either of these assignment statements can be used:

```
nPt = &nums[0];
nPt = nums;
```

Both assignment statements produce the same result because nums is a pointer constant containing the address of the first location in the array: the address of nums[0]. Figure 12.15 illustrates the memory allocation resulting from the previous declaration and assignment statements, assuming each integer requires 4 bytes of memory, and the location of the beginning of the nums array is address 18934.

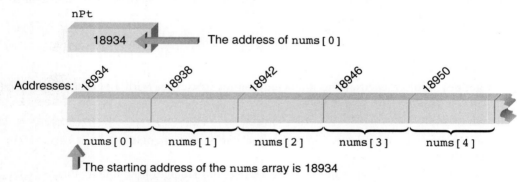

Figure 12.15   The nums array in memory

After nPt contains a valid address, values can be added and subtracted from the address to produce new addresses. When adding or subtracting numbers to pointers, the computer adjusts the number automatically to ensure that the result still "points to" a value of the correct type. For example, the statement nPt = nPt + 4; forces the computer to scale the 4 by the correct number to make sure the resulting address is the address of an integer. Assuming each integer requires 4 bytes of storage, as shown in Figure 12.15, the computer multiplies the 4 by 4 and adds 16 to the address in nPt. The resulting address is 18950, which is the correct address of nums[4].

The computer's automatic scaling ensures that the expression nPt + i, where i is any positive integer, points to the ith element beyond the one currently pointed to by nPt. Therefore, if nPt initially contains the address of nums[0], nPt + 4 is the address of nums[4], nPt + 50 is the address of nums[50], and nPt + i is the address of nums[i]. Although actual addresses are used in Figure 12.15 to illustrate the scaling process, the programmer doesn't need to be concerned with the actual addresses the computer uses. Manipulating addresses with pointers generally doesn't require knowledge of the actual addresses.

Addresses can also be incremented or decremented with the prefix and postfix increment and decrement operators. Adding one to a pointer causes the pointer to point to the next element of the type being pointed to. Decrementing a pointer causes the pointer to point to the previous element. For example, if the pointer variable p is a pointer to an integer, the expression p++ increments the address in the pointer to point to the next integer, as illustrated in Figure 12.16.

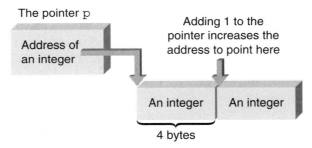

Figure 12.16 Increments are scaled when used with pointers

In reviewing Figure 12.16, notice that the increment added to the pointer is scaled to account for the pointer used to point to integers. It is, of course, up to the programmer to make sure the correct type of data is stored in the new address contained in the pointer.

The increment and decrement operators can be applied as both prefix and postfix pointer operators. All the following combinations using pointers are valid:

```
*ptNum++      // use the pointer and then increment it
*++ptNum      // increment the pointer before using it
*ptNum--      // use the pointer and then decrement it
*--ptNum      // decrement the pointer before using it
```

Of these four possible forms, the most commonly used is *ptNum++ because it allows accessing each array element as the address is "marched along" from the array's starting address to the address of the last array element. Program 12.8 shows this use of the increment operator. In this program, each element in the nums array is retrieved by successively incrementing the address in nPt. Program 12.8 produces the following output:

```
The total of the array elements is 115
```

Program 12.8

```cpp
#include <iostream>
using namespace std;

int main()
{
  const int NUMS = 5;

  int nums[NUMS] = {16, 54, 7, 43, -5};
  int i, total = 0, *nPt;

  nPt = nums;     // store address of nums[0] in nPt
  for (i = 0; i < NUMS; i++)
    total = total + *nPt++;

  cout << "The total of the array elements is " << total << endl;

  return 0;
}
```

The expression total = total + *nPt++ in Program 12.8 accumulates the values pointed to by the nPt pointer. In this expression, the *nPt part causes the computer to retrieve the integer pointed to by nPt. Next, the postfix increment, ++, adds one to the address in nPt so that nPt then contains the address of the next array element. The computer, of course, scales the increment so that the actual address in nPt is the correct address of the next element.

Pointers can also be compared, which is particularly useful when dealing with pointers that point to elements in the same array. For example, instead of using a counter in a for loop to access each array element, the address in a pointer can be compared to the array's starting and ending addresses. The expression

```cpp
nPt <= &nums[4]
```

is true (non-zero) as long as the address in nPt is less than or equal to the address of nums[4]. Because nums is a pointer constant containing the address of nums[0], the term &nums[4] can be replaced by the equivalent term nums + 4. Using either form, Program 12.8 can be rewritten in Program 12.9 to continue adding array elements while the address in nPt is less than or equal to the address of the last array element.

In Program 12.9, the compact form of the accumulating expression total += *nPt++ was used in place of the longer form, total = total + *nPt++. Also, the expression nums + 4 doesn't change the address in nums. Because nums is an array name, not a pointer variable, its value can't be changed. The expression nums + 4 first retrieves the address in nums, adds 4 to this address (scaled appropriately), and uses the result for comparison purposes. Expressions such as *nums++, which attempt to change the address, are invalid. Expressions such as *nums or *(nums + i), which use the address without attempting to alter it, are valid.

Program 12.9

```cpp
#include <iostream>
using namespace std;

int main()
{
  const int NUMS = 5;

  int nums[NUMS] = {16, 54, 7, 43, -5};
  int total = 0, *nPt;

  nPt = nums;     // store address of nums[0] in nPt
  while (nPt < nums + NUMS)
    total += *nPt++;

  cout << "The total of the array elements is " << total << endl;

  return 0;
}
```

Pointer Initialization

Like all variables, pointers can be initialized when they are declared. When initializing pointers, however, you must be careful to set an address in the pointer. For example, an initialization such as

```cpp
int *ptNum = &miles;
```

is valid only if `miles` is declared as an integer variable before `ptNum` is. This statement creates a pointer to an integer and sets the address in the pointer to the address of an integer variable. If the variable `miles` is declared after `ptNum` is declared, as follows, an error occurs:

```cpp
int *ptNum = &miles;
int miles;
```

The error occurs because the address of `miles` is used before `miles` has even been defined. Because the storage area reserved for `miles` hasn't been allocated when `ptNum` is declared, the address of `miles` doesn't exist yet.

Pointers to arrays can also be initialized in their declaration statements. For example, if `volts` has been declared as an array of double-precision numbers, either of the following declarations can be used to initialize the pointer `zing` to the address of the first element in `volts`:

```cpp
double *zing = &volts[0];
double *zing = volts;
```

The last initialization is correct because volts is a pointer constant containing an address of the correct type. (The variable name zing was selected in this example to reinforce the idea that any variable name can be selected for a pointer.)

EXERCISES 12.3

1. **(Modify)** Replace the while statement in Program 12.9 with a for statement.

2. **(Program) a.** Write a program that stores the following numbers in the array named rates: 6.25, 6.50, 6.8, 7.2, 7.35, 7.5, 7.65, 7.8, 8.2, 8.4, 8.6, 8.8, and 9.0. Display the values in the array by changing the address in a pointer called dispPt. Use a for statement in your program.

   b. Modify the program written in Exercise 2a to use a while statement.

3. **(Program)** Write a program that stores the following numbers in the array named miles: 15, 22, 16, 18, 27, 23, and 20. Have your program copy the data stored in miles to another array named dist, and then display the values in the dist array. Your program should use pointer rotation when copying and displaying array elements.

4. **(Program)** Write a program that declares three one-dimensional arrays named miles, gallons, and mpg. Each array should be capable of holding 10 elements. In the miles array, store the numbers 240.5, 300.0, 189.6, 310.6, 280.7, 216.9, 199.4, 160.3, 177.4, and 192.3. In the gallons array, store the numbers 10.3, 15.6, 8.7, 14, 16.3, 15.7, 14.9, 10.7, 8.3, and 8.4. Each element of the mpg array should be calculated as the corresponding element of the miles array divided by the equivalent element of the gallons array: for example, mpg[0] = miles[0] / gallons[0]. Use pointers when calculating and displaying the elements of the mpg array.

5. **(Program)** Define an array of 10 pointers to double-precision numbers. Then read 10 numbers into the locations referenced by the pointers. Next, have your program sum the numbers and store the result in a pointer-accessed location. Finally, have your program display the contents of all locations, again using pointer notation.

12.4 Passing Addresses

You have already seen one method of passing addresses to a function: using reference parameters in Section 6.3. Passing a reference to a function is an implied use of an address because even though the reference does provide the function with an address, the actual call statement doesn't reveal what is being passed—it could be a variable's address or the variable's value. For example, the function call swap(num1, num2); doesn't reveal whether num1 or num2 is an address. Only by looking at the declarations for the variables num1 and num2, or by examining the function header for swap() for declarations of the function's parameters, can you determine the data types of num1 and num2. If they have been defined as reference variables, an address is passed; otherwise, the value stored in the variables is passed.

In contrast to implicitly passing addresses with references, addresses can be explicitly passed with pointers. To explicitly pass an address to a function, all you need to do is place the address operator, &, in front of the variable being passed. For example, this function call

```
swap(&firstnum, &secnum);
```

passes the addresses of the variables `firstnum` and `secnum` to `swap()`, as shown in Figure 12.17. Explicitly passing addresses with the address operator is also referred to as a **pass by reference** because the called function can reference, or access, variables in the calling function by using the passed addresses. As you saw in Section 6.3, pass by references can also be made with references. In this section, you use the addresses passed with pointers to directly access the variables `firstnum` and `secnum` from `swap()` and exchange their values—a procedure accomplished in Program 6.8 with reference parameters.

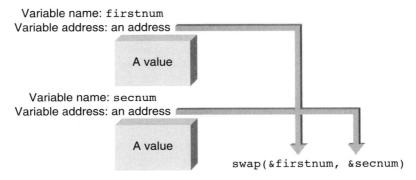

Figure 12.17 Explicitly passing addresses to `swap()`

One of the first requirements in writing `swap()` is to construct a function header that receives and stores the passed values, which in this case are two addresses. As you saw in Section 12.1, addresses are stored in pointers, which means the parameters of `swap()` must be declared as pointers.

Assuming `firstnum` and `secnum` are double-precision variables and `swap()` returns no value, a suitable function header for `swap()` is as follows:

```
void swap(double *nm1Addr, double *nm2Addr);
```

The choice of the parameter names nm1Addr and nm2Addr is, as with all parameter names, up to the programmer. The declaration `double *nm1Addr`, however, states that the parameter named nm1Addr is used to store the address of a double-precision value. Similarly, the declaration `double *nm2Addr` specifies that nm2Addr also stores the address of a double-precision value.

Before writing the body of `swap()` to exchange the values in `firstnum` and `secnum`, first check that the values accessed by using the addresses in nm1Addr and nm2Addr are correct. Program 12.10 performs this check.

The output displayed when Program 12.10 runs is as follows:

```
The number whose address is in nm1Addr is 20.5
The number whose address is in nm2Addr is 6.25
```

Program 12.10

```cpp
#include <iostream>
using namespace std;

void swap(double *, double *);        // function prototype

int main()
{
  double firstnum = 20.5, secnum = 6.25;

  swap(&firstnum, &secnum);     // call swap

  return 0;
}

// this function illustrates passing pointer arguments
void swap(double *nm1Addr, double *nm2Addr)
{

  cout << "The number whose address is in nm1Addr is "
       << *nm1Addr << endl;
  cout << "The number whose address is in nm2Addr is "
       << *nm2Addr << endl;

  return;
}
```

In reviewing Program 12.10, note two things. First, the function prototype for swap()

```cpp
void swap(double *, double *)
```

declares that swap() returns no value directly, and its parameters are two pointers that "point to" double-precision values. When the function is called, it requires that two addresses be passed, and each address is the address of a double-precision value.

Second, the indirection operator is used in swap() to access the values stored in firstnum and secnum. The swap() function has no knowledge of these variable names, but it does have the address of firstnum stored in nm1Addr and the address of secnumstored in nm2Addr. The expression *nm1Addr in the first cout statement means "the variable whose address is in nm1Addr." It is, of course, the variable firstnum. Similarly, the second cout statement obtains the value stored in secnum as "the variable whose address is in nm2Addr." Pointers have been used successfully to allow swap() to access variables in main(). Figure 12.18 illustrates storing addresses in parameters.

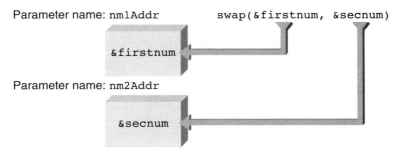

Figure 12.18   Storing addresses in parameters

Having verified that swap() can access main()'s local variables firstnum and secnum, you can now expand swap() to exchange the values in these variables. The values in main()'s variables firstnum and secnum can be interchanged from within swap() by using the three-step interchange algorithm described in Section 6.3:

1. Store firstnum's value in a temporary location.
2. Store secnum's value in firstnum.
3. Store the temporary value in secnum.

Using pointers in swap(), this algorithm takes the following form:

1. Store the value of the variable that nm1Addr points to in a temporary location by using the statement temp = *nm1Addr; (see Figure 12.19).

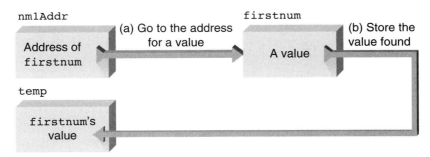

Figure 12.19   Indirectly storing firstnum's value

2. Store the value of the variable whose address is in nm2Addr in the variable whose address is in nm1Addr by using the statement *nm1Addr = *nm2Addr; (see Figure 12.20).
3. Move the value in the temporary location into the variable whose address is in nm2Addr by using the statement *nm2Addr = temp; (see Figure 12.21).

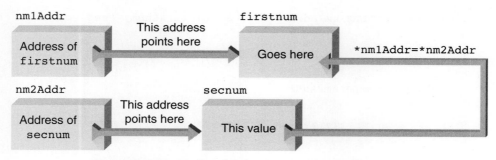

Figure 12.20 Indirectly changing `firstnum`'s value

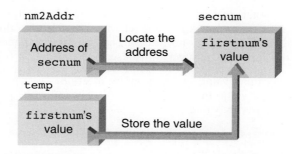

Figure 12.21 Indirectly changing `secnum`'s value

Program 12.11 contains the final form of `swap()`, written according to this description.

 ## Program 12.11

```
#include <iostream>
using namespace std;

void swap(double *, double *);      // function prototype

int main()
{
  double firstnum = 20.5, secnum = 6.25;


  cout << "The value stored in firstnum is: " << firstnum << endl;
  cout << "The value stored in secnum is: " << secnum << "\n\n";
```

☞

```
    swap(&firstnum, &secnum);         // call swap

  cout << "The value stored in firstnum is now: "
       << firstnum <<  endl;
  cout << "The value stored in secnum is now: "
       << secnum << endl;

  return 0;
}

// this function swaps the values in its two arguments
void swap(double *nm1Addr, double *nm2Addr)
{
  double temp;

  temp = *nm1Addr;        // save firstnum's value
  *nm1Addr = *nm2Addr;    // move secnum's value into firstnum
  *nm2Addr = temp;        // change secnum's value

  return;
}
```

A sample run of Program 12.11 produced this output:

```
    The value stored in firstnum is: 20.5
    The value stored in secnum is: 6.25

    The value stored in firstnum is now: 6.25
    The value stored in secnum is now: 20.5
```

As this output shows, the values stored in main()'s variables have been modified in swap(), which was made possible by using pointers. To make sure you understand, you could compare this version of swap() with the version using references in Program 6.10. The advantage of using pointers rather than references is that the function call specifies that addresses are being used, which is an alert that the function will most likely alter variables of the calling function. The advantage of using references is that the notation is much simpler. Generally, for functions such as swap(), ease of notation wins out, and references are used. In passing arrays to functions, however, which is the next topic, the compiler passes an address automatically, which dictates using pointers to store the address.

Passing Arrays

When an array is passed to a function, its address is the only item actually passed. "Address" means the address of the first location used to store the array, as shown in Figure 12.22. Because the first location reserved for an array corresponds to element 0 of the array, the "address of the array" is also the address of element 0.

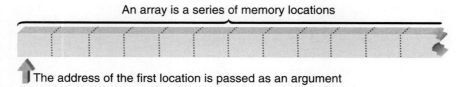

The address of the first location is passed as an argument

Figure 12.22   An array's address is the address of the first location reserved for the array

For a specific example of passing an array to a function, examine Program 12.12. In this program, the nums array is passed to the findMax() function, using conventional array notation.

Program 12.12

```
#include <iostream>
using namespace std;

int findMax(int [], int);    // function prototype

int main()
{
  const int NUMPTS = 5;

  int nums[NUMPTS] = {2, 18, 1, 27, 16};

  cout << "\nThe maximum value is "
       << findMax(nums,NUMPTS) << endl;
  return 0;
}
// this function returns the maximum value in an array of ints
int findMax(int vals[], int numels)
{
  int i, max = vals[0];

  for (i = 1; i < numels; i++)
   if (max < vals[i])
     max = vals[i];

  return max;
}
```

The following output is displayed when Program 12.12 runs:

```
The maximum value is 27
```

The parameter named `vals` in the function header declaration for `findMax()` actually receives the address of the `nums` array. Therefore, `vals` is really a pointer because pointers are variables (or parameters) used to store addresses. Because the address passed to `findMax()` is the address of an integer, the following function header for `findMax()` is also suitable:

```
int findMax(int *vals, int numels) // vals is declared as
                                   // a pointer to an integer
```

The declaration `int *vals` in the function header declares that `vals` is used to store an address of an integer. The address stored is, of course, the location of the beginning of an array. The following is a rewritten version of the `findMax()` function that uses the new pointer declaration for `vals` but retains the use of subscripts to refer to array elements:

```
int findMax(int *vals, int numels)    // find the maximum value
{
  int i, max = vals[0];

  for (i = 1; i < numels; i++)
   if (max < vals[i])
     max = vals[i];

  return max;
}
```

Regardless of how `vals` is declared in the function header or how it's used in the function body, it's truly a pointer variable. Therefore, the address in `vals` can be modified. This isn't true for the name `nums`, however. Because `nums` is the name of the originally created array, it's a pointer constant. As described in Section 12.2, this means the address in `nums` can't be changed, and the address of `nums` can't be taken. No such restrictions, however, apply to the pointer variable `vals`. All the pointer arithmetic you learned in Section 12.3 can be applied to `vals`.

Next, you see how to write two more versions of `findMax()`, both using pointers instead of subscripts. In the first version, you simply substitute pointer notation for subscript notation. In the second version, you use pointer arithmetic to change the address in the pointer. As stated previously, access to an array element with the subscript notation *arrayName*[i] can always be replaced by the pointer notation * (*arrayName* + i).

In the first modification to `findMax()`, you make use of this correspondence by simply replacing all references to `vals[i]` with the expression `* (vals + i)`:

```
int findMax(int *vals, int numels)    // find the maximum value
{
  int i, max = *vals;

  for (i = 1; i < numels; i++)
   if (max < * (vals + i) )
     max = * (vals + i);

  return max;
}
```

The second modification of `findMax()` makes use of being able to change the address stored in `vals`. After each array element is retrieved by using the address in `vals`, the address is incremented by one in the altering list of the `for` statement. The expression `max = *vals` previously used to set `max` to the value of `vals[0]` is replaced by the expression `max = *vals++`, which adjusts the address in `vals` to point to the second array element. The element this expression assigns to `max` is the array element `vals` points to before it's incremented. The postfix increment, `++`, doesn't change the address in `vals` until after the address has been used to retrieve the first array element.

```
int findMax(int *vals, int numels)    // find the maximum value
{
  int i, max = *vals++;    // get the first element and increment it
  for (i = 1; i < numels; i++, vals++)
  {
    if (max < *vals)
      max = *vals;
  }
  return max;
}
```

Review this version of `findMax()`. Initially, the maximum value is set to "the thing pointed to by `vals`." Because `vals` initially contains the address of the first array element passed to `findMax()`, the value of this first element is stored in `max`. The address in `vals` is then incremented by one. The one added to `vals` is scaled automatically by the number of bytes used to store integers. Therefore, after the increment, the address stored in `vals` is the address of the next array element, as illustrated in Figure 12.23. The value of this next element is compared to the maximum, and the address is again incremented, this time in the altering list of the `for` statement. This process continues until all array elements have been examined.

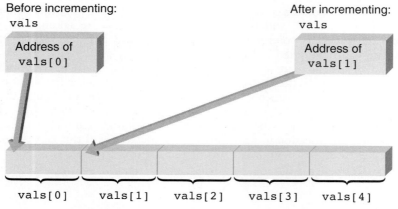

Figure 12.23   Pointing to different elements

The version of `findMax()` you choose is a matter of personal style. Generally, beginning programmers feel more at ease using subscripts rather than pointers. Also, if the program uses an array as the natural storage structure for the application and data, an array access using subscripts is more appropriate to indicate the program's intent clearly. However, as you learn more about data structures, pointers become an increasingly useful and powerful tool. In more complex data structures, there's no simple or easy equivalence for subscripts.

There's one more neat trick you can glean from this discussion. Because passing an array to a function actually involves passing an address, you can pass any valid address. For example, the function call findMax(&nums[2],3) passes the address of nums[2] to findMax(). In findMax(), the pointer vals stores the address, and the function starts the search for a maximum at the element corresponding to this address. Therefore, from findMax()'s perspective, it has received an address and proceeds appropriately.

Advanced Pointer Notation[9]

You can also access multidimensional arrays by using pointer notation, although the notation becomes more cryptic as the array dimensions increase. Pointer notation is especially useful with two-dimensional character arrays, and this section discusses pointer notation for two-dimensional numeric arrays. For example, examine this declaration:

```
int nums[0][1] = { {16,18,20},
                   {25,26,27} };
```

This declaration creates an array of elements and a set of pointer constants named nums, nums[0], and nums[1]. Figure 12.24 illustrates the relationship between these pointer constants and the elements of the nums array.

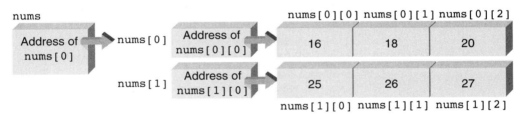

Figure 12.24 Storage of the nums array and associated pointer constants

The availability of the pointer constants associated with a two-dimensional array enables you to access array elements in a variety of ways. One way is to view a two-dimensional array as an array of rows, with each row as an array of three elements. From this viewpoint, the address of the first element in the first row is provided by nums[0], and the address of the first element in the second row is provided by nums[1]. Therefore, the variable pointed to by nums[0] is nums[0][0], and the variable pointed to by nums[1] is nums[1][0]. Each element in the array can be accessed by applying an offset to the correct pointer. Therefore, the following notations are equivalent:

Pointer Notation	Subscript Notation	Value
*nums[0]	nums[0][0]	16
*(nums[0] + 1)	nums[0][1]	18
*(nums[0] + 2)	nums[0][2]	20
*nums[1]	nums[1][0]	25
*(nums[1] + 1)	nums[1][1]	26
*(nums[1] + 2)	nums[1][2]	27

---

[9]This topic can be omitted without loss of subject continuity.

You can now go further and replace nums[0] and nums[1] with their pointer notations, using the address of nums. As shown in Figure 12.24, the variable pointed to by nums is nums[0]. That is, *nums is nums[0]. Similarly, *(nums + 1) is nums[1]. Using these relationships leads to the following equivalences:

Pointer Notation	Subscript Notation	Value
*(*nums)	nums[0][0]	16
*(*nums + 1)	nums[0][1]	18
*(*nums + 2)	nums[0][2]	20
((nums + 1))	nums[1][0]	25
((nums + 1) + 1)	nums[1][1]	26
((nums + 1) + 2)	nums[1][2]	27

The same notation applies when a two-dimensional array is passed to a function. For example, the two-dimensional array nums is passed to the calc() function by using the call calc(nums);. As with all array passes, an address is passed. A suitable function header for the calc() function is as follows:

```
calc(int pt[2][3])
```

As you have seen, the parameter declaration for pt can also be the following:

```
calc(int pt[][3])
```

Using pointer notation, the following is another suitable declaration:

```
calc(int (*pt)[3])
```

In this declaration, the inner parentheses are required to create a single pointer to arrays of three integers. Each array is, of course, equivalent to a single row of the nums array. By offsetting the pointer, each element in the array can be accessed. Notice that without the parentheses, the declaration becomes

```
int *pt[3]
```

which creates an array of three pointers, each one pointing to a single integer. After the correct declaration for pt is made (any of the three valid declarations can be used), all the following notations in the calc() function are equivalent:

Pointer Notation	Subscript Notation	Value
*(*pt)	pt[0][0]	16
*(*pt+1)	pt[0][1]	18
*(*pt+2)	pt[0][2]	20
((pt+1))	pt[1][0]	25
((pt+1)+1)	pt[1][1]	26
((pt+1)+2)	pt[1][2]	27

The last two notations using pointers are seen in more advanced C++ programs. The first occurs because functions can return any valid C++ scalar data type, including pointers to any of these data types. If a function returns a pointer, the data type being pointed to must be declared in the function's declaration. For example, the declaration

```
int *calc()
```

declares that `calc()` returns a pointer to an integer value, which means the address of an integer variable is returned. Similarly, the declaration

```
double *taxes()
```

declares that `taxes()` returns a pointer to a double-precision value, which means the address of a double-precision variable is returned.

In addition to declaring pointers to integers, double-precision numbers, and C++'s other data types, you can declare pointers that point to (contain the address of) a function. Pointers to functions are possible because function names, like array names, are pointer constants. For example, the declaration

```
int (*calc)()
```

declares `calc` to be a pointer to a function that returns an integer. This means `calc` contains the address of a function, and the function whose address is in the variable `calc` returns an integer value. If, for example, the function `sum()` returns an integer, the assignment `calc = sum;` is valid.

EXERCISES 12.4

1. **(Practice)** The following declaration was used to create the `prices` array:

   ```
   double prices[500];
   ```

   Write three different headers for a function named `sortArray()` that accepts the `prices` array as a parameter named `inArray` and returns no value.

2. **(Practice)** The following declaration was used to create the `keys` array:

   ```
   char keys[256];
   ```

   Write three different headers for a function named `findKey()` that accepts the `keys` array as a parameter named `select` and returns no value.

3. **(Practice)** The following declaration was used to create the `rates` array:

   ```
   double rates[256];
   ```

   Write three different headers for a function named `maximum()` that accepts the `rates` array as a parameter named `speed` and returns a double-precision value.

4. **(Modify)** Modify the `findMax()` function to locate the minimum value of the passed array. Write the function using only pointers.

5. **(Debug)** In the second version of `findMax()`, `vals` was incremented in the altering list of the `for` statement. Instead, you do the incrementing in the condition expression of the `if` statement, as follows:

```
int findMax(int *vals, int numels)      // incorrect version
{
  int i, max = *vals++;    // get the first element and increment

  for (i = 1; i < numels; i++)
    if (max < *vals++)
      max = *vals;
  return (max);
}
```

Determine why this version produces an incorrect result.

6. **(Program) a.** Write a program that has a declaration in `main()` to store the following numbers in an array named `rates`: 6.5, 7.2, 7.5, 8.3, 8.6, 9.4, 9.6, 9.8, and 10.0. Include a function call to `show()` that accepts `rates` in a parameter named `rates` and then displays the numbers by using the pointer notation `*(rates + i)`.

   b. Modify the `show()` function written in Exercise 6a to alter the address in `rates`. Always use the expression `*rates` rather than `*(rates + i)` to retrieve the correct element.

12.5 Common Programming Errors

In using the material in this chapter, be aware of the following possible errors:

1. Attempting to store an address in a variable that hasn't been declared as a pointer.
2. Using a pointer to access nonexistent array elements. For example, if `nums` is an array of 10 integers, the expression `*(nums + 15)` points to a location six integer locations beyond the last array element. Because C++ doesn't do bounds checking on array accesses, the compiler doesn't catch this type of error. This error is the same error, disguised in pointer notation form, that occurs when using a subscript to access an out-of-bounds array element.
3. Forgetting to use the bracket set, `[]`, after the `delete` operator when dynamically deallocating memory that was allocated previously with the `new []` operator.
4. Incorrectly applying address and indirection operators. For example, if `pt` is a pointer variable, both the expressions
   ```
   pt = &45
   pt = &(miles + 10)
   ```
   are invalid because they attempt to take the address of a value. Notice that the expression `pt = &miles + 10`, however, is valid. This expression adds 10 to the address of `miles`. It's the programmer's responsibility to ensure that the final address points to a valid data element.

5. Taking addresses of pointer constants. For example, given the declarations
   ```
   int nums[25];
   int *pt;
   ```
   the assignment
   ```
   pt = &nums;
   ```

is invalid. The constant `nums` is a pointer constant that's equivalent to an address. The correct assignment is `pt = nums`.

6. Taking addresses of a reference argument, reference variable, or register variable. The reason is that reference arguments and variables are essentially the same as pointer constants, in that they're named address values. Similarly, the address of a register variable can't be taken. Therefore, for the declarations

```
register int total;
int *ptTot;
```

the assignment

```
ptTot = &total;   // INVALID
```

is invalid. The reason is that register variables are stored in a computer's internal registers, and these storage areas don't have standard memory addresses.

7. Initializing pointer variables incorrectly. For example, the initialization

```
int *pt = 5;
```

is invalid. Because `pt` is a pointer to an integer, it must be initialized with a valid address.

8. Becoming confused about whether a variable *contains* an address or *is* an address. Pointer variables and pointer arguments contain addresses. Although a pointer constant is synonymous with an address, it's useful to treat pointer constants as pointer variables with two restrictions:

- The address of a pointer constant can't be taken.
- The address "contained in" the pointer constant can't be altered.

Except for these two restrictions, pointer constants and pointer variables can be used almost interchangeably. Therefore, when an address is required, any of the following can be used:

- A pointer variable name
- A pointer argument name
- A pointer constant name
- A non-pointer variable name preceded by the address operator (for example, `&variable`)
- A non-pointer argument name preceded by the address operator (for example, `&argument`)

Some confusion surrounding pointers is caused by careless use of the word *pointer*. For example, the phrase "a function requires a pointer argument" is more clearly understood when you realize it really means "a function requires an address as an argument." Similarly, the phrase "a function returns a pointer" really means "a function returns an address."

If you're ever in doubt as to what's contained in a variable or how it should be treated, use a `cout` statement to display the variable's contents, the "thing pointed to," or "the address of the variable." Seeing what's actually displayed often helps sort out what the variable contains.

12.6 Chapter Summary

1. Every variable has a data type, an address, and a value. In C++, you can obtain the address of a variable by using the address operator, &.

2. A pointer is a variable used to store the address of another variable. Pointers, like all C++ variables, must be declared. The indirection operator, *, is used both to declare a pointer variable and to access the variable whose address is stored in a pointer.

3. An array name is a pointer constant. The value of the pointer constant is the address of the first element in the array. Therefore, if val is the name of an array, val and &val[0] can be used interchangeably.

4. Any access to an array element with subscript notation can always be replaced with pointer notation. That is, the notation a[i] can always be replaced by the notation *(a + i). This is true whether a was initially declared as an array or a pointer.

5. Arrays can be created dynamically as a program is executing. For example, the following sequence of statements creates an array named grades of size num:

```
cout  << "Enter the array size: ";
cin   >> num;
int  *grades = new int[num];
```

The area allocated for the array can be destroyed dynamically by using the delete[] operator. For example, the statement delete[] grades; returns the allocated area for the grades array back to the computer.

6. Arrays are passed to functions as addresses. The called function always receives direct access to the originally declared array elements.

7. When a one-dimensional array is passed to a function, the function's parameter declaration can be an array declaration or a pointer declaration. Therefore, the following parameter declarations are equivalent:

```
double a[];
double *a;
```

8. Pointers can be incremented, decremented, compared, and assigned. Numbers added to or subtracted from a pointer are scaled automatically. The scale factor used is the number of bytes required to store the data type originally pointed to.

Programming Projects for Chapter 12

1. **(Program)** Write a function named trimfrnt() that deletes all leading blanks from a string. Write the function using pointers with a return type of void.

2. **(Program)** Write a function named trimrear() that deletes all trailing blanks from a string. Write the function using pointers with a return type of void.

3. **(Program)** Write a C++ program that asks for two lowercase characters. Pass the two entered characters, using pointers, to a function named capit(). The capit() function should capitalize the two letters and return the capitalized values to the calling function through its pointer arguments. The calling function should then display all four letters.

4. **(Program)** **a.** Write a program that has a declaration in main() to store the string Vacation is near in an array named message. Include a function call that accepts message in an argument named strng and then displays the contents of message by using the pointer notation *(strng + i).

b. Modify the display function written in Exercise 4a to alter the address in message. Also, use the expression *strng rather than *(strng + i) to retrieve the correct element.

5. **(Program)** Write a program that declares three one-dimensional arrays named price, quantity, and amount. Each array should be declared in main() and be capable of holding 10 double-precision numbers. The numbers to be stored in price are 10.62, 14.89, 13.21, 16.55, 18.62, 9.47, 6.58, 18.32, 12.15, and 3.98. The numbers to be stored in quantity are 4, 8.5, 6, 7.35, 9, 15.3, 3, 5.4, 2.9, and 4.8. Have your program pass these three arrays to a function called extend(), which calculates the elements in the amount array as the product of the equivalent elements in the price and quantity arrays: for example, amount[1] = price[1] * quantity[1].

After extend() has put values in the amount array, display the values in the array from within main(). Write the extend() function by using pointers.

6. **(Desk Check)** **a.** Determine the output of the following program:

```
#include <iostream.h>

void arr(int [] []);  // equivalent to void arr(int (*) []);

int main()
{
  const int ROWS = 2;
  const int COLS = 3;
  int nums[ROWS][COLS] = { {33,16,29},
                           {54,67,99}};

  arr(nums);
  return 0;
}

void arr(int (*val) [3])
{
  cout << endl << *(*val);
  cout << endl << *(*val + 1);
  cout << endl << *(*(val + 1) + 2);
  cout << endl << *(*val) + 1;
  return;
}
```

b. Given the declaration for val in the arr() function, is the notation val[1][2] valid in the function?

Chapter 13

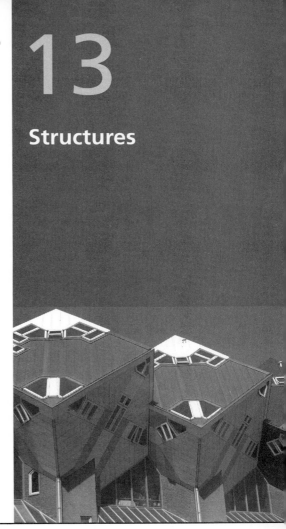

Structures

A structure is a historical holdover from C. From a programmer's perspective, a structure can be thought of as a class that has all public instance variables and no member methods. In commercial applications, a structure is referred to, and is the same thing as, a record. In C and C++, a structure provides a way to store values of different data types, such as an integer part number, a character part type, and a double-precision supply voltage.

For example, an integrated circuit (IC) manufacturer maintains a summary of information for each circuit it fabricates. The data items kept for each circuit are shown in this inventory record:

Part Number:
Integrated Circuit Family:
Function Type:
Supply Voltage:
Units in Stock:

*Each data item is a separate entity referred to as a **data field**. Taken together, the data fields form a single unit referred to as a **structure**.*

Although the IC manufacturer could keep track of hundreds of components, the form of each component's structure is identical. In dealing with structures, distinguishing between a structure's form and its contents is important. A structure's form consists of the symbolic names, data types, and arrangement of data fields in the structure. The structure's contents refer to the actual data stored in the symbolic names. The following shows acceptable contents for the structure form listed previously:

Part Number: 23421
Integrated Circuit Family: TTL
Function Type: AND
Supply Voltage: 6.0
Units in Stock: 345

This chapter describes the C++ statements required to create, fill, use, and pass structures between functions.

13.1 Single Structures

Creating and using a structure involves the same two steps for creating and using any variable. First, the record structure must be declared. Second, specific values can be assigned to the structure elements. Declaring a structure requires listing the data types, data names, and arrangement of data items. For example, the definition

```
struct
{
  int month;
  int day;
  int year;
} birth;
```

gives the form of a structure called `birth` and reserves storage for the data items listed in the structure. The `birth` structure consists of three data items or fields, which are called **members** of the structure.

Assigning actual data values to a structure's members is referred to as **populating the structure**, which is a straightforward procedure. Each structure member is accessed by giving both the structure name and data item name, separated by a period. For example, `birth.month` refers to the first member of the `birth` structure, `birth.day` refers to the second member of the structure, and `birth.year` refers to the third member. Program 13.1 shows assigning values to members of the `birth` structure. Program 13.1 produces the following output:

```
My birth date is 12/28/86
```

Program 13.1

```cpp
// a program that defines and populates a structure
#include <iostream>
using namespace std;

int main()
{
  struct
  {
    int month;
    int day;
    int year;
  } birth;

  birth.month = 12;
  birth.day = 28;
  birth.year = 86;

  cout << "My birth date is "
       << birth.month << '/'
       << birth.day   << '/'
       << birth.year  << endl;

  return 0;
}
```

As in most C++ statements, the spacing of a structure definition isn't rigid. For example, the `birth` structure could just as well have been defined as the following:

```cpp
struct {int month; int day; int year;} birth;
```

Also, as with all C++ definition statements, multiple variables can be defined in the same statement. For example, the definition statement

```cpp
struct
{
  int month;
  int day;
  int year;
} birth, current;
```

creates two structure variables having the same form. The members of the first structure are referenced by the names `birth.month`, `birth.day`, and `birth.year`, and the members of the second structure are referenced by the names `current.month`, `current.day`, and `current.year`. Notice that the form of this structure definition statement is identical to the form for defining any program variable: The data type is followed by a list of variable names.

A helpful and commonly used modification for defining structure types is to list the structure's form with no variable names following. In this case, however, the list of structure members must be preceded by a user-selected data type name. For example, in the declaration

```
struct Date
{
  int month;
  int day;
  int year;
};
```

the term `Date` is a structure type name: It defines a new data type that's a data structure of the declared form.[1] By convention, the first letter of a user-selected data type name is uppercase, as in the name `Date`, which helps identify it when it's used in subsequent definition statements. This declaration for the `Date` structure creates a new data type without actually reserving any storage locations. Therefore, it's not a definition statement. It simply declares a `Date` structure type and describes how data items are arranged in the structure. Actual storage for the structure members is reserved only when variable names are assigned. For example, the definition statement

```
Date birth, current;
```

reserves storage for two `Date` structure variables named `birth` and `current`. Each of these structures has the form previously declared for the `Date` structure.

The declaration of structure data types, like all declarations, can be global or local. Program 13.2 shows the global declaration of a `Date` data type. In `main()`, the variable `birth` is defined as a local variable of `Date` type. The output Program 13.2 produces is identical to the output of Program 13.1.

The initialization of structures follows the same rules as for initialization of arrays: Global and local structures can be initialized by following the definition with a list of initializers. For example, the definition statement

```
Date birth = {12, 28, 86};
```

can be used to replace the first four statements in `main()` in Program 13.2. Notice that the initializers are separated by commas, not semicolons.

---

[1]For completeness, it should be mentioned that a C++ structure can also be declared as a class with no member functions and all public data members. Similarly, a C++ class can be declared as a structure having all private data members and all public member functions. Therefore, C++ provides two syntaxes for structures and classes. The convention, however, is to not mix notations; in other words, always use structures for creating record types, and use classes for providing true information and implementation hiding.

Program 13.2

```cpp
#include <iostream>
using namespace std;

struct Date      // this is a global declaration
{
  int month;
  int day;
  int year;
};

int main()
{
  Date birth;

  birth.month = 12;
  birth.day = 28;
  birth.year = 86;

  cout << "My birth date is " << birth.month << '/'
       << birth.day    << '/'
       << birth.year   << endl;

  return 0;
}
```

Structure members aren't restricted to integer data types, as in the Date structure. Any valid C++ data type can be used. For example, an employee record consists of the following data items:

```
Name:
Identification Number:
Regular Pay Rate:
Overtime Pay Rate:
```

The following is a suitable declaration for these data items:

```cpp
struct PayRec
{
  string name;
  int idNum;
  double regRate;
  double otRate;
};
```

Point of Information

Homogeneous and Heterogeneous Data Structures

Both arrays and structures are structured data types. The difference between these two data structures is the types of elements they contain. An array is a **homogeneous** data structure, which means all its components must be of the same data type. A structure is a **heterogeneous** data structure, which means its components can be of different data types. Therefore, an array of structures is a homogeneous data structure with elements of the same heterogeneous type.

After the `PayRec` data type is declared, a structure variable using this type can be defined and initialized. For example, the definition

```
PayRec employee = {"H. Price",12387,15.89,25.50};
```

creates a structure named `employee` of the `PayRec` data type. The members of `employee` are initialized with the data listed between braces in the definition statement.

Notice that a single structure is simply a convenient method for combining and storing related items under a common name. Although a single structure is useful in identifying the relationship among its members, the members could be defined as separate variables. One of the real advantages of using structures is realized only when the same data type is used in a list many times over. Creating lists with the same data type is discussed in Section 13.2.

Including a structure inside a structure follows the same rules for including any data type in a structure. For example, a structure is to consist of a name and a birth date, and a `Date` structure has been declared as follows:

```
struct Date
{
  int month;
  int date;
  int year;
};
```

A suitable definition of a structure that includes a name and a `Date` structure is as follows:

```
struct
{
  string name;
  Date birth;
} person;
```

Notice that in declaring the `Date` structure, the term `Date` is a data type name, so it appears before the braces in the declaration statement. In defining the `person` structure variable, `person` is a variable name, so it's the name of a specific structure. The same is true of the variable `birth`; it's the name of a specific `Date` structure. Members in the `person` structure are accessed by using the structure name, followed by a period, followed by the member. For example, `person.birth.month` refers to the `month` variable in the `birth` structure contained in the `person` structure.

EXERCISES 13.1

1. **(Practice)** Declare a structure data type named `Stemp` for each of the following records:

   a. A student record consisting of a student identification number, number of credits completed, and cumulative grade point average

   b. A student record consisting of a student's name, birth date, number of credits completed, and cumulative grade point average

   c. An inventory record consisting of the items listed in the chapter introduction

   d. A stock record consisting of the stock's name, the stock's price, and the date of purchase

   e. An inventory record consisting of an integer part number, a part description, the number of parts in inventory, and an integer reorder number

2. **(Practice)** For the data types declared in Exercise 1, define a suitable structure variable name, and initialize each structure with the following data:

   a. Identification Number: 4672

      Number of Credits Completed: 68

      Grade Point Average: 3.01

   b. Name: Rhona Karp

      Birth Date: 8/4/60

      Number of Credits Completed: 96

      Grade Point Average: 3.89

   c. Part Number: 54002

      IC Family: ECL

      Function Type: NAND

      Supply Voltage: -5

      Units in Stock: 123

   d. Stock Name: IBM

      Stock Price: 134.5

      Date Purchased: 10/1/2009

   e. Part Number: 16879

      Part Description: Battery

      Number in Stock: 10

      Reorder Number: 3

3. **(Program) a.** Write a C++ program that prompts a user to input the current month, day, and year. Store the entered data in a suitably defined record and display the date in an appropriate manner.

   b. Modify the program written in Exercise 3a to use a record that accepts the current time in hours, minutes, and seconds.

4. **(Financial)** Write a C++ program that uses a structure for storing a stock name, its esti-mated earnings per share, and its estimated price-to-earnings ratio. Have the program prompt the user to enter these items for five different stocks, each time using the same structure to store the entered data. When data has been entered for a particular stock, have the program compute and display the anticipated stock price based on the entered earnings and price-per-earnings values. For example, if a user enters the data XYZ 1.56 12, the anticipated price for a share of XYZ stock is (1.56) × (12) = \$18.72.

5. **(Timing)** Write a C++ program that accepts a user-entered time in hours and minutes. Have the program calculate and display the time one minute later.

6. **(Dates) a.** Write a C++ program that accepts a user-entered date. Have the program cal-culate and display the date of the next day. For the purposes of this exercise, assume all months consist of 30 days.

   b. Modify the program written in Exercise 6a to account for the actual number of days in each month.

13.2 Arrays of Structures

The real power of structures is realized when the same structure is used for lists of data. For example, the data shown in Figure 13.1 must be processed. Clearly, the employee numbers can be stored together in an array of integers, the names in an array of strings, and the pay rates in an array of double-precision numbers. In organizing the data in this fashion, each column in Figure 13.1 is considered a separate list stored in its own array. The correspon-dence between data items for each employee is maintained by storing an employee's data in the same array position in each array.

Employee Number	Employee Name	Employee Pay Rate
32479	Abrams, B.	6.72
33623	Bohm, P.	7.54
34145	Donaldson, S.	5.56
35987	Ernst, T.	5.43
36203	Gwodz, K.	8.72
36417	Hanson, H.	7.64
37634	Monroe, G.	5.29
38321	Price, S.	9.67
39435	Robbins, L.	8.50
39567	Williams, B.	7.20

Figure 13.1 A list of employee data

The separation of the list into three arrays is unfortunate because all the items relating to a single employee constitute a natural organization of data into structures, as shown in Figure 13.2. Using a structure, the integrity of the data's organization as a record can be maintained and reflected by the program. With this approach, the list in Figure 13.2 can be processed as a single array of 10 structures.

	Employee Number	Employee Name	Employee Pay Rate
1st structure ➤	32479	Abrams, B.	6.72
2nd structure ➤	33623	Bohm, P.	7.54
3rd structure ➤	34145	Donaldson, S.	5.56
4th structure ➤	35987	Ernst, T.	5.43
5th structure ➤	36203	Gwodz, K.	8.72
6th structure ➤	36417	Hanson, H.	7.64
7th structure ➤	37634	Monroe, G.	5.29
8th structure ➤	38321	Price, S.	9.67
9th structure ➤	39435	Robbins, L.	8.50
10th structure ➤	39567	Williams, B.	7.20

Figure 13.2   A list of structures

Declaring an array of structures is the same as declaring an array of any other variable type. For example, if the data type `PayRec` is declared as

```
struct PayRec {int idnum; string name; double rate;};
```

then an array of 10 such structures can be defined as follows:

```
PayRec employee[10];
```

This definition statement constructs an array of 10 elements, and each element is a structure of the data type `PayRec`. Notice that creating an array of 10 structures has the same form as creating any other array. For example, creating an array of 10 integers named `employee` requires the following declaration:

```
int employee[10];
```

In this declaration, the data type is integer, and in the previous declaration for `employee`, the data type is `PayRec`.

After an array of structures is declared, a data item is referenced by giving the position of its structure in the array, followed by a period and the structure member. For example, the variable `employee[0].rate` references the `rate` member of the first `employee` structure in the `employee` array. Including structures as elements of an array permits processing a list of structures by using standard array programming techniques. Program 13.3 displays the first five employee records in Figure 13.2.

Program 13.3

```cpp
#include <iostream>
#include <iomanip>
#include <string>
using namespace std;

const int NUMRECS = 5;    // maximum number of records

struct PayRec    // this is a global declaration
{
  int id;
  string name;
  double rate;
};

int main()
{
  int i;
  PayRec employee[NUMRECS] = {
                              { 32479, "Abrams, B.", 6.72 },
                              { 33623, "Bohm, P.", 7.54},
                              { 34145, "Donaldson, S.",  5.56},
                              { 35987, "Ernst, T.", 5.43 },
                              { 36203, "Gwodz, K.", 8.72 }
                              };

  cout << endl;    // start on a new line
  cout << setiosflags(ios::left);  // left-justify the output
  for ( i = 0; i < NUMRECS; i++)
    cout << setw(7)  << employee[i].id
         << setw(15) << employee[i].name
         << setw(6)  << employee[i].rate << endl;

  return 0;
}
```

Program 13.3 displays the following output:

```
32479   Abrams, B.     6.72
33623   Bohm, P.       7.54
34145   Donaldson, S.  5.56
35987   Ernst, T.      5.43
36203   Gwodz, K.      8.72
```

In reviewing Program 13.3, notice the initialization of the array of structures. Although the initializers for each structure have been enclosed in inner braces, they aren't strictly necessary because all members have been initialized. As with all external and static variables, in the absence of explicit initializers, the numeric elements of static and external arrays or structures are initialized to 0 and their character elements are initialized to NULLs. The setiosflags(ios::left) manipulator included in the cout stream forces each name to be displayed left-justified in its designated field width.

EXERCISES 13.2

1. **(Practice)** Define arrays of 100 structures for each of the data types described in Exercise 1 of Section 13.1.

2. **(Practice) a.** Using the data type

```
struct MonthDays
{
   string name;
   int days;
};
```

define an array of 12 structures of type MonthDays. Name the array convert[], and initialize the array with the names of the 12 months in a year and the number of days in each month.

   b. Include the array created in Exercise 2a in a program that displays the names of months and number of days in each month.

3. **(Modify)** Using the data type declared in Exercise 2a, write a C++ program that accepts a month from a user in numerical form and displays the name of the month and the number of days in the month. For example, in response to an input of 3, the program would display March has 31 days.

4. **(Data Processing) a.** Declare a single structure data type suitable for an employee structure of the type shown in the following chart:

Number	Name	Rate	Hours
3462	Jones	4.62	40
6793	Robbins	5.83	38
6985	Smith	5.22	45
7834	Swain	6.89	40
8867	Timmins	6.43	35
9002	Williams	4.75	42

   b. Using the data type declared in Exercise 4a, write a C++ program that interactively accepts the chart's data in an array of six structures. After the data has been entered, the program should create a payroll report listing each employee's name, number, and gross pay. Include the total gross pay of all employees at the end of the report.

5. (Data Processing) a. Declare a single structure data type suitable for a car structure of the type in the following chart:

Car Number	Miles Driven	Gallons Used
25	1450	62
36	3240	136
44	1792	76
52	2360	105
68	2114	67

b. Using the data type declared for Exercise 5a, write a C++ program that interactively accepts the chart's data in an array of five structures. After the data has been entered, the program should create a report listing each car number and the car's miles per gallon. At the end of the report, include the average miles per gallon for the entire fleet of cars.

13.3 Structures as Function Arguments

Structure members can be passed to a function in the same manner as any scalar variable. For example, given the structure definition

```
struct
{
   int idNum;
   double payRate;
   double hours;
} emp;
```

the following statement passes a copy of the structure member emp.idNum to a function named display():

```
display(emp.idNum);
```

Similarly, the statement

```
calcPay(emp.payRate,emp.hours);
```

passes copies of the values stored in structure members emp.payRate and emp.hours to the calcPay() function. Both functions, display() and calcPay(), must declare the correct data types for their arguments.

Copies of all structure members can also be passed to a function by including the name of the structure as an argument to the called function. For example, this function call passes a copy of the emp structure to calcNet():

```
calcNet(emp);
```

Inside calcNet(), a declaration must be made to receive the structure. Program 13.4 declares a global data type for an employee structure. The main() and calcNet() functions then use this data type to define structures with the names emp and temp.

 Program 13.4

```
#include <iostream>
#include <iomanip>
using namespace std;

struct Employee        // declare a global data type
{
  int idNum;
  double payRate;
  double hours;
};

double calcNet(Employee);    // function prototype

int main()
{
  Employee emp = {6782, 8.93, 40.5};
  double netPay;

  netPay = calcNet(emp);        // pass copies of the values in emp
    // set output formats
  cout << setw(10)
       << setiosflags(ios::fixed)
       << setiosflags(ios::showpoint)
       << setprecision(2);

  cout << "The net pay for employee " << emp.idNum
       << " is $" << netPay << endl;

  return 0;
}

double calcNet(Employee temp) // temp is of data type Employee
{
  return temp.payRate * temp.hours;
}
```

The output produced by Program 13.4 is as follows:

```
The net pay for employee 6782 is $361.66
```

In reviewing Program 13.4, observe that both `main()` and `calcNet()` use the same data type to define their structure variables. The structure variable defined in `main()` and the structure variable defined in `calcNet()` are two different structures. Any changes made to the local `temp` variable in `calcNet()` aren't reflected in the `emp` variable of `main()`. In fact, because both structure variables are local to their functions, the same structure variable name could have been used in both functions with no ambiguity.

When `calcNet()` is called by `main()`, copies of `emp`'s structure values are passed to the `temp` structure. `calcNet()` then uses two of the passed member values to calculate a number, which is returned to `main()`. Because `calcNet()` returns a non-integer number, the data type of the returned value must be included in all declarations for `calcNet()`.

An alternative to the pass-by-value function call in Program 13.4, in which the called function receives a copy of a structure, is a pass by reference that passes a reference to a structure. Doing so permits the called function to access and alter values directly in the calling function's structure variable. For example, referring to Program 13.4, the prototype of `calcNet()` can be modified to the following:

```
double calcNet(Employee &);
```

If this function prototype is used and the `calcNet()` function is rewritten to conform to it, the `main()` function in Program 13.4 can be used as is. Program 13.4a shows these changes in the context of a complete program.

Program 13.4a

```
#include <iostream>
#include <iomanip>
using namespace std;

struct Employee        // declare a global data type
{
  int idNum;
  double payRate;
  double hours;
};

double calcNet(Employee&);    // function prototype

int main()
{
  Employee emp = {6782, 8.93, 40.5};
  double netPay;
```

☞

```
    netPay = calcNet(emp);          // pass a reference
      // set output formats
    cout << setw(10)
         << setiosflags(ios::fixed)
         << setiosflags(ios::showpoint)
         << setprecision(2);

    cout << "The net pay for employee " << emp.idNum
         << " is $" <<  netPay << endl;

    return 0;
}


double calcNet(Employee& temp)    // temp is a reference variable
{
    return temp.payRate * temp.hours;
}
```

Program 13.4a produces the same output as Program 13.4, except the calcNet() function in Program 13.4a receives direct access to the emp structure instead of a copy of it. This means the variable name temp in calcNet() is an alternate name for the variable emp in main(), and any changes to temp are direct changes to emp. Although the same function call, calcNet(emp), is made in both programs, the call in Program 13.4a passes a reference, and the call in Program 13.4 passes values.

Passing a Pointer

Instead of passing a reference, a pointer can be used. Using a pointer requires, in addition to modifying the function's prototype and header, modifying the call to calcNet() in Program 13.4 to the following:

```
calcNet(&emp);
```

This function call clearly indicates that an address is being passed (which isn't the case in Program 13.4a). The disadvantage is the dereferencing notation required inside the function. However, as pointers are widely used in practice, becoming familiar with this notation is worthwhile.

To store the passed address correctly, calcNet() must declare its parameter as a pointer. The following function definition for calcNet() is suitable:

```
calcNet(Employee *pt)
```

This definition declares the pt parameter as a pointer to a structure of type Employee. The pt pointer receives the starting address of a structure when calcNet() is called. In calcNet(), this pointer is used to reference any member in the structure directly. For example, (*pt).idNum refers to the idNum structure member, (*pt).payRate refers to the payRate structure member, and (*pt).hours refers to the hours structure member. These relationships are illustrated in Figure 13.3.

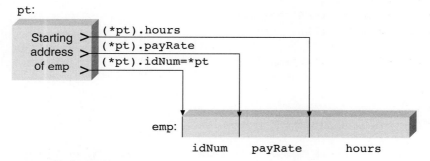

Figure 13.3   A pointer can be used to access structure members

The parentheses around the expression *pt in Figure 13.3 are necessary to access "the structure whose address is in pt." The (*pt) is followed by an identifier to access the structure member. In the absence of parentheses, the structure member operator, ., takes precedence over the indirection operator, *. Therefore, the expression *pt.hours is another way of writing *(pt.hours), which would mean "the variable whose address is in the pt.hours variable." This expression makes no sense because there's no structure named pt and hours doesn't contain an address.

As shown in Figure 13.3, the starting address of the emp structure is also the address of the first structure member. Using pointers in this manner is so common that a special notation exists for it. The general expression (*pointer).member can always be replaced with the notation pointer->member. The -> operator is a hyphen followed by a greater-than symbol. Either expression can be used to locate the member. For example, the following expressions are equivalent:

```
(*pt).idNum   can be replaced by pt->idNum
(*pt).payRate can be replaced by pt->payRate
(*pt).hours   can be replaced by pt->hours
```

Program 13.5 shows passing a structure's address and using a pointer with the new notation to reference the structure directly. The name of the pointer parameter declared in Program 13.5 is, of course, selected by the programmer. When calcNet() is called, emp's starting address is passed to the function. Using this address as a starting point, structure members are accessed by including their names with the pointer.

Program 13.5

```cpp
#include <iostream>
#include <iomanip>
using namespace std;

struct Employee    // declare a global data type
{
  int idNum;
  double payRate;
  double hours;
};

double calcNet(Employee *);    //function prototype

int main()
{
  Employee emp = {6782, 8.93, 40.5};
  double netPay;
  netPay = calcNet(&emp);         // pass an address

     // set output formats
  cout << setw(10)
       << setiosflags(ios::fixed)
       << setiosflags(ios::showpoint)
       << setprecision(2);

  cout << "The net pay for employee " << emp.idNum
       << " is $" << netPay << endl;

  return 0;
}

double calcNet(Employee *pt)    // pt is a pointer to a
{                               // structure of Employee type
  return(pt->payRate * pt->hours);
}
```

As with all C++ expressions that access a variable, the increment (++) and decrement (--) operators can also be applied to them. For example, the expression

```cpp
++pt->hours
```

adds one to the hours member of the emp structure. Because the -> operator has a higher priority than the prefix increment operator, the hours member is accessed first, and then the increment is applied. If you enclose the prefix increment operator and pointer in parentheses, as in the expression (++pt)->hours, the address in pt is incremented before the hours member is accessed. Similarly, the expression (pt++)->hours uses the postfix increment operator to increment the address in pt after the hours member is accessed. In both cases, however, there must be enough defined structures to ensure that the incremented pointers actually point to legitimate structures.

As an example, Figure 13.4 illustrates an array of three structures of type Employee. Assuming the address of emp[1] is stored in the pointer variable pt, the expression ++pt changes the address in pt to the starting address of emp[2], and the expression --pt changes the address to point to emp[0].

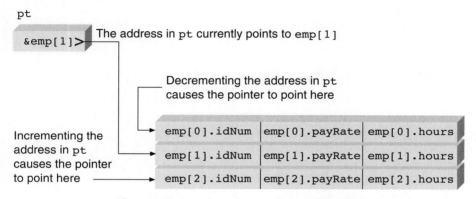

Figure 13.4   Changing pointer addresses

Returning Structures

In practice, most structure-handling functions get direct access to a structure by receiving a structure reference or address. Then any changes to the structure can be made directly from the function. If you want to have a function return a separate structure, however, you must follow the same procedures for returning data structures as for returning scalar values. These procedures include declaring the function appropriately and alerting any calling function to the type of data structure being returned. For example, the getVals() function in Program 13.6 returns a data structure to main().

The following output is displayed when Program 13.6 runs:

```
The employee id number is 6789
The employee pay rate is $16.25
The employee hours are 38
```

Program 13.6

```cpp
#include <iostream>
#include <iomanip>
using namespace std;

struct Employee        // declare a global data type
{
  int idNum;
  double payRate;
  double hours;
};

Employee getVals();    // function prototype

int main()
{
  Employee emp;

  emp = getVals();
  cout << "\nThe employee id number is " << emp.idNum
       << "\nThe employee pay rate is $" << emp.payRate
       << "\nThe employee hours are " << emp.hours << endl;

  return 0;
}

Employee getVals() // return an Employee structure
{
  Employee next;

  next.idNum = 6789;
  next.payRate = 16.25;
  next.hours = 38.0;

  return next;
}
```

Because the getVals() function returns a structure, the function header for getVals() must specify the type of structure being returned. Because getVals() doesn't receive any arguments, the function header has no parameter declarations and consists of this line:

```cpp
Employee getVals();
```

In getVals(), the variable next is defined as a structure of the type to be returned. After values have been assigned to the next structure, the structure values are returned by including the structure name in the return statement.

On the receiving side, main() must be alerted that the getVals() function will be returning a structure. This alert is handled by including a function declaration for getVals() in main(). Notice that these steps for returning a structure from a function are identical to the procedures for returning scalar data types, described in Chapter 6.

EXERCISES 13.3

1. **(Data Processing)** Write a C++ function named days() that determines the number of days from the turn of the century for any date passed as a structure. Use the Date structure:

```
struct Date
{
  int month;
  int day;
  int year;
};
```

In writing the days() function, follow the financial convention that all years have 360 days and each month consists of 30 days. The function should return the number of days for any Date structure passed to it.

2. **(Data Processing)** Write a C++ function named difDays() that calculates and returns the difference between two dates. Each date is passed to the function as a structure by using the following global data type:

```
struct Date
{
  int month;
  int day;
  int year;
};
```

The difDays() function should make two calls to the days() function written for Exercise 1.

3. **(Modify) a.** Rewrite the days() function written for Exercise 1 to receive a reference to a Date structure rather than a copy of the structure.

   b. Redo Exercise 3a, using a pointer rather than a reference.

4. **(Data Processing) a.** Write a C++ function named larger() that returns the later date of any two dates passed to it. For example, if the dates 10/9/2005 and 11/3/2005 are passed to larger(), the second date is returned.

   b. Include the larger() function written for Exercise 4a in a complete program. Store the Date structure returned by larger() in a separate Date structure and display the member values of the returned Date.

13.4 Linked Lists

A classic data-handling problem is making additions or deletions to existing structures that are maintained in a specific order. This problem is best illustrated by the alphabetical telephone list shown here:

Acme, Sam
(555) 898-2392
Dolan, Edith
(555) 682-3104
Lanfrank, John
(555) 718-4581
Mening, Stephen
(555) 382-7070
Zemann, Harold
(555) 219-9912

Starting with this set of names and telephone numbers, you want to add new structures to the list in the correct alphabetical sequence and delete existing structures in such a way that storage for deleted structures is eliminated.

Although inserting or deleting ordered structures can be accomplished by using an array of structures, these arrays aren't efficient representations for adding or deleting structures in the array. Arrays are fixed and have a specified size. Deleting a structure from an array creates an empty slot that requires special marking or shifting all elements below the deleted structure up to close the empty slot.

Similarly, adding a structure to an array of structures requires shifting all elements below the addition down to make room for the new entry, or the new element could be added to the bottom of the existing array, and the array could then be resorted to restore the structures' correct order. Therefore, adding or deleting records to or from this type of list generally requires restructuring and rewriting the list—a cumbersome, time-consuming, and inefficient practice.

A linked list provides a convenient method for maintaining a constantly changing list, without needing to reorder and restructure the entire list. A **linked list** is simply a set of structures in which each structure contains at least one member whose value is the address of the next logically ordered structure in the list. Instead of requiring each record to be physically stored in the correct order, each new structure is physically added wherever the computer has free storage space. The records are "linked" together by including the address of the next record in the record immediately preceding it. From a programming standpoint, the current structure being processed contains the address of the next record, no matter where the next structure is actually stored.

Figure 13.5 illustrates the concept of a linked list. Although the actual data for the Lanfrank structure in the figure can be physically stored anywhere in the computer, the additional member included at the end of the Dolan structure maintains the correct alphabetical order. This member provides the starting address of the location where the Lanfrank record is stored. As you might expect, this member is a pointer.

To see the usefulness of the pointer in the Dolan structure, add a telephone number for June Hagar to the alphabetical list. The data for June Hagar is stored in a data structure,

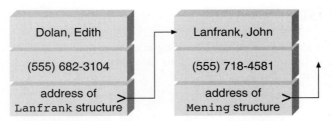

Figure 13.5   Using pointers to link structures

using the same type as for the existing structures. To make sure the telephone number for Hagar is displayed correctly after the Dolan telephone number, the address in the `Dolan` structure must be altered to point to the `Hagar` structure, and the address in the `Hagar` structure must be set to point to the `Lanfrank` structure, as illustrated in Figure 13.6. Notice that the pointer in each structure simply points to the location of the next ordered structure, even if that structure isn't physically located in the correct order.

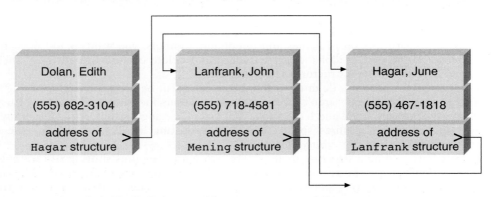

Figure 13.6   Adjusting addresses to point to the correct structures

Removing a structure from the ordered list is the reverse of adding a record. The actual record is removed from the list simply by changing the address in the structure preceding it to point to the structure immediately after the deleted record.

Each structure in a linked list has the same format; however, it's clear the last record can't have a valid pointer value that points to another record because there's no other record. C++ provides a special pointer value called `NULL` that acts as a sentinel or flag to indicate when the last record has been processed. The `NULL` pointer value, like its end-of-string counterpart, has a numerical value of 0.

Besides an end-of-list sentinel value, a special pointer must be provided for storing the address of the first structure in the list. Figure 13.7 illustrates the pointers and structures for a list consisting of three names.

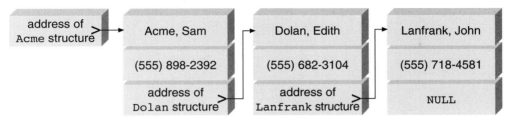

Figure 13.7   Using initial and final pointer values

Including a pointer in a structure shouldn't seem surprising. As you discovered in Section 13.1, a structure can contain any C++ data type. For example, the following structure declaration declares a structure type consisting of two members:

```
struct Test
{
  int idNum;
  double *ptPay;
};
```

The first member is an integer variable named idNum, and the second variable is a pointer named ptPay, which is a pointer to a double-precision number. Program 13.7 shows that the pointer member of a structure is used like any other pointer variable.

Figure 13.8 illustrates the relationship between members of the emp structure defined in Program 13.7 and the variable pay. The value assigned to emp.idNum is the number 12345, and the value assigned to pay is 456.20. The address of the pay variable is assigned to the structure member emp.ptPay. Because this member has been defined as a pointer to a double-precision number, placing the address of the double-precision variable pay in it is a correct use of this member. Finally, because the member operator, ., has a higher precedence than the indirection operator, *, the expression in the cout statement in Program 13.7, *emp.ptPay, is correct. This expression is equivalent to the expression *(emp.ptPay), which is translated as "the variable whose address is contained in the member emp.ptPay."

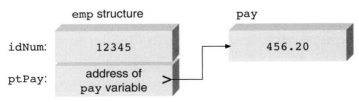

Figure 13.8   Storing an address in a structure member

Program 13.7

```cpp
#include <iostream>
#include <iomanip>
using namespace std;

struct Test
{
  int idNum;
  double *ptPay;
};

int main()
{
  Test emp;
  double pay = 456.20;

  emp.idNum = 12345;
  emp.ptPay = &pay;
    // set output formats
  cout << setw(6)
       << setiosflags(ios::fixed)
       << setiosflags(ios::showpoint)
       << setprecision(2);

  cout << "\nEmployee number " << emp.idNum << " was paid $"
       << *emp.ptPay << endl;

  return 0;
}
```

The output Program 13.7 produces is as follows:

```
Employee number 12345 was paid $456.20
```

Although the pointer defined in Program 13.7 is rather simple, the program does illustrate the concept of including a pointer in a structure. This concept can be extended easily to create a linked list of structures suitable for storing the names and telephone numbers listed at the beginning of this section. The following declaration creates a type for this structure:

```cpp
struct TeleType
{
  string name;
  string phoneNo;
  TeleType *nextaddr;
};
```

The last member in this structure is a pointer suitable for storing the address of a structure of the TeleType type. Program 13.8 shows the use of the TeleType type by defining three structures having this form. The three structures are named t1, t2, and t3, and the name and telephone members of each structure are initialized when the structures are defined, using the data in the list of names and telephone numbers.

Program 13.8

```cpp
#include <iostream>
#include <string>
using namespace std;

struct TeleType
{
  string name;
  string phoneNo;
  TeleType *nextaddr;
};

int main()
{
  TeleType t1 = {"Acme, Sam","(555) 898-2392"};
  TeleType t2 = {"Dolan, Edith","(555) 682-3104"};
  TeleType t3 = {"Lanfrank, John","(555) 718-4581"};
  TeleType *first;      // create a pointer to a structure

  first = &t1;          // store t1's address in first
  t1.nextaddr = &t2;    // store t2's address in t1.nextaddr
  t2.nextaddr = &t3;    // store t3's address in t2.nextaddr
  t3.nextaddr = NULL;   // store a NULL address in t3.nextaddr

  cout << endl << first->name
       << endl << t1.nextaddr->name
       << endl << t2.nextaddr->name
       << endl;

  return 0;
}
```

Program 13.8 produces the following output:

```
Acme, Sam
Dolan, Edith
Lanfrank, John
```

Program 13.8 demonstrates using pointers to access successive structure members. As illustrated in Figure 13.9, each structure contains the address of the next structure in the list.

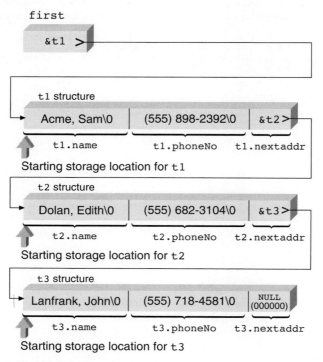

Figure 13.9 The relationship between structures in Program 13.8

The initialization of the names and telephone numbers for each structure defined in Program 13.8 is straightforward. Although each structure consists of three members, only the first two members of each structure are initialized. As both these members are arrays of characters, they can be initialized with strings. The remaining member of each structure is a pointer. To create a linked list, each structure pointer must be assigned the address of the next structure in the list.

The four assignment statements in Program 13.8 perform the correct assignments. The expression `first = &t1` stores the address of the first structure in the list in the pointer variable `first`. The expression `t1.nextaddr = &t2` stores the starting address of the t2 structure in the pointer member of the t1 structure. Similarly, the expression `t2.nextaddr = &t3` stores the starting address of the t3 structure in the pointer member of the t2 structure. To end the list, the value of the NULL pointer, which is 0, is stored in the pointer member of the t3 structure.

After values have been assigned to each structure member and correct addresses have been stored in the appropriate pointers, the addresses in the pointers are used to access each structure's `name` member. For example, the expression `t1.nextaddr->name` refers to the name member of the structure whose address is in the `nextaddr` member of the t1 structure. The member operator, `.`, and the structure pointer operator, `->`, have equal precedence and are evaluated from left to right. Therefore, the expression t1.nextaddr->name is evaluated as (t1.nextaddr)->name. Because t1.nextaddr contains the address of the t2 structure, the correct name member is accessed.

The expression t1.nextaddr->name can, of course, be replaced by the equivalent expression (*t1.nextaddr).name, which uses the more conventional indirection operator. This expression also means "the name member of the variable whose address is in t1.nextaddr."

The addresses in a linked list of structures can be used to loop through the complete list. As each structure is accessed, it can be examined to select a specific value or used to display a complete list. For example, the display() function in Program 13.9 shows the use of a while loop, which uses the address in each structure's pointer member to cycle through the list and display data stored in each structure.

Program 13.9

```cpp
#include <iostream>
#include <iomanip>
#include <string>
using namespace std;

struct TeleType
{
  string name;
  string phoneNo;
  TeleType *nextaddr;
};

void display(TeleType *);        // function prototype

int main()
{
  TeleType t1 = {"Acme, Sam","(555) 898-2392"};
  TeleType t2 = {"Dolan, Edith","(555) 682-3104"};
  TeleType t3 = {"Lanfrank, John","(555) 718-4581"};
  TeleType *first;    // create a pointer to a structure

  first = &t1;        // store t1's address in first
  t1.nextaddr = &t2;  // store t2's address in t1.nextaddr
  t2.nextaddr = &t3;  // store t3's address in t2.nextaddr
  t3.nextaddr = NULL; // store the NULL address in t3.nextaddr

  display(first);     // send the address of the first structure

  return 0;
}
```

```
void display(TeleType *contents) // contents is a pointer to a
{                                 // structure of type TeleType
  while (contents != NULL)   // display until end of linked list
  {
    cout << endl << setiosflags(ios::left)
         << setw(30) << contents->name
         << setw(20) << contents->phoneNo ;
    contents = contents->nextaddr;    // get next address
  }
  cout << endl;

  return;
}
```

The output produced by Program 13.9 is as follows:

```
Acme, Sam              (555) 898-2392
Dolan, Edith           (555) 682-3104
Lanfrank, John         (555) 718-4581
```

The important concept Program 13.9 shows is using the address in one structure to access members of the next structure in the list. When the `display()` function is called, it's passed the value stored in the variable `first`. Because `first` is a pointer variable, the actual value passed is an address (the address of the t1 structure). The `display()` function accepts the passed value in the argument `contents`. To store the passed address correctly, `contents` is declared as a pointer to a structure of the `TeleType` type. In `display()`, a `while` loop is used to cycle through the linked structures, starting with the structure whose address is in `contents`. The condition tested in the `while` statement compares the value in `contents`, which is an address, to the `NULL` value. For each valid address, the name and telephone number members of the addressed structure are displayed. The address in `contents` is then updated with the address in the pointer member of the current structure.

The address in `contents` is then retested, and the process continues as long the address in `contents` isn't equal to the `NULL` value. The `display()` function "knows" nothing about the names of structures declared in `main()` or even how many structures exist. It simply cycles through the linked list, structure by structure, until it encounters the end-of-list `NULL` address. Because the value of `NULL` is 0, the tested condition can be replaced by the equivalent expression `contents`.

A disadvantage of Program 13.9 is that exactly three structures are defined in `main()` by name, and storage for them is reserved at compile time. Should a fourth structure be required, it would have to be declared and the program recompiled. In Section 13.5, you see how to have the computer allocate and release storage for structures dynamically at runtime, as storage is required. Only when a new structure is to be added to the list, and while the program is running, is storage for the new structure created. Similarly, when a structure is no longer needed and can be deleted from the list, storage for the deleted record is relinquished and returned to the computer.

EXERCISES 13.4

1. **(Modify)** Modify Program 13.9 to prompt the user for a name. Have the program search the existing list for the entered name. If the name is in the list, display the corresponding telephone number; otherwise, display this message: The name is not in the current phone directory.

2. **(Practice)** Write a C++ program containing a linked list of 10 integer numbers. Have the program display the numbers in the list.

3. **(Data Processing)** Using the linked list of structures in Figure 13.10, write the sequence of steps for deleting the record for Edith Dolan from the list.

4. **(Modify)** Generalize the description in Exercise 3 to describe the sequence of steps for removing the nth structure from a list of linked structures. The nth structure is preceded by the $(n - 1)$st structure and followed by the $(n + 1)$st structure. Make sure to store all pointer values correctly.

5. **(Data Processing) a.** In a doubly linked list, each structure contains a pointer to both the following and previous structures in the list. Define an appropriate type for a doubly linked list of names and telephone numbers.

   b. Using the type defined in Exercise 5a, modify Program 13.9 to list the names and telephone numbers in reverse order.

13.5 Dynamic Data Structure Allocation

You have already learned about allocating and deallocating memory space with the new and delete operators (see Section 12.2). For convenience, Table 13.1 repeats the description of these operators.

Table 13.1 Operators for Dynamic Allocation and Deallocation

Operator Name	Description
new	Reserves the number of bytes required by the requested data type. Returns the address of the first reserved location or NULL if not enough memory is available.
delete	Releases a block of bytes reserved previously. The address of the first reserved location is passed as an argument to the operator.

Dynamic allocation of memory is especially useful when dealing with a list of structures because it permits expanding the list as new records are added and contracting the list as records are deleted. In requesting additional storage space, the user must provide the new operator with an indication of the amount of storage needed for a particular data type. For example, the expression new(int) or new int (the two forms can be used interchangeably) requests enough storage to store an integer number. A request for enough storage for a data structure is made in the same fashion. For example, using the declaration

```
struct TeleType
{
  string name;
  string phoneNo;
};
```

both the expressions new TeleType and new(TeleType) reserve enough storage for one TeleType data structure.

In allocating storage dynamically, you have no advance indication where the computer will physically reserve the requested number of bytes, and you have no explicit name to access the newly created storage locations. To provide access to these locations, new returns the address of the first location that has been reserved. This address must, of course, be assigned to a pointer. The return of a pointer by new is especially useful for creating a linked list of data structures. As each new structure is created, the pointer new returns to the structure can be assigned to a member of the previous structure in the list. Program 13.10 shows using new to create a structure dynamically in response to a user-input request.

Program 13.10

```
// a program illustrating dynamic structure allocation
#include <iostream>
#include <string>
using namespace std;

struct TeleType
{
  string name;
  string phoneNo;
};

void populate(TeleType *);  // function prototype needed by main()
void dispOne(TeleType *);   // function prototype needed by main()

int main()
{
  char key;
  TeleType *recPoint;    // recPoint is a pointer to a
                         // structure of type TeleType
```

☞

```cpp
  cout << "Do you wish to create a new record (respond with y or n): ";
  key = cin.get();
  if (key == 'y')
  {
    key = cin.get();       // get the Enter key in buffered input
    recPoint = new TeleType;
    populate(recPoint);
    dispOne(recPoint);

  }
  else
    cout << "\nNo record has been created.";

  return 0;
}

  // input a name and phone number
void populate(TeleType *record) // record is a pointer to a
  {                              // structure of type TeleType
    cout << "Enter a name: ";
    getline(cin,record->name);
    cout << "Enter the phone number: ";
    getline(cin,record->phoneNo);
    return;
  }

  // display the contents of one record
void dispOne(TeleType *contents)  // contents is a pointer to a
{                                 // structure of type TeleType
  cout << "\nThe contents of the record just created are:"
       << "\nName: " << contents->name
       << "\nPhone Number: " << contents->phoneNo << endl;
  return;
}
```

A sample of the output Program 13.10 produces is as follows:

```
Do you wish to create a new record (respond with y or n): y
Enter a name: Monroe, James
Enter the phone number: (555) 617-1817

The contents of the record just created are:
Name: Monroe, James
Phone Number: (555) 617-1817
```

In reviewing Program 13.10, notice that only two variable declarations are made in main(). The variable key is declared as a character variable, and the variable recPoint is declared as being a pointer to a structure of the TeleType type. Because the declaration for the type TeleType is global, TeleType can be used in main() to define recPoint as a pointer to a structure of the TeleType type.

If a user enters y in response to the first prompt in main(), a call to new is made for the required memory to store the designated structure. After recPoint has been loaded with the correct address, this address can be used to access the newly created structure.

The populate() function is used to prompt the user for data needed in filling the structure and to store the user-entered data in the correct structure members. The argument passed to populate() in main() is the pointer recPoint. Like all passed arguments, the value in recPoint is passed to the function. Because the value in recPoint is an address, populate() receives the address of the newly created structure and can access the structure members directly.

In populate(), the value it receives is stored in the argument record. Because the value to be stored in record is the address of a structure, record must be declared as a pointer to a structure. This declaration is provided by the statement TeleType *record;. The statements in populate() use the address in record to locate the structure members.

The dispOne() function displays the contents of the newly created and populated structure. The address passed to dispOne() is the same address that was passed to populate(). Because this passed value is the address of a structure, the argument used to store the address is declared as a pointer to the correct structure type.

After you understand the mechanism of calling new, you can use it to construct a linked list of structures. As described in Section 13.4, the structures used in a linked list must contain at least one pointer member. The address in the pointer member is the starting address of the next structure in the list. Additionally, a pointer must be reserved for the address of the first structure, and the pointer member of the last structure in the list is given a NULL address to indicate that no more members are being pointed to. Program 13.11 shows using new to construct a linked list of names and telephone numbers. The populate() function in Program 13.11 is the same one used in Program 13.10, and the display() function is the same one used in Program 13.9.

 Program 13.11

```
#include <iostream>
#include <iomanip>
#include <string>
using namespace std;
```

☞

```cpp
const int MAXRECS = 3;    // maximum number of records

struct TeleType
{
  char name;
  char phoneNo;
  TeleType *nextaddr;
};

void populate(TeleType *);    // function prototype needed by main()
void display(TeleType *);     // function prototype needed by main()

int main()
{
  int i;
  TeleType *list, *current; // two pointers to structures of
                            // type TeleType

    // get a pointer to the first structure in the list
  list = new TeleType;
  current = list;

    // populate the current structure and create the remaining
    // structures
  for(i = 0; i < MAXRECS - 1; i++)
  {
    populate(current);
    current->nextaddr = new TeleType;
    current = current->nextaddr;
  }

  populate(current);           // populate the last structure
  current->nextaddr = NULL;  // set the last address to a NULL address
  cout << "\nThe list consists of the following records:\n";
  display(list);   // display the structures

  return 0;
}
```

☞

```
    // input a name and phone number
void populate(TeleType *record) // record is a pointer to a
{                               // structure of type TeleType

  cout << "Enter a name: ";
  getline(cin,record->name);
  cout << "Enter the phone number: ";
  getline(cin,record->phoneNo);

  return;
}

void display(TeleType *contents) // contents is a pointer to a
{                                //    structure of type TeleType
  while (contents != NULL)       // display until end of linked list
  {
    cout << endl << setiosflags(ios::left)
         << setw(30) << contents->name
         << setw(20) << contents->phoneNo;
    contents = contents->nextaddr;
  }
  cout << endl;

  return;
}
```

The first time new is called in Program 13.11, it's used to create the first structure in the linked list. Therefore, the address new returns is stored in the pointer variable list. The address in list is then assigned to the pointer current. This pointer variable is always used to point to the current structure. Because the current structure is the first structure created, the address in the pointer list is assigned to the pointer current.

In main()'s for loop, the name and telephone number members of the newly created structure are populated by calling populate() and passing the address of the current structure to the function. At the return from populate(), the pointer member of the current structure is assigned the address of the next structure in the list, which is obtained from new. The call to new creates the next structure and returns its address to the pointer member of the current structure. This call completes the population of the current member. The final statement in the for loop resets the address in the current pointer to the address of the next structure in the list.

After the last structure has been created, the final statements in main() populate this structure, assign a NULL address to the pointer member, and call display() to display all structures in the list. The following is a sample run of Program 13.11:

```
    Enter a name: Acme, Sam
    Enter the phone number: (555) 898-2392
    Enter a name: Dolan, Edith
    Enter the phone number: (555) 682-3104
```

```
Enter a name: Lanfrank, John
Enter the phone number: (555) 718-4581
The list consists of the following records:
Acme, Sam                    (555) 898-2392
Dolan, Edith                 (555) 682-3104
Lanfrank, John               (555) 718-4581
```

Just as new creates storage dynamically at runtime, the delete operator restores a block of storage to the computer at runtime. The only argument delete requires is the starting address of a storage block that was allocated dynamically. Therefore, any address new returns can be passed subsequently to delete to restore the reserved memory to the computer. The delete operator doesn't alter the address passed to it; it simply removes the storage that the address references.

EXERCISES 13.5

1. **(Modify)** As described in Table 13.1, the new operator returns the address of the first new storage area allocated or NULL if insufficient storage is available. Modify Program 13.11 to check that a valid address has been returned before a call to populate() is made. Display an appropriate message if not enough storage is available.

2. **(Program)** Write a C++ function named remove() that removes an existing structure from the linked list of structures Program 13.11 created. The algorithm for removing a linked structure should follow the sequence for removing a structure developed in Exercise 4 in Section 13.4. The argument passed to remove() should be the address of the structure preceding the record to be removed. In the remove() function, make sure the value of the pointer in the removed structure replaces the value of the pointer member of the preceding structure before the structure is removed.

3. **(Program)** Write a function named insert() that inserts a structure in the linked list of structures Program 13.11 created. The algorithm for inserting a structure in a linked list should follow the sequence for inserting a record previously shown in Figure 13.7. The argument passed to insert() should be the address of the structure preceding the structure to be inserted. The inserted structure should follow this current structure. The insert() function should create a new structure dynamically, call the populate() function used in Program 13.11, and adjust all pointer values accordingly.

4. **(Program)** You want to insert a new structure in the linked list of structures Program 13.11 created. The function developed to do this in Exercise 3 assumes that the preceding structure's address is known. Write a function called findRec() that returns the address of the structure immediately preceding the point where the new structure is to be inserted. (*Hint:* findRec() must request the new name as input and compare the entered name to existing names to determine where to place the new name.)

5. **(Program)** Write a C++ function named modify() that can be used to modify the name and telephone number members of a structure of the type created in Program 13.11. The argument passed to modify() should be the address of the structure to be modified. The modify() function should first display the existing name and telephone number in the selected structure, and then request new data for these members.

6. **(Program) a.** Write a C++ program that presents a menu of choices for the user. The menu should consist of the following choices:

> Create a linked list of names and phone numbers
> Insert a new structure in the linked list
> Modify an existing structure in the linked list
> Delete an existing structure from the list
> Exit from the program

Based on the user's selection, the program should execute a function to satisfy the request.

b. Why is creating a linked list usually done by one program, and the options to add, modify, or delete a structure in the list provided by a different program?

13.6 Unions[2]

A **union** is a data type that reserves the same area in memory for two or more variables that can be different data types. A variable declared as a union data type can be used to hold a character variable, an integer variable, a double-precision variable, or any other valid C++ data type. Each of these types, but only one at a time, can be assigned to the union variable.

The definition of a union has the same form as a structure definition, with the keyword `union` used in place of the keyword `struct`. For example, the following declaration creates a union variable named `val`:

```
union
{
  char key;
  int num;
  double volts;
} val;
```

If `val` were a structure, it would consist of three members. As a union, however, `val` contains a single member that can be a character variable named `key`, an integer variable named `num`, or a double-precision variable named `volts`. In effect, a union reserves enough memory locations to accommodate its largest member's data type. This same set of locations is then referenced by different variable names, depending on the data type of the value currently stored in the reserved locations. Each value stored overwrites the previous value, using as many bytes of the reserved memory area as necessary.

Union members are referenced by using the same notation as structure members. For example, if the `val` union is currently being used to store a character, the correct variable name to access the stored character is `val.key`. Similarly, if the union is used to store an integer, the value is accessed by the name `val.num`, and a double-precision value is accessed by the name `val.volts`. In using union members, it's the programmer's responsibility to make sure the correct member name is used for the data type currently stored in the union.

---

[2]This topic can be omitted on first reading with no loss of subject continuity.

Typically, a second variable is used to keep track of the current data type stored in the union. For example, the following code could be used to select the appropriate member of `val` for display. The value in the `uType` variable determines the currently stored data type in the `val` union:

```
switch(uType)
{
  case 'c': cout << val.key;
            break;
  case 'i': cout << val.num;
            break;
  case 'd': cout << val.volts;
            break;
  default : cout << "Invalid type in uType : " << uType;
}
```

As in structures, a data type can be associated with a union. For example, the declaration

```
union DateTime
{
  int days;
  double time;
};
```

provides a union data type without actually reserving any storage locations. This data type can then be used to define any number of variables. For example, the definition

```
DateTime first, second, *pt;
```

creates a union variable named `first`, a union variable named `second`, and a pointer that can be used to store the address of any union having the form `DateTime`. After a pointer to a union has been declared, the same notation for accessing structure members can be used to access union members. For example, if the assignment `pt = &first;` is made, `pt->date` references the date member of the union named `first`.

Unions can be members of structures or arrays, and structures, arrays, and pointers can be members of unions. In each case, the notation used to access a member must be consistent with the nesting used. For example, in the structure defined by

```
struct
{
  char uType;
  union
  {
    char *text;
    float rate;
  } uTax;
} flag;
```

the variable `rate` is referenced as

```
flag.uTax.rate
```

Similarly, the first character of the string whose address is stored in the pointer `text` is referenced as follows:

```
*flag.uTax.text
```

EXERCISES 13.6

1. **(Practice)** Assume the following definition has been made:

```
union
{
  double rate;
  double taxes;
  int num;
} flag;
```

For this union, write `cout` statements to display the members of the union.

2. **(Practice)** Define a union variable named `car` containing an integer named `year`, an array of 10 characters named `name`, and an array of 10 characters named `model`.

3. **(Practice)** Define a union variable named `lang` that allows referencing a double-precision number by the variable names `volts` and `emf`.

4. **(Practice)** Define a union data type named `Amt` containing an integer variable named `intAmt`, a double-precision variable named `dblAmt`, and a pointer to a character named `ptKey`.

5. **(Desk Check) a.** What do you think the following section of code will display?

```
union
{
  char ch;
  double btype;
} alt;
alt.ch = 'y';
cout << alt.btype;
```

   b. Include the code in Exercise 5a in a program, and run the program to verify your answer to Exercise 5a.

13.7 Common Programming Errors

Three common errors are often made when using structures or unions. The first error occurs because structures and unions, as complete entities, can't be used in relational expressions. For example, even if `TeleType` and `PhonType` are two structures of the same type, the expression `TeleType == PhonType` is invalid. Members of a structure or union can, of course, be compared if they are of the same data type, using any of C++'s relational operators.

The second common error is actually an extension of a pointer error as it relates to structures and unions. When a pointer is used to "point to" either of these data types, or when a pointer is a member of a structure or a union, take care to use the address in the pointer to access the correct data type. If you're confused about exactly what's being pointed to, remember: "If in doubt, print it out."

The final error occurs with unions. Because a union can store only one of its members at a time, you must be careful to keep track of the currently stored variable. Storing one data type in a union and accessing it by the wrong variable name can result in an error that's particularly troublesome to locate.

13.8 Chapter Summary

1. A structure allows grouping variables under a common variable name. Each variable in a structure is accessed by its structure variable name, followed by a period, followed by its variable name. Another term for a data structure is a record. One form for declaring a structure is as follows:

```
struct
{
   // member declarations
} structureName;
```

2. A data type can be created from a structure by using this declaration form:

```
struct DataType
{
   // member declarations
};
```

Structure variables can then be defined as this `DataType`. By convention, the first letter of the `DataType` name is always capitalized.

3. Structures are particularly useful as elements of arrays. Used in this manner, each structure becomes one record in a list of records.

4. Complete structures can be used as function arguments, in which case the called function receives a copy of each element in the structure. A structure's address can also be passed, as a reference or a pointer, which gives the called function direct access to the structure.

5. Structure members can be any valid C++ data type, including other structures, unions, arrays, and pointers. When a pointer is included as a structure member, a linked list can be created. This list uses the pointer in one structure to "point to" (contain the address of) the next logical structure in the list.

6. Unions are declared in the same manner as structures. The definition of a union creates a memory overlay area, with each union member using the same memory storage locations. Therefore, only one member of a union can be active at a time.

Programming Projects for Chapter 13

1. (Code) Define a structure data type and member variables for a single kind of screw in a parts inventory, with fields for inventory number, screw length, diameter, kind of head (Phillips or standard slot), material (steel, brass, other), and cost.

2. (Code) You have a structure type defined as follows:

```
struct Inventory
{
  char description[50];
  int prodnum;
  int quantity;
  double price;
};
```

Given this structure, write code for the following:

a. A declaration for an array of 100 structures of type `Inventory`

b. An assignment of inventory number 4355 to the 83rd `Inventory` item

c. A statement that displays the price of the 15th `Inventory` item

3. (Code) Define an array of structures for up to 50 factory employees, in which each structure contains fields for name, age, social security number, hourly wage, and years with the company. Write the following:

a. Statements that display the name and number of years with the company for the 25th employee in the array

b. A loop that, for every employee, adds 1 to the number of years with the company and adds 50 cents to the hourly wage

4. (Mathematical) In two dimensions, a vector is a pair of numbers representing directed arrows in a plane, as shown by vectors V1 and V2 in Figure 13.10.

Two-dimensional mathematical vectors can be written in the form (a,b), where a and b are called the x and y components of the vector. For example, for the vectors in Figure 13.10, V1 = (9,4) and V2 = (3,5). For mathematical vectors, the following operations apply:

$$\text{If } V1 = (a,b) \text{ and } V2 = (c,d)$$
$$V1 + V2 = (a,b) + (c,d) = (a + c, b + d)$$
$$V1 - V2 = (a,b) - (c,d) = (a - c, b - d)$$

Using this information, write a C++ program that defines an array of two mathematical vector structures; each structure consists of two double-precision components, a and b. Your program should permit a user to enter two vectors, call two functions that return the sum and difference of the entered vectors, and display the results calculated by these functions.

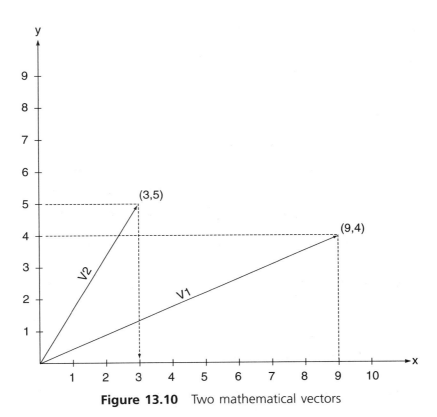

Figure 13.10 Two mathematical vectors

5. **(Modify)** In addition to the operations defined in Exercise 4, two other vector operations are negation and absolute value. For a vector V1 with components (a,b), these operations are defined as follows:

Negation: $-V1 = -(a,b) = (-a,-b)$
Absolute value: $|V1| = \text{sqrt}\,(a * a + b * b)$

Using this information, modify the program you wrote for Exercise 4 to display the negation and absolute values of both vectors input by a user as well as the negation and absolute value of the sum of the two input vectors.

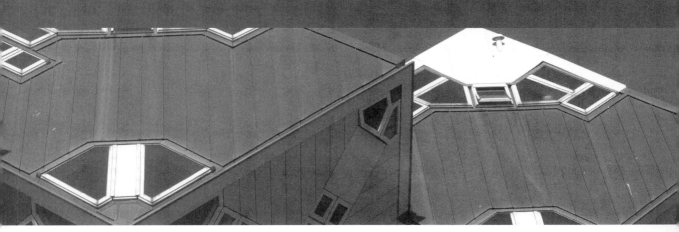

Part Four
Additional Topics

Chapter 14

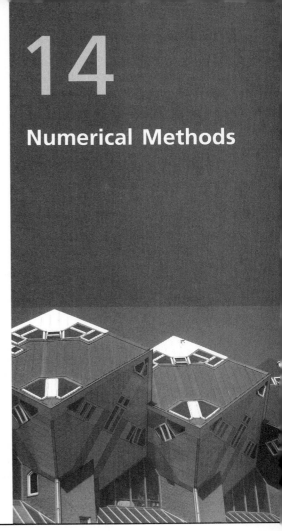

Numerical Methods

One of the most common tasks in science and engineering is finding the roots of equations—that is, given a function f(x), finding values of x such that f(x) = 0.0. This type of problem also includes determining the points of intersection of two curves. If the curves are represented by the functions f(x) and g(x), the intersection points correspond to the roots of the function F(x) = f(x) - g(x).

A second important task is numerical integration, in which approximation methods are used to determine the integral's value when exact solutions don't exist. In this chapter, you learn several programming techniques for finding the roots of equations as well as techniques commonly used in numerical integration.

14.1 Introduction to Root Finding

Root-finding techniques are important for a number of reasons. They are useful, easy to understand, and usually easy to carry out. By using them, you can solve genuine problems in engineering with a minimum of instruction. Vital elements in numerical analysis are appreciating what can or can't be solved and clearly understanding the accuracy of the answers found. Because this appreciation and understanding come mostly from experience, you need to begin solving numerical problems immediately. Besides, root-solving problems can be fun.

The following list shows some examples of the types of functions encountered in root-solving problems:

$$ax^2 + bx + c = 0 \qquad \text{(Equation 14.1)}$$
$$2x^4 - 7x^3 + 4x^2 + 7x - 6 = (x - 2)(x - 1)(x + 1)(2x - 3) = 0 \quad \text{(Equation 14.2)}$$
$$x^5 - 2x^3 - 5x^2 + 2 = 0 \qquad \text{(Equation 14.3)}$$
$$\sin^5(x) + \sin^3(x) + 5\cos(x) - 7 = 0 \qquad \text{(Equation 14.4)}$$
$$100e - x - \sin(2\pi x) = 0 \qquad \text{(Equation 14.5)}$$

The general quadratic equation, Equation 14.1, can be solved easily and exactly by using this quadratic formula:

$$r = \frac{-b \pm \sqrt{(b^2 - 4ac)}}{2a}$$

Equation 14.2 can be solved for x exactly by factoring the polynomial. The roots are then clearly 1, -1, 2, and 3/2. However, most polynomials can't be factored so easily, and other more general techniques are required. There are formulas for the exact solution of general cubic or quartric equations, but they are cumbersome and, therefore, seldom used. No exact formula is possible for a polynomial such as Equation 14.3, in which the highest power of x is greater than 4. For these polynomials, numerical means must generally be used to determine the roots.

Recall from high school algebra that a polynomial of degree n (that is, the highest power of x^n) has precisely n roots, of which some can be complex numbers and others can be multiple roots. Therefore, Equation 14.3 has three real roots

$$r_1 = -0.712780744625. . .$$
$$r_2 = 0.57909844162. . .$$
$$r_3 = 2.0508836199. . .$$

and two complex roots:

$$r_4 = 0.757225433526 + i(0.57803468208)$$
$$r_5 = 0.757225433526 - i(0.57803468208)$$

The equation

$$x^2 - 2x + 1 = 0$$

can be factored as

$$(x - 1)^2 = 0$$

and has two real roots, both of which happen to be the same. In this case, the root is said to be a multiple root with multiplicity 2.

Equations 14.4 and 14.5 are called **transcendental equations** and represent an entirely different class of functions. Typically, transcendental equations involve trigonometric, exponential, or logarithmic functions and can't be reduced to any polynomial equation in x. The real roots of polynomials are usually classified as being rational numbers (a simple fraction) or irrational (for example, $\sqrt{2}$). The roots of transcendental equations are often transcendental numbers, such as π or e.

Irrational numbers and transcendental numbers are represented by nonrepeating decimal fractions and can't be expressed as simple fractions. These numbers are important to mathematics because they're responsible for the real number system being dense or continuous. Therefore, classifying equations as polynomials or transcendental and the roots of these equations as rational or irrational is vital to traditional mathematics; however, the distinction is of less consequence to the computer. In fact, the number system available to the computer is not only continuous, but is also a finite set.

At any rate, when finding the roots of equations, the distinction between polynomials and transcendental equations is unnecessary, and the same numerical procedures are applied to both. The distinction between the two types of functions is, however, important in other regards. Many of the theorems you learned for roots of polynomials don't apply to transcendental equations. For instance, both Equations 14.4 and 14.5 have an infinite number of real roots.

All the root-solving techniques discussed in this chapter are interactive; that is, you specify an interval that's known to contain a root or simply provide an initial guess for the root, and the various routines return a more limited interval or a better guess. Some schemes discussed in this chapter are guaranteed to find a root eventually, but arriving at the answer might take considerable computer time. Others might converge to a root much faster but are more susceptible to problems of divergence; in other words, they come with no guarantees.

The common ingredient in all root-solving recipes is that potential computational difficulties can be avoided by providing the best possible choice of a method and the initial guess, based on your knowledge of the problem. This part of the solution is often the most difficult and time consuming. The art of numerical analysis consists of balancing time spent optimizing the problem's solution before computation against time spent correcting unforeseen errors during computation.

If possible, you should sketch the function before you attempt root solving; you can use graphing routines or generate a table of function values that are then graphed by hand. These graphs are useful to programmers in estimating the first guess for the root as well as anticipating potential difficulties. If a sketch isn't feasible, you must use some method of monitoring the function to understand what the function is doing before you start the actual computation. As an example of the general procedure to follow, take a look at this transcendental function:

$$f(x) = e^{-x} - \sin(\tfrac{1}{2}\pi x)$$

This equation, as you'll see shortly, has an infinite number of positive roots. For the moment, concentrate on obtaining an initial guess for the first root, and then use this initial guess to find a more precise root value.

Begin by gathering as much information as possible before trying to construct a C++ program. This step almost always involves making a rough sketch of the function. The previous equation can be written as follows:

$$e^{-x} = \sin(\tfrac{1}{2}\pi x)$$

A root of this equation then corresponds to any value of x so that the left side and right side are equal. If the left and right sides are plotted separately, the roots of the original equation are then given by the points of intersection of the two curves (see Figure 14.1). From the sketch, you can see that the roots are the following:

Roots $\approx$ 0.4, 1.9, 4.0, . . .

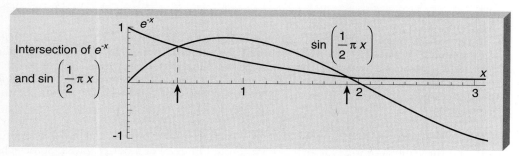

Figure 14.1 Graph of e^{-x} and $\sin(\tfrac{1}{2}\pi x)$ for locating the intersection points

Because the sine oscillates, there are an infinite number of positive roots. First, you should concentrate on improving the estimate of the first root near 0.4. You begin by establishing a procedure, or algorithm, that's based on the most obvious method of attack when using a pocket calculator; that is, begin at some value of x just before the root (say, 0.3) and step along the x-axis, carefully watching the magnitude and particularly the sign of the function, as shown:

Step	x	e^{-x}	$\sin(\tfrac{1}{2}\pi x)$	$f(x) = e^{-x} - \sin(\tfrac{1}{2}\pi x)$
0	0.3	0.741	0.454	0.297
1	0.4	0.670	0.588	0.082
2	0.5	0.606	0.707	-0.101

Notice that the function has changed sign between 0.4 and 0.5, indicating a root between these two x values. For the next approximation, you use the midpoint value, x = 0.45, for the next step:

Step	x	e^{-x}	$\sin(\tfrac{1}{2}\pi x)$	$f(x) = e^{-x} - \sin(\tfrac{1}{2}\pi x)$
3	0.45	0.638	0.649	-0.012

The function is again negative at 0.45, indicating that the root is between 0.4 and 0.45. The next approximation, therefore, is the midpoint of this interval, 0.425. In this way, you can proceed systematically to a computation of the root to any degree of accuracy.

Step	x	e^{-x}	$\sin(\tfrac{1}{2}\pi x)$	$f(x) = e^{-x} - \sin(\tfrac{1}{2}\pi x)$
4	0.425	0.654	0.619	0.0347
5	0.4375	0.6456	0.6344	0.01126
6	0.44365	0.6417	0.6418	-0.00014

The key element in this procedure is monitoring the sign of the function. When the sign changes, specific action is taken to refine the estimate of the root. This change in the function's sign, indicating the vicinity of a root has been located, forms the key element in the computer code for locating roots. In the next three sections, you learn several root-finding methods based on this procedure.

EXERCISES 14.1

1. **(Practice)** Use the iterative technique presented in this section to find a root of the equation

   $f(x) = \sin x - x/3 = 0$ (x is in radians)

   To do this, first rewrite the equation as

   $\sin x = x/3$

   and plot the left and right sides separately on the same graph.

14.2 The Bisection Method

The root-solving procedure explained in Section 14.1 is suitable for hand calculations; however, a slight modification makes it more systematic and easier to adapt to computer coding. This modified computational technique is known as the **bisection method**. Suppose you already know there's a root between $x = a$ and $x = b$; that is, the function changes sign in this interval. For simplicity, assume there's only one root between $x = a$ and $x = b$ and the function is continuous in this interval.

The function might then resemble the sketch in Figure 14.2. If you then define $x_1 = a$ and $x_3 = b$ as the left and right ends of the interval, respectively, and $x_2 = \tfrac{1}{2}(x_1 + x_3)$ as the midpoint, in which half-interval does the function cross the x-axis? In the figure, the crossing is on the right, so you replace the full interval by the right half-interval. Therefore,

x_2 now becomes x_1.

x_3 remains as it is.

x_2 is recalculated as the value $\tfrac{1}{2}(x_1 + x_3)$.

and again, the question is "In which half-interval does the function cross the x-axis?"

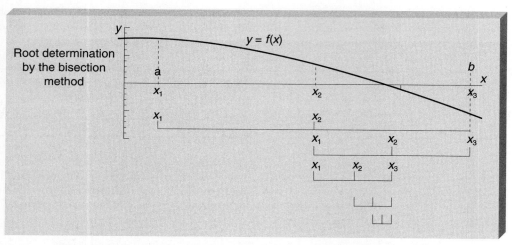

Figure 14.2 A sketch of a function with one root between *a* and *b*

After determining a second time whether the left half or right half contains the root, the interval is again replaced by the left or right half-interval. This process is continued until you narrow in on the root to a previously assigned accuracy. Each step halves the interval, so after *n* iterations, the interval's size containing the root is $(b - a)/2n$. If you're required to find a root to within a tolerance δ (that is, $|x - \text{root}| < \delta$), the number of iterations, *n*, required can be determined from this equation:

$$\frac{b-a}{2^n} < \delta$$

For example, the initial search interval in the example in the previous section was $(b - a) = 0.1$. If the root is required to an accuracy of $\delta = 10^{-5}$, then

$$\frac{0.1}{2^n} < 10^{-5}$$

or

$$2^n > 10^4$$

This equation can be solved for *n* as follows:

$$n > \frac{\log(10^4)}{\log(2)} > 13$$

Therefore, the calculation reveals that the degree of accuracy is achieved after the 13th application of the interval-halving procedure. The only element of the method that has been omitted is how the computer determines which half of the interval contains the axis crossing.

To that end, consider the product of the function evaluated at the left, $f_1 = f(x_1)$, and the function evaluated at the midpoint, $f_2 = f(x_2)$, as shown:

If	Then
$f_1 f_2 > 0.0$	f_1 and f_2 are both positive or both negative. In either case, there's no crossing between x_1 and x_2, and no root lies within the interval.
$f_1 f_2 < 0.0$	$f(x)$ has changed sign between x_1 and x_2. In this case, there's a root within the interval bounded by x_1 and x_2.

Program 14.1 computes the roots of an equation by using this procedure. In reviewing this program, note the following features:

- In each iteration after the first, there's only one function evaluation. Reevaluating $f(x_1)$, $f(x_2)$, and $f(x_3)$ for each iteration would be inefficient because two of them are already known. If the function is extremely complicated, redundant computations such as this one would be a serious problem. Unnecessary function evaluations can waste a great deal of computer time.
- The program contains several checks for potential problems along with diagnostic messages (such as excessive iterations, no roots in interval, and so forth), even though the programmer might think these possibilities are remote. Generally, the more of these checks a program contains, the better. They take only a few minutes to code and can save hours of debugging.
- The criterion for success is based on the interval's size. Therefore, even if the function isn't close to zero at a point, x changes very little, and continuing the iterations wouldn't improve the accuracy of the root substantially.

 ## Program 14.1

```cpp
#include <iostream>
#include <cmath>
using namespace std;

void bisection(double, double, double, int); // function prototype
double f(double); // function prototype
using namespace std;

int main()
{
    int imax;          // maximum number of iterations
    double a, b;       // left and right ends of the original interval
    double epsilon;    // convergence criterion

    // obtain the input data
    cout << "Enter the limits of the original search interval, a and b: ";
```

```
  cin  >> a >> b;
  cout << "Enter the convergence criteria: ";
  cin  >> epsilon;
  cout << "Enter the maximum number of iterations allowed: ";
  cin  >> imax;

  bisection(a, b, epsilon, imax);

  return 0;
}


// A bisection function that finds roots of a function
// The interval a < x < b is known to contain a root of f(x). The estimate
// of the root is improved successively by finding in which half of the
// interval the root lies and then replacing the original interval by that
// half-interval.

void bisection(double a, double b, double epsilon, int imax)
{
  int i;                 // current iteration counter
  double x1, x2, x3; // left, right, and midpoint of current interval
  double f1, f2, f3; // function evaluated at these points
  double width;        // width of original interval = (b - a)
  double curwidth;     // width of current interval = (x3 - x1)

  // echo back the passed input data
  cout << "\nThe original search interval is from "
       << a << " to " << b << endl;
  cout << "The convergence criterion is: interval < " << epsilon << endl;
  cout << "The maximum number of iterations allowed is " << imax << endl;

  // calculate the root
  x1 = a;
  x3 = b;
  f1 = f(x1);
  f3 = f(x3);
  width = (b - a);

  // verify there is a root in the interval
  if (f1 * f3 > 0.0)
    cout << "\nNo root in the original interval exists" << endl;
  else
  {
```

☞

```
  for (i = 1; i <= imax; i++)
  {
    // find which half of the interval contains the root
    x2 = (x1 + x3) / 2.0;
    f2 = f(x2);
    if (f1 * f2 <= 0.0) // root is in left half-interval
    {
      curwidth = (x2 - x1) / 2.0;
      f3 = f2;
      x3 = x2;
    }
    else // root is in right half-interval
    {
      curwidth = (x3 - x2) / 2.0;
      f1 = f2;
      x1 = x2;
    }
    if (curwidth < epsilon)
    {
      cout << "\nA root at x = " << x2 << " was found "
           << "in " << i << " iterations" << endl;
      cout << "The value of the function is " << f2 << endl;
      return;
    }
  }
  cout << "\nAfter " << imax << " iterations, no root was found "
       << "within the convergence criterion" << endl;

  return;
}

// function to evaluate f(x)
double f(double x)
{
  const double PI = 2*asin(1.0); // value of pi

  return (exp(-x) - sin(0.5 * PI * x));
}
```

A sample run of Program 14.1 produced the following:

```
Enter the limits of the original search interval, a and b: .4 .5
Enter the convergence criteria: .00001
Enter the maximum number of iterations allowed: 25
```

☞

```
The original search interval is from 0.4 to 0.5
The convergence criterion is: interval < 1e-005
The maximum number of iterations allowed is 25


A root at x = 0.443567 was found in 13 iterations
The value of the function is 1.22595e-005
```

Although Program 14.1 is used to evaluate the roots of the equation $f(x) = e^{-x} - \sin(\pi x/2)$, by changing the calculation in the `return` statement in the last function, `f()`, this program can be used for any function.

One final comment: The bisection method used in Program 14.1 is an example of a so-called brute-force method, meaning it has a minimum of finesse. Although it illustrates fundamental C++ techniques, more powerful and clever numerical procedures are available. These techniques are explained in Section 14.3.

EXERCISES 14.2

1. **(Practice)** Use the bisection method for finding the roots of an equation. First, construct a table of the following form:

Step	x_1	x_2	x_3	$f(x_1)$	$f(x_2)$	$f(x_3)$	Crossing Left	Crossing Right
0	a	½(a + b)	b					
1								
.	.	.	.	.	.	.	.	.
.	.	.	.	.	.	.	.	.
.	.	.	.	.	.	.	.	.

Next, use the bisection method and a pocket calculator to obtain the roots of the following functions to an accuracy of five significant figures:

a. $f(x) = x^2 + 2x - 15$ (Use $a = 2.8$ and $b = 3.1$. The exact answer = 3.0.)

b. $g(x) = \frac{1}{2}\sin(x)(e^x - e^{-x}) + 1$ (This is the elliptic gear equation, with x in radians. Use $a = 1$ and $b = 4$.)

c. $E(x) = \sqrt{(R^2 - x^2)} - x\tan(x)$ (This is the equation for quantum energies of a particle in a box. Use $R = 10$, $a = 4.0$, and $b = 4.7$.)

d. Predict the number of steps needed to find the answer to the specified accuracy of five significant figures in Exercises 1a through 1c.

2. **(Modify)** Modify Program 14.1 to solve for the indicated roots of each function in Exercise 1.

3. **(Modify)** Modify Program 14.1 to produce a table similar to the one required in Exercise 1 for each function listed in Exercise 1.

14.3 Refinements to the Bisection Method

The bisection method described in Section 14.2 presents the basics on which most root-finding methods are constructed. This brute-force method is rarely used in practice because for almost any problem, an alternative method that's faster, more accurate, and only slightly more complex is available. All refinements of the bisection method that might be devised are based on attempts to use as much information as available about the function's behavior at each iteration. In the ordinary bisection method, the only feature of the function that's monitored is its sign. Therefore, if you're searching for roots of the function

$$f(x) = e^{-x} - \sin(\tfrac{1}{2}\pi x)$$

you begin the search, as described in Section 14.1, by stepping along the x-axis and watching for a change in sign of the function, as follows:

i	x_i	$f(x_i)$
0	0.0	2.0
1	0.1	1.33
2	0.2	0.75
3	0.3	0.29
4	0.4	-.05

The next step in the bisection method is reducing the step size by half; that is, try $x_5 = 0.35$. However, from the magnitude of the preceding numbers, you would expect the root to be closer to 0.4 than 0.3. By using information about the size of the functional value in addition to its sign, you can speed up the convergence. In this example, you might interpolate the root to be approximately

$$\frac{0.29 - 0.0}{0.29 - (-0.05)} = \frac{f_3 - 0}{f_3 - f_4} = 0.853$$

of the distance from $x_3 = 0.3$ to $x_4 = 0.4$ or $x_5 = 0.3853$. Continuing in this manner and interpolating at each step, you get the following results:

i	x_i	$f(x_i)$
3	0.30	0.29
4	0.40	-0.05
5	0.385	-0.0083
6	0.3823	-0.0013
7	0.3819	-0.00019
8	0.38185	-0.000028
9	0.38184	-0.000004

Comparing these results with the bisection method applied to a similar function in Section 14.2, you can see that the convergence rate for this method is much faster. The next task is to formalize this procedure into a method suitable for a general function.

Regula Falsi Method

The basic idea in the first refinement of the bisection method is that it's essentially the same as bisection, except instead of using the interval's midpoint at each step of the calculation, you use an interpolated value for the root. This method is illustrated in Figure 14.3. In this figure, a root is known to exist in the interval $(x_1 \leftrightarrow x_3)$, and in the drawing, f_1 is negative, and f_3 is positive. The interpolated position of the root is x_2. Because the two triangles ABC and CDE are similar, the lengths of the sides are related by

$$\frac{DE}{AB} = \frac{CD}{BC}$$

or

$$\frac{0.0 - f_1}{f_3 - f_1} = \frac{x_2 - x_1}{x_3 - x_1}$$

which can be solved for the unknown position x_2 to yield the following:

$$x_2 = x_1 - (x_3 - x_1)\frac{f_1}{f_3 - f_1}$$

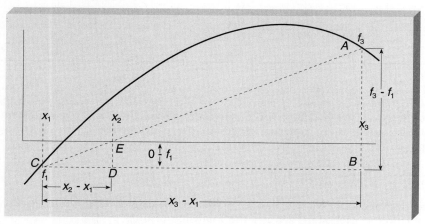

Figure 14.3   Estimating the root by interpolation

This value of x_2 then replaces the midpoint used in the bisection method, and the rest of the procedure remains the same. Therefore, the next step is determining whether the actual root is to the left or to the right of x_2, as before:

If $f_1 \times f_2 < 0$, then the root is on the left.
If $f_2 \times f_3 < 0$, then the root is on the right.

In the figure, the root is to the left of x_2, so the interval used for the next iteration is as follows:

$$x_3 = x_2$$
$$f_3 = f_2$$
$$f_2 = f(x_2)$$

In other words, to use this slightly faster algorithm, the only change that has to be made to the previous bisection code is replacing statements of the form

$$x_2 = (x_1 + x_3) / 2$$

by a statement of this form:

$$x_2 = x_1 - (x_3 - x_1)\frac{f_1}{f_3 - f_1}$$

This method is still guaranteed to obtain a root eventually and almost always converges faster than the conventional bisection method. You do, however, pay a small price. The values of f_1 and f_3 used in solving for x_2 might be nearly equal, and you could be plagued by round-off errors in their difference. Also, in the bisection method, you could predict with some precision the number of iterations required to find the root to a certain accuracy (see Section 14.1). This prediction is no longer possible if you use the interpolated values, so the code must include a check for excessive iterations.

This method shows that a simple change in the algorithm, which is based on more intelligent monitoring of the function, can reap considerable rewards in more rapid convergence. The formal name of this method is the **regula falsi method** (the method of false position).

Are there any other improvements in the basic bisection method that can be implemented easily? To answer this question, you must examine how the regula falsi method arrives at a solution. This examination is best done graphically. Figure 14.4 continues the calculation begun in Figure 14.3.

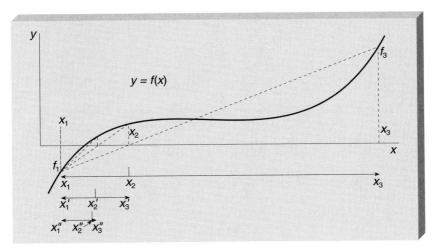

Figure 14.4 Illustration of several iterations of the regula falsi method

Notice that in Figure 14.4, in which the function is concave downward near the root, the value of the search interval's left limit near the root, x_1, never changes. The actual root always remains in the left segment in each iteration. The right segment of the interval, $x_3 - x_2$, shrinks quite rapidly, but the left segment, $x_2 - x_1$, doesn't. If the function were concave upward, the converse would be true. Therefore, a drawback of the regula falsi method is that even though it converges more rapidly to a value of x that results in a "small" $|f(x)|$, the interval containing the root does *not* diminish significantly.

Modified Regula Falsi Method

Perhaps the procedure can be made to converge more rapidly if the interval can be made to collapse from both directions. Figure 14.5 shows one way to accomplish this. The idea is as follows:

If the root is determined to lie in the left segment ($x_2 - x_1$)
  The interpolation line is drawn between the points (x_1, ½f_1) and (x_3, f_3)
Else If the root is in the right segment
  The interpolation line is drawn between the points (x_1, f_1) and (x_3, ½f_3)
Endif

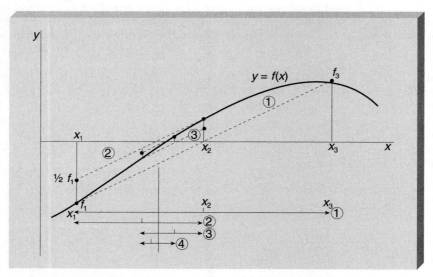

Figure 14.5   Illustration of the modified regula falsi method

Using this algorithm, the slope of the line is reduced *artificially*. The effect of this reduction is that if the root is in the left of the original interval, it eventually turns up in the right segment of a later interval and subsequently alternates between left and right. This modification to the bisection method combined with the regula falsi method is known as the **modified regula falsi method**, a powerful and popular procedure for finding roots of equations. The alternatives to the original bisection code in Program 14.1 are straightforward and are incorporated into Program 14.2. The C++ code in Program 14.2 requires some explanation, however:

1. The function $f(x)$ is evaluated only once per cycle. If the function is complicated and, therefore, costly to compute, this measure of efficiency is often a deciding factor in choosing the method of solution.
2. The code can terminate in only three ways:
   a. One success path: The current fractional size of the search interval—that is, (current interval) / (original interval)—is less than the user-supplied convergence criterion. If so, the program's original aim to bracket a root narrowly has been achieved. There's no guarantee that this criterion will result in a value of $f(x)$ that's "small." The point, however, is that successive iterations have resulted in only small changes in the interval containing the root, so continuing the process isn't necessary or productive.
   b. Two failure paths: 1) If the number of iterations is greater than I_{max}, the maximum number of iterations set by the programmer, the process is stopped. This test allows the programmer to specify the maximum cost accepted for an attempted solution. Because the number of iterations isn't predictable in the regula falsi and modified regula falsi methods, this safeguard is essential. It's also a prudent precaution against unforeseen errors in constructing the problem that could cause the program to cycle forever and not find a solution. Statements of this type are required in any program in which there's a danger of infinite looping. 2) If the function doesn't change sign ($f_1 \times f_3 > 0$), the process is stopped. Because the original interval is known to contain a root, the only way this condition can happen is by error. Usually, the error is in the code for the function $f(x)$; that is, you're attempting to find a root of a function different from the one intended.

Program 14.2

```cpp
#include <iostream>
#include <cmath>
using namespace std;

void modregfalsi(double, double, double, int); // function prototype
double f(double); // function prototype

int main()
{
    int imax;          // maximum number of iterations
    double a, b;       // left and right ends of the original interval
    double epsilon;    // convergence criterion
```

☞

```
   // obtain the input data
   cout << "Enter the limits of the original search interval, a and b: ";
   cin  >> a >> b;
   cout << "Enter the convergence criterion: ";
   cin  >> epsilon;
   cout << "Enter the maximum number of iterations allowed: ";
   cin  >> imax;

   modregfalsi(a, b, epsilon, imax);

   return 0;
}

// A modified regula falsi function that finds roots of a function
// The maximum number of iterations permitted is imax. The convergence
// criterion is that the fractional size of the search interval
// (x3 - x1) / (b - a) is less than epsilon. A relaxation factor,
// RELAX, is used.
void modregfalsi(double a, double b, double epsilon, int imax)
{
   const double RELAX = 0.9; // the relaxation factor

   int i;                 // current iteration counter
   double x1, x2, x3; // left, right, and midpoint of current interval
   double f1, f2, f3; // function evaluated at these points
   double width;       // width of original interval = (b - a)
   double curwidth;    // width of current interval = (x3 - x1)
   // echo back the passed input data
   cout << "\nThe original search interval is from " << a << " to " << b
        << "\nThe convergence criterion is: interval < " << epsilon
        << "\nThe maximum number of iterations allowed is " << imax << endl;

   // calculate the root
   x1 = a;
   x3 = b;
   f1 = f(x1);
   f3 = f(x3);
   width = abs(b - a);

   // iterations
   for (i = 1; i <= imax; i++)
   {
     curwidth = (x3 - x1) / width;
     x2 = x1 - width * curwidth * f1 / (f3 - f1);
```

☞

```
      f2 = f(x2);
      if (abs(curwidth) < epsilon) // root is found
      {
        cout << "\nA root at x = " << x2 << " was found "
             << "in " << i << " iterations" << endl;
        cout << "The value of the function is " << f2 << endl;
        return;
      }
      else // check for left and right crossing
      {
        if(f1 * f2 < 0.0) // check for crossing on the left
        {
          x3 = x2;
          f3 = f2;
          f1 = RELAX * f1;
        }
        else if (f2 * f3 < 0.0) // check for crossing on the right
        {
          x1 = x2;
          f1 = f2;
          f3 = RELAX * f3;
        }
        else // no crossing in the interval
        {
          cout << "The search for a root has failed due to no root in "
               << "the interval\n"
               << "In step " << i << " of the iteration the function "
               << "does not change sign" << endl;
        }
      }
    }
  cout << "\nAfter " << imax << " iterations, no root was found "
       << "within the convergence criterion\n"
       << "The search for a root has failed due to excessive iterations\n"
       << "after the maximum number of " << imax << " iterations" << endl;
  return;
}
// function to evaluate f(x)
double f(double x)
{
  const double PI = 2*asin(1.0); // value of pi

  return (exp(-x) - sin(0.5 * PI * x));
}
```

A sample run of Program 14.2 produced the following:

```
Enter the limits of the original search interval, a and b: .4 .5
Enter the convergence criterion: .00001
Enter the maximum number of iterations allowed: 25

The original search interval is from 0.4 to 0.5
The convergence criterion is: interval < 1e-005
The maximum number of iterations allowed is 25

A root at x = 0.443574 was found in 7 iterations
The value of the function is -2.25374e-009
```

In comparing the results of Program 14.2 to those of Program 14.1, notice that the modified regula falsi method located a more exact root in six fewer iterations (7 instead of 13). The exactness of the root is indicated by the functional value at the root, which is closer to 0.0 in Program 14.2's output. Table 14.1 shows a more complete comparison of the rate of convergence for all three root-finding methods discussed so far, as these methods apply to this function:

$$f(x) = 2e^{-2x} - \sin(\pi x)$$

Table 14.1   Comparison of Root-Finding Methods Using the Function $f(x) = 2e^{-2x} - \sin(\pi x)$

i	Bisection x_2	Regula Falsi Bisection x_2	Modified Regula Falsi Bisection x_2
1	0.35	0.385	0.385
2	0.375	0.3823	0.3820
3	0.3875	0.3819	0.38183
4	0.38125	0.38185	0.381843
5	0.38438	0.381844	0.38184267
6	0.38281	0.381843	0.38184276
7	0.38203	0.3818428	0.38184275
8	0.38164	0.38184275	0.38184275

A slope-reduction factor of one-half was used in constructing Figure 14.5 and is an example of what's called a **relaxation factor**, a number used to alter the results of one iteration before inserting them into the next. Determining the optimum relaxation factor is usually a complex problem in any calculation and is well beyond the scope of this book. However, in this instance, a little trial and error shows that a less drastic decrease in the slope results in improved convergence. Using a relaxation factor of 0.9 should be adequate for most problems; this factor was used to generate the values in Table 14.1.

Summary of the Bisection Methods

The characteristic features of the three methods discussed so far are as follows:

Bisection	Success based on size of interval
	Slow convergence
	Predictable number of iterations
	Interval halved in each iteration
	Guaranteed to bracket a root
Regula falsi	Success based on size of function
	Faster convergence
	Unpredictable number of iterations
	Interval containing the root is not small
	Monitors size of function as well as its sign
Modified regula falsi	Success based on size of interval
	Faster convergence
	Unpredictable number of iterations

Of the three methods, the modified regula falsi is probably the most efficient for common problems and is recommended when the only information available is that the function changes sign between x_1 and x_3.

The requirement that the initial search interval be one in which the function changes sign (only once) can be troublesome occasionally. For example, the problem of finding the root of the function

$$f(x) = x^2 - 2x + 1 = (x - 1)^2$$

isn't suited to any of the bisection methods because the function never changes sign. This difficulty occurs when the root of the function is a multiple root of even multiplicity. A method that overcomes this limitation is the secant method, discussed in Section 14.4.

EXERCISES 14.3

1. **(Practice)** Execute Program 14.2.

2. **(Practice)** Roughly reproduce the sketch in Figure 14.6, and then graphically apply the regula falsi method for three iterations.

3. **(Practice)** Using a pocket calculator, apply the regula falsi method for three iterations to the following functions:

   a. $f(x) = xe^{-x^2} - \cos(x)$; $a = 0$, b = 2; exact root = 1.351491185. . .

   b. $g(x) = x^2 - 2x - 3$; $a = 0$, $b = 4$; exact root = 3.0

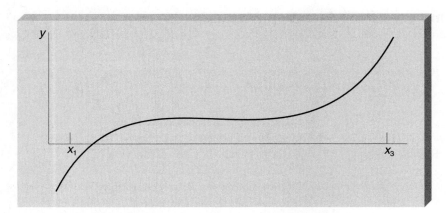

Figure 14.6   Function for Exercise 2

4. **(Practice)** Using a pocket calculator, apply the regula falsi method for three iterations to the following functions:

   a. $h(x) = e^x - (1 + x + x^2/2)$; $a = -1$, $b = 1$; exact root = 0.0

   b. $F(x) = x^3 - 2x - 5$; $a = 1$, $b = 3$; exact root = 2.0945514815. . .

   c. $G(x) = 10 \ln(x) - x$; $a = 1$, $b = 2$; exact root = 1.1183255916. . .

5. **(Practice)** Roughly reproduce Figure 14.6, and then graphically apply the modified regula falsi method for three iterations.

14.4 The Secant Method

The **secant method** is identical to the regula falsi method, except the sign of $f(x)$ doesn't need to be checked at each iteration. As in the regula falsi method, the values of x_0 and x_1 are required to start the procedure, but then the following algorithm is used to obtain an improvement for the next value of x:

Step 1: Start with the interval defined by (x_0,x_1)
Step 2: Compute the next value of x as

$$x_2 = \frac{f(x_0)}{f(x_0) - f(x_1)}(x_1 - x_0)$$

Step 3: Replace the pair of values (x_0,x_1) by the pair (x_1,x_2)
Step 4: Repeat Steps 2 and 3 until the value of f(x) is within an acceptable limit of zero

The secant method can be shown (see Exercise 2 at the end of this section) to be equivalent to replacing the function repeatedly by straight lines drawn through the points $[x_0, f(x_0)]$ and $[x_1, f(x_1)]$—that is, secant lines. Program 14.3 includes the C++ code for a function using the secant method.

Program 14.3

```cpp
#include <iostream>
#include <cmath>
using namespace std;

void secant(double, double, double, int); // function prototype
double f(double); // function prototype

int main()
{
   int imax;            // maximum number of iterations
   double a, b;         // left and right ends of the original interval
   double epsilon;      // convergence criterion

   // obtain the input data
   cout << "Enter the limits of the original search interval, a and b: ";
   cin  >> a >> b;
   cout << "Enter the convergence criteria: ";
   cin  >> epsilon;
   cout << "Enter the maximum number of iterations allowed: ";
   cin  >> imax;

   secant(a, b, epsilon, imax);

   return 0;
}

// This function implements the secant method for finding
// a root of a function
void secant(double a, double b, double epsilon, int imax)
{

   int i;               // current iteration counter
   double x0, x1;       // left and right x values of current interval
   double f0, f1;       // function evaluated at these points
   double dx0;          // delta x0
   double dx1;          // delta x1
```

☞

```cpp
   // echo back the passed input data
   cout << "\nThe original search interval is from " << a << " to " << b
        << "\nThe convergence criterion is: interval < " << epsilon
        << "\nThe maximum number of iterations allowed is " << imax << endl;
   // determine the root
   x0 = a;
   f0 = f(x0);
   dx0 = abs(b - a);

   // iterations
   for (i = 1; i <= imax; i++)
   {
     x1 = x0 + dx0;
     f1 = f(x1);
     if (abs(f1) < epsilon) // root is found
     {
       cout << "\nA root at x = " << x1 + dx1 << " was found "
            << "in " << i << " iterations" << endl;
       cout << "The value of the function is " << f1 << endl;
       return;
     }
     else // do next iteration
     {
       dx1 = ( f1/(f0 - f1) ) * dx0;
       x0 = x1;
       dx0 = dx1;
       f0 = f1;
     }
   }
   cout << "\nAfter " << imax << " iterations, no root was found "
        << "within the convergence criterion\n"
        << "The search for a root has failed due to excessive iterations\n"
        << "after the maximum number of " << imax << " iterations" << endl;

   return;
}


// function to evaluate f(x)
double f(double x)
{
   const double PI = 2*asin(1.0); // value of pi

   return (exp(-x) - sin(0.5 * PI * x));
}
```

A sample run of Program 14.3 produced the following:

```
Enter the limits of the original search interval, a and b: .4 .5
Enter the convergence criteria: .00001
Enter the maximum number of iterations allowed: 25


The original search interval is from 0.4 to 0.5
The convergence criterion is: interval < 1e-005
The maximum number of iterations allowed is 25


A root at x = 0.443628 was found in 4 iterations
The value of the function is -9.01417e-008
```

Although the secant method is probably the most popular method for finding the root of a function, it does pose divergence problems. For this reason, a check should be built into this method's C++ code that detects when successive intervals start to become larger rather than smaller.

EXERCISES 14.4

1. **(Practice)** Execute Program 14.3.

2. **(Practice)** Use Program 14.3 to find the root of the function $f(x) = x^2 - 2x + 0.9$, starting with an initial guess of $x_0 = 0.6$ and $x_1 = 0.9$.

3. **(Practice)** The secant() function in Program 14.3 was used to find a root of the function $f(x) = x^2 - 2x + 0.9$. Starting with an initial guess of $x_0 = 0.6$, $x_1 = 0.9$, the values of x_0 and $x_1 - x_0$ were displayed for each iteration as follows:

Step	x_0	$x_1 - x_0$
0	0.600	0.300
1	0.900	-0.180
2	0.720	-0.057
3	0.663	0.022
4	0.685	-0.001

Carefully graph the function for $0.5 \leq x \leq 1.0$ and use the numbers in the preceding chart to show how the secant method arrives at a root of the function.

4. **(Numerical)** Use Program 14.3 to find a root of the function $f(x) = x^2 - 2x - 3$.

14.5 Introduction to Numerical Integration

The integration of a function of a single variable can be thought of as the opposite of differentiation—that is, the antiderivative—or as the area under a curve. Antiderivatives are ordinarily discussed in depth in a calculus course. In this section, you concentrate instead on the less analytic, more visual approach of interpreting a definite integral as an area. The integral of the function $f(x)$ from $x = a$ to $x = b$, designated as

$$I = \int_a^b f(x)\,dx$$

will be evaluated by devising schemes for measuring the area under the graph of the function over this interval (see Figure 14.7). This method of evaluating an integral lends itself so naturally to numerical computation that the most effective way to understand the process of integration is to learn the numerical approach first and later have these ideas reinforced by the more formal concepts of the antiderivative.

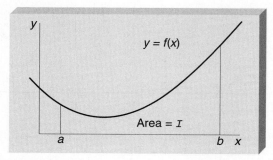

Figure 14.7 An integral as an area under a curve

Another reason for studying numerical integration at this stage is that it's a stable process. It almost always works because numerical integration consists of expressing the area as the sum of areas of smaller segments, a procedure that's fairly safe from problems such as division by zero or a round-off error caused by subtracting numbers of approximately the same magnitude.

Finally, it's unfortunately true that many, perhaps most, of the integrals occurring in actual engineering or science problems can't be expressed in any closed form.

Formally integrating a function—obtaining a closed expression for the answer—often takes considerable training and experience. Dozens of "tricks" must be learned and understood. On the other hand, the procedures of numerical integration are few, and all are easy to understand and remember. As in many other numerical procedures, you begin by replacing the function over a limited range by straight-line segments. The interval $x = a$ to $x = b$ is divided into subintervals or panels of size Δx, the function is replaced by line segments over each subinterval, and the area under the function is then approximated by the area under the line segments. This procedure is the trapezoidal rule approximation for an integral and is described in the next section. The next order approximation is replacing the function by parabolic segments, known as Simpson's rule, and is explained in Section 14.7.

14.6 The Trapezoidal Rule

An approximation to the area under a complicated curve is obtained by assuming the function can be replaced by simpler functions over a limited range. A straight line, the simplest approximation to a function, is the first to be considered and leads to what's called the **trapezoidal rule.**

The area under the curve $f(x)$ from $x = a$ to $x = b$ is approximated by the area beneath a straight line drawn between the points $xa, f(a)$ and $xb, f(b)$ (see Figure 14.8). The lighter area is then the approximation to the integral and is the area of a trapezoid, which is

$\quad I \approx$ (average value of f over interval) (width of interval)

or

$\quad I \approx \frac{1}{2}\,[f(a) + f(b)]\,(b - a) = T_0$ (**Equation 14.6**)

This is the trapezoidal rule for one panel, identified as T_0.

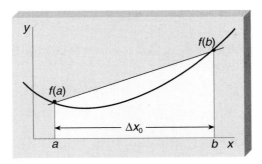

Figure 14.8   Approximating the area under a curve by a single trapezoid

To improve the accuracy of the approximation to the area under a curve, the interval is next divided in half, and the function is approximated by straight-line segments over each half. The area in this example is approximated by the area of two trapezoids, as illustrated in Figure 14.9.

$$I \approx T_1 = \left[\tfrac{1}{2}\left(f(a) + f_1\right)\Delta x_L\right] + \left[\tfrac{1}{2}\left(f_1 + f(b)\right)\Delta x_L\right]$$

or

$$T_1 = \frac{\Delta x_L}{2}\left[f(a) + 2f_1 + f(b)\right] \qquad (\textbf{Equation 14.7})$$

where

$$\Delta x_L = \frac{(b - a)}{2}$$

$$f_1 = f\left(x = a + \Delta x_L\right)$$

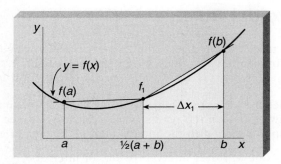

Figure 14.9   Two-panel approximation to the area

Notice that when adding the areas of the trapezoids, the sides at $f(a)$ and $f(b)$ are sides of only the first and last trapezoid, but the side at f_1 is a side of two trapezoids and, therefore, "counts twice," explaining the factor of 2 in Equation 14.7. Furthermore, the two-panel approximation, T_1, can be related to the one-panel results, T_0, as shown:

$$T_1 = \frac{T_0}{2} + \Delta x_1 f_1 \qquad \text{(Equation 14.8)}$$

To increase the accuracy, the interval is simply subdivided into a large number of panels. The result for n panels is clearly

$$I \approx T_1 = \tfrac{1}{2}\,\Delta x_n \left[f(a) + 2\sum_{i=1}^{n-1} f_i + f(b) \right] \quad \text{(Equation 14.9)}$$

where $\Delta x_n = (b - a)/n$, and f_i is the function evaluated at each of the interior points:

$$f_i = f\left(x = a + i\,\Delta x_n\right)$$

The reason for the extra factor of 2 in Equation 14.9 is the same as in the two-panel example. Equation 14.9 is known as the trapezoidal rule.

Computational Form of the Trapezoidal Rule Equation

Equation 14.9 was derived assuming that the widths of all panels are the same and equal to Δx_n. However, equal panel widths aren't required in the derivation, and the equation can be generalized easily to a partition of the interval into unequal panels of width Δx_i, $i = 1, \ldots, n - 1$. However, for reasons to be explained a bit later, you'll restrict the panel widths to be equal and the number of panels to be a power of 2, as shown:

$$n = 2^k$$

The number of panels is n, the order of the calculation is called k, and the corresponding trapezoidal rule approximation is labeled as T_k. Therefore, T_0 is the result for $n = 2^0 = 1$ panel. The situation for $k = 2$ or $2^2 = 4$ panels is illustrated in Figure 14.10. In this figure, the width of a panel is $\Delta x_2 = (b - a)/2^2$, and the value of the $k = 2$ trapezoidal rule approximation is the following:

$$T_2 = \left(\Delta x_2/2\right)\left[f(a) + 2f\left(a + \Delta x_2\right) + 2f\left(a + \Delta x_2\right) + 2f\left(a + 3\Delta x_2\right) + f(b) \right]$$

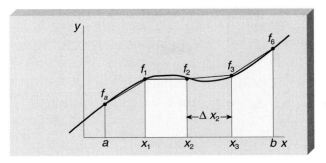

Figure 14.10 Four-panel trapezoidal approximation, T_2

However, because $2\triangle x_2 = \triangle x_1$, you can see that

$$f\left(a + 2\triangle x_2\right) = f\left(a + x_1\right)$$

and $f(a + \triangle x_1)$ was already determined in the previous calculation of T_1 (Equation 14.8). The point is that by successively doubling the number of panels in each stage, the only new information required to proceed to the next order trapezoidal rule approximation is the evaluation of the function at the midpoints of the current intervals.

To exploit this fact further, Equations 14.7 and 14.8 can be used to rewrite Equation 14.10 in this form:

$$T_2 = \left(\triangle x_1 / 4\right)\left[f\left(a\right) + 2f\left(a + \triangle x_1\right) + f\left(b\right)\right] + \triangle x_2 \left[f\left(a + \triangle x_2\right) + f\left(a + 3\triangle x_2\right)\right]$$

$$= T_1 / 2 + \triangle x_2 \left[f\left(a + \triangle x_2\right) + f\left(a + 3\triangle x_2\right)\right] \qquad \textbf{(Equation 14.10)}$$

This equation can be generalized to yield

$$T_k = \tfrac{1}{2} T_{k-1} + \triangle x_k \sum_{\substack{i=1 \\ \text{odd only}}}^{n-1} f\left(a + i\,\triangle x_k\right) \qquad \textbf{(Equation 14.11)}$$

where

$$\triangle x_k = \frac{b - a}{2^k}$$

The procedure for using Equation 14.11 to approximate an integral by the trapezoidal rule is then:

1. Compute T_0 by using Equation 14.6.
2. Repeatedly apply Equation 14.11 for $k = 1, 2, \ldots$ until sufficient accuracy is obtained.

Example of a Trapezoidal Rule Calculation

To illustrate this section's concepts, the following integral is used:

$$I = \int_1^2 \left(1/x\right) dx$$

The function $f(x) = 1/x$ can, of course, be integrated analytically to give $\ln(x)$, and because $\ln(1) = 0$, the value of the integral is $\ln(2) = 0.69314718$. The trapezoidal rule approximation to the integral with $a = 1$ and $b = 2$ begins with Equation 14.6 to obtain T_0:

$$T_0 = \frac{1}{2}\left(\frac{1}{1} + \frac{1}{2}\right)(2 - 1) = 0.75$$

Repeated use of Equation 14.11 then yields the following:

$k = 1$ $\Delta x_1 = \frac{1}{2}$

$$T_1 = T_0/2 + \frac{1}{2}\left[f\left(1 + \frac{1}{2}\right)\right] = 0.75/2 + \frac{1}{2}\left(1/1.5\right)$$

$$= 0.708333$$

$k = 2$ $\Delta x_2 = \frac{1}{4}$

$$T_2 = T_1/2 + \frac{1}{4}\left(1/1.25 + 1/1.75\right)$$

$$= 0.6970238$$

$k = 3$ $\Delta x_3 = \frac{1}{8}$

$$T_3 = T_2/2 + \frac{1}{8}\left(1/1.25 + 1/1.375 + 1/1.625 + 1/1.875\right)$$

$$= 0.69412185$$

Continuing the calculation through $k = 5$ yields the following:

k	T_k
0	0.75
1	0.70833
2	0.69702
3	0.69412
4	0.69339
5	0.693208
.	.
.	.
.	.
Exact	0.693147. . .

The convergence of the computed values of the trapezoidal rule isn't particularly fast, but the method is quite simple.

EXERCISES 14.6

1. **(Practice)** Evaluate the following integrals by using the trapezoidal rule:
   a. Evaluate T_0 for one panel by using Equation 14.6.

b. Compute T_1 by using the value of T_0 and Equation 14.11.

c. Continue the calculation through T_4.

Collect your results in the form of a table. (Be careful: Errors in one step carry over into the next.)

i. $\displaystyle\int_0^8 x^2\,dx$ (Exact result = 170.667)

ii. $\displaystyle\int_0^8 x^4\,dx$ (Exact result = 6553.6)

2. **(Practice)** Evaluate the following integrals by using the trapezoidal rule:

a. Evaluate T_0 for one panel by using Equation 14.6.

b. Compute T_1 using the value of T_0 and Equation 14.11.

c. Continue the calculation through T_4.

Collect your results in the form of a table. (Be careful: Errors in one step carry over into the next.)

i. $\displaystyle\int_0^1 xe^{-x}\,dx$ (Exact result = $1-2/e$ = .2642411175. . .)

ii. $\displaystyle\int_0^{\pi/2} x(\sin x)\,dx$ (Exact result = 1.0)

3. **(Practice)** Evaluate the following integrals by using the trapezoidal rule:

a. Evaluate T_0 for one panel by using Equation 14.6.

b. Compute T_1 using the value of T_0 and Equation 14.11.

c. Continue the calculation through T_4.

Collect your results in the form of a table. (Be careful: Errors in one step carry over into the next.)

i. $\displaystyle\int_0^1 (1+x^2)^{3/2}\,dx$ (Exact result = 1.567951962. . .)

ii. $\displaystyle\int_0^1 e^{-x^2}\,dx$ (Exact result = 0.74682404. . .)

14.7 Simpson's Rule

The trapezoidal rule is based on approximating the function by straight-line segments. To improve the method's accuracy and convergence rate, an obvious approach is approximating the function by parabolic segments in place of straight lines. This approach results in an approximation for the integral known as **Simpson's rule**; a simple example is shown in Figure 14.11. Specifying a parabola uniquely requires three points, so the lowest-order Simpson's rule has two panels.

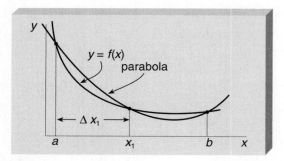

Figure 14.11   Area under a parabola drawn through three points

To proceed, you need to know the area under a parabola drawn through three points. Note that the corresponding step in the derivation of the trapezoidal rule was simple: The area under a line through two points is simply $\Delta x[f(a) + f(b)])/2$.

If the curve $f(x)$ drawn in Figure 14.11 is approximated by a parabola drawn through the three points—$f(a)$, $f(b)$, and the value of $f(x)$ at the midpoint of the interval f_{mid}—it can be shown with calculus that the area under this parabola, denoted as S_1, is

$$S_1 = \tfrac{1}{3}\Delta x_1 \left[f(a) + 4f(a + \Delta x_1) + f(b) \right]$$

where

$$\Delta x_1 = \frac{b - a}{2}$$

This is the first-order Simpson's rule approximation, where $k = 1$ and $n = 2^1$ panels. The next level of approximation is to halve the interval width and partition the interval into four panels, as shown in Figure 14.12. The area under the function $f(x)$ is then approximated as the area under the two parabolas shown in the figure. Again, using calculus, it can be shown that the area under the two parabolas is

$$S_2 = \tfrac{1}{3}\Delta x_2 \left\{ \left[f(a) + 4f(x_1) + f(x_2) \right] + \left[f(x_2) + 4f(x_3) + f(b) \right] \right\}$$

$$= \tfrac{1}{3}\Delta x_2 \left\{ f(a) + 4\left[f(x_1) + f(x_3) \right] + 2f(x_2) + f(b) \right\} \qquad \textbf{(Equation 14.12)}$$

where

$$\Delta x_2 = \frac{b - a}{2^2}$$

and

$$f_i = f\left(x = a + i\Delta x_2 \right)$$

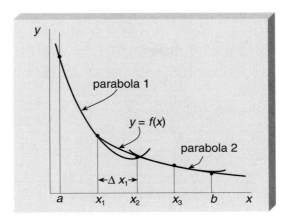

Figure 14.12   The second-order Simpson's rule approximation is the area under two parabolas

This procedure can be extended to 8, 16, 32, and so on panels. The result is a rather simple generalization of Equation 14.12, and for $n = 2^k$ panels is the following:

$$S_k = \tfrac{1}{3}\Delta x_k \left[f(a) + 4\sum_{\substack{i=1 \\ \text{odd only}}}^{n-1} f(a + i\,\Delta x_k) + 2\sum_{\substack{i=2 \\ \text{even only}}}^{n-2} f(a + i\,\Delta x_k) + f(b) \right] \qquad \textbf{(Equation 14.13)}$$

Equation 14.13, known as Simpson's rule, is a popular method of evaluating integrals of functions that are smooth, and rightly so. As you see later in this chapter, Simpson's rule converges nicely in most instances and is easy to use. Also, Equation 14.13 can be adapted easily to handle an odd number of unevenly spaced points and is the most common method for estimating the integral of experimentally obtained data.

Example of Simpson's Rule as an Approximation to an Integral

Again, consider this integral:

$$I = \int_1^2 (1/x)\,dx$$

Using Equation 14.13 first for $k = 1$ yields the following:

$k = 1$

$n = 2^1 = 2$

$\Delta x_1 = \dfrac{b - a}{2^2} = \dfrac{1}{2}$

$S_1 = \tfrac{1}{3}(\tfrac{1}{2})[1 + 4(1/1.5) + \tfrac{1}{2}] = 0.6944444$

Repeating for $k = 2$ yields the following results:

$k = 2$

$n = 2^2 = 4$

$\Delta x_2 = \tfrac{1}{4}$

$S_2 = \tfrac{1}{3}(\tfrac{1}{4})[1 + 4(1/1.25 + 1/1.75) + 2(1/1.5) + \tfrac{1}{2}] = 0.69325397$

Continuing the calculation, you get the values listed in Table 14.2. For comparison, results are also included for the same integral obtained in Section 14.6 when using the trapezoidal rule. Clearly, Simpson's rule converges much faster that the trapezoidal rule, at least for this example.

Table 14.2 Trapezoidal and Simpson's Rule Results for the Integral $\int_1^2 (1/x)\, dx$

Order k	Number of Panels n	T_k	S_k
0	1	0.75	–
1	2	0.7083	0.6944
2	4	0.69702	0.69325
3	8	0.69412	0.69315
4	16	0.69339	0.6931466
5	32	0.693208	0.6931473
6	64	0.693162	0.6931472

EXERCISES 14.7

1. **(Practice)** Using Equation 14.13, calculate the two-panel and four-panel Simpson's rule results, S_1 and S_2, for the following integrals:

a. $\int_0^8 x^2\, dx$ (Exact result = 170.667)

b. $\int_0^8 x^4\, dx$ (Exact result = 6553.6)

2. **(Practice)** Using Equation 14.13, calculate the two-panel and four-panel Simpson's rule results, S_1 and S_2, for the following integrals:

a. $\int_0^1 xe^{-x}\, dx$ (Exact result = 1-2/e = .2642411175...)

b. $\int_0^{\pi/2} x(\sin x)\, dx$ (Exact result = 1.0)

3. **(Practice)** Using Equation 14.13, calculate the two-panel and four-panel Simpson's rule results, S_1 and S_2, for the following integrals:

a. $\int_0^1 (1+x^2)^{3/2}\, dx$ (Exact result = 1.567951962. . .)

b. $\int_0^1 e^{-x^2}\, dx$ (Exact result = 0.74682404. . .)

4. **(Practice)** Using Equation 14.13, calculate S_1 through S_4 for the integrals listed in Exercise 1.

14.8 Common Programming Errors

In using the modified bisection root-finding method, two problems can occur. The first problem is round-off error, which can occur when the values of $f(x_1)$ and $f(x_3)$ used in the computation are nearly equal. The second problem occurs because a prediction of the exact number of iterations required to achieve a specific accuracy isn't available. To counter these two problems successfully, the code used in these two methods must detect their occurrence to prevent excessive and possibly infinite iterations.

In numerical integration, excessive computation times can also be a problem. This problem typically occurs when the number of iterations exceeds 50. Often you can reduce runtime quite a bit by inspecting each program loop to ensure that only calculations that must be computed iteratively are included in the loop, and moving all other calculations to be computed before or after the loop is completed.

14.9 Chapter Summary

All the root-solving methods described in this chapter are of an iterative nature and can be categorized in two classes of root-finding algorithms, depending on whether you're starting with an interval containing a root or an initial estimate of the root. The bisection-based procedures begin with an interval that's known to contain a root and are guaranteed to converge to within a prescribed tolerance bracketing the root. Of the bisection methods, the modified regula falsi is the fastest converging and is recommended.

In algorithms based on the bisection method, the initial interval is refined by evaluating the function repeatedly at points within the interval, and then by monitoring the sign of the function and determining in which subinterval the root lies. If the left and right ends of the current interval are x_1 and x_3, respectively, the standard bisection method uses the function evaluated at the midpoint, $x_2 = \frac{1}{2}(x_1 + x_3)$. The sign of the function at x_2 is compared with that at either end of the interval to determine which half of the interval contains the root. The full interval is then replaced by this half, and the process is repeated. After n iterations, the root is contained in an interval of size $(x_3 - x_1)/2n$.

In the regula falsi method, the conditions are the same as for the bisection method. Instead of using the interval's midpoint, however, a straight line connecting the points at the ends of the interval is used to interpolate the position of the root. The intersection of this line with the x-axis determines the value of x_2 used in the next step. This value of x_2 is given by the equation

$$x_2 = x_1 - \left(x_3 - x_1\right) \frac{f\left(x_1\right)}{f\left(x_3\right) - f\left(x_1\right)}$$

in place of the equation for the midpoint. Convergence is faster than with the bisection method. However, the interval will likely converge to the root from one side only.

The modified regula falsi method is the same as the regula falsi method, except for the following change: In each iteration, when the full interval is replaced by the subinterval containing the root, a relaxation factor is used to modify the function's value at the fixed end of the subinterval. A relaxation factor of approximately 0.9 is suggested. This added feature causes the interval to converge from both ends, and convergence is then based on interval size. This method is the preferred procedure for finding a root of a function that isn't too expensive to evaluate and is known to have a root in a specified interval.

The secant method replaces the function by a secant line through two points and then finds the point of intersection of the line with the x-axis. The algorithm requires two input numbers, x_0 and Δx_0, corresponding to initial guesses for the root and for an interval containing the root. This pair of values is then replaced by the pair $(x_1, \Delta x_1)$, where

$$x_1 = x_0 + \Delta x_0$$

and

$$\Delta x_1 = \frac{f(x_1)}{f(x_0) - f(x_1)} \Delta x_0$$

and the process is continued until the new interval Δx is sufficiently small.

Root-solving methods are amenable to C++ coding. However, the success of a program in finding the root of a function usually depends on the quality of information supplied by the user. That is, how accurate is the initial guess or search interval, and how well does the method chosen match the circumstances of the problem? Execution-time problems are usually traceable to errors in coding the function or to inadequate user-supplied diagnostics for potential problems.

The integral of $f(x)$ from $x = a$ to $x = b$, written as

$$I = \int_a^b f(x)\, dx$$

is evaluated numerically by computing the area under the curve $f(x)$ over the specified range of x. The procedures for estimating this area consist of partitioning the interval $a \le x \le b$ into n panels of width $\Delta x_i (i = 1, n)$ and approximating the function $f(x)$ over each panel by a simpler function.

The trapezoidal rule results from replacing the function $f(x)$ by straight-line segments over the panels Δx_i. The approximate value for the integral is then given by the following formula, which is known as the trapezoidal rule:

$$\int_a^b f(x)\, dx \approx \tfrac{1}{2} \Delta x_n \left(f(a) + 2 \sum_{i-1}^{n-1} f_i + f(b) \right)$$

If the panels are of equal size *and* the number of panels is $n = 2^k$, where k is a positive integer, the trapezoidal rule approximation is then labeled as T_k and satisfies the equation

$$T_k = \tfrac{1}{2} T_{k-1} + \Delta x_k \sum_{\substack{i=1 \\ \text{odd only}}}^{n-1} f(a + i\Delta x_k)$$

where

$$\Delta x_k = \frac{b-a}{2^k}$$

In the next level of approximation, the function $f(x)$ is replaced by $n/2$ parabolic segments over pairs of equal-size panels, $\Delta x = (b - a)/n$, and results in the formula for the area known as Simpson's rule:

$$\int_a^b f(x)\, dx \approx \tfrac{1}{3} \Delta x_k \left[f(a) + 4 \sum_{\substack{i=1 \\ \text{odd only}}}^{n-1} f(a + i\Delta x_k) + 2 \sum_{\substack{i=2 \\ \text{even only}}}^{n-2} f(a + i\Delta x_k) + f(b) \right]$$

Programming Projects for Chapter 14

1. **(Numerical)** Write a C++ program to find the maximum of a function $f(x)$ over an interval $a \le x \le b$ by starting at $x = a$ with a step size of Δx. Evaluate $f_1 = f(x)$ and $f_2 = f(x + \Delta x)$. If $f_1 < f_2$, replace x with $x + \Delta x$ and continue; otherwise, reduce the step size by half and repeat the comparison. The program should terminate successfully when $\Delta < 10^{-6}$.

2. **(Numerical)** **a.** Use Program 14.2 to find the root of the following function to an accuracy of 10^{-5}:

   $f(x) = x^3 - 2x - 5$ ($a = 1$, $b = 3$; exact root = 2.0945514815)

   b. Change the relaxation factor from 0.9 to 0.75 and rerun the program. Comment on the difference between the two calculations.

3. **(Numerical)** Use Program 14.3 to find a root of the function $f(x) = e^x - (1 + x + x^2/2)$ ($a = -1$, $b = 1$; exact root = 0.0).

4. **(Numerical)** Given a number, n, and an approximation for its square root, a closer approximation to the actual square root can be obtained by using this formula:

   $$new\ approximation = \frac{\left(n\ /\ previous\ approximation\right) + previous\ approximation}{2}$$

   Using this information, write a C++ program that prompts the user for a number and an initial guess at its square root. Using this input data, your program should calculate an approximation to the square root that's accurate to 0.00001 (*Hint:* Stop the loop when the difference between the two approximations is less than 0.00001.)

5. **(Numerical)** The Newton-Raphson method can be used to find the roots of any equation $y(x) = 0$. In this method, the $(i + 1)$st approximation, x_{i+1}, to a root of $y(x) = 0$ is given in terms of the ith approximation, x_i, by this formula:

   $$x_{i+1} = x_i - \frac{y(x_i)}{y'(x_i)}$$

   For example, if $y(x) = 3x^2 + 2x - 2$, then $y'(x) = 6x + 2$, and the roots are found by making a reasonable guess for a first approximation, x_1, and iterating by using this equation:

   $x_{i+1} = x_i - (3x_i^2 + 2x_i - 2) / (6x_i + 2)$

   a. Using the Newton-Raphson method, write a program to find the two roots of the equation $3x^2 + 2x - 2 = 0$. (*Hint:* There's one positive root and one negative root.)

   b. Extend the program written for Exercise 5a so that it finds the roots of any function $y(x) = 0$, when the function for $y(x)$ and the derivative of $y(x)$ are placed in the code.

Chapter 15

Bit Operations

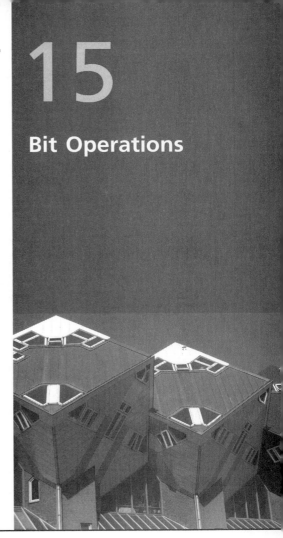

C++ operates with data entities stored as one or more bytes, such as character, integer, and double-precision constants and variables. In addition, C++ provides for the manipulation of bits of character and integer values and variables. The operators used to perform bit manipulations are called bit operators and are listed in Table 15.1.

All the operators listed in Table 15.1, except ~, are binary operators, requiring two operands. Each operand is treated as a binary number consisting of a series of 1s and 0s. The bits in each operand are then compared on a bit-by-bit basis, and the result is determined based on the selected operation.

Table 15.1 Bit Operators

Operator	Description
&	Bit-by-bit AND
|	Bit-by-bit inclusive OR
^	Bit-by-bit exclusive OR
~	Bit-by-bit ones complement
<<	Left shift
>>	Right shift

15.1 The AND Operator

The AND operator, &, causes a bit-by-bit AND comparison between its two operands. *The result of each bit-by-bit comparison is a 1 only when both bits being compared are 1s; otherwise, the result of the AND operation is a 0.* For example, the following two 8-bit numbers are to be ANDed:

```
1 0 1 1 0 0 1 1
1 1 0 1 0 1 0 1
– – – – – – – –
```

To perform an AND operation, each bit in one operand is compared to the bit occupying the same position in the other operand. This sample AND operation illustrates the correspondence between bits for these two operands:

```
   1 0 1 1 0 0 1 1
 & 1 1 0 1 0 1 0 1
   – – – – – – – –
   1 0 0 1 0 0 0 1
```

As shown, when both bits being compared are 1s, the result is a 1; otherwise, the result is a 0. The result of each comparison is, of course, independent of any other bit comparison.

Program 15.1 shows the use of an AND operation. In this program, the variable op1 is initialized to the octal value 325, which is the octal equivalent of the binary number 1 1 0 1 0 1 0 1, and the variable op2 is initialized to the octal value 263, which is the octal representation of the binary number 1 0 1 1 0 0 1 1. They are the same two binary numbers used in the preceding example.

 Program 15.1

```cpp
#include <iostream>
using namespace std;

int main()
{
  int op1 = 0325, op2 = 0263;

  int op3 = op1 & op2;
  cout << oct << op1 << " ANDed with "<< op2 << " is " << op3 << endl;

  return 0;
}
```

Program 15.1 produces the following output:

```
325 ANDed with 263 is 221
```

The AND Operator

The result of ANDing the octal numbers 325 and 263 is the octal number 221. The binary equivalent of 221 is the binary number 1 0 0 1 0 0 0 1, which is the result of the AND operation shown previously.

AND operations are useful for masking, or eliminating, selected bits from an operand because ANDing any bit (1 or 0) with a 0 forces the resulting bit to be a 0, and ANDing any bit (1 or 0) with a 1 leaves the original bit unchanged. For example, the variable op1 has the bit pattern x x x x x x x x, where each x can be 1 or 0, independent of any other x in the number. The result of ANDing this binary number with the binary number 0 0 0 0 1 1 1 1 is as follows:

```
op1    =    x x x x x x x x
op2    =    0 0 0 0 1 1 1 1
            - - - - - - - -
Result =    0 0 0 0 x x x x
```

As you can see in this example, the 0s in op2 mask the bits in op1, and the 1s in op2 filter, or pass, the bits in op1 through with no change in their values. In this example, the variable op2 is called a **mask**. By choosing the mask appropriately, any bit in an operand can be selected, or filtered, out of an operand for inspection. For example, ANDing the variable op1 with the mask 0 0 0 0 0 1 0 0 forces all bits of the result to be 0, except the third bit. The third bit of the result is a copy of the third bit of op1. Therefore, if the result of the AND is 0, the third bit of op1 must have been 0, and if the result of the AND is a non-zero number, the third bit must have been 1.

Program 15.2 uses this masking property to convert lowercase letters into their uppercase form, assuming the letters are stored with the ASCII code. The algorithm for converting letters is based on binary codes for lowercase and uppercase letters in ASCII being the same except for bit five, which is a 1 for lowercase letters and a 0 for uppercase letters.[1]

For example, the binary code for the letter a is 01100001 (hex 61), and the binary code for the letter A is 01000001 (hex 41). Similarly, the binary code for the letter z is 01111010 (hex 7A), and the binary code for the letter Z is 01011010 (hex 5A). (See Appendix B for the hexadecimal values of uppercase and lowercase letters.) Therefore, a lowercase letter can be converted into its uppercase form by forcing the fifth bit to 0. Program 15.2 does this by masking the letter's code with the binary value 11011111, which has the hexadecimal value DF.

A sample run of Program 15.2 follows:

```
Enter a string of both uppercase and lowercase letters:
abcdefgHIJKLMNOPqrstuvwxyz
The string of letters just entered is:
abcdefgHIJKLMNOPqrstuvwxyz
This string, in uppercase letters, is:
ABCDEFGHIJKLMNOPQRSTUVWXYZ
```

---

[1]This algorithm assumes the conventional numbering scheme, starting with bit 0 as the rightmost bit, is used. Using this convention, the rightmost bit (bit 0) is referred to as the last significant bit (LSB), and the leftmost bit is referred to as the most significant bit (MSB). In this example, the MSB is bit 7.

Program 15.2

```cpp
#include <iostream>
using namespace std;

const int TOUPPER = 0xDF;
void upper(char *);   // function prototype

int main()
{
  char word[81];      // enough storage for a complete line

  cout << "Enter a string of both uppercase and lowercase letters:\n";
  cin.getline(word,80,'\n');
  cout << "\nThe string of letters just entered is:\n"
       << word << endl;
  upper(word);
  cout << "\nThis string, in uppercase letters, is:\n"
       << word << endl;
  return 0;
}
void upper(char *word)
{
  while (*word != '\0')
    *word++ &= TOUPPER;
}
```

In reviewing Program 15.2, first notice that the input string has been stored and passed to upper() as a C-string, which is an array of characters. Doing so permits the function to receive and operate on the original character values instead of receiving a copy of these values. Second, notice that the lowercase letters are converted to uppercase form, and uppercase letters are unaltered. This result happens because bit five of all uppercase letters is 0, so forcing this bit to 0 with the mask has no effect. Only when bit five is a 1, as for lowercase letters, is the input character altered.

15.2 The Inclusive OR Operator

The inclusive OR operator, |, performs a bit-by-bit comparison of its two operands in a similar fashion as the bit-by-bit AND. The result of the OR comparison, however, is determined by the following rule: *The result of the comparison is 1 if either bit being compared is a 1; otherwise, the result is a 0.*

You can see this rule in the following sample OR operation. As with all bit operations, the result of each comparison is, of course, independent of any other comparison.

```
   1 0 1 1 0 0 1 1
 | 1 1 0 1 0 1 0 1
   - - - - - - - -
   1 1 1 1 0 1 1 1
```

Program 15.3 shows the use of an OR operation, using the octal values of the operands shown in the preceding example.

 Program 15.3

```cpp
#include <iostream>
using namespace std;

int main()
{
   int op1 = 0325, op2 = 0263;

   int op3 = op1 | op2;
   cout << oct << op1 << " ORed with " << op2 << " is " << op3 << endl;

   return 0;
}
```

Program 15.3 produces the following output:

```
325 ORed with 263 is 367
```

The result of ORing the octal numbers 325 and 263 is the octal number 367. The binary equivalent of 367 is 1 1 1 1 0 1 1 1, which is the result of the OR operation shown previously.

Inclusive OR operations are useful for forcing selected bits to take on a 1 value or for passing through other bit values unchanged. The reason is that ORing any bit (1 or 0) with a 1 forces the resulting bit to be a 1, and ORing any bit (1 or 0) with a 0 leaves the original bit unchanged. For example, the variable op1 has the bit pattern x x x x x x x x; each x can be 1 or 0, independent of any other x in the number. The result of ORing this binary number with the binary number 1 1 1 1 0 0 0 0 is as follows:

```
op1  =    x x x x x x x x
op2  =    1 1 1 1 0 0 0 0
          - - - - - - - -
Result =  1 1 1 1 x x x x
```

As you can see in this example, the 1s in op2 force the resulting bits to 1, and the 0s in op2 filter, or pass, the bits in op1 through with no change in their values. By using an OR operation, a masking operation similar to an AND operation can be produced, except the masking bits are set to 1s rather than 0s. Another way of looking at it is to say that ORing with a 0 has the same effect as ANDing with a 1.

Program 15.4 uses this masking property to convert uppercase letters in a word into their lowercase form, assuming the letters are stored with the ASCII code. The algorithm for converting letters is similar to the one in Program 15.2 and converts uppercase letters into their lowercase form by forcing the fifth bit in each letter to 1. Program 15.4 does this by masking the letter's code with the binary value 00100000, which has the hexadecimal value 20.

Program 15.4

```cpp
#include <iostream>
using namespace std;

const int TOLOWER = 0x20;
void lower (char *);   // function prototype

int main()
{
  char word[81];        // enough storage for a complete line

  cout << "Enter a string of both uppercase and lowercase letters:\n";
  cin.getline(word,80,'\n');
  cout << "\nThe string of letters just entered is:\n"
       << word << endl;
  lower(word);
  cout << "\nThis string, in lowercase letters, is:\n"
       << word << endl;
  return 0;
}

void lower(char *word)
{
  while (*word != '\0')
    *word++ |= TOLOWER;
}
```

A sample run of Program 15.4 follows:

```
Enter a string of both uppercase and lowercase letters:
abcdefgHIJKLMNOPqrstuvwxyz
The string of letters just entered is:
abcdefgHIJKLMNOPqrstuvwxyz
This string, in lowercase letters, is:
abcdefghijklmnopqrstuvwxyz
```

In reviewing Program 15.4, first notice that the input string has been stored and passed to lower() as a C-string, which is an array of characters. This permits the called function to receive and process the original character values instead of a copy of the values. Second, notice that uppercase letters are converted to lowercase form, and lowercase letters are unaltered. This result happens because bit five of all lowercase letters is 1, so forcing this bit to 1 with the mask has no effect. Only when bit five is 0, as for uppercase letters, is the input character altered.

15.3 The Exclusive OR Operator

The exclusive OR operator, ^, performs a bit-by-bit comparison of its two operands. The result of the comparison is determined by the following rule: *The result of the comparison is 1 if one, and only one, of the bits being compared is a 1; otherwise, the result is 0.*
   As shown in the following example of an exclusive OR operation, when both bits being compared are the same value (both 1 or both 0), the result is 0. Only when both bits have different values (one bit a 1 and the other a 0) is the result 1. Again, each pair or bit comparison is independent of any other bit comparison.

```
  1 0 1 1 0 0 1 1
^ 1 1 0 1 0 1 0 1
  _ _ _ _ _ _ _ _
  0 1 1 0 0 1 1 0
```

An exclusive OR operation can be used to create the opposite value, or complement, of any bit in a variable. The reason is that exclusive ORing any bit (1 or 0) with 1 forces the resulting bit to be the opposite value of its original state, and exclusive ORing any bit (1 or 0) with 0 leaves the original bit unchanged. For example, the variable op1 has the bit pattern x x x x x x x x; each x can be 1 or 0, independent of any other x in the number. Using the notation that $\bar{x}$ is the complement (opposite) value of x, the result of exclusive ORing this binary number with the binary number 0 1 0 1 0 1 0 1 is as follows:

```
op1 =   x x x x x x x x
op2 =   0 1 0 1 0 1 0 1
        _ _ _ _ _ _ _ _

        _   _   _   _
Result = x x x x x x x x
```

As you can see in this example, the 1s in op2 force the resulting bits to be the complement of their original bit values, and the 0s in op2 filter, or pass, the bits in op1 through with no change in their values.

Many encryption methods use the exclusive OR operation to code data by exclusive ORing each character in the string with a mask value. The choice of the mask value, which is referred to as the **encryption key**, is arbitrary, and any key value can be used. Program 15.5 uses an encryption key of 52 to code a user-entered message.

 Program 15.5

```cpp
#include <iostream>
using namespace std;

void encrypt(char *); // function prototype

int main()
{
  char message[81];   // enough storage for a complete line

  cout << "\nEnter a sentence:\n";
  cin.getline(message,80,'\n');
  cout << "\nThe sentence just entered is:\n"
       << message << endl;
  encrypt(message);
  cout << "\nThe encrypted version of this sentence is:\n"
       << message << endl;

  return 0;
}

void encrypt(char *message)
{
  while (*message != '\0')
    *message++ ^= 52;
}
```

Following is a sample run of Program 15.5:

```
Enter a sentence:
Good morning
The sentence just entered is:
Good morning
The encrypted version of this sentence is:
s[[P¶Y[FZ]ZS
```

Decoding an encrypted message requires exclusive ORing the coded message with the original encryption key, which is left for you to try as an exercise (see Programming Projects for Chapter 15, Exercise 12, at the end of this chapter).

15.4 The Complement Operator

The complement operator, ~, is a unary operator that changes each 1 bit in its operand to 0 and each 0 bit to 1. For example, if the variable op1 contains the binary number 11001010, ~op1 replaces this binary number with the number 00110101. The complement operator is used to force any bit in an operand to 0, independent of the actual number of bits used to store the number. For example, the statement

```
op1 = op1 & ~07;    // 07 is an octal number
```

or its shorter form

```
op1 &= ~07;     // 07 is an octal number
```

sets the last three bits of op1 to 0, regardless of how op1 is stored in the computer. Either statement can, of course, be replaced by ANDing the last three bits of op1 with 0s, if the number of bits used to store op1 is known. In a computer that uses 16 bits to store integers, the AND operation is

```
op1 = op1 & 0177770;      // in octal
```

or

```
op1 = op1 & 0xFFF8;     // in hexadecimal
```

For a computer that uses 32 bits to store integers, the preceding AND also sets the leftmost or higher order 16 bits to 0, which is an unintended result. The following is the correct statement for 32 bits:

```
op1 = op1 & 027777777770;     // in octal
```

or

```
op1 = op1 & 0xFFFFFFF8;     // in hexadecimal
```

Using the complement operator in this situation frees the programmer from having to determine the operand's storage size and, more important, makes the program portable between machines by using different integer storage sizes.

15.5 Different-Size Data Items

When the bit operators &, |, and ^ are used with operands of different sizes, the shorter operand is always increased in bit size to match the larger operand's size. Figure 15.1 illustrates extending a 16-bit unsigned integer into a 32-bit number. As the figure shows, the additional bits are added to the left of the original number and filled with 0s. This is the equivalent of adding leading 0s to the number, which has no effect on the number's value.

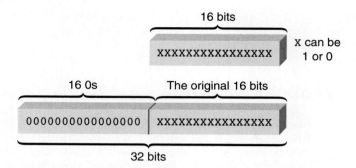

Figure 15.1   Extending 16-bit unsigned data to 32 bits

When extending signed numbers, the original leftmost bit is reproduced in the extra bits added to the number. As illustrated in Figure 15.2, if the original leftmost bit is 0, corresponding to a positive number, 0 is placed in each of the additional bit positions. If the leftmost bit is 1, which corresponds to a negative number, 1 is placed in the additional bit positions. In either case, the resulting binary number has the same sign and magnitude of the original number.

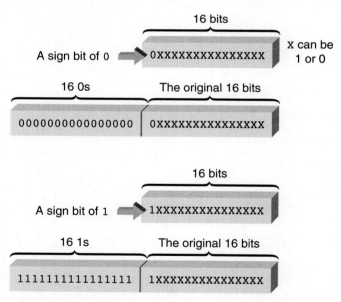

Figure 15.2   Extending 16-bit signed data to 32 bits

15.6 The Shift Operators

The left shift operator, <<, causes the bits in an operand to be shifted to the left by a given amount. For example, the statement

```
op1 = op1 << 4;
```

causes the bits in op1 to be shifted four bits to the left, filling any vacated bits with a 0. Figure 15.3 illustrates the effect of shifting the binary number 1111100010101011 to the left by four bit positions.

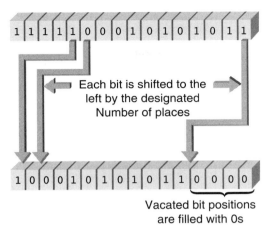

Figure 15.3 An example of a left shift

For unsigned integers, each left shift corresponds to multiplication by two. This is also true for signed numbers using twos complement representation, as long as the leftmost bit doesn't switch values. Because a change in the leftmost bit of a twos complement number represents a change in both the sign and magnitude represented by the bit, this shift doesn't represent a simple multiplication by two.

The right shift operator, >>, causes the bits in an operand to be shifted to the right by a given amount. For example, the statement

```
op2 = op1 >> 3;
```

causes the bits in op1 to be shifted to the right by three bit positions. Figure 15.4a illustrates the right shift of the unsigned binary number 1111100010101011 by three bit positions. As shown, the three rightmost bits are shifted "off the end" and are lost.

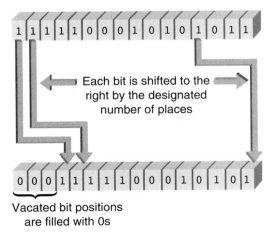

Figure 15.4a An unsigned arithmetic right shift

For unsigned numbers, the leftmost bit isn't used as a sign bit. For this type of number, the vacated leftmost bits are always filled with 0s, as shown in Figure 15.4a. For signed numbers, what's filled in the vacated bits depends on the computer. Most computers reproduce the number's original sign bit. Figure 15.4b illustrates the right shift of a negative binary number by four bit positions, and the sign bit is reproduced in the vacated bits. Figure 15.4c illustrates the equivalent right shift of a positive signed binary number.

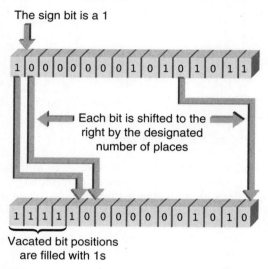

Figure 15.4b   The right shift of a negative binary number

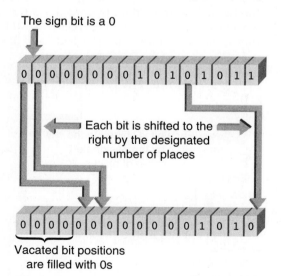

Figure 15.4c   The right shift of a positive binary number

The type of fill shown in Figures 15.4b and 15.4c, where the sign bit is reproduced in vacated bit positions, is called an **arithmetic right shift**. In an arithmetic right shift, each single shift to the right corresponds to a division by two.

Instead of reproducing the sign bit in right-shifted signed numbers, some computers fill the vacated bits with 0s automatically. This type of shift is called a **logical shift**. For positive signed numbers, in which the leftmost bit is 0, both arithmetic and logical right shifts produce the same result. The results of these two shifts are different only when negative numbers are involved.

15.7 Chapter Summary

1. Bits of character and integer variables and constants can be manipulated by using C++'s bit operators: AND, inclusive OR, exclusive OR, ones complement, left shift, and right shift operators.

2. The AND and inclusive OR operators are useful in creating masks that can be used to pass or eliminate bits from the selected operand. The exclusive OR operator is useful in complementing an operand's bits.

3. When the AND and OR operators are used with operands of different sizes, the shorter operand is always increased in bit size to match the size of the larger operand.

4. The shift operators produce different results, depending on whether the operand is a signed or an unsigned value.

Programming Projects for Chapter 15

1. (**Practice**) Determine the results of the following operations:

```
a.    11001010          b.    11001010          c.    11001010
    & 10100101              | 10100101              ^ 10100101
      --------                --------                --------
```

2. (**Practice**) Write the octal representations of the binary numbers given in Exercise 1.

3. (**Practice**) Determine the octal results of the following operations, assuming unsigned numbers:

   a. The octal number 0157 shifted left by one bit position

   b. The octal number 0701 shifted left by two bit positions

   c. The octal number 0673 shifted right by two bit positions

   d. The octal number 067 shifted right by three bit positions

4. (**Practice**) Repeat Exercise 3, assuming the numbers are treated as signed values.

5. **(Practice) a.** The arbitrary bit pattern xxxxxxxx, where each x can represent 1 or 0, is stored in the integer variable `flag`. Determine the octal value of a mask that can be ANDed with the bit pattern to reproduce the third and fourth bits of `flag` and set all other bits to 0. The rightmost bit in `flag` is considered bit 0.

   b. Determine the octal value of a mask that can be inclusively ORed with the bit pattern in `flag` to reproduce the third and fourth bits of `flag` and set all other bits to 1. Again, the rightmost bit in `flag` is considered bit 0.

   c. Determine the octal value of a mask that can be used to complement the values of the third and fourth bits of `flag` and leave all other bits unchanged. Determine the bit operation that should be used with the mask value to produce this result.

6. **(Practice) a.** Write the twos complement form of the decimal number -1, using 8 bits. (*Hint*: Refer to Section 1.5 for a review of twos complement numbers.)

   b. Repeat Exercise 6a, using 16 bits to represent the decimal number -1, and compare your answer to your previous answer. Could the 16-bit version have been obtained by sign-extending the 8-bit version?

7. **(Desk Check)** As noted in the chapter, Program 15.2 has no effect on uppercase letters. Using the ASCII codes listed in Appendix B, determine what other characters are unaffected by Program 15.2.

8. **(Modify)** Modify Program 15.2 so that a complete sentence can be read in and converted to lowercase values. (*Hint*: When a space is masked in Program 15.2, the resulting character is \0, which terminates the output.)

9. **(Modify)** Modify Program 15.4 to allow a complete sentence to be input and converted to uppercase letters. Make sure your program doesn't alter any other characters or symbols that are entered.

10. **(Modify)** Modify Program 15.5 to permit the encryption key to be a user-entered input value.

11. **(Modify)** Modify Program 15.5 to have its output written to a file named `coded.dat`.

12. **(Program)** Write a C++ program that reads the encrypted sentence produced by the program written for Exercise 10, decodes the sentence, and displays the decoded values.

13. **(Program)** Write a C++ program that displays the first 8 bits of each character value entered in a variable named `ch`. (*Hint*: Assuming each character is stored with 8 bits, start by using the hexadecimal mask 80, which corresponds to the binary number 10000000. If the result of the masking operation is a 0, display a 0; otherwise, display a 1. Then shift the mask one place to the right to examine the next bit, and so on until all bits in the variable `ch` have been processed.)

14. **(Program)** Write a C++ program that reverses the bits in an integer variable named `okay` and stores the reversed bits in the variable named `revokay`. For example, if the bit pattern 11100101, corresponding to the octal number 0345, is assigned to `okay`, the bit pattern 10100111, corresponding to the octal number 0247, should be produced and stored in `revokay`.

Appendix A

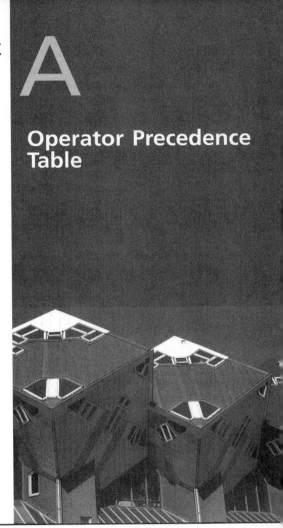

Operator Precedence Table

Table A.1 lists the symbols, precedence, descriptions, and associativity of C++'s operators. Operators toward the top of the table have a higher precedence than those toward the bottom. Operators in each section of the table have the same precedence and associativity.

Table A.1 Summary of C++ Operators

Operator	Description	Associativity
() [] –> .	Function call Array element Structure member pointer reference Structure member reference	Left to right

Table A.1 Summary of C++ Operators (continued)

Operator	Description	Associativity
++ -- – ! ~ (type) sizeof & *	Increment Decrement Unary minus Logical negation One's complement Type conversion (cast) Storage size Address of Indirection	Right to left
* / %	Multiplication Division Modulus (remainder)	Left to right
+ –	Addition Subtraction	Left to right
<< >>	Left shift Right shift	Left to right
< <= > >=	Less than Less than or equal to Greater than Greater than or equal to	Left to right
== !=	Equal to Not equal to	Left to right
&	Bitwise AND	Left to right
^	Bitwise exclusive OR	Left to right
|	Bitwise inclusive OR	Left to right
&&	Logical AND	Left to right
||	Logical OR	Left to right
?:	Conditional expression	Right to left
= += -= *= /= %= &= ^= |= <<= >>=	Assignment Assignment Assignment Assignment Assignment	Right to left
,	Comma	Left to right

Appendix B

ASCII Character Codes

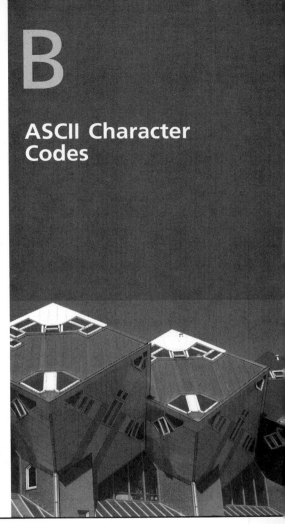

Key(s)	Dec	Oct	Hex	Key(s)	Dec	Oct	Hex	Key(s)	Dec	Oct	Hex
Ctrl 1	0	0	0	Ctrl K	11	13	B	Ctrl V	22	26	16
Ctrl A	1	1	1	Ctrl L	12	14	C	Ctrl W	23	27	17
Ctrl B	2	2	2	Ctrl M (Ret)	13	15	D	Ctrl X	24	30	18
Ctrl C	3	3	3	Ctrl N	14	16	E	Ctrl Y	25	31	19
Ctrl D	4	4	4	Ctrl O	15	17	F	Ctrl Z	26	32	1A
Ctrl E	5	5	5	Ctrl P	16	20	10	Esc	27	33	1B
Ctrl F	6	6	6	Ctrl Q	17	21	11	Ctrl <	28	34	1C
Ctrl G	7	7	7	Ctrl R	18	22	12	Ctrl /	29	35	1D
Ctrl H	8	10	8	Ctrl S	19	23	13	Ctrl =	30	36	1E
Ctrl I	9	11	9	Ctrl T	20	24	14	Ctrl -	31	37	1F
Ctrl J (line feed)	10	12	A	Ctrl U	21	25	15	Space	32	40	20

Key(s)	Dec	Oct	Hex	Key(s)	Dec	Oct	Hex	Key(s)	Dec	Oct	Hex
!	33	41	21	A	65	101	41	a	97	141	61
"	34	42	22	B	66	102	42	b	98	142	62
#	35	43	23	C	67	103	43	c	99	143	63
$	36	44	24	D	68	104	44	d	100	144	64
%	37	45	25	E	69	105	45	e	101	145	65
&	38	46	26	F	70	106	46	f	102	146	66
'	39	47	27	G	71	107	47	g	103	147	67
(	40	50	28	H	72	110	48	h	104	150	68
)	41	51	29	I	73	111	49	i	105	151	69
*	42	52	2A	J	74	112	4A	j	106	152	6A
+	43	53	2B	K	75	113	4B	k	107	153	6B
,	44	54	2C	L	76	114	4C	l	108	154	6C
-	45	55	2D	M	77	115	4D	m	109	155	6D
.	46	56	2E	N	78	116	4E	n	110	156	6E
/	47	57	2F	O	79	117	4F	o	111	157	6F
0	48	60	30	P	80	120	50	p	112	160	70
1	49	61	31	Q	81	121	51	q	113	161	71
2	50	62	32	R	82	122	52	r	114	162	72
3	51	63	33	S	83	123	53	s	115	163	73
4	52	64	34	T	84	124	54	t	116	164	74
5	53	65	35	U	85	125	55	u	117	165	75
6	54	66	36	V	86	126	56	v	118	166	76
7	55	67	37	W	87	127	57	w	119	167	77
8	56	70	38	X	88	130	58	x	120	170	78
9	57	71	39	Y	89	131	59	y	121	171	79
:	58	72	3A	Z	90	132	5A	z	122	172	7A
;	59	73	3B	[	91	133	5B	{	123	173	7B
<	60	74	3C	\	92	134	5C	|	124	174	7C
=	61	75	3D	]	93	135	5D	}	125	175	7D
>	62	76	3E	^	94	136	5E	~	126	176	7E
?	63	77	3F	-	95	137	5F	del	127	177	7F
@	64	100	40	'	96	140	60				

Appendix C

Floating-Point Number Storage

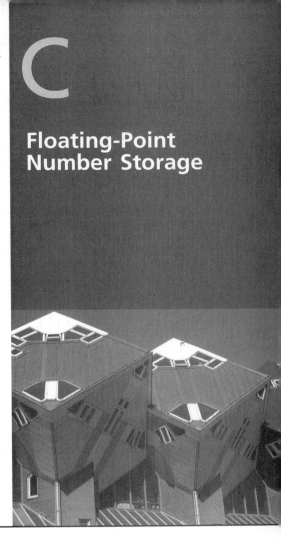

The twos complement binary code used to store integer values was introduced in Section 1.5. This appendix covers the binary storage format typically used in C++ to store single-precision and double-precision numbers, which are stored as floats and doubles, respectively. Collectively, single- and double-precision values are commonly referred to as floating-point values.

Like their decimal number counterparts that use a decimal point to separate the integer and fractional parts of a number, floating-point numbers are represented in a conventional binary format with a binary point. For example, in the binary number 1011.11, the digits to the left of the binary point (1011) represent the integer part and the digits to the right of the binary point (11) represent the fractional part.

To store a floating-point binary number, a code similar to decimal scientific notation is used. To obtain this code, the conventional binary number format is separated into a mantissa and an exponent. The following examples show floating-point numbers expressed in this scientific notation:

Conventional Binary Notation	Binary Scientific Notation
1010.0	1.01 exp 011
-10001.0	-1.0001 exp 100

Conventional Binary Notation	Binary Scientific Notation
0.001101	1.101 exp -011
-0.000101	-1.01 exp -100

In binary scientific notation, the term "exp" stands for exponent. The binary number in front of the exp term is the mantissa, and the binary number following the exp term is the exponent value. Except for the number 0, the mantissa always has a single leading 1 followed by a binary point. The exponent represents a power of 2 and indicates the number of places the binary point should be moved in the mantissa to obtain the conventional binary notation. If the exponent is positive, the binary point is moved to the right. If the exponent is negative, the binary point is moved to the left.

For example, the exponent 011 in the number

```
1.01 exp 011
```

means move the binary point three places to the right so that the number becomes 1010. The -011 exponent in the number

```
1.101 exp -011
```

means move the binary point three places to the left so that the number becomes the following:

```
.001101
```

In storing floating-point numbers, the sign, mantissa, and exponent are stored in separate fields. The number of bits used for each field determines the number's precision. The Institute of Electrical and Electronics Engineers (IEEE) Standard 754-1985 defines single-precision (32-bit), double-precision (64-bit), and extended-precision (80-bit) floating-point data formats to have the characteristics in Table C.1. Figure C.1 illustrates the format for a single-precision floating-point number.

Table C.1   IEEE Standard 754-1985 Floating-Point Specification

Data Format	Sign Bits	Mantissa Bits	Exponent Bits
Single-precision	1	23	8
Double-precision	1	52	11
Extended-precision	1	64	15

The sign bit shown in Figure C.1 refers to the mantissa's sign. A sign bit of 1 represents a negative number, and a 0 sign bit represents a positive value. Because all mantissas, except the number 0, have a leading 1 followed by their binary points, these two items are never stored explicitly. The binary point resides immediately to the left of mantissa bit 22, and a leading 1 is always assumed. The binary number 0 is specified by setting all mantissa and exponent bits to 0. For this number only, the implied leading mantissa bit is also 0.

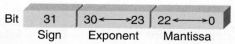

Figure C.1   Single-precision floating-point number storage format

The exponent field contains an exponent that's biased by 127. For example, an exponent of 5 is stored by using the binary equivalent of the number 132 (127 + 5). Using eight exponent bits, it's coded as 100000100. The addition of 127 to each exponent allows coding negative exponents in the exponent field without needing an explicit sign bit. For example, the exponent -011, which corresponds to -3, is stored by using the binary equivalent of +124 (127 - 3).

Figure C.2 illustrates encoding and storing the decimal number 59.75 as a 64-bit single-precision binary number. The sign, exponent, and mantissa are determined as follows. The conventional binary equivalent of

```
-59.75
```

is

```
-111011.11
```

| 1 | 10000100 | 1101111000000000000000000 |

Figure C.2 Encoding and storing the decimal number 59.75

Expressed in binary scientific notation, it becomes

```
-1.1101111 exp 101
```

The minus sign is signified by setting the sign bit to 1. The mantissa's leading 1 and binary point are omitted, and the 23-bit mantissa field is encoded as follows:

```
11011110000000000000000
```

The exponent field encoding is obtained by adding the exponent value of 101 to 1111111, which is the binary equivalent of the 127_{10} bias value:

```
 1 1 1 1 1 1 1    = 127₁₀
       + 1 0 1    =   5₁₀
 1 0 0 0 0 1 0 0  = 132₁₀
```

Appendix D

Command-Line Arguments

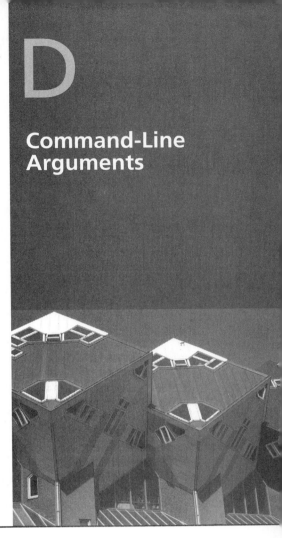

Arguments can be passed to any function in a program, including the main() function. This appendix describes the procedures for passing arguments to main() when a program is initially invoked and having main() correctly receive and store the arguments passed to it. Both the sending and receiving sides of the transaction must be considered. Fortunately, the interface for transmitting arguments to a main() function has been standardized in C++, so sending and receiving arguments can be done almost mechanically.

All the programs run so far can be invoked by typing the name of the program's executable version in a DOS window after the operating system prompt. The command line for these programs consists of a single word: the name of the program. For computers using UNIX, the prompt is usually the $ symbol and the program's executable name is a.out. For these systems, the simple command line

```
$a.out
```

begins program execution of the last compiled source program currently residing in a.out.

If you're using a Windows-based C++ compiler, the equivalent operating system prompt is typically C:\>, and the executable program's name is usually the same as the source program but with an .exe extension rather than a .cpp extension. For this type of system, the command line for running an executable program named `PGMD-1.exe` is `C:\>PGMD-1`. As illustrated in Figure D.1, this command line causes the executable version of the `PGMD-1` program to begin execution with its `main()` function, but no additional arguments are passed to `main()`.

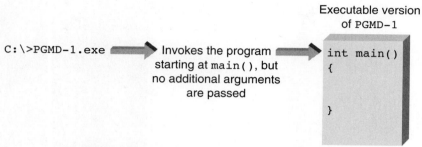

Figure D.1   Invoking the `PGMD-1.exe` program

Now assume you want to pass three separate string arguments—three blind mice—to `PGMD-1`'s `main()` function. Sending arguments to a `main()` function is easy; you simply include the arguments on the command line used to begin program execution. Because the arguments are typed on the command line, they're called **command-line arguments**. To pass the arguments `three blind mice` to the `main()` function of the `PGMD-1` program, add them after the program name, as shown:

`C:\>PGMD-1 three blind mice`

When the operating system encounters this command line, it stores the strings after the prompt as a sequence of four strings. (Some systems also store the prompt as part of the first string.) Figure D.2 illustrates the storage of these strings, assuming each character uses 1 byte of storage. As shown, each string terminates with the standard C++ null character, `\0`.

| P | G | M | D | - | 1 | \0 | t | h | r | e | e | \0 | b | l | i | n | d | \0 | m | i | c | e | \0 |

Figure D.2   The command-line arguments stored in memory

Sending command-line arguments to `main()` is always this simple. Type the arguments on the command line, and the operating system stores them as a sequence of separate strings. Next, you see how to handle the receiving side of the transaction and let `main()` know that arguments are being passed to it.

Arguments passed to `main()`, like all function arguments, must be declared as part of the function's definition. To standardize passing arguments to a `main()` function, only two items are allowed: a number and an array. The number is an integer variable, typically named `argc` (short for argument counter), and the array is a one-dimensional list, which is, by convention, named `argv` (short for argument values). Figure D.3 illustrates these two arguments.

The integer passed to `main()` is the total number of items on the command line. In this example, the value of `argc` passed to `main()` is 4, which includes the name of the program plus the three command-line arguments. The one-dimensional array passed to `main()` is a list of pointers containing the starting storage address of each string typed on the command line, as illustrated in Figure D.4.

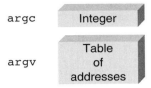

Figure D.3   An integer and an array are passed to `main()`

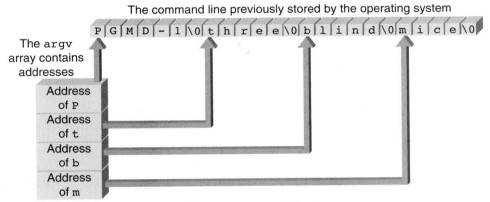

Figure D.4   Addresses are stored in the `argv` array

You can now write the complete function definition for `main()` to receive arguments by declaring their names and data types. For `main()`'s two arguments, the names used by convention are `argv` and `argc`.[1] Because `argc` stores an integer value, its declaration is `int argc`. Because `argv` is the name of an array whose elements are addresses pointing to where the actual command-line arguments are stored, its proper declaration is `char *argv[]`. This statement is nothing more than the declaration of an array of pointers. It's read as "`argv` is an array whose elements are pointers to characters." Putting all this together, the full function header for a `main()` function that receives command-line arguments is as follows:

```
int main(int argc, char *argv[])
```

No matter how many arguments are typed on the command line, `main()` needs only the two standard pieces of information provided by `argc` and `argv`: the number of items on the command line and the list of starting addresses indicating where each argument is actually stored.

Program D.1 verifies this description by displaying the data actually passed to `main()`. The variable `argv[i]` used in Program D.1 contains an address that's displayed by the first `cout` statement in the `for` loop. For ease of reading the output, this address is cast into an integer value. The string notation `*argv[i]` in the second `cout` statement refers to "the character pointed to" by the address in `argv[i]`.

---

[1] These names aren't required, and any valid C++ identifier can be used in their place.

Program D.1

```cpp
#include <iostream>
using namespace std;
int main(int argc, char *argv[])
{
  int i;

  cout << "\nThe number of items on the command line is "
       << argc << endl << endl;

  for(i = 0; i < argc; i++)
  {
    cout << "The address stored in argv[" << i <<"] is "
         << int(argv[i]) << endl;    // display address as an integer number
    cout << "The character pointed to is " << *argv[i] << endl;
  }

  return 0;
}
```

Assuming the executable version of Program D.1 is named PGMD-1.exe, a sample output for the command line C:\>PGMD-1 three blind mice is the following:

```
The number of items on the command line is 4
The address stored in argv[0] is 3280388
The character pointed to is P
The address stored in argv[1] is 3280395
The character pointed to is t
The address stored in argv[2] is 3280401
The character pointed to is b
The address stored in argv[3] is 3280407
The character pointed to is m
```

The addresses Program D.1 displays clearly depend on the machine used to run the program. Figure D.5 illustrates storage of the command line as displayed by the sample output. As anticipated, the addresses in the argv array "point" to the starting characters of each string typed on the command line.

After command-line arguments are passed to a C++ program, they can be used like any other C-strings. Program D.2 causes its command-line arguments to be displayed from main().

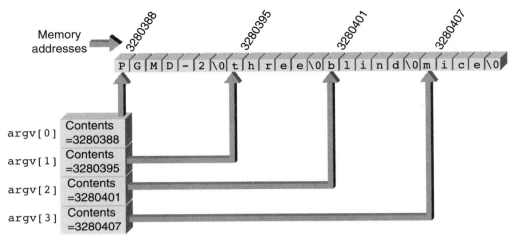

Figure D.5 The command line stored in memory

Program D.2

```cpp
// A program that displays its command-line arguments
#include <iostream>
using namespace std;

int main(int argc, char *argv[])
{
  int i;

  cout << "\nThe following arguments were passed to main(): ";

  for (i = 0; i < argc; i++)
    cout << argv[i] << " ";

  cout << endl;

  return 0;
}
```

Assuming the executable version of Program D.2 is named PGMD-2.exe, the output for the command line C:\>PGMD-2 three blind mice is the following:

```
The following arguments were passed to main(): PGMD-2 three blind mice
```

Notice that when addresses in `argv[]` are inserted in the `cout` stream in Program D.2, the C-strings these addresses point to are displayed. As mentioned previously, this display occurs because `cout` dereferences these addresses automatically and performs the required indirection to locate the actual string that's displayed.

One final comment about command-line arguments: Any argument typed on a command line is considered a C-string. If you want numerical data passed to `main()`, it's up to you to convert the passed string into its numerical counterpart. This is seldom an issue, however, because most command-line arguments are used as flags to pass processing control signals to an invoked program.

Index

Special Characters

A